I0049856

SharePoint Online Administrator Playbook

A step-by-step approach to
SharePoint Online administration

Deviprasad Panda

bpb

www.bpbonline.com

First Edition 2025

Copyright © BPB Publications, India

ISBN: 978-93-65897-333

All Rights Reserved. No part of this publication may be reproduced, distributed or transmitted in any form or by any means or stored in a database or retrieval system, without the prior written permission of the publisher with the exception to the program listings which may be entered, stored and executed in a computer system, but they can not be reproduced by the means of publication, photocopy, recording, or by any electronic and mechanical means.

LIMITS OF LIABILITY AND DISCLAIMER OF WARRANTY

The information contained in this book is true and correct to the best of author's and publisher's knowledge. The author has made every effort to ensure the accuracy of these publications, but the publisher cannot be held responsible for any loss or damage arising from any information in this book.

All trademarks referred to in the book are acknowledged as properties of their respective owners but BPB Publications cannot guarantee the accuracy of this information.

To View Complete
BPB Publications Catalogue
Scan the QR Code:

www.bpbonline.com

Dedicated to

My parents
elder brother **Prabhu Prasad Panda**
younger brother **Hara Prasada Panda**
wife **Saranga** *and*
Lord Jagannath – most important in my life
Thanks for everything you do

About the Author

Deviprasad Panda is currently working as a senior lead infrastructure/cloud architect expertise in SharePoint and Power Platform, having almost 14 years of experience. He has strong experience in SharePoint on-premises production farm, SharePoint online, hosting SharePoint in Azure, Power Platform. He is a Microsoft certified SharePoint professional and Power Platform architect, having certifications including PL-600: Microsoft Power Platform Solution Architect. He has a huge production experience in multiple reputed companies in India. He is the founder of SharePointTechnicalSupport a website to support SharePoint related queries. He is a trainer, and a YouTuber as well. He is very passionate about the work that he steps into, and his dedication to providing quality work as a committed professional is highly appreciated.

About the Reviewer

Salaudeen Rajack is an accomplished IT professional with over 20 years of experience, specializing in SharePoint, PowerShell, Microsoft 365, and related technologies. Throughout his career, he has excelled in various roles, including SharePoint architect, administrator, developer, and consultant, enabling organizations to overcome complex IT challenges and optimize their solutions.

Renowned for his deep technical expertise, Salaudeen is passionate about sharing his knowledge through practical, real-world articles that empower IT professionals. His dedication to helping others and his ability to simplify intricate concepts have made him a respected voice in the technology community.

Acknowledgement

I would like to acknowledge my parents and my elder brother, Prabhu Prasad Panda, for their small sacrifices to give me a higher education and put me in a place where I am capable enough to make the right decisions and drive my life for a better future. I can never forget and fully fulfill your sacrifices in my life. Thank you!

I would like to acknowledge my younger brother, Hara Prasada Panda, who is my best friend and guide at every step in my career. Thank you!

I would like to acknowledge my lovely wife, who has been with me through all the ups and downs in life. All her encouragement and support have brought me success. Thank you!

Most importantly, I believe we need blessings from Lord Jagannath to share true values with society and grow together. I strongly believe that without god's blessings, nothing is possible.

Finally, I thank the BPB team for giving me this wonderful opportunity to write my first book for them. Thank you!

Preface

We are moving very fast towards the digital world. The digital revolution and content is important to manage content effectively, make content secure, targeted, collaborate more to work together to save cost, time, and improve quality with more productive works. SharePoint is the giant of collation tools when managing everything related to content comes into the picture. SharePoint online by Microsoft is one of the finest softwares as a solution service that provides smart features and keep on upgrading tools, rolling out new features to manage content smartly, with more security.

The primary goal of this book is to provide a clear concept of SharePoint online administration settings step-by-step, so that even a new user having no SharePoint subscription can learn and understand better. The book covers all SharePoint admin center settings, like a user manual or field guide that admin can follow to administer SharePoint online, with very simple words but advanced level production task experience as outcome. Every setting in SharePoint is covered with screenshots, so there will not be any problem if you are not accessing the admin center. You will not face any problem since all images are taken considering user understanding step-by-step. This book is divided into 13 chapters, and it provides a detailed description on SharePoint online administration to an advanced level. Over the 13 chapters in this book, you will learn the following:

Chapter 1: SharePoint Admin Center Home - Covers, introduction to SharePoint admin center, accessing SharePoint admin center, accessing Microsoft 365 admin center, SharePoint admin center tour, scope of administrator.

Chapter 2: Site Administration - Covers about the active sites, creating site with a modern approach, export site information, search sites, views, manage membership, hub, sharing, delete site, edit site, your recent actions, storage, deleted site, restore site, permanently delete site.

Chapter 3: Policies Administration - Covers specifics about policies administration, content sharing settings, access control settings.

Chapter 4: Settings - Focusing specific to home sites, notifications, pages, site creation, site storage limits, application management, stream app launcher tile, OneDrive notifications, retention, storage limit, sync, classic settings page.

Chapter 5: Content Services - Covers introduction to managed metadata, term store administration, content type gallery administration.

Chapter 6: Migration - Describes about file shares to microsoft 365 migration, install Microsoft 365 agent, connect migration agent to Microsoft 365 tenant, add source path, scans, migration, agents, stream classic to Microsoft 365 migration, Google Workspace to Microsoft 365 migration.

Chapter 7: User Profiles Administration - Covers more features, people management, and My Site Settings management.

Chapter 8: Search Administration - Focus specific to manage search schema, manage search dictionaries, query suggestion settings, manage result sources, manage query rules, remove search results, view usage reports, search center settings, export search configuration, import search configuration, crawl log permissions.

Chapter 9: App Administration - Focuses specifically on SharePoint store, manage apps, API access, app requests, and more features.

Chapter 10: BCS Administration - Focuses specifically on how to manage BDC models and external content types, manage connections to online services, and manage connections to on-premises services.

Chapter 11: Secure Store Administration - Focuses specifically on how to create new target application, set credential for target application, edit target application, delete target application.

Chapter 12: Record Management Administration - Describes how to create send-to connections, edit or remove connection.

Chapter 13: Hybrid Picker - Explains how to run hybrid picker, hybrid OneDrive, hybrid sites, hybrid app launcher, hybrid business to business sites, hybrid self-service site creation, hybrid taxonomy and content type, hybrid search.

Coloured Images

Please follow the link to download the
Coloured Images of the book:

https://rebrand.ly/d884fht

We have code bundles from our rich catalogue of books and videos available at **https://github.com/bpbpublications**. Check them out!

Errata

We take immense pride in our work at BPB Publications and follow best practices to ensure the accuracy of our content to provide with an indulging reading experience to our subscribers. Our readers are our mirrors, and we use their inputs to reflect and improve upon human errors, if any, that may have occurred during the publishing processes involved. To let us maintain the quality and help us reach out to any readers who might be having difficulties due to any unforeseen errors, please write to us at :

errata@bpbonline.com

Your support, suggestions and feedbacks are highly appreciated by the BPB Publications' Family.

Did you know that BPB offers eBook versions of every book published, with PDF and ePub files available? You can upgrade to the eBook version at www.bpbonline. com and as a print book customer, you are entitled to a discount on the eBook copy. Get in touch with us at :

business@bpbonline.com for more details.

At **www.bpbonline.com**, you can also read a collection of free technical articles, sign up for a range of free newsletters, and receive exclusive discounts and offers on BPB books and eBooks.

Piracy

If you come across any illegal copies of our works in any form on the internet, we would be grateful if you would provide us with the location address or website name. Please contact us at **business@bpbonline.com** with a link to the material.

If you are interested in becoming an author

If there is a topic that you have expertise in, and you are interested in either writing or contributing to a book, please visit **www.bpbonline.com**. We have worked with thousands of developers and tech professionals, just like you, to help them share their insights with the global tech community. You can make a general application, apply for a specific hot topic that we are recruiting an author for, or submit your own idea.

Reviews

Please leave a review. Once you have read and used this book, why not leave a review on the site that you purchased it from? Potential readers can then see and use your unbiased opinion to make purchase decisions. We at BPB can understand what you think about our products, and our authors can see your feedback on their book. Thank you!

For more information about BPB, please visit **www.bpbonline.com**.

Join our book's Discord space

Join the book's Discord Workspace for Latest updates, Offers, Tech happenings around the world, New Release and Sessions with the Authors:

https://discord.bpbonline.com

Table of Contents

CHAPTER 1
SharePoint Admin Center Home

Introduction

Every software application has a central location to manage or control all the settings or configurations in a single place. For example, we can manage the settings of Windows 10 operating system from the **All Settings** option. Similarly, in SharePoint on-premises, **Central Administration** is the central location to manage all settings or configurations. In SharePoint online, it is called **SharePoint admin center**. You will find all settings in the SharePoint admin center to configure and manage SharePoint sites centrally at one place. The admin center home page will be the landing page in the SharePoint admin center. In this chapter, we will discuss the settings available in the admin center and a few more basic information.

Structure

In this chapter, you will understand the following topics:

- Introduction to SharePoint admin center
- Accessing SharePoint admin center
- Creating Office 365 account
- SharePoint admin center tour

- Microsoft 365 active users report
- Scope of administrator

Objectives

By the end of the chapter, you will get a clear understanding of SharePoint admin center. You will also learn how to create an Office 365 account and navigate the SharePoint admin center. This chapter will help you learn how to set up the default domain, primary email address, and username. The types of roles available in the Microsoft 365 admin center, the SharePoint Online administrator roles and responsibilities, and how to assign SharePoint admin roles will also be discussed. After you complete reading the chapter, you will clearly understand the user interface and different options available in the SharePoint admin center.

Introduction to SharePoint admin center

SharePoint is based on sites with one top-level site, and multiple subsites below that top-level site. Under each subsite, we can create multiple subsites, and this hierarchy continues. In SharePoint online, the first site is the SharePoint admin center which the administrators can access through a specific URL. The SharePoint Online Administrator creates multiple sites in the Admin center, called **Site** (Site collection in SharePoint On-Premises), that remain at the top level in the site hierarchy accessible by the end users. If any requirement comes to create a top-level site in SharePoint Online, then you understand it is a new Site request (site collection requirement in SharePoint On-Premises). If you think from a site point of view, the site will be end-users facing, but the SharePoint admin center is isolated from the end-users and limited to administrators only.

Once the site is created, users are added or assigned to it to access the site. The users or user properties in SharePoint are managed by a specific service. Once this service is configured, only end users will be available to be added to sites. So, this service is considered as a backend task. Settings to manage user properties are available in the SharePoint admin center only.

The end users contribute content, create records, search content on-site, access apps, and access external content from SharePoint sites. All these activities are end-user-facing but are configured and managed from a central location at the backend, called the **admin center**. These backend activities are administrator-facing tasks, so the end-user cannot access these settings. Many service configurations are managed from the backend to make the features available for end-users. Now, you must have a clear idea that **SharePoint admin center** is the central location or site where administrators can configure and control all backend services and features.

Accessing SharePoint admin center

SharePoint Online is included under **Software as a Service (SaaS)**. Services under SaaS can be accessed over the internet with web browser, anytime, anywhere using any device. Organizations do not need to worry about infrastructure, software, maintenance, and so on. All data resides in the service provider's data center. In the traditional organizational process, each software, such as SharePoint, Exchange, office applications, and so on, has an on-premises environment in its organizations' data center. Now, these on-premises servers reside in a Microsoft data center and are configured to make this software available as a service through the internet using a browser with added security and compliance. An organization needs to take subscriptions and charges applied based on the type of services and usage. If SharePoint Online is included in that subscription, we can only access the admin center.

Creating Office 365 account

Different services are bundled up and called **Office 365**. There are several types of plans in Office 365 based on the various types of services offered. The organization needs to subscribe to a plan. This section will explain the background of making SharePoint admin center available. Let us perform the following steps to subscribe to Office 365 plan:

1. If you search for `Office 365 plans for enterprise` in Google, you will get the option to navigate the URL **https://www.microsoft.com/en-in/microsoft-365/enterprise/compare-office-365-plans**. Check plans and proceed to **Buy now,** any one of the plans, as per your requirement, as seen in the following screenshot:

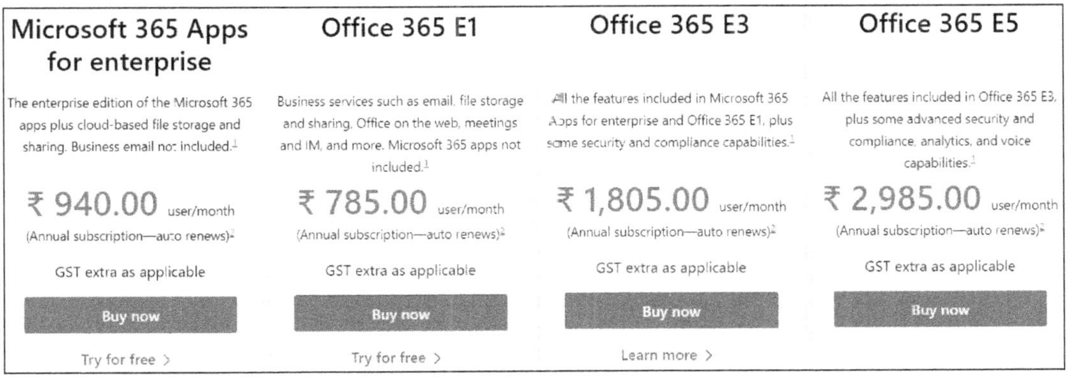

Figure 1.1: Office 365 plans

2. Once you click on **Buy now**, you will be redirected to another page to set up your account. On the right of the page, you will find the list of services included in the selected plan. The first step to proceed with account setup is entering the e-mail ID. For example, enter mail ID `support@spmcse.com`, and click on **Next**, as shown in the following screenshot:

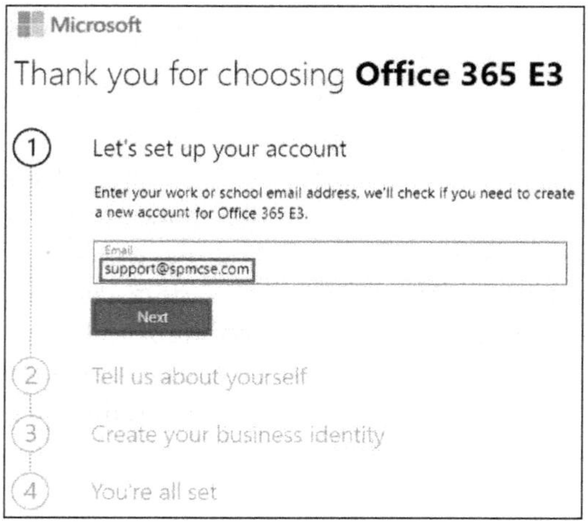

Figure 1.2: Set up your account

3. The mail ID will be verified on the backend to confirm whether any office account exists with this mail ID. If there is no office account linked to that mail ID, you will see options to confirm (**Not you?**) and proceed to the next step of account creation by clicking on **Set up account** as shown in the following figure:

Figure 1.3: Existing Office 365 account validation

If any office account is already linked to that mail ID, then you will be asked to **Sign in** or **Create a new account instead** as shown in the following figure:

Figure 1.4: Sign into existing Office 365 account

4. Let us consider a mail ID which is not linked to any office account. In that case, click on **Set up account**. You will get an option to fill in details about yourself. Enter **Name**, Valid **Business phone number**, **Company name**, **Company size**, and **Country or region**. Click on **Next** as shown in the following figure:

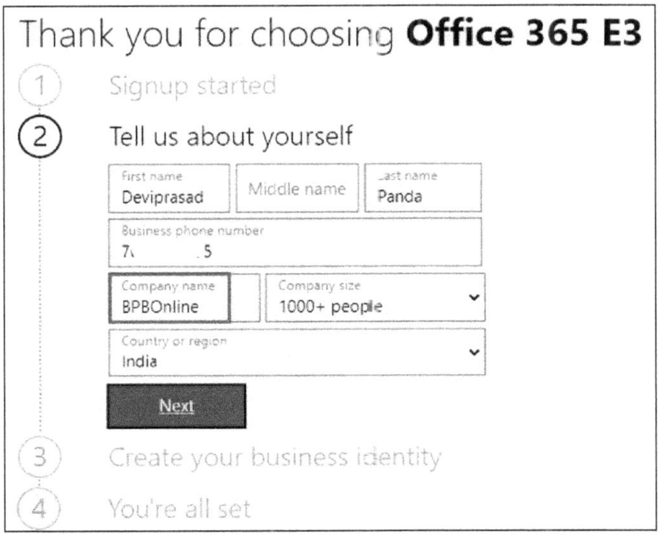

Figure 1.5: Fill details about yourself

5. The next step is OTP verification which can be in the form of Text or Call. Select the mode of OTP verification method, and click on **Send Verification Code** as shown in the following figure:

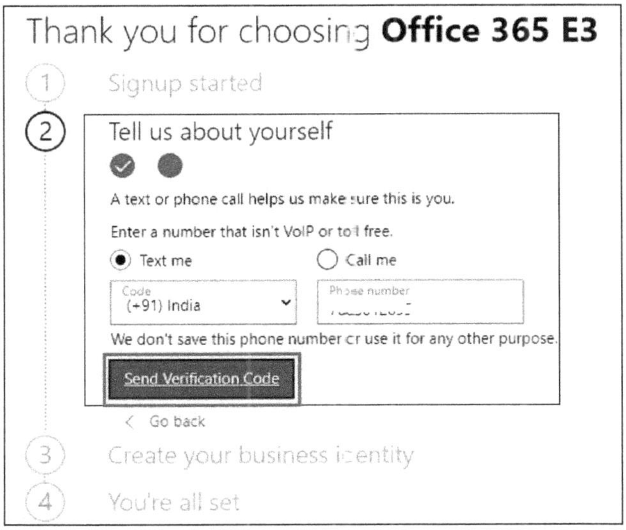

Figure 1.6: Send verification code

6. Once you receive the OTP, enter it in the **Verification code** field, and click on **Verify** as shown in the following figure:

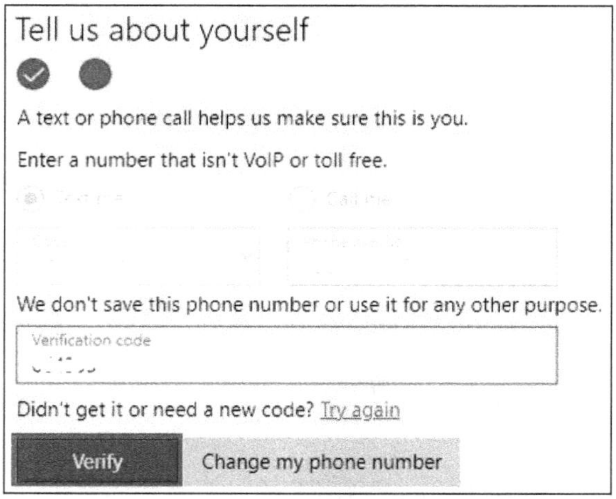

Figure 1.7: OTP verification

7. The next option will be to enter Business Identity. Corporate domain name should be used in this place. We are working for the organization BPB Publication and the organization's domain is BPBOnline.com. We will enter **BPBOnline** under the field **yourbusiness**. Click on **Check availability**. You will see the availability status of the domain as **BPBOnline.onmicrosoft.com is available**. Click on **Next** as shown in the following figure:

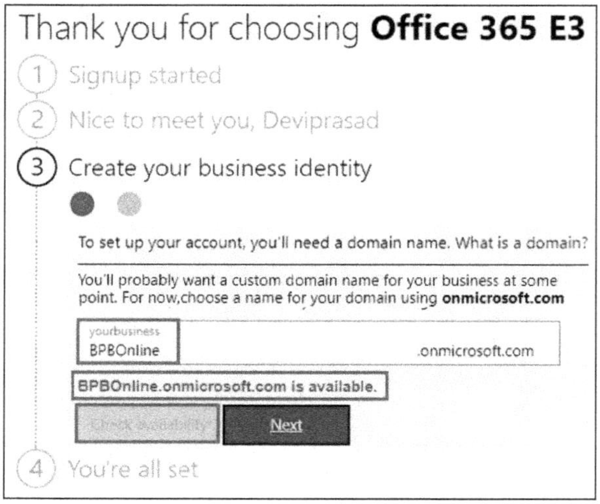

Figure 1.8: Business identity details

8. The next window is to create a **user Id** and **Password**, which will be the global administrator account. You should give a proper name, as per best practice,

while creating the user. Enter the **user Id** and **Password** under the fields **Name**, **Password, Confirm password,** respectively. Click on **Sign up** to complete the account creation process as shown in the following figure:

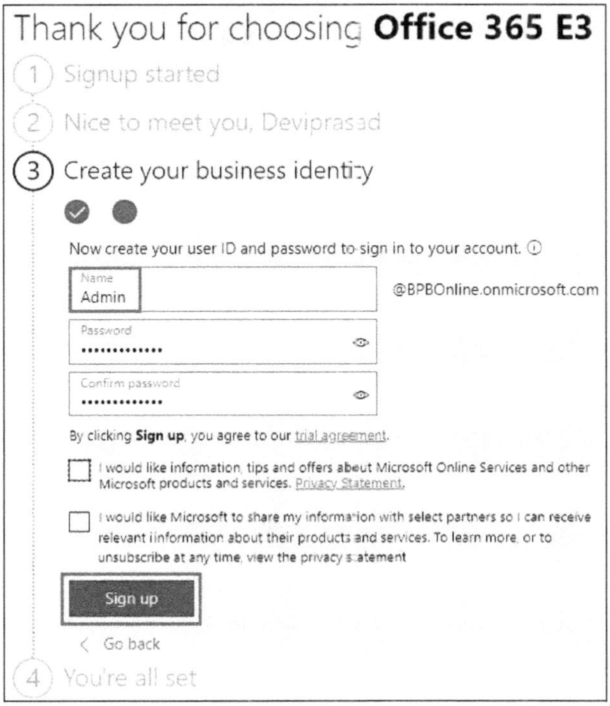

Figure 1.9: Select user Id and password

9. Your account is now created. You will see the **username Admin@BPBOnline. onmicrosoft.com** with message regarding a mail sent to the mail ID **support@ spmcse.com** with sign-in information. Click on **Go to Setup** now to proceed towards setting up Microsoft 365 admin center as shown in the following figure:

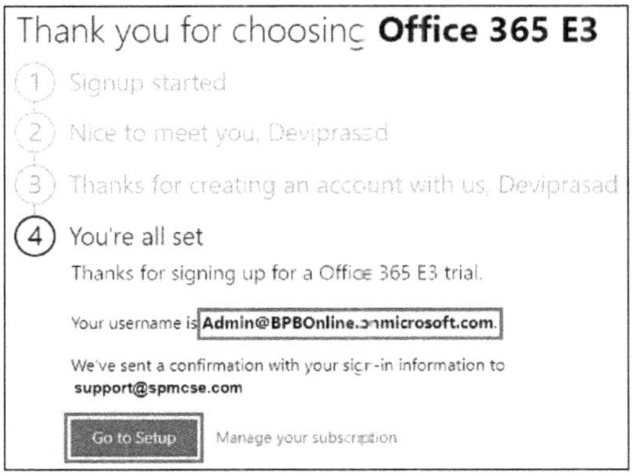

Figure 1.10: Office 365 account created

10. Next, you will get **m365setupwizard** page where you need to install Office 365 apps. Click on **Continue** to proceed without installing **Office apps** as shown in the following figure:

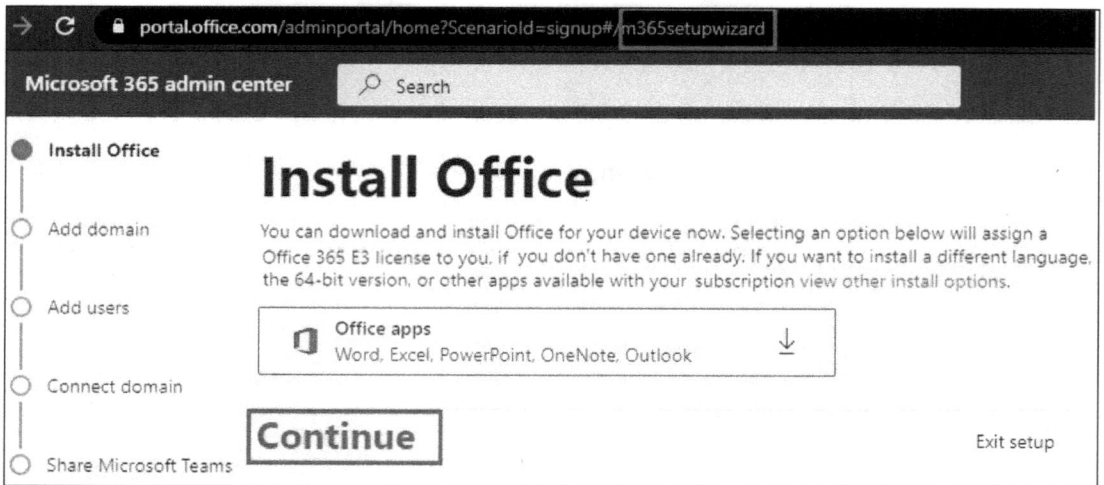

Figure 1.11: Install Office apps

11. Next, you will be redirected to enter the domain of the organization and set up Microsoft 365 admin center. Select the radio button **Yes, add this domain now**. Enter domain name, for example, **bpbonline.com** and click on **Use this domain** as shown in the following figure:

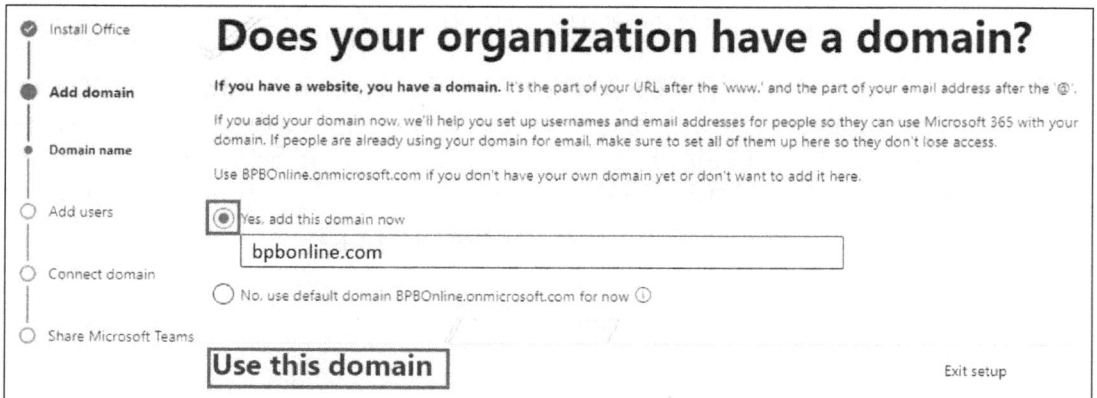

Figure 1.12: Domain setup

12. After this, certain steps need to be done by different teams related to network entries to add domain in office 365. After that, Microsoft 365 admin center (**https://admin.microsoft.com/Adminportal/#/homepage**) can be accessed.

Accessing Microsoft 365 admin center

Once Microsoft 365 admin center is opened, you will see multiple options in left navigation pane like **Home, Users, Groups, Roles, Resources, Billing, Support, Settings, Setup, Reports, Health** and **all admin centers** like **Security, Compliance, Azure Active Directory, Exchange, SharePoint**, and **Teams** as shown in the following figure:

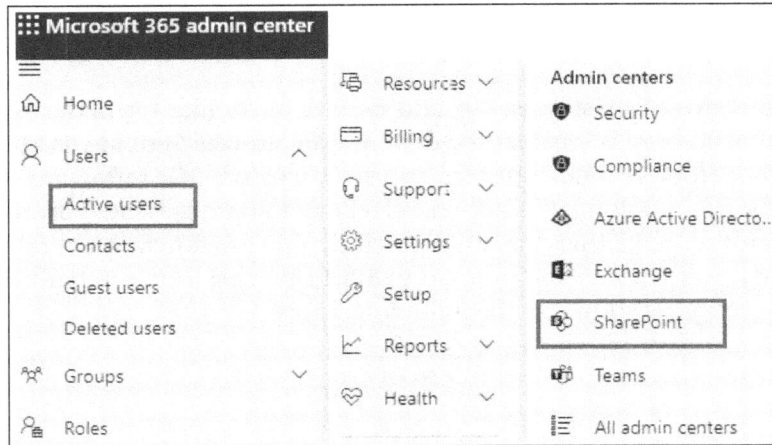

Figure 1.13: *Microsoft 365 admin center*

Default Microsoft 365 domain

Once Office 365 account set up is completed, you will find the default domain available in Microsoft 365 admin center under left navigation **Domains**. As per requirement, domains can be added or removed from Microsoft 365 admin center. Let us perform the following steps to set custom domain as default domain:

1. Click on **Domains** from left navigation. It will expand and you will find additional options like **Domains, Search & intelligence, Org settings, Add-ins**, and **Partner relationships**. Click on **Domains**.

2. You will notice that the default domain as **BPBOnline.onmicrosoft.com** with status as **Healthy** will get reflected. If you have added custom organization domain, for example **BPBOnline.com**, as discussed previously under *Creating Office 365 account step 11*, you will find the domain (BPBOnline.com) here as well.

3. The default domain will be **BPBOnline.onmicrosoft.com**. You need to change the default domain from **BPBOnline.onmicrosoft.com** to **BPBOnline.com**.

4. We can add or manage additional domains by clicking on **Add domain** as shown in the following figure:

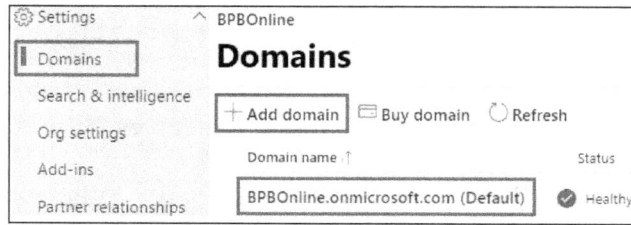

Figure 1.14: Domains

5. Let me show an existing setup and how it looks like for better understanding. When the account is created, the default domain was **SPmcse.onmicrosoft.com**. Added custom domain **spmcse.com** to Microsoft 365 following specific steps. Once the custom domain is added, select the domain **spmcse.com** and click on **Set as default** to make this domain the default one as shown in the following figure. Similarly, we can add the domain **BPBOnline.com** as the default domain in the current setup, as shown in the following figure:

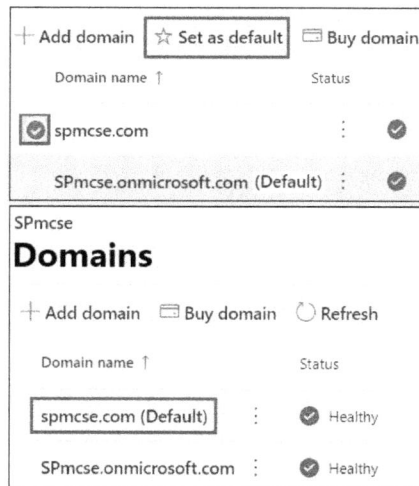

Figure 1.15: Setting custom domain as default

Primary email address and username

The user created during the Office 365 account set up will be available under the left navigation option, **Active users**. The user is linked with a default mail ID with a default domain **BPBOnline.onmicrosoft.com**. We can create our username and mail ID with the custom domain, as default. Let us perform the following steps to create a username and mail ID with the custom domain, as default:

1. Click on **Active users** from the left navigation pane. It will expand and you will find additional options like **Active users**, **Contacts**, **Guest users**, and **Deleted users**.

2. Click on **Active users**, you will find only one user under username, that is, **Admin@BPBOnline.onmicrosoft.com**. Select the user and click on **Manage username and email** as shown in the following figure:

Figure 1.16: Active users

3. Another dialog box will open on the right side of the page. You see the option **Primary email address and username** as **Admin@BPBOnline.onmicrosoft.com**, which is created by default. You can create your own **Username** and **email ID** using the custom domain as default.

4. In the field **Username** under the **Aliases** section, enter your custom name, for example **Admin**. To the right, you will find the option **Domain**. Clicking the drop-down button will display the custom domain **BPBOnline.com**. Select that domain from the drop-down.

5. Click on **Add** and then **Save changes** to apply the setting, as shown in *Figure 1.17*.

6. After that, you will see the email address under the section **Primary email address and username** are **Admin@BPBOnline.com**. The previous mail ID **Admin@BPBOnline.onmicrosoft.com** will be found at the bottom. Refer to *Figure 1.17*:

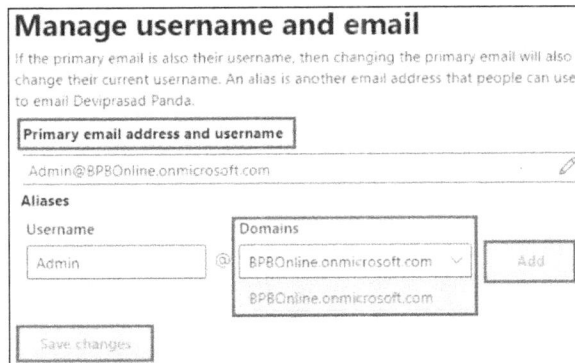

Figure 1.17: Manage username and email

7. Let us now see an existing setup and how it looks like for better understanding. In this example, **primary email address and username** is changed from the default **Devi.Panda@SPmcse.onmicrosoft.com** to **Devi.Panda@spmcse.com** as

shown in the following figure. This username is configured for personal use. For organization, you can choose as **Admin**, or something based on your company naming convention, as shown in the following figure:

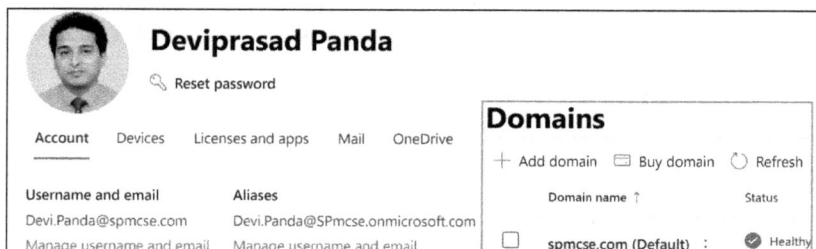

Figure 1.18: Setting custom domain and username

Manage roles

Each user is assigned specific roles in the Microsoft 365 admin center. Let us perform the following steps to understand different roles available in the Microsoft 365 admin center:

1. If you select the only user present under **Active users** and click on **Manage roles**, you will notice that the access given to this default username is **Global admin** as shown in the following figure. This is the top-level permission for Microsoft 365 admin center tenant. Refer to *Figure 1.19*:

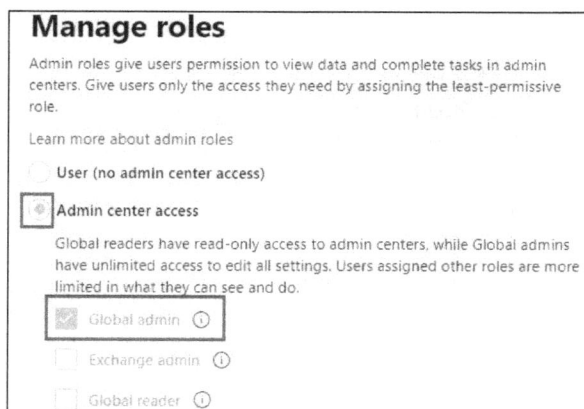

Figure 1.19: Manage roles

2. Click on **Roles** from the left navigation pane, you will see the list of all Microsoft 365/Office 365 **Roles** categorized based on business function.

3. Under the **Category Security & Compliance**, you will find **Roles** like **Attack Payload Author**, **Attack Simulation Administrator**, **Azure Information Protection admin**, **Compliance admin**, **Compliance data admin**, **Customer Lockbox access approver**, **Security admin**, and **Security operation** as shown in the following figure:

	Name	☆	Description	Category ↑
☐	Attack Payload Author	⋮ ★	Create attack payloads, but not launch or schedule them. Attack payloads are then available to all administrators who have permission to create an attack simulation.	Security & Compliance
☐	Attack Simulation Administrator	⋮ ★	Create and manage all aspects of attack simulation creation, launch and scheduling of a simulation, and the review of simulation results. Members of this role have this access for all simulations in the organization.	Security & Compliance
☐	Azure Information Protection Administrator	⋮ ★	Manages labels for the Azure Information Protection policy, manages protection templates, and activates protection.	Security & Compliance
☐	Compliance Administrator	⋮ ★	Manages regulatory requirements and eDiscovery cases, maintains data governance for locations, identities, and apps.	Security & Compliance
☐	Compliance Data Administrator	⋮ ★	Keeps track of data, makes sure it's protected, gets insights into issues, and helps mitigate risk.	Security & Compliance
☐	Customer Lockbox Access Approver	⋮ ★	Manages Customer Lockbox requests, can turn Customer Lockbox on or off.	Security & Compliance
☐	Security Administrator	⋮ ★	Controls organization's security, manages security policies, reviews security analytics and reports, monitors the threat landscape.	Security & Compliance
☐	Security Operator	⋮ ★	Investigates and responds to security alerts, manages features in Identity Protection center, monitors service health.	Security & Compliance

Figure 1.20: Security and compliance roles

4. Under the category **Devices**, you will find roles like **Cloud device administrator, Desktop Analytics administrator, Intune administrator, Printer administrator, Printer Technician, Windows 365 Administrator** as shown in the following figure:

	Name	☆	Description	Category
☐	Cloud Device Administrator	⋮	Enables, disables, and deletes devices and can read Windows 10 BitLocker keys.	Devices
☐	Desktop Analytics Administrator	⋮ ☆	Can access and manage Desktop management tools and services.	Devices
☐	Intune Administrator	⋮	Full access to Intune, manages users and devices to associate policies, creates and manages groups.	Devices
☐	Printer Administrator	⋮	Manages network printers and connectors, configures printer access and preferences, manages print status and queues, and accepts admin consent permissions.	Devices
☐	Printer Technician	⋮	Can register and unregister printers and update printer status.	Devices
☐	Windows 365 Administrator	⋮	Provision and manage all aspects of Cloud PCs.	Devices

Figure 1.21: Devices roles

5. Under the category **Identity**, you will find roles like **Application admin, Application developer, Authentication administrator, Cloud application administrator, Conditional Access administrator, Domain Name Administrator, External identity provider administrator, Guest inviter, Helpdesk administrator,**

Hybrid Identity administrator, License administrator, Password administrator, Privileged **authentication administrator, Privileged role administrator, User administrator,** and **Global admin** as shown in the following figure:

	Name	☆	Description	Category
☐	Global Administrator	⋮ ☆	Has unlimited access to all management features and most data in all admin centers.	Global
☐	Application Administrator	⋮	Full access to enterprise applications, application registrations, and application proxy settings.	Identity
☐	Application Developer	⋮	Create application registrations and consent to app access on their own behalf.	Identity
☐	Authentication Administrator	⋮	Can require users to re-register authentication for non-password credentials, like MFA.	Identity
☐	Cloud Application Administrator	⋮	Full access to enterprise applications and application registrations. No application proxy.	Identity
☐	Conditional Access Administrat...	⋮	Manages Azure Active Directory conditional access settings, but not Exchange ActiveSync conditional access policy.	Identity
☐	Domain Name Administrator	⋮	Add and remove domain names for both on-premises and cloud deployments, and read and update all properties for domains.	Identity
☐	External Identity Provider Admi...	⋮	Configure identity providers for use in direct federation.	Identity
☐	Guest Inviter	⋮	Manages Azure Active Directory B2B guest user invitations.	Identity
☐	Helpdesk Administrator	⋮	Resets passwords and re-authenticates for all non-admins and some admin roles, manages service requests, and monitors service health.	Identity
☐	Hybrid Identity Administrator	⋮	Full access to manage Azure AD Connect cloud provisioning.	Identity
☐	License Administrator	⋮	Assigns and removes licenses from users and edits their usage location.	Identity
☐	Password Administrator	⋮	Resets passwords for all non-admin users and some admin roles.	Identity
☐	Privileged Authentication Admi...	⋮	Resets passwords, updates non-password credentials, forces users to sign out, monitors service health, and manages service requests.	Identity
☐	Privileged Role Administrator	⋮	Manages role assignments and manages all access control features of Privileged Identity Management.	Identity
☐	User Administrator	⋮	Resets user passwords, creates and manages users and groups, including filters, manages service requests, and monitors service health.	Identity

Figure 1.22: Identity and global roles

6. Under the category **Read-only**, you will find roles like **Global Reader, Message Center Privacy Reader, Message Center Reader, Reports Reader, Security Reader, Usage Summary Reports Reader** and under category **Other** you will find roles like **Domain Name Administrator, Attribute Assignment Reader, Attribute Definition Administrator, Attribute Definition Reader, Authentication Extensibility Administrator, Billing Admin, Edge Administrator, Microsoft Hardware Warranty Administrator, Microsoft Hardware Warranty Specialist, Organizational Messages Writer, Service support administrator, User Experience Success Manager, Viva Pulse Administrator** as shown in the following figure:

Name		Description	Category ↑
☐ Attribute Assignment Administrator	⋮	Assigns and removes custom security attribute keys and values for objects such as users, devices, and service principals.	Other
☐ Attribute Assignment Reader	⋮	Reads custom security attribute keys and values for objects such as users, devices, and service principals.	Other
☐ Attribute Definition Administrator	⋮	Defines, activates, and deactivates custom security attributes that can be assigned to objects such as users, devices, and service principals.	Other
☐ Attribute Definition Reader	⋮	Reads the definitions of custom security attributes that can be assigned to objects such as users, devices, and service principals.	Other
☐ Authentication Extensibility Administrator	⋮	Customize sign in and sign up experiences for users by creating and managing custom authentication extensions.	Other
☐ Billing Administrator	⋮	Makes purchases, manages subscriptions, manages service requests, and monitors service health.	Other
☐ Edge Administrator	⋮ ☆	Manage the site list for Internet Explorer mode in Microsoft Edge	Other
☐ Microsoft Hardware Warranty Administr...	⋮	Create and manage all aspects warranty claims and entitlements for Microsoft manufactured hardware, like Surface and HoloLens.	Other
☐ Microsoft Hardware Warranty Specialist	⋮	Create and read warranty claims for Microsoft manufactured hardware, like Surface and HoloLens.	Other
☐ Organizational Messages Writer	⋮	Write, publish, manage, and review the organizational messages for end-users through Microsoft product surfaces.	Other
☐ Service Support Administrator	⋮	Creates service requests for Azure, Microsoft 365, and Microsoft 365 services, and monitors service health.	Other
☐ User Experience Success Manager	⋮	View product feedback, survey results, and reports to find training and communication opportunities.	Other
☐ Viva Pulse Administrator	⋮	Can manage all settings for Microsoft Viva Pulse app	Other
☐ Global Reader	⋮	Can view all administrative features and settings in all admin centers.	Read-only
☐ Message Center Privacy Reader	⋮	Access to data privacy messages in Message Center, gets email notifications, has read-only access to users, groups, domains, and subscriptions.	Read-only
☐ Message Center Reader	⋮	Reads and shares regular messages in Message Center, gets email notifications, has read-only access to users, groups, domains, and subscriptions.	Read-only
☐ Reports Reader	⋮	Reads usage reporting data from the reports dashboard, Power BI adoption content pack, sign-in reports, and Microsoft Graph reporting API.	Read-only
☐ Security Reader	⋮	Read-only access to security features, sign-in reports, and audit logs.	Read-only
☐ Usage Summary Reports Reader	⋮	Reads Usage reports and Adoption Score, but can't access user details.	Read-only

Figure 1.23: Read-only and other roles

7. Under category **Collaboration**, you will find roles like **Authentication Policy Administrator, Cloud App Security Administrator, Dynamics 365 Admin, Exchange Admin, Exchange Recipient Administrator, Fabric Administrator, Groups Admin, Identity Governance Administrator, Insights Administrator, Insights Analyst, Insight Business Leader, Kaizala Admin, Knowledge Administrator, Knowledge Manager, Network Admin, Office Apps Admin, Power Platform Admin, Search Admin, Search Editor, SharePoint Admin, Skype For Business Admin, Teams Administrator, Teams Communication Admin,**

Teams Communication Support Engineer, Teams Communication Support Specialist, Teams Device Administrator, Virtual Visits Administrator, Viva Goals Administrator, Windows Update Deployment Administrator, Yammer Administrator as shown in the following figure:

☑ Name		Description	Category ↑
☐ Authentication Policy Administrator		Configures the authentication methods policy, organization-wide MFA settings, and password protection policies.	Collaboration
☐ Cloud App Security Administrator	⋮	Manages all aspects of Microsoft Cloud App Security.	Collaboration
☐ Dynamics 365 Administrator	⋮	Full access to Microsoft Dynamics 365 Online, manages service requests, monitors service health.	Collaboration
☐ Exchange Administrator	⋮	Full access to Exchange Online, creates and manages groups, manages service requests, and monitors service health.	Collaboration
☐ Exchange Recipient Administrator	⋮	Manages all aspects of recipients, message tracking, and the migration of recipients to Exchange Online.	Collaboration
☐ Fabric Administrator	⋮	Full access to Microsoft Fabric management tasks, manages service requests, and monitors service health.	Collaboration
☐ Groups Administrator		Creates and manages groups, including group naming and expiration policies, views activity and audit reports, monitors service health.	Collaboration
☐ Identity Governance Administrator	⋮	Manages access to resources in Azure AD entitlement management	Collaboration
☐ Insights Administrator	⋮	Full access to the Microsoft 365 Insights application, reads Azure AD properties, monitors service health, and manages service requests.	Collaboration
☐ Insights Analyst	⋮	Access the analytical capabilities in Microsoft Viva Insights and run custom queries.	Collaboration
☐ Insights Business Leader	⋮	Reads Microsoft 365 Insights application reports and insights.	Collaboration
☐ Kaizala Administrator	⋮	Full access to all Kaizala management features and data, manages service requests.	Collaboration
☐ Knowledge Administrator	⋮	Can configure the knowledge network and content understanding.	Collaboration
☐ Knowledge Manager	⋮	Creates and manages content and content centers, maintains the quality and structure of knowledge, and manages taxonomies for term store management.	Collaboration
☐ Network Administrator		Manage network locations and view network performance recommendations and insights.	Collaboration
☐ Office Apps Administrator	⋮	Manages settings, policies, and deployment of Office apps.	Collaboration
☐ Power Platform Administrator	⋮	Full access to Microsoft Dynamics 365, PowerApps, data loss prevention policies, and Power Automate.	Collaboration
☐ Search Administrator	⋮	Full access to Microsoft Search, assigns the Search Administrator and Search Editor roles, manages editorial content, monitors service health, and creates service requests.	Collaboration
☐ Search Editor	⋮	Can only create, edit, and delete content for Microsoft Search, like bookmarks, Q&A, and locations.	Collaboration
☐ SharePoint Administrator	⋮	Full access to SharePoint Online, manages Microsoft 365 groups, manages service requests, and monitors service health.	Collaboration
☐ Skype for Business Administrator	⋮	Full access to all Teams and Skype features, Skype user attributes, manages service requests, and monitors service health.	Collaboration
☐ Teams Administrator	⋮	Full access to Teams & Skype admin center, manages Microsoft 365 groups and service requests, and monitors service health.	Collaboration
☐ Teams Communication Administrator	☆	Assigns telephone numbers, creates and manages voice and meeting policies, and reads call analytics.	Collaboration
☐ Teams Communication Support Engineer	⋮	Reads call record details for all call participants to troubleshoot communication issues.	Collaboration
☐ Teams Communication Support Specialist	⋮	Reads user call details only for a specific user to troubleshoot communication issues.	Collaboration
☐ Teams Device Administrator	⋮	Configure and manage devices used for Microsoft Teams services, like Teams Rooms, Teams displays, and phones.	Collaboration
☐ Virtual Visits Administrator	⋮	Manage and share Virtual Visits information and metrics from admin centers or the Virtual Visits app.	Collaboration
☐ Viva Goals Administrator	⋮	Manage and configure all policies of Microsoft Viva Goals.	Collaboration
☐ Windows Update Deployment Administr..	⋮ ☆	Create and manage all aspects of Windows Update deployments through the Windows Update for Business deployment service.	Collaboration
☐ Yammer Administrator	⋮	Manage all aspects of the Yammer service.	Collaboration

Figure 1.24: Collaboration roles

Assigning SharePoint admin role

Only Global administrators can manage permission for the user account, and central admin. Based on roles and responsibility in business function, admin access is assigned to specific service. SharePoint admin roles are present under the category of Collaboration. Users identified as SharePoint administrators are given access from here. Follow these steps to assign SharePoint Admin role:

1. Select Active users | Manage roles | User

2. Select Admin center access

3. Click the checkbox SharePoint admin and click on Save changes to provide access to SharePoint admin center as shown in the following figure. It is only after the access is given, that the user can access SharePoint admin center, as shown in Figure 1.25:

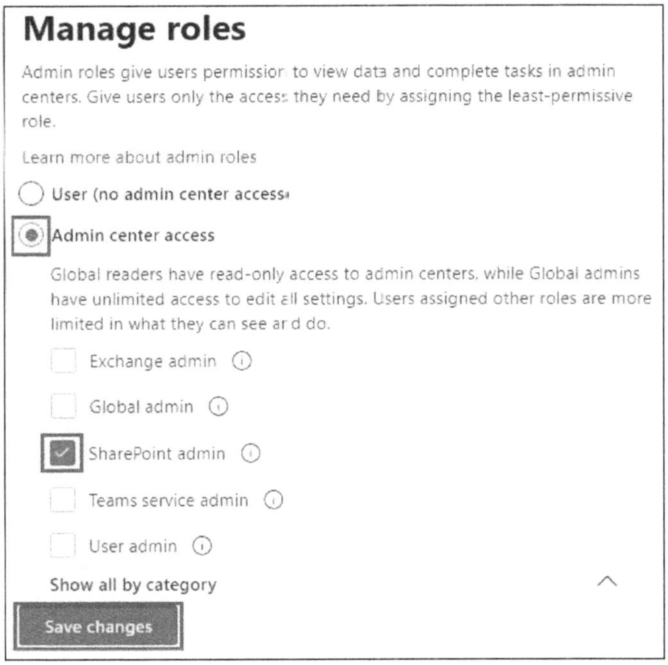

Manage roles

Admin roles give users permission to view data and complete tasks in admin centers. Give users only the access they need by assigning the least-permissive role.

Learn more about admin roles

◯ User (no admin center access)

◉ Admin center access

Global readers have read-only access to admin centers, while Global admins have unlimited access to edit all settings. Users assigned other roles are more limited in what they can see and do.

☐ Exchange admin ⓘ

☐ Global admin ⓘ

☑ SharePoint admin ⓘ

☐ Teams service admin ⓘ

☐ User admin ⓘ

Show all by category ︿

Save changes

Figure 1.25: Assign SharePoint admin permission

SharePoint admin center tour

After the SharePoint admin access is provided, click on **SharePoint** from the **Microsoft 365 admin center** present under **Admin centers** in the left navigation pane. You will be redirected to **SharePoint admin center** in a new tab from your browser. We added **BPBOnline.com** as a domain while setting up Office 365 account. So, URL of SharePoint admin center will be **https://bpbonline-admin.sharepoint.com/**. In our personal setup, we have added **spmcse.com** as a domain so my SharePoint admin center URL will be **https://spmcse-admin.sharepoint.com/**. From now on, we will use this Admin center URL throughout this book.

In this section, we will discuss the home page/landing page of SharePoint admin center. Please find the step-by-step information mentioned further to understand this better.

Once the admin center is open, you will see the **SharePoint admin center** home page (**AdminHome.aspx**). The home page includes a navigation section and the content section. The left side of the home page contains navigation options, and the right side of the page contains the content section, as shown in the following figure:

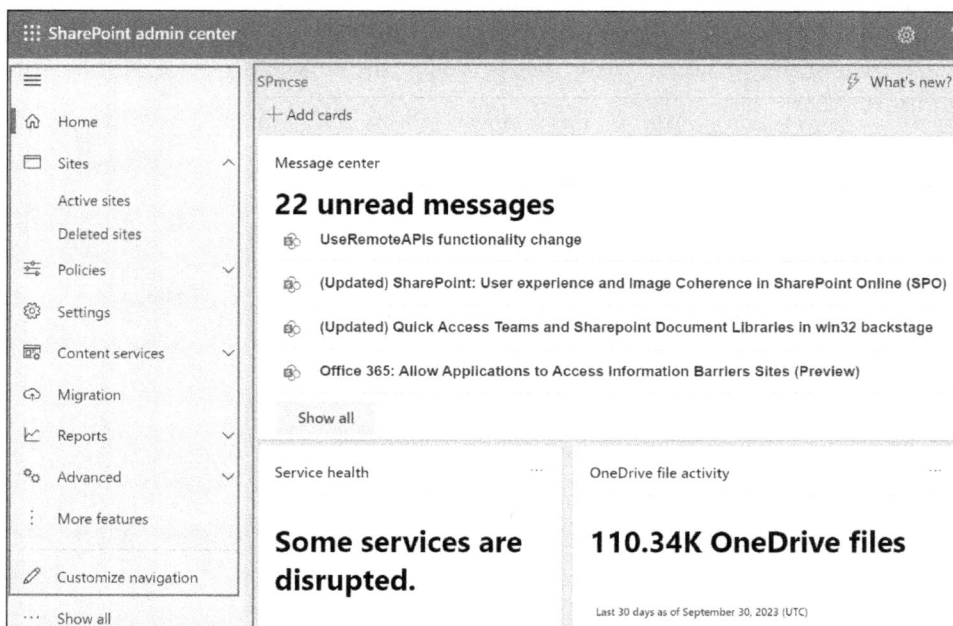

Figure 1.26: SharePoint admin center home page

Navigation section

The navigation section of SharePoint admin center includes options like **Home**, **Sites**, **Policies**, **Settings**, **Content Services**, **Migration**, **Reports**, **Advanced**, **More features**, and **Customize navigation**. Let us perform the following steps to understand SharePoint admin center better:

1. Click the first option in the left navigation, **Sites**. It will expand and you will see two options: **Active sites**, **Deleted sites**. **Active sites** contain all the site collections that are active or live, and the **Deleted sites** contain all site collections that got deleted. These options can be seen in the following figure:

Figure 1.27: Active sites and Deleted sites

2. The next option in the left navigation will be **Policies**. Clicking on **Policies** will expand, and you will find options like **Sharing** and **Access control** as shown in the following figure:

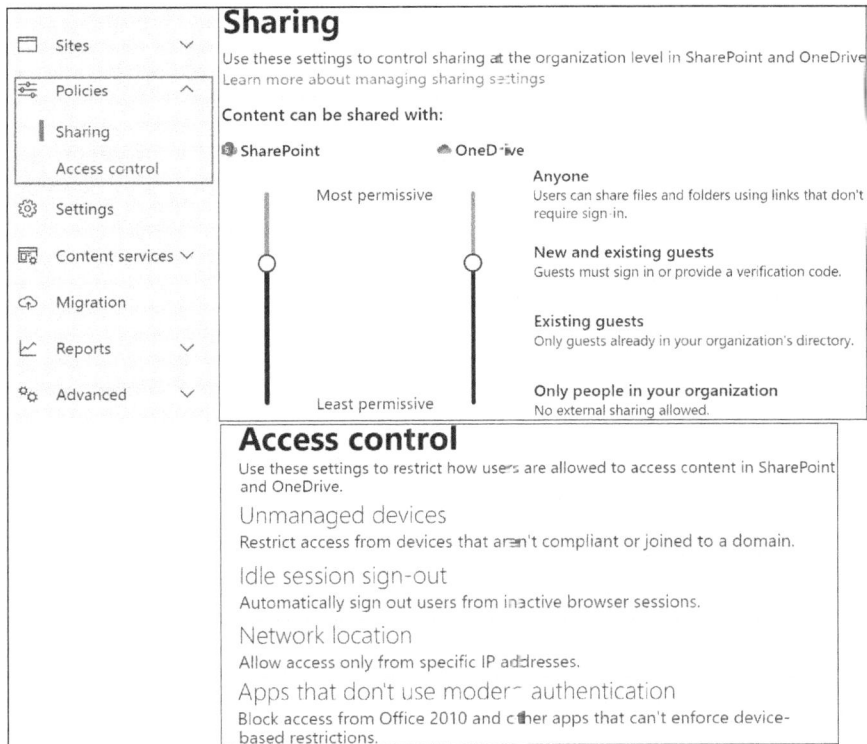

Figure 1.28: Sharing and access control under policies

3. The next option will be **Settings**. Clicking on that will show you options like **Default admin center**, **Pages**, **SharePoint notifications**, **Site creation**, and **Site storage limits** as shown in the following figure:

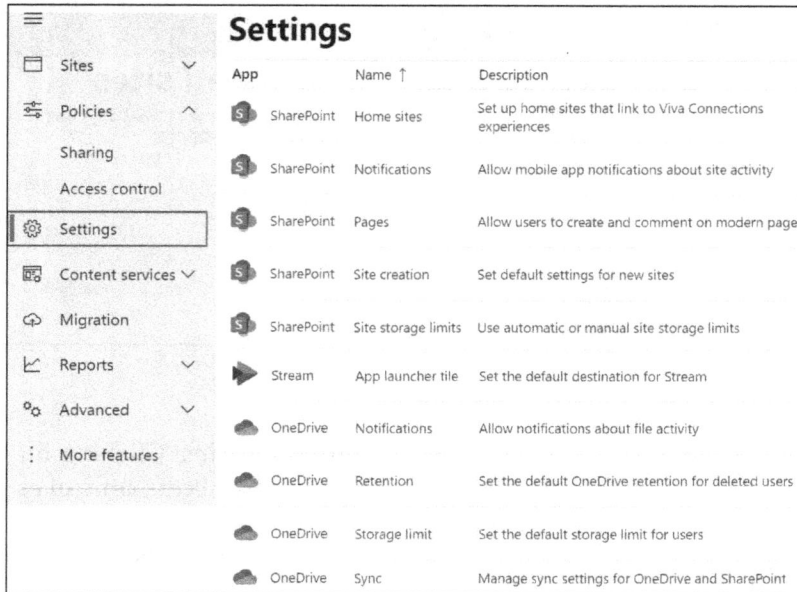

Figure 1.29: Settings

4. Further, we have **Content services**. Clicking on **Content services**, it will expand, and you will find options like **Term store**, and **Content type gallery** as shown in the following figure:

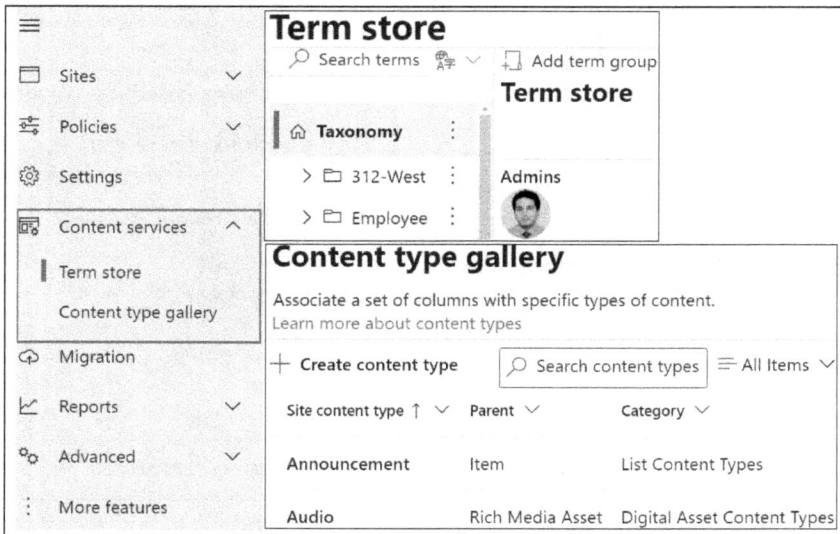

Figure 1.30: Term store and content type gallery under content source

5. Next option in the left navigation is **Migration** which on clicking gives the list of supported applications (contents of which can be migrated to Microsoft 365)

categorized as **Migration Manager**, and **Other migration solutions**, as shown in the following figure:

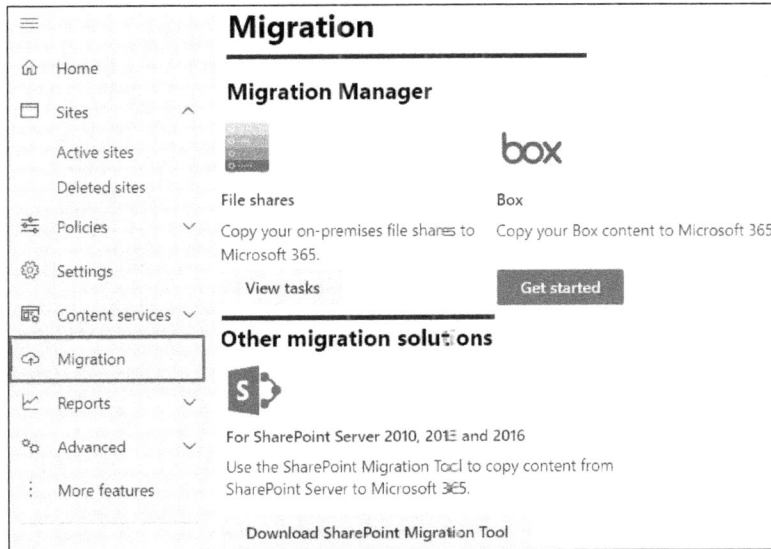

Figure 1.31: Migration

6. The next option in left navigation **More features**. Clicking on that will show you all features available in SharePoint like **Term store**, **User profile**, **Search**, **Apps**, **BCS**, **Secure store**, **Record management**, **InfoPath**, and **Hybrid picker** as shown in the following figure:

Figure 1.32: More features

7. Next, we have **Customize navigation**. Clicking on that will provide you with the list of options to show or hide in the left navigation. Uncheck any option and click on **Save** to apply the changes as shown in the following figure:

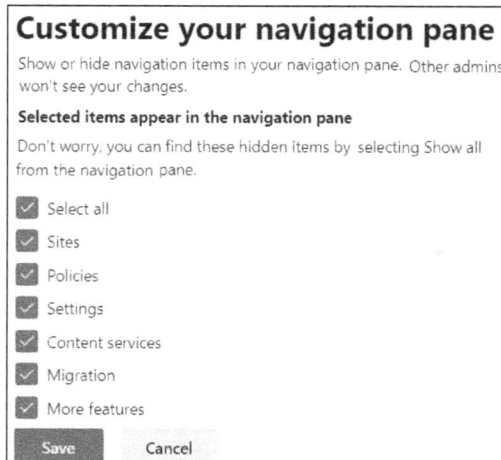

Figure 1.33: *Customize navigation*

Content section

The content section of the home page represents a dashboard that holds all activity or usage details in the form of a graphical representation. You will see different blocks or zones of dashboard in the home page holding a specific set of details. Each block in this section is called Cards. We can customize the home page dashboard by adding or removing cards, as per the requirement. Several types of cards are available like **OneDrive file activity**, **Service health**, **SharePoint file activity report**, and **Message center** as shown in the following figure:

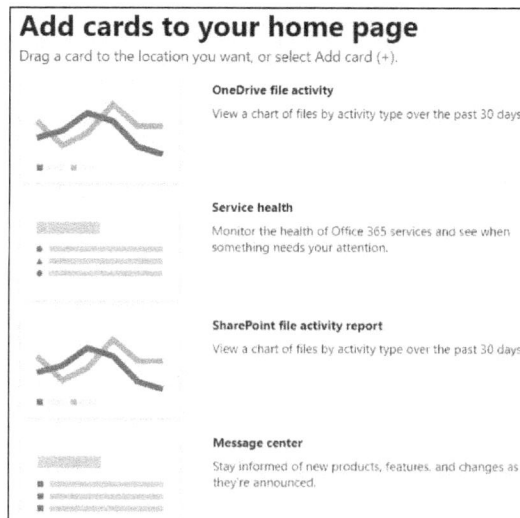

Figure 1.34: *OneDrive file activity, service health, SharePoint file activity report, message center card*

More cards that can be added are **SharePoint site search, Microsoft 365 active users report, Information barriers in OneDrive,** and **SharePoint storage usage** as shown in the following figure:

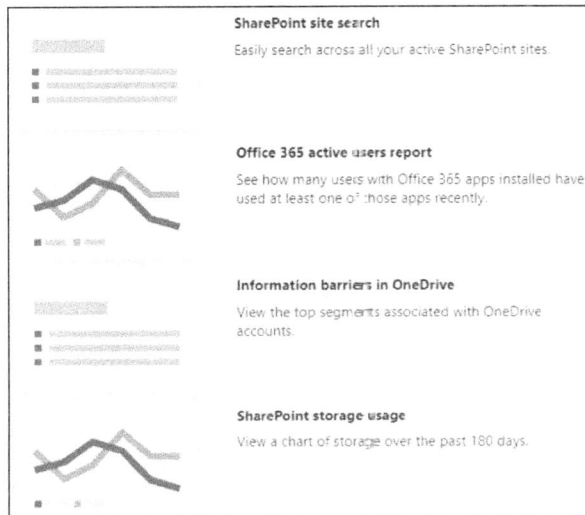

Figure 1.35: *SharePoint site search, Office 365 active users report, information barriers in OneDrive, SharePoint storage usage card*

Some other cards include **SharePoint site usage report, Sensitivity labels, OneDrive usage, Information barriers in SharePoint,** and **Track views** as shown in the following figure:

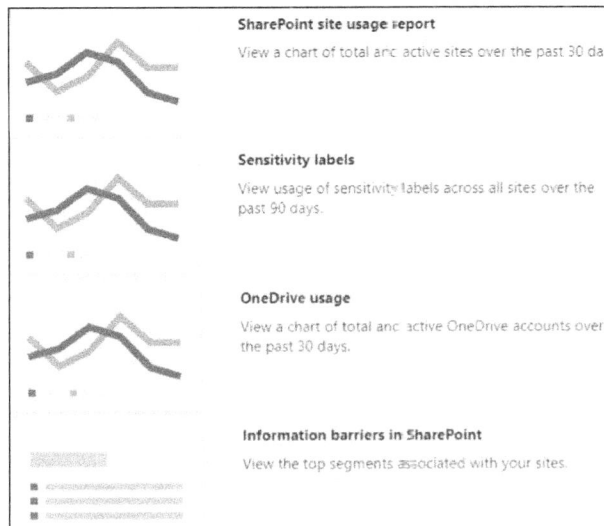

Figure 1.36: *SharePoint site usage report, sensitivity labels, OneDrive usage, information barriers in SharePoint*

These cards are helpful to monitor SharePoint usage or other activities to manage SharePoint sites better.

Message center

Message center acts as a primary mode of communication with users to share any update. Microsoft uses this card to send information related to your Microsoft 365 service like upcoming features that are going to be rolled out to your tenant, changes in existing features, announcements, any planned maintenance activity, and so on. Users who have **Message center** Reader Role can access these messages. Message center Card will be available in SharePoint admin center as shown in the following figure:

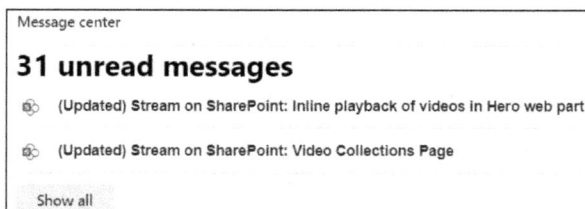

Figure 1.37: Message center card

You will see the latest unread messages on the card. Click on the **Message**. You will see more details of that message like **Message Summary**, **When this will happen**, **How this affects your organization**, and **What you can do to prepare** as shown in the following figure:

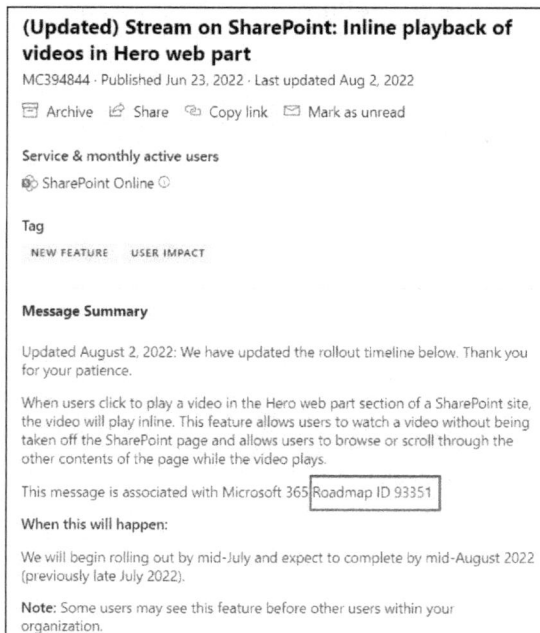

Figure 1.38: Message details

This will help users remain updated with the latest changes in SharePoint. The administrator will be updated about the impact of this change on tenant level, so that they can prepare accordingly to proceed for the next action on this change. The effect of this change is mentioned in the following figure:

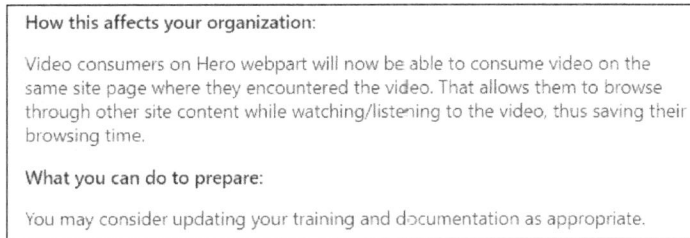

How this affects your organization:

Video consumers on Hero webpart will now be able to consume video on the same site page where they encountered the video. That allows them to browse through other site content while watching/listening to the video, thus saving their browsing time.

What you can do to prepare:

You may consider updating your training and documentation as appropriate.

Figure 1.39: Effect of change in message detail

Service health

Service health card will display the Microsoft Service Health. From this status, administrators can know if the SharePoint service is healthy or if an advisory is present. If there is any issue, you will see the advisories in the card **Service health** as shown in the following figure:

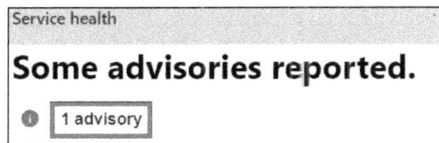

Service health

Some advisories reported.

● 1 advisory

Figure 1.40: Service health card

Click on the message **Advisory**. You will be redirected to the page **Microsoft service health**. Under the section **Active issues**, you will find advisories along with issue subject line under the column **Issue title** as shown in the following figure:

Active issues		
∨ Issue title	Affected service	Issue type
∨ Microsoft service health (4)		
Admins are unable to utilize search verticals via SharePoint ...	SharePoint Online	Advisory
Users may encounter crashes when launching the Skype for...	Skype for Business	Advisory
Admins don't receive Data Loss Prevention (DLP) alerts in th...	Exchange Online	Advisory
Some users intermittently can't send or open email messag...	Exchange Online	Advisory
Issues in your environment that require action (0)		

Figure 1.41: Advisory

If service health is good, then you will find the status column under the section **Microsoft service health** as **Healthy** as shown in the following figure:

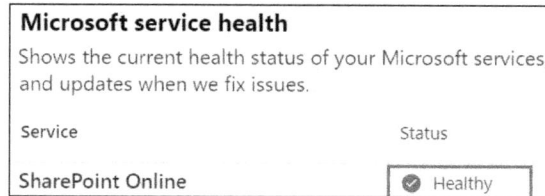

Figure 1.42: *Microsoft service health status*

Microsoft 365 active users report

Microsoft 365 services and app usage information by number of unique active users is stored in this card. You will find the number of active users' usage reports on various applications like **Microsoft Teams, Exchange, Office 365, OneDrive, SharePoint, Skype for Business** and **Yammer** are displayed in different color code as shown in the following figure:

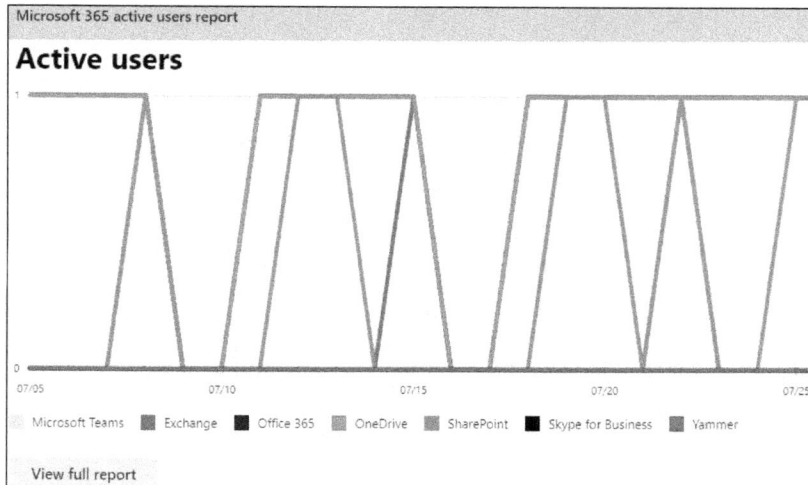

Figure 1.43: *Microsoft 365 active users*

Click on the option **View full report** present in the card to see more details on report.

SharePoint file activity report

Activities happening on SharePoint files are displayed by this card. This indicates how many SharePoint files got viewed or edited by users, how many files synchronized (total number of SharePoint files present), how many SharePoint files shared internally and how many shared to external users in 30 days as shown in the following figure:

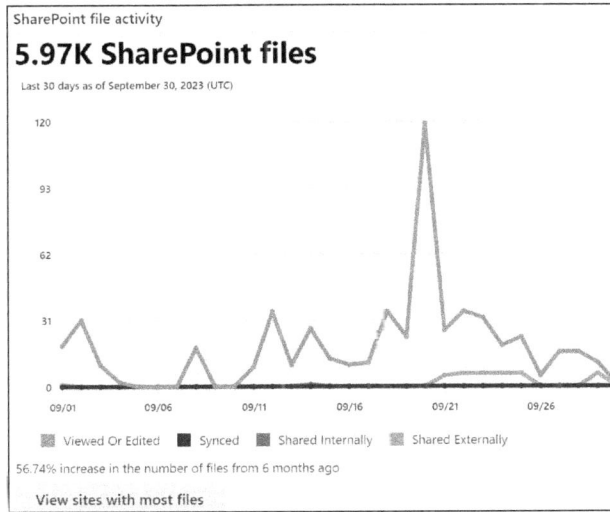

Figure 1.44: SharePoint file activity

OneDrive file activity

Activities happening on OneDrive files are displayed by this card. This indicates how many OneDrive files got viewed or edited by users, how many files synchronized (total number of OneDrive files present) how many OneDrive files shared to internal users and how many shared to external users in last 30 days as shown in the following figure:

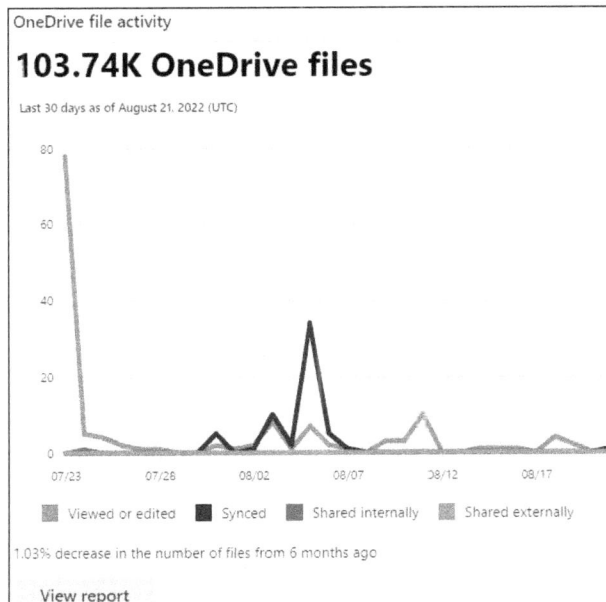

Figure 1.45: OneDrive file activity

SharePoint site usage report

Activities happen on the sites are called active sites. This card displays the percentage of active sites. You can see total sites present as well as active sites in last 30 days as shown in the following figure:

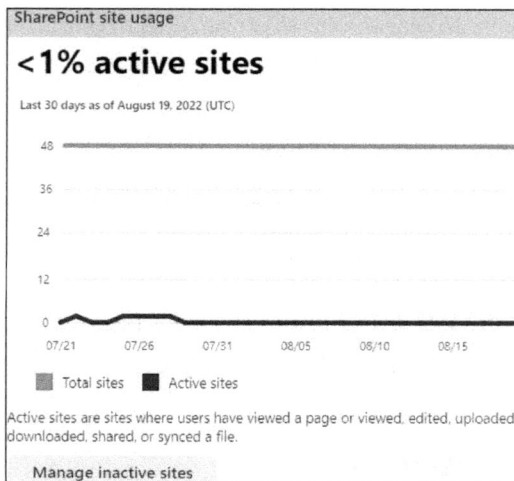

Figure 1.46: *SharePoint site usage*

OneDrive usage

The number of users who did any activity in OneDrive are called active users. This card displays the percentage of active OneDrive accounts. You can see the total OneDrive accounts present as well as active accounts in the last 30 days as shown in the following figure:

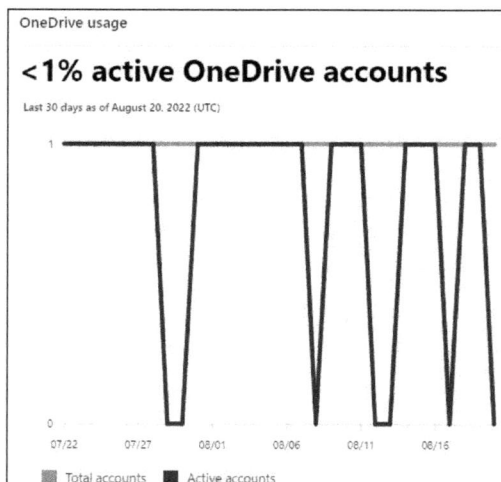

Figure 1.47: *OneDrive usage*

SharePoint storage usage

This card displays SharePoint storage usage details over the last 180 days. The percentage of space consumed over the allocated storage. This will be helpful to analyze and monitor the rate of memory spaces required in SharePoint as shown in the following figure:

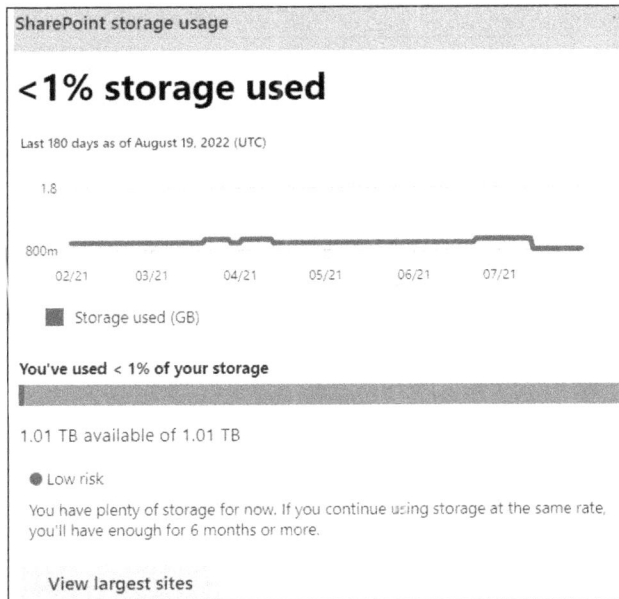

Figure 1.48: *SharePoint storage usage*

Sensitivity labels

This card holds information about the usage of labels applied in the sites. If sensitivity label is configured, then information will be displayed here as shown in the following figure:

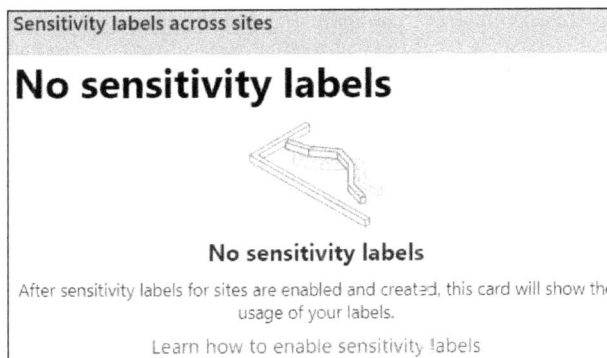

Figure 1.49: *Sensitivity labels*

SharePoint site search

There will be thousands of sites in SharePoint admin center. As an administrator you must take action on any specific site from that list of sites present in the organization. This card makes it easy for you to search the site. Enter the keyword to search as shown in the following figure:

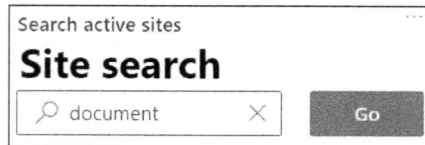

Figure 1.50: *Enter search query in search bar*

You will find a list of active sites related to the keyword as search result as shown in the following figure. You can pass more specific details to get more specific result:

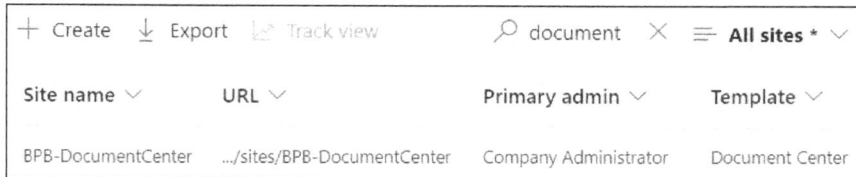

Figure 1.51: *Search result*

Information barriers in SharePoint

Information barriers are additional compliance policies that can be configured to prevent unauthorized collaboration and communication. This is configured where compliance requirements are very strict like finance, legal, and government. When the information barrier is configured and applied in organizations, activity reports will be displayed on this card, as shown in the following figure:

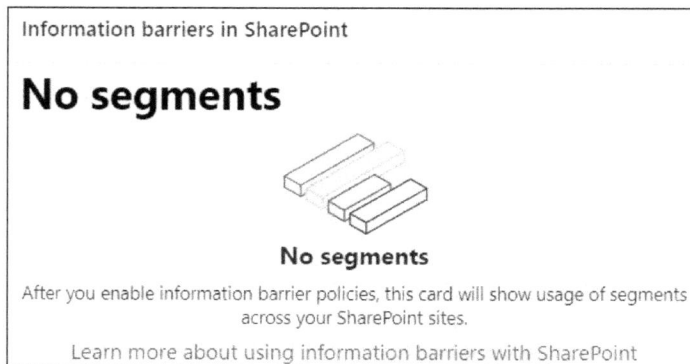

Figure 1.52: *Information barriers in SharePoint*

Information barriers in OneDrive

Information barriers are additional compliance policies that can be configured to prevent unauthorized collaboration and communication. This is configured where compliance requirements are very strict, mostly in finance, legal, and government. Activity reports will be displayed on this card when the information barrier is configured and applied in organizations, as shown in the following figure:

Figure 1.53: Information barriers in OneDrive

Track views

This card displays the percentage of inactive sites, the percentage of external sharing sites and the percentage of sites connected to Microsoft 365 group as shown in the following figure:

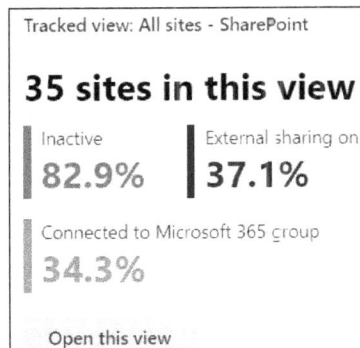

Figure 1.54: Tracked views of all sites

Scope of administrator

SharePoint Online Administrator is responsible for managing all backend activities in SharePoint Online from central admin since it is accessible only by administrator. If you think from central admin left navigation point of view, the following are the list of activities that come under SharePoint admin scope:

- Creating and Deleting Site collection.
- Manage site admins for site collections.
- Applying policies related to Sharing and Access control.
- Manage Settings related to Pages, Storage, Notification, Site creation.
- Managing Term store and Content type gallery.
- Migration of sites to SharePoint Online.
- Manage other features like User profile, Search, Apps, BCS, Secure store, Records management, Hybrid picker.

Conclusion

In this chapter, we discussed the basics of the SharePoint admin center, created an Office 365 account, and configured the default organizational domain. We understood the process of setting up a primary email address and username and got clarity about the options available in the Microsoft 365 admin center. We got an overall idea about the roles available in the Microsoft 365 admin center and how to assign users an administrator role. We finally explained the roles and responsibilities of an administrator.

In the next chapter, *Chapter 2, Site Administration*, we will discuss the options available under the left navigation **Sites** and its application.

Points to remember

- Regular changes are applied in Office 365 and SharePoint Online. There may be changes in the template or some other features with time.

Join our book's Discord space

Join the book's Discord Workspace for Latest updates, Offers, Tech happenings around the world, New Release and Sessions with the Authors:

https://discord.bpbonline.com

CHAPTER 2
Site
Administration

Introduction

In the previous *Chapter 1, SharePoint Admin Center Home*, we got a clear idea about the Office 365 account setup, custom domain setup, assigning admin permission to the users to access the SharePoint admin center, and the options available in the SharePoint admin center. In this chapter, we will discuss one of the options, Sites from left navigation in the SharePoint admin center, and understand how to administer the site using this option from the admin center. As we have already discussed, SharePoint is all about sites. A site is a container of content types, and each contains a specific type of content. In SharePoint online, the site resides at the top-level, which can be created and managed in the central admin. This chapter focuses on the options available under the left navigation Sites and its applications.

Structure

In this chapter, we will discuss the following topics:

- Active sites
- Creating site with a modern approach
- Export site information
- Search sites
- Views

- Manage membership
- Hub
- Sharing
- Delete site
- Edit site
- Your recent actions
- Storage
- Deleted site
- Restore site
- Permanently delete site

Objectives

By the end of this chapter, you will get a clear understanding about various options available under the left navigation option, Sites, Active sites, Deleted sites in SharePoint admin center. You will get an idea about the types of site templates available in SharePoint and how site templates are helpful towards creation of sites. You will learn how to export sites list to `.csv` file, search sites smartly for quick results. You will understand about view, save and delete view, how to set any view as a default. You will get to know the types of membership available to manage permission on site and everything related to sharing. You will understand what hub site is, how to edit site and storage. You will get to know the types of site activities that you can check and all about deleting and restoring sites.

Active sites

The first option in the left navigation is Home, the landing page of the SharePoint admin center. Next to Home, you will find an option Site that holds all information or actions related to sites. The information or actions related to site is categorized into two options Active sites and Deleted sites. In this section, we will discuss which option under Sites holds what information or actions, in detail. Let us discuss the following steps to understand it better:

1. Click on Sites from the left navigation. It will expand, and you will find two options, **Active sites** and **Deleted sites**, as shown in *Figure 2.1*:

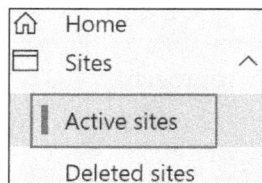

Figure 2.1: *Left navigation option sites*

2. As the name suggests, Active sites hold information about active, live, or working sites in SharePoint.

3. Click on Active sites from the left navigation, and you will find all sites in the tenant as a list, and options like **Create**, **Export**, **Track view**, **Your recent actions**, **Search**, **Views**, **Membership**, **Hub**, **Sharing**, **Delete**, and **Storage** in the command bar as seen in *Figure 2.2*. The options present in the command bar are used to take different actions related to the site.

4. Options like Membership, Hub, Sharing, Delete, and Storage will be available in the command bar once you select a site from the list.

5. The sites present under the **Active sites** list hold properties like Site name, URL, Teams, Channel sites, Storage used (GB), Primary admin, Hub, Template, Last activity (UTC), Date created, Created by, Storage limit (GB), Storage used (%), Files viewed or edited, Page views, Page visits, Files, and Sensitivity.

In the next section, we will discuss the actions that can be taken using the command bar:

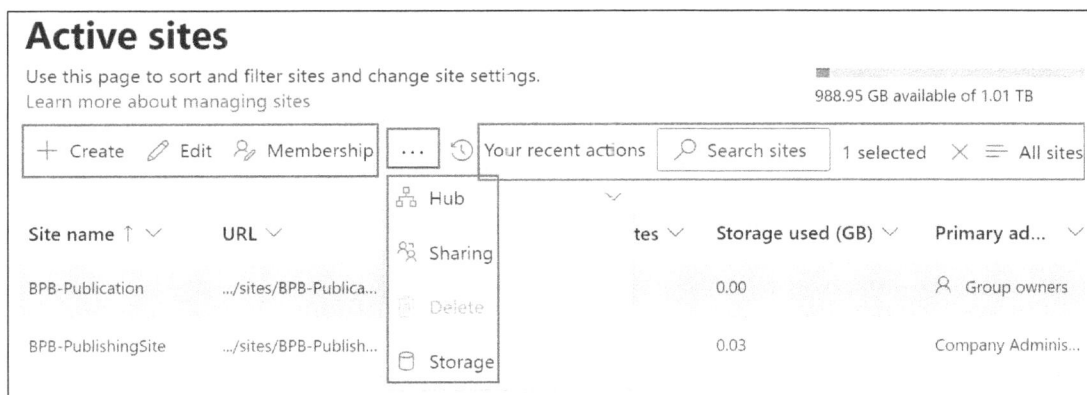

Figure 2.2: Active sites list

Creating site with a modern approach

In the previous section, *Active sites*, we learned about different options available under Active sites. In this section, we will discuss one of the options, **Create**, which is used to create site from admin center. As per the process, after business approval, a user must create a request for the site with details like the Name of Site, Type of Site, and Site Owner or Site Administrator. SharePoint administrators are responsible for creating top-level sites and handing them to the site owner. Before creating a site, you need to understand the different site templates available in SharePoint. Let us discuss different site templates first and then create types of sites.

Site templates out of the box

SharePoint provides default templates considering the types of uses by customers and keeps introducing new templates by time based on customer demand. Here we will discuss different types of site templates available out of the box, which you need to select during new site creation. The different templates have different layouts and features, and the purpose of the requirement is different. Let us perform the following steps to create a new site:

1. When users want to create a new site, the user will get an option to select either a modern Team site, Communication site, Syntex content center, or any site templates present under the option Browse more sites. Modern Team site, Communication site, and Syntex content center are the new templates introduced to collaborate and communicate better. The following figure is a screenshot of the default site template options:

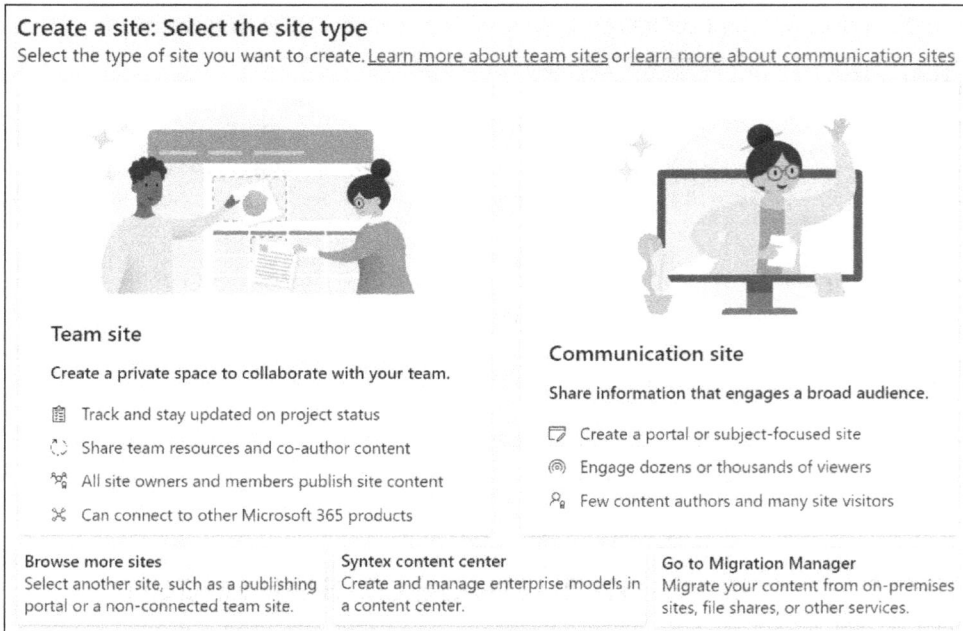

Create a site: Select the site type
Select the type of site you want to create. Learn more about team sites orlearn more about communication sites

Team site

Create a private space to collaborate with your team.

- Track and stay updated on project status
- Share team resources and co-author content
- All site owners and members publish site content
- Can connect to other Microsoft 365 products

Communication site

Share information that engages a broad audience.

- Create a portal or subject-focused site
- Engage dozens or thousands of viewers
- Few content authors and many site visitors

Browse more sites
Select another site, such as a publishing portal or a non-connected team site.

Syntex content center
Create and manage enterprise models in a content center.

Go to Migration Manager
Migrate your content from on-premises sites, file shares, or other services.

Figure 2.3: Default site template options

2. Click on the option Team site and you will get list of team site templates like **Standard team, Crisis communication team, Employee onboarding team, Event planning, IT help desk, Project management, Retail management team, Store collaboration, Training course, Training design team.**

3. Click on the option Communication site and you will get list of communication site templates like **Standard communication, Brand central, Crisis management, Department, Event, Human resources, Leadership connection, Learning central, New employee onboarding, Organization home, Showcase, Volunteer center, Blank**.

4. Proceeding further, click on **Browse more sites**. You will see templates like **Document Center, Enterprise Wiki, Publishing Portal, Content center** and option for **More templates** as shown in *Figure 2.4*:

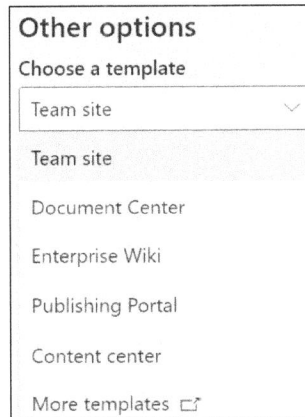

> **Other options**
>
> Choose a template
>
> | Team site ⌄ |
>
> Team site
>
> Document Center
>
> Enterprise Wiki
>
> Publishing Portal
>
> Content center
>
> More templates ⌐✓

Figure 2.4: Default site template options

5. Click on **More templates**; you will see additional templates in form of categories like **Collaboration, Enterprise, Publishing,** and **Custom**.

6. Click on the category **Collaboration** under the option **Create Site Collection | Template Selection**; you will see **Team Site (classic experience), Developer Site, Project Site,** and **Community Site** templates, which are called **Collaboration** site templates.

7. Click on the category **Enterprise**: you will see **Document Center, eDiscovery Center, Records Center, Team Site - SharePoint Online configuration, Business Intelligence Center, Compliance Policy Center, Enterprise Search Center, My Site Host, Community Portal, Basic Search Center, Visio Process Repository** templates, which are called **Enterprise site** templates.

8. Click on the category **Publishing**: you will see **Publishing Portal,** and **Enterprise Wiki** templates, which are called **Publishing** templates.

9. Click on **Custom,** where you can find customized templates implemented by developers. All site templates can be seen in the following figure:

Figure 2.5: Default site template options

Now, you got an idea about default site templates available in SharePoint, out of which you need to select any one while creating a site.

Create modern communication site

You got an idea what the site template is and what types of site templates are available in SharePoint by default. In this section, we will create a site using any one of the templates. Let us create a modern communication site. A communication site is a new template that is introduced, and it focuses more on representing content with a visually stunning format, widescreen without any left navigational element. Users can create and share news, events, reports, and showcase products with images. Mainly content is consumed by and targeted at a large audience but contributed by very few selected people. The primary purpose of communication site is to inform a broad range of people and engage. This site comes with many design templates. Topic design is mostly used for visual content related to news, events, and reports. Showcase design is used during launch and marketing-related content that is visually stunning. Similarly, each temple has its own purpose for the business requirements. However, it is important to ensure the site creation process follows the organization's governance guidance. Communication sites you can create specific to each service, topic, program, or function. The following is the step-by-step procedure to create a newly introduced communication site:

1. From the SharePoint admin center, navigate to **Active sites** present under Site in the left navigation. Click on **Create** from the command bar as shown in *Figure 2.6*:

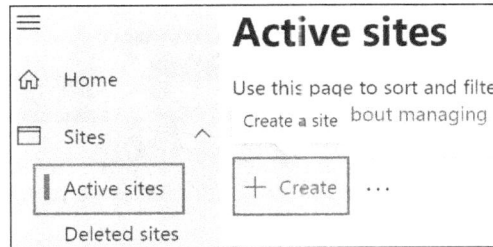

Figure 2.6: Create site

2. You will get a dialog box to select one type of site template to proceed. Click on the **Communication site** to create a new communication site, as shown in *Figure 2.7*:

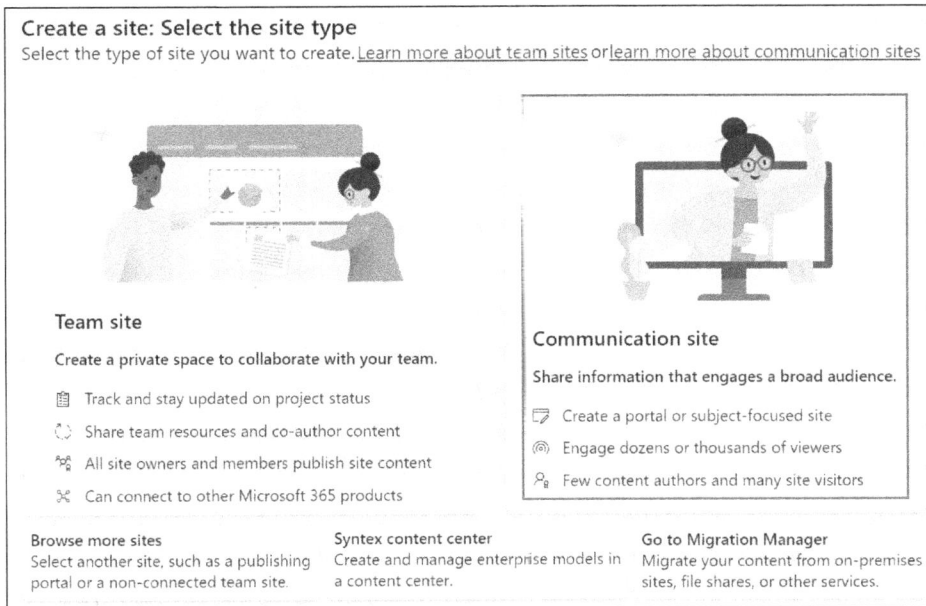

Figure 2.7: Communication site

3. The site creation wizard will open. You will get a list of communication site templates like **Standard communication, Brand central, Crisis management, Department, Event, Human resources, Leadership connection, Learning central, New employee onboarding, Organization home, Showcase, Volunteer center,** and **Blank**. Each template has a specific user interface and holds specific site capabilities. As per user requirement, the admin can suggest a template or select the template as per user requirement to proceed in the site creation process. Select one communication site template as shown in the following *Figure 2.8*:

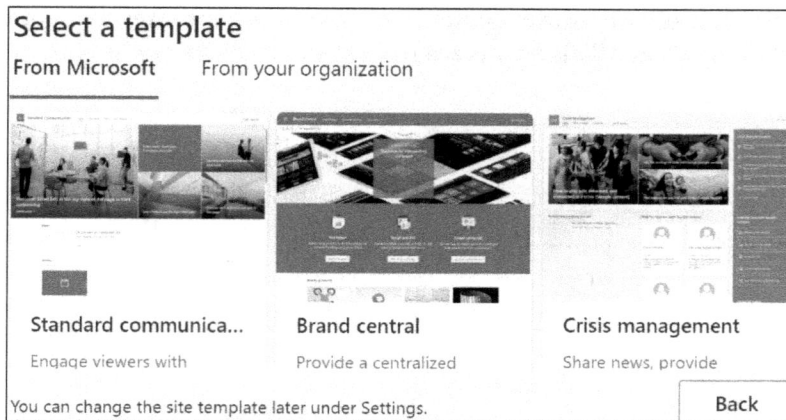

Figure 2.8: Communication site designs and fills up all fields during site creation

4. You will find more details about the site template, like **Site capabilities, What's included, Preview site,** and the button. Use the template to proceed with site creation. Click on the button **Use template** as shown in *Figure 2.9*:

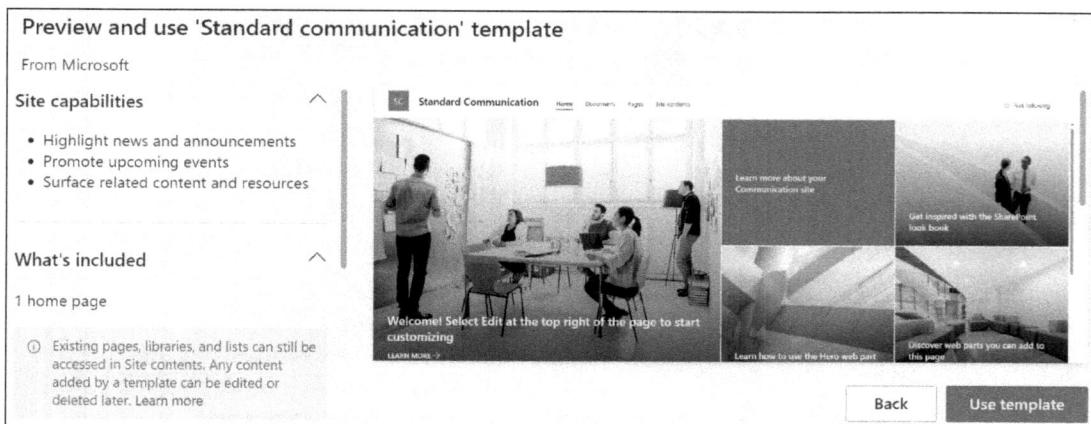

Figure 2.9: Use template

5. Enter the **Site name,** for example **BPB-ModernCommunication**.

6. Enter a few details about the site in the field. **Site description** will give an idea to the users, like what this site is for.

7. You will find the field **Site address** is automatically taken as the same name as of the site name **BPB-ModernCommunication** by default under the managed path **/sites** as shown in *Figure 2.10*. You can change the managed path of the site address from **/sites** to **/teams**. You can change the site address as per your requirement, but default is taken same as the site name. If any site with the same name and default URL already exists in the active sites list, then the new site address will be

auto-suggested close to the site name you entered. You can use the symbols in the site address, like periods, single quotes, underscores, and dashes. Other symbols are not allowed, and make sure the site address does not start or end with a period.

8. Enter the **user ID** under the field **Site owner,** who will own and manage the site and select the site's language. Click on **Next**, as shown in *Figure 2.10*:

Figure 2.10: *Enter site details*

9. Next, you will get the option to **Select a language**, **Time zone**, **Storage limit**. After selecting the detail, click on the button **Create site** as shown in *Figure 2.11*:

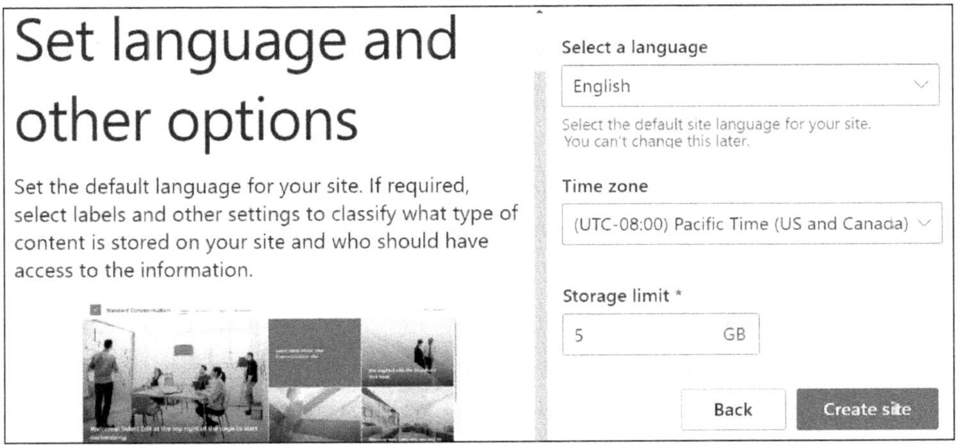

Figure 2.11: *Site a language, time zone, storage limit*

10. A standard communication site will be created with a hero web part at the top as per the following figure:

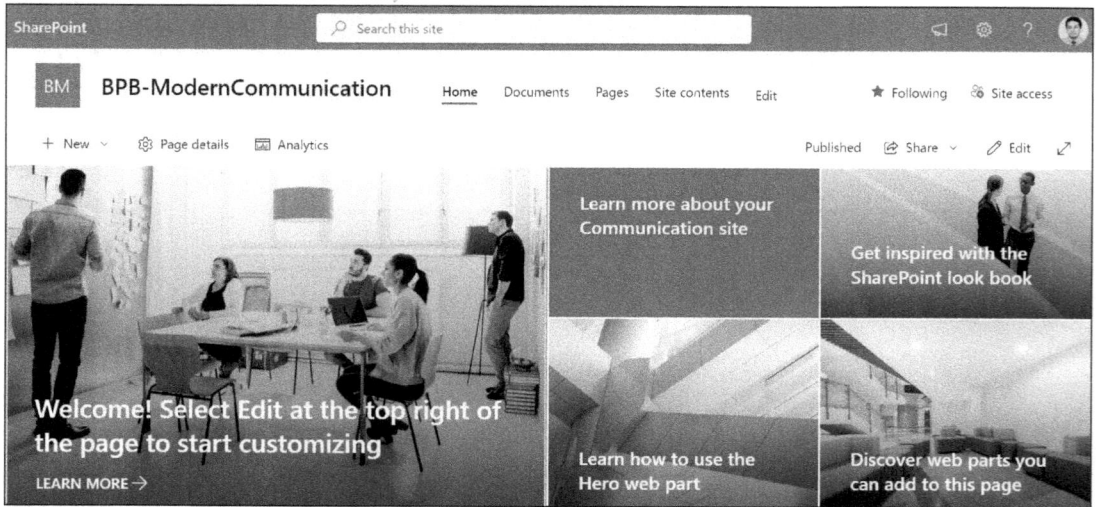

Figure 2.12: Communication site home page hero web part

11. Next to hero web part, you will find **News,** as shown in *Figure 2.13*:

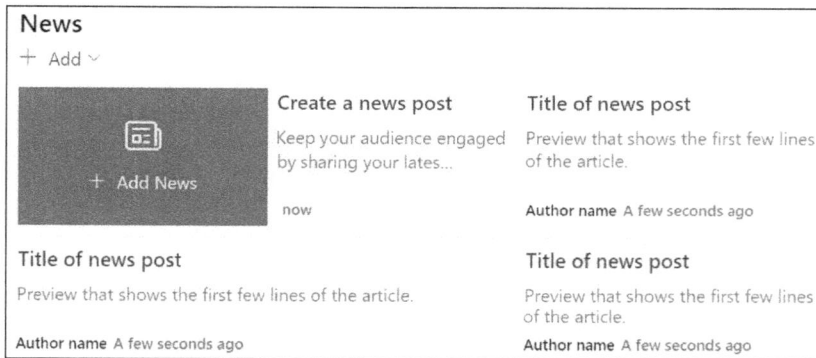

Figure 2.13: News web part in communication site

12. Next to the news web part, you will find **Events** as shown in *Figure 2.14*:

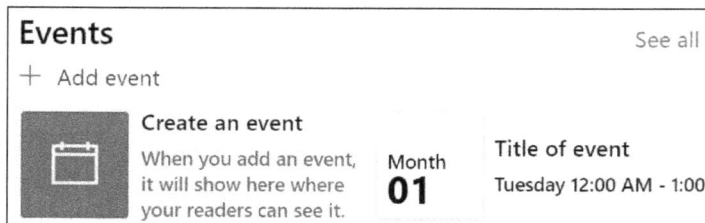

Figure 2.14: Events zone in communication site

13. Further, you will find the **Documents** web part as shown in *Figure 2.15*:

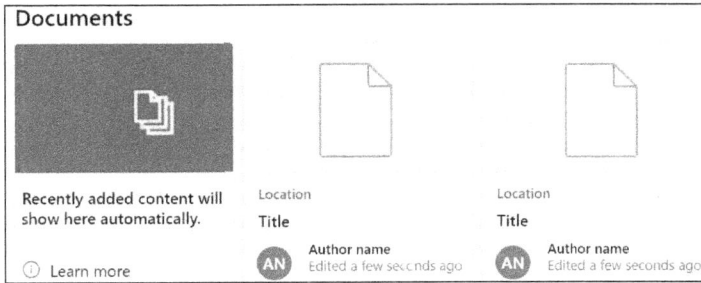

Figure 2.15: Documents zone in communication site

Create modern team site

A modern team site is one of the most used template in SharePoint Online. This site provides a collaborative platform with a brand-new template, where users can share documents within team members, organize their activities in the list, share news within a team by creating news post, share news links, create a plan for the team, assign tasks and check the progress of tasks. It also integrates with OneNote, which allows users to keep critical notes in the notebook. If the user requirement is limited, then you should suggest users for a new modern team site. The following is the step-by-step process to create a **Modern team site**:

1. From the **SharePoint** admin center, navigate to **Active sites** present under **Site** in the left navigation.

2. Click on **Create** from the command bar. You will get a dialog box to select one type of site template to proceed. Click on the **Team site** to create a new team site, as shown in *Figure 2.16*:

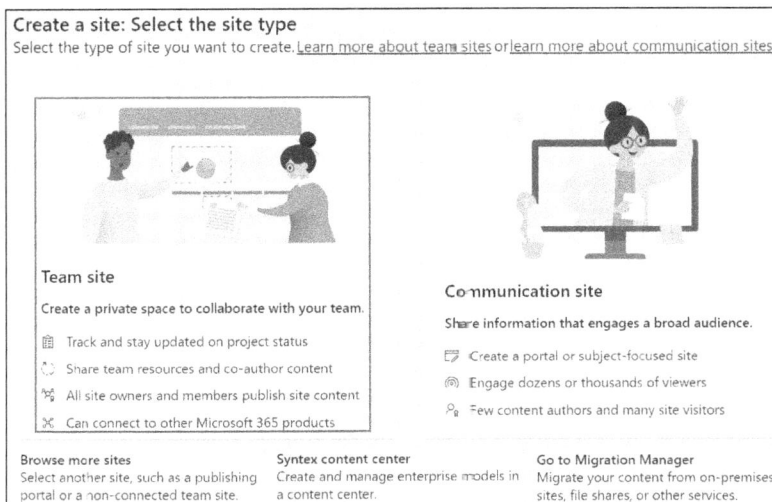

Figure 2.16: Team site template

3. The site creation wizard will open. You will get a list of team site templates like **Standard team, Crisis communication team, Employee onboarding team, Event planning, IT help desk, Project management, Retail management team, Store collaboration, Training course, Training design team**. Each template has a specific user interface and holds specific site capabilities. As per user requirement, the admin can suggest a template or select the template as per user requirement to proceed in the site creation process. Select one team site template as shown in the following *Figure 2.17*:

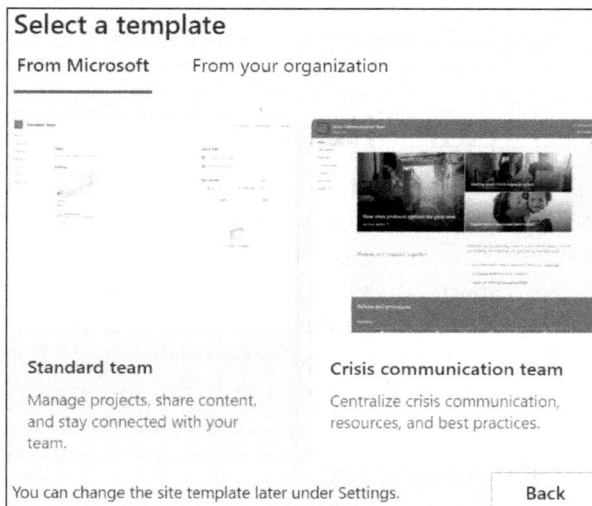

Figure 2.17: Team site template

4. You will find more details about the site template, like **Site capabilities, What's included, Preview site,** and the button. **Use the template** to proceed with site creation. Click on the button **Use template** as shown in *Figure 2.18*:

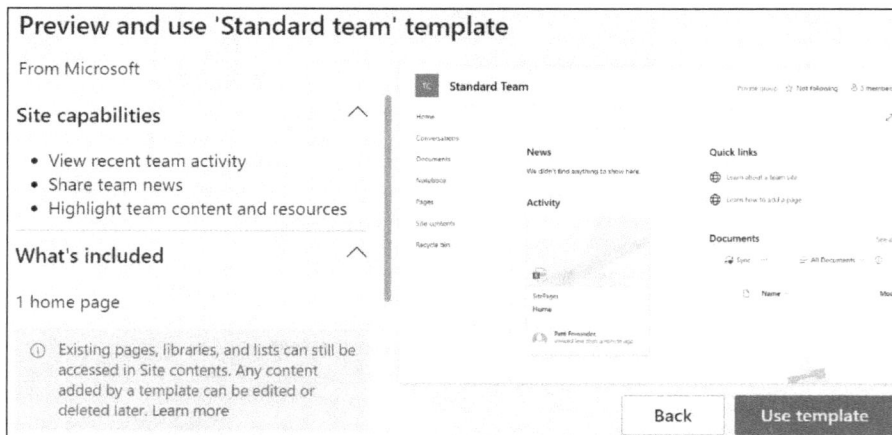

Figure 2.18: Use team site template

5. The site creation wizard will open. Enter **Site name** as `BPB-ModernTeamSite`, enter **Site description**. One Office 365 group will be created, and the **Group email address** will be the same as the site name (`BPB-ModernTeamSite`) by default, but you can change it as per user requirement. The **site address** will be the same as the site name, which will come up automatically after entering the site name. You can change or edit the site address at any time as per user requirements. Then, click **Next**, as shown in *Figure 2.19*:

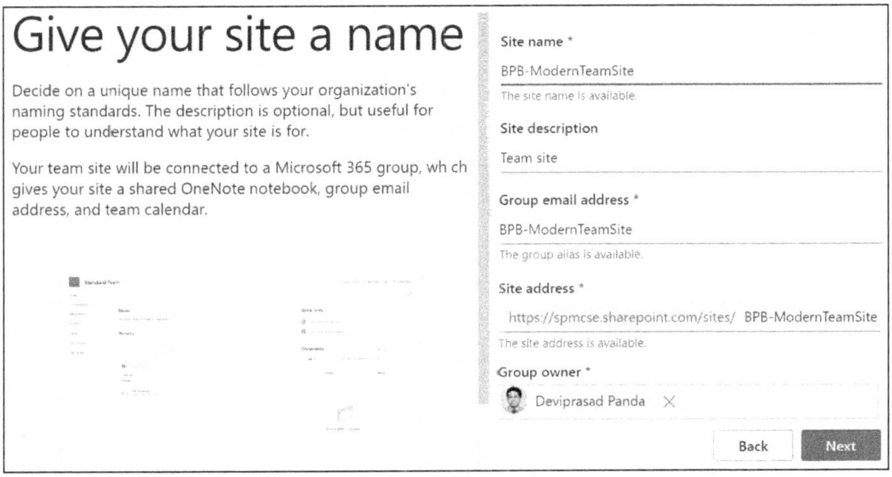

Figure 2.19: Fill team site details

6. In the next window, you need to select **Privacy settings** as **Private - only members can access this site** or **Public - anyone in the organization can access this site** as per the user requirement. Choose one language from the drop-down option. **Select a language**, select **Time zone,** and assign a **Storage limit** to the site. Click on the button **Create site** as shown in *Figure 2.20*:

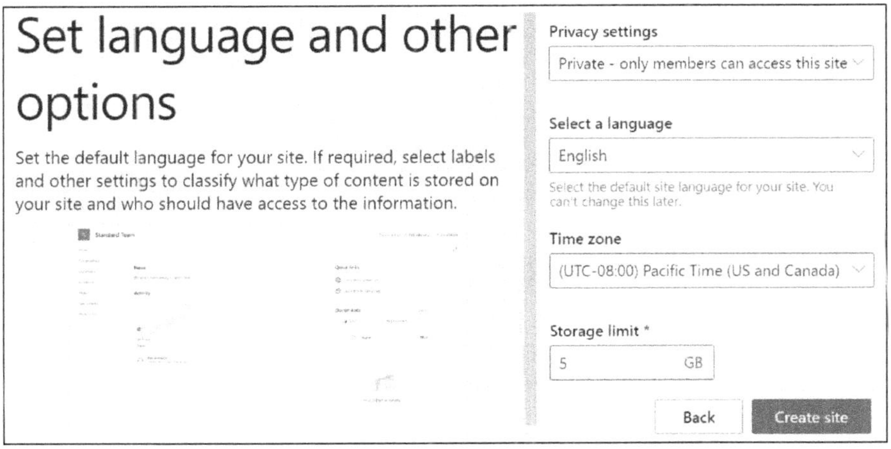

Figure 2.20: Click on create site

7. The next window will provide the option to **Add members**. Either you can add users as per owner requirements else skip this and click on the button **Finish**, as shown in *Figure 2.21*:

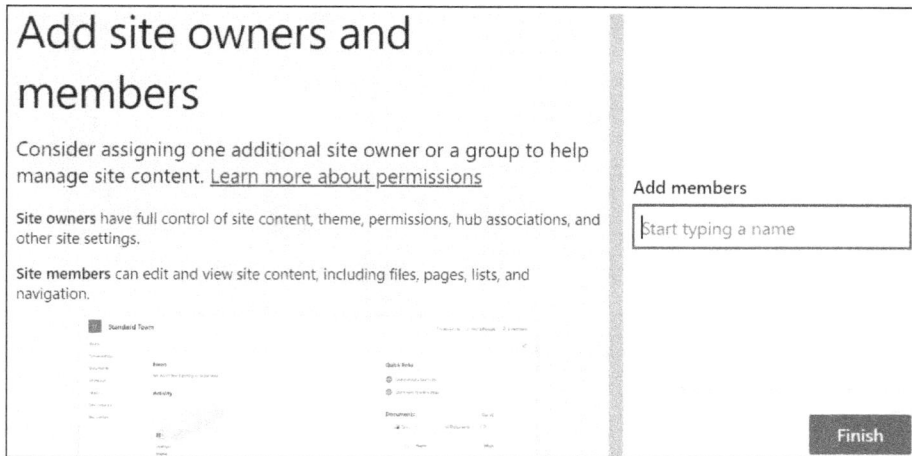

Figure 2.21: *Finish the team site creation process*

8. A new modern team site, `BPB-ModernTeamSite,` is created, and the URL will be **https://spmcse.sharepoint.com/sites/BPB-ModernTeamSite**. You will find the team site with the standard team site template, as shown in *Figure 2.22*:

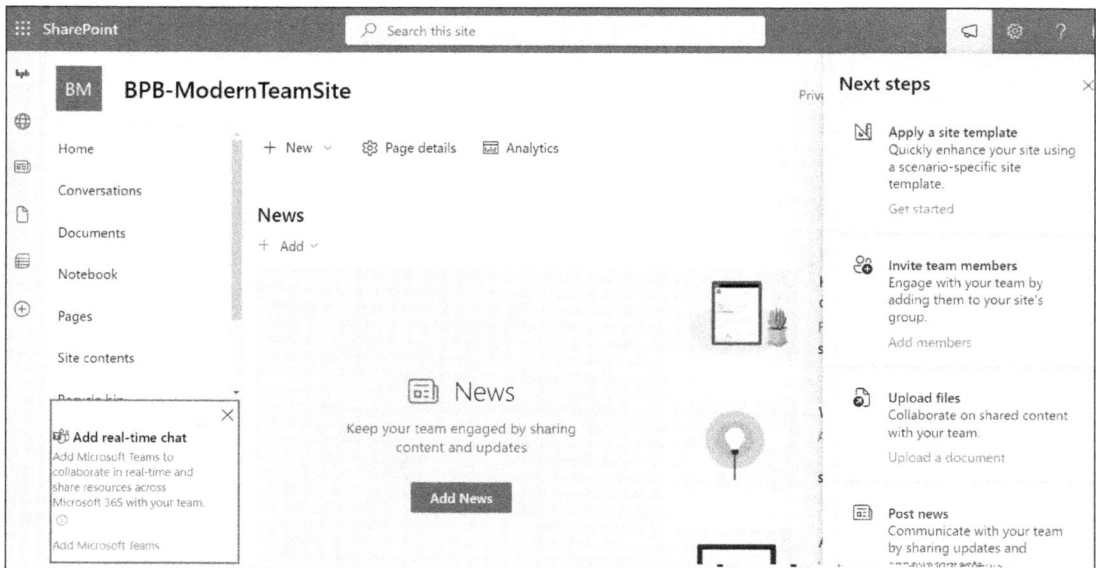

Figure 2.22: *Team site created*

9. Since you are creating a team site, you will get an option to create a Teams group. You will notice an option **Add Microsoft Teams** at the bottom left corner of the site. Click on **Add Microsoft Teams**.

10. You will get a new window to continue and follow a few steps to create Microsoft Teams group and channel. Click on the button **Continue** as shown in the following *Figure 2.23*:

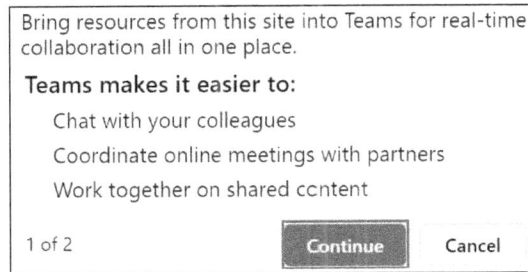

Figure 2.23: Continue to create teams group

11. As shown in *Figure 2.24*, you will find four tabs **Recommended, Pages, Lists,** and **Document Libraries**. You can select resources from these tabs, which will be pinned in the Teams channel. The **Recommended** Resources tab will open by default, and you will find resources like **Documents** and **Home** selected.

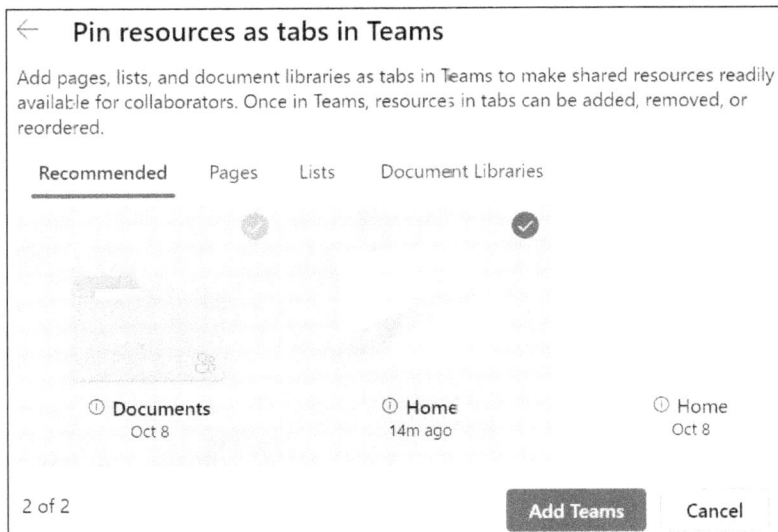

Figure 2.24: Recommended pin resources as tabs in Teams

12. Click on the tab **Pages**. You will find the page Home selected, as shown in the following *Figure 2.25*:

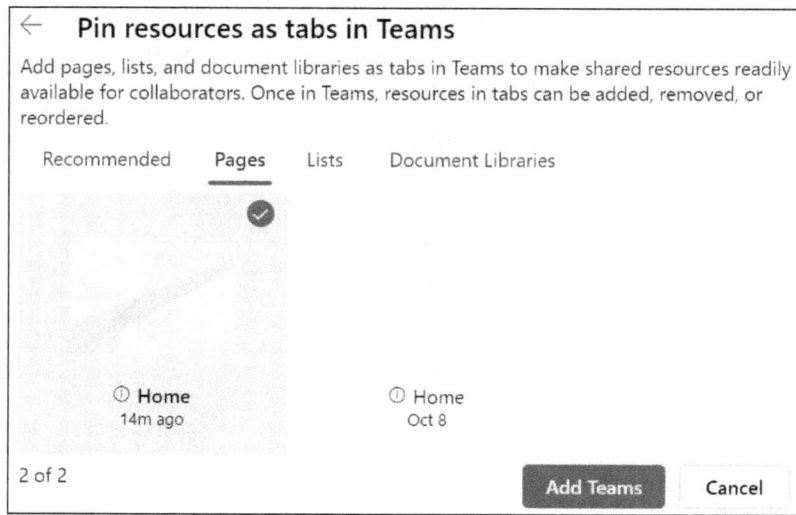

Figure 2.25: Pin pages resource as tabs in Teams

13. Click on the tab **Document Libraries** to find the resource **Document** selected, as shown in *Figure 2.26*. Click on the **Add Teams** button:

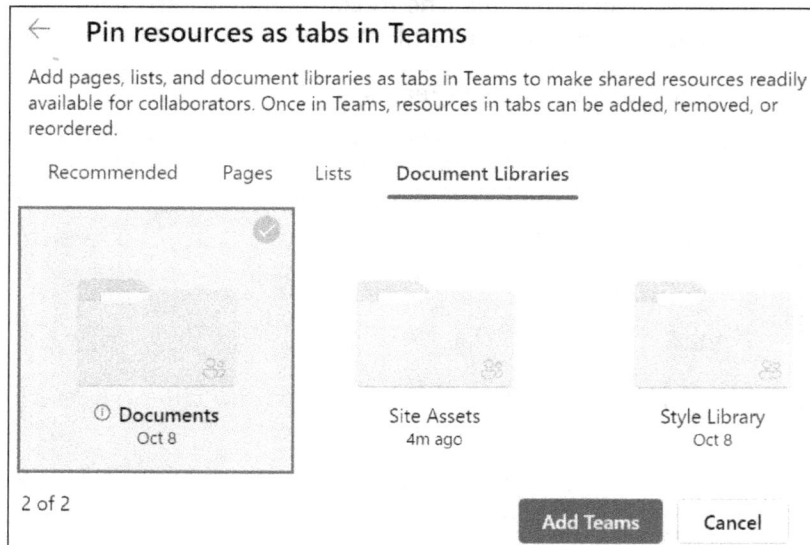

Figure 2.26: Pin Document libraries resources as tabs in Teams

14. Teams group with the same name as the site created. Teams channel is created with the resources pinned in the **Teams** tab to share content and collaborate with the team, as shown in *Figure 2.27*. Expand the group, and you will notice one folder, **General**. The actual location of this folder is inside the site collection document library **Documents**:

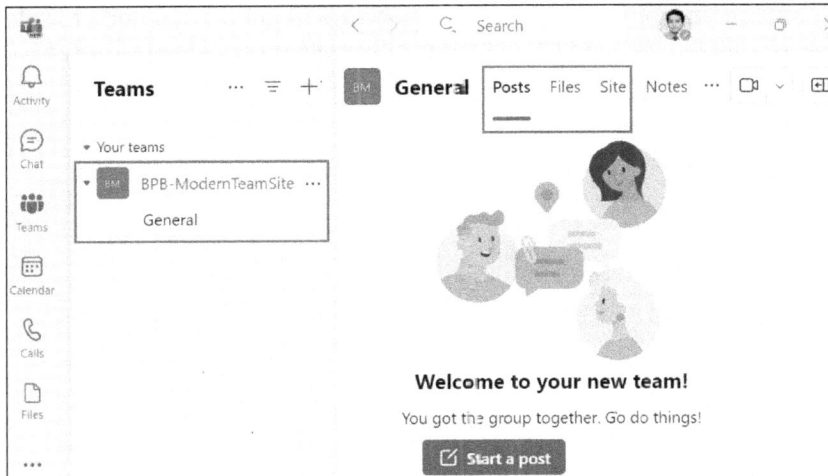

Figure 2.27: Teams group and channel created

15. On the **Site** home page, under the left navigation, you will notice one more quick launch **Teams** is added. You will find the **General** folder under the document library **Documents**, as shown in the following figure:

Figure 2.28: ModernTeamSite home page and folder for storing files by a private group in Microsoft Teams

SharePoint administrator should create the site and hand it over to the site owner, but we intend to show you how to create a new modern team site and how it is different from the classic team site. When you create a subsite of a template Team Site (no Office 365 group), it will be a modern Team site only, but no Office 365 group is created.

Create other site

We discussed creating modern team sites and communication sites. In this section, we will discuss creating site collections other than teams and communication sites. Every individual template has a different layout and features, and the purpose of the requirement is also different. Let us perform the following steps to see what other site templates are available and will create a site other than the teams and communication site:

1. From the SharePoint admin center, navigate to **Active sites** present under **Site** in the left navigation.

2. Click on **Create** from the command bar. You will get a dialog box to select one type of site template to proceed. Click on the **Browse more sites** as shown in *Figure 2.29*:

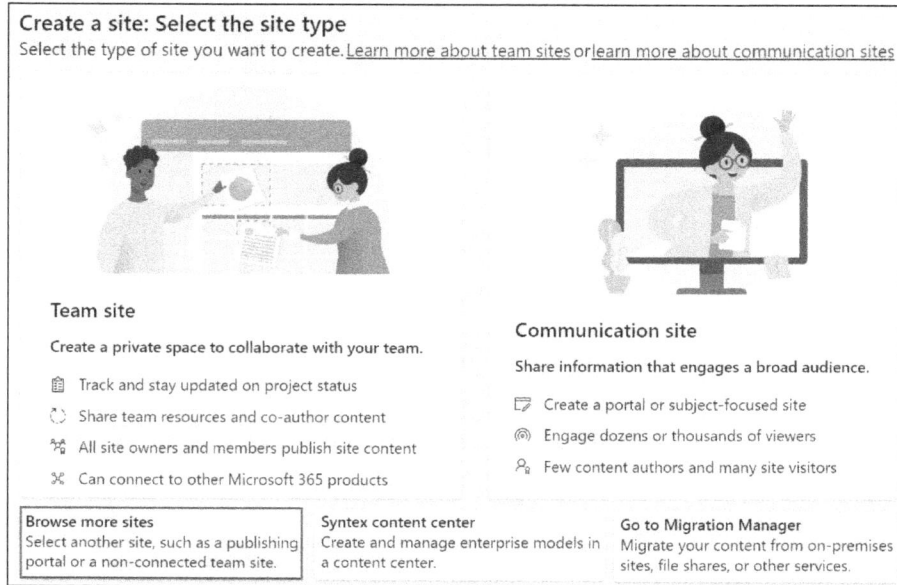

Create a site: Select the site type
Select the type of site you want to create. Learn more about team sites or learn more about communication sites

Team site
Create a private space to collaborate with your team.

- 📖 Track and stay updated on project status
- ⟨⟩ Share team resources and co-author content
- ⚯ All site owners and members publish site content
- ✂ Can connect to other Microsoft 365 products

Communication site
Share information that engages a broad audience.

- 📑 Create a portal or subject-focused site
- ⦿ Engage dozens or thousands of viewers
- ⧒ Few content authors and many site visitors

Browse more sites	Syntex content center	Go to Migration Manager
Select another site, such as a publishing portal or a non-connected team site.	Create and manage enterprise models in a content center.	Migrate your content from on-premises sites, file shares, or other services.

Figure 2.29: Default site template options

3. Proceeding further, click on the **Other options**. You will see templates like **Document Center, Enterprise Wiki, Publishing Portal, Content Center,** and **More templates** to check more default templates available, as shown in the following figure:

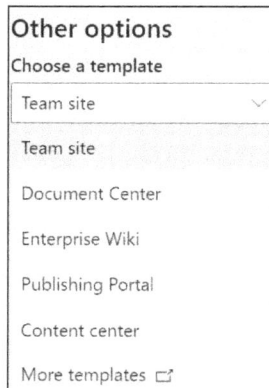

Other options
Choose a template

Team site ⌄
Team site
Document Center
Enterprise Wiki
Publishing Portal
Content center
More templates ⌐

Figure 2.30: Default site template options

4. Click on **More templates**, and you will see an additional template in the form of categories like **Collaboration, Enterprise, Publishing,** and **Custom,** as shown in the following figure:

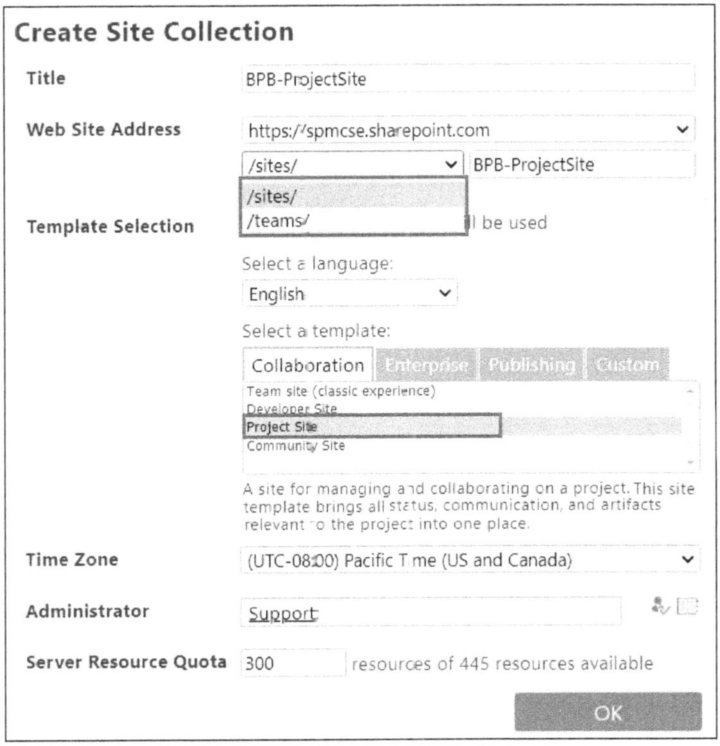

Figure 2.31: Create a site other than the team and communication site

5. Select one template as per the requirement. Enter site **Title**, **Web Site Address** by choosing any one of the managed paths (**sites/teams**), **Language**, **Time Zone**, **Administrator ID**, **Server Resource Quota** and finally click on **OK** to complete site creation process.

Export site information

In the preceding section, we discussed the first option, **Create** present under **Active sites** in the left navigation of central admin. Understood how to create different types of sites from central admin in SharePoint Online. Once a site is created, you can find the site under Active sites list. You will notice all the properties of the site. This section will discuss the site information present under the Active site and how to export bulk site information. It is equally important to manage and administrate the site by analyzing or monitoring specific site information at certain intervals of time. In that case, site information plays an important role. The more information about the site is available, the better management administrator can do. We can avoid the issues and plan something before upgrading the services. SharePoint Online allows the export of site information details from the admin center as an **out of box** feature. Let us follow the step-by-step process to export site collection information from the central admin:

1. Open **SharePoint admin center**.

2. Click on **Active sites** present under **Sites** from the left navigation.

3. Click on **Export** from the command bar present at the top of site list, as shown in the following figure:

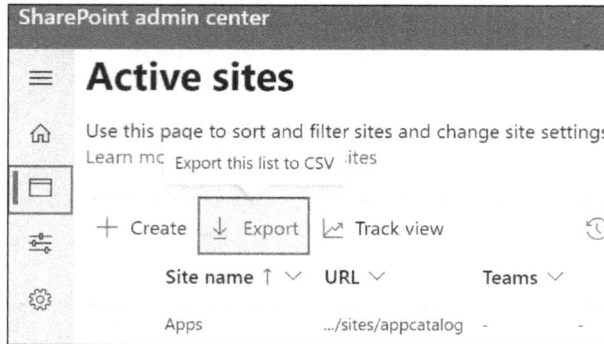

Figure 2.32: Export site collection information

4. Site information will be downloaded in CSV format that includes fields like **Site name, URL, Teams, Channel sites, Storage used (GB), Primary admin, Hub, Template, Last activity (UTC), Date created, Created by, Storage limit (GB), Storage used (%), Files viewed or edited, Page views, Page visits, Files, Sensitivity, External sharing, Segments, Microsoft 365 group** as shown in the following figure:

"Site name"	URL	Teams	Channel sites	Storage used (GB)
BPB-Moderr	https	TRUE		0.28

Primary admin	Hub		Template	Last activity (UTC)
	BPB-Moderi		Team site	10/20/2023 5:00:00 PM

Date created	Created by	Storage limit (GB)	Storage used (%)
11/22/2019 9:	Deviprasad F	25600	0

Files viewed or edited	Page views	Page visits	Files	Sensitivity
5	6	6	2124	

External sharing	Segments	Microsoft 365 group
Off		TRUE

Figure 2.33: Export site information

Search sites

There can be two million sites present in the admin center. It is impossible to find a specific site manually. SharePoint online provides a simplified way to find specific site collections from the search box present in the command bar. Click on the search box **Search sites** in the command bar and enter the possible name of your site collection. The search result will be displayed as a site/sites related to the word entered in the search box, as seen in the following figure. The possible site name entered in the search box will be considered a keyword to be searched from the list of sites and their related information. Refer to *Figure 2.34*:

Figure 2.34: Search site collection from Active sites list

Views

SharePoint **Active sites** list has **Standard views** to display site collections meeting specific criteria. It works as a type of filter. Selecting the option **Change view** from the command bar will display **Standard views** as a drop-down like **All sites, Classic sites, Microsoft 365 Group sites, Sites without a group, Largest sites, Least active sites, and Most popular shared sites**. Click on **view Classic sites**, and it will display all classic site collections present in the active sites list. Clicking on the view Sites connected to Teams will display sites connected to Teams. Similarly, clicking any other view from the drop-down will display the respective site list. Refer to *Figure 2.35*:

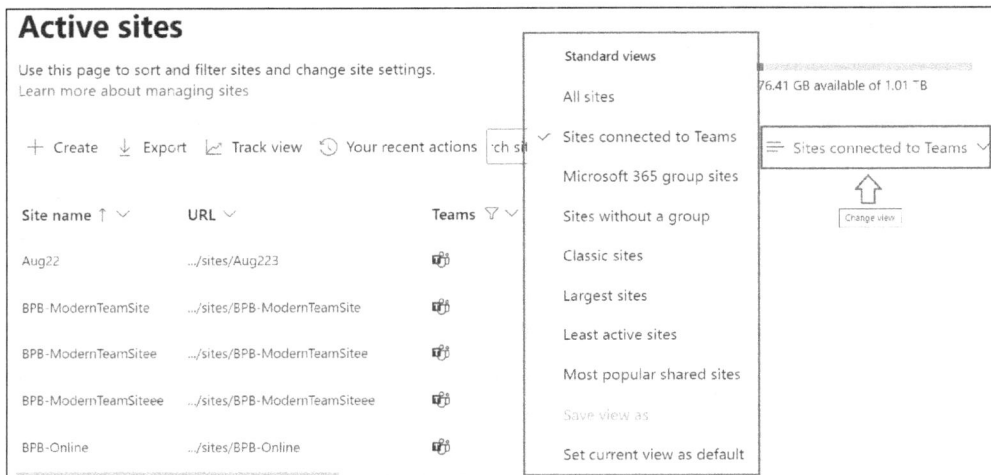

Figure 2.35: Change view

Set current view as default

Sites matching the default view will appear first once you open the **SharePoint admin center**. **All sites** is the default view in **the Active sites** list. We can use any other view per our requirement and set it as default. Open any other view apart from the default view and then select the option **Set current view as default** to make that view default. Refer to *Figure 2.36*:

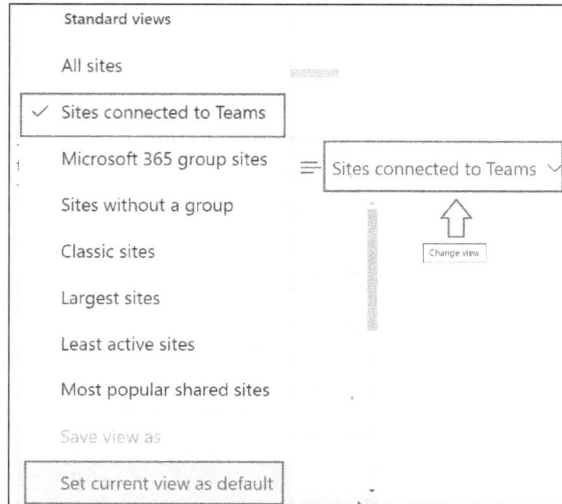

Figure 2.36: Set current view as default

Save view as

Apart from the default view **All sites**, we can create **Custom views** by selecting the option **Save view as** from the drop-down **Change view** in the command bar. Following is the step-by-step procedure to create custom views.

1. Navigate to Site collection list from **Active sites** present in left navigation under **Sites**.

2. Choose one condition as per your requirement. Let us say, we are checking sites connected to teams. Click on the option **Change view** from the command bar and select the view **Sites connected to Teams** from the **Standard views** drop-down list.

3. Filter any of the columns from active sites list. You will find the option **Save view as** got enabled.

4. Click the option **Save view as** from the drop-down. Refer to *Figure 2.37*:

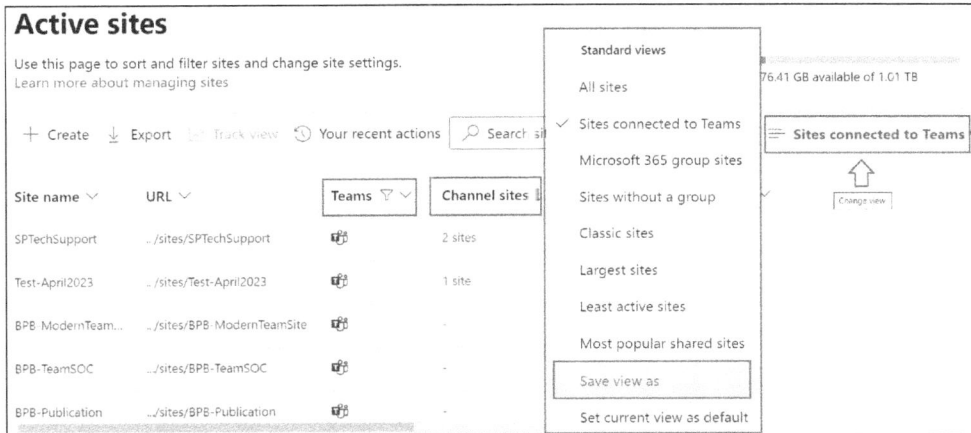

Figure 2.37: Save view as

5. The dialog box will open. Enter view name **BPB-ConnectedTeams** and click on **Save**, as shown in *Figure 2.38*:

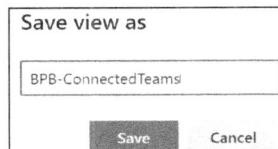

Figure 2.38: Save view

6. Custom view will be added under **Custom views** category. Next time onwards, you can filter sites by clicking on the custom view, as shown in the following figure:

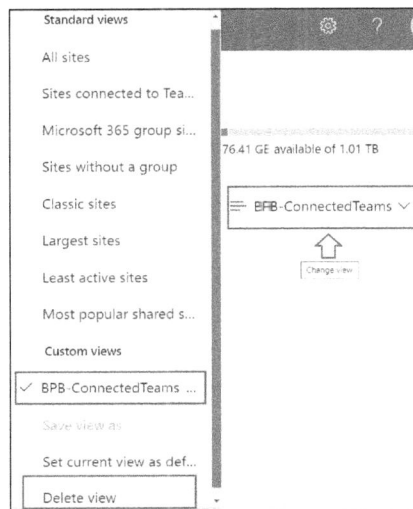

Figure 2.39: Custom view added

7. You will notice a new option, **Delete view** that is enabled in the **Change view** list.

Delete view

You can delete any unwanted custom view present in active sites list by following these steps:

1. Navigate to **Site collection** list from **Active sites** present in the left navigation under **Sites.**

2. Click on **Change view** from the drop down from command bar. It will expand and display all views.

3. Click on the custom view **BPB-ConnectedTeams** as discussed in the preceding section **Save view as**. The related sites will open.

4. Now, click on **Delete view** from the drop-down option. **Change views** are present in the command bar, as shown in *Figure 2.40*.

5. Confirm deletion of view by clicking **Delete** from the dialog box opened next. View **BPB-ConnectedTeams** will be deleted.

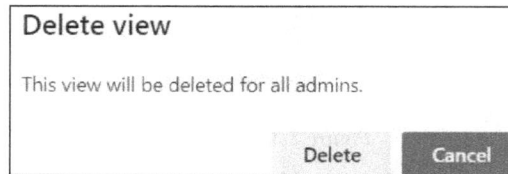

Figure 2.40: Delete view

Manage membership

Every site in SharePoint is assigned a group of people having specific permission levels, roles to manage and collaborate better. Administrators can manage permission using the option Membership by adding or removing users from a specific role. There are specific roles present in site Membership by default. While creating a new team site, we also added Microsoft teams. There are classic team sites and other sites with no groups or teams linked to them. You will find more roles in the sites that have Microsoft 365 groups or are connected to teams compared to the sites that have no groups or are not linked to teams. Let us discuss this in detail.

Membership of sites without group

In this section, we will discuss the membership roles present in sites that are not linked to Microsoft 365 groups or teams. Let us follow the step-by-step procedure below to understand the roles better.

1. Navigate to **Active sites** list and click on the option **Change view** present in the command bar. Select any one of the views like **Sites without a group,** as shown in *Figure 2.41*:

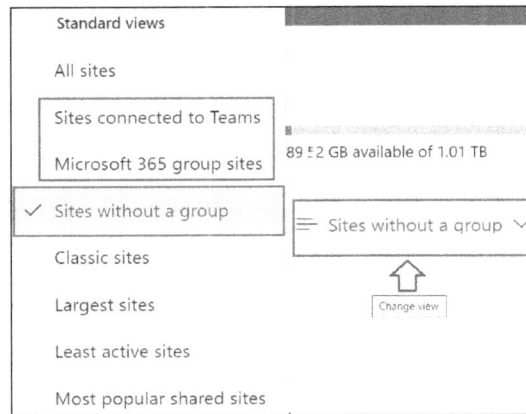

Figure 2.41: Filter by Microsoft 365 group

2. Sites not connected to Teams or Microsoft 365 group will be displayed in the active sites list. Select any one of the sites and click on **Membership** from the command bar, as shown in *Figure 2.42*:

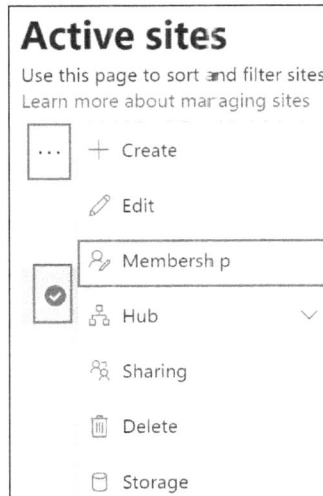

Figure 2.42: Manage group owners in the command bar

3. Another window will open with the tab **Membership** selected default. You will find roles or permission levels like **Site admins (Traditionally called site collection administrators in on-premises SharePoint), Site owners, Site members,** and **Site visitors,** as shown in *Figure 2.43*. Select the permission level or role **Site admins** and click on **Add site admins**:

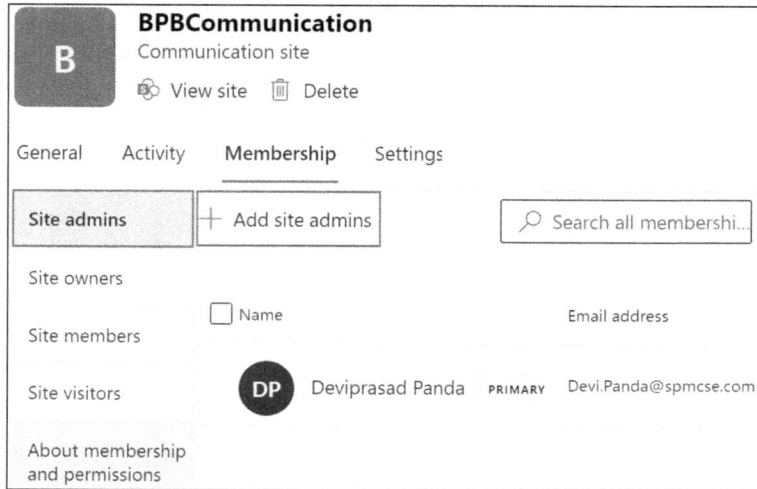

Figure 2.43: Add Microsoft 365 group owners

4. In the next window, enter the name or email address of the user. Select the user from drop-down and click on **Add**, as shown in *Figure 2.44*:

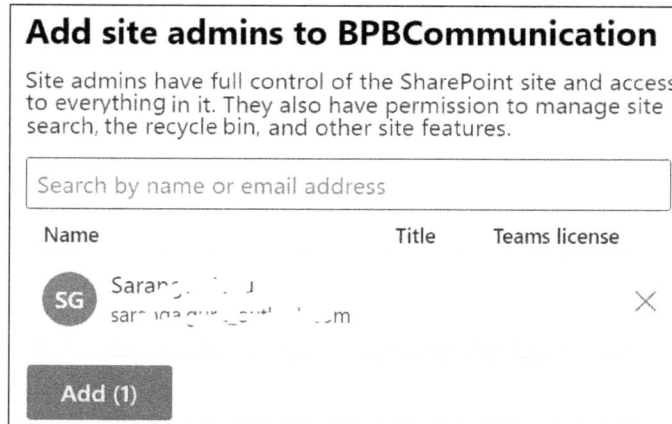

Figure 2.44: Add site admins to site

5. The user is now a member of the Site admins group. Site admins have the highest permission levels on the site, including all permissions of the Site owner as well as additional permissions like managing search, recycle bin, site features, etc. These permissions are applied to item levels in the subsite, although permissions inheritance stopped at any level in the site hierarchy. Similarly, administrators can add users to other groups or roles like **Site owners**, **Site members**, **Site visitors**. Site owners have full control over the site. Site members have edit permissions to the site so that members can add, remove, and edit files present in the list or library. Site visitors have view only permissions over the site.

Membership of sites linked to group

In the previous section, we will discuss the membership roles present in the sites that are not linked to Microsoft 365 groups or teams. In this section, we will discuss the membership roles present in the sites that are linked to Microsoft 365 groups or teams. Let us follow the step-by-step procedure below to understand better:

1. Follow *steps 1* and *2* discussed in the previous section **Membership of sites without group,** and click on **Membership** from the command bar, as shown in *Figure 2.45*:

2. Another window will open with the tab Membership selected default. You will find two more roles or permission levels, like **Owners** and **Members**, and other site roles like **Site admins**, **Site owners**, **Site members**, **Site visitors**, as shown in *Figure 2.45*. Since the site is connected to Microsoft 365 group or teams, you will get teams group owners and teams group members as additional.

3. Select the permission level or role **Owners** and click on **Add Owners**.

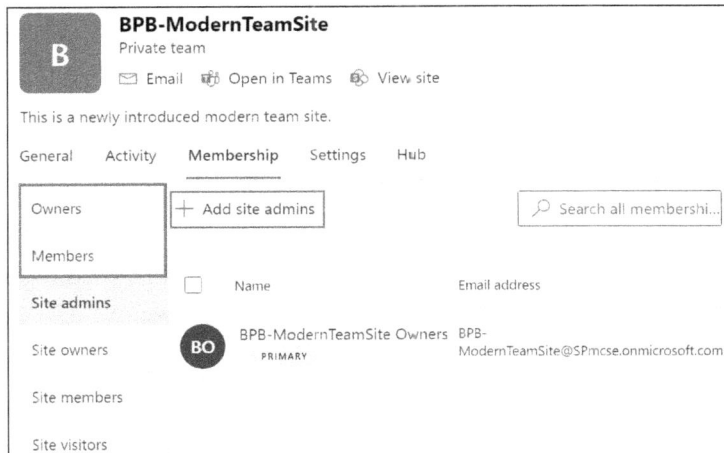

Figure 2.45: *Manage additional admins on command bar*

4. You will get a similar window to enter user details add, as shown in *Figure 2.44* in the previous section. Follow the same procedure to add users in the **Owners** group.

5. We need to understand what these two groups' **Owners** and **Members** are. Owners group is nothing but the Microsoft 365 group owner. If the Microsoft team is linked to the Microsoft 365 group, then group owners are also team owners. If a site is linked with a team, then team owners are automatically added as site owners.

6. Similarly, **Members** are the Microsoft 365 group members. If the Microsoft team is linked to the Microsoft 365 group, then group members are also team members. If a site is linked with a team, then team members are automatically added as site members.

Hub

Hub site provides a building block for intranet sites by which multiple sites can be associated with one site as links. The purpose of the hub site is to build connections. It helps better governance, branding, securing and faster access to sites for intranet users at any time. Traditionally, in SharePoint on-premises, the organization created multiple site collections, sites, and subsites, and a few features activated at the site collection level were applied to the subsite level as well, although owners do not want to apply at the subsite level. This was the blockage towards flexibility and adapting to change in today's dynamic changing world. SharePoint online brings the model such that each unit of work can create a dedicated site that allows applying own governance, flexibility, as well as adapt to change. SharePoint hub brings those dedicated sites associates with one site as links. Let us say one organization, BPB Publications, has multiple sites like **BPB-ModernTeamSite**, **Marketing, HR, Author, Social, Career**, and **News**. In total, seven sites with different URLs. Now, we can register the **BPB-ModernTeamSite** site as a hub site and associate the rest six sites with the hub site **BPB-ModernTeamSite** as shown in *Figure 2.46*. Any change in the organization's business model has no impact on the site since governance is applied to each site separately. It is recommended to use a modern team site or communication site as a hub site. You can remove the site from the hub site or associate it with a new hub site at any point in time during need, which provides better flexibility and adapts to change over time. Whenever a user accesses any of these six sites, the hub site link will appear at the top of all sites for quick redirection. Similarly, one organization can create up to 2000 hub sites per tenant when the number of sites is huge and wants to collaborate with a group of sites for a common purpose. In this section, we will discuss how to register the site as a hub site, and associate other sites with a hub site.

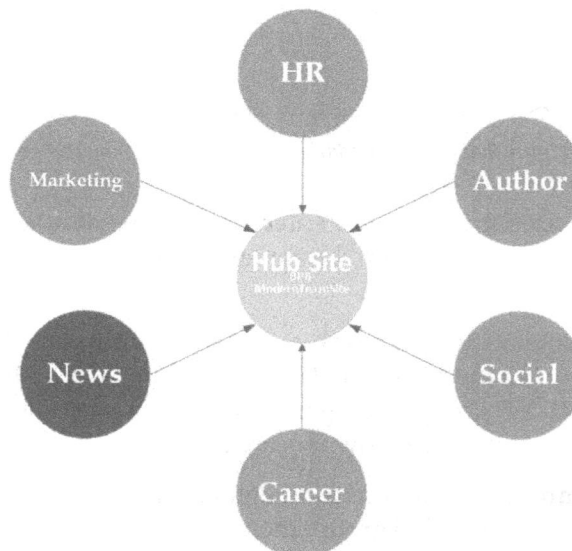

Figure 2.46: Hub site

Register as a hub site

The first step to proceed with the hub feature is registering one site as a hub site. Let us follow the following steps to understand better:

1. Select one site from the **Active sites** list from **SharePoint admin center** and click on **Hub** from the command bar.

2. You will get dropdown options like **Register as hub site** and **Associate with a hub**. Select the option **Register as hub site** as shown in the following figure:

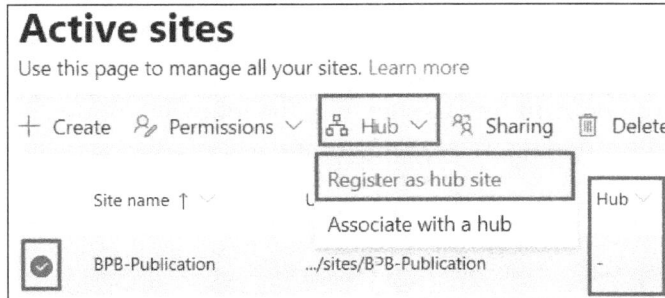

Figure 2.47: *Register as hub site*

3. Another window will open where you need to enter **Hub name** and the **People who can associate site with this hub site**. In the future, when other site owners want to associate their sites with the hub sites, the user added here can only do it. Enter people's details and click on **Save** to apply changes, as shown in the following figure:

Figure 2.48: *Assign a user who can associate the site with the hub site*

4. Once the site is registered as a hub site, you will find the column **Hub** related to the site and will be marked as a **Hub site**, as shown in the following figure:

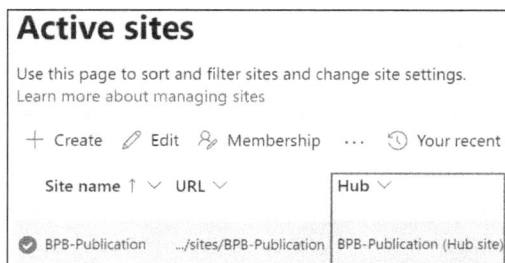

Figure 2.49: Hub site created

5. Open the hub site, and you will find a top link navigation bar has been added. The hub site will be added as the first link in the hub site navigation bar with the additional option **Add link** as shown in the following figure:

Figure 2.50: Top hub site navigation updated

Associate with a hub

In the previous section, we discussed registering a site as a hub site. If you have already registered a site as hub site, then you can associate any site with the hub site using the option **Associate with a hub**. The following is the step-by-step procedure for linking any site with a hub site.

1. Select one site from the **Active sites** list from the SharePoint admin center.

2. Click on **Hub** from the command bar.

3. Select the option **Associate with a hub** from the drop-down menu, as shown in the following figure:

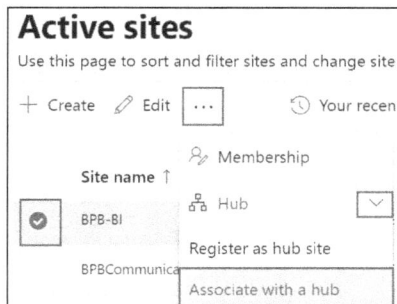

Figure 2.51: Associate with a Hub

4. **Edit hub association** dialog box will open. Expand the drop-down field. **Select a hub** and choose one hub site (for example: **BPB-ModernTeamSiteHub**) present in the tenant to which you want to link. Click on **Save** to apply changes. Refer to *Figure 2.52*:

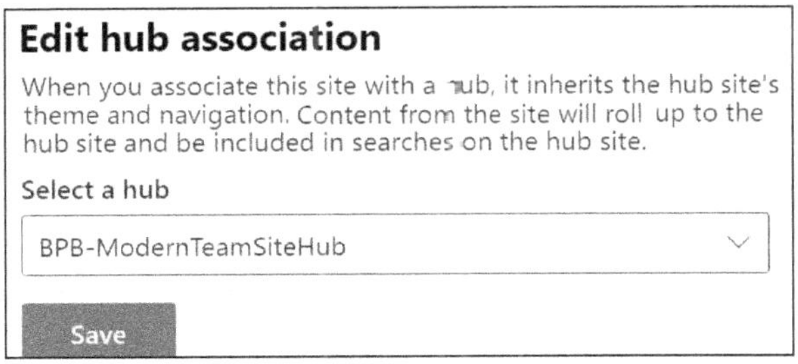

> **Edit hub association**
>
> When you associate this site with a hub, it inherits the hub site's theme and navigation. Content from the site will roll up to the hub site and be included in searches on the hub site.
>
> Select a hub
>
> BPB-ModernTeamSiteHub ∨
>
> Save

Figure 2.52: Associate site with a hub

5. Now site (For example: **BPB-BI**) is associated with the hub site (For example: **BPB-ModernTeamSiteHub**).

Change hub association

In the future, if there is any change in the business plan and you are planning to restructure the hub site associations or connections, you can use the option **Change hub** association. This option allows the sites to change the association from the current hub site to a different hub site at any time. This is what we were talking about: flexibility and adapting to change. The following is the step-by-step procedure to change the hub association:

1. Select one site from the **Active sites** list from SharePoint admin center which is already associated with any one of the hub sites.

2. Click on **Hub** from the command bar and select the drop-down option **Change hub association** as shown in *Figure 2.53*:

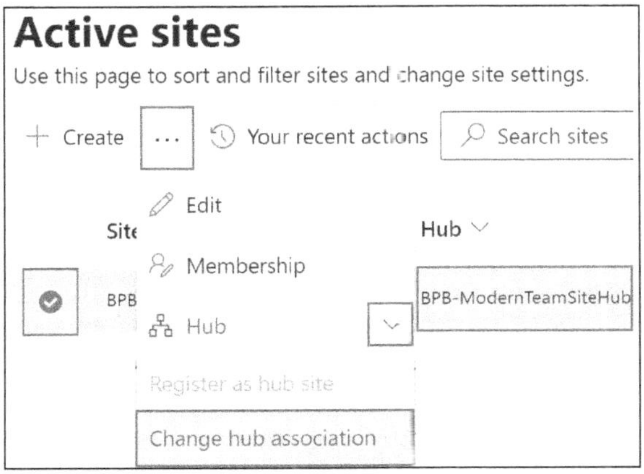

> **Active sites**
>
> Use this page to sort and filter sites and change site settings.
>
> + Create   …   🕙 Your recent actions   🔍 Search sites
>
> ✏ Edit
> Site   Hub ∨
> 👥 Membership
> ✓ BPB   BPB-ModernTeamSiteHub
> ⛗ Hub   ∨
>
> Register as hub site
>
> Change hub association

Figure 2.53: Change hub association

3. **Edit hub association** dialog will open. You will find the existing hub site linked to it with the button **Save** greyed out. Click on the drop-down field **Select a hub** and choose any other hub site that you want to associate with. Click on **Save** to apply changes as shown in the following *Figure 2.54*:

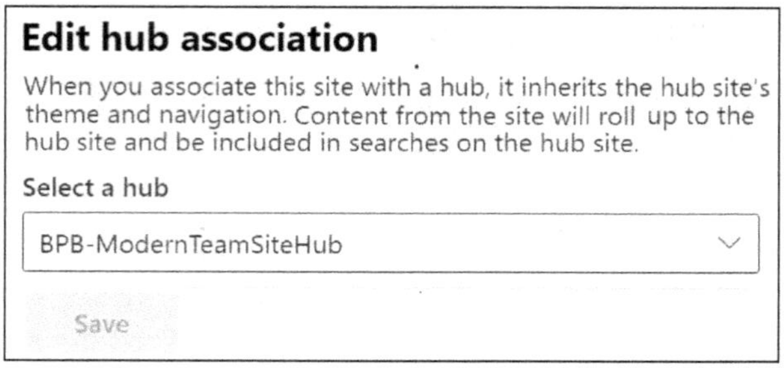

Edit hub association

When you associate this site with a hub, it inherits the hub site's theme and navigation. Content from the site will roll up to the hub site and be included in searches on the hub site.

Select a hub

BPB-ModernTeamSiteHub

Save

Figure 2.54: Edit hub association

4. You can get this **Edit hub association** dialog box by following another way. Click on **Site name** for any site collection. One dialog box will open at right side.

5. Identify the option **Hub association** under category **General**. Click on the **Edit** option. Edit **Hub association** dialog box will open to switch hub site. Refer to the following figure:

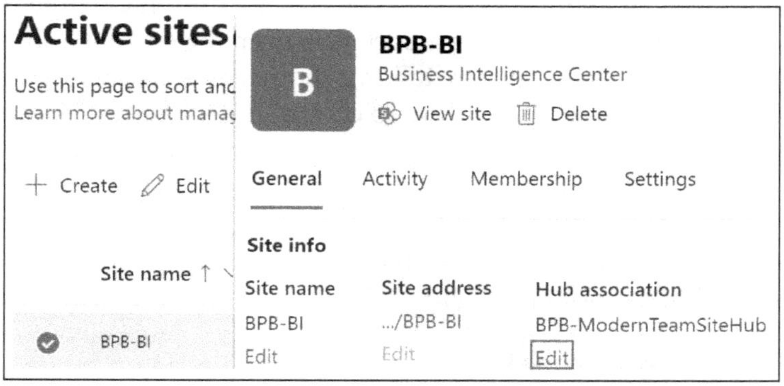

Figure 2.55: Edit hub association under general tab

Sharing

SharePoint is a collaboration tool, and sharing content is the primary feature or requirement. SharePoint keeps improving the sharing experience as well as security related to sharing. Now, sharing sites with intranet users (within the organization) and extranet users (outside the organization) is made easy with predefined settings at the tenant level. Select one site from **Active sites** present in the left navigation under **Sites** and click on **Sharing** from the command bar, as shown in *Figure 2.56*:

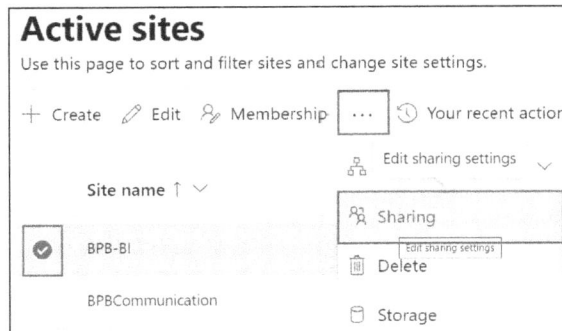

Figure 2.56: Sharing from command bar

A dialog box will open that ultimately suggests the actions can be taken related to the site sharing. You will notice all **Sharing** actions are categorized into **External sharing (Site content can be shared with)**, **Advanced settings for external sharing**, **Default sharing link type**, **Advanced settings for Anyone links**, **Default link permission**. Refer Let us discuss each category of options in detail.

External sharing

The first category under **Sharing** is **External sharing (Site content can be shared with)** which signifies site content will be shared to which users. Users are categorized into four types, like **Anyone (User can share files and folders using links that do not require sign-in)**, **New and existing guests (Guests must sign in or provide verification code)**, **Existing guests only (Only guests already in your organization's dictionary)**, **Only people in your organization (No external sharing allowed)**. The default option selected is **Only people in your organization (No external sharing allowed)**. This means only the organization's internal employees (same domain as Office 365 tenant) can access the site. Sharing site and its content to external users is prevented. Refer to *Figure 2.57*:

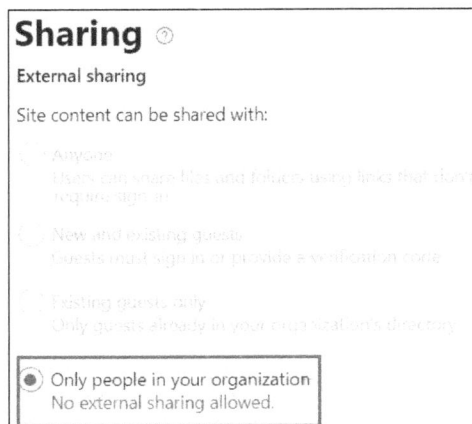

Figure 2.57: Site content can be shared with

You need to understand each of the four options and its application, then only you can select the appropriate option as per the requirement. Let us discuss the types of users to whom site content can be shared with:

- **Anyone**: This option is applicable for public facing sites that do not require user login. Any internal or external user to the organization can access the site and contents if they have the site or file. The link can be shared by any user since this option allows all users to have control over the link to share with anyone. You cannot track details about the changes. Security is another point you need to consider before choosing.

- **New and existing guests**: This option allows external users to access sites but authenticated by a specific process so that users accessing sites can be identified during audit. External users can be of Microsoft account or from any other organization. The site can be only accessed by the user whose mail ID the site is shared with. Select this option when the site needs to be shared with a new external user (users with personal mail ID or from another organization). To access shared content, the user should be added as a member of the group in the Azure Active Directory; else the user must enter a new verification code every time while trying to access shared content (files or folders). Users having full control can share the site only. The user will receive mail with a link to access the site once it is shared. The user can follow the link to access the site with that mail ID account credentials. After the user accesses the site, a new guest user account will be created in Azure Active Directory with the same mail ID.

- **Existing guests only**: This option allows external users to access the site with proper authentication, but the user must be added as a member of a group in the Azure Active Directory to access any shared content (site, folder, or file). If any user accepted the previous sharing invitation, then the user already exists in the guest users list in the Azure Active Directory.

- **Only people in your organization**: This option prevents sharing sites to external user. The site can only be shared or accessed within your organization (intranet users). Accessing content is applied as per the permission applied in site.

Advanced settings for external sharing

The second category under **Sharing** is **Advanced settings for external sharing,** which is disabled initially. We will discuss this in more detail in *Chapter 3, Policies Administration*. Under this category, you will find options like **Limit sharing by domain** and settings related to **Expiration of guest access**, as seen in *Figure 2.58*:

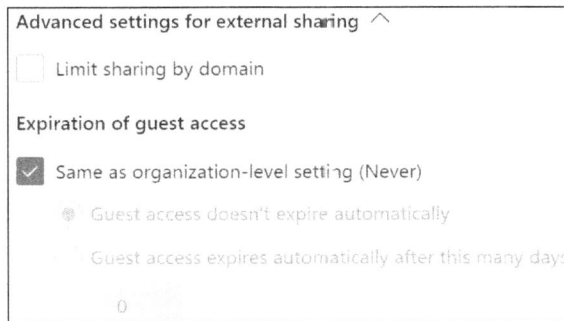

Figure 2.58: Advanced settings for external sharing

Sharing link type

The third category under **Sharing** is **Default sharing link type**. This option signifies the sharing link that will be shared by default. There are four options with whom it can be shared:

- People with existing access
- specific people (only the people the user specifies)
- only people in your organization
- Anyone with the link

You will find a checkbox option like **Same as organization-level settings (specific people)** present at the top of these four options. This checkbox is selected by default and applies the default organizational level setting, which is currently **Specific people (only the people the user specifies)**. Refer to the following *Figure 2.59*:

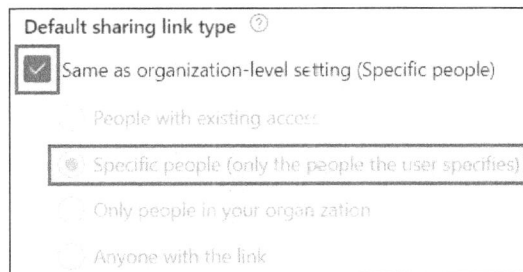

Figure 2.59: Default sharing link type

Changing the default organizational level setting will change the default selected option. We will discuss changing the default sharing link type in *Chapter 3, Policies Administration*. You can switch to link-sharing options from the default options selected. Uncheck the option **Same as organization-level settings (Specific people)**, you will notice the following options:

- People with existing access

- Specific people (only the people the user specifies)

- Only people in your organization are enabled apart from the default option specific people (only the people the user specifies)

Select the option that fits your requirements and click on **Save** to apply changes. The option **Anyone with the link** is still disabled. Refer to the following *Figure 2.60*:

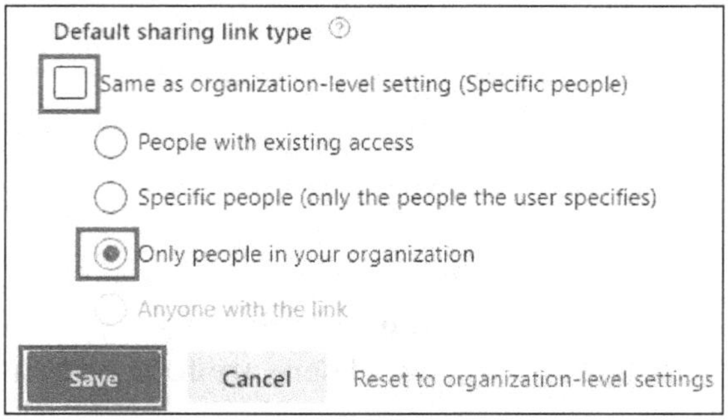

Figure 2.60: Edit sharing link type

You need to understand the use of the default sharing link. When you share any site content (file or folder), the link to the content is shared with the user. The option selected here will appear as the default option while sharing any specific content (file or folder). You can change the option further, but the default selected option will be chosen here. You will notice options under the default sharing link type.

- **People with existing access**: This option allows sending the link of content (files or folders) to users who are already added to the Azure Active Directory group either manually or by the user from previously shared content as per process.

- **Specific people (only the people the user specifies)**: This option is selected to send link of content (files or folders) to specific users as well as external users who pass through the authentication process to access the site contents.

- **Only people in your organization**: This option is to send link of content (files or folders) to users within your organization but not with external users.

- **Anyone with the link**: This option enables links to be shared with any user, whether internal or external, without any authentication process.

Advanced settings for Anyone links

You will find the fourth category at the bottom **Default sharing link type** as **Advanced settings for Anyone links** which is disabled currently. This option allows you to select the **Expiration of Anyone links**. Refer to *Figure 2.61*: We will discuss this in *Chapter 3, Policies Administration*:

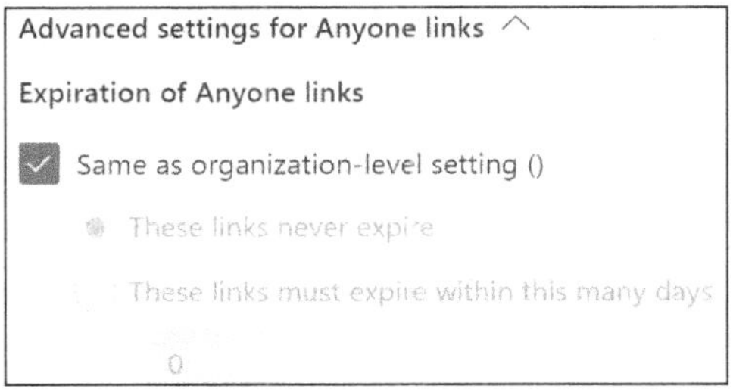

Figure 2.61: *Advanced settings for anyone links*

Default link permission

The fifth category under **Sharing** is **Default link permission**. This defines the default link permission that is applied to the sharing content and what type of action they can take. The user can **View** and **Edit** following the default link. The default option is the same as organization-level settings, i.e., **View**. Refer to *Figure 2.62*:

Figure 2.62: *Default link permission*

You can change the **Default link permission**. Uncheck the **Same as organization-level settings.** Select the radio button **Edit** and click on **Save** to apply changes as shown in the following figure:

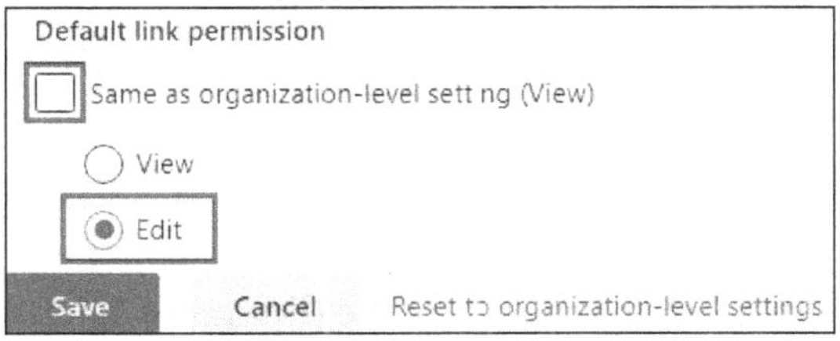

Figure 2.63: *Edit link permission*

Delete site

The next option in the command bar is **Delete**. The owner creates a site deletion request when there is no need for the site. The administrator will delete the site from the admin center by following these steps:

1. Navigate to the site list from **Active sites,** which are present in the left navigation under **Sites**.

2. Select one site from the list.

3. Click on **Delete** from the command bar, as shown in the following figure:

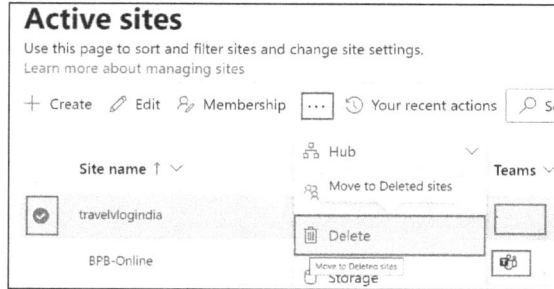

Figure 2.64: Delete site

4. A new dialog box will appear as a warning. You need to confirm and click on **Delete** as seen in the following *Figure 2.65*. The site will be deleted. It will be removed from the active sites list and moved to the **Deleted sites** list.

5. You can click on the **Close button** the cross mark to discard site deletion. Refer to the following figure:

Figure 2.65: Delete site other than Team site

6. Deleted sites retained for 93 days (about three months). If the site owner thinks of using it again then administrator can restore the site within that time. After 93 days (about three months) it will be deleted permanently.

7. If you are deleting any site connected to Microsoft 365 group, you will get a dialog to delete the Teams group related to that site, as shown in *Figure 2.66*.

8. Click on **Delete** to complete the team site (linked to Microsoft 265 group) deletion process. Refer to *Figure 2.66*:

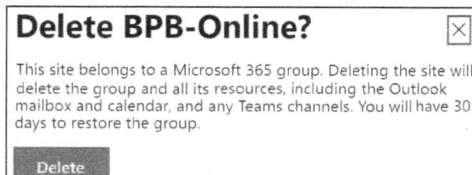

Figure 2.66: Delete Team site

Edit site

You can still change the properties of sites after they are created. You can change properties like site **Name**, **Description**, **Site address**, **Aliases**, **Hub association**, **Storage limit**, **Membership**, **Email Settings**, **Privacy Settings**, **External file sharing**, and **Teams conversations**. Let us discuss how to change site properties and understand other options available under the **Edit** option.

Change site name

SharePoint online made it simpler to rename an existing site. There might be a situation in the future when the site owner may ask to change the display name of the site, justifying the business requirement. In this section, we will discuss the step-by-step procedure to change the name of a site from SharePoint admin center:

1. Navigate to the site list from **Active sites** present in the left navigation under **Sites**.

2. Select one site from the list and click cn **Edit** from the command bar, as seen in *Figure 2.67*:

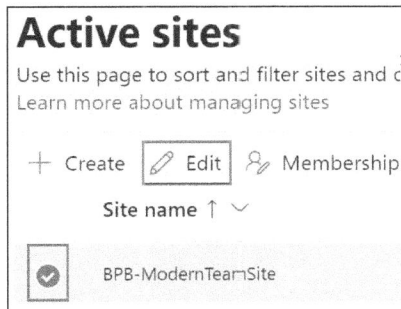

Figure 2.67: Edit site

3. Alternatively, click on the **Site name** directly. You will get a dialog box. You find site information categorized into tabs like **General**, **Activity**, **Membership**, **Settings**, **and Hub**. By default, **General** tab is selected. Refer to *Figure 2.68*.

4. If you are editing a team site and a Microsoft 365 group linked to it, you will find general information categorized as **Basic info**, **Email address**, **Other info**, and **Site info**.

5. **Basic info** contains the site name and site description. The email address contains information related to the group mail ID and alias details. Other info includes information on the site created date and created by.

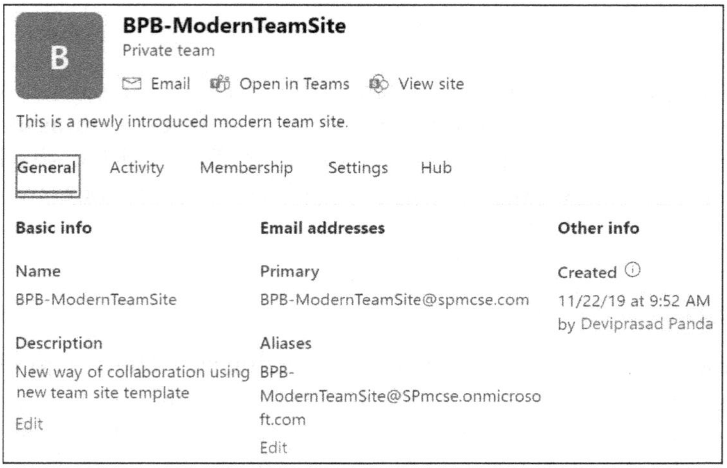

Figure 2.68: Site information from command bar

6. **Site info** holds information like **Site name**, **Site address**, **Hub association**, **Description**, **Storage limit**, **Domain**, **Template**, and **Channel sites**. If the site is marked as a hub site, you will find the site name marked as a Hub site inside the bracket, as shown in *Figure 2.69*. Storage limit holds the site quota limit. Domain holds information about the site domain. The template indicates what type of site it is. Option **Channel sites** hold the number of channel sites present in the site, as shown in *Figure 2.69*:

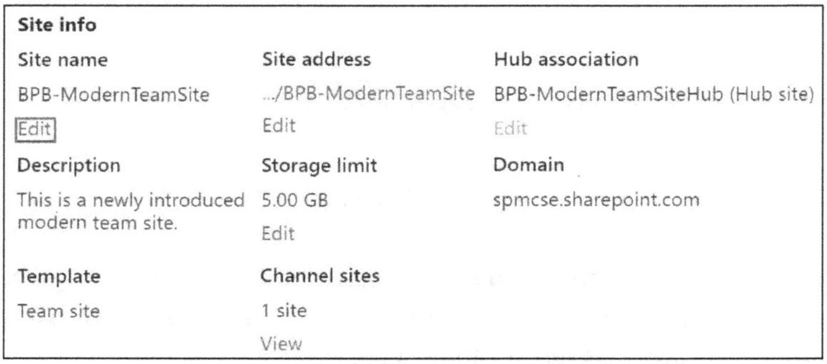

Figure 2.69: Site information

7. If you are trying to edit a communication site or a site with no Microsoft 365 group linked to it, then you will find only the **Site Info** option. You will find **Basic info**, **Email address**, and **Other info**.

8. Click on **Edit** present at the bottom of the field **Site name** under the **Site info**. Refer to *Figure 2.69*.

9. The **Edit site name** dialog box will open. Enter the preferred name you want to change under the filed **Site name**. You will notice the site name availability status

at the bottom of the field **SharePoint Site name** as **The site name is available.** Refer to *Figure 2.70*:

Figure 2.70: *Enter the preferred site name*

10. Click on **Save** to apply changes.

11. The site name will be updated immediately, but the URL of the site will remain unchanged as usual. Refer to *Figure 2.71*:

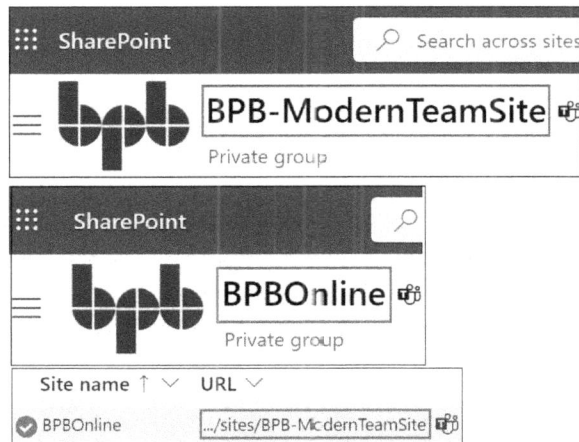

Figure 2.71: *Site name updated*

Change site URL

SharePoint online provides an easy option to change site URL. Due to any business requirement change in the future, the site owner might ask to change the URL of the site. It is recommended to change the site address when site usage is less. Once you enter the new site address and save apply to changes, it will take up to ten minutes to update at the back end. Till the site address update is finished, the state of the site will be read only. At a time 100 sites you can change the address. You cannot move the site from **/sites** to **/ teams**. Changing the site URL or address usually creates a redirect at the previous URL or address. If you want the old address to be used again, delete the redirect.

Before changing the site address, you, as an administrator, need to make the requester aware and get confirmation about the impacts due to this change. Apps referring to the old site need to be republished, recreate the custom forms created in power apps, edit the folder path in list view web part if used in the site, any upload questions in Microsoft forms need to be fixed, reassociate the site with the hub site, site customization, and embedded code fixing is required after changing the site address. Follow the step-by-step procedure below to edit the site address:

1. Follow the *steps 1* to *7* as discussed in the section *Change site name*.

2. Click on **Edit** present at the bottom of the field **Site address** under the **Site info**. Refer to *Figure 2.72*:

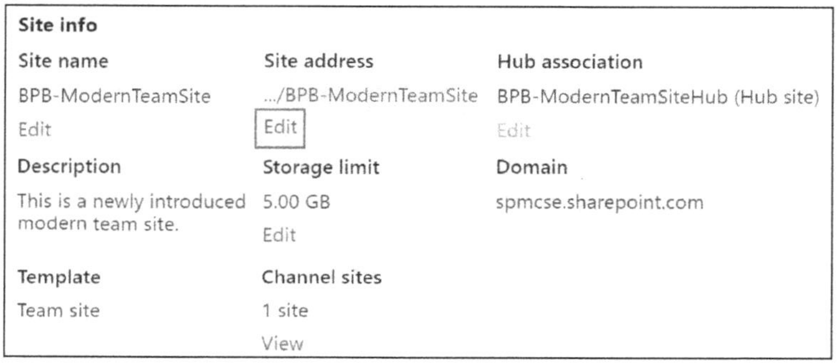

Site info		
Site name	Site address	Hub association
BPB-ModernTeamSite	.../BPB-ModernTeamSite	BPB-ModernTeamSiteHub (Hub site)
Edit	Edit	Edit
Description	Storage limit	Domain
This is a newly introduced modern team site.	5.00 GB	spmcse.sharepoint.com
	Edit	
Template	Channel sites	
Team site	1 site	
	View	

Figure 2.72: Edit site address

3. Edit SharePoint site address **dialog box will open**. Enter the preferred SharePoint site address that you want to change under the **SharePoint site address** field. You will notice the site address availability status at the bottom of the field **SharePoint Site address** as **available.** Refer to the following *Figure 2.73*:

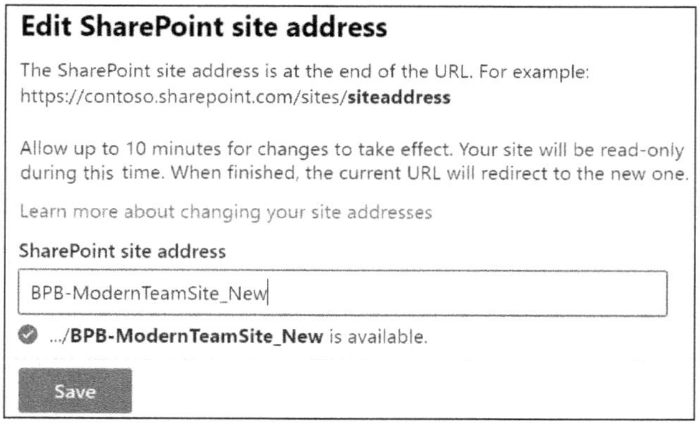

Edit SharePoint site address

The SharePoint site address is at the end of the URL. For example:
https://contoso.sharepoint.com/sites/**siteaddress**

Allow up to 10 minutes for changes to take effect. Your site will be read-only during this time. When finished, the current URL will redirect to the new one.

Learn more about changing your site addresses

SharePoint site address

> BPB-ModernTeamSite_New|

✅ .../**BPB-ModernTeamSite_New** is available.

`Save`

Figure 2.73: Change SharePoint site address

4. You cannot change the site URL of a Hub site unless you unregister it as a hub site. You will get a message, as seen in *Figure 2.74*. Similarly, you cannot change

the site URL of Project Web App sites, BCS-connected sites, or sites in a locked or hold state.

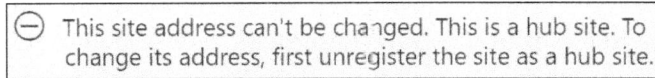

Figure 2.74: Change site URL hub site

5. Click on **Save** to apply changes.

6. You will get another dialog box to change **Site name**. If you wish to change the site name, click **Yes**. It will show you the same option as we saw in the preceding section **Change site name**. If you wish to change only site address, click on **No**, as shown in *Figure 2.75*:

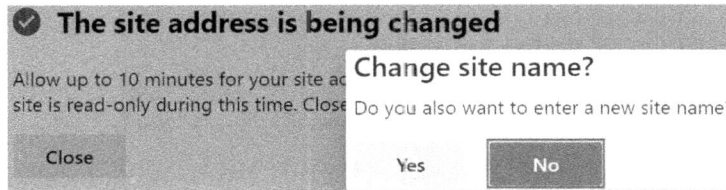

Figure 2.75: Change site name

7. You will notice the status of the field **Site address** as **Updating**, as shown in *Figure 2.76*:

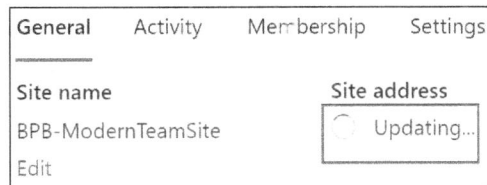

Figure 2.76: Updating URL

8. After a few seconds, you will see the **URL** of the site has changed to the preferred name, as shown in the following figure:

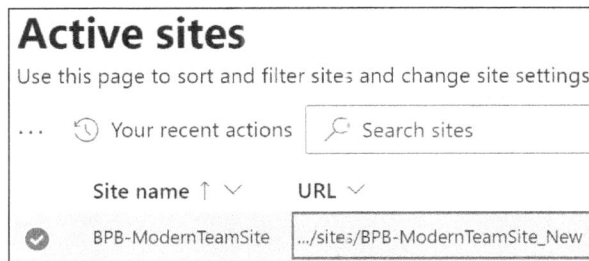

Figure 2.77: Site URL changed

Site activity

Site activity information provides a quick idea about site usage, which is helpful in planning any action in the future. Follow these steps to check site activity in detail:

1. Navigate to site list from **Active sites** present in the left navigation under **Sites**.

2. Click on the site whose activity details you want to check and click on **Edit** from command bar. Alternatively, click on the **Site name** directly. You will get a dialog box. You find site information categorized into tabs like **General**, **Activity**, **Membership**, **Settings**, and **Hub**.

3. Select the tab **Activity**.

4. You will get details related to **Last site activity**, **Files stored**, **Page views in the last 30 days**, **Page visits in the last 30 days**, **Files viewed/edited in the last 30 days**, and **Storage usage** as shown in *Figure 2.78*:

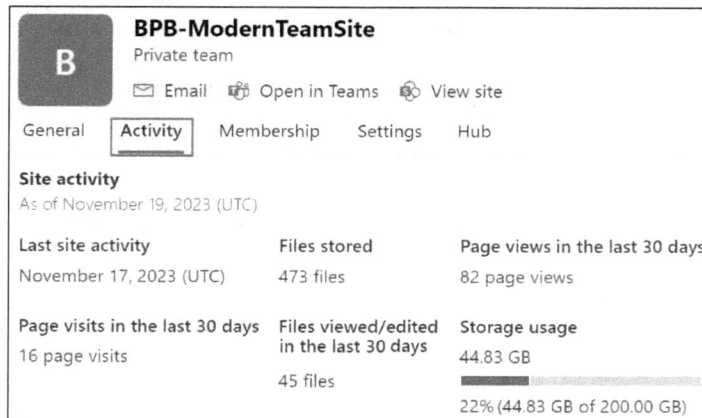

Figure 2.78: Site activity

5. The last site activity holds the date (November 17, 2023) when the last time any activity happened on the site. The file stored contains the number of files (473 files) stored on the site. Page views in the last 30 days hold information about the number of views (82 page views) of the pages. Pages visits in the last 30 days hold information about a number of pages visited (16 pages visits) in the last 30 days, which means 16 pages viewed 82 times. Files viewed/edited holds information about the number of files viewed or edited in the last 30 days. Storage usage holds information about the total space occupied by the files.

Membership

Membership tab provides an alternate way to manage different types of site roles, Microsoft 365 Group owners and additional admins from the edit site dialog box. In the preceding section, *Manage membership*, we already discussed how to manage **Owners**, **Members**, **Site admins**, **Site Owners**, **Site members**, **Site visitors**. Once you select the site, click on **Edit** from the command bar and select the tab Membership. You will get the same window as discussed in the section *Manage Membership*. After that, you can follow the steps discussed in the same section.

Edit site settings

Settings is the fourth tab present in the edit site tabs. It provides options to manage individual settings related to **Email**, **Privacy**, **External sharing**, **Sensitivity label**, and **Team conversation** for the teams related to the site. It is mostly team settings related to the site. Follow these steps to understand the procedure to change various settings for team settings linked to a specific site:

1. Navigate to the site list from **Active sites** present in the left navigation under **Sites**.

2. Click on the site to which you want to edit and click on the tab **Settings**. You will get setting options categorized as **Email**, **Privacy**, **External sharing**, **Sensitivity label**, and **Team conversation**.

3. Under the category **Email**, you will find three options, as seen in *Figure 2.79*. The first option: **Let people outside the organization email this team** to enable or disable the outside people sending emails to the team related to the SharePoint site. The second option is **Send copies of team emails and events to team members' inboxes.** This allows us to enable or disable sending a copy of emails to each team member's inboxes that are sent to team emails. The third option, **Don't show the team email address in Outlook,** allows enabling or disabling showing the team email address in Outlook.

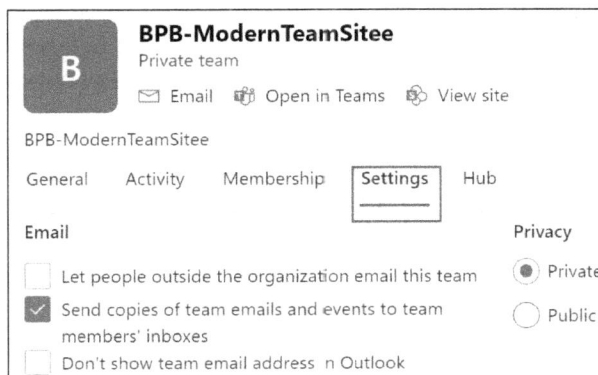

Figure 2.79: Edit site settings email and privacy options

4. Next to Email, you will notice the second category, **Privacy**. You will find two options, **Private** and **Public**, as shown in the above *Figure 2.79*. Privacy indicates the type of Teams group that is linked to the site. If privacy is selected as **Private**,

then approval is required if anyone needs to join the Teams group. If **Privacy** is selected as **Public**, then anyone in the organization can join the team group, and no approval is required from the Teams owner. If you notice in the Teams admin center under **Manage teams**, you will find the status under privacy as **Private** as selected as shown in the following *Figure 2.80:*

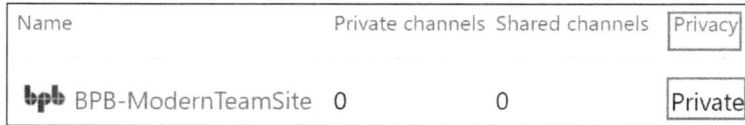

Name	Private channels	Shared channels	Privacy
ᵇᵖᵇ BPB-ModernTeamSite	0	0	Private

Figure 2.80: Privacy settings in manage teams from admin center end

5. Next to **Privacy**, you will find the option **External file sharing**. This option defines the site content that can be shared with which types of users, whether **only people in your organization**, **Existing guests only**, **New and existing guests**, or **Anyone**. We have already discussed site sharing under the section *Sharing*. This is another location that reflects the same setting as site sharing. Refer to *Figure 2.81*:

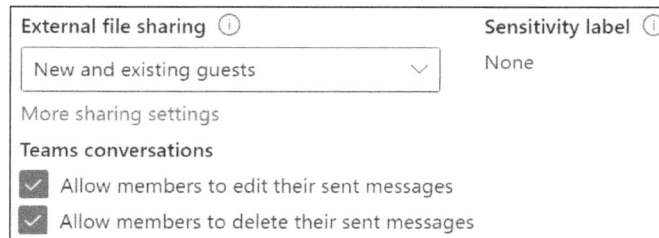

External file sharing ⓘ	Sensitivity label ⓘ
New and existing guests ⌄	None
More sharing settings	
Teams conversations	
☑ Allow members to edit their sent messages	
☑ Allow members to delete their sent messages	

Figure 2.81: Edit site settings external sharing, sensitivity label, team conversations

6. Next, you will find the option **Sensitivity label** as shown in *Figure 2.81*. If a Sensitivity label is configured, you will find the type of Sensitivity label here. You will find the option to change by clicking on **Edit** present below the **Sensitivity label**.

7. The next option you will find is **Team conversations,** as shown in *Figure 2.81*. You will find check box options: **Allow members to edit their sent messages, Allow members to delete their sent messages** to enable or disable edit sent messages, and delete sent messages respectively.

Your recent actions

Any changes in site properties under the active sites list will be captured under **Your recent actions**. This gives quick information about all the site activities that happened recently like any change in site properties like name, URL, storage, settings, site deletion, etc. Bulk action will be displaced as one item in Your recent actions. Your recent action data is dependent on the user's current session, which means until the current session is continued, data on recent action is available. Once the browser is closed or signed out, the recent action data will be cleared, and you will not find the details. If you want to capture data for a few days, then Microsoft Syntex needs to be applied. After that, you can find the recent actions data for specific dates. Refer to *Figure 2.82,* which gives an idea of the details captured and what they look like in a real-time view. You can also export the recent action details as **.csv** file.

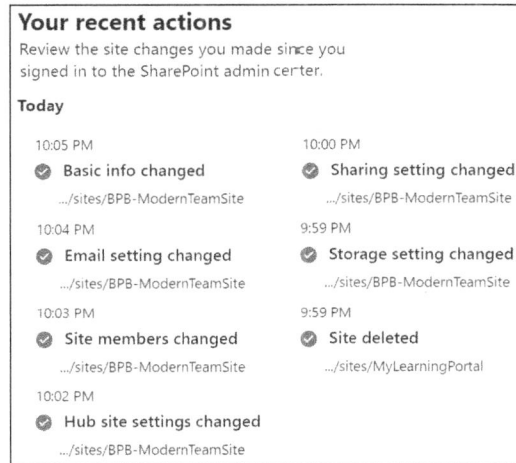

Your recent actions
Review the site changes you made since you signed in to the SharePoint admin center.

Today

10:05 PM	10:00 PM
Basic info changed	Sharing setting changed
.../sites/BPB-ModernTeamSite	.../sites/BPB-ModernTeamSite
10:04 PM	9:59 PM
Email setting changed	Storage setting changed
.../sites/BPB-ModernTeamSite	.../sites/BPB-ModernTeamSite
10:03 PM	9:59 PM
Site members changed	Site deleted
.../sites/BPB-ModernTeamSite	.../sites/MyLearningPortal
10:02 PM	
Hub site settings changed	
.../sites/BPB-ModernTeamSite	

Figure 2.82: Your recent site actions

Storage

Each site in SharePoint is assigned a storage limit. You can edit the storage limit and change to higher or lower as per requirements. In this section, we will discuss how to change the storage limit of a site. Follow these steps to change the storage limit:

1. Navigate to the option **Active Sites** from the left navigation present under **Sites**.

2. Select one site and click on the option **Storage** from the command bar as shown in *Figure 2.83*:

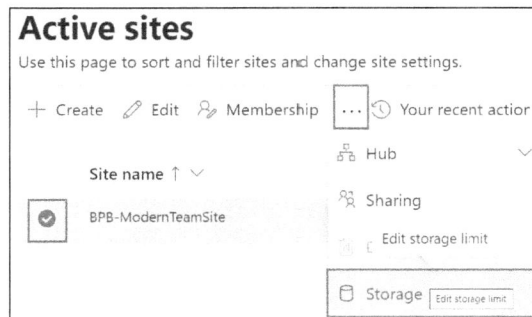

Active sites
Use this page to sort and filter sites and change site settings.

+ Create   ⟋ Edit   ⅗ Membership   ···   ⟳ Your recent action

                         ⬚ Hub   ⌄

Site name ↑ ⌄

☑   BPB-ModernTeamSite   ⅗ Sharing

                           Edit storage limit

                     🗄 Storage   Edit storage limit

Figure 2.83: Edit storage limit from command bar option

3. You will get the **Edit storage limit** window with options like **Maximum storage for this site, Allow notifications, Email owners when this much of the storage limit is used** as shown in *Figure 2.84*.

4. Allocate the storage limit for the site by entering a value from 1 GB to maximum 25600 GB in the field **Maximum storage for this site**.

5. You will find the percentage limit 98% auto suggested in the field **Email owners when this much of the storage limit is used**. When the site storage limit reaches 98%, you will get notified. You can modify this percentage to any value as per your requirements.

6. Select the checkbox option **Allow notifications** to receive email notifications on reaching the percentage storage limit used.

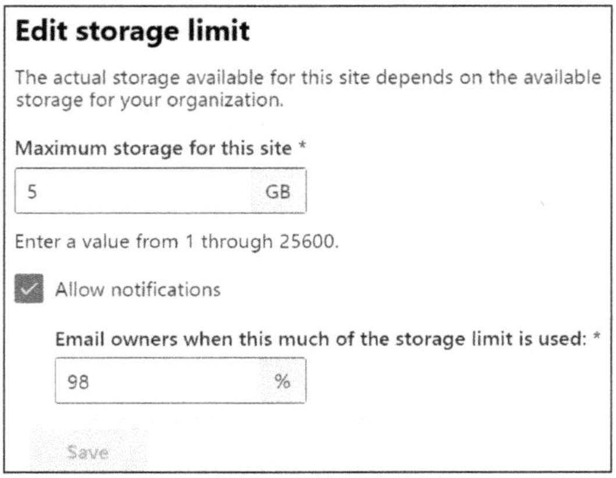

Edit storage limit

The actual storage available for this site depends on the available storage for your organization.

Maximum storage for this site *

| 5 | GB |

Enter a value from 1 through 25600.

☑ Allow notifications

Email owners when this much of the storage limit is used: *

| 98 | % |

Save

Figure 2.84: Configure maximum storage limit and warning notification

7. Alternatively, you can edit the storage from another window. Follow the steps from *1* to *6* as discussed in the previous section *Change site name*. Under **Site info**, you will find an option **Storage limit**. Click on the option **Edit**, as shown in *Figure 2.85*. You will get the same window as shown in *Figure 2.84*. You can edit the storage limit in any one of these ways:

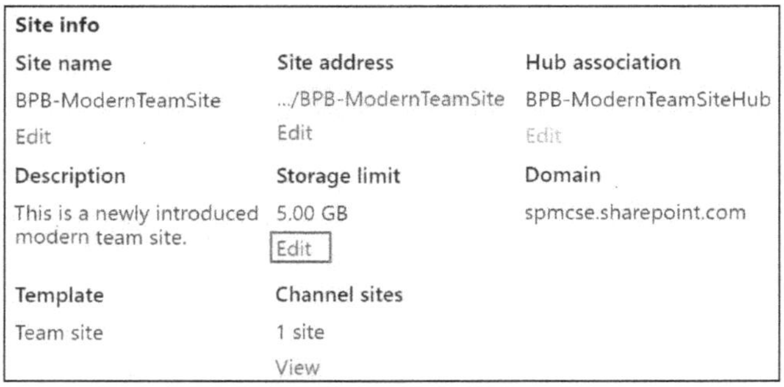

Site info

Site name	Site address	Hub association
BPB-ModernTeamSite	.../BPB-ModernTeamSite	BPB-ModernTeamSiteHub
Edit	Edit	Edit
Description	**Storage limit**	**Domain**
This is a newly introduced modern team site.	5.00 GB	spmcse.sharepoint.com
	Edit	
Template	**Channel sites**	
Team site	1 site	
	View	

Figure 2.85: Edit storage limit from edit site tab

Deleted sites

Active sites that are in use will be found under the **Active sites** list. Once the site is of no use, the site owner requests to delete the site. Once a site is deleted from the **Active site** tab, it will be moved to the **Delete sites** list present under the left navigation under **Sites**. Deleted sites are retained for 93 days (about 3 months) so the administrator can restore them during need. After 93 days (about 3 months), sites will be deleted permanently. Let us discuss the various options available under **Delete** and its applications.

Restore site

There might be a situation where the site got deleted by mistake or deleted as per the site owner's request, but now the site owner wants to restore the site to use it again. In that case, the administrator can restore the site only if the site falls under those 93 days (about three months) retained period. If the site is deleted for more than 93 days (about three months), then the administrator cannot restore the site. Follow these steps to restore site:

1. Navigate to **Deleted sites** from the left navigation present under **Sites**. Refer to *Figure 2.86*:

Figure 2.86: Navigate to deleted sites

2. Select one site that you want to restore

3. Click on the option **Restore** from the command bar as shown in *Figure 2.87*:

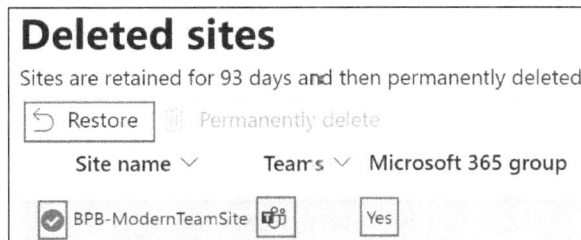

Figure 2.87: Restore site

4. If you are restoring a team site with a teams group linked to it, then you will get an additional dialog box, as shown in *Figure 2.88*, which indicates that you have to restore teams and all resources like conversations, calendars, and notebooks. You

need to confirm by clicking **Restore** to finish the restoration of the site. If there is no teams group linked to the site that you are trying to restore, then the site will be moved back to **Active sites** list without any further dialog box:

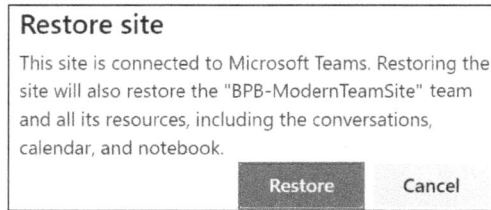

Figure 2.88: Restore site confirmation

Permanently delete site

Although deleted sites will be permanently removed from the tenant after 93 days (about three months), you can delete them at any moment within these 93 days. Follow these steps to delete a site permanently:

1. Navigate to **Deleted sites** from left navigation present under **Sites**.

2. Select one site that you want to delete.

3. Click on option **Permanently delete** from the command bar to delete the site permanently, as shown in the following figure:

Figure 2.89: Permanently delete site

4. You will get a dialog box to confirm and click on **Delete**. Once site collection is deleted, it cannot be restored. Refer to *Figure 2.90*:

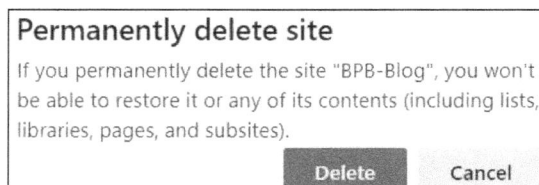

Figure 2.90: Confirm to delete sites permanently

5. If you select any team site and try to **Permanently delete** it, you will find the option **Permanently delete** is not enabled, as shown in the following figure:

Deleted sites

Sites are retained for 93 days and then permanently deleted. Learn more

↺ Restore | 🗑 Permanently delete

	Site name ˅	URL ˅	Template
✔	TeamSIte1	.../sites/TeamSIte1	Team site

Figure 2.91: Permanently delete sites disabled

6. You need to use PowerShell command, as mentioned, to permanently delete the team site from **Deleted sites** list since Microsoft Teams groups are linked to it.

Remove-SPODeletedSite -Identity https://spmcse.sharepoint.com/sites/ TeamSIte1 as shown in *Figure 2.92*:

Figure 2.92: Delete Teams site using PowerShell

Conclusion

In this chapter, we discussed creating sites, searching, filtering, and exporting site list to CSV file. We discussed step-by-step procedures to manage permissions by adding Microsoft 365 group owners and additional admins on site. We also got an idea about sharing sites, files, and links. Understood how to register a site as a hub site and associate any site with a hub site. We learned how to edit the site and check recent actions. Shared information on deleting and restoring sites. In *Chapter 3, Policies Administration,* we will discuss managing sharing and access control policies.

Points to remember

- The modern team site is linked with the Microsoft 365 group. You will notice a slight difference while creating a site, deleting a site, and permission management.

- Deleting the team site permanently before 93 days must be done using PowerShell only.

- Regular changes are applied in Office 365 and SharePoint Online. There may be changes in the template or some other features with time.

Join our book's Discord space

Join the book's Discord Workspace for Latest updates, Offers, Tech happenings around the world, New Release and Sessions with the Authors:

https://discord.bpbonline.com

CHAPTER 3
Policies Administration

Introduction

In the previous *Chapter 2, Site Administration,* we discussed multiple settings related to SharePoint online sites to administrate and the basic understanding of sharing options available on the site. In this chapter, we will discuss the policies that can be applied at the tenant level to control the sharing of sites, folders, and files. We will have a high-level discussion on sharing and access control. You will understand how to create policies at the tenant level to control content sharing with external users and set permission for the links shared with external users or internal users. You will understand the policy and its impact on site-sharing options at the tenant level, site level, and document-sharing level and how to control the way we can access content in SharePoint and OneDrive.

Structure

In this chapter, we will discuss the following topics:

- Policies administration
- Sharing
- File and folder links settings

Objectives

By the end of this chapter, you will get a clear understanding of various options available under the left navigation option *Policies, Sharing, Access control* in the SharePoint admin center. You will get a clear understanding of the external sharing policies available in SharePoint and how to apply policies to control the external sharing of sites. You will learn how to limit sharing of site with the people in your organization or external users who already exist in the organization directory or new external user or anyone having the link. You will understand the policy's impact at the tenant, site, and item level. You will understand about configuring permission of the link that can be shared to the users. You will get to know the use of access control settings to restrict how users are allowed to access content in SharePoint and OneDrive. You will understand about managing unmanaged devices, allow or block app access based on modern authentication, network locations.

Policies administration

SharePoint is a content management tool that provides a collaborative platform to access content and work on it. It provides multiple options to manage permission and authorize users to access content. We can further limit the permission and sharing content by applying policies. By applying policies, we can disable certain sharing options available for files and folders. It also enables additional options to control and limit sharing as well. Let us discuss the options available under **Policies** in the following steps:

1. Navigate to SharePoint admin center.

2. Expand the option **Policies** present under left navigation.

3. You will notice two options: **Sharing** and **Access control**. We can use these two options to configure and manage policies that are applicable at the organizational level. In this chapter, we will focus on the types of options available under policies and their applications in detail. Refer to *Figure 3.1*:

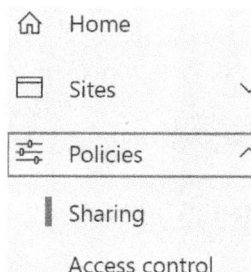

Figure 3.1: Policies and options available under policy

Let us discuss more about this in the next section.

Sharing

Sharing is the first category present under **Policies**. Once you click on Sharing from left navigation as shown in *Figure 3.1*, you will notice the options are categorized into three: **External sharing, File and folder links**, and **Other settings**. Sharing allows the admin to create organizational-level policies, like **External sharing,** to control with whom the content can be shared. **File and folder links** allow the admin to create policies related to default links, which will be selected during the sharing of content. We can also control the type of permission that can be assigned by default when a link is shared with the user. **Other settings** to enable or disable additional information related to sharing. Let us discuss each option in detail.

External sharing settings

External sharing is the first option under sharing. We can control and apply organizational level policies from the setting: **External sharing**. This provides options to apply policies and limit sharing of contents from SharePoint site and OneDrive at tenant level. Administrators can find options to limit content sharing policy from least permissive (highly secure) to most permissive (lowest secure) from admin center.

Let us discuss the options available in the following steps:

1. Navigate to the **SharePoint admin center**.

2. Expand **Policies** from the left navigation. You will find two options: **Sharing** and **Access control**. Click on **Sharing** as shown in the following *Figure 3.2*:

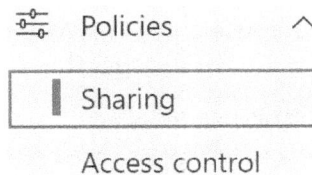

Figure 3.2: *Policies navigation option*

3. You will find the first option category as **External sharing (Content can be shared with)**.

4. You will notice slider (graphical format) for the applications **SharePoint** and **OneDrive** and right to that all permissive levels that we can set for the applications SharePoint and OneDrive. Refer to *Figure 3.3*.

5. You will notice four permissive levels like **Only people in your organization** (Least permissive level), **Existing guests, New and existing guests, Anyone** (Most permissive level). Refer to *Figure 3.3*:

Sharing

Use these settings to control sharing at the organization level in SharePoint and OneDrive.

External sharing

Content can be shared with:

🔷 SharePoint   ☁ OneDrive

| | | |
Most permissive

Anyone
Users can share files and folders using links that don't require sign-in.

New and existing guests
Guests must sign in or provide a verification code.

Existing guests
Only guests already in your organization's directory.

Least permissive

Only people in your organization
No external sharing allowed.

You can further restrict sharing for each individual site and OneDrive. Learn how

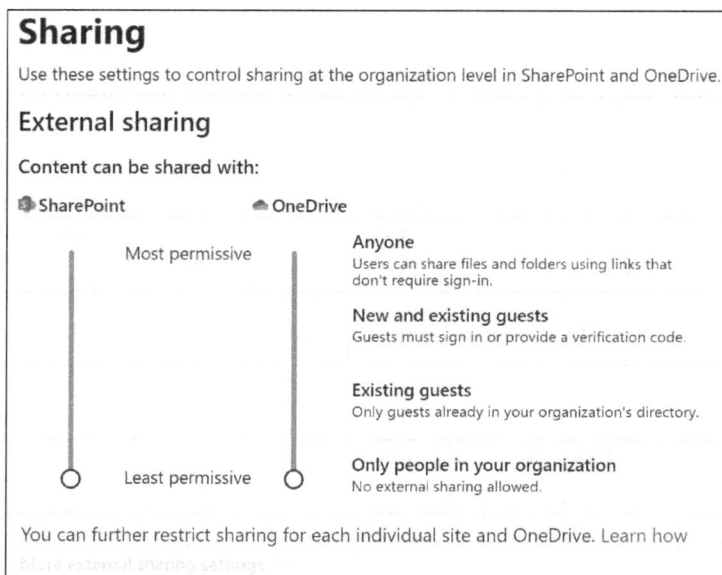

Figure 3.3: External sharing options

6. You can use the slider to drag and select any one of the four permissive levels to apply tenant/organizational level policy settings.

7. By default, the permissive level selected as **Only people in your organization** the **Least permissive** level. You can use the slider to drag and select the permissive level as per your requirement.

8. Below the slider, you will notice an option **More external sharing settings**. This setting is disabled initially. We will discuss this later.

Let us discuss in detail about permissive levels, its application, and changes in options upon selecting different permissive levels.

Only people in your organization

Only people in your organization are one of the four permissive levels, the least permissive level that admin can choose under the **External Sharing** settings. This setting will limit users in sharing sites and content to people within their organization, and it will block sharing the content to people residing out of the organization, that is, external users. Accessing content is applied as per the permission applied in site. In this section, we will discuss how to apply the policy at the tenant level and understand its impact on sharing a site at the tenant level, individual site settings at site sharing level, document sharing level. Let us discuss the following steps to understand better:

1. Select the slider from applications **SharePoint** and **OneDrive,** drag to the permissive level: **Only people in your organization,** as seen in *Figure 3.4*:

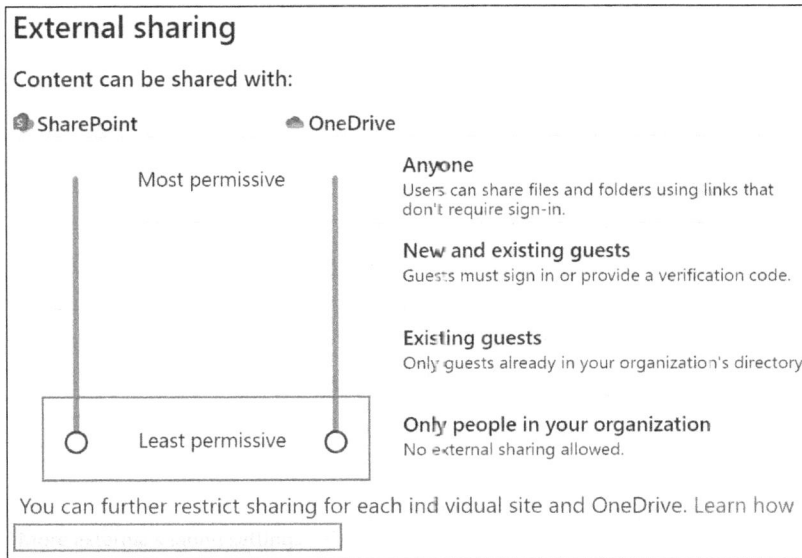

External sharing

Content can be shared with:

SharePoint   OneDrive

Most permissive

Anyone
Users can share files and folders using links that don't require sign-in.

New and existing guests
Guests must sign in or provide a verification code.

Existing guests
Only guests already in your organization's directory.

Only people in your organization
No external sharing allowed.

Least permissive

You can further restrict sharing for each individual site and OneDrive. Learn how

Figure 3.4: Only people in your organization

2. You will notice an option **More external sharing settings**, below the slider, in disabled state as shown in *Figure 3.4*. Next to **External sharing**, you will get the **File and folder links** category and the option **Only people in your organization** selected. The default shared link permission is **View**, refer to *Figure 3.5*. We will discuss more about the option category, **File and folder links,** later.

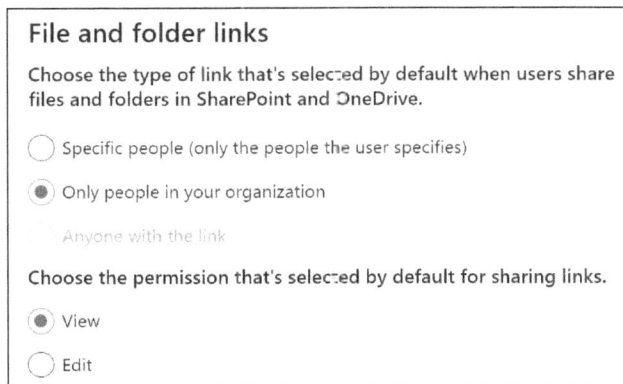

File and folder links

Choose the type of link that's selected by default when users share files and folders in SharePoint and OneDrive.

( ) Specific people (only the people the user specifies)

(●) Only people in your organization

( ) Anyone with the link

Choose the permission that's selected by default for sharing links.

(●) View

( ) Edit

Figure 3.5: File and folder links

3. Next to **Files and folder links**, you will get the **Other settings** category. Keep all the settings as default. Refer to *Figure 3.6*:

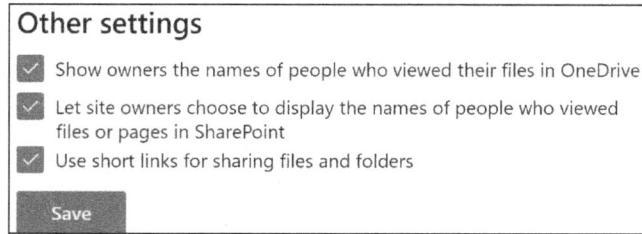

Figure 3.6: *Other settings*

We just applied the tenant/organizational level policy. Let us see its impact in sharing a site at the tenant level. Let us discuss the following steps to understand better:

1. Expand the option **Sites** present under the left navigation in SharePoint admin center.

2. Click on **Active sites**.

3. Select any one site and click on **Sharing** from the command bar.

4. A new dialog box related to **Sharing** will open. Under the first category, **External sharing,** you will notice that the permissive level, **Only people in your organization** (Least permissive), is selected, and the remaining three permissive levels, like **Existing guests**, **New and existing guests**, and **Anyone,** are disabled due to the sharing policy applied at the tenant level. So, we cannot choose any other option except **Only people in your organization**. Refer to *Figure 3.7*:

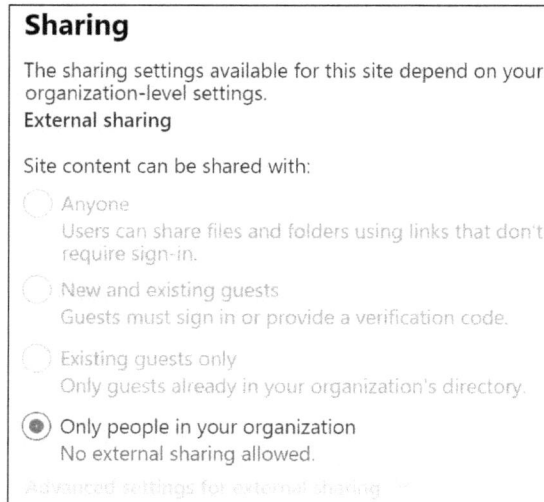

Figure 3.7: *Impact of policy only people in your organization in external sharing*

5. At the bottom of **External sharing,** you will find the option **Advanced settings for external sharing** in the disabled state as shown in *Figure 3.7*.

6. In the next category, **Default sharing link type,** you will find the checkbox **Same as organization-level setting (Only people in your organization)** is selected. Since we configured the policy only people in your organization, you will find the option **Only people in your organization** applied by default here. Refer to *Figure 3.8*:

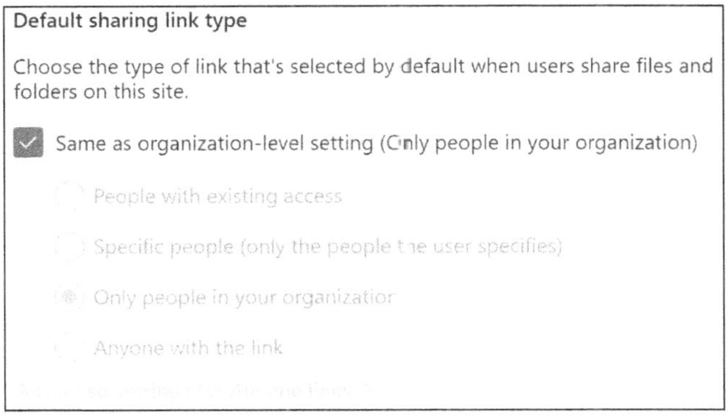

Default sharing link type

Choose the type of link that's selected by default when users share files and folders on this site.

☑ Same as organization-level setting (Only people in your organization)

○ People with existing access

○ Specific people (only the people the user specifies)

⦿ Only people in your organization

○ Anyone with the link

Figure 3.8: Impact of policy on default sharing link type

7. In the next category, **Default link permission,** you will find the default permission applied to the link shared to the user, which is **View** and **Same as the organization-level setting (View).** We configured this setting while configuring policy. Refer to *Figure 3.9*:

Default link permission

☑ Same as organization-level setting (View)

⦿ View

○ Edit

Save   Reset to organization-level settings

Figure 3.9: Impact of policy on default link permission

We discussed the impact of configured policy on sharing a site at the tenant level. Let us see the impact on individual site settings at the site sharing level. Let us discuss the following steps to understand better:

1. Access any site.

2. Click on **Settings**, the gear icon at the top right corner of the site, and click on **Site permissions**.

3. A new dialog box **Permissions** will open. Click on **Add members**. You will get drop down with options like **Add members to group** and **Share site only** as seen in *Figure 3.10*.

4. Click on the option **Share site only**.

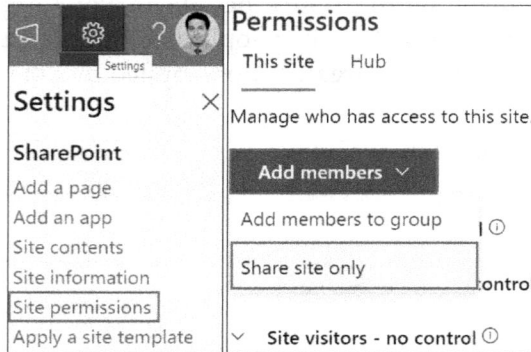

Figure 3.10: Impact of policy on share site only

5. Enter the mail ID of any internal user who is employed by your organization and has the same email address as your organization's domain. Here, the tenant domain is spmcse.com. So, enter any email ID with the domain **spmcse.com**. You can add internal users and share the site.

6. Now, enter the mail ID of an external user (outside your organization) with a domain other than spmcse.com (existing guest user whose external mail ID already exists in Azure Active Directory). You will get a message like: **The mail ID entered is outside of your organization**. As soon as you click on **Add**, you will see an error: **Couldn't resolve user** as seen in *Figure 3.11*. This means the site can be shared with internal users only who are part of your organization's domain:

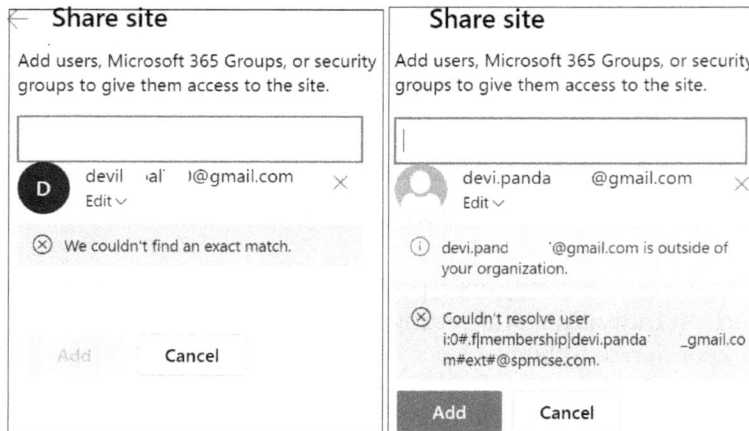

Figure 3.11: Impact of policy on external sharing

7. Now enter the mail ID of an external user (outside your organization) with a domain other than **spmcse.com** (a user whose external mail ID does not exist in Azure Active Directory is not a guest user yet, also called a new guest). You will

get a message like the **mail id entered is outside of your organization**. As soon as you click on **Add**, you will see an error: **We couldn't find an exact match**, as seen in *Figure 3.11*.

We discussed the impact of configured policy on individual site settings at site sharing level. Now let us discuss the impact of configured policy at document sharing level. Let us discuss the following steps to understand better.

1. Open the document library.

2. Select any document and click on **Share** from the command bar, as shown in *Figure 3.12*:

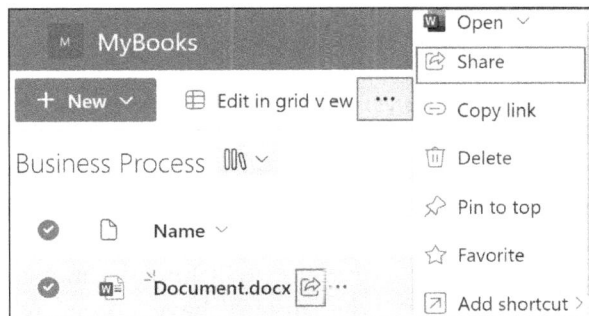

Figure 3.12: Impact of policy on document sharing

3. You will get another window to enter sharing details. In the people picker field, enter the email ID of the internal user with the organizational domain, e.g., Spmcse. com. You will see the option **Send** is enabled and allowed to share documents with internal company users. Refer to *Figure 3.13*. This means you can share the file with an internal user.

4. You will also notice that the default link permission is set as **Can view**. Refer to *Figure 3.13*:

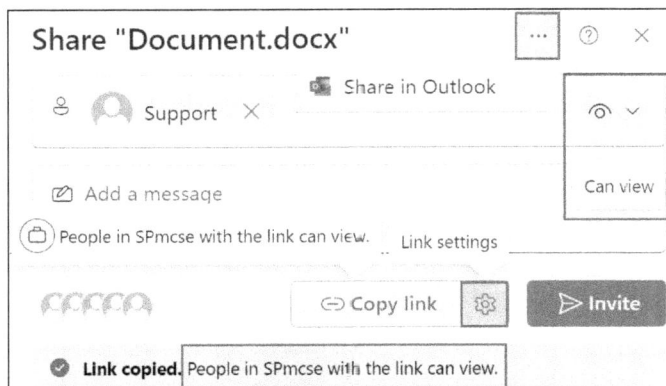

Figure 3.13: Option send is enabled for internal user

5. Now enter the mail ID of the external user (new guest or existing guest) outside of your organization, then you will get an error like **We couldn't find an exact match**. Refer to *Figure 3.14*:

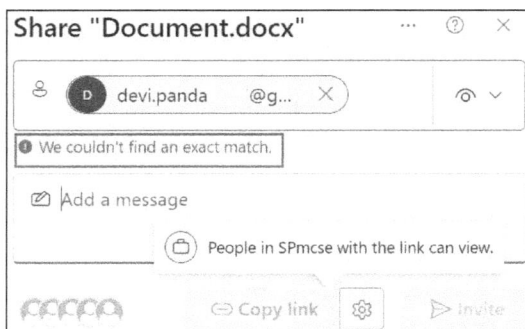

Figure 3.14: Option send is disabled for external user

6. Click on **Link settings**, the gear icon as seen in *Figure 3.13*. You will find the default option under the category **Share the link with** as **People in organization domain**. Refer to *Figure 3.15*. You can change to other options from the default option. If you select **People with existing access**, you will find the message like **Reshare with people in your organization who already have access**, which also indicates to internal users. If you are selecting the option **People you choose**, you will find the message like **Share with specific people you choose inside of SPmcse, using their name, group, or email** which also indicates to internal users only. Refer to *Figure 3.15*:

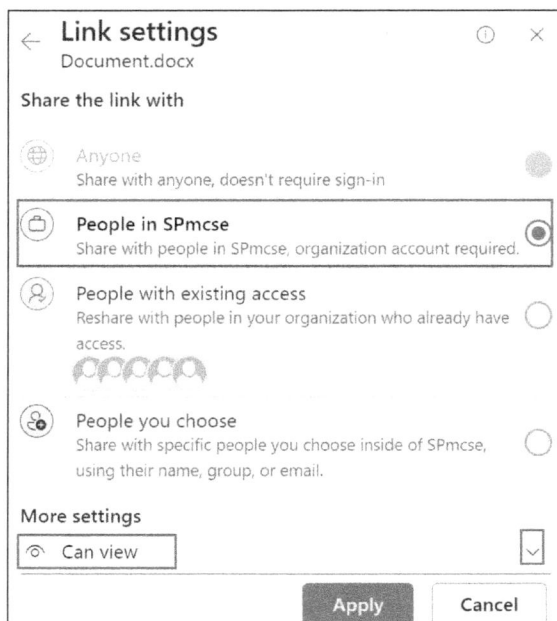

Figure 3.15: Impact of policy on document sharing settings

7. Regardless of any options selected, the shared content can only be accessed by internal users with an organizational comain and will be blocked for external users.

8. Next, under the category **More settings**, you will find the default link permission selected as **Can view** which can be changed to other permission as per requirement.

Existing guests

We discussed the external sharing policy option **Only people in your organization** out of four options as discussed in the section **External sharing settings**, *Step 5*. Let us discuss the second external sharing policy option: **Existing guests** under the category of external sharing. This option allows external users to access sites with proper authentication, but the user must be added as a member of the group in Azure Active Directory to access any shared content, such as a site, folder, or file. If the user accepted the previous sharing invitation, then the user might be available in the Azure Active Directory. This means that any site content was shared with the external user previously, and the user must have accessed the content at least once. The option **existing guests** is applicable to those users. In this section, we will discuss how to apply the policy at the tenant level and understand its impact on sharing a site at the tenant level, individual site settings at the site sharing level, and the document sharing level. Let us discuss the following steps to understand better:

1. Under **External Sharing** settings, select the slider from applications SharePoint and OneDrive, and drag to the permissive level **Existing Guests** as seen in *Figure 3.16*. You will notice that another category **More external sharing settings** got enabled:

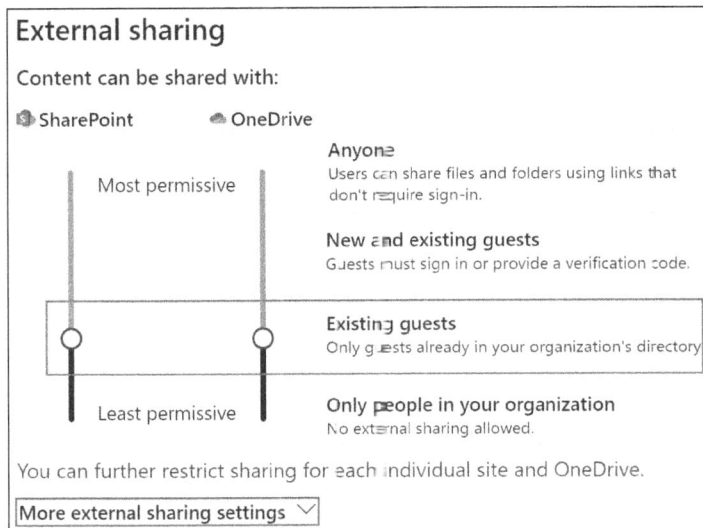

Figure 3.16: *Apply external sharing policy to existing guests*

2. Expand the option **More external sharing settings**, you will find five options like **Limit external sharing by domain, Allow only users in specific security groups to share externally, Guests must sign in using the same account to which sharing invitations are sent, Allow guests to share items they don't own, People who use a verification code must reauthenticate after this many days**, to manage external sharing better, as seen in *Figure 3.17*:

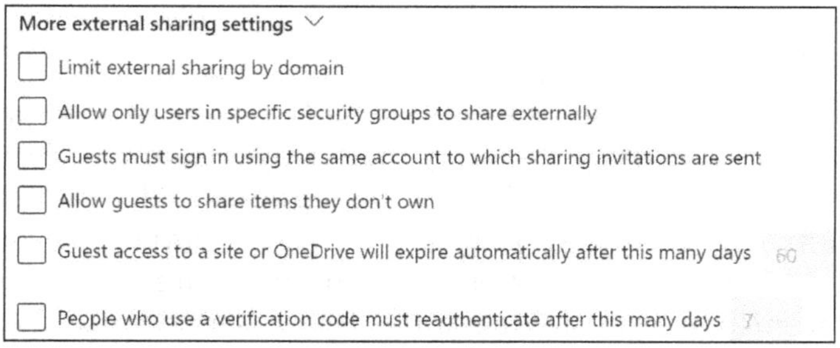

Figure 3.17: More external sharing settings got enabled

We just applied another tenant/organizational level policy. Let us see its impact in sharing a site at the tenant level. Let us discuss the following steps to understand better:

1. Select any site from **Active sites** present in left navigation of SharePoint admin center under **Sites**.

2. Click on **Sharing** from the command bar. A **Sharing** dialog box will open.

3. You will find one more option **Existing guests only** is enabled in addition to **Only people in your organization** present under **External sharing (Site content can be shared with)**. Refer to *Figure 3.18*.

4. Below the external sharing, you will notice another category of options, **Advanced settings for external sharing**, gets enabled too.

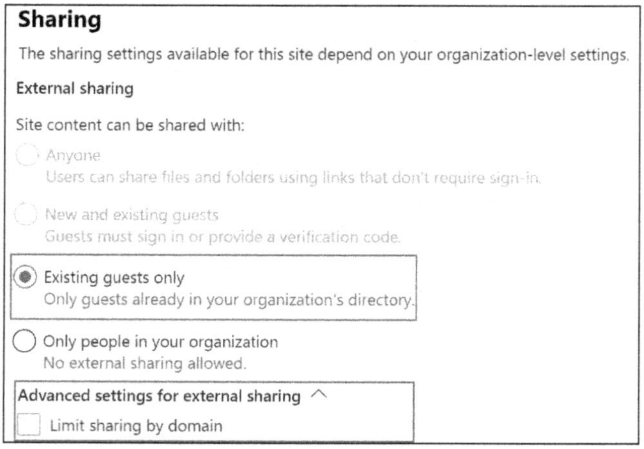

Figure 3.18: Existing guests only, Advanced settings for external sharing options got enabled

We discussed the impact of configured policy in sharing a site at the tenant level. Let us see the impact on individual site settings at the site sharing level:

1. Access any site.

2. Click on **Settings**, the gear icon at the top right corner of the site, and click on **Site permissions**.

3. A new dialog box **Permissions** will open. Click on **Add members**. You will get drop down with options like **Add members to group** and **Share site only** as shown in *Figure 3.19*.

4. Click on the option **Share site only**.

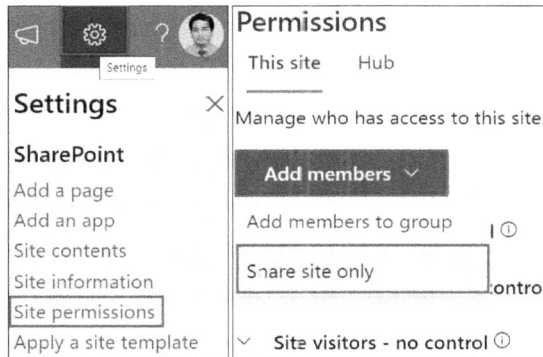

Figure 3.19: Share site only

5. Let us say the external user **devi.panda@gmail.com** already accepted one site invitation request before and guest account already exists in Azure AD. Share the site to this ID **devi.panda@gmail.com** now. When you enter mail ID under the field **Share site**, you will see a message like **devi.panda@gmail.com is outside of your organization** as seen in *Figure 3.20*.

6. Click on **Add** present at the bottom to share site, as shown in the following figure:

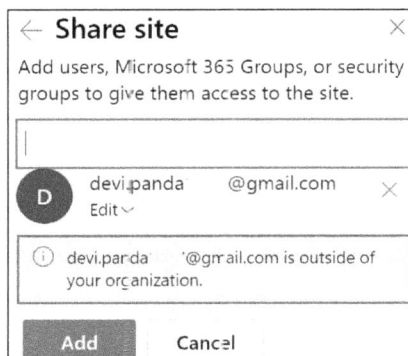

Figure 3.20: Sharing site to existing guest users enabled

7. The user will receive mail with messages like **Go to Sitename (MyBooks)**. Since that user already exists in Azure AD, user can access the site by clicking the site name from the link received in mail. Refer to *Figure 3.21*:

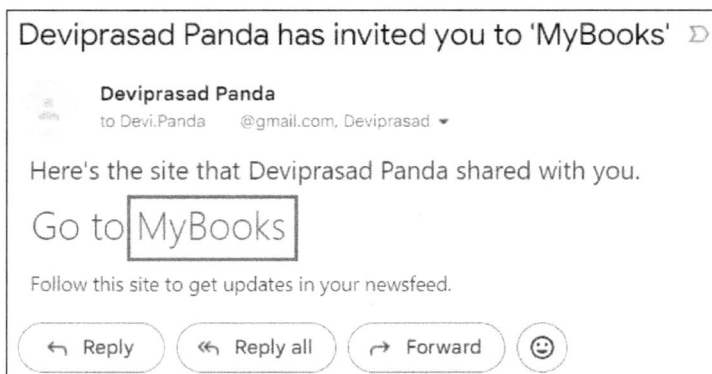

Figure 3.21: Existing guest user will receive mail on sharing content

8. Now, enter the mail ID of the external user whose external mail ID does not exist in Azure Active Directory. Since policy is applied so that only existing guests and this user are not existing guest users, you will get an error message like **We couldn't find an exact match**. Sharing is not possible other than for existing guest users. Refer to *Figure 3.22*:

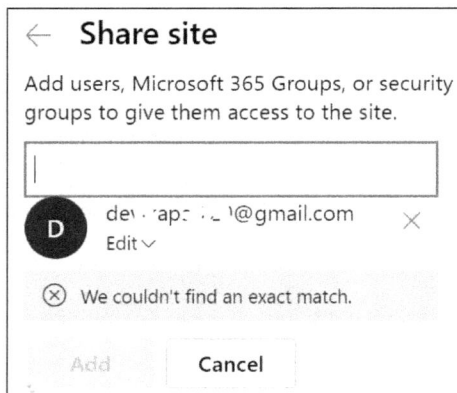

Figure 3.22: External user not an existing guest

We discussed the impact of the configured policy on individual site settings at the site sharing level. Now let us discuss the impact of the configured policy at the document sharing level. Let us discuss the following steps to understand better:

1. Open the document library.

2. Select any document and click on **Share** from the command bar. Refer to *Figure 3.23*:

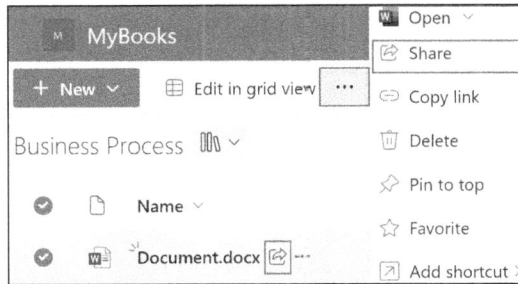

Figure 3.23: Share the document to existing user

3. Click on **Link settings** from the sharing window next. Refer to *Figure 3.24*:

Figure 3.24: Link settings while sharing document

4. Select the option **People with existing access** and click on **Apply**. Refer to *Figure 3.25*:

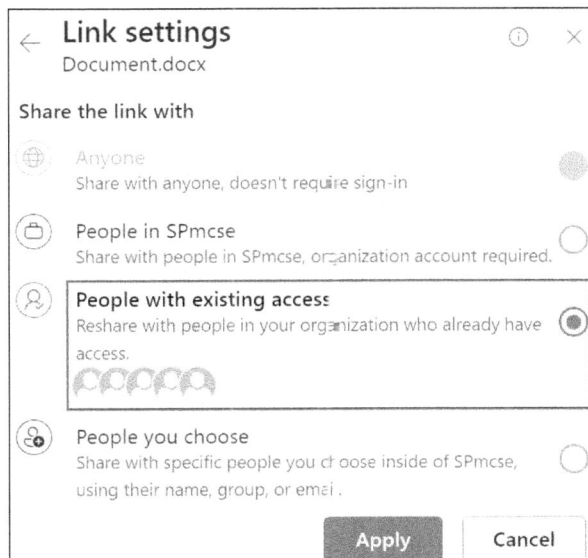

Figure 3.25: People with existing access

5. Now, enter the external mail already added to the organization Azure Active Directory (Existing guest user). Click on the **Copy link**. You will get a message like **People with existing access can use the link** as expected. Refer to *Figure 3.26.* Existing guest users to whom the link is shared can access the file:

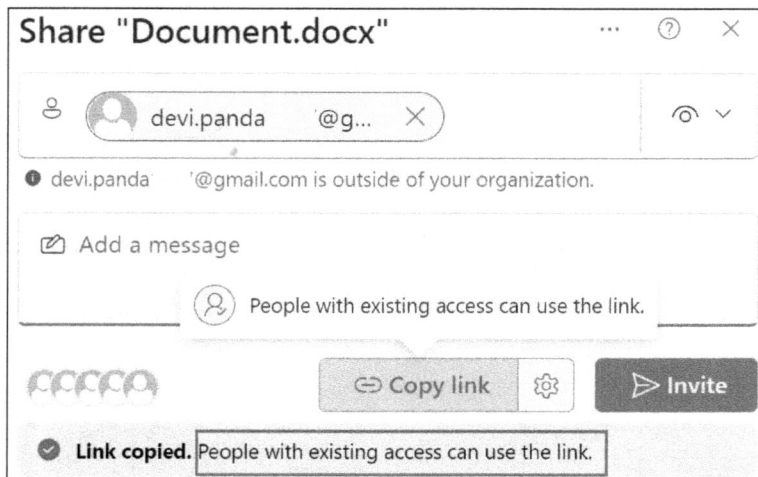

Figure 3.26: People with existing access can use the link

6. If you try to share the document to new external mail ID not added to Azure Active Directory, you will get an error like We could not find an exact match as seen in Figure 3.27:

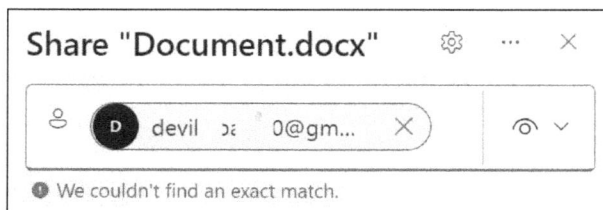

Figure 3.27: Document sharing error to new external users

We discussed the impact switching of External Sharing (Content can be shared with) to Existing guests. We noticed the additional option category **More external sharing settings** was enabled due to this change. Let us discuss the option category **More external sharing settings** and its impact on external sharing after selecting different options in it.

Admin can limit the sharing of site or content by allowing or blocking specific domain. The user's part of that domain can access the site or content only. Admin can add or block domain at tenant level or at the site collection level. Let us discuss the following steps to understand better:

1. Navigate to **More external sharing settings** which got enabled on switching the policy to Existing guests present under **External sharing**.

2. Select the check box **Limit external sharing** settings and click on **Add domains**. Refer to *Figure 3.28*:

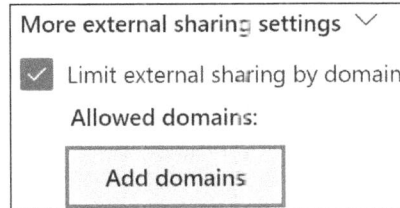

Figure 3.28: Limit external sharing by domain got enabled

3. Add domains dialog box will open. Select the radio button **Allow only specific domains**.

4. Enter the domain (example, `SharePointTechnicalSupport.com`) that you want to allow sharing in the field. If you want to allow multiple domains, then enter all domains in separate line, as shown in *Figure 3.29*.

5. Click on **Save** to apply changes.

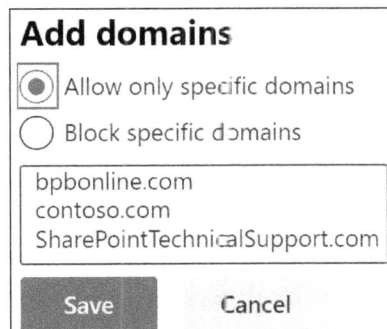

Figure 3.29: Add domains

Let us see its impact in sharing a site at the tenant level.

6. Navigate to **Active sites** present in the left navigation of SharePoint admin center under **Sites**.

7. Select any one of the sites and click on **Sharing** from the command bar.

8. The sharing dialog box will open. You will find the option **Advanced settings for external sharing** is enabled now. You can enable the option **Limit sharing by domain** present under Advanced settings for external sharing by selecting the checkbox as seen in *Figure 3.30*. You will see **Allowed domains** that we added:

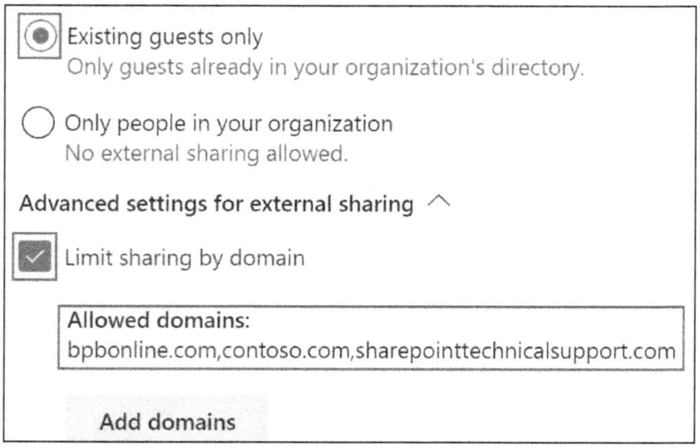

Figure 3.30: *Allowed domains under limit sharing by domains*

9. You can also modify the allowed domains for specific sites at the site sharing level by following the button **Add domains**, as shown in *Figure 3.30*.

10. Remove any domains applied at the tenant level following the cross icon and click on **Save** to apply changes. You will not find that specific domain under allowed domain for that site only.

Figure 3.31: *Edit allowed domains at site sharing, tenant level*

11. The user's part of the allowed domains can access the shared site or content.

12. Now, share the site with the existing guest user whose mail ID already exists in Azure Active Directory. You will get a message like: **xxx@abc.com is outside of your organization**. Refer to *Figure 3.32*:

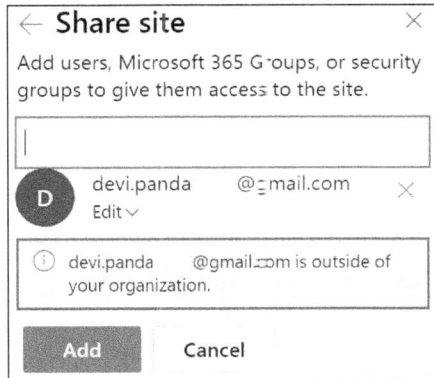

Figure 3.32: Sharing site outside domain

13. The user will receive a mail but when the user will try to access the site, a message will appear like **Something went wrong. The organization that owns this resource has a policy that prevents access from people in the domain you are currently signed in to**. Refer to *Figure 3.33*. This is due to the domain policy applied, as this domain is restricted by the admin. This setting gives an additional option to prevent external sharing by allowing specific domain, although you allowed existing guest user access:

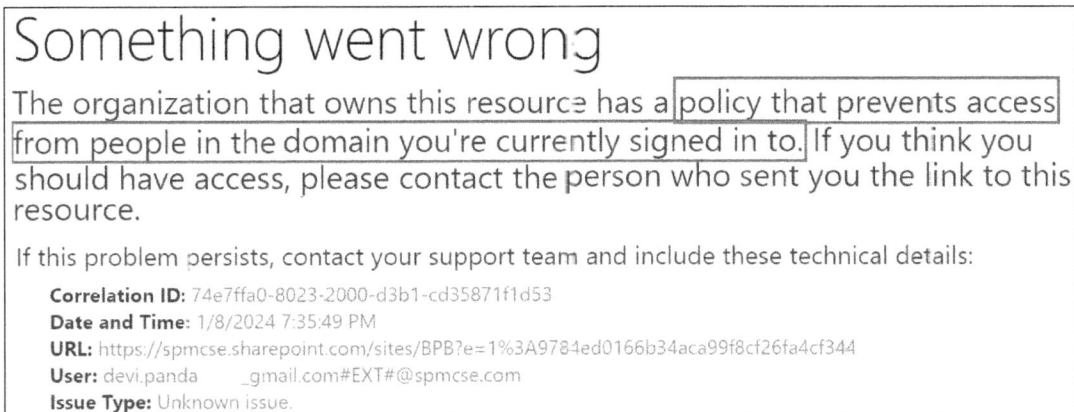

Figure 3.33: Error while external user other than allowed domain try to access content

14. The way we allow content sharing to external users of a specific domain, we can block content sharing to specific domain external users. Follow the same steps that we discussed while allowing specific domain. The only change will be to select the option **Block specific domains**. Refer to *Figure 3.34*:

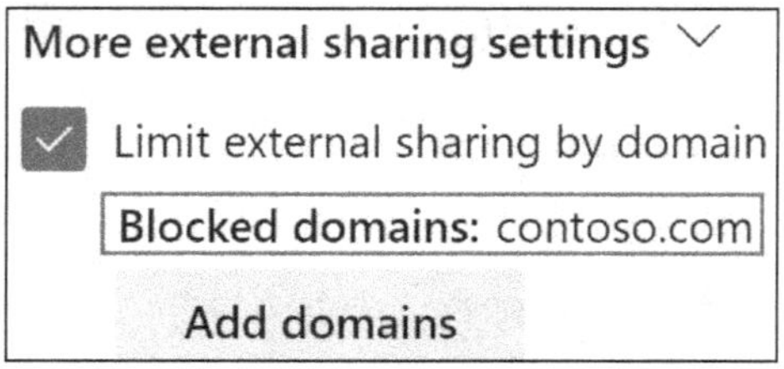

Figure 3.34: Blocked domains

Let us discuss the second option, **Allow only users in specific security groups to share externally**, present under the category **More external sharing settings** and its impact on external sharing. We can further control which security group users only can share sites, content, OneDrive files to external users by using this option. Let us discuss the following steps to understand better:

1. Select the checkbox **Allow only users in specific security groups to share externally** present under the category **More external sharing settings**. Refer to *Figure 3.35*:

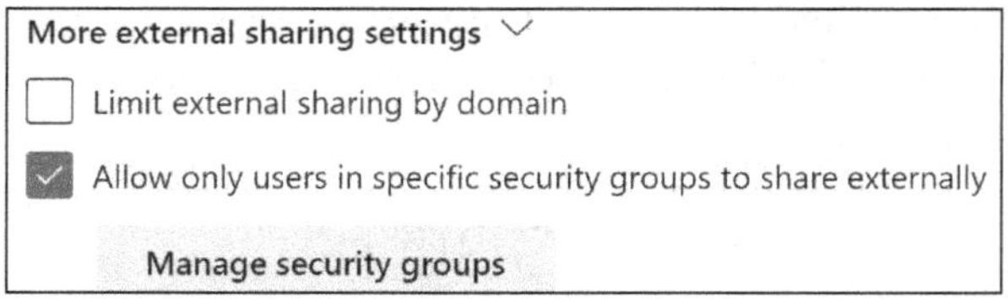

Figure 3.35: Enable the option, allow only users in specific security groups to share externally

2. You will find the **Manage security groups** button. Click on **Manage security groups**.

3. **Manage security groups** dialog box will open. Enter the name of security group in the field **Add a security group**. Refer to *Figure 3.36*:

Figure 3.36: Add security group members of which can only share to external users

4. You will find two fields like **Name** and **Can share with** that define the security group name and the users to whom those security group members can share content respectively. Users who are present in this group only can share site, content, OneDrive files to external users. Selecting the option **Can share with Anyone** will allow users present in that security group to share the site, content, and OneDrive files with external users who do not need authentication to access. Selecting the option **Can share with** as **Authenticated guests only** will allow users present in that security group to share the site, content, and OneDrive file with external users who need to pass through the authentication process by entering a verification code to verify their identity.

Let us discuss the third option, **Guests must sign in using the same account to which sharing invitation sent**, present under the category **More external sharing settings**. Refer to *Figure 3.37*. This can be applied to manage security better. This will make sure users need to sign in using the same account to which site or content or OneDrive file is shared.

Let us discuss the fourth option, **Allow guests to share items they don't own**, present under the category **More external sharing settings**. Refer to *Figure 3.37*. Selecting this option will let guests share items further, although the guest is not the content's owner. Let this option be unchecked for better security management.

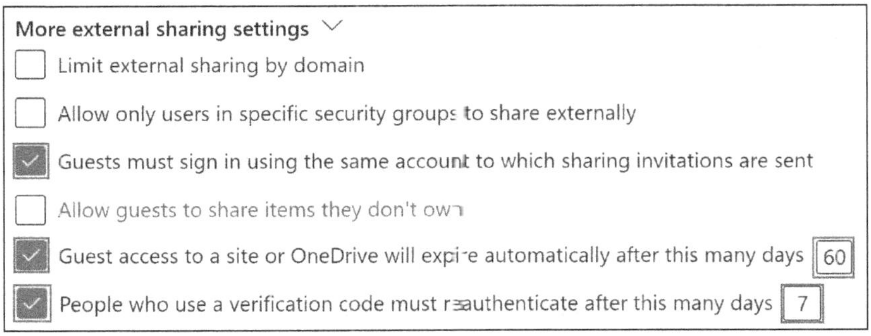

Figure 3.37: Enable options from more external sharing settings

Let us discuss the fifth option, **Guest access to a site or OneDrive will expire automatically after this many days**, present under the category **More external sharing settings**. Refer to *Figure 3.37*. Select the checkbox and enter the number of days after which access will expire, as per the requirement. Users cannot access the content after the specified number of days.

The final sixth option is **People who use a verification code that must reauthenticate after this many days**. Refer to *Figure 3.37*. Selecting this option will configure such that guest users need to reauthenticate after that configured days to access shared site, content, or OneDrive file. The default value for this option is selected as 7. This is the maximum limit we can set. Admin can decrease the value from 7 to lower as per requirement.

New and existing guests

We discussed the external sharing policy options **Only people in your organization** and **Existing guests** out of four options as discussed in the section **External sharing settings**, *Step 5*. Let us discuss the third external sharing policy option **New and existing guests** under the category external sharing. This option allows users to share the content to new external users (users with personal mail ID or people from another organization) whose mail IDs do not exist in the Azure Active Directory. Once the new external user accesses the shared content, that external user's email ID will be added as a guest user in the Azure Active Directory, and that user will be considered as an existing guest next time onwards. So, the **New and existing guests** policy opens an option to invite new guest users (external users) to access shared content. If your organization has no plan to include any new extern users, then you can switch the policy from **New and existing guests** to **Existing guests**. The new users who have already accepted the invitation are already part of existing guest users now, so there will be no issue in exceeding shared content. This option allows new external users to access sites, but authentication is done by a specific process. This way the users accessing sites can be identified during audit. Sites can be accessed only by the user to which the mail ID site is shared. Only users who have full control can share the site. In this section, we will discuss how to apply the policy **New and existing guests** at the tenant level and understand its impact on sharing a site at the tenant level, individual site settings at site sharing level, document sharing level:

1.   Under **External Sharing settings**, select the slider from applications SharePoint and OneDrive, and drag to permissive level **New and existing guests** as seen in *Figure 3.38*. You will notice that another category **More external sharing settings** got enabled same as we discussed in the section **Existing guests**.

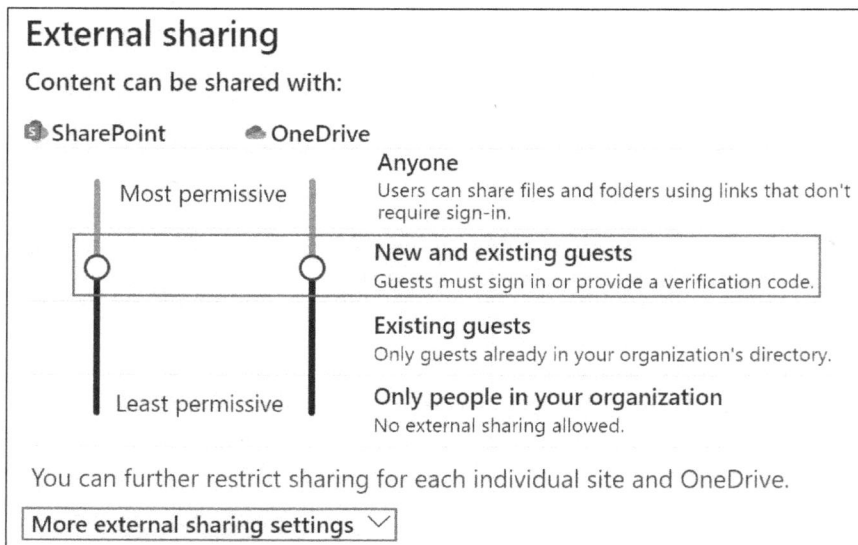

Figure 3.38: Switch external sharing settings to new and existing guests

2. As an impact, when you select any site and click on **share** from admin center command bar, you will find the option **New and existing guests** enabled and can be selected. Refer to *Figure 3.39*:

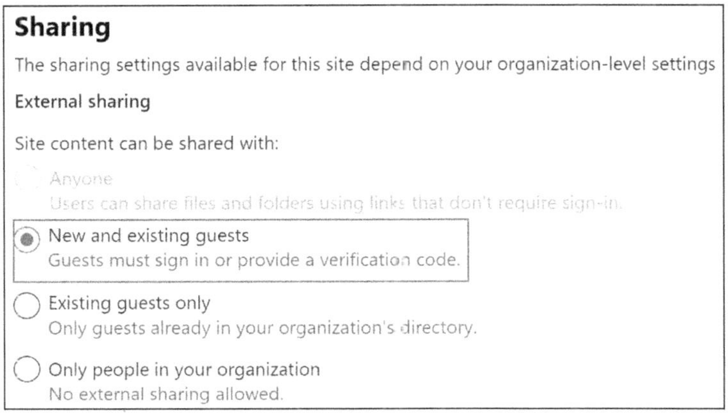

Sharing

The sharing settings available for this site depend on your organization-level settings

External sharing

Site content can be shared with:

○ Anyone
Users can share files and folders using links that don't require sign-in.

● New and existing guests
Guests must sign in or provide a verification code.

○ Existing guests only
Only guests already in your organization's directory.

○ Only people in your organization
No external sharing allowed.

Figure 3.39: New and existing guests enabled as per tenant level settings applied

3. Now, back to **More external sharing settings** under **Content can be shared with** under **External sharing**. Select the options as per requirement. You can select the checkbox **Limit external sharing by domain** and add domains under as per requirement as discussed under section **Existing guest policy**. Refer to *Figure 3.40*.

4. Select the option, **Guests must sign in using the same account to which sharing invitations are sent** so that new user must access using the same account to which content is shared. Refer to *Figure 3.40*.

5. You can select the option, **People who use a verification code must reauthenticate after this many days** to add additional security. Refer to *Figure 3.40*:

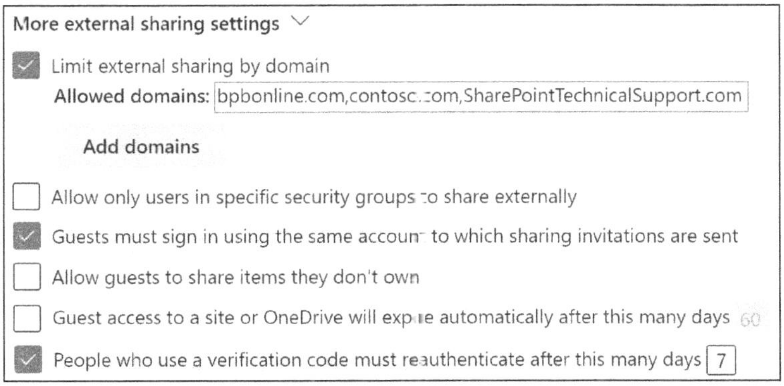

More external sharing settings ∨

☑ Limit external sharing by domain
Allowed domains: bpbonline.com,contosc.com,SharePointTechnicalSupport.com

Add domains

☐ Allow only users in specific security groups to share externally

☑ Guests must sign in using the same account to which sharing invitations are sent

☐ Allow guests to share items they don't own

☐ Guest access to a site or OneDrive will expire automatically after this many days 60

☑ People who use a verification code must reauthenticate after this many days 7

Figure 3.40: More external settings policy can be selected

6. As an impact, when you select any site and click on **Share** from command bar, you will find the option **Advanced settings for external sharing** is available to

be applied. You can select the checkbox option **Limit sharing by domain** to limit sharing within these allowed domains. Refer to *Figure 3.41*.

7. You will find the option **Expiration of guest access** also available under advanced settings for external sharing which is selected as **Same as organization-level setting (Never)**. Refer to *Figure 3.41*.

8. Since you have not selected the option **Guest access to a site or OneDrive will expire automatically after this many days**, it is being reflected as guest access never expires. Refer to *Figure 3.41*. If you select any custom day to expire, the same will be reflected under this option.

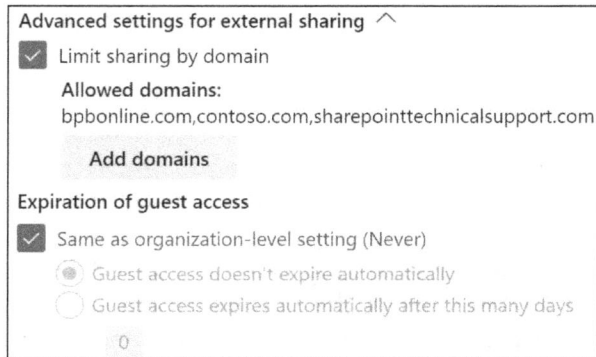

Figure 3.41: Advanced settings for external sharing when the policy is New and existing guests

9. Now, try to access any site and share the site with the new external user whose mail ID does not exist in Azure Active Directory yet and the mail ID (example, Gmail) you are sharing is not coming under allowed domains. You will get a message like **Your organization doesn't allow sharing with users from this domain**. Refer to *Figure 3.42*:

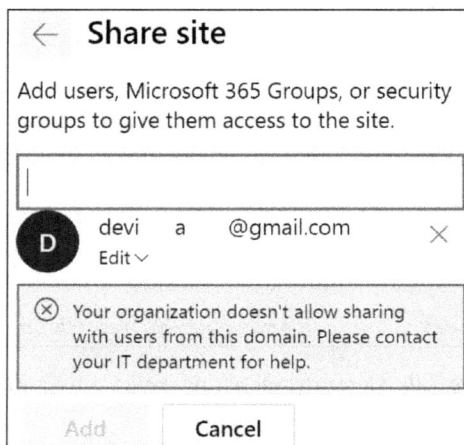

Figure 3.42: Sharing site to other domains blocked

10. Now, try to access any site and share the site with new external user whose mail ID does not exist in Azure Active Directory yet and the mail ID (example, **bpbonline**) you are sharing is coming under allowed domains. You can share the site now. Refer to *Figure 3.43*.

11. The user will receive a mail. When the user tries to access the site, the browser will be redirected to a page where the user will have to enter the user ID and password to access shared content. Once the user accesses the shared content, that user will be added as a guest user in Azure Active Directory, if that user did not accept any shared content previously.

Figure 3.43: Content sharing to allowed domains enabled

12. If you are disabling the option **Limit external sharing by domain** under external sharing and trying to share the site to any external user, you will just get a warning message like the domain is outside of your organization, but sharing is possible. Refer to *Figure 3.44*:

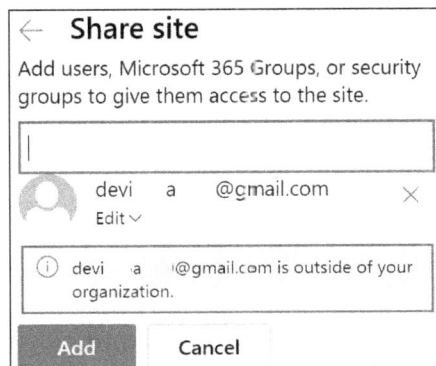

Figure 3.44: Share content to any user by unchecking limit external sharing domain

13. Now try to share any document and click on **Sharing settings** from the sharing dialog box. In the next window select the option **People you choose** under **Share the link with** and you will notice the information mentioned below the option as

Share with specific people you choose inside or outside of domain, using their name, group, or email. Refer to *Figure 3.45*:

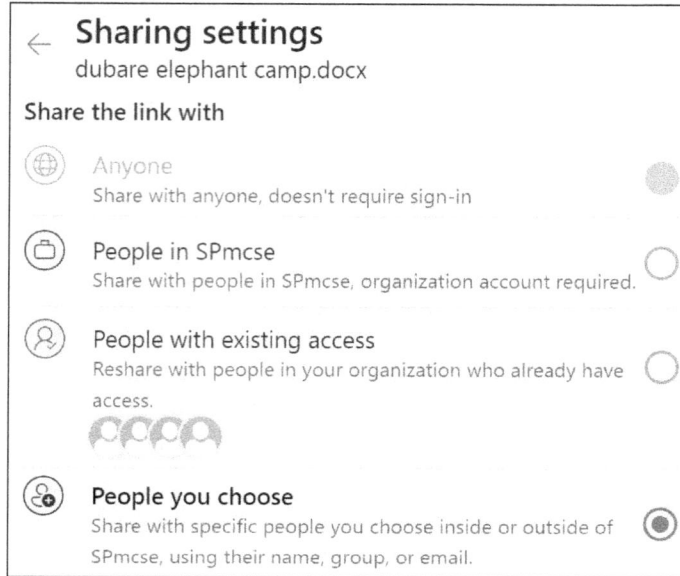

Figure 3.45: Document level sharing settings when policy is anyone

14. Now, back to **Files and folder links** under **More external sharing**. Keep the option **Specific people (only the people the user specifics)** selected under **Choose the type of link that's selected by default when users share files and folders in SharePoint and OneDrive.** Refer to *Figure 3.46*:

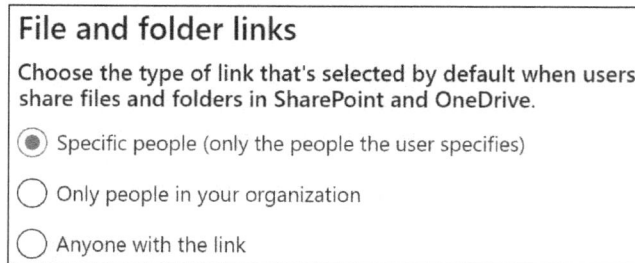

Figure 3.46: File and folder links setting can be selected

15. As an impact, when you try to share a site from central admin, you will find the **Default sharing link type** as **Same as organization-level settings (Specific people)**. Refer to *Figure 3.47*:

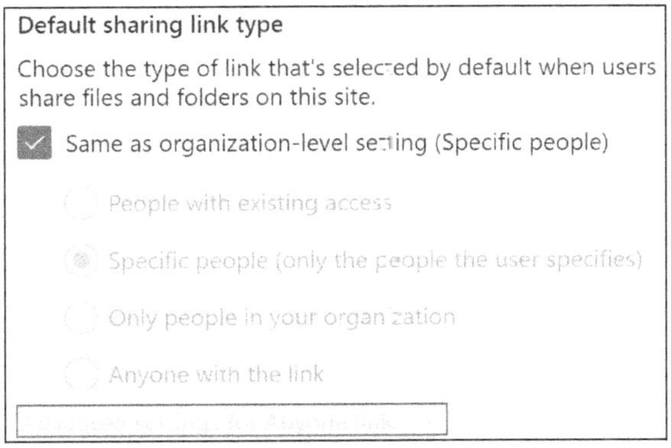

Default sharing link type

Choose the type of link that's selected by default when users share files and folders on this site.

☑ Same as organization-level setting (Specific people)

    ◯ People with existing access

    ◉ Specific people (only the people the user specifies)

    ◯ Only people in your organization

    ◯ Anyone with the link

Figure 3.47: Default sharing link type

16. Now, back to **Files and folder links** under **More external sharing**. Keep the options **Choose the permission that's selected by default for sharing links** and **Other settings** as default. Refer to *Figure 3.48*:

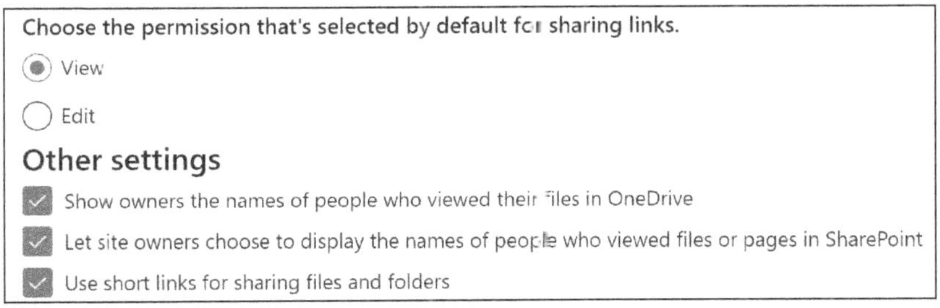

Choose the permission that's selected by default for sharing links.

◉ View

◯ Edit

Other settings

☑ Show owners the names of people who viewed their files in OneDrive

☑ Let site owners choose to display the names of people who viewed files or pages in SharePoint

☑ Use short links for sharing files and folders

Figure 3.48: Choose the permission that's selected by default for sharing links and other settings

Anyone

We discussed the external sharing policy options **Only people in your organization**, **Existing guests** and **New and existing guests** out of four options as discussed in the section **External sharing settings**, *Step 5*. Let us discuss the fourth external sharing policy option **Anyone** under the category external sharing. This option is like anonymous access (no authentication process followed by user) in on-premises SharePoint site and applicable for public facing sites. Any user, no matter internal user of your organization or external user outside of your organization, can access the site and contents present on the site if they have site or file link available with them. That link can be shared by any user to anyone since this option allows control over link to all users to share with anyone. So, you cannot really track details about changes, security which ultimately is another point you need to consider before choosing. In this section we will discuss how to apply the policy at tenant level and understand its impact on sharing a site at the tenant level, individual site settings at site sharing level, document sharing level. Let us discuss the following steps to understand better:

1. Under **External Sharing** settings, select the slider from applications SharePoint and OneDrive, and drag to permissive level **Anyone** as seen in *Figure 3.49*. You will notice that another category **More external sharing settings** got enabled as happened while selecting policy **New and existing guests** and **Existing guests**:

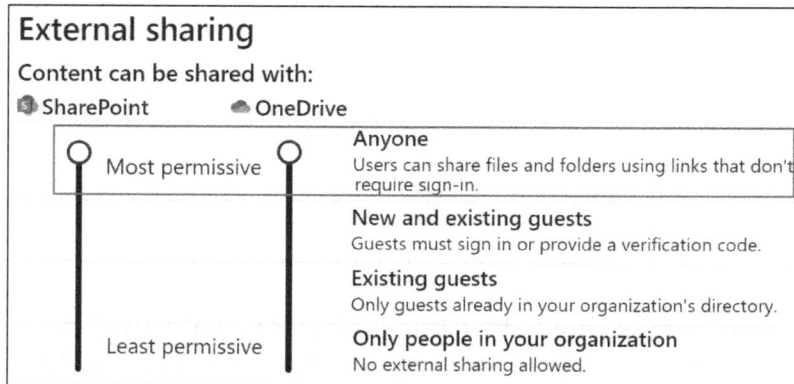

Figure 3.49: External sharing policy anyone

2. As an impact, when you select any site and click on **Share** from command bar, you will find the option **Anyone** is available now for selection. Refer to *Figure 3.50*:

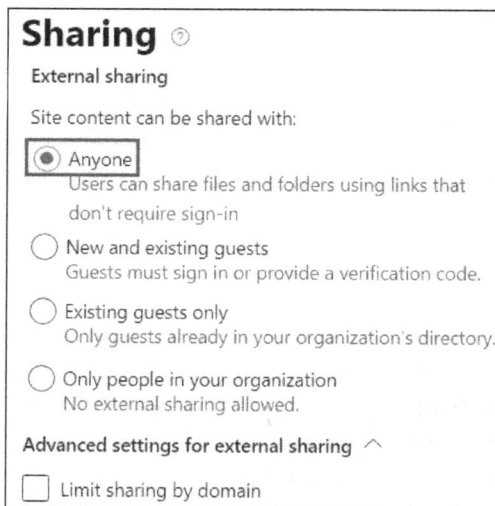

Figure 3.50: Anyone option enabled

3. Now, back to **More external sharing settings** under **Content can be shared with** under **External sharing**. Refer to *Figure 3.51*. Admin can further control the sharing of site content or OneDrive files by allowing or blocking specific domains. You may select the checkbox **Limit external sharing by domain** and follow the same steps as discussed in the above section, **Existing guests** to add or block domains with whom external users are allowed or blocked to share contents, respectively.

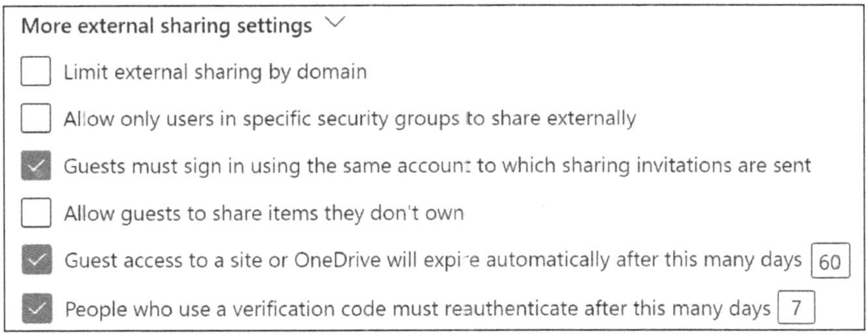

Figure 3.51: More external sharing settings

4. You may apply a policy to allow users of specific groups only can share files to external users by selecting the option **Allow only users in specific security groups to share externally** if required as per organization's requirement. Refer to *Figure 3.51*. Follow the same steps as discussed in the section **Existing guests**.

5. Select the checkbox **Guest must sign in using the same account to which sharing invitations are sent**. Refer to *Figure 3.51*. This ensures that the user needs to sign in with the same account to which the content is shared. Other users cannot access the content, although they have the link available with them forwarded by another user. This ensures maintaining a secure track for content access for anyone.

6. It is good to uncheck the option **Allow guests to share items they don't own**. If this option is selected, guest users can share content to any other external user. This means that a user who has access to any content, can share that content to any other external user. This way, we cannot keep track of who has access to which content and whether that user is really authorized to access that content or not.

7. Select the checkbox for the option next **People who use a verification code must reauthenticate after this many days** and set number of days, for example, 7 days. Refer to *Figure 3.51*. This will ensure that users to whom content is shared need to reauthenticate with verification code again after the number of days configured. This will help with improved security.

8. Check the option **Choose the type of link that's selected by default when users share files and folders in SharePoint and OneDrive** under the next category **File and folder links** under you will notice the option **Anyone with the link** got enabled. Refer to *Figure 3.52*. You will notice the option **Anyone with the link** got enabled under **File and folder links**:

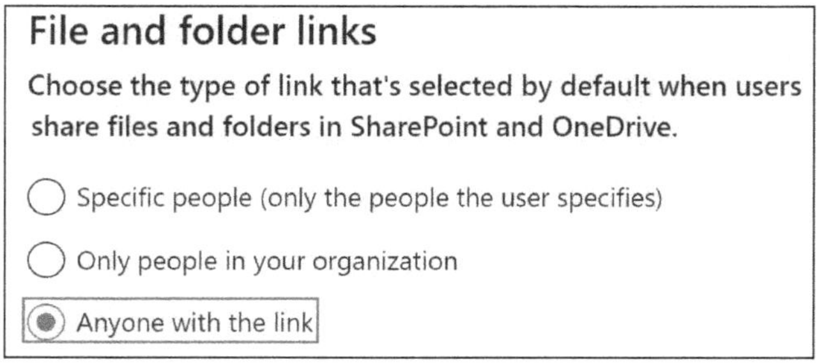

Figure 3.52: *Anyone with the link enabled in files and folder links*

9. You will find additional options like **Choose expiration and permissions options for Anyone links,** including the permission settings for **Files** and **Folders, which are** enabled under the category **File and folder links**. Refer to *Figure 3.53.*

10. We can configure expiration days for the link shared with the user as well as the permission for **Anyone links** for **Files** and **Folders**. Permissions configured under this will work only when **Anyone** link is selected. Options present under **Choose the permission that's selected by default for sharing links** will not be effective. Permission for **Files** can be selected as either **View** or **View and edit**. Similarly, permission for **Folder** can be selected as either **View** or **view, edit and upload**.

11. Select the checkbox **These links must expire within this many days** and enter the value as **7**. Select the permission for **Files** as **View** and the permission for **Folders** as **View** for the moment. Refer to *Figure 3.53*:

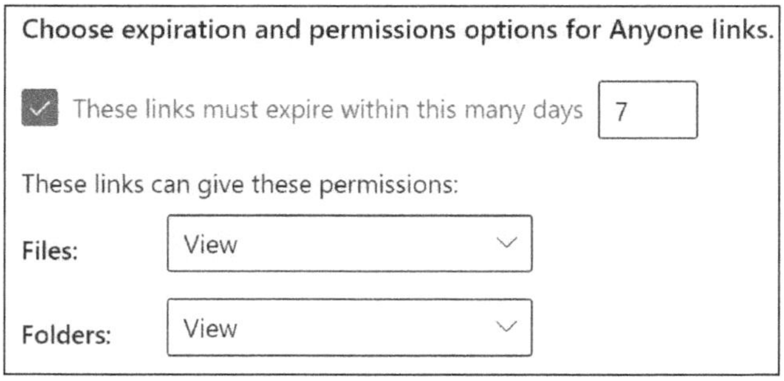

Figure 3.53: *Choose expiration and permissions options for Anyone links enabled*

12. Now, back to the **Active sites** list in SharePoint admin center. Select any site and click on **Share** from the command bar. You will get the sharing window. You will find the option **Anyone with the link** enabled under category **Default sharing link type**. Refer to *Figure 3.54:*

Default sharing link type

Choose the type of link that's selected by default when users share files and folders on this site.

☑ Same as organization-level setting (Anyone with the link)

○ People with existing access

○ Specific people (only the people the user specifies)

○ Only people in your organization

◉ Anyone with the link

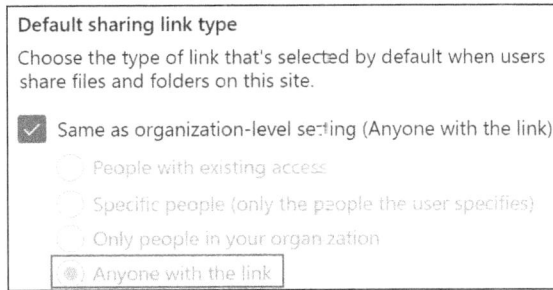

Figure 3.54: Default sharing link type

13. Next to the **Default sharing link type**, you will notice an additional category, **Advanced settings for Anyone links,** has been enabled. Refer to *Figure 3.55*. You can either accept the organizational level policy for **Expiration of Anyone links** for site by selecting **Same as organization-level settings (7 Days)**, or you can change to custom days by selecting the option, **These links must expire within this many days**. You can select the option; **These links never expire** if required. The changes made here apply to that specific site only, not to all sites in tenant.

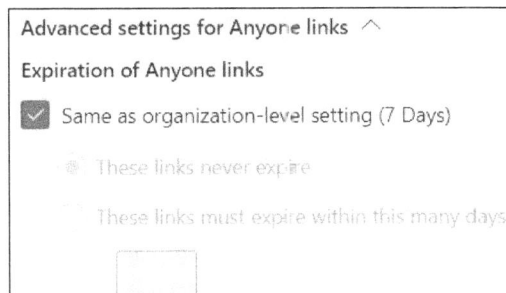

Advanced settings for Anyone links ⌃

Expiration of Anyone links

☑ Same as organization-level setting (7 Days)

◉ These links never expire

○ These links must expire within this many days

Figure 3.55: Advanced settings for Anyone links enabled

14. Now, back to **Choose the permission that's selected by default for sharing links** under **File and folder links** under **External sharing**. Keep the option selected as **View**. Refer to *Figure 3.56*:

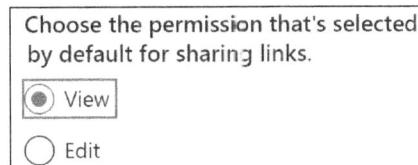

Choose the permission that's selected by default for sharing links.

◉ View

○ Edit

Figure 3.56: Default sharing link permission

15. Now, back to SharePoint document library and share any document. You will get the sharing window. You will notice the default link permission as **Can view**. Hover mouse over the **Copy link**, you will see a message as **Anyone with the link**

can view. Click on the option **Copy link** now. You will find a message like **Link copied Anyone with the link can view**. Refer to *Figure 3.57*:

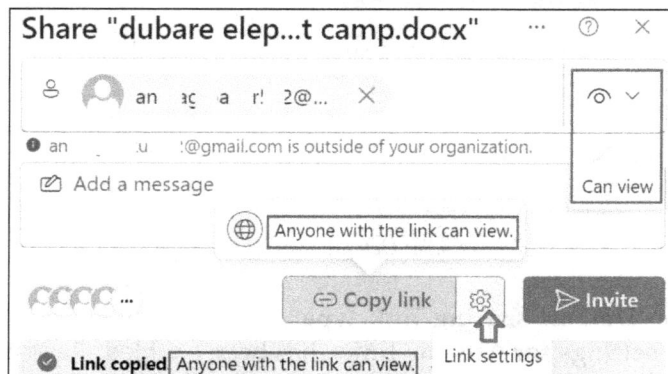

Figure 3.57: Share files from document library, anyone can view

16. Click on the **Link settings**. From the window next, you will find the option **Anyone** selected under **Share the link with** category.

17. Next under the category **More settings,** you will notice the default permission **Can view** selected. Refer to *Figure 3.58*:

Figure 3.58: Link setting, anyone can view

18. Click on the drop-down option **Can view**. You will find four options in the drop down like **Can edit, Can review, Can view, Can't download** as seen in *Figure 3.59*.

You will notice the option **Can edit** disabled since we selected the **File** permission as **View**. Refer to *step 12* and *Figure 3.59*:

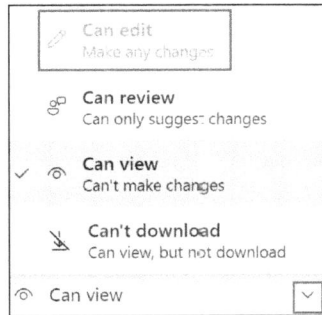

Figure 3.59: Can edit disabled

19. Next to that, you will find the expiry date which is seven days as per the number of days entered. Refer to *Step 12* and *Figure 3.53*.

20. Next, you will find the option **Set password**. You can configure it by entering the password while sharing the file. Click on the button **Apply**. Click on the **Invite** button to share the file.

21. After sharing you will get a message like **You've invited user to view the file**. Refer to *Figure 3.60*:

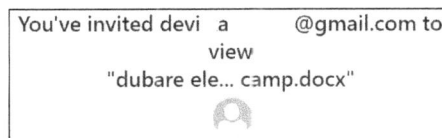

Figure 3.60: Shared link displaying the type of permission assigned

22. The user will receive a mail with file name and a button **Open** to access the file. Click on the button **Open**. Refer to *Figure 3.61*:

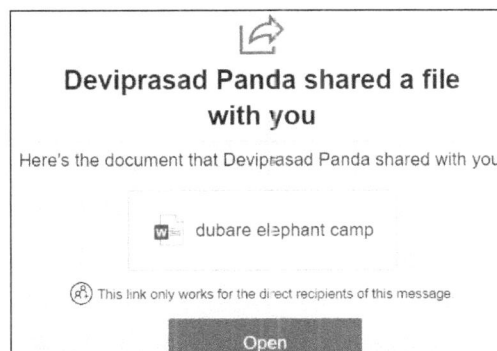

Figure 3.61: Shared link received in mail

23. The user needs to verify identity by entering mail ID from the window **Verify Your Identity** next, and click on **Next**. Refer to *Figure 3.62*:

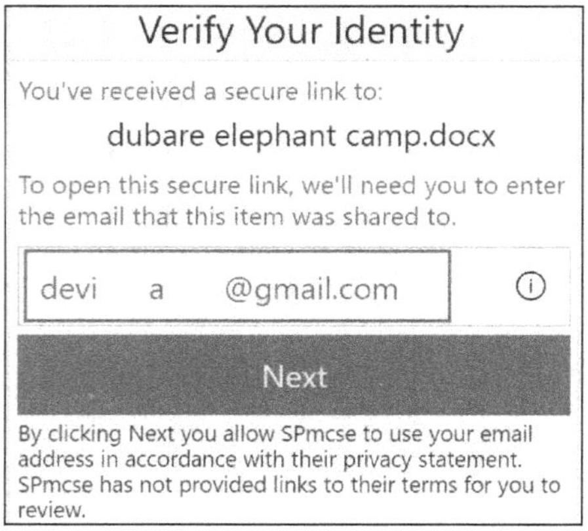

Figure 3.62: Verify your identity while accessing link

24. The user will receive a code by mail to which document is shared. Enter the code in the **Enter Verification Code** window to access the file. Refer to *Figure 3.63*:

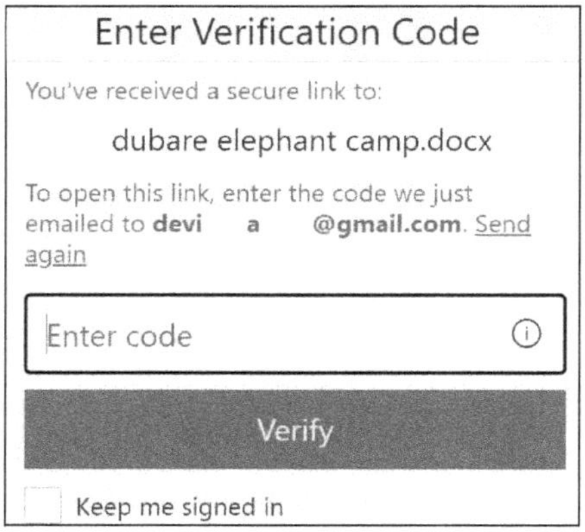

Figure 3.63: Enter verification code to verify identity

25. The file will open with a **View-only** permission icon to the side of the file name. In the top left corner, when the user tries to rename the file, the user will get a message like `You don't have permission to rename this file`. Refer to *Figure 3.64*:

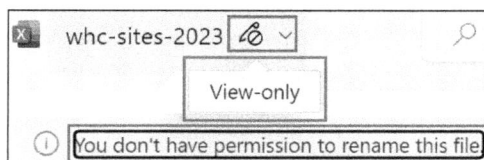

Figure 3.64: Document permission having view permission

26. In the top right corner, below the mail ID, you will find the icon **Viewing** that indicates the type of permission given to the file. Refer to *Figure 3.65*:

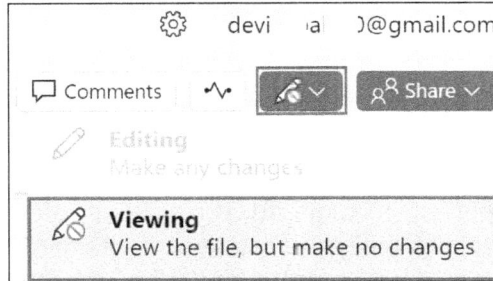

Figure 3.65: Document viewing mode

27. If the user tries to edit the file, the user will get a message: **This file was opened in read-only mode**. Refer to *Figure 3.66*:

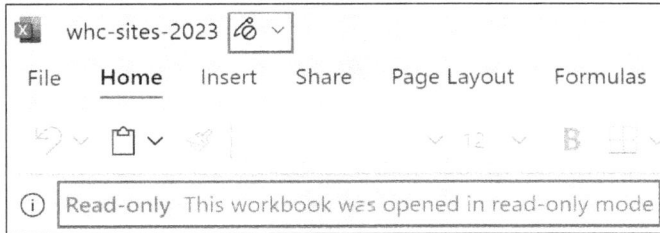

Figure 3.66: This workbook was opened in read-only mode

28. The way a document is shared and accessed by the user, share anyone link of a folder to any external user. When the user tries to access the folder link, the user will not find the **Upload** button in the command bar. The user will have view permission in the folder. Refer to *Figure 3.67*:

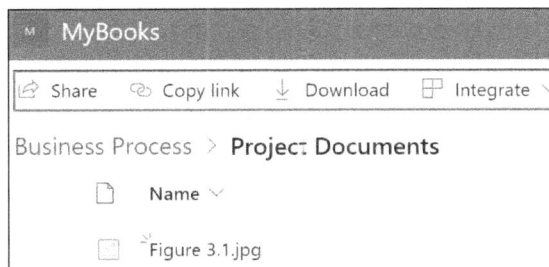

Figure 3.67: Upload button does not present in the folder

29. Now, back to **Choose the permission that is selected by default for sharing links** under **File and folder links** under **External sharing**. Select the option selected as **Edit**. Refer to *Figure 3.68*:

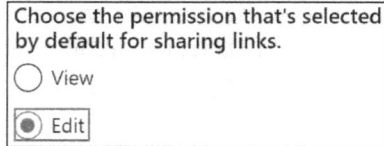

Figure 3.68: Default sharing link permission Edit

30. Now try to share one document from the document library. You will find the default link permission changed to **Can edit**. If you hover mouse over the button **Copy link** and click on it, you will get a message like **People in domain (organization domain means internal user only) with the link can edit**. Refer to *Figure 3.69*:

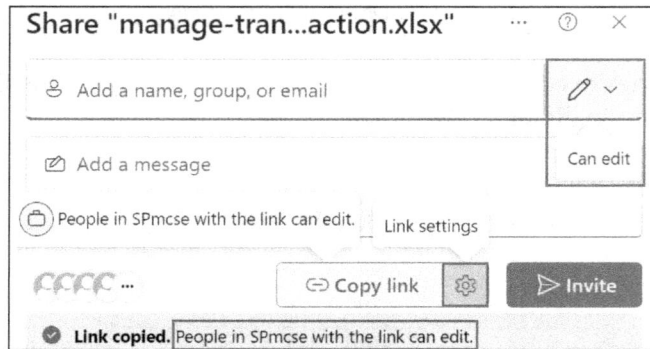

Figure 3.69: Edit mode while sharing the document

31. Click on **Link settings**. You will find the option **Share the link** has changed from **Anyone** to People in the domain (organization/internal user). Link permission under **More settings** is **Can edit** as selected default. Refer to *Figure 3.70*:

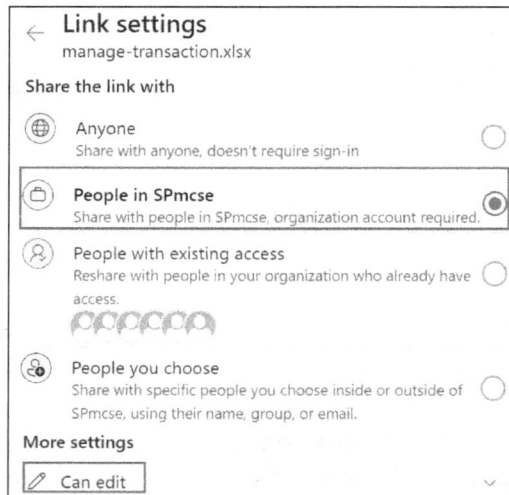

Figure 3.70: Link setting switch to people in your organization

32. Now, click on the drop-down option from **More settings** and select **Can view**. You will notice the option **Share the link with** changed to **Anyone**. Refer to *Figure 3.71*:

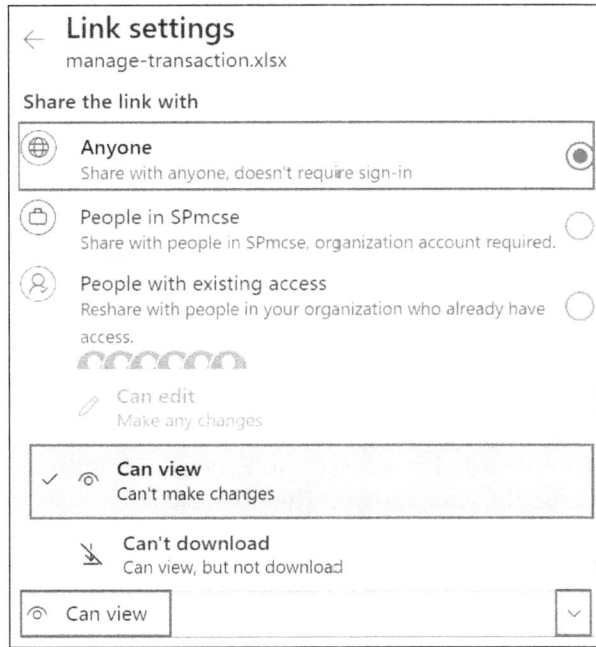

Figure 3.71: Switching to Anyone change the permission to view mode

33. Now, back to **Choose expiration and permissions options for Anyone links** under **File and folder links** under **External sharing**. Select the permission for **Files** as **View and edit**. Permission for **Folders** as **View** for the moment. Refer to *Figure 3.72*:

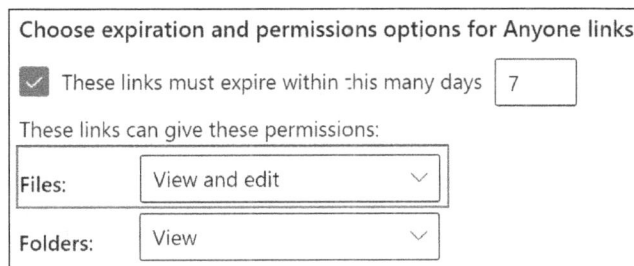

Figure 3.72: Link permission View and Edit

34. Now try to share one document from the document library. You will find the default link permission changed to **Can edit**. If you hover mouse over the button **Copy link** and click on it, you will get a message like **Anyone with the link can edit**. Refer to *Figure 3.73*:

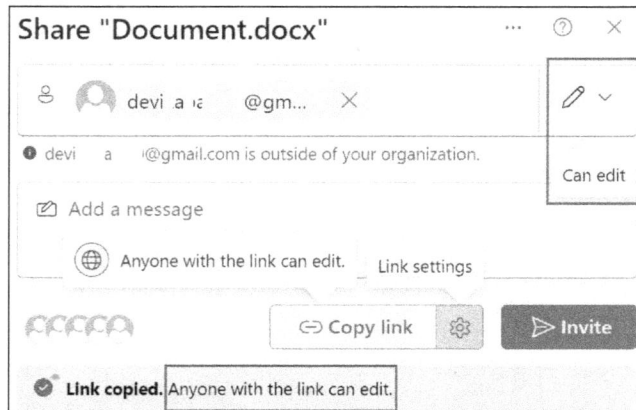

Figure 3.73: Default permission of document changed to can edit

35. Now click on the drop-down option from **More settings** and you will notice the option **Can edit** is enabled now. Refer to *Figure 3.74*. If the user is trying to access the document link, the user can edit the file now:

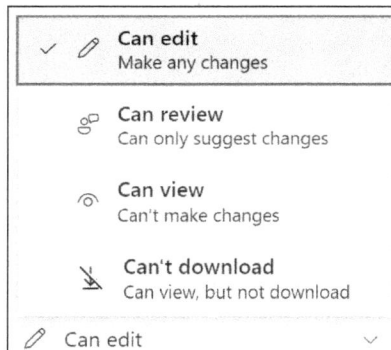

Figure 3.74: Can edit mode enabled

36. Now, back to **Choose expiration and permissions options for Anyone links** under **File and folder links** under **External sharing**. Select the permission for **Files** as **View and edit**. Permission for **Folders** as **View, edit and upload**. Refer to *Figure 3.75*:

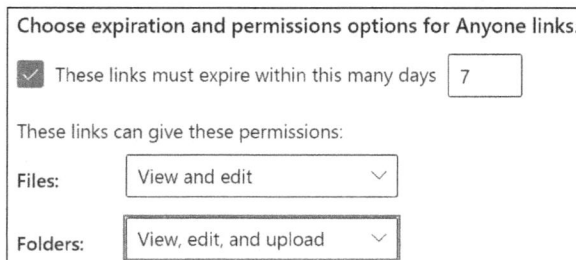

Figure 3.75: Folders permission set as View, edit and upload

37. If you share any folder and the user follows that to link for accessing that folder, user will find the button **Upload** in the command bar. Refer to *Figure 3.76*:

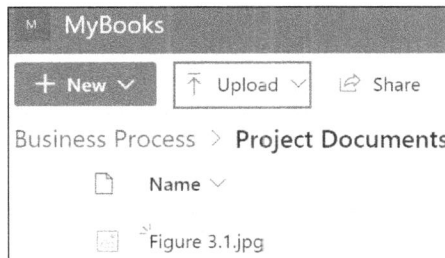

Figure 3.76: *Upload button enabled in the folder*

File and folder links settings

First in the section **Sharing**, we already said that sharing options are categorized into three: **External sharing**, **File and folder links**, **Other settings**. We discussed **External sharing**, the first category of options till now. Let us discuss the second category **File and folder links**.

File and folder links are divided into three categories as follows:

- Choose the type of link that is selected by default when users share files and folders in SharePoint and OneDrive.

- Choose the permission that is selected by default for sharing links.

- Choose expiration and permissions options for Anyone links.

The first category under **File and folder links** is **Choose the type of link that's selected by default when users share files and folders in SharePoint and OneDrive**. Refer to *Figure 3.77*. It signifies the default sharing link type that will be shared to user. You will find three options under this category as follows:

- Specific people (only the people the user specifies)

- Only people in your organization

- Anyone with the link

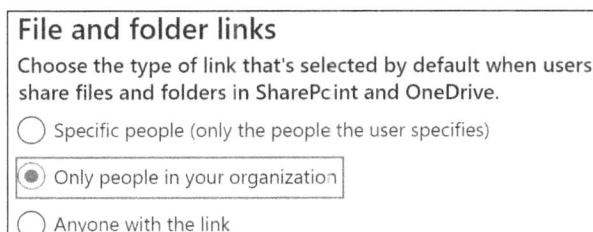

Figure 3.77: *Files and folder links*

The second category under **File and folder links** is **Choose the permission that's selected by default for sharing links**. This signifies the default permission that users have over the shared link. There are two types of permission that can be given to the user. Users can either **View** the content or **Edit** the content shared over the link. Refer to *Figure 3.78*:

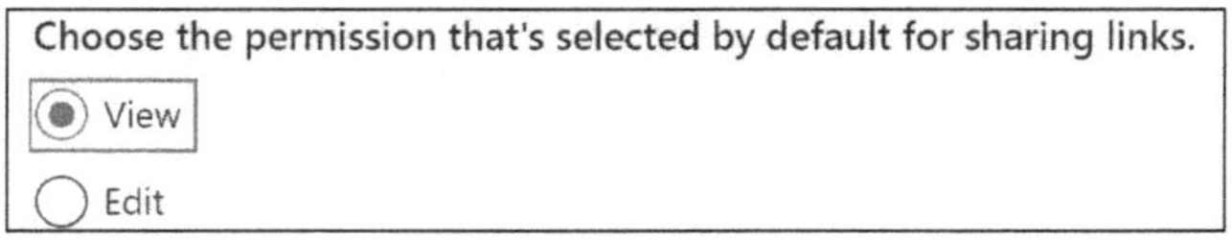

Figure 3.78: Choose the permission that's selected by default for sharing links

The third category is **Choose expiration and permissions options for Anyone links**, which is available only when the **Content can be shared with** under **External sharing** as **Anyone** as discussed in the section **Anyone**. Refer to *Figure 3.79*. We can configure expiration days for the link shared to user as well as the permission for **Anyone links** for **Files** and **Folders**. Permissions configured under this will work only when Anyone link is selected. Permission for **Files** can be selected either **View** or **View and edit**. Similarly, permission for Folder can be selected either **View** or **view, edit and upload**.

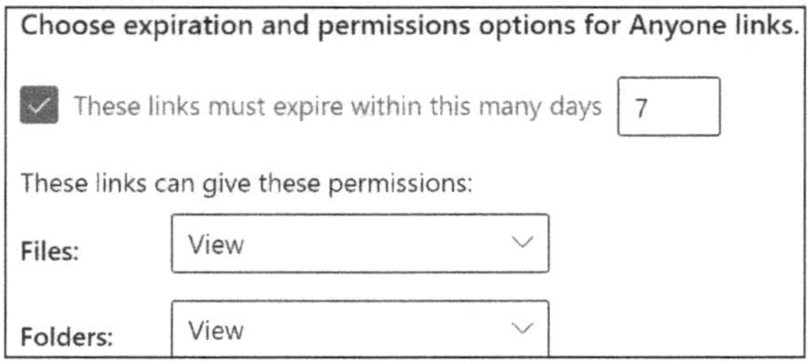

Figure 3.79: Choose expiration and permissions options for Anyone links

Other settings

The final category of setting under **Sharing** is **Other settings**, where the admin can control the activity details for files and pages in OneDrive and SharePoint, respectively. You will find different options like **Show owners the names of people who viewed their files in OneDrive, Let site owners choose to display the names of people who views files or pages in SharePoint, Use short links for sharing files and folders** as seen in the following *Figure 3.80*:

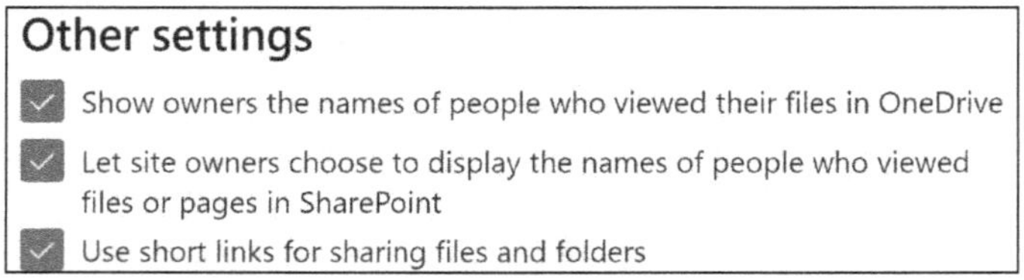

Figure 3.80: Other settings

Here is what the **Other settings** contain:

- Select the checkbox **Show owners the names of people who viewed their files in OneDrive** to enable file tracking in OneDrive. This will capture the user details who viewed files in OneDrive. When owners hover over a file, they can see the user's name in the file card.

- Select the checkbox **Let site owners choose to display the names of people who views files or pages in SharePoint** to enable tracking of files and Pages in SharePoint. This will capture the user details like who viewed files in SharePoint. When owners hover over the file or a page, they can see users name in file card.

- Select the checkbox **Use short links for sharing files and folders**. This will allow users to send a short link instead of the long traditional link.

Access control

This is the second option under the category **Policies** in the SharePoint admin center. We can configure the settings present under this category to control how to access content in SharePoint and OneDrive. Expand the option **Policies** from the left navigation in the admin center. Click on **Access control**, as shown in *Figure 3.81*:

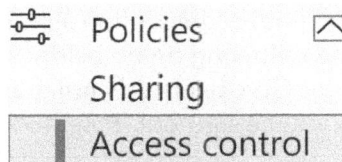

Figure 3.81: *Click on access control*

You find four categories of options like **Unmanaged devices, Idle session sign-out, Network location, Apps that don't use modern authentication,** as shown in *Figure 3.82*:

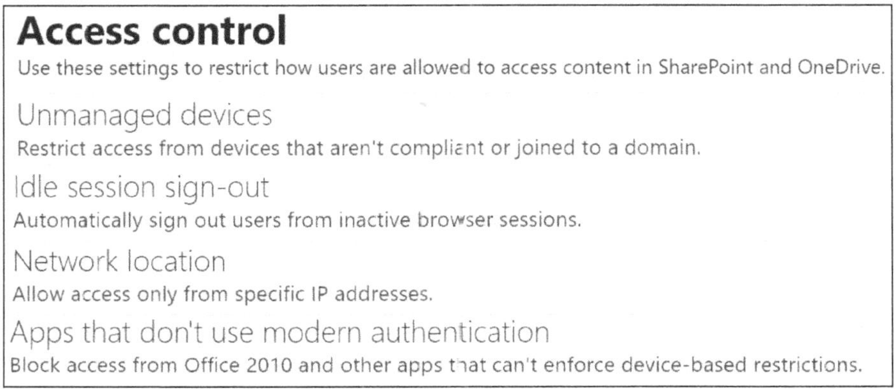

Figure 3.82: *Access control options*

Unmanaged devices

We can manage user devices to access contents. User devices can be managed from **Enterprise Mobility + Security** admin center as shown in *Figure 3.83*. This provides additional security to contents by allowing only registered devices to access contents.

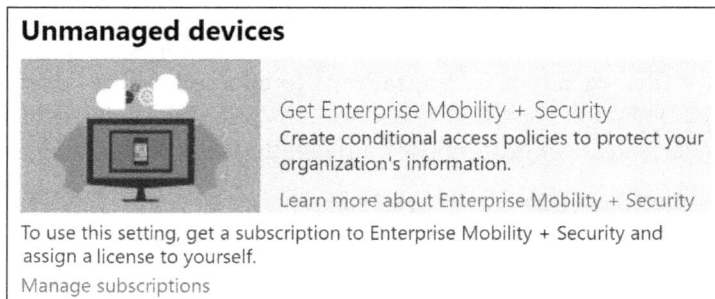

Figure 3.83: Unmanaged devices

Idle session sign-out

This setting is used to manage content access on unmanaged devices. Turning on **Sign out inactive users automatically**, under Idle session sign-out will make the user sign-out after a specific time as seen in the following figure below. The user will get an alert before a specific time as configured under **Give users this much notice before signing them out**. After that time, the user session will be sign-out. Refer to *Figure 3.84*:

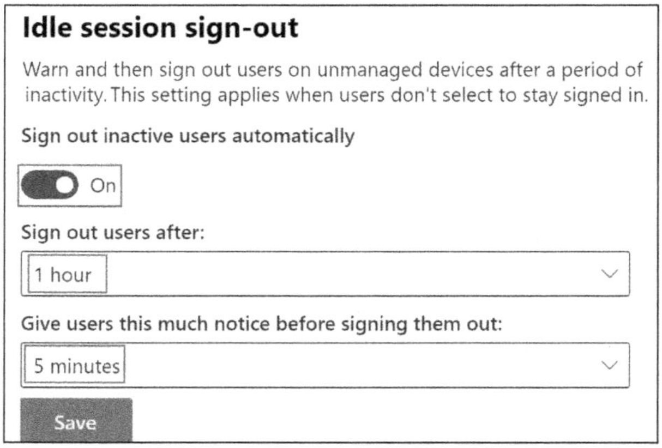

Figure 3.84: Idle session sign-out

Network location

We can add a trusted range of IP addresses under this setting as seen in the following *Figure 3.85*. Users whose locations fall under this trusted IP range boundary can access the content and outside this boundary will be blocked from accessing content. Please refer to the following figure:

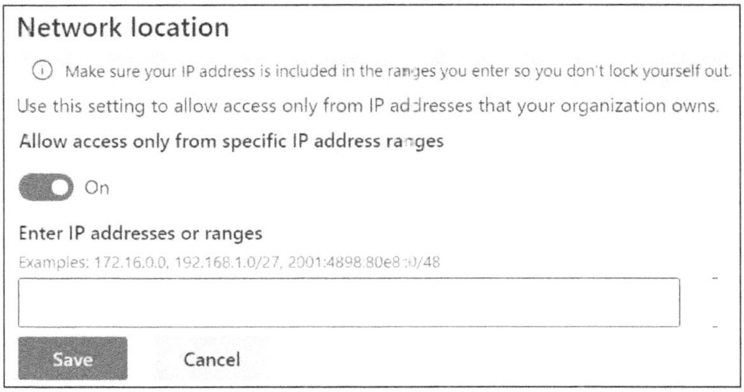

Figure 3.85: Network location

Apps not using modern authentication

This setting is used to allow or block access to third-party apps not using modern authentication. Refer to the following *Figure 3.86*:

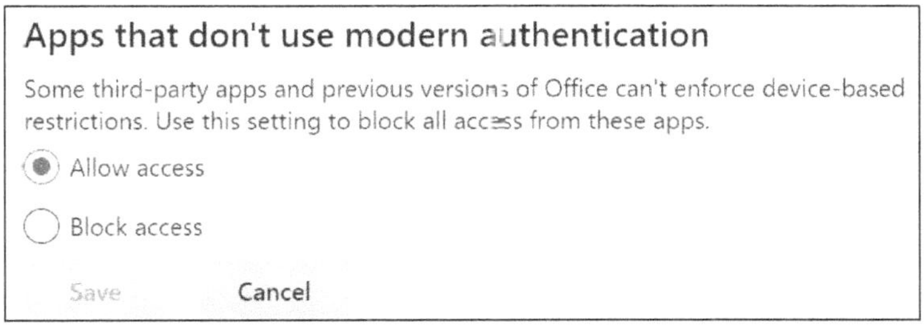

Figure 3.86: Apps that don't use modern authentication

Conclusion

In this chapter, we had a glance at applying policies for secure access of content that are shared to external users. We discussed different permissive levels to apply and restrict whom the content can be shared with. We discussed the impact of policy on sharing sites, files, folder at tenant level, site level and item level. We also discussed the step-by-step procedure of external sharing control, File and folder links configuration, configure permission that is selected by default for sharing links, configure by choosing expiration and permissions options for Anyone links. Finally discussed managing unmanaged devices, allow or block app access based on modern authentication, network locations.

In the next *Chapter 4, Settings*, we will discuss the SharePoint settings and its applications.

Points to remember

- Changing permissive level will enable additional options at site sharing level at tenant, site level and item level. So, plan better before changing the permissive level from admin center.

- Changing default link permission from tenant level might have a high security impact on all sites in tenant. You should plan better before configuring.

- Permissive level Anyone is normally not enabled for large enterprises. You should be careful while enabling it.

- Allow guests to share items they don't own option is usually not enabled for better security and track the content sharing.

- Regular changes are applied in Office 365 and SharePoint Online. There might be slight change after some days compared to the contents mentioned in this chapter.

Join our book's Discord space

Join the book's Discord Workspace for Latest updates, Offers, Tech happenings around the world, New Release and Sessions with the Authors:

https://discord.bpbonline.com

CHAPTER 4

Settings

Introduction

In the previous *Chapter 3, Policies Administration*, we discussed how to create policies that can be applied at tenant level to control the sharing of sites, folders and files with external users. In this chapter, we will discuss the settings present in the admin center. Settings is the fourth category in left navigation in SharePoint admin center. Once you click on settings, you will find options namely, **Home sites**, **Notifications**, **Pages**, **Site creation**, **Site storage limits**, **Application management**, **App launcher tile**, **Notifications**, **Retention**, **Storage limit**, **Sync**. These are the settings used to set up home sites that are linked to viva connection experiences, manage notifications related to app SharePoint and OneDrive, organization-level settings for creating and commenting on modern pages, settings for new sites including site and OneDrive storage limit.

Structure

In this chapter we will discuss the following topics:

- Home sites
- Notifications
- Pages

- Site creation
- Site storage limits
- Application management
- Stream app launcher tile
- OneDrive notifications
- Retention
- Storage limit
- Sync
- Classic settings page

Objective

By the end of this chapter, you will get a clear understanding of various options available under the left navigation option Settings. You will learn how to set up home sites that link to Viva Connections experiences, default site creation settings, manage storage limits, control the notifications, create modern site pages, and comment on modern site pages. You will get to know how to configure the retention period for OneDrive files for the deleted user accounts, default OneDrive storage limits, and enabling OneDrive notifications. You will get clarity on the classic settings page options available and their functions.

Home sites

Microsoft Viva Connection provides a modern experience to access announcements, news, resources, and links from Teams to the targeted audiences and a gateway to Viva apps and services. Once you open the Viva Connection app from Microsoft Teams, the default landing page will open. Viva Connection allows you to create new experiences and use the SharePoint intranet portal as the primary or secondary landing page or home page in the Viva Connection app. The option **Home sites** is the first option under **Settings** to create new home site targeted user experiences. Let us discuss the following steps to understand better:

1. Click on **Settings** from the left navigation option in **SharePoint admin center**. Refer to *Figure 4.1*:

App		Name ↑	Description	Value
🟦	SharePoint	Home sites	Set up home sites that link to Viva Connections experiences	/sites/Home
🟦	SharePoint	Notifications	Allow mobile app notifications about site activity	Allow notifications
🟦	SharePoint	Pages	Allow users to create and comment on modern pages	Multiple values
🟦	SharePoint	Site creation	Set default settings for new sites	Multiple values
🟦	SharePoint	Site storage limits	Use automatic or manual site storage limits	Manual storage limits
🟦	SharePoint Embedded	Application management	Allow access to build and use document centric applications	Enabled
▶	Stream	App launcher tile	Set the default destination for Stream	Recommended
☁	OneDrive	Notifications	Allow notifications about file activity	Allow notifications
☁	OneDrive	Retention	Set the default OneDrive retention for deleted users	30 days
☁	OneDrive	Storage limit	Set the default storage limit for users	1024 GB
☁	OneDrive	Sync	Manage sync settings for OneDrive and SharePoint	Multiple values

Figure 4.1: Settings

2. Click on the option **Home sites** related to **the** app **SharePoint**. Refer to *Figure 4.2*:

App		Name ↑	Description	Value
🟦	SharePoint	Home sites	Set up home sites that link to Viva Connections experiences	/sites/Home

Figure 4.2: Home sites option in settings

3. You will get a message like **Home site set up has moved to Viva Connections in the Microsoft 365 admin center**. Click on the button **Go to Microsoft 365 admin center**. Refer to *Figure 4.3*:

Home site set up has moved to Viva Connections in the Microsoft 365 admin center

Home sites can be created when you set up a new Viva Connections experience. Use Viva Connections to create a company branded app where employees can explore news, discover resources, and easily access the tools and apps they need to get their work done.

Use an existing intranet portal to set up a Viva Connections experience and home site together.

Go to Microsoft 365 admin center

Figure 4.3: Go to Microsoft 365 admin center

4. You will be redirected to the **Viva Connections experiences** window where you can create and manage viva connections experiences. You will find an entry in the viva connection experience list with columns namely, **Home Status** as **Enabled**, **Home site as Yes** along with other columns **Order, Audience, License type**. Refer to *Figure 4.4*:

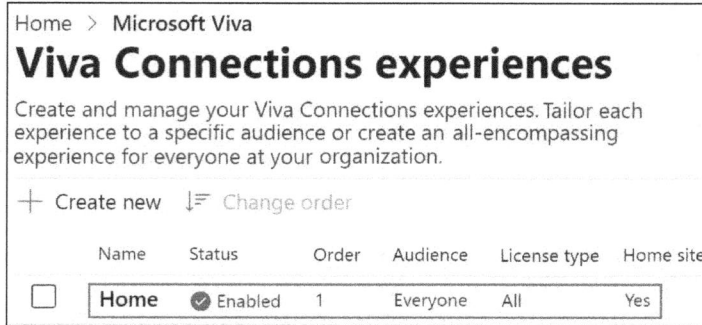

Figure 4.4: Viva connections experiences

5. Click on the item anywhere in the row. You will find an additional dialog box with tabs namely **General, Audience, Permissions** as seen in *Figure 4.5*. Tab **General** is selected by default, and you will find properties namely, **Experience name, URL, Status, License type, Default language, Experience description, Creation details**. Click on the link present under the property **URL**. You will be redirected to the SharePoint site configured as a home site for the organization, linked to viva connection experience. Refer to *Figure 4.5*:

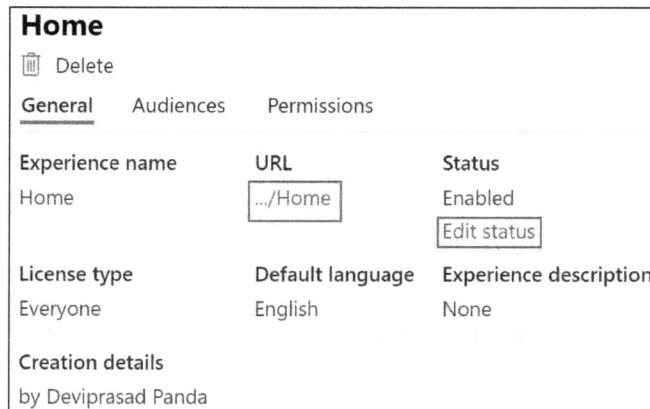

Figure 4.5: Edit viva connection experience dialog box

6. Now, log in to **Microsoft teams** and open the **Viva Connections** app. You will find the **Home site** link in the navigation bar on the top-right corner, linked to Viva Connection experience. Refer to *Figure 4.6*:

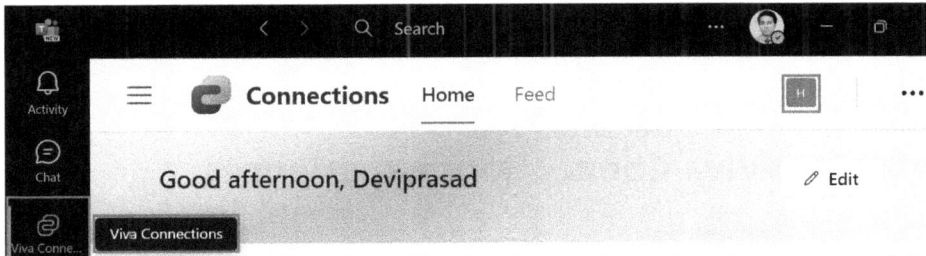

Figure 4.6: *Viva connection home page experience enabled default*

7. Now, click on the option **Edit status** present below the property **Status**. Refer to *Figure 4.5*. The **Enable experience** dialog box will open. You can select or deselect the checkbox to enable or disable the experience in Microsoft Teams, respectively. Deselect the checkbox **Enable experience** and click on **Save**, as shown in the following figure:

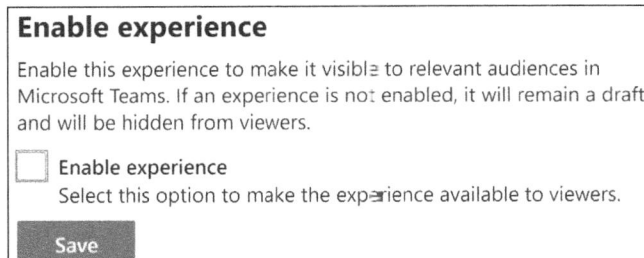

Figure 4.7: *Enable or Disable experience*

8. Now, log in to **Microsoft Teams** and open the **Viva Connections** app. You will not find the **Home site** link in the navigation bar on the top-right corner, linked to viva connection experience. Refer to *Figure 4.8*:

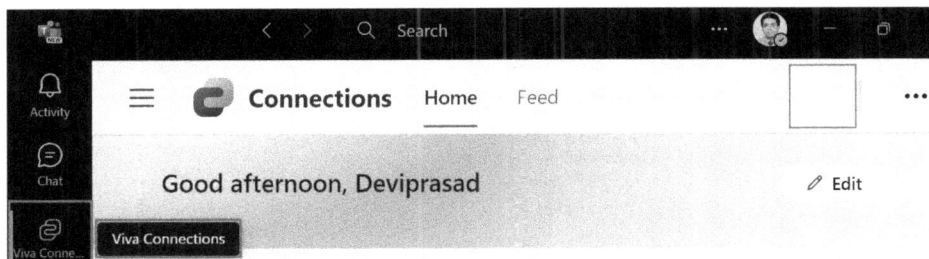

Figure 4.8: *Viva connection home page experience disabled*

9. We discussed an existing viva experience and its properties. We can create a new experience from SharePoint portal and make it available for targeted users as a link in the navigation bar to switch the experience as per user requirements. Sometimes, organizations need to customize the viva experience and set specific

customized site as the primary landing page or home site. Click on the button **Create new** from the **Viva Connections experiences** window to create Viva Connections experiences. Refer to *Figure 4.9*:

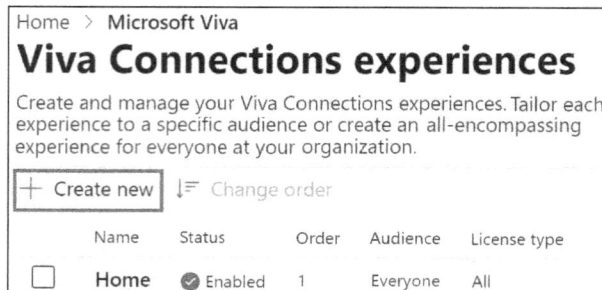

Figure 4.9: Create new home site viva experience

10. The **Create a new Viva Connection experience** window will appear. You will find two experience types **Create a Connections experience** and **Build from an existing portal to set a home site**. Select the experience type **Build from an existing portal to set a home site** and click on **Next**, as shown in the following figure:

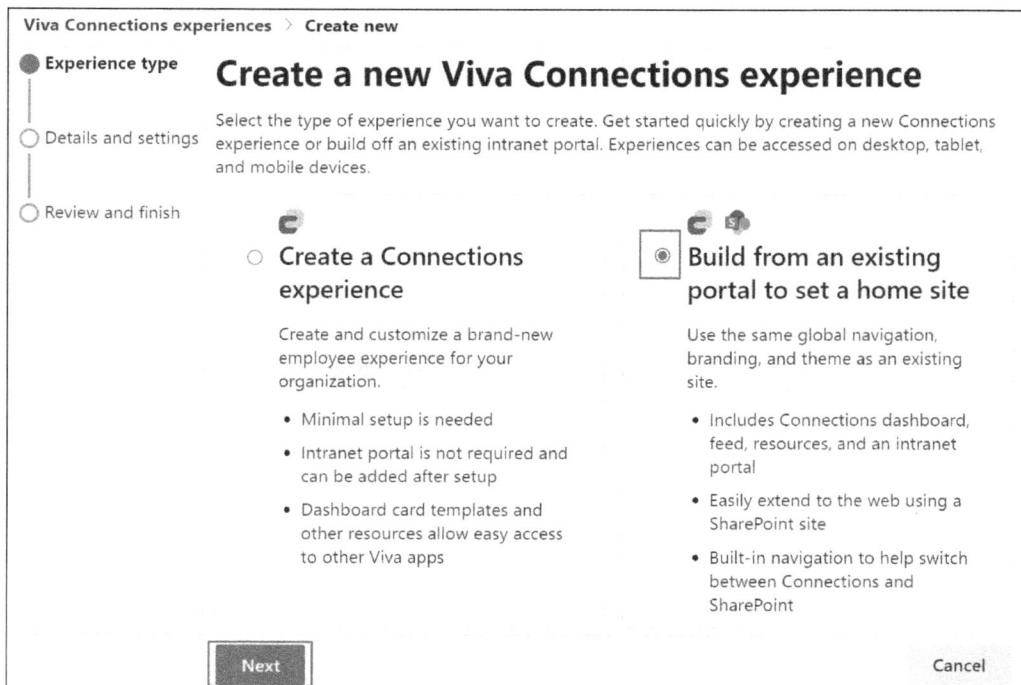

Figure 4.10: Create a new Viva Connections experience home page

11. Enter the URL of the communication site to use and click on **Next**. Refer to *Figure 4.11*:

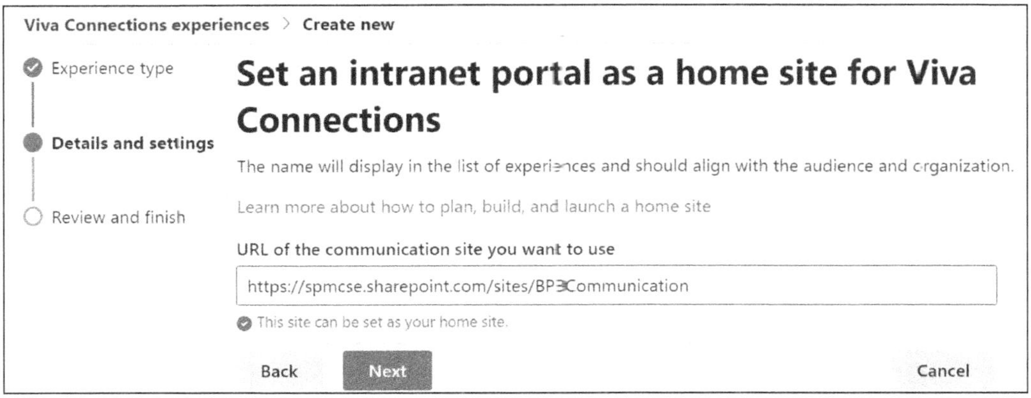

Figure 4.11: *Enter intranet portal URL to set as a home site for Viva Connections*

12. Finally review and click on the button **Create experience**. Refer to *Figure 4.12*:

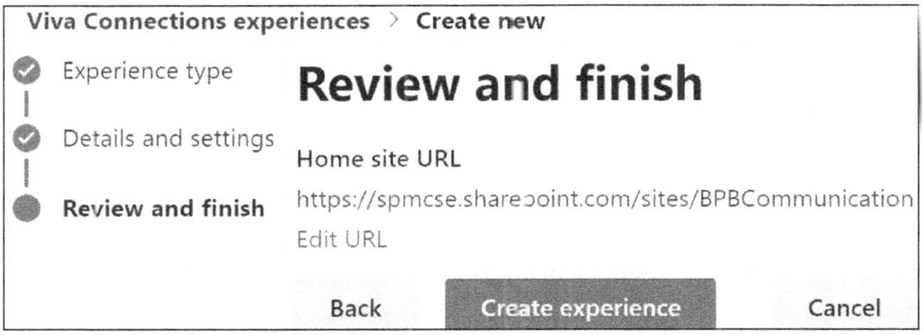

Figure 4.12: *Review and finish to create experience*

13. You will get confirmation that the new experience has been created successfully. Refer to *Figure 4.13*. Enable the experience following the step as discussed in *Step 7*:

Figure 4.13: *New Viva Connection experience created*

14. Now, open the viva connection app in Microsoft Teams. Click on the three dots and select the option **Switch experience**. Please refer to the following figure:

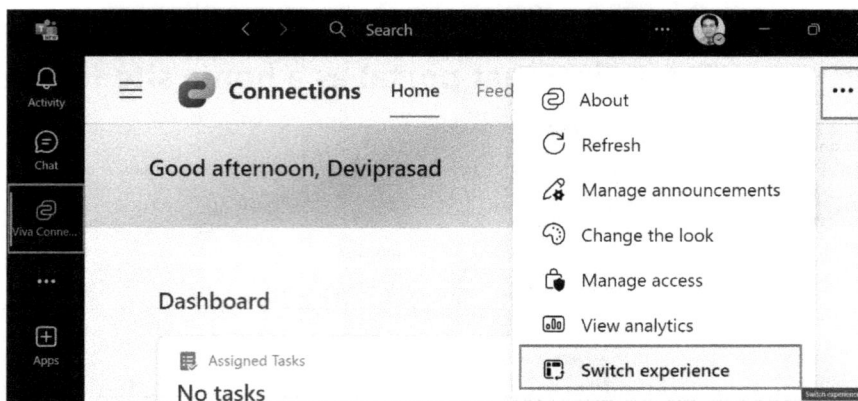

Figure 4.14: Switch experience

15. You will find the new home site experience created. Select the new home and click on the button **Switch**, as shown in the following figure:

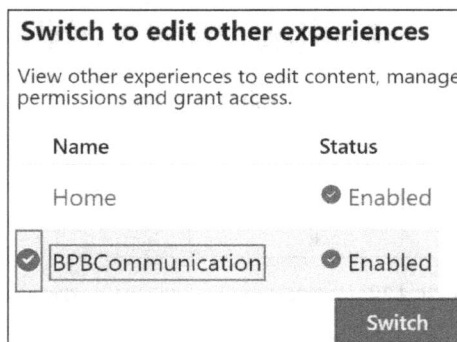

Figure 4.15: Select a new home page to switch experience

16. Now, log in to Microsoft Teams and open the Viva Connections app. You will find the new home site link in the navigation bar on the top-right corner, as shown in the following figure:

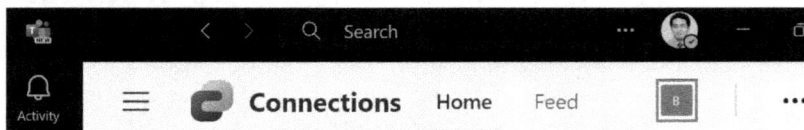

Figure 4.16: New home page added to team Viva Connections app navigation

17. Now, back to *Step 5*. We discussed already there will be three tabs like **General**, **Audience, Permissions**. We discussed the options related to the tab **General**. Now, let us discuss the second tab **Audiences**. You will notice the properties **Audience details** and **License type**. Refer to *Figure 4.17*:

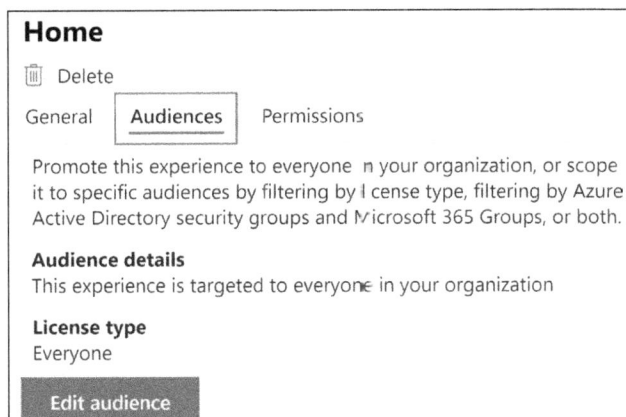

Figure 4.17: Edit Audience

18. Click on the button **Edit audience**. You will get two options related to the audience namely **Everyone in the organization** and **Scope down the audience for this experience**. By default, the option is selected as **Everyone in the organization**. This means the viva connection experience is targeted to every user in the organization. Refer to *Figure 4.18:*

Figure 4.18: Everyone in the organization should be associated with this experience

19. We can target the viva experience to all users present in a security group or group of users based on specific license type present in a security group or only users of specific license types by selecting option **Scope down the audience for this experience**.

20. Select the option **Scope down the audience for this experience**, enter group details in the field **Filter by group**. The option **Filter by license type** will be applied as **Everyone** present in that group, by default. The Viva Connection home site experience is targeted to everyone present in that group now. Refer to *Figure 4.19:*

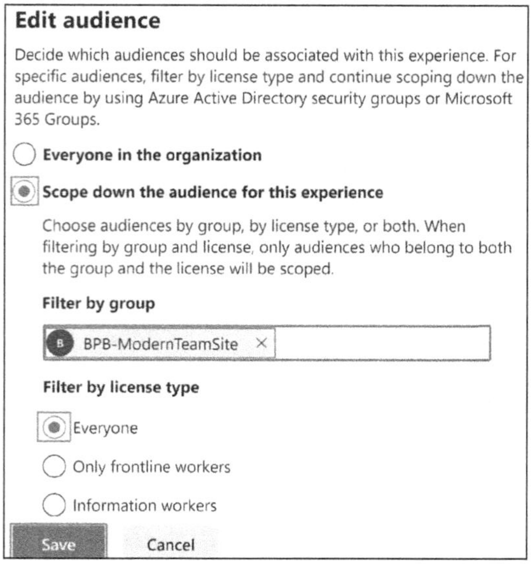

Figure 4.19: Security group by license type, Everyone

21. Select the option **Scope down the audience for this experience,** and enter group details in the field **Filter by group**. Select the option **Filter by license type** as **Only frontline workers**. The Viva Connections home site experience is targeted to only frontline workers present in that group now. Refer to *Figure 4.20*:

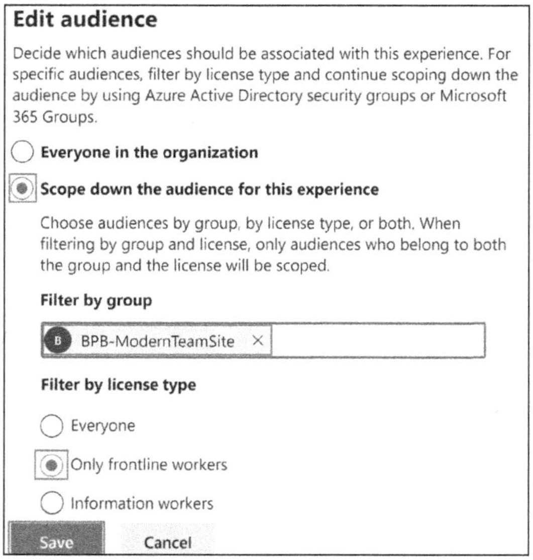

Figure 4.20: Security group by license type only frontline workers

22. Select the option **Scope down the audience for this experience**, enter group details in the field **Filter by group**. Select the option **Filter by license type** as

Information workers. The Viva Connections home site experience is targeted to only Information workers present in that group now. Refer to *Figure 4.21:*

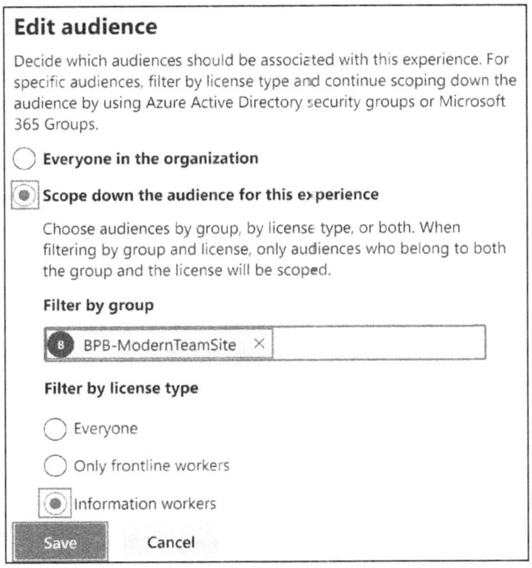

Figure 4.21: Security group by license type only information workers

23. Select the option **Scope down the audience for this experience**. Select the option **Filter by license type** as **Only frontline workers**. The Viva Connections home site experience will be targeted only at frontline workers in the organization. Similarly, selecting the option **Information workers** will lead to targeting the viva experience to only information workers in the organization. Refer to *Figure 4.22:*

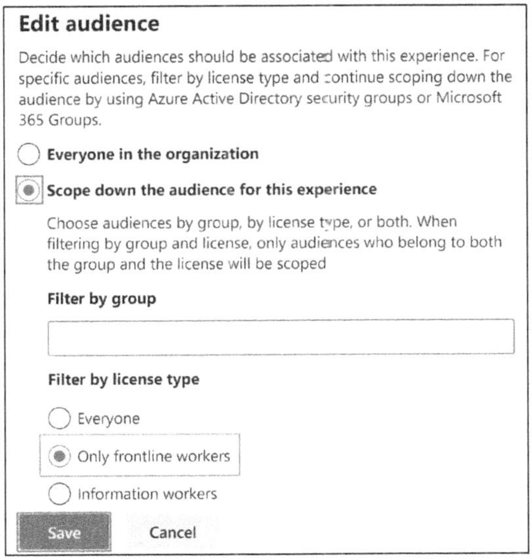

Figure 4.22: Audiences by license type

24. Now back to *Step 5*. We discussed already that there will be three tabs, namely **General**, **Audience**, and **Permissions**. We discussed the options related to the tab **General, Audience**. Now, let us discuss the third tab **Permissions**. Once you click on the tab **Permissions**, you will find information about the site owners. You will get the option to add or remove site owners. Refer to *Figure 4.23*:

Figure 4.23: Home site owner

Notifications

We discussed the first option **Home sites** present under **Settings** in the SharePoint admin center. The next option under settings is SharePoint **Notifications**, which provides options to enable or disable notifications related to site activities like published site news, comments on a page, or replies to page comments or page likes. You can select or deselect the checkbox to enable or disable the SharePoint notifications, respectively. Refer to *Figure 4.24*:

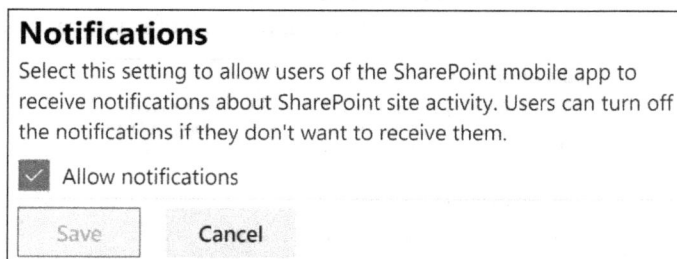

Figure 4.24: Site notifications

Pages

This is the third option present under **Settings** in the SharePoint admin center. Pages provide tenant level settings to allow or prevent users from creating modern pages and commenting on them. You will find options **Allow users to create new modern pages** and **Allow commenting on modern pages**. You can select or deselect the checkboxes to enable or disable as per the organization's requirement. Refer to *Figure 4.25*:

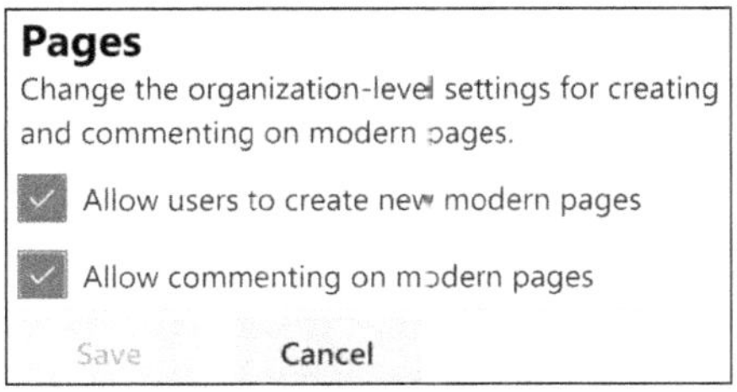

Figure 4.25: Pages

Site creation

Site creation is the fourth option present under **Settings**, in SharePoint admin center, related to the app SharePoint. By default, users are allowed to create Microsoft 365 group connected team sites and communication sites. Site creation setting allows admin to control creation of own sites. Administrators can select or deselect the checkbox to allow or restrict users creating their own sites. Select the checkbox **Users can create SharePoint sites** to enable site creation using APIs, PNP, and PowerShell. Select or deselect the second option **Show the options to create a site in SharePoint and create a shared library from OneDrive** to enable or disable site creation using UX options respectively, as shown in *Figure 4.26*:

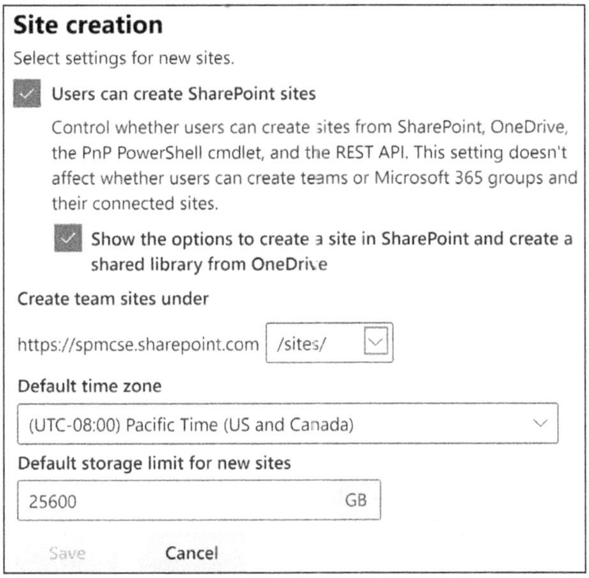

Figure 4.26: Site creation

Click on the drop-down present under the field **Create team sites under** and you will find two options like **sites** and **teams** as seen in *Figure 4.27*. SharePoint on-premises is called as managed path. Selecting the option **sites** will create a new site under the specific path sites like **https://spmcse.sharepoint.com/sites/**, for example, **https://spmcse.sharepoint.com/sites/BPB-ModernTeamSite**. If you are selecting **teams**, then default path for site creation will be under **teams**, for example, **https://spmcse.sharepoint.com/teams/BPB-ModernTeamSite**.

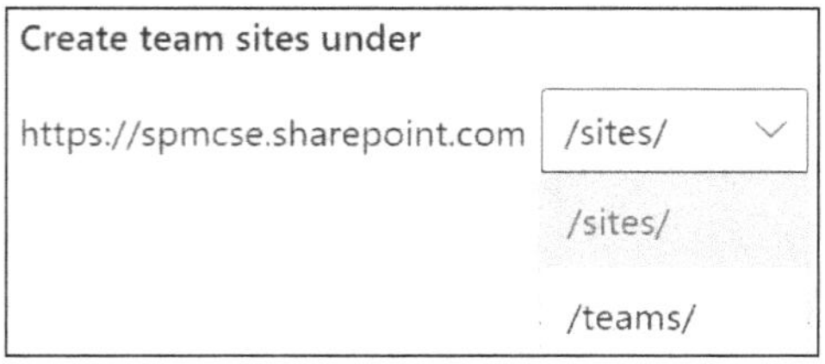

Figure 4.27: Site URL

The next option under **Site creation** is the Default time zone. You can select the time zone you want to keep as the default for the tenant. You can set the default storage limit for newly created sites by entering a limit in GB in the field **Default storage limit for new sites**. Refer to *Figure 4.26.*

Site storage limits

Every site is provided with a specific storage limit. The option **Site storage limits** offers options to control site space automatically or manually by selecting the options **Automatic** or **Manual** respectively. Select the option **Automatic** to allow sites to use as much tenant storage as possible. Refer to *Figure 4.28:*

Figure 4.28: Site storage limit

Select the option **Manual** to limit site storage to a specific amount. Once this option is enabled, you will find a mandatory option **Storage limit** under **Advanced settings** while creating site. Select the GB storage you want to set for the site. Refer to *Figure 4.29*:

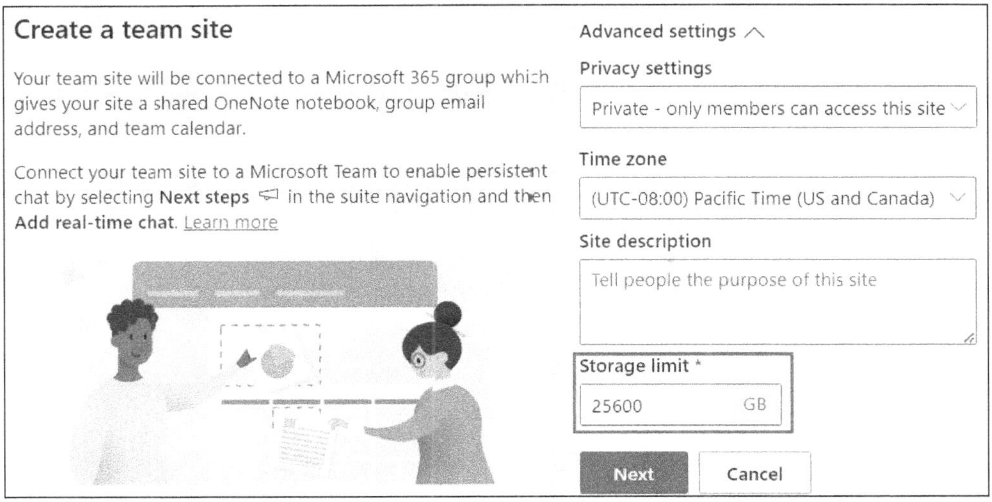

Figure 4.29: Site storage limit: Manual limit

Application management

Application management provides an option to enable the **SharePoint Embedded** feature. Once you open the option **Application management** related to SharePoint Embedded app, you will get the option to select the check box and apply changes to enable tenant level. Once it is enabled, you will get a confirmation, as seen in *Figure 4.30*:

Figure 4.30: Enable SharePoint Embedded application management

Stream app launcher tile

The stream app launcher tile is the default video player. Currently, you will find the new stream app called Stream (on SharePoint) and the classic version of Stream. Classic stream will be removed after a few months. Once you click on the option Stream app launcher tile, you will find options, namely, **Stream (Classic)**, **Stream (on SharePoint)**, and **Automatically switch to Stream (on SharePoint) when recommended,** as seen in

Figure 4.31. By default, the option **Automatically switch to Stream (on SharePoint) when recommended** is selected, which will redirect to the play video with the new experience **Stream** (on SharePoint). In the future, the default option will be **Stream (on SharePoint)**. Please refer to the following figure:

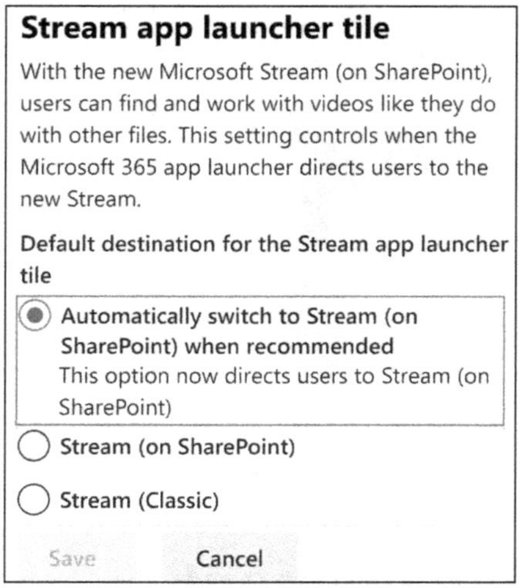

Figure 4.31: Stream app launcher tile

OneDrive notifications

OneDrive notifications options allow the admin to enable or disable notifications related to file activity in OneDrive, as shown in *Figure 4.32:*

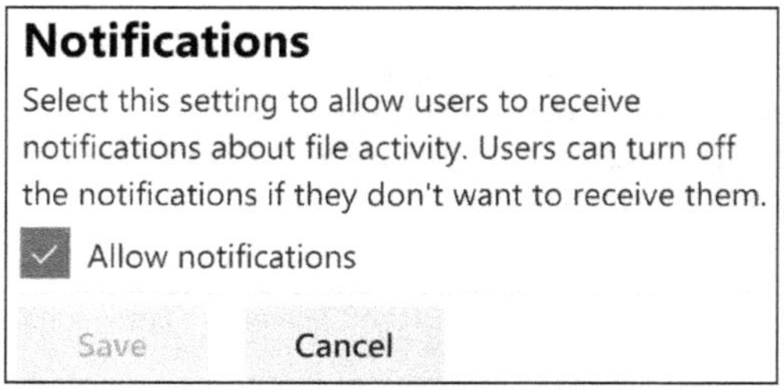

Figure 4.32: OneDrive notifications

Retention

If any user account is deleted, then OneDrive files will move to a recoverable state and are preserved for specific days. Option **Retention** allows admin to configure the number of days to retain deleted user's OneDrive. Enter the number of days from 30 to 3650 in the field **Days to retain a deleted user's OneDrive**. After that number of days, deleted user OneDrive files will be deleted permanently and cannot be recovered. Refer to *Figure 4.33:*

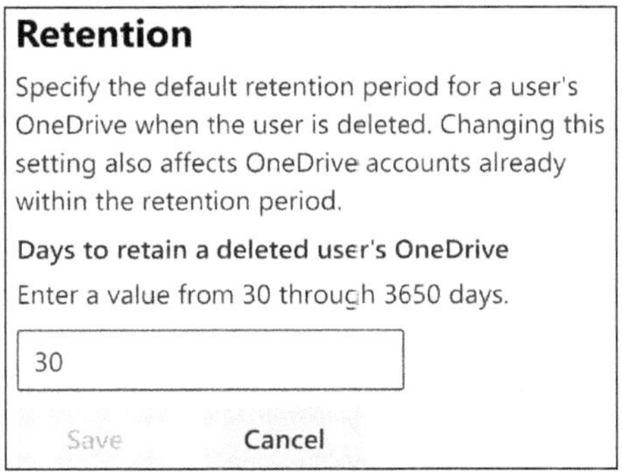

Retention

Specify the default retention period for a user's OneDrive when the user is deleted. Changing this setting also affects OneDrive accounts already within the retention period.

Days to retain a deleted user's OneDrive

Enter a value from 30 through 3650 days.

30

Save   **Cancel**

Figure 4.33: Retention

Storage limit

The **storage limit** option related to the app OneDrive provides an option to control the default OneDrive space allocated to each user account. Based on the subscription, there is default space of 1 TB allocated which can be modified up to 5 TB using this option as seen in *Figure 4.34*:

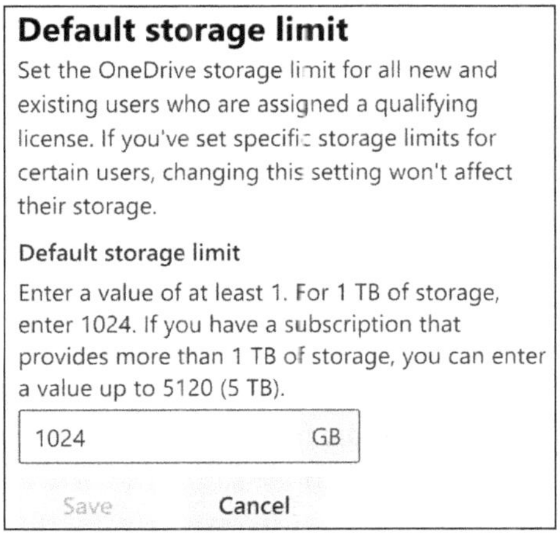

Default storage limit

Set the OneDrive storage limit for all new and existing users who are assigned a qualifying license. If you've set specific storage limits for certain users, changing this setting won't affect their storage.

Default storage limit

Enter a value of at least 1. For 1 TB of storage, enter 1024. If you have a subscription that provides more than 1 TB of storage, you can enter a value up to 5120 (5 TB).

1024   GB

Save   **Cancel**

Figure 4.34: OneDrive storage limit

Sync

Sync settings allow admin to control syncing of SharePoint and OneDrive files. There will be three options under sync namely, **Show the sync button on the OneDrive website**, **Allow syncing only on computers joined to specific domains** and **Block upload of specific file types** as seen in *Figure 4.35*. Select or unselect the option **Show the sync button on the OneDrive website** to show or hide **Sync** button on the OneDrive website. Please refer to the following figure:

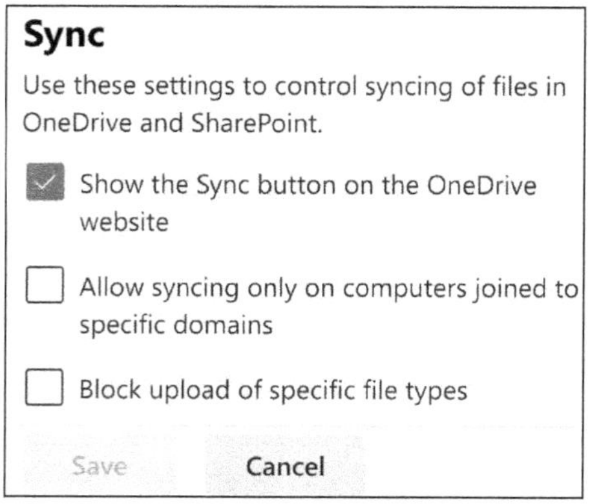

Figure 4.35: Sync

Select the option **Allow syncing only on computers joined to specific domains** to control sync of files on specific devices that are called as managed devices which are joined to specific domains. Enter the **GUID** of Active Directory domain in the box to enable this configuration. For multiple domains, enter GUID for each domain as new line as seen in the following *Figure 4.36*:

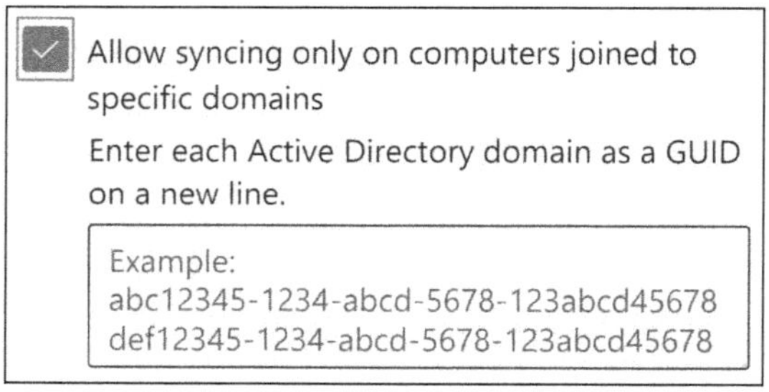

Figure 4.36: Sync managed devices

Select the option **Block upload of specific file types** to block uploading specific file types. Enter the file extensions in the field and those file types will be blocked from uploading. Refer to *Figure 4.37*:

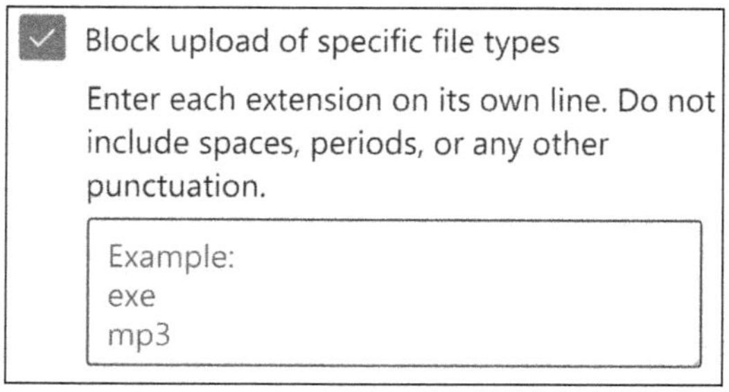

Figure 4.37: Block uploading files

Classic settings page

At the bottom of the settings page, you will find an option called **Classic settings page**. A few more settings fall under this category and can be controlled from here. Let us discuss these settings in this section.

Show or hide app tiles

Show or Hide App Tiles is the first category of options present in the classic settings page. This setting allows you to show or hide OneDrive and SharePoint app tiles in the app launcher on the Microsoft 365 portal. Select the radio button **Show** or **Hide** for each app (OneDrive or SharePoint Apps) to display or **Hide** in the all launcher, respectively. Refer to *Figure 4.38*:

Show or Hide App Tiles			
Show or hide app tiles in the app launcher and on the Microsoft 365 portal.	OneDrive and Office Online	◉ Show	○ Hide
	SharePoint	◉ Show	○ Hide

Figure 4.38: Show or Hide App Tiles

Site collection storage management

We already discussed on site storage management in the previous section **Site storage limits**. You can select site collection storage management from here as well. You can select any one of the options **Automatic** or **Manual** to manage storage automatically or manually allocating storage respectively. Refer to *Figure 4.39*:

Site Collection Storage Management	
Automatic storage management provides worry free operation by removing the overhead of having to manage individual storage limits. Manual override allows the tenant admin to set usage limits on a per site collection level.	○ Automatic ◉ Manual

Figure 4.39: Site Collection Storage Management

OneDrive for business experience

OneDrive for business experience provides options to choose the type of OneDrive experience that you want to give users. You can select the option **Classic experience** for the older version and the option **New experience** provides the latest OneDrive experience with improved features and performances. Refer to *Figure 4.40*:

OneDrive for Business experience	○ Classic experience ◉ New experience
The new experience gives people improved performance, additional phone and tablet features, and a simplified UI. If you select the new experience, users can still switch to the classic experience if they want. Select the classic experience if you're not ready for your users to switch to the new experience. Note that eventually, the classic experience will no longer be available.	

Figure 4.40: OneDrive for Business Experience

Admin center experience

You can switch between simple or advanced admin center user experience by selecting **Use Simple** or **Use Advanced** respectively. Refer to *Figure 4.41*:

Admin Center Experience	○ Use Simple ◉ Use Advanced
Use this setting to switch between a simple or advanced admin center user experience. The simple experience displays only the essential options. The advanced experience shows everything.	

Figure 4.41: Admin Center Experience

Delve

You can enable or disable **Delve** by selecting the options **Enable Delve** or **Disable Delve,** respectively. Refer to *Figure 4.42*:

Delve	◉ Enable Delve ○ Disable Delve
Delve helps users discover relevant content based on who they work with and what they're working on. By default, users in your organization can access Delve. If you disable Delve, users will only see profile properties, and the Delve app tile in the app launcher will be removed.	

Figure 4.42: Delve

Enterprise social collaboration

You can select the primary social experience as **Yammer** or **SharePoint Newsfeed** by selecting options from **Use Yammer.com service** or **Use SharePoint Newsfeed (default)**, respectively. Refer to *Figure 4.43*:

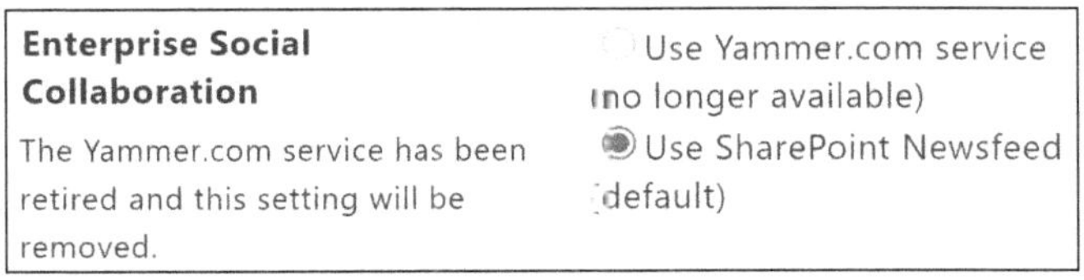

Enterprise Social Collaboration	○ Use Yammer.com service (no longer available)
The Yammer.com service has been retired and this setting will be removed.	◉ Use SharePoint Newsfeed (default)

Figure 4.43: *Enterprise social collaboration*

Personal blogs

Select one option from **Enable Personal Blogs** or **Disable Personal Blogs** to enable or disable personal blogs. Refer to *Figure 4.44*:

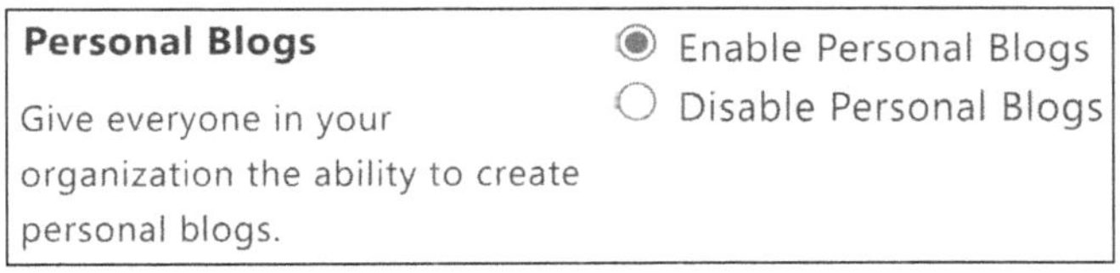

Personal Blogs	◉ Enable Personal Blogs
Give everyone in your organization the ability to create personal blogs.	○ Disable Personal Blogs

Figure 4.44: *Personal Blogs*

Site pages

We can control the creation of site pages by user. Select the option **Allow users to create Site Pages** to enable site pages creation and select the option **Prevent users from creating Site Pages** to restrict the same. Refer to *Figure 4.45*:

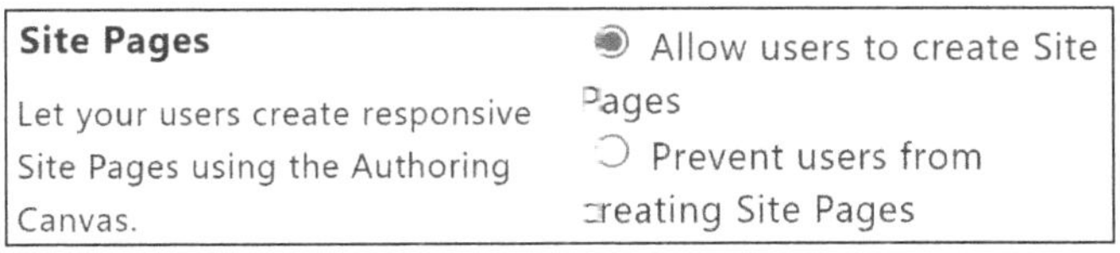

Site Pages	◉ Allow users to create Site Pages
Let your users create responsive Site Pages using the Authoring Canvas.	○ Prevent users from creating Site Pages

Figure 4.45: *Site Pages*

Global experience version settings

This setting provides options namely **Allow creation of old version site collections but prevent creation of new version site collections, Prevent opt-in upgrade to the new version site collections, Allow creation of old version site collections, and creation of new version site collections, Allow opt-in upgrade to the new version site collections** and **Prevent creation of old version site collections but allow creation of new version site collections, Allow opt-in upgrade to the new version site collections**. The last option is selected by default currently. Refer to *Figure 4.46*:

Global Experience Version Settings	Allow creation of old version site collections, but prevent creation of new version site collections. Prevent opt-in upgrade to the new version site collections.
Control which version of site collections can be created by end users, and whether users can upgrade them.	Allow creation of old version site collections, and creation of new version site collections. Allow opt-in upgrade to the new version site collections.
	Prevent creation of old version site collections, but allow creation of new version site collections. Allow opt-in upgrade to the new version site collections.

Figure 4.46: Global experience version settings

Information rights management

In **Information Rights Management (IRM),** select one of the options **Use the IRM service specified in your configuration** or **Do not use IRM for this tenant** to enable or disable IRM service, respectively. Refer to *Figure 4.47*:

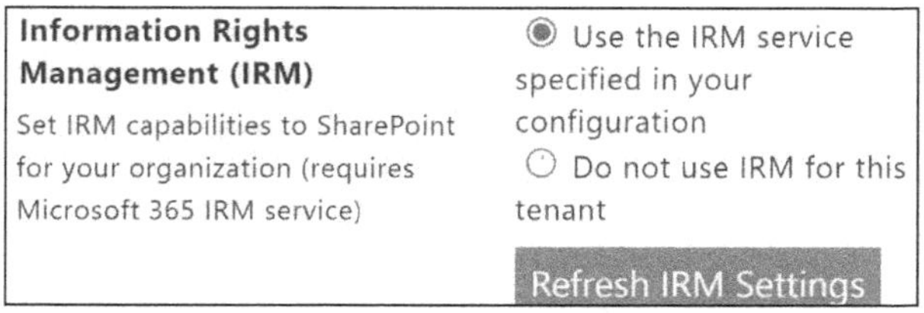

Information Rights Management (IRM)	● Use the IRM service specified in your configuration
Set IRM capabilities to SharePoint for your organization (requires Microsoft 365 IRM service)	○ Do not use IRM for this tenant
	Refresh IRM Settings

Figure 4.47: Information Rights Management

Site creation

Next, you will find the option **Site creation** that allows admin to show or hide the create site command, controls to create new team site, communication site or classic team sub site, create sites from a custom form.

Select one of the options **Hide the Create site command** or **Show the Create site command** to hide or display create site command on SharePoint home page and in the sites list in OneDrive.

Select the option **A new team site or communication site** to make a new team site, communication site as default when a user clicks on Create site command. Select the option **A classic team subsite** to enable creating classic team subsites.

Select the option **Use the form at this URL** to create sites from a custom form by entering the form URL. Refer to *Figure 4.48*:

Site Creation	○ Hide the Create site command
Display the Create site command on the SharePoint home page and in the sites list in OneDrive so users can create new sites.	◉ Show the Create site command
The first option lets users create a Microsoft 365 group-connected team site or a communication site. Users who don't have permission to create Microsoft 365 groups can still create new team sites without the Microsoft 365 group.	When users select the Create site command, create: ◉ A new team site or communication site ○ A classic team subsite
The second option lets users create a classic team subsite.	Create groups under: https://spmcse.sharepoint.com ˅ Secondary contact: Not required ˅
For both options, you can let users create sites from a custom form by entering the form URL. If you selected the first option, users can access the form by clicking "See other options" when they're creating the site.	☐ Use the form at this URL:

Figure 4.48: Site Creation

Subsite creation

Select one of the options from **Disable subsite creation for all sites** or **Enable sub site creation for classic sites only** or **Enable subsite creation for all sites** to disable or enable subsite creation based on requirement, as shown in *Figure 4.49*:

Subsite Creation	○ Disable subsite creation for all sites
Control subsite creation for people who have permission to create sites. This controls visibility of the Subsite option on the Site contents page and enables new subsite creation. Use hub sites to connect related sites instead of using subsites.	○ Enable sub site creation for classic sites only ◉ Enable subsite creation for all sites

Figure 4.49: Subsite Creation

Connections from sites to Microsoft 365 groups

Select one of the options from Prevent site collection administrators from connecting sites to new Microsoft 365 groups or Allow site collection administrators to connect sites to new Microsoft 365 groups to disable to enable the option Connect site to New Microsoft 365 groups. Refer to *Figure 4.50*:

Connections from sites to Microsoft 365 groups	○ Prevent site collection administrators from connecting sites to new Microsoft 365 groups
Control whether site collection administrators can use the "Connect to a new Microsoft 365 Group" command on the Settings menu to connect classic team sites to new Microsoft 365 groups.	◉ Allow site collection administrators to connect sites to new Microsoft 365 groups

Figure 4.50: Connections from sites to Microsoft 365 groups

Custom script

The Custom script option controls running custom script. Select one of the options from **Prevent users from running custom script on personal sites** or **Allow users to run custom script on personal sites** to block or allow running custom script on personal sites.

Select one of the options from **Prevent users from running custom script on self-service created sites** or **Allow users to run custom script on self-service created sites** to block or allow running custom script on self-service created sites, as shown in *Figure 4.51*:

Custom Script	○ Prevent users from running custom script on personal sites
Control whether users can run custom script on personal sites and self-service created sites. Note: changes to this setting might take up to 24 hours to take effect.	◉ Allow users to run custom script on personal sites
For more information, see https://go.microsoft.com/fwlink/?LinkId=397546	○ Prevent users from running custom script on self-service created sites
	◉ Allow users to run custom script on self-service created sites

Figure 4.51: Custom script

Preview features

Select one of the options from **Enable preview features** or **Disable preview features** to enable or disable the preview features, as shown in *Figure 4.52*:

Preview Features	◉ Enable preview features
Turning off this setting will disable Preview features making them inaccessible to your users. Preview features have limited support in SharePoint Online and do not yet meet all service requirements. A full list of the Preview features and support details can be found at the O365 website.	○ Disable preview features Learn more about Preview Features

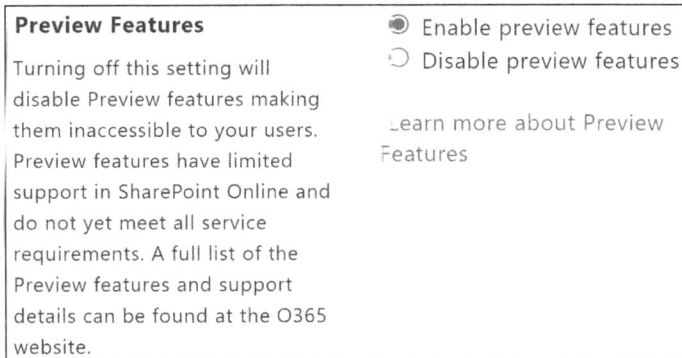

Figure 4.52: Preview Features

Connected services

Connected services allows limiting SharePoint features that attempt to connect to other services. You see the fixed setting applied as **Use SharePoint Online Management Shell to block SharePoint 2013 workflows**. Refer to *Figure 4.53*:

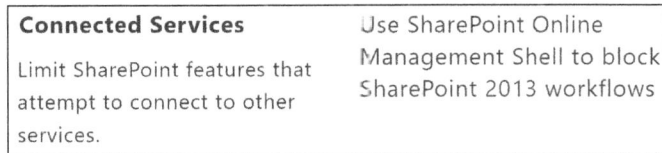

Connected Services	Use SharePoint Online Management Shell to block SharePoint 2013 workflows
Limit SharePoint features that attempt to connect to other services.	

Figure 4.53: Connected Services

Mobile push notifications: OneDrive for business

Select one of the options from **Allow notifications** or **Don't allow notifications** to enable or disable mobile push notifications for OneDrive for business, as shown in *Figure 4.54*:

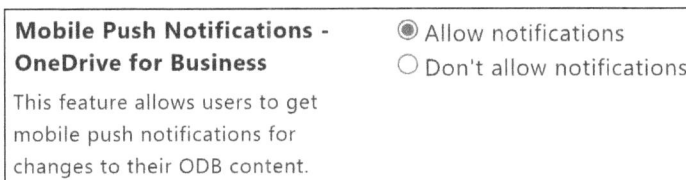

Mobile Push Notifications - OneDrive for Business	◉ Allow notifications
This feature allows users to get mobile push notifications for changes to their ODB content.	○ Don't allow notifications

Figure 4.54: Mobile push notifications OneDrive for business

Mobile push notifications: SharePoint

Select one of the options from **Allow notifications** or **Don't allow notifications** to enable or disable the mobile push notifications for SharePoint, as shown in *Figure 4.55*:

Mobile Push Notifications – SharePoint	◉ Allow notifications
This feature allows users to get mobile push notifications for changes to their SharePoint content.	○ Don't allow notifications

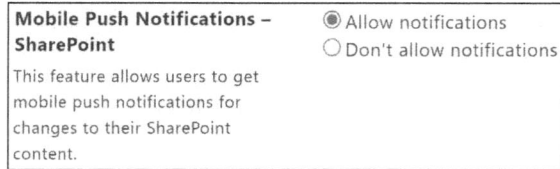

Figure 4.55: Mobile Push Notifications: SharePoint

Comments on site pages

Select one of the options from **Enable comments on Site Pages** or **Disable comments on Site Pages** enable or disable comments on site pages, as shown in *Figure 4.56*:

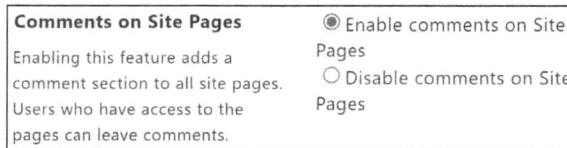

Comments on Site Pages	◉ Enable comments on Site Pages
Enabling this feature adds a comment section to all site pages. Users who have access to the pages can leave comments.	○ Disable comments on Site Pages

Figure 4.56: Comments on site pages

Conclusion

In this chapter, we had a glance at various options available under the left navigation option Settings. We discussed the step-by-step procedure to understand setting up the home site experience related to Viva connection, switching to different user home sites, targeting the Viva experience by providing permission to a specific group of users. The chapter also discussed the settings for creating and commenting on modern pages. We discussed the default site creation settings, managing storage limits, and controlling the notifications for SharePoint sites. We also had a look at configuring the retention period for OneDrive files for the deleted user accounts, default OneDrive storage limits, enabling OneDrive notifications, and finally, the classic settings page options available and their functions.

In the next chapter, *Chapter 5, Content Services,* we will discuss the term store and the content type gallery.

Points to remember

- By default, users are allowed to create Microsoft 365 group connected team sites and communication sites. Using the **Site creation** setting we can restrict users creating their own communication sites. Creating Microsoft 365 group connected sites can be restricted by different methods not from SharePoint admin center.

- Regular features are getting updated on SharePoint Online. You might find slight changes after some days.

CHAPTER 5

Content Services

Introduction

In *Chapter 4, Settings,* we discussed settings, the fourth navigation option available in the SharePoint admin center. In this chapter, we will discuss terms, managed metadata, and content types that are part of the SharePoint content services (fifth navigation option in SharePoint admin center) categorized as **Term store and Content type gallery**. Terms, structured under taxonomy, are managed centrally using the term store management tool. Taxonomy is the central repository of terms, words, and labels arranged into a structured hierarchy and defined as a formal classification system. Metadata is the information or data, and plays an important role in quick and most relevant content searching, refining content, and building global navigation that can apply to all sites under one site collection for better user experience. We can create metadata and keywords by tagging, which is ultimately helpful in searching and getting information quickly and most relevantly. Let us start discussing terms store, content type gallery, and its management from the admin center.

Structure

In this chapter we will discuss the following:

- Term store administration
- Content type gallery administration

Objectives

By the end of this chapter, you will get a clear understanding about various options available under the left navigation namely content services, term store, content type gallery in SharePoint admin center. You will understand the term store taxonomy hierarchy and terminologies used in that hierarchy. You will get a clear understanding of the term group and know the step-by-step procedure to add a term group in the taxonomy, rename the term group, delete the term group, and manage permissions in the term group. You will learn how to add a term set, import a term set, rename a term set, delete a term set, copy a term set, and move a term set. You will understand the settings available as tabs namely, general tab, usage settings, navigation, advanced for term set. You will understand how to add a term, rename a term, copy a term, copy a term with children, move a term, delete a term, pin a term, reuse a term, merge a term, and deprecate a term. You will get in-depth information about the settings available as tabs, namely, general tab, usage settings, navigation, advanced for term. You will learn the default term group and its application in term store. You will get a clear understanding of content types and how to create content type, edit content type, and manage publishing. You will get to know about the content type settings, namely advanced settings, policy settings and other general settings and will understand how to delete the content type.

Term store administration

Term is a predefined, reusable word or phrase in SharePoint. Term has a unique ID but many labels for different languages apply to multilingual sites. Terms are of two types, **Managed terms** and **Enterprise keywords**. Managed terms are organized hierarchically into term set and Enterprise keywords used as tagging. A group of terms is called a **Term Set,** and a group of Term Sets is called a **Term Group**. Terms can be managed centrally from the **Term Store** present under the **SharePoint Admin Center**. Think of a situation where an organization needs to use specific details like band, business unit, horizontal tag, total experience, relevant experience, skill related to employees in many authorized sites in the tenant. In that case, you can create a term group namely **Employee**. Under the term group Employee, you can create multiple term sets, namely **Band, Business Unit, Horizontal Tag, Total Experience, Relevant Experience, Skill**. Each term set can have multiple options. **Azure, networking, database, office 365, SharePoint, storage, windows** are the different skills that employees work on in the project. You can include these skills under the term set **Skill,** which are called terms. You can create terms under term set Skill. Similarly, you can create terms within terms. All created term groups, term set, terms are structured as a hierarchy. These terms will be available globally to apply to all sites in the tenant. Similarly, you can categorize, plan, and create related terms in other term sets, etc. Let us perform the following steps to understand the options available under content services:

1. Click on **Content services** present under the left navigation of SharePoint admin center.

2. The navigation option will expand, and you will notice two categories of options, namely **Term store** and **Content type gallery**. Refer to *Figure 5.1*:

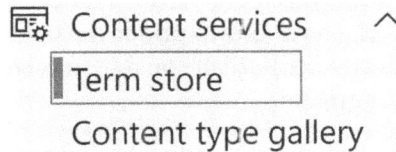

Figure 5.1: Content services

3. Click on **Term Store**. You will be redirected to the term store admin center (**https://< SharePoint admin center url>/ _layouts/15/online/AdminHome. aspx?modern=true#/termStoreAdminCenter**), which is the central location for creating, storing, configuring, and managing terms, taxonomies, or metadata. You will notice three default term groups, namely **People**, **Search Dictionaries**, and **System**, structured as a hierarchy under Taxonomy.

4. The default option will be selected as **Taxonomy**, as shown in *Figure 5.2*:

Figure 5.2: Term Store in SharePoint admin center

5. On the right pane, you will find information about the term store, such as term store Admins, Default language, Working languages, Unique identifier, and the option Add term group to create a new term group as per business requirement.

Let us proceed to the next part in this section to create a new term group and its related options.

Term group

Term group is a top-level folder in the taxonomy hierarchy that we can create based on usability and to keep related term sets and terms in one place. It is a group of term sets that share common security requirements, with each term group maintaining unique access and being created to meet unique requirements. Let us proceed to the next part of this section to understand term group better.

Adding term group

The term group is positioned at the top level in the taxonomy hierarchy. In this section, we will discuss how to create or add a term group under the taxonomy. Users with permission from the term store administrator can create or add a term group. Let us perform the following steps to create a term group:

1. Click on **Content services** present under the left navigation of SharePoint admin center. The navigation option will expand.

2. Click on Term Store. You will be redirected to the term store admin center from where you can manage terms. It is also called the term store management tool.

3. You will notice the default option, Taxonomy, selected. Click on the option Add term group from the right pane or from the show action option. Enter the Name of the term group as Employee and press *ENTER* on the keyboard. Refer to *Figure 5.3*:

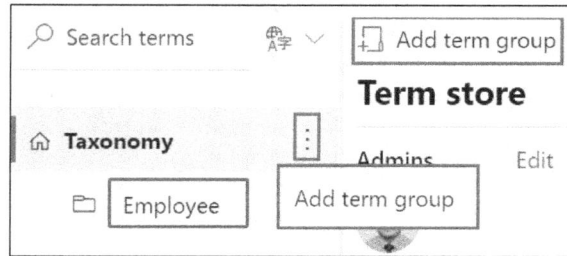

Figure 5.3: Create term group

4. Term group Employee will be created and added to the tree-view pane under **Taxonomy** as shown in *Figure 5.4*:

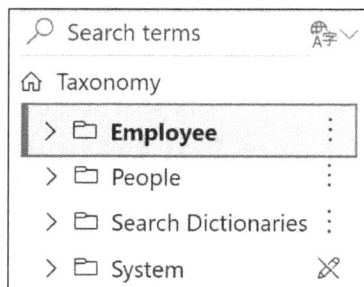

Figure 5.4: Term group added to Taxonomy

5. Click on the term group **Employee**. On the right pane, you will find more details related to the term group. At the top of the right pane, you will find options related to the actions that can be taken on the term group, namely Add term set, Rename term group, Delete term group, and Import term set in the form of a command bar. Refer to *Figure 5.5*:

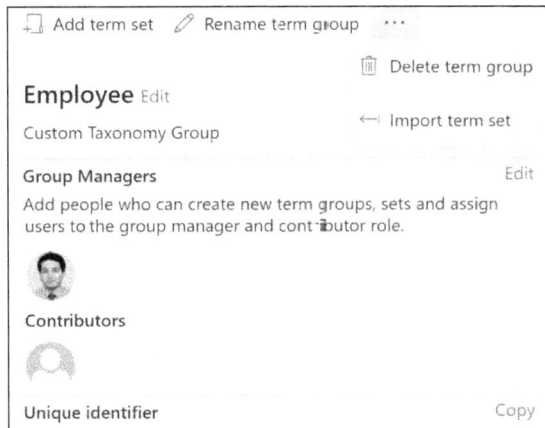

Figure 5.5: Term group setting

6. Below that you will find the name and description of the term group.

7. Below the term group name, you will find the users assigned to roles and permissions to the term group.

8. Below that, you will find the unique identifier ID related to the term group.

Renaming term group

Let us proceed to the next action that can be taken related to term group. We can change the name and description of term group. Let us perform the following steps to modify name and description of term group:

1. Select the term group **Employee** from **Taxonomy**.

2. From the right pane, click on Rename term group from command bar or click on Edit option present side to the term group name Employee.

3. You will get a new window to modify **Term group name** and **Description**. Enter details and click on **Save** to apply changes. Refer to *Figure 5.6*:

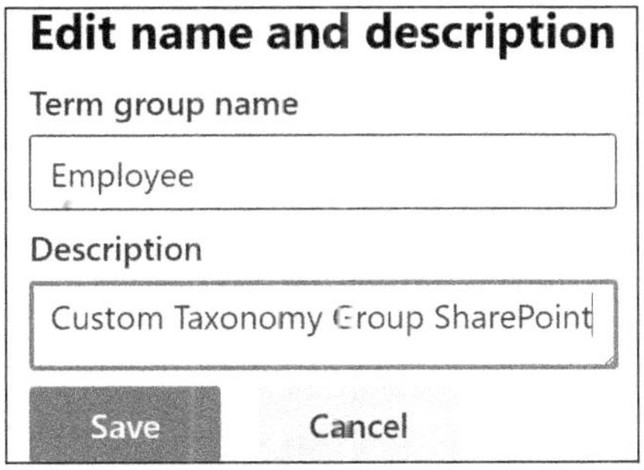

Figure 5.6: Edit name and description of term group

Deleting term group

Let us proceed to the next action that can be taken related to the term group. You can delete the term group, if not required, as per business requirement. Identify the term group that you want to delete. Click on show action option present side to the term group. You will get the option Delete term group. Alternatively, you can select the same option **Delete term group** from right pane in the command bar. Refer to *Figure 5.7*:

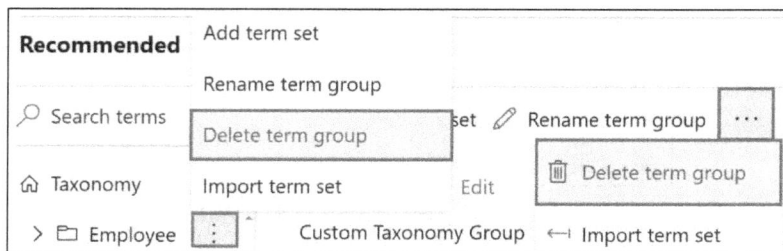

Figure 5.7: Delete term group

You will get **This action is permanent and cannot be undone** as a warning message. If you agree, click on the button **Delete,** and the Term group will be deleted. Refer to *Figure 5.8*:

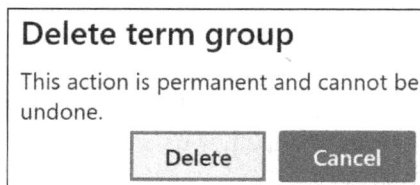

Figure 5.8: Confirm to delete the term group

Managing permissions term group

Let us proceed to the next action that can be taken related to term group. Term store defines security boundaries. When we create a term group, the term set will be created under the term group. So, we need to assign permissions to business users who can manage term group. Click on the term group Employee from **Taxonomy**. On the right pane, below term group name, you will find two roles, namely Group Managers, and Contributors. The Term store administrator can create new term group. Users having contributor permission in the term group can create and manage term sets specific to that term group only. The group Managers can add or remove contributors in the term group permission list. So, the group manager has this additional permission along with the contribute permission. Term store administrators can add group managers. Let us perform the following steps to add or modify user permissions in the term group as per business requirements:

1. Click on the **Edit** option present next to **Group Managers**. Refer to *Figure 5.5*.

2. You will get a new window called **Edit properties**. Refer to *Figure 5.9*.

3. Enter the name or email of the user in the field. Enter a name or email address whom you want to give permission to this term group.

4. The user will be added to the list with default permission as Contributor. Click on **Save** to apply changes.

5. Click on the drop-down option present on the side to the user and select the option Manager if you want to change permission assigned to that user in future as per business requirement.

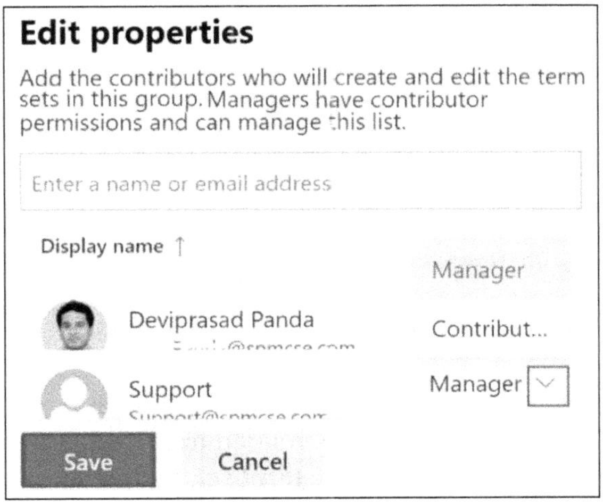

Figure 5.9: Term group permission

Term set

We discussed the term store and understood the terminologies, namely taxonomy and term group. Under taxonomy we created term group Employee. Similarly, under the term group **Employee**, we can create a group of Term Set. Under the Term set, we can create multiple terms. So, term set is a group of terms. Each employee in an organization has **Band** based on experience, **Business Unit**, **Horizontal Tag**, **Total Experience**, **Relevant Experience**, **Skill**. Since these are linked to an employee, we can categorize and create them as term set under the term group Employee. Let us proceed to the next section to understand the term set better.

Adding term set

Term set is positioned at the second level in taxonomy hierarchy, next to term group. In this section, we will discuss and understand how to create or add a term set under the term group. Users having contribute permission (Added as a Contributor in term group) can create or add term set. Let us perform the following steps to create a term set:

1. Click on the term group **Employee** under which you want to create the term set.

2. Click on Add term set from the right or the action pane, as shown in *Figure 5.10*:

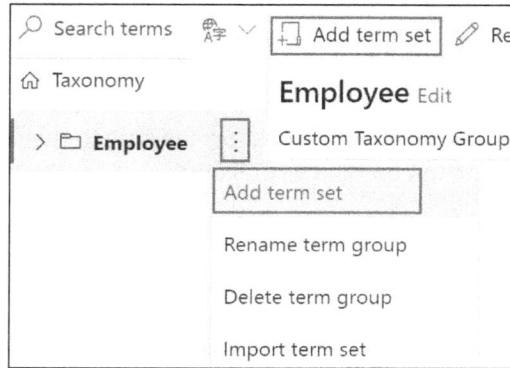

Figure 5.10: Adding term set

3. Type the name of term set as Business Unit and press *Enter* from the keyboard.

4. The new term set Business Unit created added to tree-view pane under term group Employee.

5. On the right pane, you will find more details related to the term set. At the top of the right pane, you will find options related to the actions that can be taken on the term set, namely **Add term**, **Rename term set**, **Delete term set**, **Copy term set**, and **Move term set** in the form of a command bar. Refer to *Figure 5.11*.

6. Under the command bar, you will find the name and description of the term set.

7. Following that you will find four tabs namely **General**, **Usage settings**, **Navigation**, **Advanced** with default tab selected as **General**.

8. We created a single term set **Business Unit**. Similarly, create a few more term sets namely Band, Horizontal Tag, Relevant Experience, Skill, Total Experience, under term group Employee.

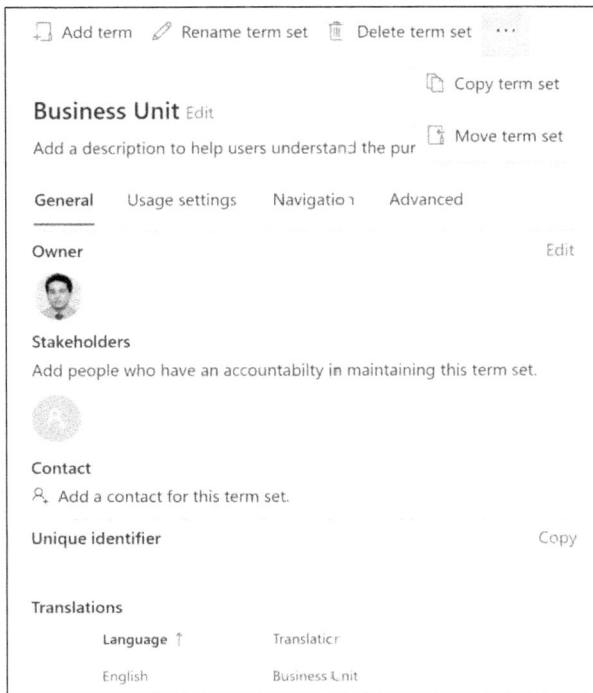

Figure 5.11: Test set settings

Importing term set

Let us proceed to the next action that can be taken related to term group. You can import the term set instead of creating manually as per business requirement. Let us perform the following steps to create a term set:

1. Identify the term group Employee under which you want to import term set.

2. Click on the **Show action** option that is present to the right of the term group. You will get the option **Import term set**. Alternatively, you can select the same option, Import term set, from the right pane in the command bar. Refer to *Figure 5.12*:

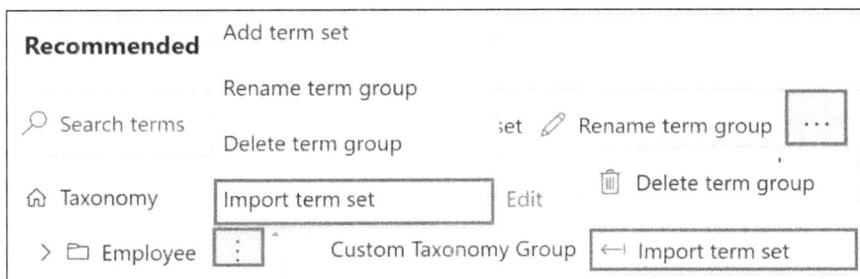

Figure 5.12: Import term set

3. You will get the Import new term set window.

4. Click on the option Browse and select the CSV file that is updated with tern set names in a specific format as suggested by Microsoft. You can download the sample file for reference, fill it.

5. Select the CSV file from the device and click on Import. Term set will be created under **Term group**.

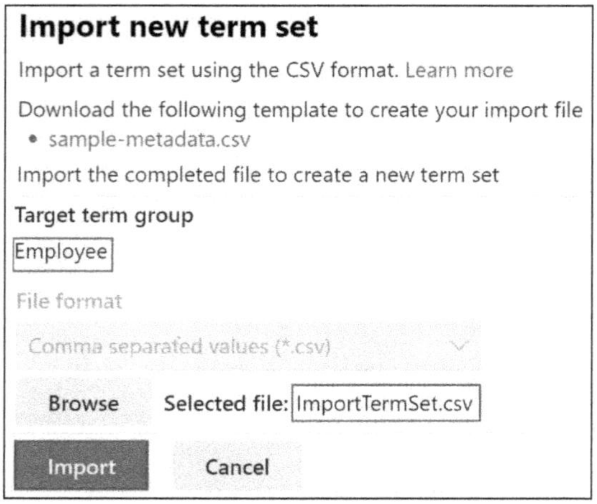

Import new term set

Import a term set using the CSV format. Learn more

Download the following template to create your import file
• sample-metadata.csv

Import the completed file to create a new term set

Target term group

Employee

File format

Comma separated values (*.csv)

Browse   Selected file: ImportTermSet.csv

Import   Cancel

Figure 5.13: Import new term set from CSV file

Renaming term set

Let us proceed to the next action that can be taken related to the term set. We can change the name and description of term set. Let us perform the following steps to modify name and description of term group:

1. Select the term set Business Unit from the tree-view pane under the term group Employee.

2. From the right pane, click on Rename term set from the command bar or click on the Edit option present on the side of the term set name Business Unit.

3. You will get a new window **Edit properties** to modify **Term set name** and **Description**. Enter details and click on Save to apply changes.

Deleting term set

Let us proceed to the next action that can be taken related to the term set. You can delete the term set if not required as per business requirement, follow these steps to do so:

1. Identify the term set that you want to delete. Click on the **Show action** option present side to the term set. You will get the option **Delete term set**. Alternatively,

you can select the same option Delete term set from the right pane in the command bar. You will get a message like If you delete this term set, all terms below it will also be deleted. Terms in this set shared with other term sets will be placed in the Orphaned term set under System. Refer to *Figure 5.14*:

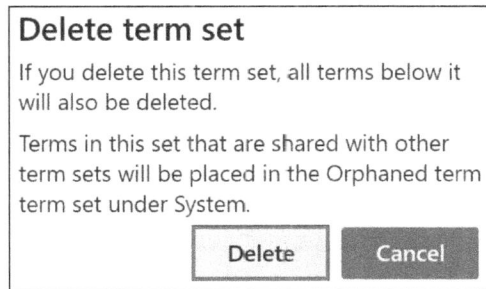

Delete term set

If you delete this term set, all terms below it will also be deleted.

Terms in this set that are shared with other term sets will be placed in the Orphaned term term set under System.

Delete   Cancel

Figure 5.14: Delete term set

2. If you agree, click on the button **Delete**. The term set will be deleted, and the terms that were present in this term set and shared with other term sets will be placed in the **Orphaned Terms**. Refer to *Figure 5.15*:

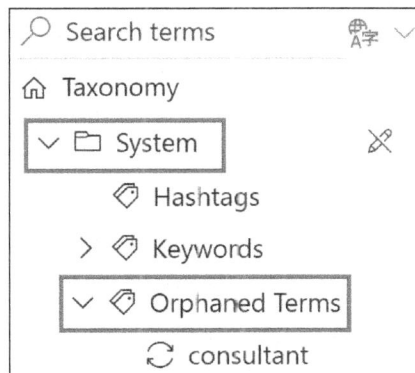

Search terms

Taxonomy

System

Hashtags

> Keywords

Orphaned Terms

consultant

Figure 5.15: Orphaned Terms

Copying term set

Let us proceed to the next action that can be taken related to the term set. You can copy the term set as per business requirement by following these steps:

1. Identify the term set that you want to copy.

2. Click on the **Show action** option on the side of the term set. You will get the option Copy term set. Alternatively, you can select the same option **Copy term set** from right pane in the command bar.

3. You will notice the new term set **Business Unit - Copy** created. Refer to *Figure 5.16*:

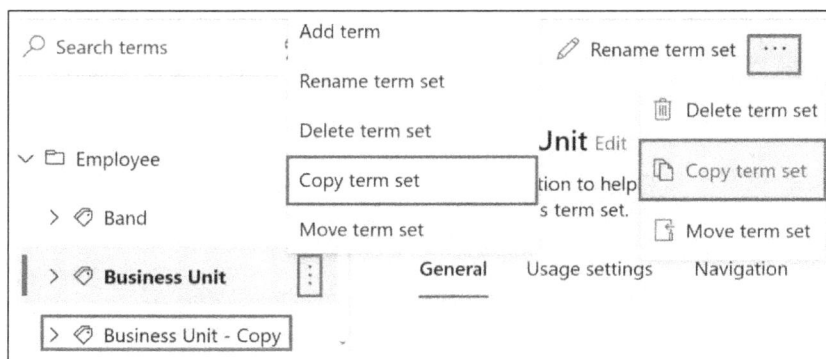

Figure 5.16: Copy term set

Moving term set

You can move the term set as per the business requirement. Identify the term set that you want to move, and click on the **Show action** option present on the side of term set. You will get the option **Move term set**. Alternatively, you can select the same option **Move term set** from right pane in the command bar. You will get another window to select the destination term group. Select the destination term group to which this term set is to be moved. Further, click on **Move**, as shown in the following figure:

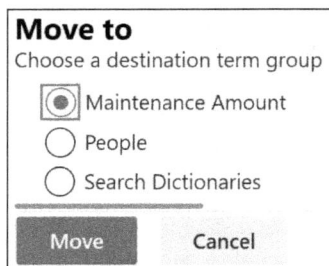

Figure 5.17: Move term set

General tab in term set

Next to the term set name Business Unit on the right pane, you will find four tabs, namely, General, Usage settings, Navigation, and Advanced. Each tab contains a specific set of information and related settings. In this section, we will discuss the first tab, General, and understand its application. Let us perform the following steps to understand it better:

1. Click on the term set Business Unit and click on the first tab, **General**, from the right pane.

2. Under the tab **General**, you will find details related to **Owner, Stakeholders, Contact, Unique identifier**, and **Translations**. Refer to Figure 5.18:

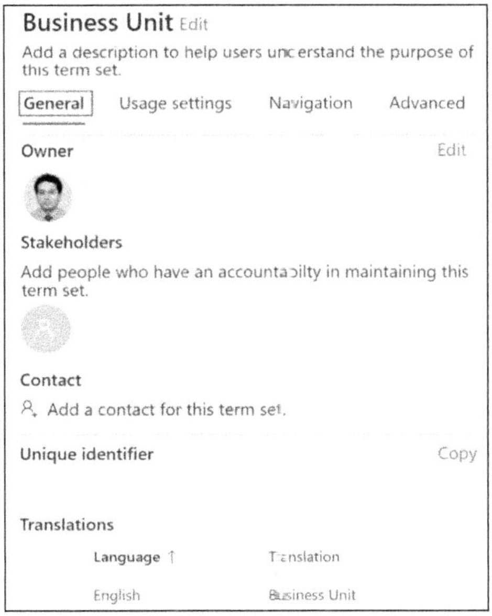

Figure 5.18: General tab in term set

3. Click on the option **Edit** present next to Owner.

4. The **Edit** properties window will open. You will find three roles, namely, Term set owner, Stakeholders, and Contact with people picker fields inside each in collapsed format, by default.

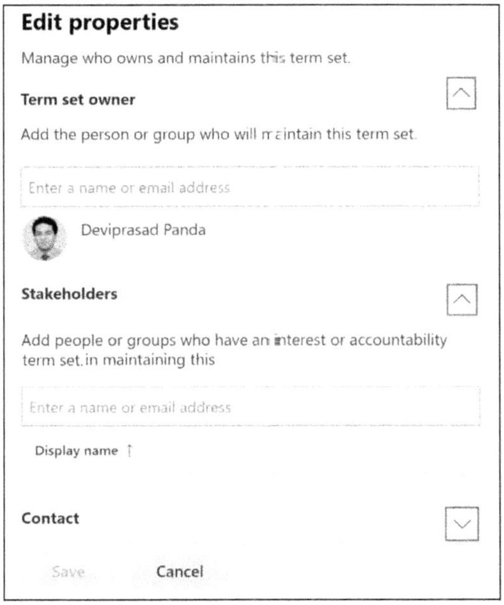

Figure 5.19: Term set permission levels

5. Expand the option **Term set owner**.

6. Enter the name or email of the user or group in the field Term set owner, who is/ are going to be the owner of the term set.

7. Expand the option **Stakeholders**. Enter the name or email of user or group under the field Stakeholders who will receive notification mail before any major changes happening in term set.

8. Expand the option **Contact**. Enter the name or email of one user or group under the field Contact if you want to enable site owners who can provide feedback on term set.

9. Once you have assigned user roles or permissions, click on the button Save to apply changes. Roles are defined for the term set.

10. Next to the user roles category, you will find the unique identifier ID of the term set.

11. Next to the unique identifier, you will find the category Translations that contain information related to current configured languages.

Usage settings tab in term set

Next to the term set name **Business Unit** on the right pane, you will find four tabs, namely **General**, **Usage settings**, **Navigation**, and **Advanced**. Each tab contains a specific set of information and related settings. In this section, we will discuss the second tab, **Usage settings**, and understand its application. Let us perform the following steps to understand it better:

1. Click on the term set **Business Unit** and click on the second tab **Usage settings** from the right pane.

2. Under the tab **Usage settings**, you will find settings like Submission policy, Available for tagging, and Sort order. Refer to Figure 5.20:

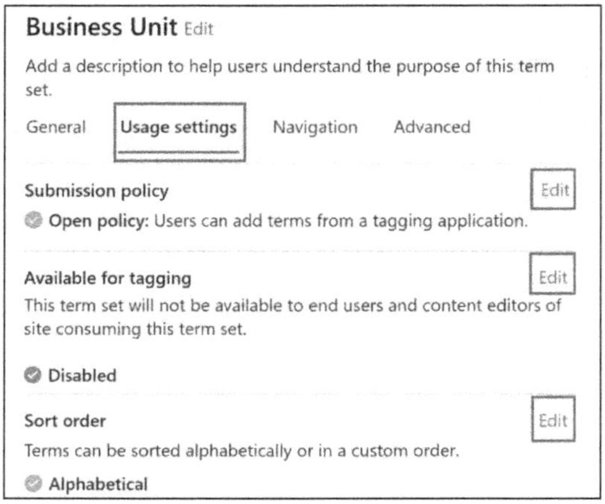

Figure 5.20: Usage settings tan term set

3. The term set can be **Open** or **Closed** type. **Submission policy** control to make the term set open or closed. It enables those who can add terms to the term set. Click on **Edit** present side to Submission policy.

4. You will get the **Edit submission policy** window. Select an option, **Open** or **Closed,** as per requirement, and click on **Save** to apply changes. Refer to *Figure 5.21*.

5. Selecting the option **Closed** will allows only administrators, contributors, metadata managers to add terms. Selecting the option **Open** will allow all users to add terms in the column mapped to the term set.

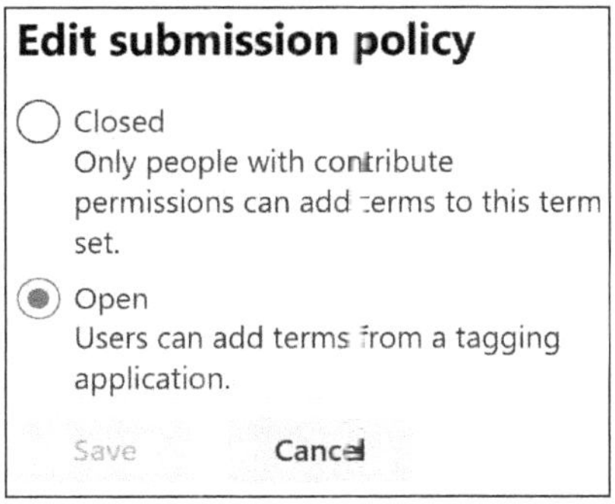

Edit submission policy

◯ Closed
   Only people with contribute
   permissions can add terms to this term
   set.

◉ Open
   Users can add terms from a tagging
   application.

   Save   Cancel

Figure 5.21: Edit submission policy

6. Let us proceed to the second option category, **Available for tagging**, under **Usage settings**. Click on Edit present side to Available for tagging. You will get a new window. Select the checkbox Enable, as seen in *Figure 5.22*. This will enable the term set to be available for tagging. End users and content editors from the site can consume that term set.

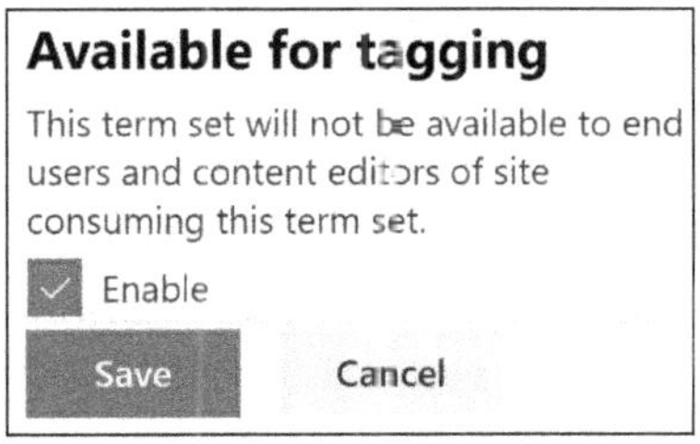

Available for tagging

This term set will not be available to end
users and content editors of site
consuming this term set.

☑ Enable

   Save   Cancel

Figure 5.22: Enable or disable term set tagging

7. Let us proceed to the third option category, Sort order, under **Usage settings**. By default, the terms in the term set are sorted in alphabetical order. The option **Sort order** allows you to select an order in which to display the terms in the term set.

8. Click on **Edit** present side to the option Sort order.

9. You will get the **Edit sort order** panel. Select the option **Custom sort order** to change the sorting order as per your requirement.

10. Click on the **Action** menu side of each term.

11. You will get options, namely, **Move to top**, **Move up**, **Move down**, **Move to bottom**.

12. Choose any option to change the current order. Finally, click on **Save** to apply changes, as shown in the following figure:

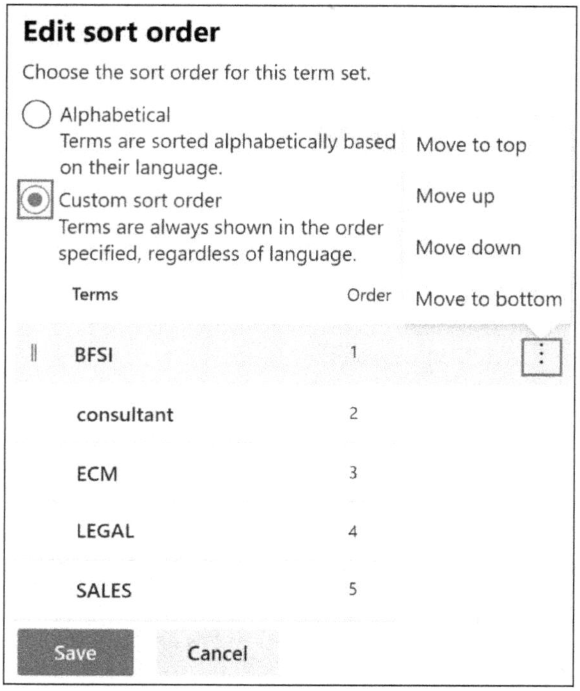

Edit sort order

Choose the sort order for this term set.

○ Alphabetical
Terms are sorted alphabetically based on their language.

◉ Custom sort order
Terms are always shown in the order specified, regardless of language.

Terms	Order
BFSI	1
consultant	2
ECM	3
LEGAL	4
SALES	5

Move to top

Move up

Move down

Move to bottom

Save   Cancel

Figure 5.23: Sort order

Navigation tab in term set

Next to the term set name Business Unit on the right pane, you will find four tabs, namely, General, Usage settings, Navigation, and Advanced. Each tab contains a specific set of information and related settings. In this section, we will discuss the third tab, Navigation, and understand its application. Let us perform the following steps to understand it better:

1. Click on the term set Business Unit and the third tab, **Navigation**, from the right pane.

2. Under the tab **Navigation**, you will find settings, namely, Use term set for site navigation, Use term faceted navigation, as shown in *Figure 5.24*:

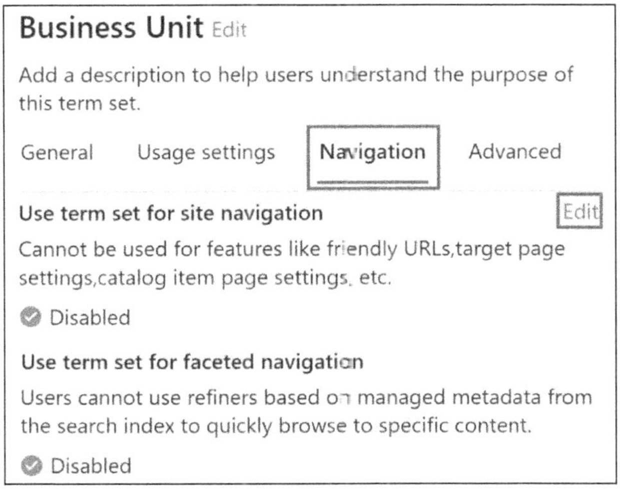

Figure 5.24: *Navigation option in the term set business unit*

3. Click on the Edit option present next to the Use term set for site navigation. You will get the **Edit Properties** window that includes two options, namely, Use term set for site navigation and Use term set for faceted navigation. Refer to *Figure 5.25*.

4. Select the checkbox Use term set for site navigation to enable, and click on Save to apply changes.

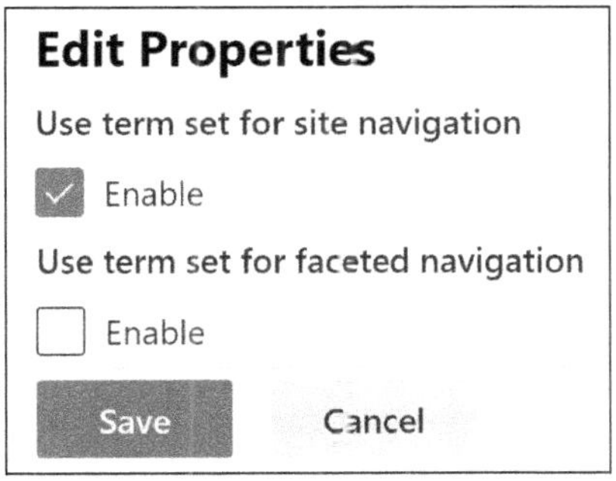

Figure 5.25: *Enable or disable use term set for site navigation*

5. You will notice two additional options, Custom target page and Custom catalog item page, added under the tab Navigation, as shown in *Figure 5.26*:

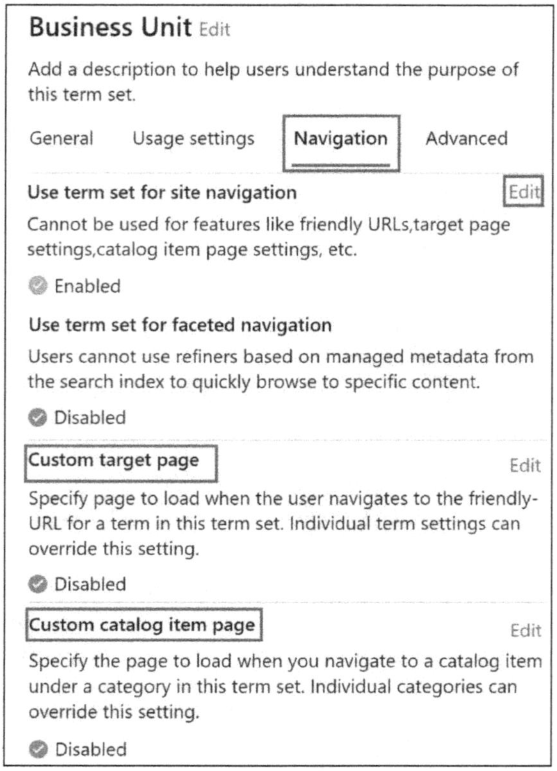

Figure 5.26: Term set Navigation options

6. Click on **Edit** present next to the option **Custom target page** as shown in *Figure 5.26*. You will get the **Edit term target page** panel.

7. Enable the option **Use a custom target page**, as shown in the following figure. You will get another option, **Select**:

Figure 5.27: Term set target page

8. Click on **Select**. You will get the **Select asset** panel.

9. Enter the custom page URL. Click on **Select** as seen in *Figure 5.28*.

10. Finally, click on **Save** to apply changes.

Select asset

/sites/BPB-ModernTeamSite/SitePages/Business-Unit.aspx

⥮ Sort ∨   ≡ ∨

Site contents

🗋 Name ∨

Style Library

DO_NOT_DELETE_SPLIST_TENANTADMIN_AGGREGATED_POLICYINSIGHTS_STORAGE

DO_NOT_DELETE_SPLIST_TENANTADMIN_AGGREGATED_SITECOLLECTIONS

DO_NOT_DELETE_SPLIST_TENANTADMIN_ALL_SITES_AGGREGATED_SITECOLLECTIONS

Form Templates

DO_NOT_DELETE_SPLIST_TENANTADMIN_USERSTORAGE

Documents

Select   Cancel

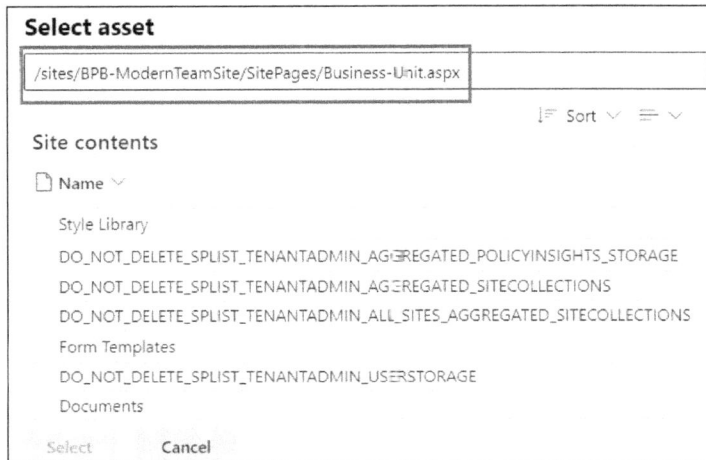

Figure 5.28: Set target page for term set

11. You will find that the custom target page is added, as shown in *Figure 5.29*:

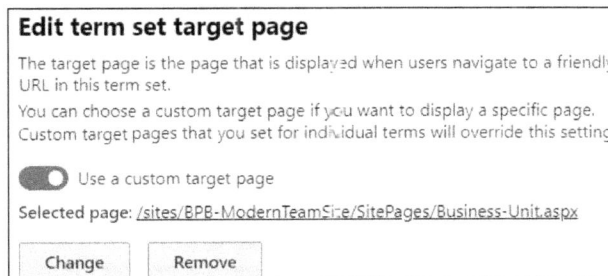

Edit term set target page

The target page is the page that is displayed when users navigate to a friendly URL in this term set.

You can choose a custom target page if you want to display a specific page. Custom target pages that you set for individual terms will override this setting.

⬤ Use a custom target page

Selected page: /sites/BPB-ModernTeamSite/SitePages/Business-Unit.aspx

Change   Remove

Figure 5.29: Target page for term set configured

12. Similarly, you can check or uncheck the option Use term set for faceted navigation to enable or disable faced navigation, respectively.

13. You can also click on Edit side to option **Custom catalog item page**. Enter custom URL as per business requirement.

Advanced tab in term set

Next to the term set name Business Unit on the right pane, you will find four tabs, namely General, Usage settings, Navigation, and Advanced. Each tab contains a specific set of information and related settings. In this section, we will discuss the fourth tab Advanced and understand its application. Let us perform the following steps to understand better:

1. Click on the term set **Business Unit** and the fourth tab **Advanced**, from the right pane.

2. Under the tab **Advanced**, you will find settings, namely, Translation, and Custom properties. Refer to *Figure 5.30*:

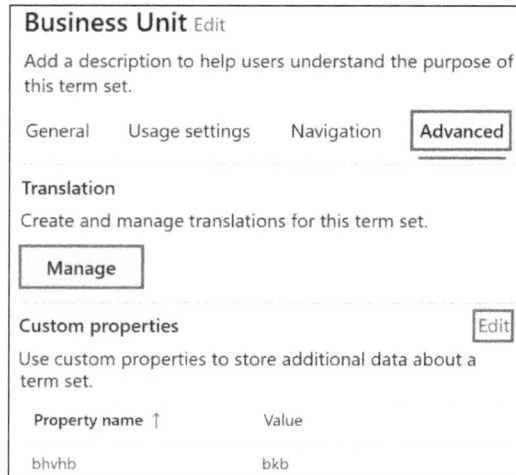

Figure 5.30: Advanced settings

3. Click on **Manage present** under **Translation**. You will get the translation panel.

4. You will find two options **Machine translation** and **Manual translation**. Click on Start present under **Machine translation**, as shown in *Figure 5.31*:

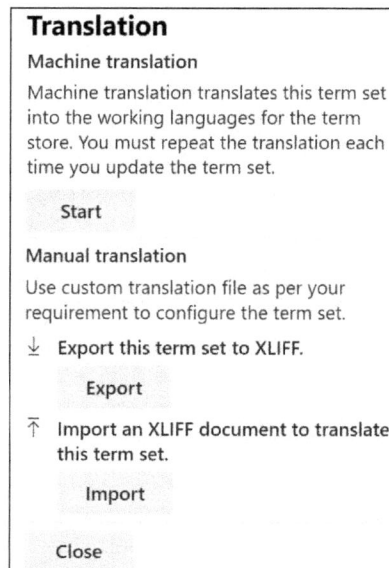

Figure 5.31: Translation

5. Select **all terms** to translate all terms present under that term set, else select the other option. Only the terms updated since the last translation.

6. Select Translate from and Translate to language, and click on Translate. Translation of the term set to working languages will start, as shown in *Figure 5.32*:

Machine translation

What terms do you want to translate?

◉ All terms

◯ Only the terms updated since the last translation

Translate from

| English ⌄ |

Translate to

| Select a language ⌄ |

Translate   Cancel

Figure 5.32: *Select terms to translate*

7. You can export translated file and import custom translation file as per the requirement.

8. Let us discuss the second category of options Custom properties present under tab Advanced. Custom properties store additional data about term set. Click on **Edit** present side to Custom properties.

9. Enter details under the fields Property name and Value to add custom properties. You can edit the properties by clicking the **Edit** option present on the side to the custom property, as shown in *Figure 5.33*:

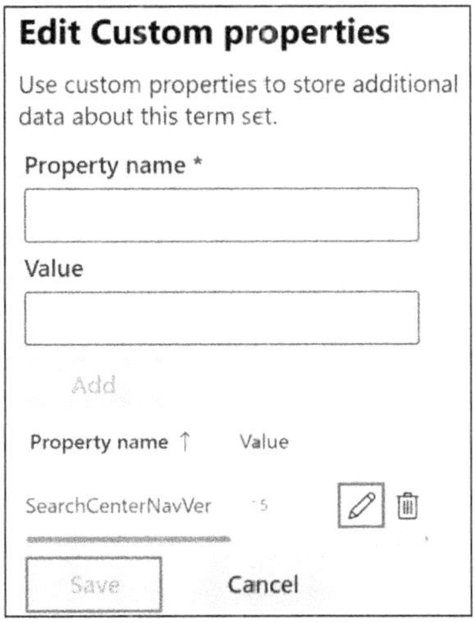

Edit Custom properties

Use custom properties to store additional data about this term set.

Property name *

| |

Value

| |

Add

Property name ↑   Value

SearchCenterNavVer   5   ✎ 🗑

Save   Cancel

Figure 5.33: *Edit custom properties term set*

10. We created a single term set Business Unit under term group Employee and discussed all options present under term set. Let us proceed to the next section to discuss and understand the terminology **Term**.

Term

We discussed term store and understood the terminologies, namely taxonomy, term group, and term set. Under taxonomy, we created term group Employee. Similarly, under the term group we created Term Set (Business Unit). Under **Term set**, we can create multiple terms. Term is a predefined, specific reusable word or phrase in SharePoint, and has a unique ID but many labels for different languages applicable to multilingual sites. Terms are of types Managed terms and Enterprise keywords. Managed terms are organized hierarchically into term set and Enterprise keywords, used as tagging. Under each term set, we can create a group of terms. Let us proceed to the next part of this section to understand the term better.

Adding term

Term is positioned at the third level in taxonomy hierarchy, next to term set. Each business is categorized into different units, for example BFSI, ECM, MARKETING, SALES, LEGAL. We can create these units as terms under the term set Business Unit. In this section, we will discuss and understand how to create or add a term under the term set. Perform the following steps to create a term:

1. Click on the term set Business Unit present under the term group Employee.

2. Click on Add term from the right pane or from the action pane.

3. Enter the name of the term as `BFSI`. The new term BFSI created is added to the tree-view pane under the term set. Refer to *Figure 5.34*:

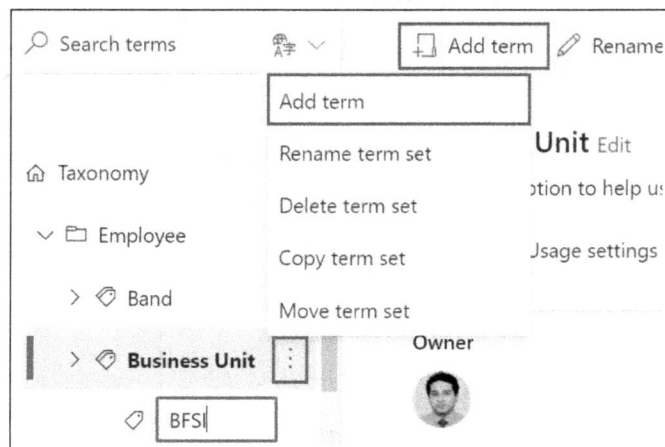

Figure 5.34: Add term

4. Similarly, create a few more terms like ECM, MARKETING, SALES, and LEGAL under the term set Business Unit.

5. Create terms MAS, DIGITAL, INSURANCE, FINANCE under the term set Horizontal Tag.

6. Create terms SHAREPOINT, OFFICE 365, WINDOWS, DATABSE, STORAGE, NETWORKING, and AZURE under the term set Skill.

7. Create terms 0-3, 3-6, 6-9, and 9-12 under the term set Relevant Experience.

8. Create terms 0-3, 3-6, 6-9, and 9-12 under the term set Total Experience.

9. Create terms A, B, C, and D under the term set Band. Refer to *Figure 5.35*:

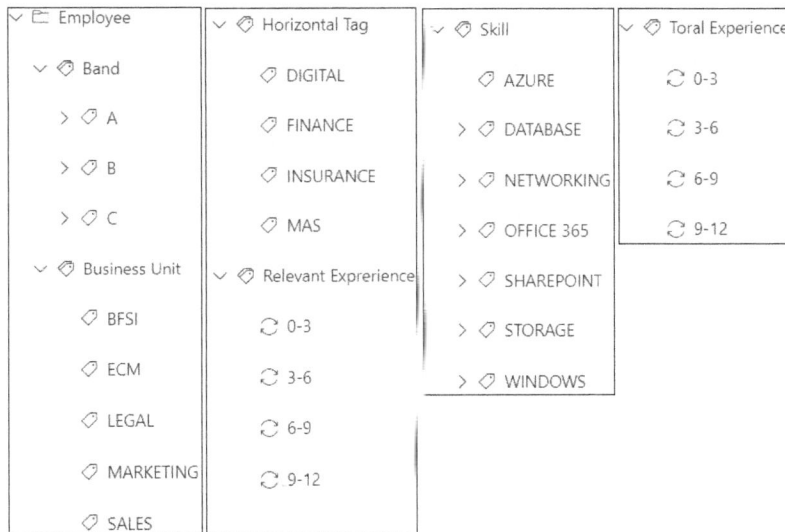

Figure 5.35: More terms created example

10. Click on the term BFSI present under the term set Business Unit.

11. On the right pane, you will find more details related to the term. Top of the right pane, you will find options related to the actions that can be taken on the term, namely Add term, Rename term, Copy term, Copy term with children, Move term, Delete term, Pin term, Reuse term, Merge term, Deprecate term in the form of command bar. Refer to Figure 5.36.

12. Under the command bar, you will find the name of the term.

13. Following that, you will find four tabs, namely, **General**, **Usage settings**, **Navigation**, and **Advanced**, with the default tab selected as **General**.

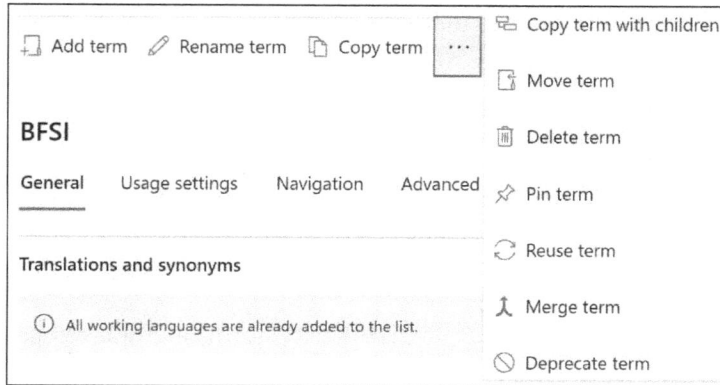

Figure 5.36: Term Navigation Pane

14. Each term can be further categorized, and the employee bands have a hierarchy. For example, **A** (Term) has lower-level bands like **A1, A2, A3**. We can create terms under terms as well. Under the term, **A** creates more terms **A1, A2, A3**. Similarly, create terms further under each term **B, C, D** and follow the same for all other terms to create relevant terms under the terms, as shown in the following screenshot:

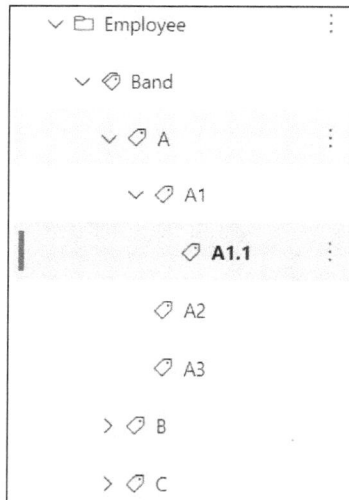

Figure 5.37: Term under a Term Created

Renaming term

Let us proceed to the next action that can be taken related to term. We can change the name, description, and synonyms of a term. Let us perform the following steps to do the same:

1. Select the term **BFSI** from tree-view pane under the term set **Business Unit**.

2. Click on the show action option that is present on the side of the term **BFSI**. You will get the option, **Rename term**. Alternatively, you can select the same option **Rename term** from the right pane in the command bar. Refer to *Figure 5.38*:

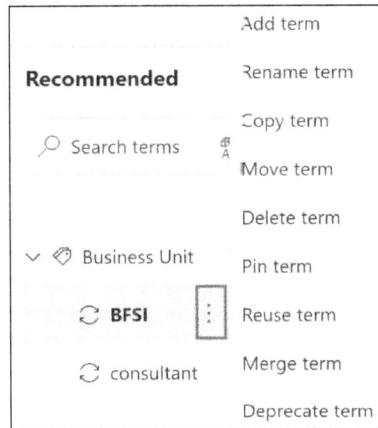

Figure 5.38: Show action options in the term

3. You will get a new window **Edit translation and synonyms** with fields, namely, **Translation**, **Description**, **Synonyms**.

4. Modify the name present in the field **Translation** to change the term name. Modify the details present in the description field. You can edit synonyms for this term by adding or removing them in the field **Synonyms**. Click on **Save** to apply changes.

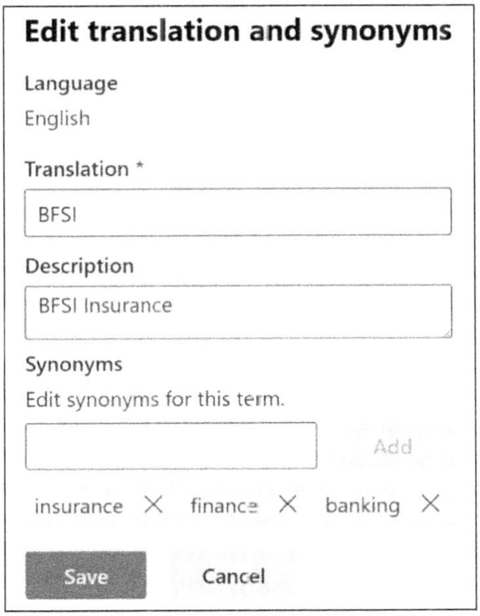

Figure 5.39: Rename term from edit translation and synonyms window

Copying term

Let us proceed to the next action that can be taken related to term. You can copy the term as per business requirements. Identify the term (example, A) that you want to copy. Term A has child term A1, and following that is another child term A1.1 present. Click on the show action option on the side of the term A. You will get the option **Copy term**. Alternatively, you can select the same option **Copy term,** from the right pane in the command bar. You will notice the new term **A - Copy** created in the same term set. Only term **A** got copied, but the children terms present below that were not copied. Refer to *Figure 5.40*:

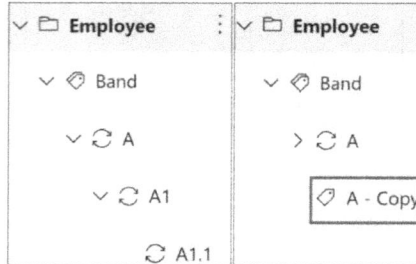

Figure 5.40: Copy term

Copying term with children

Let us proceed to the next action that can be taken related to term. You can copy the term with children terms present under that, as per business requirement. Identify the term (example, A) that you want to copy. Term A has child term A1, and below that, another child term A1.1 is present. Click on the show action option on the side of term A. You will get the option **Copy term with children**. Alternatively, you can select the same option **Copy term with children** from the right pane in the command bar. You will notice the new term **A - Copy** created including all children terms present under that in the same term set. Refer to *Figure 5.41*:

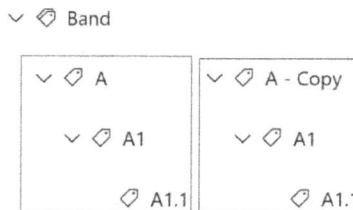

Figure 5.41: Copy term with children

Moving term

Let us proceed to the next action that can be taken related to term. You can move the term as per business requirement by following these steps:

1. Identify the term that you want to move.

2. Click on the show action option on the present side of the term. You will get the option **Move term**. Alternatively, you can select the same option.

3. Move term set from the right pane in the command bar. You will get another window to select the destination, Term set, Term or Child term.

4. Select the destination Term set or Term or Child term. Click on **Move**.

5. Term will be moved out of the source location and will be added to destination location. Refer to *Figure 5.42*:

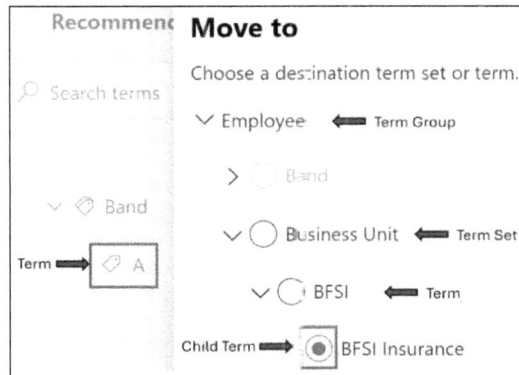

Figure 5.42: Move term

Deleting term

Let us proceed to the next action that can be taken related to term. You can delete the term if not required as per business requirement. Identify the term that you want to delete. Click on the show action option on the right side of the term. You will get the option **Delete term**. Alternatively, you can select the same option, **Delete term** from right pane, in the command bar. You will get a message like **If you delete this term, any terms below it will also be deleted. Terms that are shared with other term sets will be placed in the Orphaned terms** term set **under System.** Confirm that you can delete the term by clicking **Delete** or click on **Cancel** to stop deleting. Refer to *Figure 5.43*:

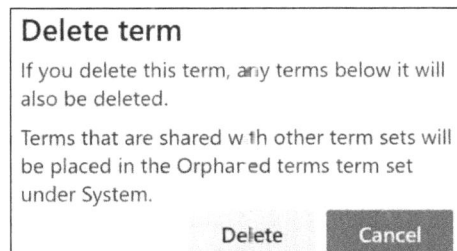

Figure 5.43: Delete term

Pin term

Let us proceed to the next action that can be taken related to the term. You can pin the term. Identify the term that you want to pin. Click on the show action option on the side of term A. You will get the option **Pin term**. Alternatively, you can select the same option **Pin term**, from the right pane in the command bar. You will get **Pin term to** the panel. Select the destination term set or term and click on **Pin** as shown in *Figure 5.44*. A copy of the terms will be available at the destination for use. Editing a pinned term can be done from the source location only, and the updated term will reflect in the destination terms.

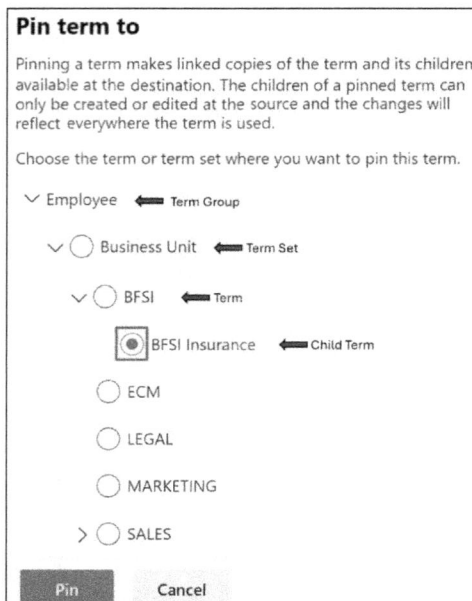

Figure 5.44: Select destination term to pin

Reusing term

You can reuse the term instead of creating manually. Let us perform the following steps to create a term set:

1. Identify the term that you want to reuse. Let us say the term **A** you want to reuse. Term **A** has child terms **A1, A2, A3. A1, A2, A3** have child terms **A1.1, A2.1, A3.1** respectively.

2. Click on show action option present side to the term **A**. You will get the option **Reuse term**. Alternatively, you can select the same option **Reuse term** from the right pane in the command bar.

3. You will get the panel **Reuse term to**. Select the destination term where you want to reuse. Refer to *Figure 5.45*:

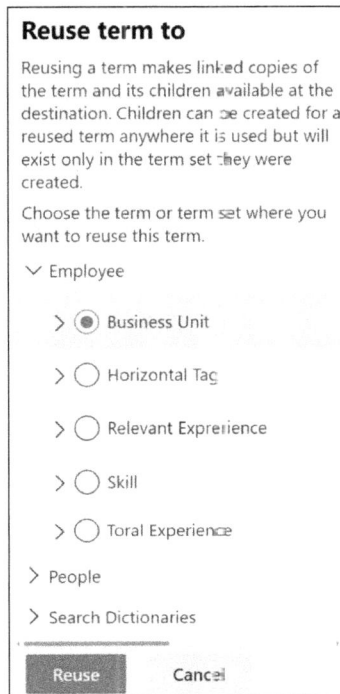

Figure 5.45: Select Destination term set or term to reuse

4. Click on **Reuse** after selection to apply changes. You will find term **A** including child terms (A, A1, A1.1, A2, A2.1, A3, A3.1) got copied from **Source** and placed under the **Destination**. Refer to *Figure 5.46*.

5. You will find the status of the icon present on each term changed. Find and compare the same on both the Source and Destination from *Figure 5.46*.

6. Reused terms at the destination are just linked copies. Both Source and Destination terms are two-way sync. This means that changing from any place will reflect in all other places where that term is reused.

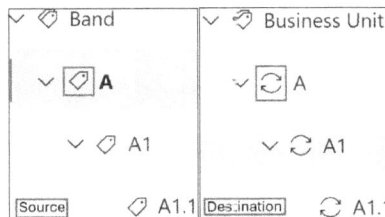

Figure 5.46: Reuse term includes child term at destination location

7. Term **A** is reused in another test set **Business Unit**. Now, create another term **A4** under term **A**. You will find the icon is different than that of the reused term. This

means the new term **A4** is not reused. You need to follow the steps again for A4 to reuse in other term sets, terms, or child terms. If you are creating any child term **A4.1** under the term **A4**, the behavior of A4.1 will be the same as that of A4. At the destination's end, you will find each reused term A4, A4.1 displayed separately. It is not like A4.1 is collapsed under A4 and A4 is collapsed under A. Refer to *Figure 5.47*:

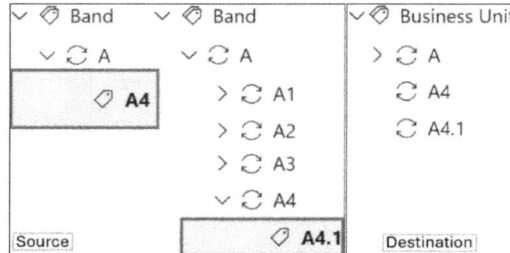

Figure 5.47: New child term status after reusing parent term

8. If you delete the reused term at source location, that term will be added to the orphaned terms under system.

Merge term

You can merge the term by following these steps:

1. Select the source term **D** present under the term set **Band**.

2. Click on **Merge term** from the right pane or action menu as seen in *Figure 5.48*:

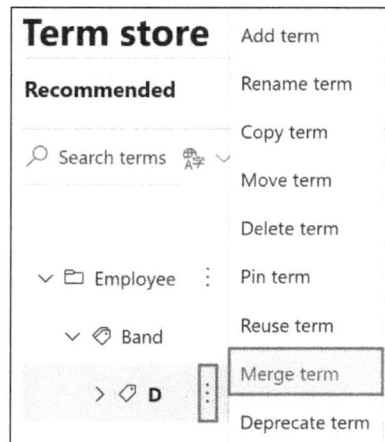

Figure 5.48: Merge term

3. You will get the **Merge to** panel. Select the destination term **ECM** present under the term set **Business Unit**, term group **People**.

4. Click on **Merge**, as shown in *Figure 5.49*:

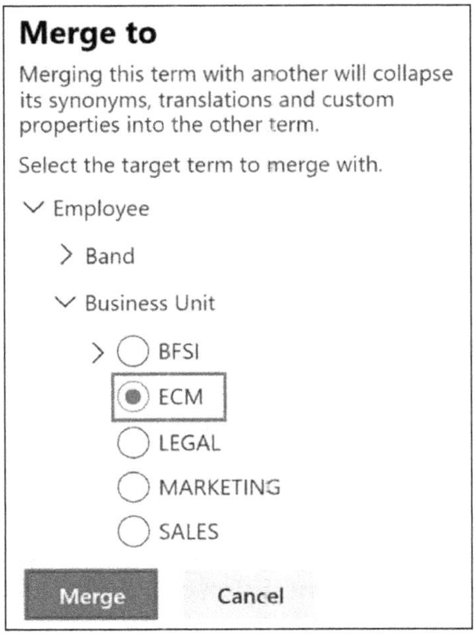

Figure 5.49: Select destination term

5. You will notice the source end term **D** is merged and the name changed from **D** to **ECM**. Refer to *Figure 5.50*:

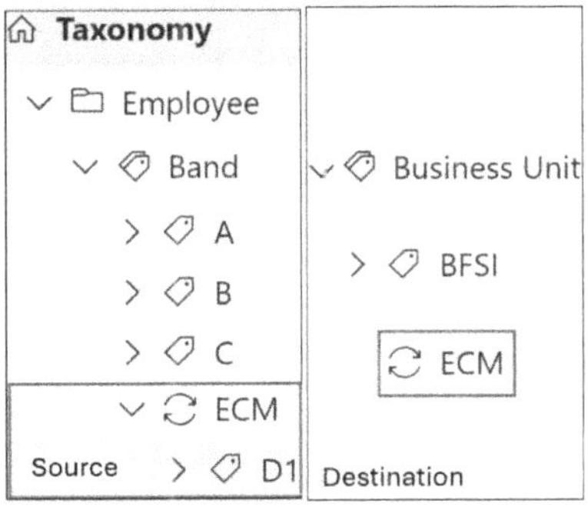

Figure 5.50: Merged term

6. Under the tab **General,** you see the translation as **ECM** and synonyms as **D**. Refer to *Figure 5.51*:

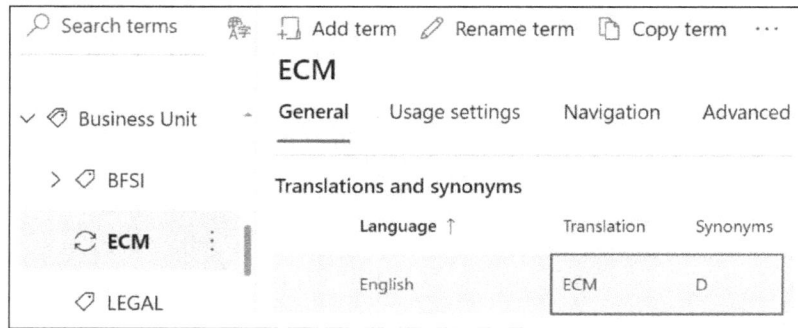

Figure 5.51: Destination term after merge

Deprecate term

You can deprecate the term. This makes the term and related child terms disable and not available for tagging. The term and its child terms are hidden, and you can enable them if required. So, instead of deleting the term, it is better to deprecate. Select the term **BFSI** present under the term set **Business Unit**. Upon clicking on **Deprecate term** from the right pane or action menu, you will see that the term will be disabled and the status will change as shown in *Figure 5.52*. You need to enable the term if you want to use it in the future.

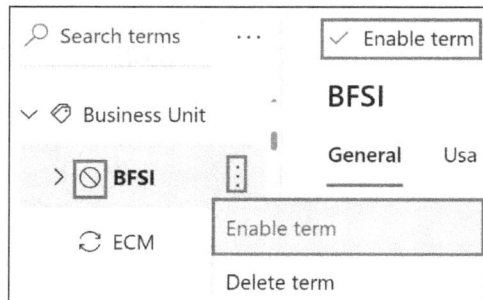

Figure 5.52: Deprecate term

General tab in term

Select the term ECM that is merged and present under the term set Band. Next to the term name **ECM** on the right pane, you will find four tabs, namely **General**, **Usage settings**, **Navigation**, and **Advanced**. Each tab contains a specific set of information and related settings. The term that we are using here is merged with term from other term set. In this section, we will discuss the first tab, **General**, and understand its application. Let us perform the following steps to understand it better:

1. Click on the merged term **ECM** present under the term set **Band** and click on the first tab **General** from the right pane.

2. Under the tab **General**, you will find details related to **Translations and synonyms**. Refer to *Figure 5.53*:

Figure 5.53: General tab for term

3. You will find translation language, translation term and its synonyms under the general tab.

Usage settings tab in term

Next to the General tab, you will find the second tab **Usage settings**. Each tab contains a specific set of information and related settings. In this section, we will discuss the second tab, **Usage settings,** and understand its application. Let us perform the following steps to understand better:

1. Click on the second tab **Usage settings** from the right pane.

2. Under the tab **Usage settings**, you will find the settings **Available for tagging, Unique identifier, Sort order,** and **Member of**. Refer to *Figure 5.54*.

3. Click on **Edit on the** present side to the option **Available for Tagging**. You will get a checkbox. Selecting the checkbox option **Enable** will make the term available for consumption by end users and site content editors.

4. Next to the option **Available for tagging**, you will find the option **Unique identifier** ID of the term.

5. Next to the option **Unique identifier**, you will find the option **Sort order** that holds information related to sorting order of terms.

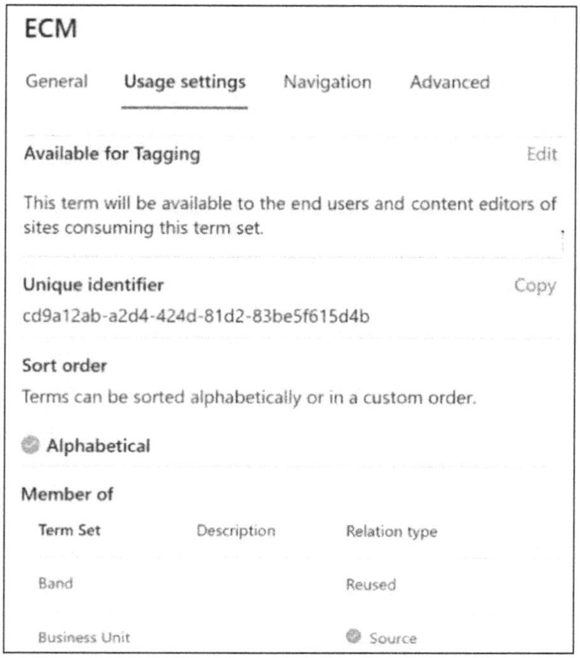

Figure 5.54: Usage Settings for term

6. Next to **Sort order,** you will find the option **Member of**. It holds information about the term and its relation type. Refer to *Figure 5.54.*

Navigation tab in term

The navigation tab is the third tab that holds specific settings related to metadata navigation. In this section, we will discuss the settings present in the tab **Navigation** for the term and understand its application. Let us perform the following steps to understand it better:

1. Click on the third tab **Navigation** from right pane for the term merged **ECM** present under term set **Band**.

2. Under the tab **Navigation,** you will find four categories of settings namely **Navigation node, Visibility in menus, Target page settings, Associated folder, Catalog item page settings, Category image**.

3. In the first category of setting, you will find the navigation node details, namely **Navigation node title, Navigation hover text**, and **Navigation node type**. The navigation node title will be the name of the term. Refer to *Figure 5.55:*

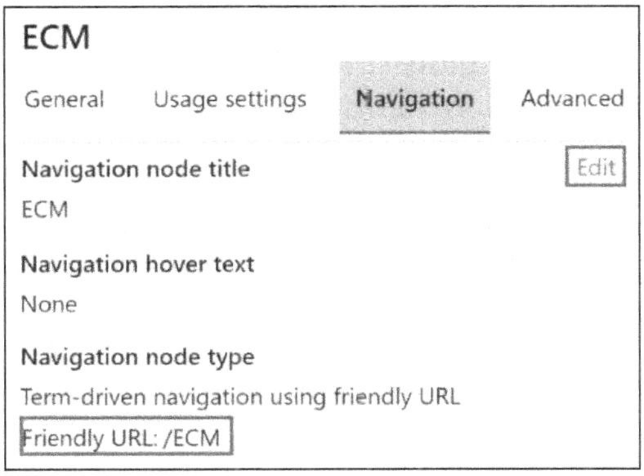

Figure 5.55: *Navigation node type for term*

4. Click on the option **Edit** present under the **Navigation node**. You will get the **Edit navigation node** window. You can enter text in the field **Navigation hover text**, which will be displayed when hovering over the navigation menus where this term is used. Refer to *Figure 5.55*.

5. Next to that, you will find the option **Navigation Node type** that includes two options, namely **Simple link or header,** and **Term-driven navigation with a friendly URL**. Select the second option **Term-driven navigation with friendly URL**. You will find the field Friendly URL with default path **/Term name** which is **/ECM** currently. Refer to *Figure 5.56*:

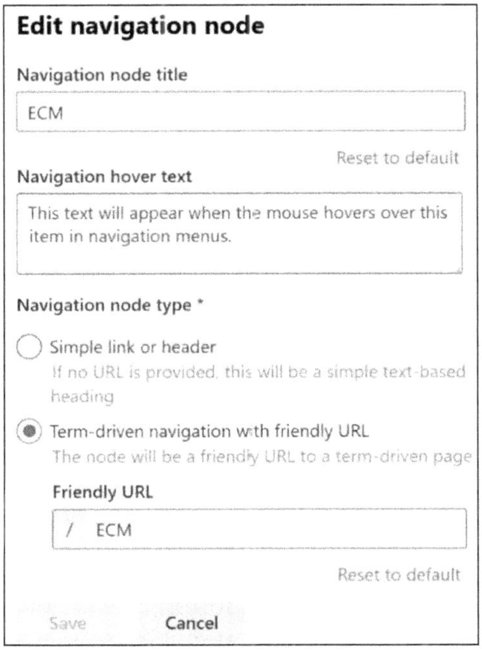

Figure 5.56: *Edit navigation mode*

6. Next, you will find the second category of setting namely **Visibility in menus**. This allows to control, show, or hide this node and its children in the global navigation menu and current navigation menu. Click on the option **Edit** as seen in *Figure 5.57*:

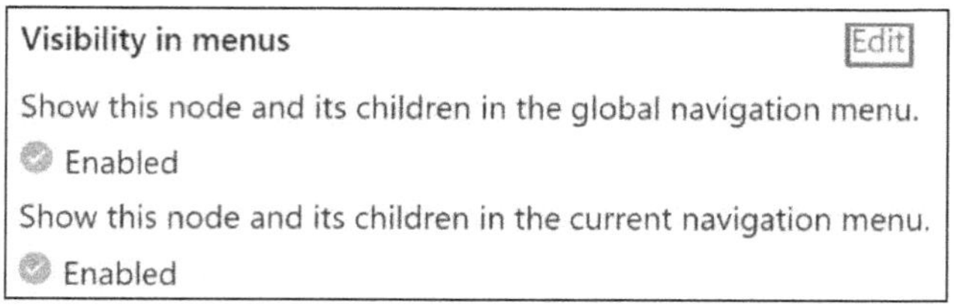

Figure 5.57: Visibility in menus

7. You will get the **Edit visibility** window. You will find two toggle buttons that can be used to enable or disable showing the node and its children in the global navigation menu and the current navigation menu. Refer to *Figure 5.58*:

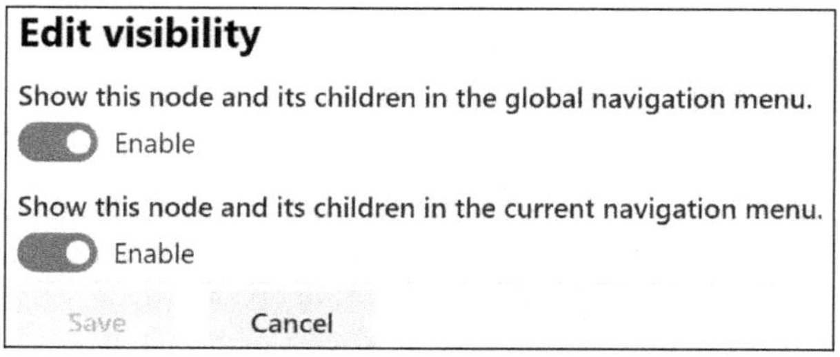

Figure 5.58: Edit visibility

8. Next, you will find the third category of setting namely **Target page settings**. Click on the option **Edit** as shown in *Figure 5.59*:

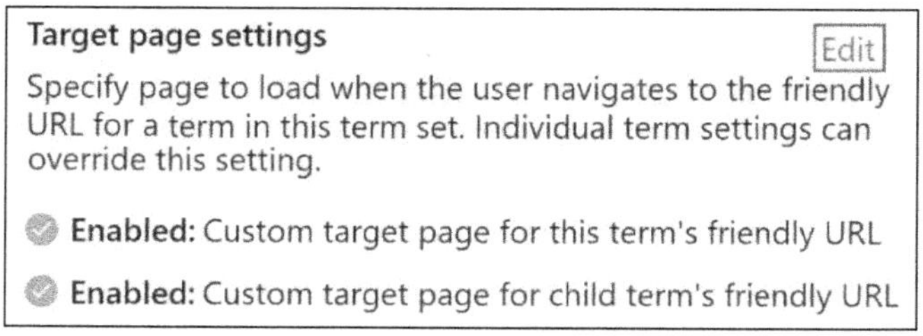

Figure 5.59: Target page settings

9. You will get the **Edit target pages** window with two toggle button fields, namely **Use a custom target page for this term** and **Use a custom target page for child terms**.

10. Enable both options by toggling the buttons. Select one site page (example, **ECM.aspx**) for term from the first option and select one page (example, **D1.aspx**) for child terms from the second option. Refer to *Figure 5.60*:

Figure 5.60: *Edit target pages*

11. We are discussing **Navigation** option for the term ECM. ECM has child term D1 and D1 has further child term D1.1, as shown in *Figure 5.61*:

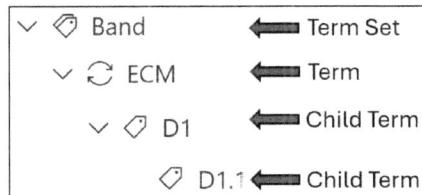

Figure 5.61: *Term hierarchy*

12. We enabled one target page for the term ECM and another page for child term. When those terms are used as navigation in the site, clicking the term ECM from site will open the site page **ECM.aspx**. On clicking child term D1 will open the page **D1.aspx**. Clicking the child term **D1.1** will open the page **D1.aspx**.

13. Now go back to *Step 5*. If you select the option **Simple link or header,** you are passing the site page URL directly for the term. You can select this option and pass a direct URL to each term. If you select the option **Term-driven navigation with friendly URL,** you should enable **Target page settings** and select pages to make a target page for the term.

14. Next, you will find the fourth settings category, the **Associated folder**. This folder contains the pages that are associated with this navigation node. Refer to *Figure 5.62*:

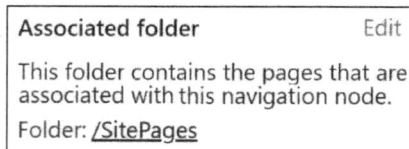

Figure 5.62: Associated folder

15. You can select the site pages folder from where you can choose the target pages as discussed in *Step 10*, as shown in *Figure 5.63*:

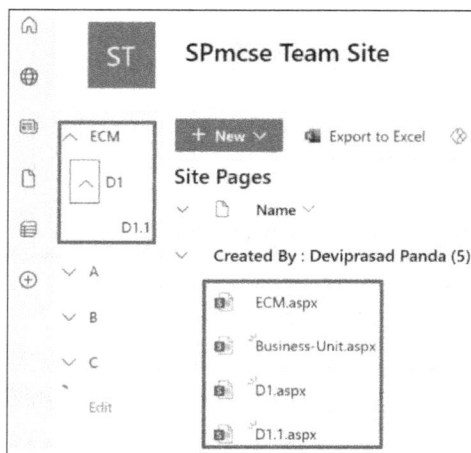

Figure 5.63: Associated folder contains pages

16. Click on the option **Edit** present side to the associated folder as shown in the following *Figure 5.62*. You can select the associated folder, change, or remove it. Refer to *Figure 5.64*:

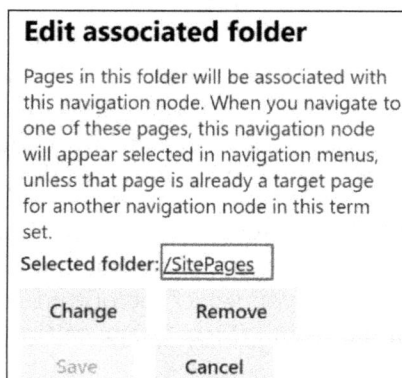

Figure 5.64: Edit associated folder

17. Next, you will find the fifth category of settings, namely **Catalog item page settings**. The way you selected the page for target page settings, you can select pages for catalog items of this category of term and child terms. Click on **Edit**, as shown in *Figure 5.65*:

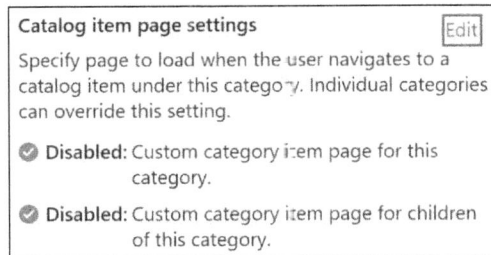

Figure 5.65: Catalog item page settings

18. You will get the **Edit target pages** window. You can enable the options and select the site page for the catalog item category and child category. Refer to *Figure 5.66*:

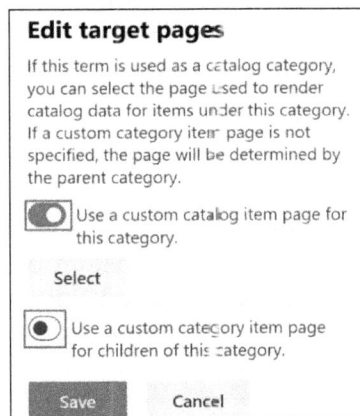

Figure 5.66: Edit target pages

19. Next, you will find the sixth category of settings namely **Category image**. You can select an image that you want to associate with this term. Click on the option **Edit** as shown in *Figure 5.67*:

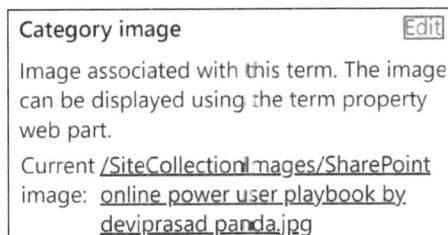

Figure 5.67: Category image

20. You will get the **Category image** window where you can change or remove the image associated with the term. Refer to *Figure 5.68*:

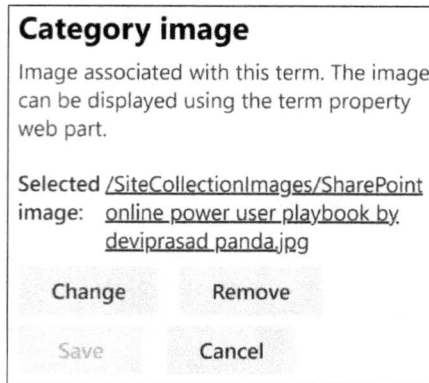

> **Category image**
>
> Image associated with this term. The image can be displayed using the term property web part.
>
> **Selected** /SiteCollectionImages/SharePoint
> **image:** online power user playbook by
> deviprasad panda.jpg
>
> Change   Remove
>
> Save   Cancel

Figure 5.68: Edit category image

We discussed the category of options present in the third tab **Navigation** for the term merged **ECM** present under term set **Band**. The next part of this section will discuss the fourth tab, **Advanced**.

Advanced tab in term

Advanced is the fourth tab for the term that holds all shared custom properties and local custom properties. Shared custom properties are available on all reused or pinned instances of this term anywhere in the term store. Local custom properties are only available for this term in this term set. You can click the option **Edit** present side to **Shared custom properties** or **Local custom properties** to edit the property name and value. Refer to *Figure 5.69*:

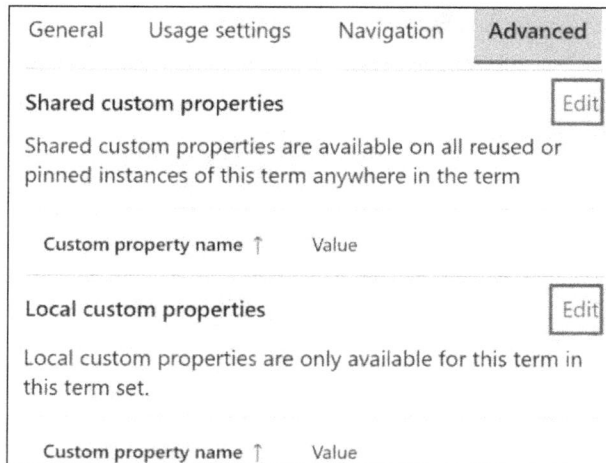

> General   Usage settings   Navigation   **Advanced**
>
> **Shared custom properties**   Edit
>
> Shared custom properties are available on all reused or pinned instances of this term anywhere in the term
>
> **Custom property name** ↑   Value
>
> **Local custom properties**   Edit
>
> Local custom properties are only available for this term in this term set.
>
> **Custom property name** ↑   Value

Figure 5.69: Advanced tab for term

We discussed everything about custom term group. In the next section, **System term group**, we will discuss about the system term group which is present by default in term store.

System term group

System term group is the default term group present in the term store. We are not creating that term group manually. You will find three terms set under System term group namely **Hashtags**, **Keywords** and **Orphaned Terms**. As the name suggests, Hashtags holds hashtag terms used in newsfeed, blog posts, and discussions. Keywords hold the tags used in documents and pages. Orphaned Terms contains terms that are in the orphan state. Refer to Figure 5.70:

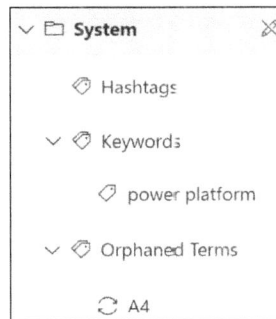

Figure 5.70: *Orphaned Term, Keywords, Hashtag under System term group*

Content type gallery administration

We discussed the first option **Term store**, present under **Content services**. Let us move forward towards the second option **Content type gallery**. This is the central location to create, store content types, and publish to make available to consume by sites in the tenant. In this section, we will discuss the options present in the Content type gallery and their application. Let us perform the following steps to understand it better:

1. Click on **Content services** present under the left navigation of SharePoint admin center. The navigation option will expand, and you will notice two categories of options, namely **Term store** and **Content type gallery**. Click on the option **Content type gallery**. Refer to *Figure 5.71*:

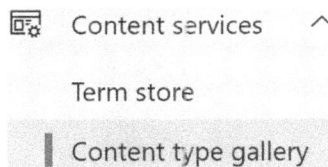

Figure 5.71: *Content type gallery navigation option*

2. You will get the **Content type gallery** administration page. You will find the content type list that holds tenant level content types with properties namely **Site content type, Parent, Category, Last published,** as shown in *Figure 5.72*. Option **Create content type** is to create a new content type in the tenant. Next to that is the **Search content types** field, which allows you to search for content types from the list of available content types. Next to that is the **View options** with the default view as **All items**.

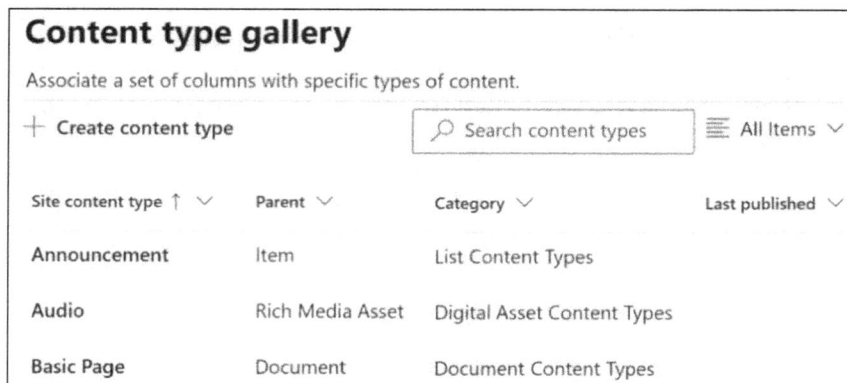

Content type gallery

Associate a set of columns with specific types of content.

+ Create content type		🔍 Search content types	≡ All Items ⌄
Site content type ↑ ⌄	Parent ⌄	Category ⌄	Last published ⌄
Announcement	Item	List Content Types	
Audio	Rich Media Asset	Digital Asset Content Types	
Basic Page	Document	Document Content Types	

Figure 5.72: Content type gallery

Creating content type

We can create a content type from the admin center and make it available to be consumed by all sites in the tenant. In this section, we will discuss how to create a content type. Let us perform the following steps to create content type:

1. Navigate to **Content services** from navigation option in admin center. Click on the option **Create content type**. You will get a new window to enter details and choose your preferred options to create a new content type.

2. Enter the name and description of the content type in the **Name** and **Description** fields, respectively.

3. The next option is **Category**. You can select an existing category by following the radio button option **Use an existing category** or create your own category by following the option **Create a new category**. Refer to *Figure 5.73*.

4. Select the option **Use an existing category** and choose one category from the drop-down option **Name**.

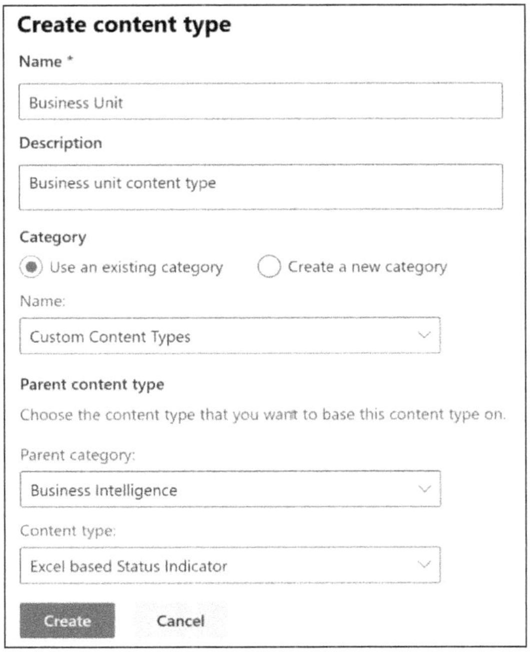

Create content type

Name *

Business Unit

Description

Business unit content type

Category

◉ Use an existing category   ○ Create a new category

Name:

Custom Content Types ⌄

Parent content type

Choose the content type that you want to base this content type on.

Parent category:

Business Intelligence ⌄

Content type:

Excel based Status Indicator ⌄

[Create]   Cancel

Figure 5.73: Create content type

5. Once you click on the drop-down field Name, you will find existing content type categories to select namely **Business Intelligence, Community Content Types, Custom Content Types, Digital Asset Content Types, Display Template Content Types, Document Content Types, Document Set Content Types, Folder Content Types, Group Work Content Types, List Content Types, Special Content Types**. Refer to *Figure 5.74*:

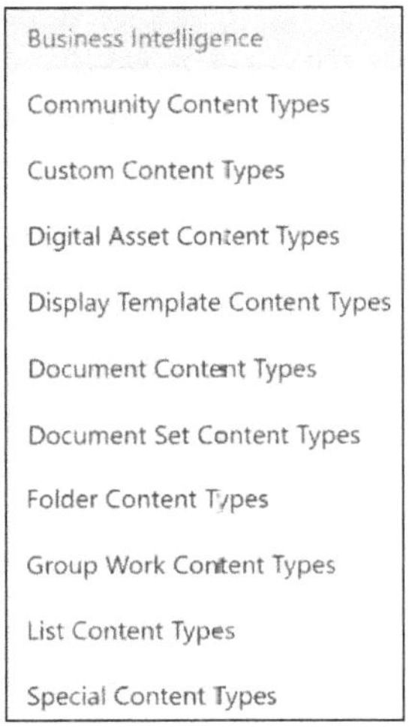

Business Intelligence

Community Content Types

Custom Content Types

Digital Asset Content Types

Display Template Content Types

Document Content Types

Document Set Content Types

Folder Content Types

Group Work Content Types

List Content Types

Special Content Types

Figure 5.74: Default existing content type categories

6. Go back to *Step 6* and select the second option, **Create a new category**, this time to create a new content type category.

7. Enter the name of the new category as **Business Unit**. Refer to *Figure 5.75*:

Figure 5.75: Create new content type categories

8. The next option category is parental content type. You will find two drop-down fields, namely **Parent category** and **Content type**. Refer to *Figure 5.76*:

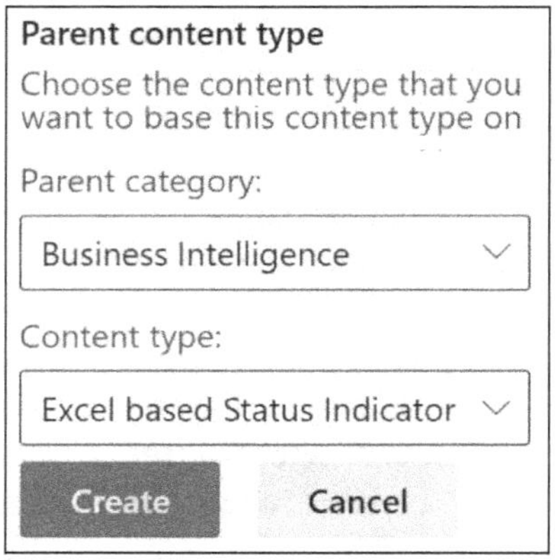

Figure 5.76: Parent content type

9. Click on the drop-down field **Parent category** under the category **Parent content type**. You will find categories, namely **Business Intelligence, Community Content Types, Custom Content Types, Digital Asset Content Types, Display Template Content Types, Document Content Types, Document Set Content Types, Folder Content Types, Group Work Content Types, List Content Types, Special Content Types**. The categories you will get are the same as discussed in *Step 7*. Select the parent category as **Business Intelligence**. Refer to *Figure 5.77*:

Business Intelligence

Community Content Types

Digital Asset Content Types

Display Template Content Types

Document Content Types

Document Set Content Types

Folder Content Types

Group Work Content Types

List Content Types

Special Content Types

Figure 5.77: Parent category

10. Click on the second drop-down field **Content type** under the category **Parent content type**. You will find the content types related to the selected parent category. Refer to *Figure 5.78*. You will find different content types for different parent category. Based on your requirement, select the parent category and content type.

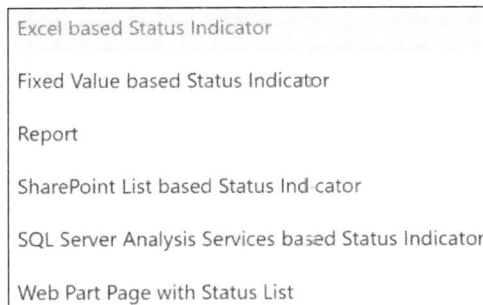

Excel based Status Indicator

Fixed Value based Status Indicator

Report

SharePoint List based Status Indicator

SQL Server Analysis Services based Status Indicator

Web Part Page with Status List

Figure 5.78: Existing content type present under the parent category

11. Click on the button **Create** once you have filled all necessary fields. Content type will be created. You will get a window that contains all details related to it namely content type **Name** that you preferred, **Category**, **Parent**, **Content Type ID**, **Site columns** present in the content type. Refer to *Figure 5.79*:

Content type gallery > **Business Unit**

✎ Edit   ⬆ Publish   ⚙ Settings ∨   🗑 Delete content type

Business Unit
Business Unit

Category
Business Unit

Parent
Excel based Status Indicator ⓘ

Content Type ID
0x00A7470EADF4194E2E9ED1031B61DA088403008332FEEE93CD114
A92C C9EE460E5F182

Site columns
Add and manage the site columns that are a part of this content type.

+ Add site column ∨

Name	Type
Description	Multiple lines of text
Indicator Comments	Multiple lines of text
Indicator Value	Number

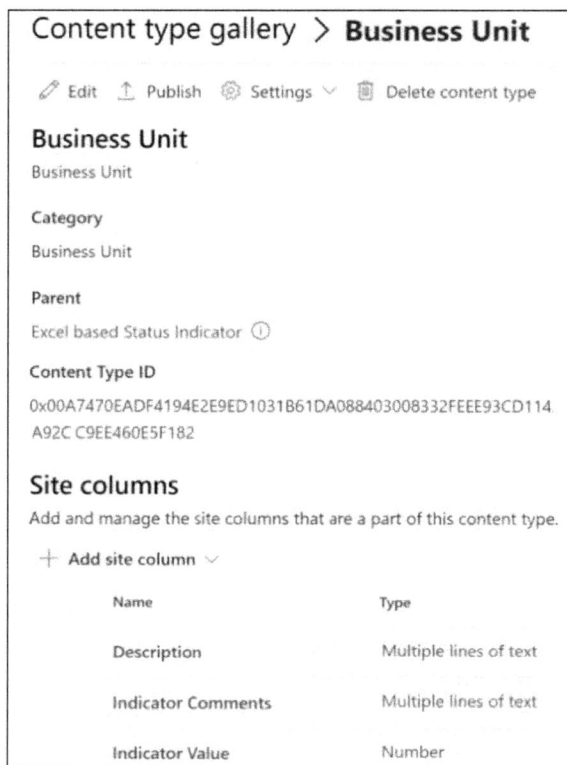

Figure 5.79: New content type created

Editing content type

You can edit the existing content type at any time as per business requirement. Click on the option **Edit** from command bar. Refer to *Figure 5.79*. **Modify** the content type and click on **Save** to apply changes.

Managing publishing

Once the content type is created, you need to publish the content type to make it available for all sites in tenant to consume. You are creating content type in one place at tenant level and reusing it on all sites. Perform these steps to understand the publishing option better:

1. Navigate to **Content services** from navigation option in admin center. Click on the content type that you created newly.

2. You will find command bar options, namely **Edit**, **Publish**, **Settings**, and **Delete content type**, at the top. Click on the option **Publish.**

Figure 5.80: Content type command bar options

3. You will get the **Manage Publishing** window. You will find three options, namely, **Publish**, **Unpublish**, and **Republish,** with the default option **Publish** selected. Click on the option **Save** to publish the content type. Refer to *Figure 5.81*:

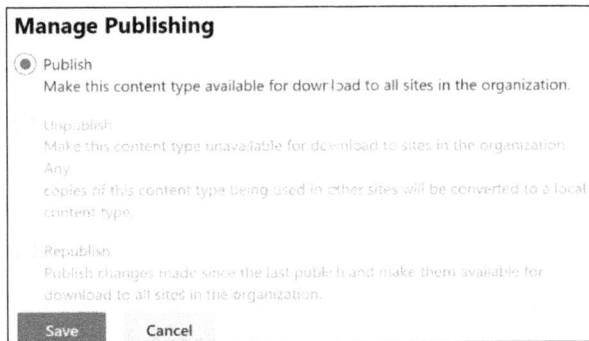

Figure 5.81: Publish content type

4. If you are editing the content type, then you need to republish it to make the updated content type available. Follow *Step 1* and *Step 2*, and click on the option **Publish** from the command bar. Select the radio button option **Republish** and click on **Save**. Refer to *Figure 5.82*.

5. You can unpublish the content type. Select the radio button **Unpublish** and click on **Save**. This will make the content type not available for use by the site. Content types used in any site will be converted to the local content type.

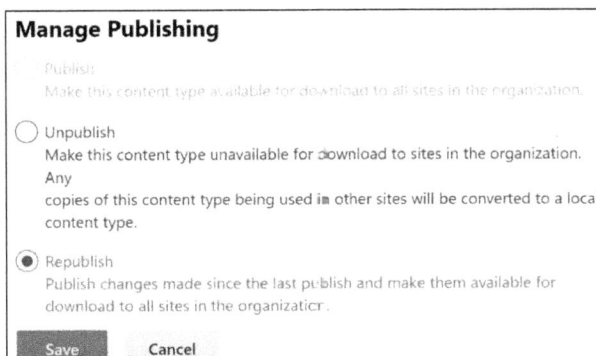

Figure 5.82: Manage publishing

Content type settings

The third option you will find in the content type command bar is **Settings**. Settings include **Advanced settings** and **Policy settings** options. Let us proceed to the next sections to discuss Advanced settings and Policy settings to understand it better.

Advanced settings

In this section, we will discuss the options available under **Advanced settings** and understand its application. Let us perform the following steps to understand the Advanced settings option better:

1. Click on the option **Settings** from the command bar. You will get two dropdown options namely, **Advanced settings** and **Policy settings**.

2. Click on the option **Advanced settings**. You will get a new window with two settings namely **Permissions, Update sites and lists**. Refer to *Figure 5.83*. Click on the first option **Permissions**.

3. You can make the content type **Edit** or **Read** mode. Selecting **Edit** will enable the content type to be modifiable. Selecting **Read** will restrict editing the content type and will be only in read mode.

4. Select the checkbox present under the second option **Update sites and lists** to enable updating all site and list content types inheriting from this content type with the settings on this page.

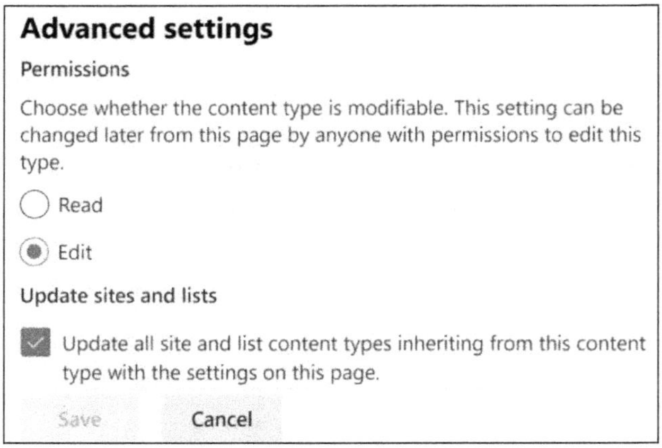

Figure 5.83: Advanced settings

Policy settings

We can enable the content type policies to manage security better. Let us perform the following steps to understand the Policy settings option better:

1. Click on the option **Settings** from command bar. You will get two dropdown options namely **Advanced settings** and **Policy settings**.

2. Click on the option **Policy settings**. You will be redirected to the content type hub **policyconfig** page.

3. First, you will find **Name** and **Administrative Description** of the content type policy. Refer to *Figure 5.84*:

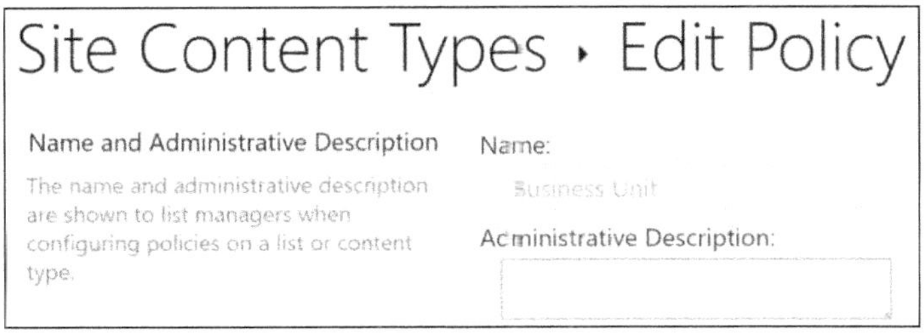

Figure 5.84: *Edit policy name and description*

4. Next you will find the field to enter **Policy Statement** details. Refer to *Figure 5.85*:

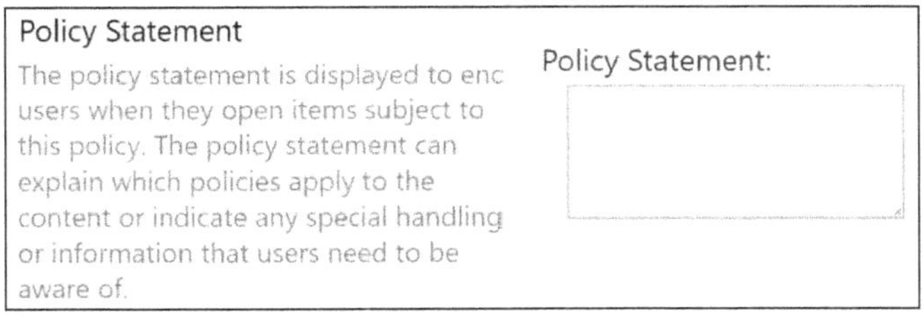

Figure 5.85: *Policy statement*

5. Next, you will find the policy related to **Retention**. You can select the check box **Enable Retention** to enable the retention policy as per business requirement. Refer to *Figure 5.86*:

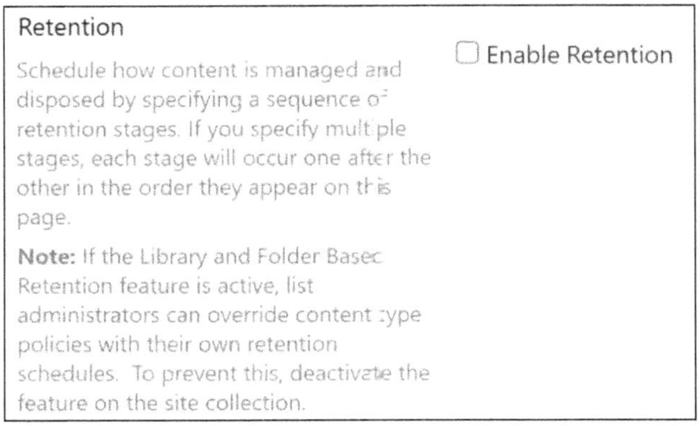

Figure 5.86: *Retention policy*

6. Next, you will find the option to enable **Auditing**. Select the check box **Enable Auditing** to enable the Auditing policy as per business requirement. Refer to *Figure 5.87*:

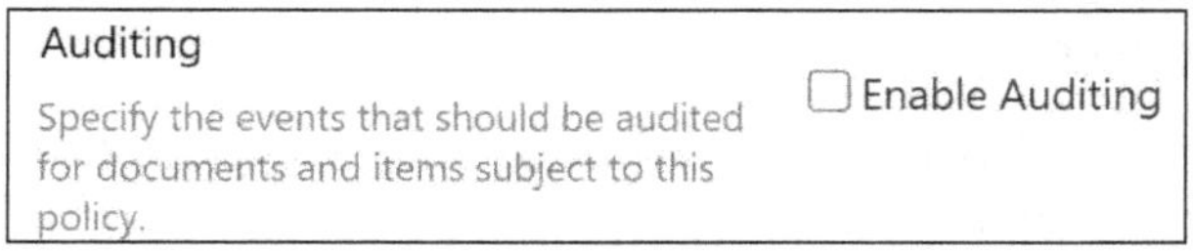

Figure 5.87: Auditing policy

7. You will find the option to enable **Barcodes**. Select the check box **Enable Barcodes** to enable the barcode policy as per business requirement. Refer to *Figure 5.88*:

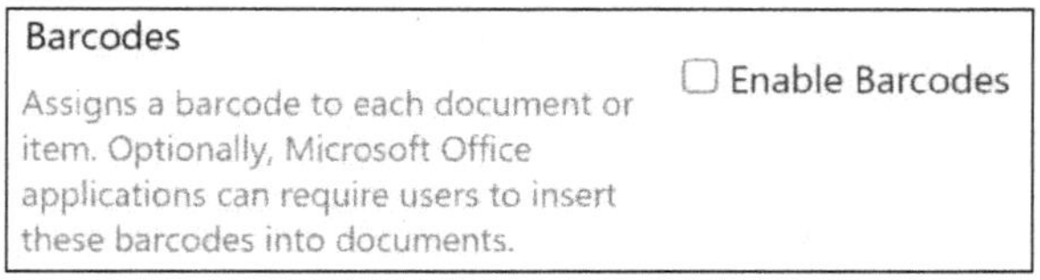

Figure 5.88: Barcodes

8. You will find the option to enable **Labels**. Select the check box **Enable Labels** to enable the label policy as per business requirement. Refer to *Figure 5.89*:

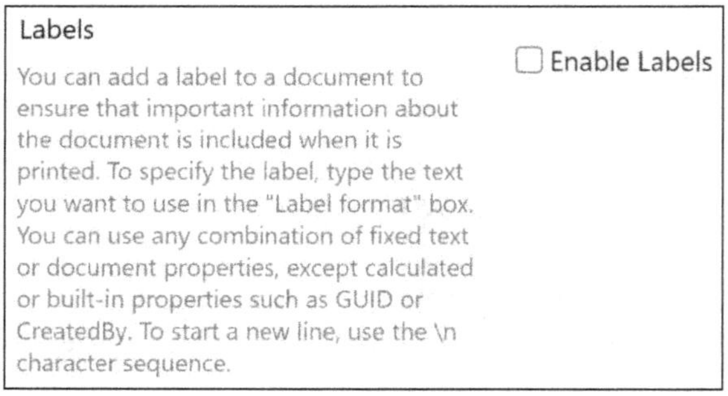

Figure 5.89: Labels

Deleting content type

You can delete a content type if not required as per business requirement. Click on the option Delete content type from content type command bar. Refer to *Figure 5.90*:

Figure 5.90: Delete content type

You will get a message as a warning to confirm the deletion. Click on the checkbox **Yes, delete this content type** and click on **Delete**. Refer to *Figure 5.91*. Sites where this content type is used will not be an issue since the content type will be unpublished automatically first. Then it will be deleted. As discussed in *Step 5* under the section **Manage publishing**, unpublished content type will be converted to local content type, so deleting the content type has no impact on the sites that already use it.

Figure 5.91: *Confirm to delete content type*

Other general settings

You can filter the content type parent field, categories and quickly find content type using search functionality. View options provide different views to show items in the content type list. Refer to *Figure 5.92*:

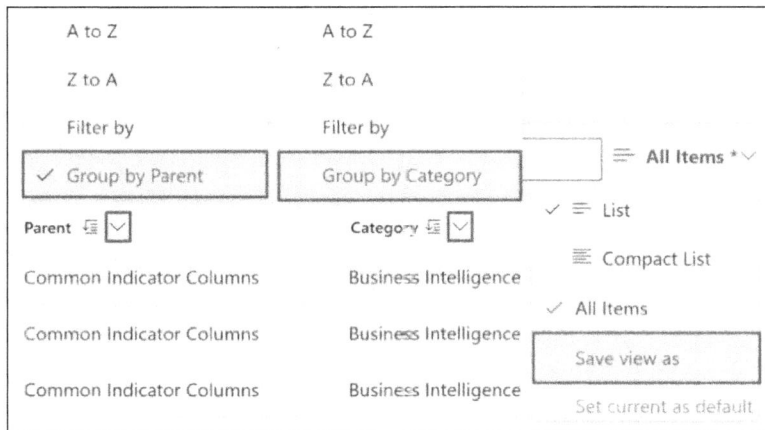

Figure 5.92: *Filter by, group by and view as options*

Conclusion

In this chapter, we had a glance at the term store administration and content services administration. We discussed terminologies, namely, taxonomy, term group, term set, term, and child term. You got a clear understanding of term group and understood the step-by-step procedure to add term group in the taxonomy, rename the term group, delete the term group, and manage permission in the term group. You learned how to add a term set, import a term set, rename a term set, delete a term set, copy a term set, move a term set, and understand the settings available as tabs, namely the general tab, usage settings, navigation, and advanced for term set. You need to know how to add a term, rename a term, copy a term, copy a term with children, move a term, delete a term, pin a term, reuse a term, merge a term, deprecate a term, and in-depth information about the settings available as tabs, namely the general tab, usage settings, navigation, and advanced for terms. We discussed the default term group and its application in the term store. You have a clear understanding of content types and how to create content types, edit content types, manage publishing, delete content types, and content type settings, namely advanced settings, policy settings, and other general settings.

In the next chapter, *Chapter 6, Migration,* we will discuss migrating content from various applications to Microsoft 365.

Points to remember

- Regular changes are applied in Office 365 and SharePoint Online, so, there might be small changes in templates and user interfaces by the time you are reading.

Join our book's Discord space

Join the book's Discord Workspace for Latest updates, Offers, Tech happenings around the world, New Release and Sessions with the Authors:

https://discord.bpbonline.com

CHAPTER 6
Migration

Introduction

In *Chapter 5, Content Services,* we discussed content services, the fourth navigation option available in the SharePoint admin center. In this chapter, we will discuss how to migrate content from different data sources to Microsoft 365. Migration is the process of moving content from one data source to Microsoft 365. Storing content in Microsoft 365, all in one place, will improve the management of content centrally for better collaboration. Microsoft provides an option to store content all in one place by moving content from File shares, Box, Stream, Google Workspace, Dropbox, Egnyte, SharePoint Server 2010, 2013, and 2016 to Microsoft 365. In this chapter, we will discuss how to move content from different sources to Microsoft 365.

Structure

In this chapter, we will discuss the following topics:

- File shares to Microsoft 365 migration
- Stream classic to Microsoft 365 migration
- Google Workspace to Microsoft 365 migration

Objectives

By the end of this chapter, you will get a clear understanding of the terminology, migration, and services available in the SharePoint admin center. You will also understand the supported data sources which can be migrated to Microsoft 365, and the step-by-step procedure to migrate content from content sources, namely file Shares, Stream, Google Workspace, Box, Dropbox, and Egnyte to Microsoft 365.

File shares to Microsoft 365 migration

The traditional way of storing files in network drives is nothing but shared folders present on any server in a common network. We are moving very fast to the new way of storing content in the cloud, which can be accessed anywhere, anytime, on any device, and on any network that provides a better user experience. Microsoft keeps on improving security as per the organization's standards so that security is assured, and organizations will be confident enough to move content to the cloud. In this section, we will discuss migrating the file share to Microsoft 365. Migration of content from file share to Microsoft 365 is a five-step process:

1. The first step is to install the migrating agent.

2. After the agent gets installed, the second step is to connect the agent to the Microsoft 365 tenant.

3. The third step is to add the source path.

4. The fourth step is to scan the content present in the content source.

5. The fifth step in this process is to add the task for migration.

Let us discuss all steps one by one to migrate file share content to Microsoft 365.

Installing Microsoft 365 agent

You need to install a migration agent on each on-premises computer source or server that needs to connect with the migration manager to initiate the first step in the migration process. The agent builds the connection between Microsoft 365 and the on-premises source. In this section, we will discuss installing a migration agent. Let us perform the following steps to install a migration agent in the on-premises source server:

1. Open the **SharePoint admin center** and click on the option **Migration** from the left navigation.

2. You will find different supported application sources that can be migrated to Microsoft 365 categorized into two, namely, **Migration Manager** and **Other migration solutions**.

3. Under the category **Migration Manager,** you will find application sources like **File shares**, **Box**, **Stream**, **Google Workspace**, **Dropbox**, **Egnyte**. Under the category **Other migration solutions**, you will find on-premises application source, namely **SharePoint Server 2010, 2013,** and **2016**.

4. Identify the application source **File shares** and click on the button **Get started.** Refer to *Figure 6.1*:

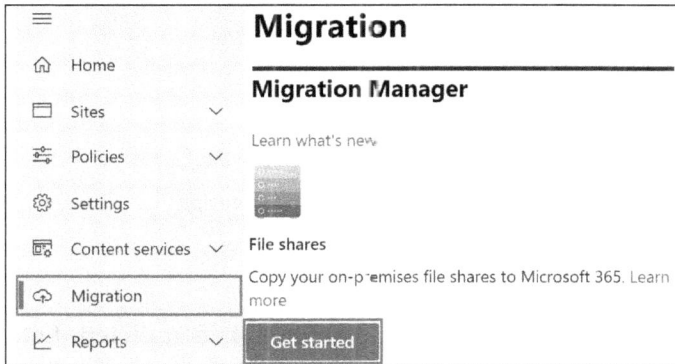

Figure 6.1: Getting started migration manager

5. In the next window, you will find two categories, namely **Download agent** and **Let's scan your source**. Click on the button **Download agent** as shown in *Figure 6.2*:

Figure 6.2: Download agent

6. **Agentsetup.exe** will be downloaded. Run the **Agentsetup.exe** file and click on the option **Install as an app**, as shown in *Figure 6.3*:

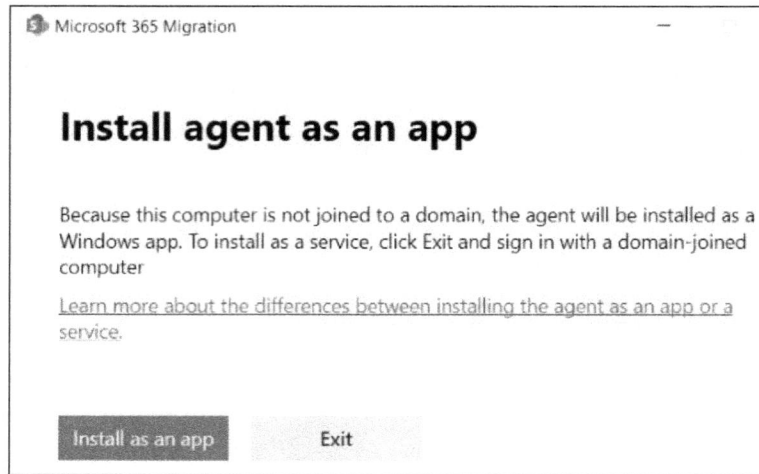

Figure 6.3: Install agent as an app

7. The agent will be installed in a few seconds.

The first step in the process of file shares migration is completed. Let us proceed to the next section to discuss the second step and understand connecting the migration agent to Microsoft 365 tenant.

Connect migration agent to Microsoft 365 tenant

As said before, the agent builds the connection between Microsoft 365 and on-premises sources. Once agent installation is completed, the **Migration Manager agent** application will open as seen in *Figure 6.4*. We will move to the second step of the file share migration process, which is connecting migration manager agent with Microsoft 365 tenant. Let us perform the following steps to understand the process better:

1. Open **Migration Manager agent**.

2. Click on the option **Sign in with SharePoint admin credentials**. Refer to *Figure 6.4*:

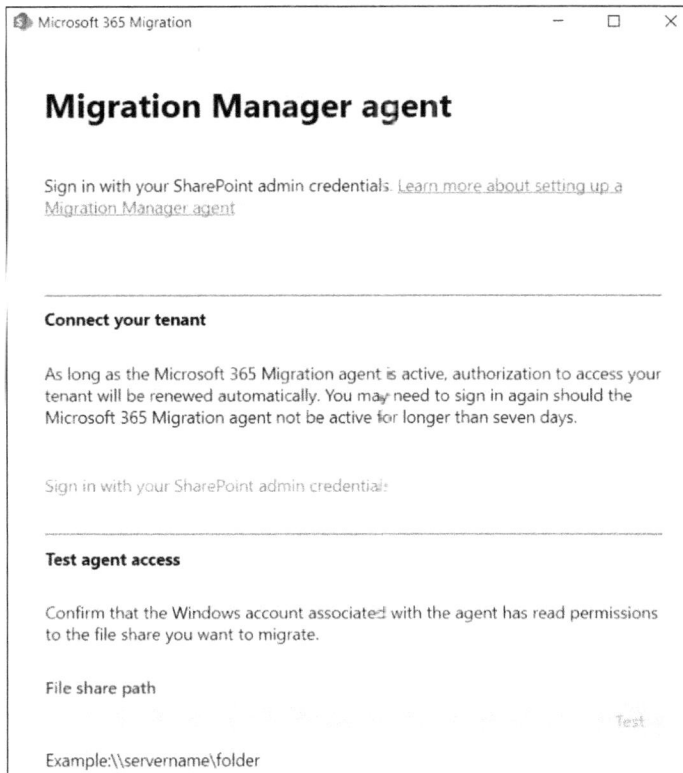

Figure 6.4: Sign in with your SharePoint admin credentials

3. You will be redirected to a new window to enter the SharePoint admin credentials as seen in *Figure 6.5*. Enter credentials and click on **Sign in**.

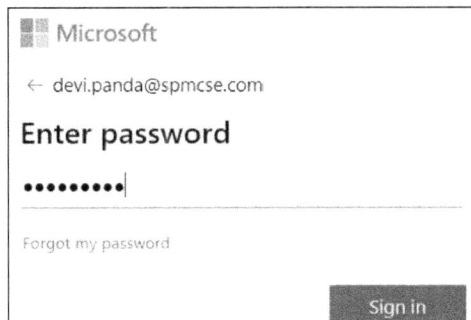

Figure 6.5: Enter Credentials

4. After successful authentication with Microsoft 365, you will find the migration agent status as **Agent connected**, and the option **Add source path** will be enabled as seen in *Figure 6.6*:

Migrate your file shares content to Microsoft 365

Download agent	Let's scan your source
Congratulations! You have an agent configured and ready for your migration tasks. The next step is to scan your source.	Enter the complete path to your file share source location. The scan looks for issues to correct before migrating your content.
● Agent connected	Add source path

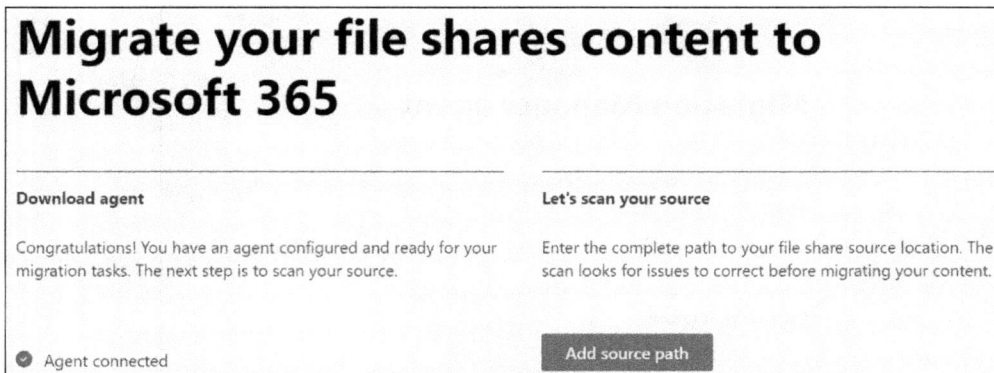

Figure 6.6: Agent connected successfully

The second step in the process of file shares migration is completed. Let us proceed to the next section to discuss the third step and understand how to add source path.

Add source path

Let us move to the third step of the file share content migration process, which is adding source path (shared file URL). Traditionally, network drive or file share folders present under a common network was used to store content, and users having permission to the network drive or shared folder can access it. There is one condition that users need to be under the configured network to access the file, which is not very user-friendly. Now, we have moved to the next level of accessing files from the cloud anywhere, anytime, any device, any network with improved security and user friendliness. This provides a better user experience with improved performance, productivity of the user as well as the organization. In this section, we will discuss how to add the file share path as a source. Let us perform the following steps to add source path for file share migration:

1. Once Microsoft 365 agent installation and connecting migration agent to Microsoft 365 tenant are completed, you will notice the option **Add source path** is enabled.

2. Click on the button **Add source path** as seen in the preceding *Figure 6.6*.

3. You will get a new dialog box to enter the source path. There will be two options, namely, **Specify a single source path**, **Upload a CSV file**. You can select the option **Specify a single source path**, if you want to migrate a single shared network folder and its subfolders present under the folder.

4. For bulk task creation (multiple file share sources), you can choose the option **Upload a CSV file**. You can download the CSV template, fill in the details, and upload.

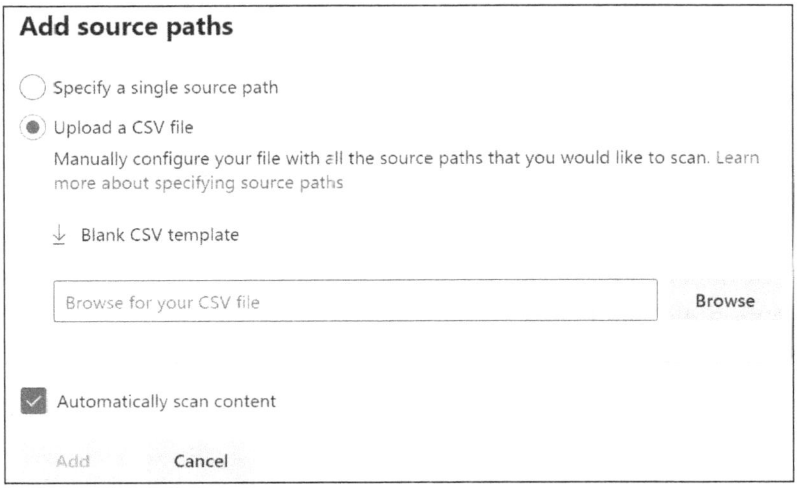

Figure 6.7: *Upload a CSV file to add source path in bulk*

5. Select the first option, **Specify a single source path**, for the moment. Enter the file share path in the same format as mentioned in *Figure 6.8*:

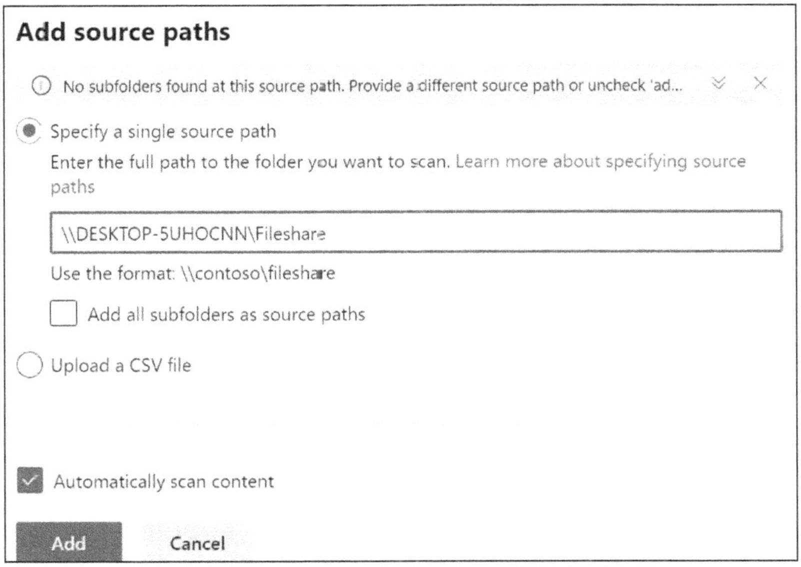

Figure 6.8: *Specify a single source path*

6. Select the checkbox **Automatically scan content** and click on **Add** as seen in the preceding figure.

7. The next step is to add scan file share content present in source path, which we will discuss in the next section.

The third step in the process of file shares migration is completed. Let us proceed to the next section to discuss the fourth step and understand how to scan file share and the content present in the data source.

Scans

Once the source path is added, the next step is to scan the content present in the source path. This is the fourth step in the file share content migration process. If you are not selecting the option **Automatically scan content** as discussed in the previous section, *Add source path* in *Step 6*, you need to scan the contents manually. In this section, we will discuss how to scan manually and post the scan results. Let us perform the following steps to understand better:

1. Once you open file share migration, you will find three tabs like **Scans**, **Migrations**, and **Agents** with the default tab selected as **Scans,** as seen in *Figure 6.9*:

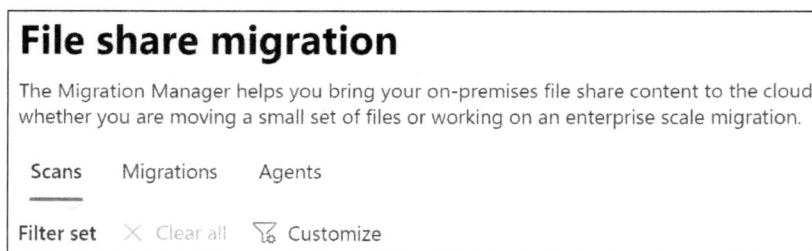

File share migration

The Migration Manager helps you bring your on-premises file share content to the cloud whether you are moving a small set of files or working on an enterprise scale migration.

Scans   Migrations   Agents
────
Filter set   ╳ Clear all   ▽ Customize

Figure 6.9: File share migration tabs

2. Under the tab **Scans**, you will find navigation options like **Add source path**, **Scan content**, **Download summary report**, and **Import tags**, which reflect all the actions that can be taken on the data source. Refer to *Figure 6.10*.

3. Select the data source and click on the option **Scan content** from the navigation options.

4. Scan results are stored in the form of a list that includes information, namely, **Source path**, **Tags**, **Scan result**, **Data size**, **File count**, **Folder count**, **Max path length**, **Root permissions**, **Last accessed**, and **Created on** in a list format. Refer to *Figure 6.10*.

5. You will find the **Scan result** column change to **Queued** and then change to **Ready to migrate** with a green mark, which indicates that the user is good to proceed for the next step, which is migration.

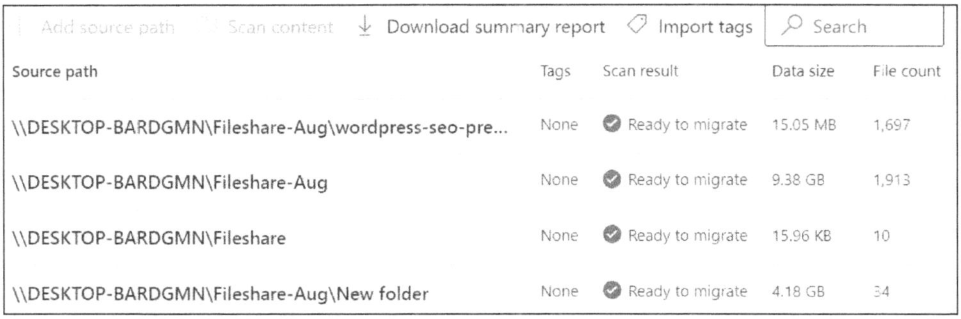

Figure 6.10: Data source options and extracted metadata information

6. You will find the contents scanned automatically, metadata will be extracted for analysis, planning, and filtering, and results are stored in list format as well as displayed in graphical format.

7. You can add data sources later by following the option **Add source path**, and scan manually by following the option **Scan content** at any time as per requirement.

8. You can download the Summary report present in the list in .csv format by following the navigation option **Download summary report**.

9. You will find the content scan details in graphical format in categories like **Overview**, **Source paths by migration readiness**, **Source paths by files and folders count**, **Source paths by data size**, and **Warnings needing attention**.

10. Category **Overview** contains the total number of files and folders present in the data source. If you have multiple data sources added and a scan completed, you will find the total number of files and folders present in all the data sources. Similarly, you will find the size of the contents present in the data source or all data sources scanned as seen in *Figure 6.11*:

Figure 6.11: Volume of content, files, and folder count

11. Category **Source paths by migration readiness** will display the status of migration readiness. If there are errors or warnings, they will be displayed here with color codes red or orange. If there is no error, it will display the green color, which indicates ready to migrate as seen in *Figure 6.12*:

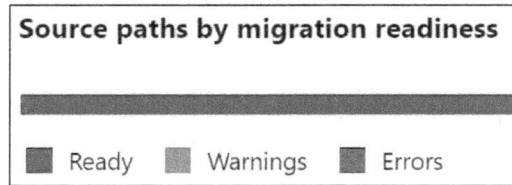

Figure 6.12: *Source paths by migration readiness*

12. If you see *Figure 6.10*, you will notice there are two data sources with files and folders counts 10 to 1k, and two data sources with files and folder counts 1k to 5k. Category **Source paths by files and folders count** displays data in graphical format as seen in *Figure 6.13*. You see different color codes for different ranges of file and folders counts. If you hover over the color, it will display the data source count falling under each range of file and folder count, as seen in *Figure 6.13*:

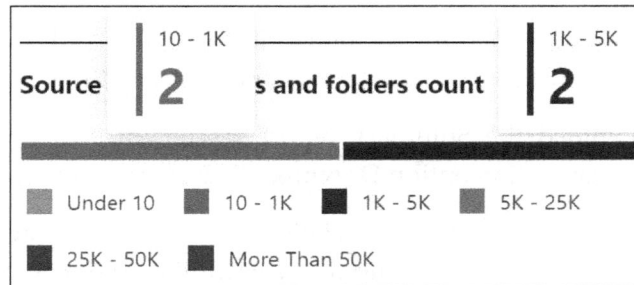

Figure 6.13: *Source paths by files and folders count*

13. If you see *Figure 6.10*, you will notice there are two data sources having data size less than 1 GB and two data sources having data size between 1 GB to 20 GB. The next category **Source paths by data size** displays data in a graphical format as seen in *Figure 6.14*. You see different color codes for different ranges of data size. If you hover over the color, it will display the data source count falling under each range of data size, as seen in the following figure:

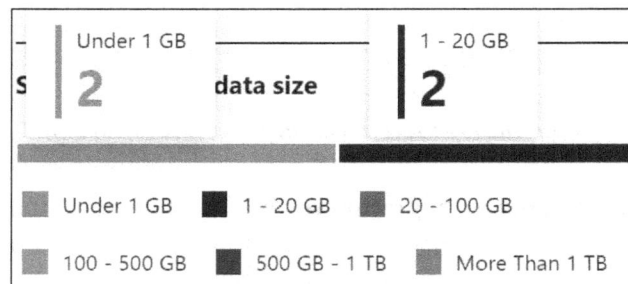

Figure 6.14: *Source paths by data size*

14. The next category is **Warnings needing attention**. If there is any warning, it will be displayed here that needs to be resolved to proceed further in migration.

15. In the next category, **Files and folders by last modified date**, you will find the total number of files and folders based on the last modified date in graphical format, as seen in *Figure 6.15*:

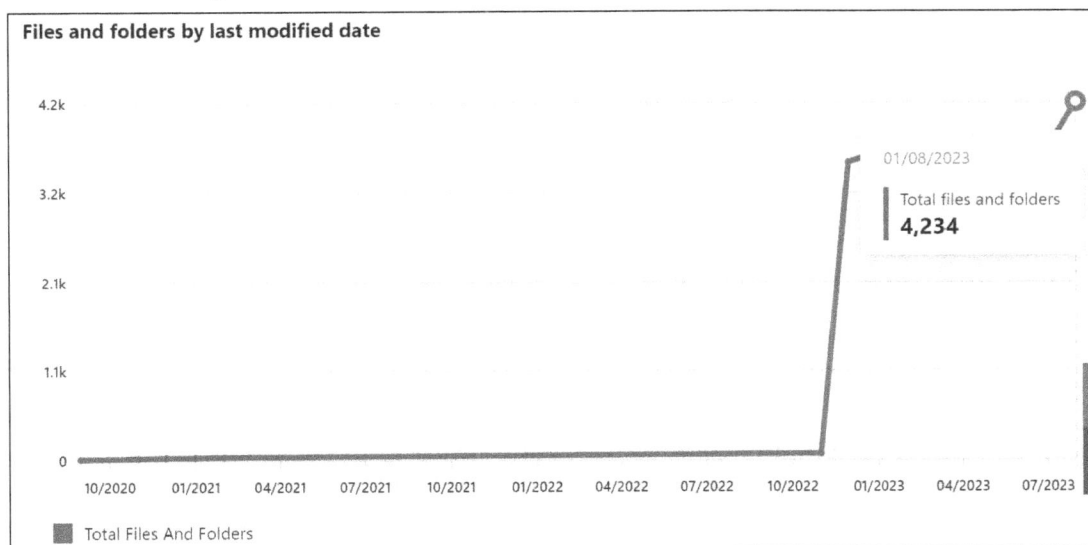

Figure 6.15: Files and folders by last modified date

16. Scanning of the file source content is completed now. You are good to proceed to the next step, migration.

Migration

Let us move to the fifth step of the file share content migration process, which is migrations. This is the step where the actual migration of content happens. Let us follow the step-by-step procedure to understand the settings present under the tab migration and migrate the scanned content sources:

1. Click on the navigation option **Migrations**. You will get a window that holds all actions that can be taken on the task.

2.   Click on the option **Add task** as seen in *Figure 6.16*:

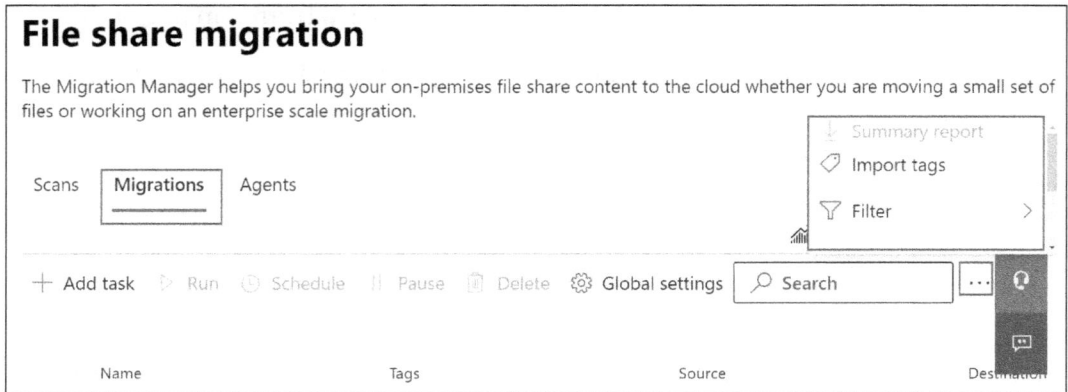

Figure 6.16: *Add migration task*

3.   You will get the option to pick a method. There are two methods you will find. The first method is to select **Single source and destination,** and the second method is to upload CSV or JSON file for **Bulk migration**. Select the first option, **Single source and destination**, for the moment and click on **Next**, as shown in *Figure 6.17*:

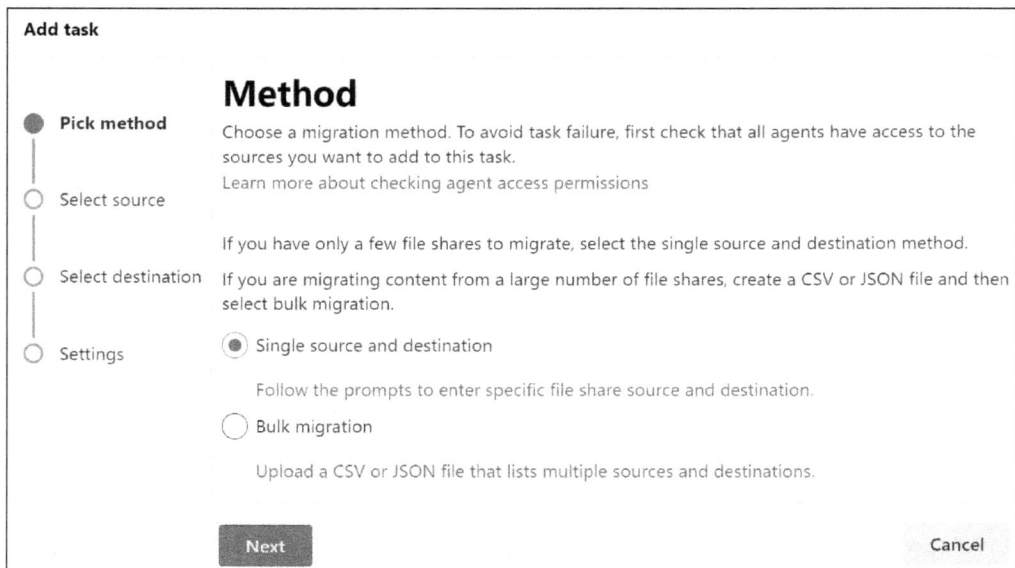

Figure 6.17: *Pick method*

4.   Enter the data source in the format as seen in the following figure and click on **Next**:

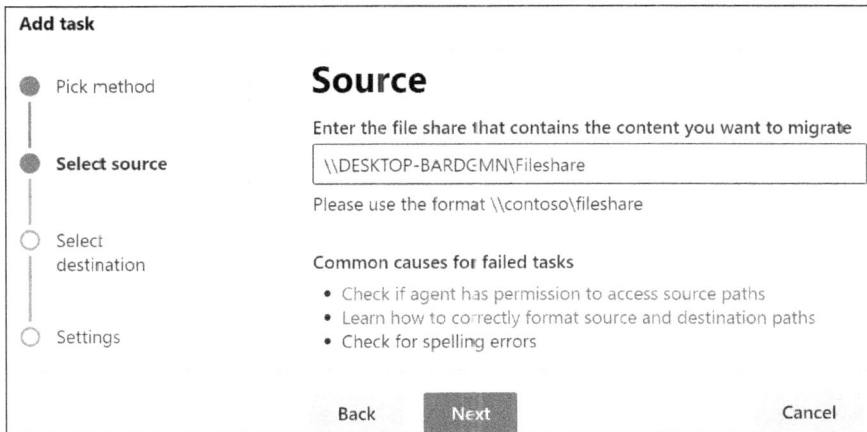

Figure 6.18: Select source

5. You need to select the destination to migrate content. You can select **SharePoint** site, **OneDrive**, or **Teams** as the destination. Select **SharePoint** site as the destination and click on **Next**, shown as follows:

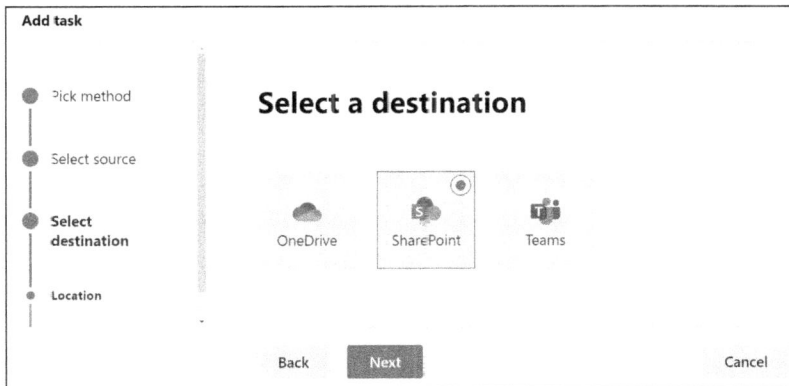

Figure 6.19: Select destination as SharePoint

6. Enter the URL of the SharePoint site, and select the document library present in that site, as seen in the following figure. Click on **Next** once the selection is completed.

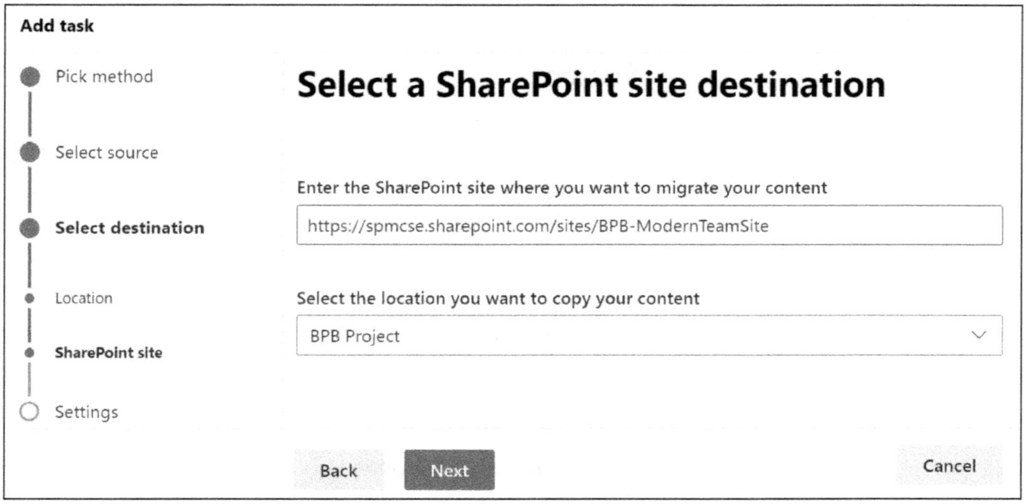

Figure 6.20: Select SharePoint site destination

7. Enter the name of the task in the field, **Task name**.

8. You can select the **Task schedule** to **Run now** or **Run later**. Select the option **Run now** for the moment, as shown in *Figure 6.21*:

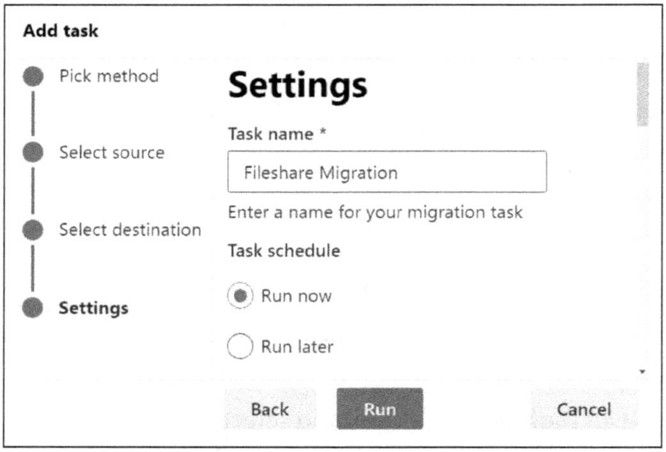

Figure 6.21: Task name and task schedule

9. If you are selecting **Run later**, then you will get the **Date** and **Time** option to schedule as seen in *Figure 6.22*:

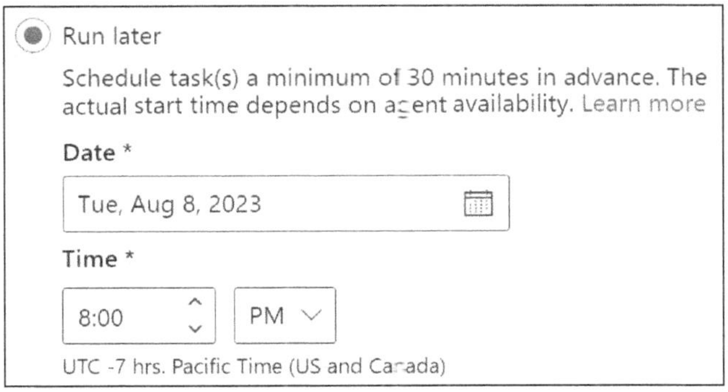

Figure 6.22: Schedule migration task

10. The next option you will find is **Agent group assignment**. The default agent will be selected.

11. Next, under **Common settings**, you will find two options like **Perform scan only** and **Preserve file share permissions** as seen in *Figure 6.23*. If you are selecting **Perform scan only**, then scanning of the data source will happen, not the migration. Since we have already completed scanning, keep this option unchecked. Select the option **Preserve file share permissions** option so that the destination document library will inherit the permissions configured in the source file location (file share).

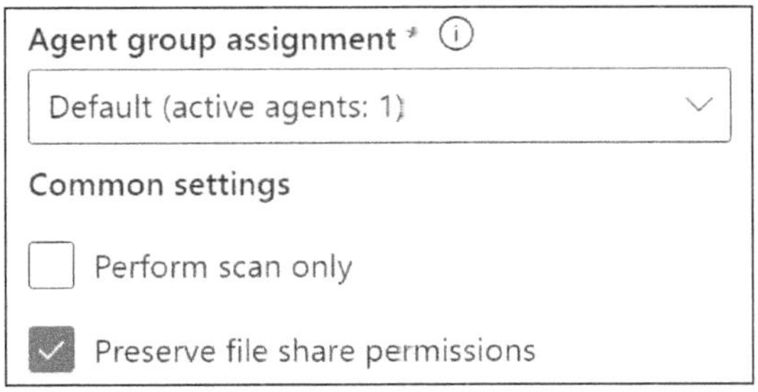

Figure 6.23: Common settings

12. Next, expand the **All settings** category. You will have three categories of options, like **Filters, Users,** and **other**.

13. Select the check box option **Migrate hidden files** present under the category filters, as seen in *Figure 6.24*, to migrate the files that are hidden in the data source file share folder.

14. You can select the option **Migrate files created after**, present under the category filters, and choose a date to migrate files created after the selected date.

15. You can select the option **Migrate files modified after**, present under the category filters, and choose a date to migrate files modified after the selected date.

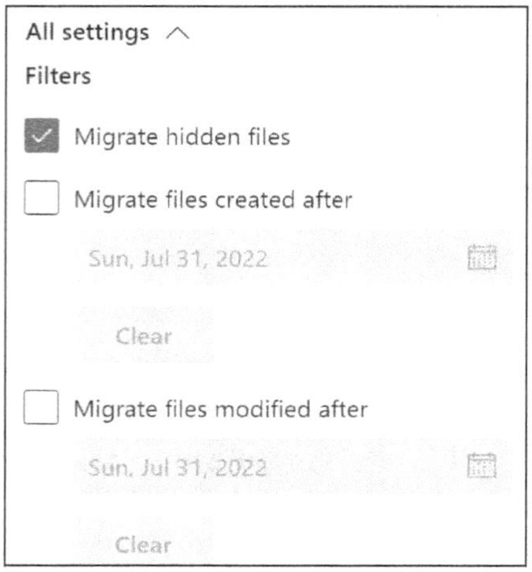

All settings ∧

Filters

☑ Migrate hidden files

☐ Migrate files created after

    Sun, Jul 31, 2022   📅

    Clear

☐ Migrate files modified after

    Sun, Jul 31, 2022   📅

    Clear

Figure 6.24: All settings option

16. You can select the check box option **Do not migrate files with these extensions,** present under the category filters, and enter file extensions manually separated by **Colon** to exclude those files from migration.

17. Select the option **Replace invalid file name characters**, present under the category filters, and enter a valid file name character manually. This will replace all the files having invalid file name characters with a valid file name character. This will help avoid migration errors. Refer to *Figure 6.25*:

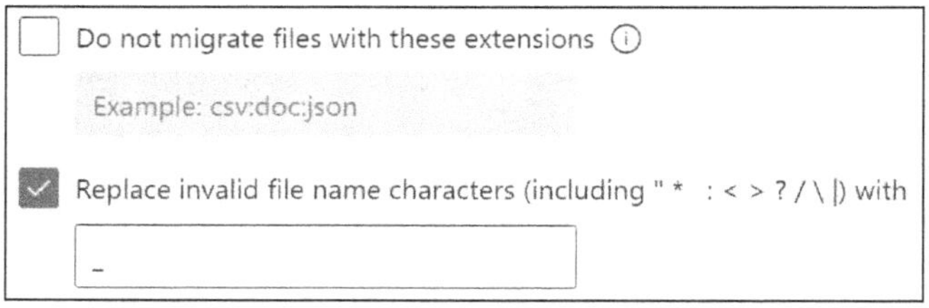

☐ Do not migrate files with these extensions ⓘ

    Example: csv:doc:json

☑ Replace invalid file name characters (including " * : < > ? / \ |) with

    _

Figure 6.25: Replace invalid characters and block specific files from migration

18. Next, select the check box **Azure Active Directory lookup** present under **Users** in the **All settings** category.

19. You can choose a **User mapping file** as seen in *Figure 6.26*. Enter **log-in name of the user, user principal name (UPN),** and **True/False** (If the user principal name on the target site is an **Active Directory (AD)** group, enter **TRUE**, else enter **FALSE**) in three columns of the CSV file that you will choose here.

20. Next, select the check box **Automatically rerun failed tasks up to 4 times** present under **Other** in the **All settings** category, shown as follows:

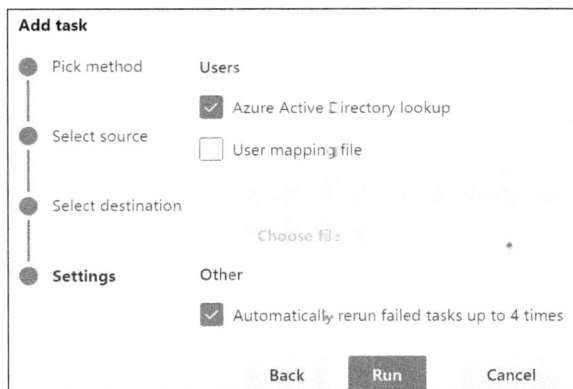

Figure 6.26: *User setting and rerun failed task option*

21. After all the settings are configured, click on the button **Run**, as shown in *Figure 6.26*.

22. Migration will start, and the status will change from **Waiting for agent** to **Percentage completed,** and will finally show **Completed**, as shown in *Figure 6.27:*

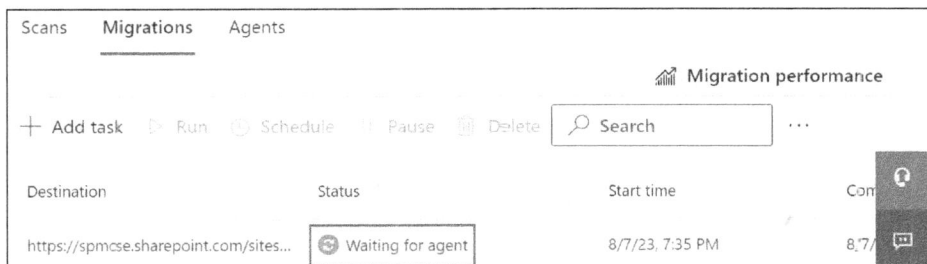

Figure 6.27: *Status column changes during migration*

23. You can proceed for migration from the previous window **Scans** as well. If you want to proceed from the previous window **Scans**, then select any one of the data sources with the scan result status as completed. Click on the option **Copy to migration** as seen in *Figure 6.28*:

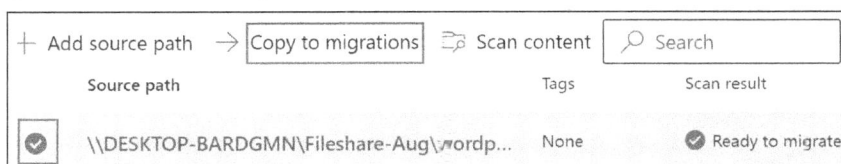

Figure 6.28: *Copy to migration*

24. You will get the option to choose a destination source. Then, follow the same steps discussed from the aforementioned *Step 5* to *Step 21*.

25. Once migration is completed, select the check box present next to the task and click on the **Summary report** from the navigation option as seen in *Figure 6.29*: A summary report will be downloaded, which you can analyze.

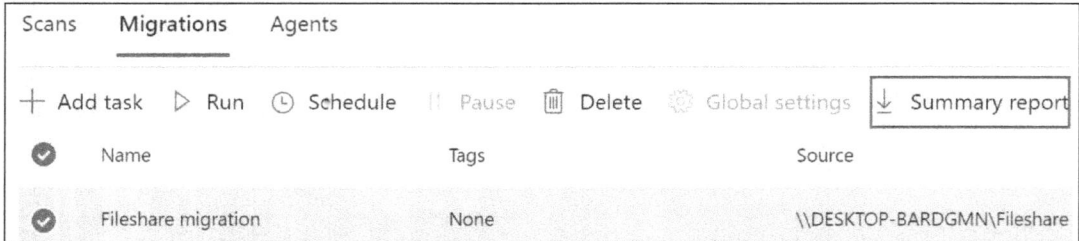

Scans	Migrations	Agents		
+ Add task	▷ Run	ⓒ Schedule ‖ Pause 🗑 Delete ⚙ Global settings	↓ Summary report	
✅	Name	Tags	Source	
✅	Fileshare migration	None	\\DESKTOP-BARDGMN\Fileshare	

Figure 6.29: Summary report

26. You will find a detailed summary report with columns like **Task name, Task ID, Status, Created date, Started date, Completed date, Source, Destination, Total scanned items, Total to be migrated items, Migrated items, Items not migrated, Total bytes, Total GB, Migrated bytes, Migrated GB, Agent, Agent group, Duration, Error message**. The following *Figure 6.30* illustrates the summary report:

Task name	Task ID	Status	Created date	Started date	Completed date
Fileshare migration	0836341f	Complete	8/7/23, 7:33	8/7/23, 7:35	8/7/23, 7:36 PM

Source	Destination
\\DESKTOP-BARDGMN\Fileshare	https://spmcse.sharepoint.com/sites/BPB-ModernTeamSite/BPB Project

Total scanned items	Total to be migrated items	Migrated items	Items not migrated	Total bytes	Total GB
10	10	10	0	16345	0

Migrated bytes	Migrated GB	Agent	Agent group	Duration	Error message
16345	0	\DESKTOP-BARDGMN - devip	Default	00:00:50	

Figure 6.30: Summary report

27. Click on the migration task, you will get quick details like **Source, Destination, Tags, Status, Start time** as seen in *Figure 6.31*:

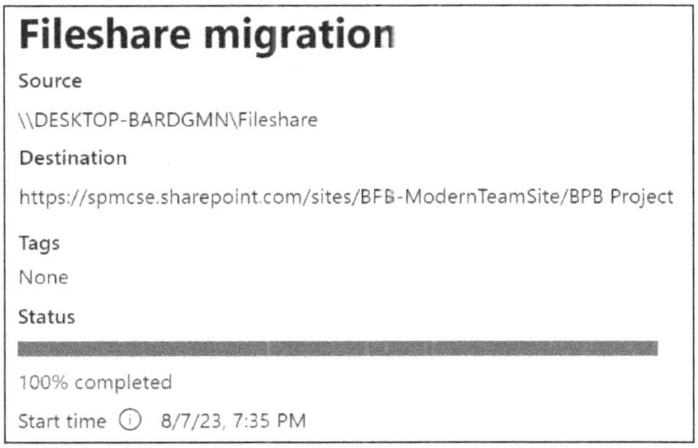

Fileshare migration

Source

\\DESKTOP-BARDGMN\Fileshare

Destination

https://spmcse.sharepoint.com/sites/BFB-ModernTeamSite/BPB Project

Tags

None

Status

100% completed

Start time ⓘ 8/7/23, 7:35 PM

Figure 6.31: Details of the migration task

28. You will find more details like **Download task report, Scan history, Scheduled start time, Files scanned, SharePoint Administrator credentials** as seen in *Figure 6.32*:

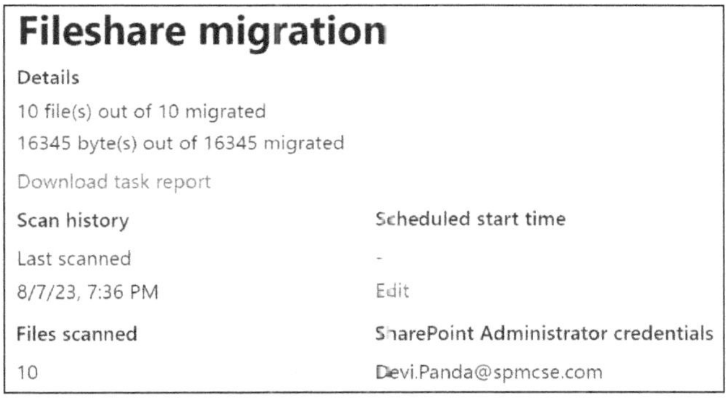

Fileshare migration

Details

10 file(s) out of 10 migrated

16345 byte(s) out of 16345 migrated

Download task report

Scan history	Scheduled start time
Last scanned	-
8/7/23, 7:36 PM	Edit
Files scanned	**SharePoint Administrator credentials**
10	Devi.Panda@spmcse.com

Figure 6.32: Task report, scan history, files scanned, schedule start time

29. You will find more information like **Files scanned with issues, Agent, Files ready to migrate, Friendly agent name, Windows credentials** as seen in *Figure 6.33*:

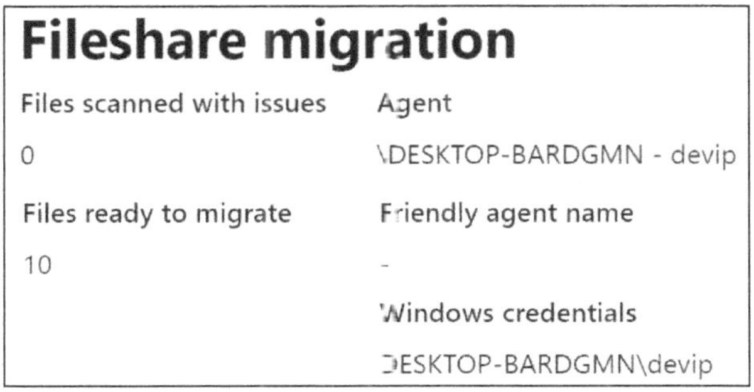

Fileshare migration

Files scanned with issues	Agent
0	\DESKTOP-BARDGMN - devip
Files ready to migrate	**Friendly agent name**
10	-
	Windows credentials
	DESKTOP-BARDGMN\devip

Figure 6.33: Files ready to migrate, files scanned with issues, agent information

30. Click on the option **Download task report** as discussed in *Step 27*. One zip file will be downloaded with multiple CSV files in it, like **GlobalSettings, ItemReport_R1, ItemReport_R2, ItemSummary, ScanSummary, StructureReport_R1, StructureReport_R2, TaskInfoSummary, UserMapped_R1, UserNotMapped_R1,** as seen in *Figure 6.34*:

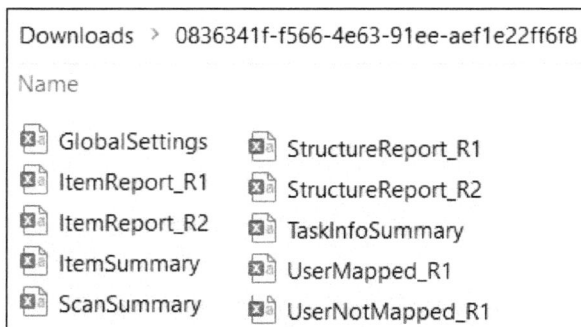

Figure 6.34: Task Report

31. Open the **GlobalSettings** task report, and you will find details as seen in the following *Figure 6.35*:

Setting	Value		
Migration auto re-run	TRUE		
User mapping file			
Use custom Azure storage	FALSE	Start Migration If No Scan Issue	FALSE
Migrate file version history	TRUE	Preserve Permission Inheritance	FALSE
Keep all versions	FALSE	Migrate Site Settings	PRESERVE_ALL_SETTINGS
Number of versions preserved	10		
Filter out created date before		Skip List With Audience Enabled	TRUE
Filter out modified date before		Migrate All Web Fields ContentTypes	FALSE
Filter out files with extensions		Migrate Navigation	TRUE
Filter out sites with names		Migrate Managed Metadata	TRUE
Filter out lists with names		Migrate Pages Options	RENAME
Filter out content types with names		Replace invalid characters in files and folder	FALSE
Automatic user mapping	TRUE		
Preserve user permission for SharePoint Server	TRUE	Replacement of invalid characters in files and folder	
Preserve user permission for File Share	TRUE	Lookup Reference Scan Policy	FIND_ALL_REFERENCE
Filter out hidden files	FALSE	Migrate Root Folder	FALSE
Temporarily allow migration of scripts	FALSE	Working Directory Path	C:\Users\devip\AppData\Roaming\Microsoft\SPMigration\Logs\Migration
Only Perform Scan	FALSE		
Start Migration If No Scan Issue	FALSE		

Figure 6.35: Global settings

32. Open **ItemReport** task report. You will find **Source, Destination, Item name** as seen in *Figure 6.36*:

Source	Destination	Item name
\\DESKTOP-BARDGMN\Fileshare\SharePoint Online Power user Playbook.txt	https://spmcse.sharepoint.com/sites/BPB-ModernTeamSite/BPB Project/SharePoint Online Power user Playbook.txt	SharePoint Online Power user Playbook.txt
\\DESKTOP-BARDGMN\Fileshare\test file.docx	https://spmcse.sharepoint.com/sites/BPB-ModernTeamSite/BPB Project/test file.docx	test file.docx
\\DESKTOP-BARDGMN\Fileshare\17e74781-cd47-44a2-981b-43ddedb1ec6a	https://spmcse.sharepoint.com/sites/BPB-ModernTeamSite/BPB Project/17e74781-cd47-44a2-981b-43ddedb1ec6a	17e74781-cd47-44a2-981b-43ddedb1ec6a
\\DESKTOP-BARDGMN\Fileshare\17e74781-cd47-44a2-981b-43ddedb1ec6a\GlobalSettings.csv	https://spmcse.sharepoint.com/sites/BPB-ModernTeamSite/BPB Project/17e74781-cd47-44a2-981b-43ddedb1ec6a/GlobalSettings.csv	GlobalSettings.csv

Figure 6.36: Item report source, destination, item name information

33. **ItemReport** task report contains more details like **Extension, Item size (bytes), Type, Status, Result category, Message, Source item ID** as seen in *Figure 6.37*:

Extension	Item size (bytes)	Type	Status	Result category	Message	Source item ID
.txt	22	File	Migrated	MIGRATION SKIP	The file was skipped because destination has newer file	80a37813-5215-55d4-9ef6-8b95adaa35a3
.docx	####	File	Migrated	MIGRATION SKIP	The file was skipped because destination has newer file	4faccbfc-2e6e-5b76-b9e0-0d1922420b26
	0	Folder	Migrated	MIGRATION SKIP	The file was skipped because destination has newer file	58485df3-4cf7-594c-b0b8-14d1809f4fde
.csv	1201	File	Migrated	MIGRATION SKIP	The file was skipped because destination has newer file	6aa20f01-f501-5201-9c59-8658c8dfae54

Figure 6.37: Item report more information

34. **ItemReport** task report contains more details, such as **Destination item ID, Package number, Migration job ID, Incremental round, Task ID, Device name** as seen in *Figure 6.38*:

Destination item ID	Package number	Migratio n job ID	Increme ntal round	Task ID	Device name
80a37813-5215-55d4-9ef6-8b95adaa35a3	N/A	N/A	R1	0836341f-f566-4e63-91ee-aef1e22ff6f8	DESKTOP-BARDGMN
4faccbfd-2e6e-5b76-b9e0-0d1922420b26	N/A	N/A	R1	0836341f-f566-4e63-91ee-aef1e22ff6f8	DESKTOP-BARDGMN
58485df3-4cf7-594c-b0b8-14d1809f4fde	N/A	N/A	R1	0836341f-f566-4e63-91ee-aef1e22ff6f8	DESKTOP-BARDGMN
6aa20f01-f501-5201-9c59-8658c8dfae54	N/A	N/A	R1	0836341f-f566-4e63-91ee-aef1e22ff6f8	DESKTOP-BARDGMN

Figure 6.38: Item report more information

35. Open **ItemSummary** task report and you will find information about **Incremental round, Scanned, Item scan, Filtered out items, Expected migrated file count, Read, Packaged, Uploaded, ReUploaded, Submitted, ReSubmitted, Migrated, Failed reading, Failed packaging, Failed uploading, Failed submitting, Failed querying, Device name**. The following figure illustrates the same:

Increm ental round	Scanned	Item scan	Filtered out items	Expected migrated file count	Read	Packaged	Uploaded	ReUploaded	Submitted
R1	10	0	0	0	0	0	0	0	0
R2	10	0	0	0	0	0	0	0	0

ReSubmitted	Migrated	Failed reading	Failed packaging	Failed uploadin g	Failed submitting	Failed queryin g	Device name
0	0	0	0	0	0	0	DESKTOP-BARDGMN
0	0	0	0	0	0	0	DESKTOP-BARDGMN

Figure 6.39: Item summary report

36. Open **ScanSummary** task report and you will find information about **Incremental round, Total scanned items, Total scanned folders, Total scanned list items, Total scanned files, Folders with issues, Items with issues, Items filtered out, Folders to be migrated, Items to be migrated, Total items to be migrated, WarningDetails, ErrorDetails, Device name**. The following figure illustrates the same:

Incremental round	Total scanned items	Total scanned folders	Total scanned list items	Total scanned files	Folders with issues	Items with issues
R1	11	1	0	10	0	0
R2	11	1	0	10	0	0

Items filtered out	Folders to be migrated	Items to be migrated	Total items to be migrated	WarningDetails	ErrorDetails	Device name
0	0	0	0			DESKTOP-BARDGMN
0	0	0	0			DESKTOP-BARDGMN

Figure 6.40: Scan summary report

37. Open **StructureReport** task report and you will find information about **Structure type**, **Structure title**, **Operation**, **Status**, **Details**, **Code** as seen in *Figure 6.41*:

Structure type	Structure title	Operation	Status	Details	Code
Site collection		Skipped		The object property is consistent between the source and the destination. Skip update	0x03000013
Site	BPB-ModernTeamSite	Skipped		The object property is consistent between the source and the destination. Skip update	0x03000013
List	BPB Project	Skipped		The object property is consistent between the source and the destination. Skip update	0x03000013

Figure 6.41: Structure report

38. You will find more information like **Source structure URL**, **Destination structure URL**, **Source structure ID**, **Destination structure ID**, **Time stamp** in the task report StructureReport as seen in *Figure 6.42*:

Source structure URL	Destination structure URL	Source structure ID	Destination structure ID	Time stamp
file:///	https://spmcse.sharepoint.com/sites/BPB-ModernTeamSite		9365390c-fa26-4eeb-bbfb-58f261f25661	
file:///	https://spmcse.sharepoint.com/sites/BPB-ModernTeamSite		0ab3fee7-ae05-455f-9bdc-6efed918d53c	
file:///	https://spmcse.sharepoint.com/sites/BPB-ModernTeamSite/BPB Project		f2542b87-a9e7-4f89-8827-e67b5fa00299	

Figure 6.42: Structure report more information

39. Open **TaskInfoSummary** task report. You will find information about **Task Name**, **TaskId**, **Machine Name**, **Workflow Path** as seen in *Figure 6.43*:

Task Name	TaskId	Machine Name	Workflow Path
Fileshare migration	0836341f-f566-4e63-91ee-aef1e22ff6f8	\DESKTOP-BARDGMN	C:\Users\devip\AppData\Roaming\Microsoft\SPMigration\Logs \Migration\MigrationTool\spmcse.com\WF_80324d4a

Figure 6.43: Task info summary

40. Similarly, you will get two more reports like **UserMapped & UserNotMapped** in task report that hold details related to user mapping.

Migration performance

Option **Migration performance** under the category **Migration** holds migration performance history. Data source read speed, computer speed, connectivity to Microsoft 365 and Azure, network infrastructure, file size, migration time, and throttling are the primary reasons that impact migration. Migration performance will display files and folders, bytes migrated in the last 7, 14, and 30 days. You can get the migration performance report for specific custom dates as seen in the following *Figure 6.44*:

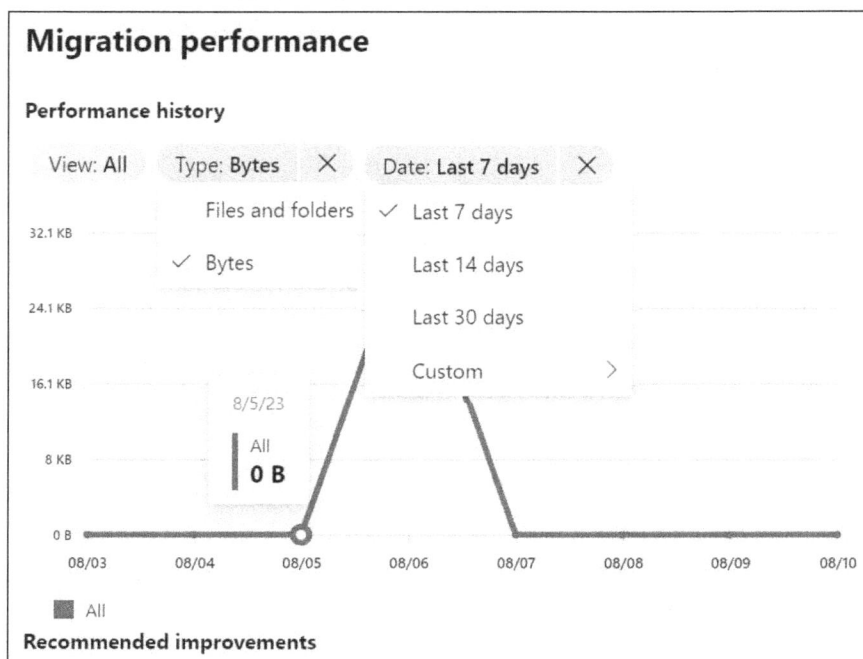

Figure 6.44: Migration performance

Agents

Agent is the third option in file share migration navigation. When you sign in after installing the agent, there will be an entry here. You will find the state is **Enabled** for the agents linked to the tenant. Agents which are not linked to the tenants will be displayed as **Disconnected** as seen in *Figure 6.45*:

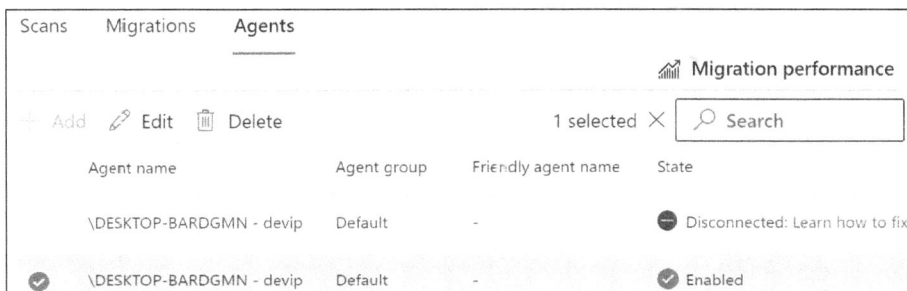

Figure 6.45: Agent state

After you click on agent, you will find details like **Agent name**, **Friendly agent name**, **State**, **Available local storage space**, **Working folder**, **Agent group** as seen in *Figure 6.46*:

Figure 6.46: Agent details

Stream classic to Microsoft 365 migration

Stream is one of the migration features that provides a service to migrate Stream Classic content to Microsoft 365 to use Stream on SharePoint. Let us discuss the step-by-step procedure to migrate Stream Classic content to Microsoft 365 and understand better:

1. Navigate to the option **Migration** present under the left navigation in **SharePoint admin center**.

2. Identify the feature **Stream** and click on the button **Get started** present below the feature as seen in *Figure 6.47*:

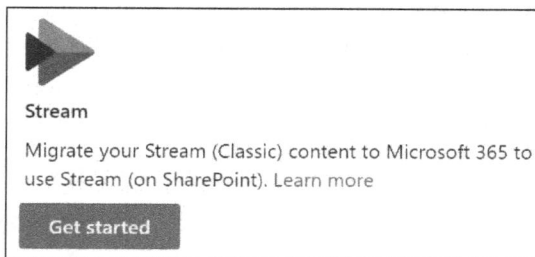

Figure 6.47: Stream migration get started

3. You will find two tabs with options like **Scans**, **Migrations** with the default option selected as **Scans** as seen in *Figure 6.48*. These two tabs contain all settings that can be used for the stream content migration.

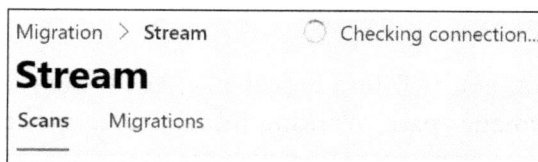

Figure 6.48: Number of tabs in stream file migration

4. Stream content migration is a three-step process. The first step is to **Scan** for videos. The second step is **Add to Migrations**. The third step is **Migrations**. All these steps can be managed from these two tabs, namely, **Scan** and **Migrations**. Let us discuss all steps one by one to migrate Stream Classic content to Microsoft 365.

Scans

Scanning is the first step in the process of Stream Classic content migration. Contents present in the stream classic will be discovered via containers. The tab **Scans** holds information about containers and actions that can be taken on containers. You will find a collapsible **Tutorial** that gives basic information about the number of steps related to stream classic content migration. Let us discuss the actions that can be taken under the tab Scan:

1. Once you access the stream as described in *Step 1* and *Step 2* under the section *Stream*, you will notice the auto-discovery of containers has started. You can see the status showing as **Loading containers**, as seen in *Figure 6.49*. Containers will be discovered automatically, and the number of containers will be displayed under **Table summary** Section **Overview**.

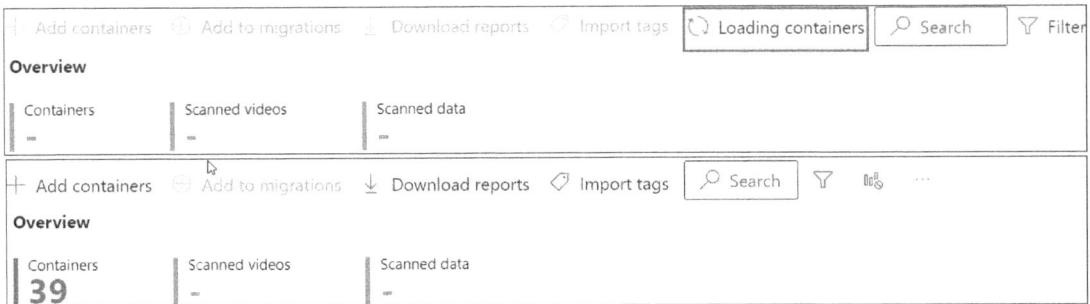

Figure 6.49: *Auto discovery of containers*

2. The next step is to scan the contents present in Stream Classic via containers.

3. You will find navigation with options like **Add containers**, **Add to migrations**, **Scan**, **Stop scan**, **Delete**, **Download reports**, **Download scan log**, **Import tags**, **Search**, **Filter**, **Show/Hide table summary** as seen in *Figure 6.50*. Few options will be visible initially, a few will be visible after selecting the container, and a few after stream content scan.

4. Select the container or containers that you want to migrate to Microsoft 365 to use **Stream (on SharePoint)**. You will get an option **Scan** in the navigation. Click on **Scan** as seen in *Figure 6.50*:

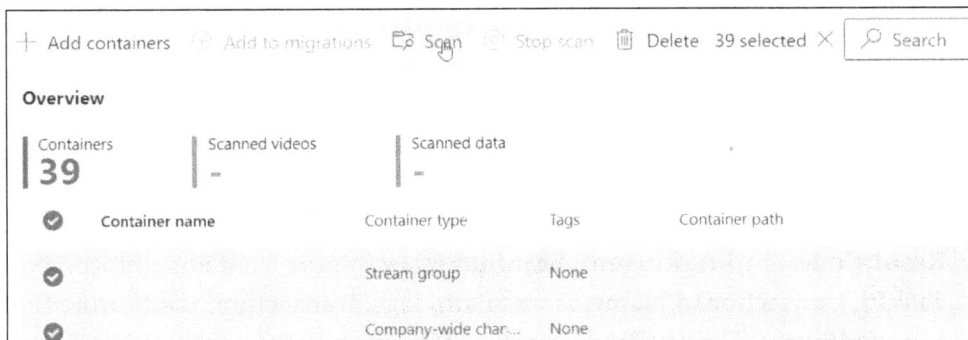

Figure 6.50: *Scan container*

5. Scanning of containers will start. You will notice that the **Scan** status column will change from **Queued, In Progress,** to **Completed**. In the **Overview** section, you will find the details like the number of **Containers**, **Scanned videos**, **Scanned data** as seen in *Figure 6.51*.

6. Click on the option **Download scan log** from the navigation to download the scan report from analysis.

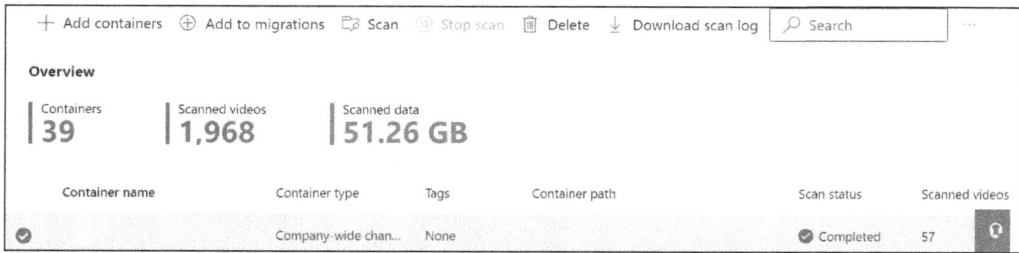

Figure 6.51: Post scan details and scan log

7. Click on the option **Download reports** from navigation.

8. You will get a `.zip` file named **Scan reports** with `.csv` files like **FileExtensions, LargeFileSizes, LongPaths, ScanErrors, ScanSummary**.

9. **FileExtensions** report contains information like **TaskId, Name, SourcePath, FullPath, SourceExtension, TotalSize**. The following figure represents the same:

TaskId	Name	SourcePath
02aea7cd-b363-491e-8f88-ace2dee18515	SharePoint online power user playbook	SharePoint online power user playbook|0cbf1a7d-2172-4a68-9f19-268aa5d04699|CompanywideChannel

FullPath	Source	TotalSize
SharePoint online power user playbook|0cbf1a7d-2172-4a68-9f19-268aa5d04699|CompanywideChannel	mp4	552387625

Figure 6.52: File extension report

10. **LargeFileSizes** report contains information like **TaskId, Name, SourcePath, FullPath, SourceSize, SourceSizeInGB. LongPaths** report contains information like **TaskId, Name, SourcePath, FullPath, SourcePathLength. ScanErrors** report contains information like **TaskId, Name, SourcePath, FullPath, Action, ResultCode, FailureReason. ScanSummary** report contains information like **TaskId, TransactionId, Name, SourcePath, Tags, TransactionSize, ScannedFolders, ScannedFiles, UniquePermissions, MaximumPathLength, TotalDataBytes, TotalDataMB, TotalFiles, ScanStatusCode, ScanStatus, MostRecentScan, ResultCode, TopFailureReason**. The following figure represents the same:

TaskId	TransactionId	Name	SourcePath	Tags
ccbc9c24-e53a-48bb-959a-bc6a9b4ac946	15861303-31b0-4167-bd87-570b8721c224	Networking TCP/IP	Networking TCP/IP|8132e948-b2cd-4dac-8391-7ae8f7ff089f|CompanywideChannel	

TransactionSize	ScannedFolders	ScannedFiles	UniquePermissions	MaximumPathLength	TotalDataBytes	TotalDataMB	TotalFiles
329547306	3	5	12	124	329547306	314	5

ScanStatusCode	ScanStatus	MostRecentScan	ResultCode	TopFailureReason
101	Success	2023-08-25T01:41:49Z		

Figure 6.53: Large file size report

11. You can analyze the reports. Select the container that got scanned and click on **Add to migration** from the navigation. You will get a dialog box with the number of containers selected, as seen in *Figure 6.54*:

Add containers to "Migrations" tab

39 containers selected

Adding containers to the "Migrations" tab allows you to set their destination paths. Once paths are set, containers are ready to migrate.

Continue   Cancel

Figure 6.54: Add containers to migration

12. Containers will be added to the **Migration** tab.

In the following section, we will discuss the options available in the tab **Migrations**.

Migrations

Once you select the container and click on the option **Add to migrations,** you will notice the containers added to the migrations tab. Click on the **Migration** tab. This tab holds options that can be used to take actions on containers. Let us discuss the actions that can be taken under the tab **Migrations**:

1. In the migration tab, you will find navigation with options like **Migrate, Upload destinations, Download reports, Import tags, Search, Filter, Show/Hide table summary** as seen in *Figure 6.55*.

2. Under that, you will find the containers and their properties like **Container name, Container type, Tags, Container path, Destination, Migration status, Task state, Videos skipped, Videos failed, Videos successful, Data skipped, Data failed, Data successful, Created on, Most recent migration**.

3. You will find that the destination for the container is not assigned. A warning message shows like **Assign destination**, under the container property **Destination**.

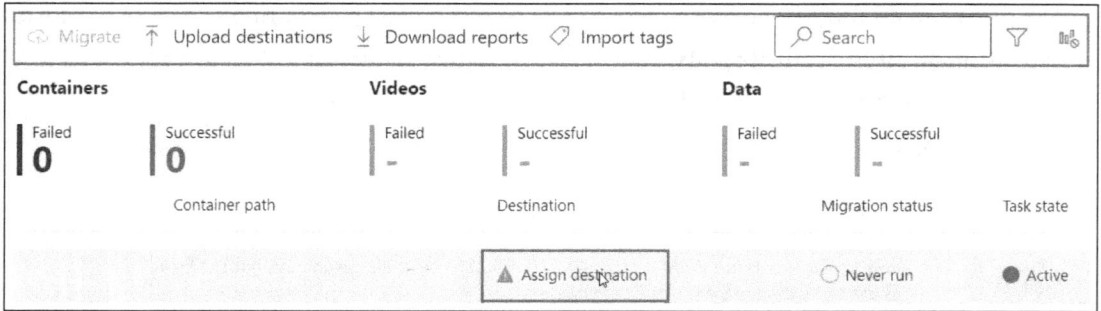

Figure 6.55: Navigation options and migration information list properties

4. Click on the warning message **Assign destination**. You will find properties in tabs like **Overview, Folders, Files, Data** as seen in *Figure 6.56*. Under the category tab **Overview,** click on the button **Edit** present below **Destination** property.

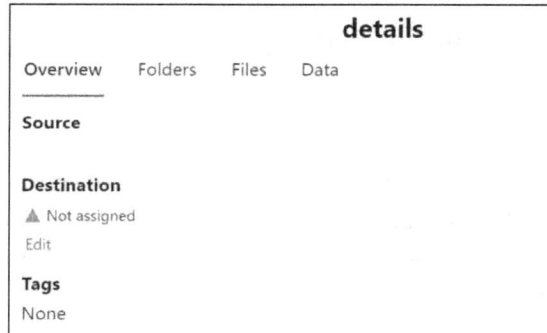

Figure 6.56: Item properties

5. You will get a window to select the destination path as **OneDrive** or **SharePoint**.

6. Select **OneDrive** as the destination path.

7. In the next field, **Select a OneDrive account** and enter your OneDrive account email address.

8. Select one folder or create a new folder in OneDrive and click on **Save path**, shown as follows:

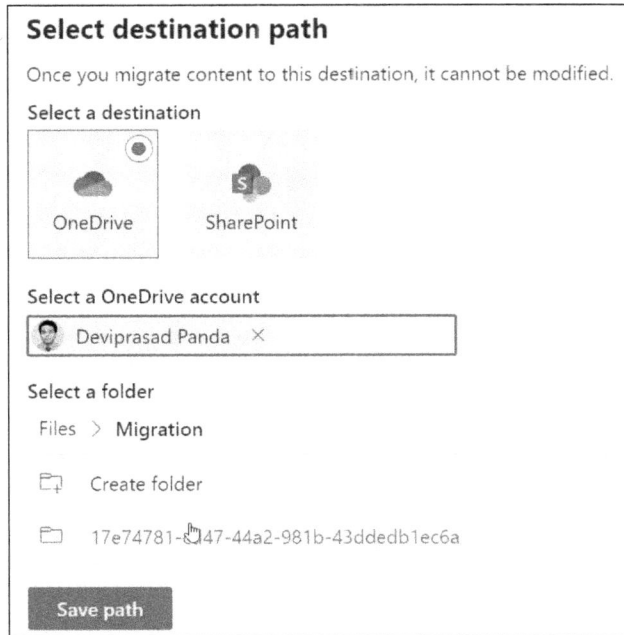

Figure 6.57: *Select OneDrive as destination path*

9. Once the destination path is selected for the containers, click on the option **Migrate**, as seen in *Figure 6.58*:

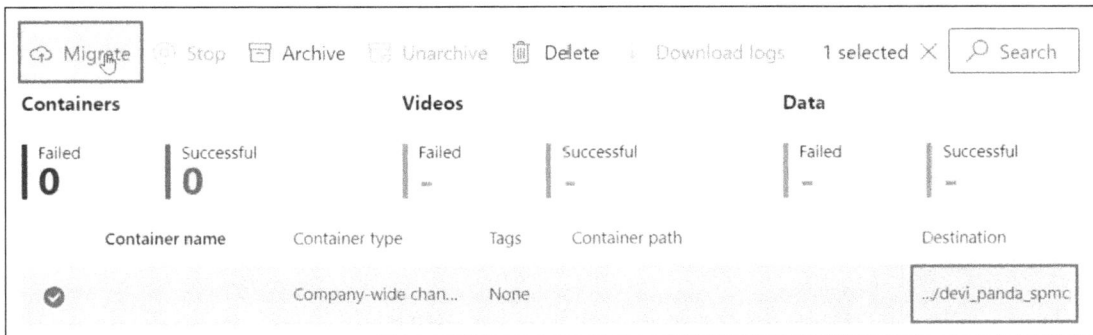

Figure 6.58: *Migrate option from navigation*

10. You will get a dialog box that contains **a Note** before proceeding to the final step in the migration process. Click on the button **Migrate** to start the migration.

Migrate

Note:

1. Some Stream (Classic) features may not be supported on Stream (on SharePoint). View supported features

   ⓘ Only some metadata migrate with videos. Learn more about it.

2. Migration transfers content from Stream (Classic) to assigned destinations on Stream (on SharePoint). These destination paths cannot be modified once migration begins for a container.

3. During migration, a video can be played in view mode only. Once a video, group or channel completely migrates, it will no longer be visible in Stream (Classic). In order to provide video status information, the video content will not be deleted from Classic until the service is fully deprecated. Learn more

[Migrate]   Cancel

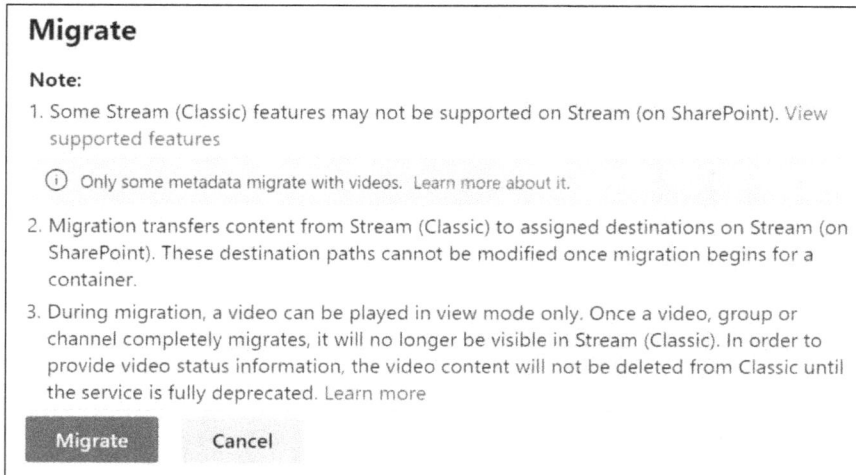

Figure 6.59: Migration note to confirm and proceed to start migration

11. Migration of content will start. The status of the column **Migration status** column will change from **Queued** to **In progress** to **Finalizing** to **Completed**.

12. Click on the container once the migration is completed. You will find details in four tabs like **Overview, Folders, Files, Data** with default tab selected as **Overview**.

13. The **Overview** tab hold information like **Source, Destination, Tags** as seen in *Figure 6.60*:

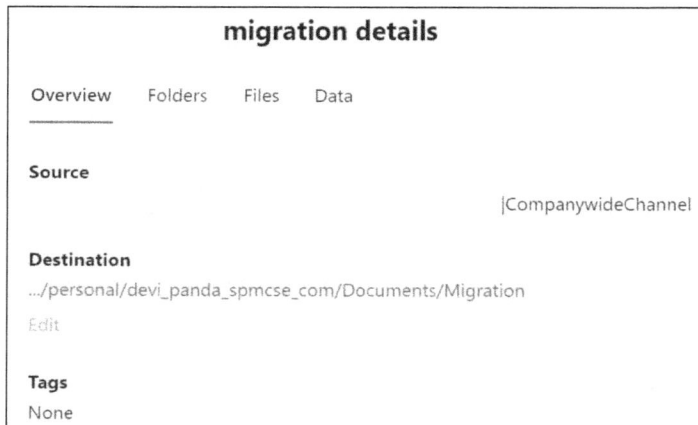

migration details

Overview   Folders   Files   Data
_____

Source

                                              |CompanywideChannel

Destination
.../personal/devi_panda_spmcse_com/Documents/Migration
Edit

Tags
None

Figure 6.60: Overview tab

14. Next, you will find **History** that contains information like **Last run, Scheduled start time, Date created, Total folders, Total files, Total data, Transaction ID, Task ID** as seen in *Figure 6.61*:

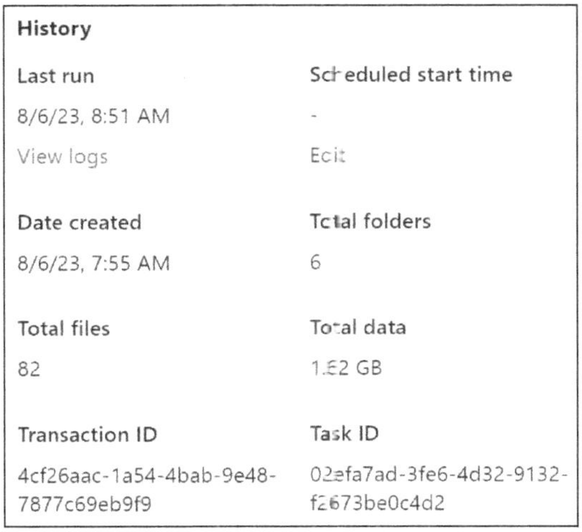

History

Last run	Scheduled start time
8/6/23, 8:51 AM	-
View logs	Edit
Date created	Total folders
8/6/23, 7:55 AM	6
Total files	Total data
82	1.52 GB
Transaction ID	Task ID
4cf26aac-1a54-4bab-9e48-7877c69eb9f9	02efa7ad-3fe6-4d32-9132-f2673be0c4d2

Figure 6.61: Migration history

15. The folders tab contains information related to **Failed** and **Successful** items. Under the category failed, you will find details like **Failed to list in stream, Failed to list in Microsoft 365, Failed to create in Microsoft 365**. Under the category **Successful,** you will find details like **Successfully listed in stream, Successfully listed in Microsoft 365, Successfully created in Microsoft 365** as seen in *Figure 6.62*:

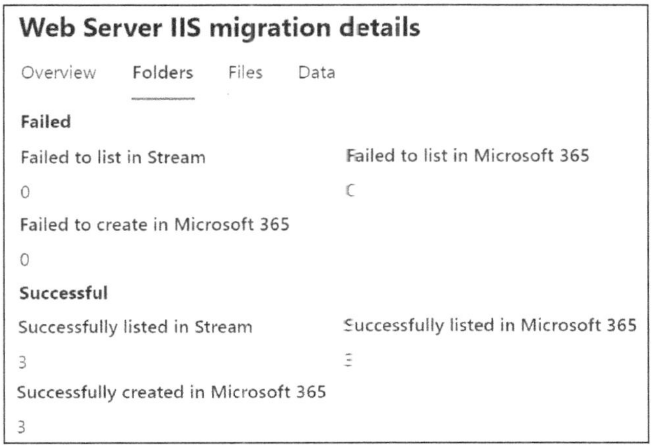

Web Server IIS migration details

Overview   Folders   Files   Data

Failed

Failed to list in Stream	Failed to list in Microsoft 365
0	C
Failed to create in Microsoft 365	
0	

Successful

Successfully listed in Stream	Successfully listed in Microsoft 365
3	3
Successfully created in Microsoft 365	
3	

Figure 6.62: Folders tab

16. The files tab contains information categorized as **Failed, Successful, Skipped**. Under the category **Failed**, you will find details like **Overall failures, Failed to downloaded from stream, Failed to upload to Microsoft 365, Failed during job processing**. Under the category **Successful**, you will find details like **Successfully**

downloaded from Stream, Successfully copied to Microsoft 365. Under the category **Skipped**, you will find the details like **Already copied or created by stream, Unsupported** as seen in *Figure 6.63*:

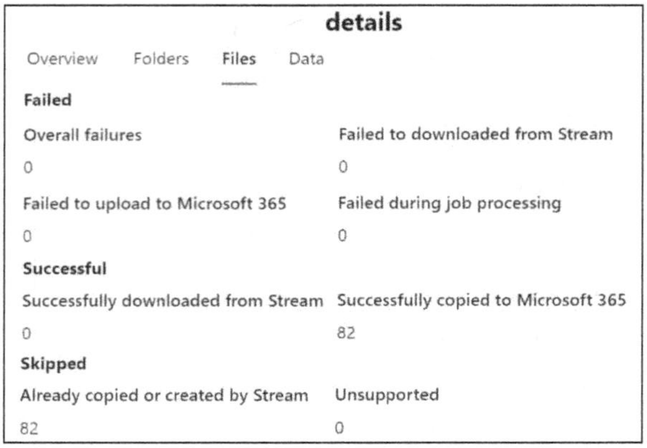

details	
Overview　　Folders　　**Files**　　Data	
Failed	
Overall failures	Failed to downloaded from Stream
0	0
Failed to upload to Microsoft 365	Failed during job processing
0	0
Successful	
Successfully downloaded from Stream	Successfully copied to Microsoft 365
0	82
Skipped	
Already copied or created by Stream	Unsupported
82	0

Figure 6.63: Files tab

17. The **Data** tab contains information categorized as **Failed, Successful, Skipped**. Under the category **Failed**, you will find details like **Overall failures, Failed to downloaded from stream, Failed to upload to Microsoft 365, Failed during job processing**. Under the category **Successful,** you will find details like **Successfully downloaded from stream, Successfully copied to Microsoft 365**. Under the category **Skipped**, you will find details like **Already copied or created by stream, Unsupported,** as seen in *Figure 6.64*:

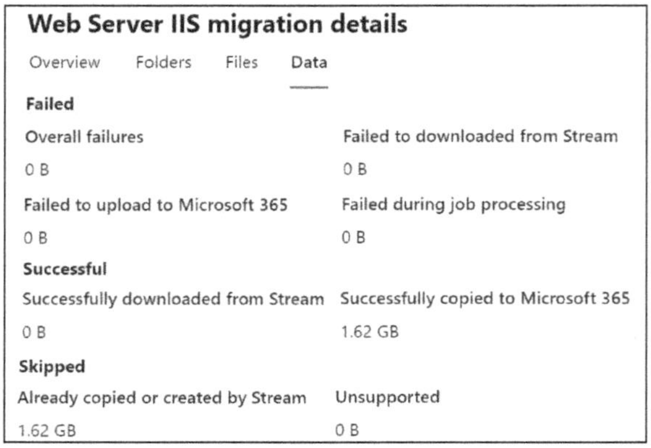

Web Server IIS migration details	
Overview　　Folders　　Files　　**Data**	
Failed	
Overall failures	Failed to downloaded from Stream
0 B	0 B
Failed to upload to Microsoft 365	Failed during job processing
0 B	0 B
Successful	
Successfully downloaded from Stream	Successfully copied to Microsoft 365
0 B	1.62 GB
Skipped	
Already copied or created by Stream	Unsupported
1.62 GB	0 B

Figure 6.64: Data tab

18. Similarly, you can transfer all contents discovered by container. You will get the summary in the **Migration** tab as per the following screenshot. This completes the migration of the stream classic contents to Microsoft 365.

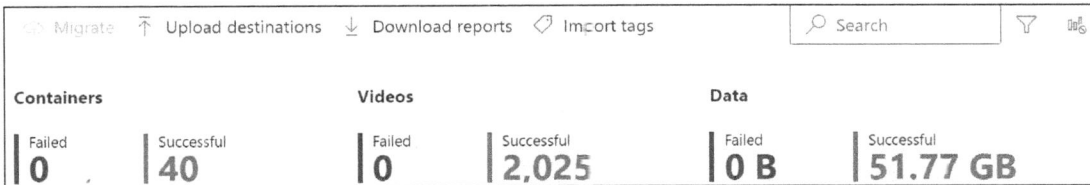

Figure 6.65: *Summary in the Migration tab*

Google Workspace to Microsoft 365 migration

Google Workspace is one of the migration features that provides a service to migrate content present in Google Workspace to Microsoft 365. Let us discuss step-by-step procedure to migrate Google Workspace content to Microsoft 365.

1. Navigate to the option **Migration** present under the left navigation in **SharePoint admin center**.

2. Identify the feature **Google Workspace** and click on the button **Get started** present below the feature, as seen in *Figure 6.66*:

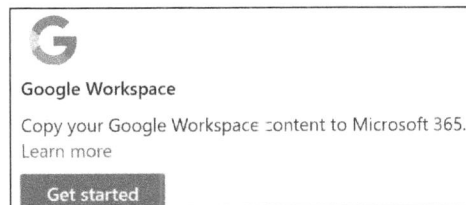

Figure 6.66: *Google Workspace get started*

3. You will be redirected to the **Connect to Google Workspace** dialog box. Click on the link **Install and authorize** as seen in *Figure 6.67*:

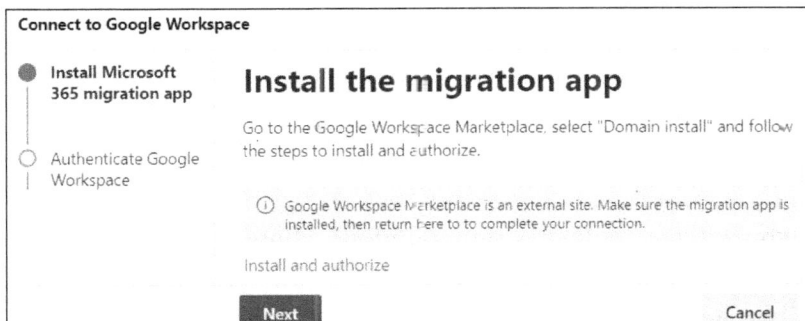

Figure 6.67: *Install Microsoft 365 migration app and authorize*

4. You will be redirected to the **Google Workspace marketplace** page to download and install the **Microsoft 365 migration app**. Click on the button **Admin install** as seen in *Figure 6.68*:

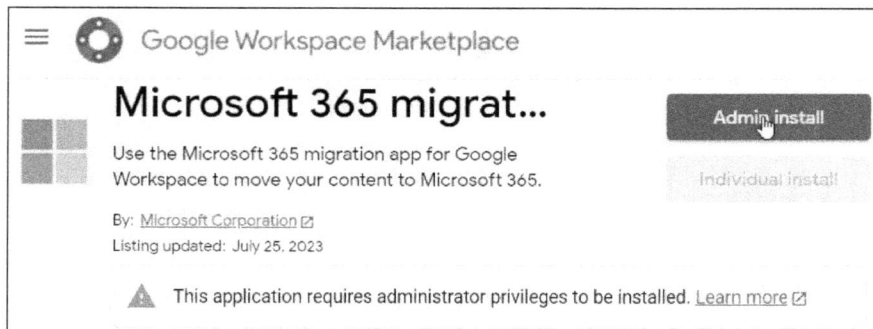

Figure 6.68: Admin installation

5. You will get **Admin install** pop up window, which includes additional information. Verify information and click on the button **Continue** as seen in *Figure 6.69*:

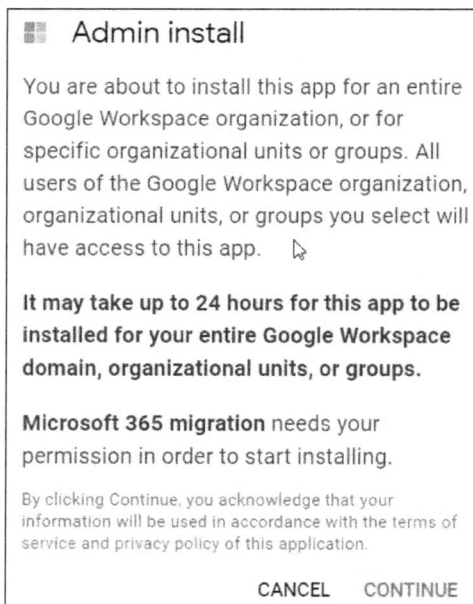

Figure 6.69: Continue towards installation

6. Next, you will get another pop-up window, **Allow data access**, to give permission for accessing data in the workspace. Select the check box related to terms and conditions and click on **Finish**. You will get a confirmation window that Microsoft 365 migration has been installed. Click on **Done** to finish the installation process.

7. Now switch to the migration wizard screen and click on the button **Next** as seen in *Figure 6.70*:

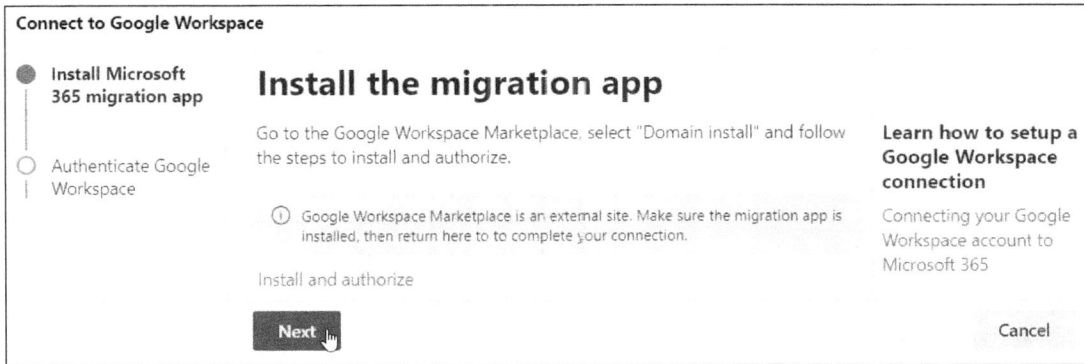

Connect to Google Workspace

● **Install Microsoft 365 migration app**

○ Authenticate Google Workspace

Install the migration app

Go to the Google Workspace Marketplace, select "Domain install" and follow the steps to install and authorize.

ⓘ Google Workspace Marketplace is an external site. Make sure the migration app is installed, then return here to to complete your connection.

Install and authorize

Next

Learn how to setup a Google Workspace connection

Connecting your Google Workspace account to Microsoft 365

Cancel

Figure 6.70: Proceed to install and authorize by clicking next

8. An authentication link will be generated, and you will get the link for signing into Google Workspace. Click on the button **Sign in to Google Workspace** from the next window, as seen in *Figure 6.71*:

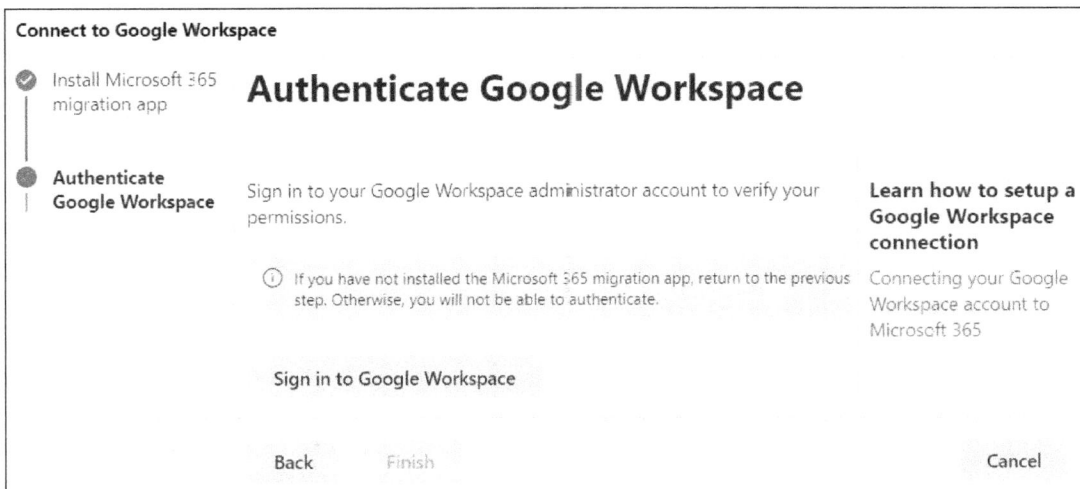

Connect to Google Workspace

✓ Install Microsoft 365 migration app

● **Authenticate Google Workspace**

Authenticate Google Workspace

Sign in to your Google Workspace administrator account to verify your permissions.

ⓘ If you have not installed the Microsoft 365 migration app, return to the previous step. Otherwise, you will not be able to authenticate.

Sign in to Google Workspace

Back   Finish

Learn how to setup a Google Workspace connection

Connecting your Google Workspace account to Microsoft 365

Cancel

Figure 6.71: Sign in to Google Workspace

9. Select an account to continue migration. You will get confirmation that the account is **Connected to Google Workspace** as seen in *Figure 6.72*. Click on the button **Finish**.

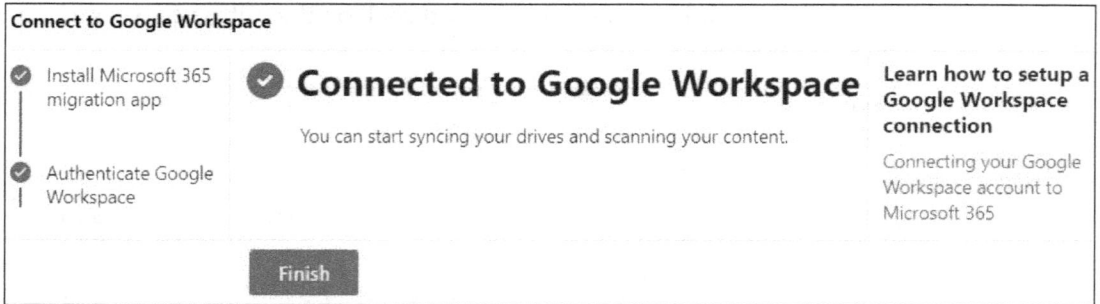

Figure 6.72: Connected to Google Workspace

10. You will be redirected to the **GooleWorkspaceMigration** page. There will be three tabs in the **GooleWorkspaceMigration** page, like **Overview, Drives, Drive migrations,** with the **Overview** tab selected by default, as seen in *Figure 6.73*. You will find information categories like **Scan result, Copy to Drive migrations, Destination planning, Migration Progress, Migration result.**

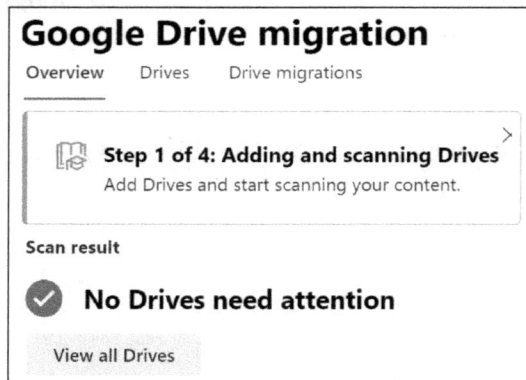

Figure 6.73: Google drive overview tab

11. Click on the tab **Drives.** You will get navigation options like **Add Drives, Scan, Stop scan, Download reports, Import tags, Copy to Drive migrations, Change Drive, Delete,** as seen in *Figure 6.74*. Few options will be available initially, and a few will be available on selecting the drive, once available.

12. Click on **Add Drivers** from the navigation.

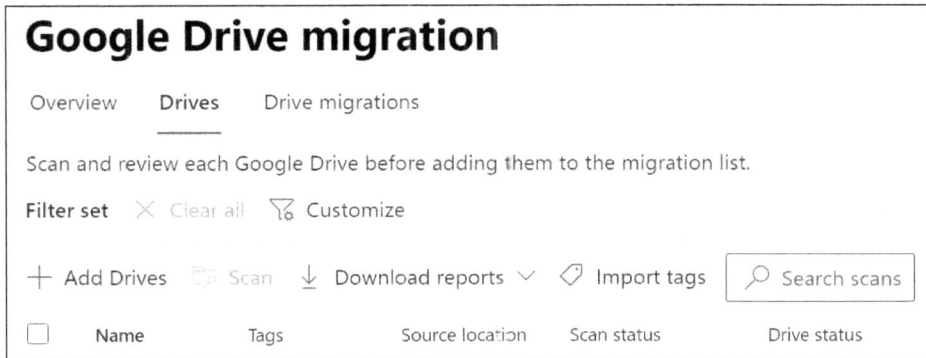

Figure 6.74: Drives tab

13. You will get three options like **All new Drives**, **Single Drive**, and **Multiple specific Drives**. If you select the first option, **All new Drives**, then all the personal and shared drives will be scanned automatically.

14. If you are selecting the second option **Single Drive**, then you need to enter the folder path as per the following shared format:

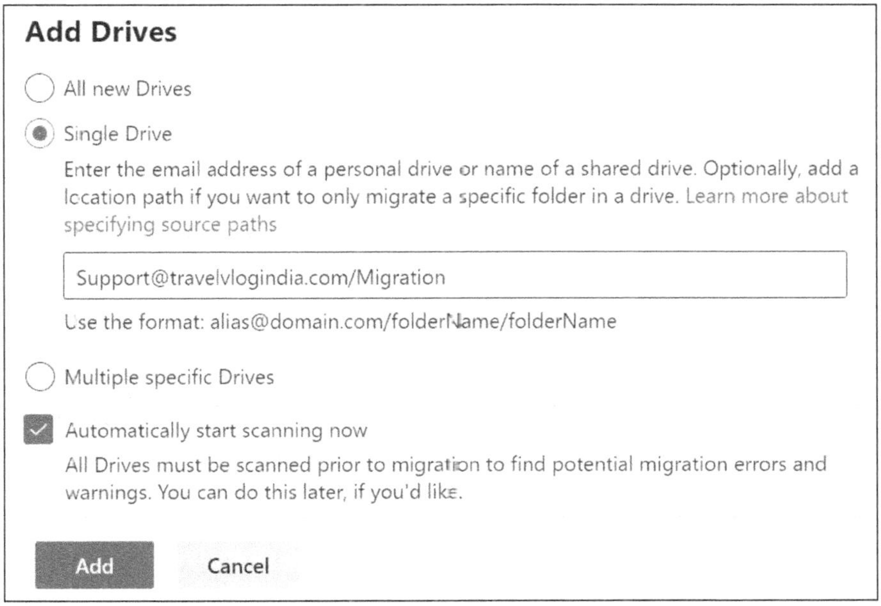

Figure 6.75: Add single drive

15. Select the option **Multiple specific Drives** if you want to include multiple drives. You can download the CSV template as seen in *Figure 6.76*. Fill in the template and upload it.

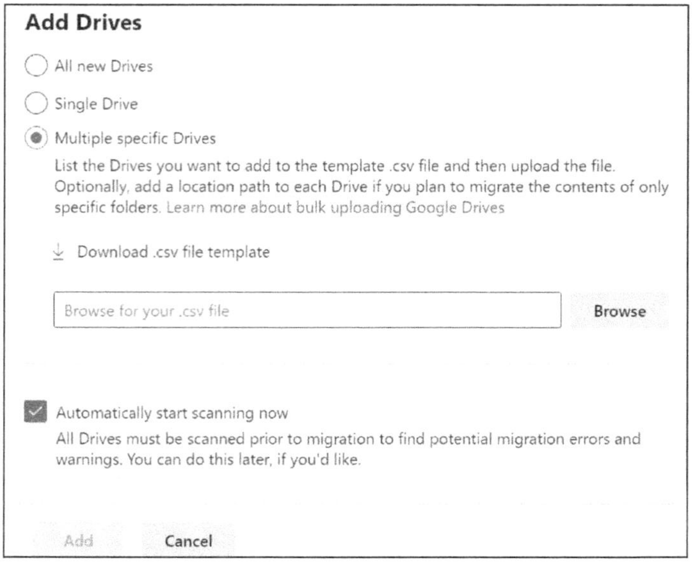

Add Drives

○ All new Drives

○ Single Drive

● Multiple specific Drives

List the Drives you want to add to the template .csv file and then upload the file. Optionally, add a location path to each Drive if you plan to migrate the contents of only specific folders. Learn more about bulk uploading Google Drives

↓ Download .csv file template

| Browse for your .csv file | Browse |

☑ Automatically start scanning now

All Drives must be scanned prior to migration to find potential migration errors and warnings. You can do this later, if you'd like.

Add   Cancel

Figure 6.76: Add multiple specific drives

16. Once drives are added, select the drive from the list and click on **Scan** from navigation as seen in *Figure 6.76*:

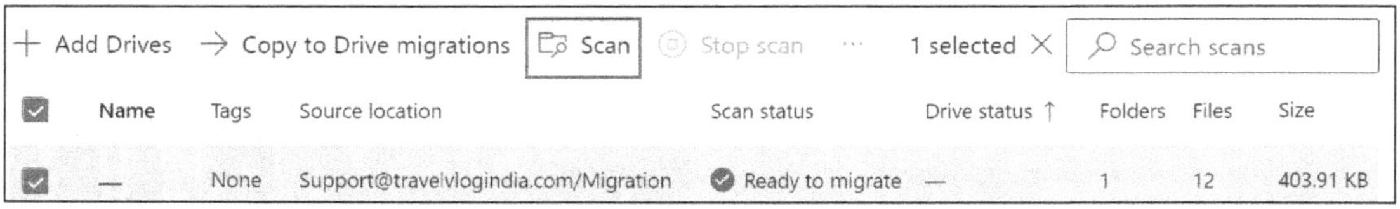

+ Add Drives	→ Copy to Drive migrations	🗗 Scan	⊘ Stop scan	···	1 selected ✕	🔍 Search scans

	Name	Tags	Source location	Scan status	Drive status ↑	Folders	Files	Size
☑	—	None	Support@travelvlogindia.com/Migration	✅ Ready to migrate	—	1	12	403.91 KB

Figure 6.77: Scan

17. Scanning and content discovery will start, and the status will change to completed once finished. A summary will be generated and will be available under the table summary. You will find details like **Volume**, **Files and folder count** under the category **Overview**. Any **Errors**, **Warnings**, or **Ready** to migrate status will be displayed in color code under the category **Migration readiness** as seen in *Figure 6.78*:

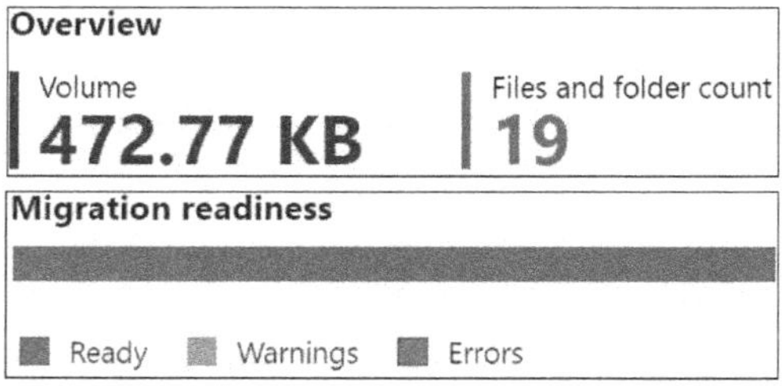

Overview

Volume	Files and folder count
472.77 KB	**19**

Migration readiness

⬛ Ready   ⬛ Warnings   ⬛ Errors

Figure 6.78: Overview and Migration readiness

18. Item counts in the drives based on sizes will be found under the category **Drive item counts**, and size of the drives based on size will be found under the category **Drive sizes** in graphical format and color codes, as seen in *Figure 6.79*:

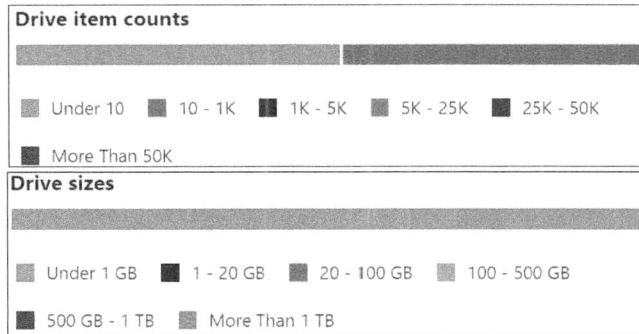

Figure 6.79: Drive items counts and drive size

19. You can download the scan reports by following the option **Download reports** from the navigation. Refer to *Figure 6.80*. You will get reports like **Detailed** report and **Summary** report as seen in the following figure:

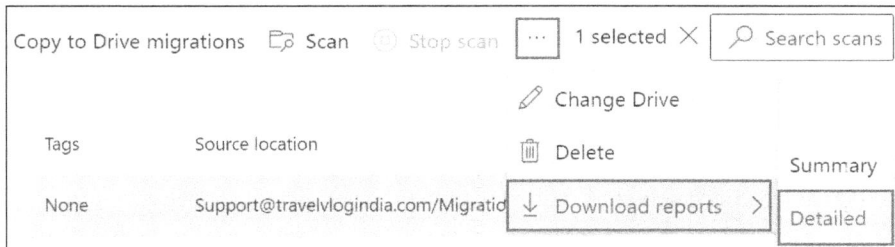

Figure 6.80: Download detailed reports

20. If you check the detailed report, you will find details like **taskid**, **transactionid**, **name**, **sourcepath**, **operationstep**, **status**, **resultcode**, **failurereason**, **fullpath**, **sourcepathdepth**, **sourcebasename**, **sourceextension**, **sourcetype**, **sourcesize**, **sourceaclstotal**, **sourceaclsunique**, **destinationpath**, **destinationpathdepth**, **destinationbasename**, **destinationextension**, **destinationlocation**, **destinationtype**, and **destinationsize**, as seen in *Figure 6.81*:

TaskId	TransactionId	Name	SourcePath	OperationStep	Status	ResultCode	FailureReason
d293c9ab-ca03-49d6-a93c-ef2f4ae890e9	195ad06c-e13b-43bf-8941-C229481eab30		Support@travelvlogindia.com/Migration	item/scan	Success	none	

FullPath	SourcePathDepth	SourceBasename	SourceExtension	SourceType	SourceSize	SourceAclsTotal
/1_ol6B7-vOKmpv1NMvx3Q8xA.jpg	1	1_ol6B7-vOKmpv1NMvx3Q8xA.jpg	jpg	file	157125	1

SourceAclsUnique	DestinationPath	DestinationPathDepth	DestinationBasename	DestinationExtension	DestinationLocation	DestinationType	DestinationSize
0		0					0

Figure 6.81: Detailed report properties

21. If you download the **Summary** report, you will get similar kinds of reports as discussed before in stream classic content migration.

22. Now, you select the drive and click on the option **Copy to Drive Migrations** from the navigation.

23. You will get a new dialog to select the **Migration settings**. You will get two options, **User default settings** and **Custom settings,** as shown in *Figure 6.82*:

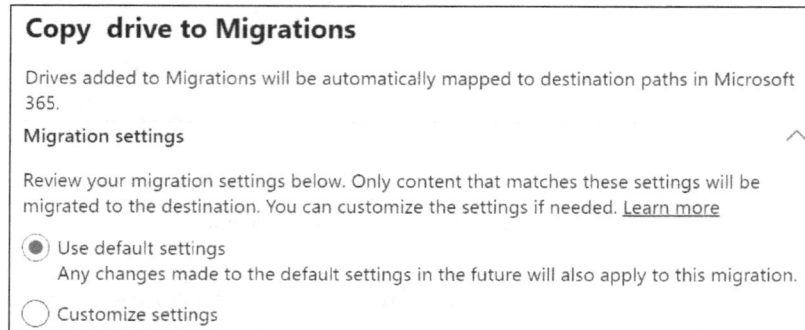

Copy drive to Migrations

Drives added to Migrations will be automatically mapped to destination paths in Microsoft 365.

Migration settings   ⌃

Review your migration settings below. Only content that matches these settings will be migrated to the destination. You can customize the settings if needed. Learn more

◉ Use default settings
  Any changes made to the default settings in the future will also apply to this migration.

◯ Customize settings

Figure 6.82: Use default settings in copy drive to migration

24. If you are selecting the option, **Use default settings,** then you will find the option **Migrate items with invalid characters** is selected as migrate and replace invalid characters with "_". Other options like **Exclude file by extension, Exclude folders by name, Exclude file and folders by date created, Exclude files and folders by date modified** are selected as none excluded, shown as follows:

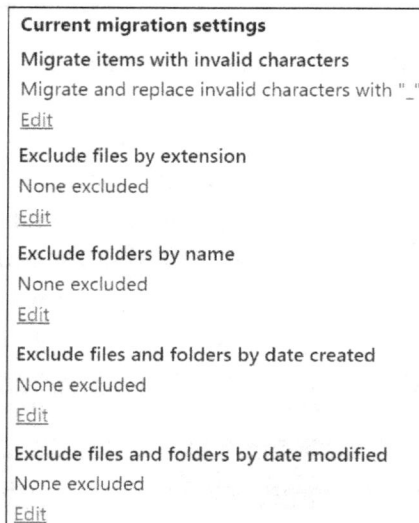

Current migration settings

Migrate items with invalid characters
Migrate and replace invalid characters with "_"
Edit

Exclude files by extension
None excluded
Edit

Exclude folders by name
None excluded
Edit

Exclude files and folders by date created
None excluded
Edit

Exclude files and folders by date modified
None excluded
Edit

Figure 6.83: Migration settings

25. If you are selecting the option **Custom settings,** then you will find the option **Edit** on each category of options, as seen in the preceding *Figure 6.83*. Click on **Edit** present under the option **Migrate items with invalid characters**. It will switch to edit mode. You can select the option **Migrate and replace invalid characters with**, and enter a valid character to be replaced with, as seen in *Figure 6.84*. Then click on the button **Use this setting** to apply the selection.

Migrate items with invalid characters

SharePoint reserves the use of certain characters and disallows them from being used in file or folder names. However, these characters can be automatically replaced with another valid character to avoid migration failures. Invalid characters include " * : < > ? / \ |
Learn more about the complete list of invalid characters and other limitations

ⓘ We recommend replacing invalid name characters to minimize migration failures and maximize the number of files and folders migrated.

Migrate items with invalid characters

◯ Do not migrate items with invalid characters

◉ Migrate and replace invalid characters with

[_] *

Only a single character can be used as a replacement.

[Use this setting]

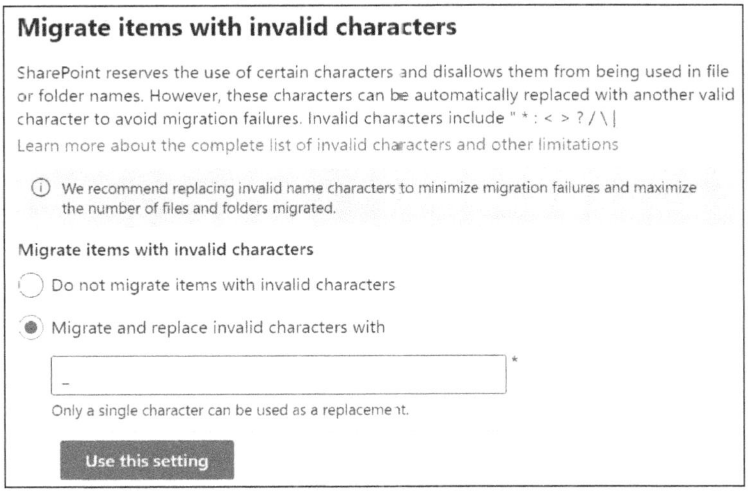

Figure 6.84: *Migrate items with invalid characters*

26. Click on **Edit** present under the option **Exclude files by extension**. It will switch to edit mode. You can select the option **Exclude some file extensions** and enter a file extension that you want to exclude. Click on **Add**. Then click on the button **Use this setting** to apply the selection as seen in *Figure 6.85*:

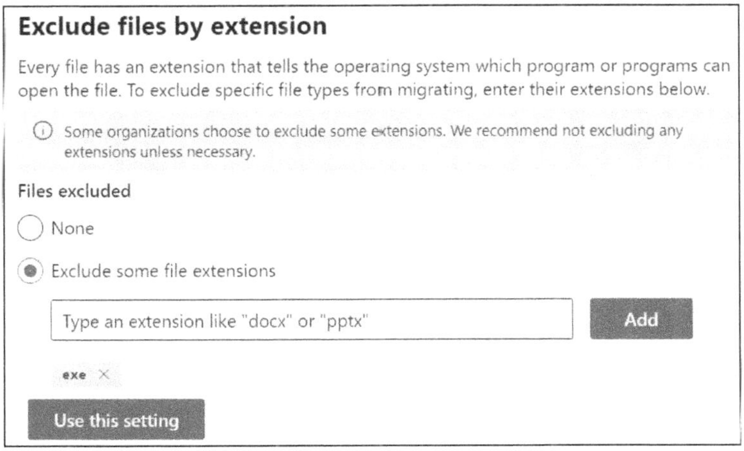

Exclude files by extension

Every file has an extension that tells the operating system which program or programs can open the file. To exclude specific file types from migrating, enter their extensions below.

ⓘ Some organizations choose to exclude some extensions. We recommend not excluding any extensions unless necessary.

Files excluded

◯ None

◉ Exclude some file extensions

[Type an extension like "docx" or "pptx"] [Add]

exe ✕

[Use this setting]

Figure 6.85: *Exclude files by extension*

27. Clicking on **Edit** present under the option **Exclude folders by name** will switch to edit mode. You can select the option **Exclude some folders** and enter the folder name that you want to exclude. Click on **Add**. Then click on the button **Use this setting** to apply the selection as seen in *Figure 6.86*:

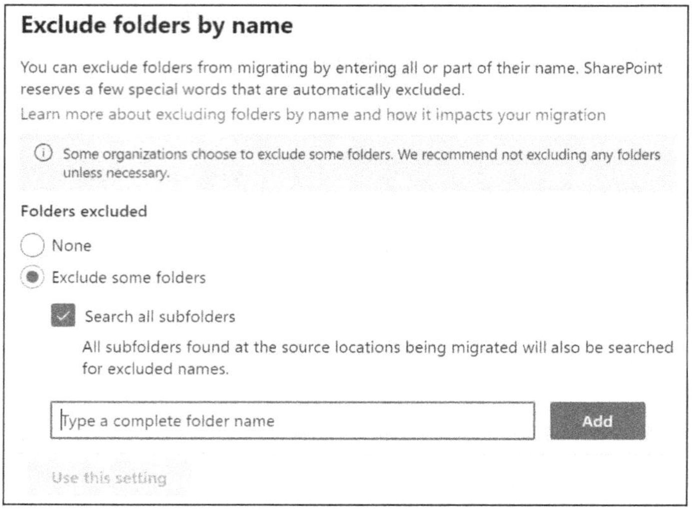

Figure 6.86: Exclude folders by name

28. Click on **Edit** present under the option **Exclude files and folders by date created**. It will switch to edit mode. You can select the option **Do not migrate files and folders outside this date range** and select **Earliest creation date** and **Latest creation date**. Then click on the button **Use this setting** to apply the selection, as seen in *Figure 6.87*:

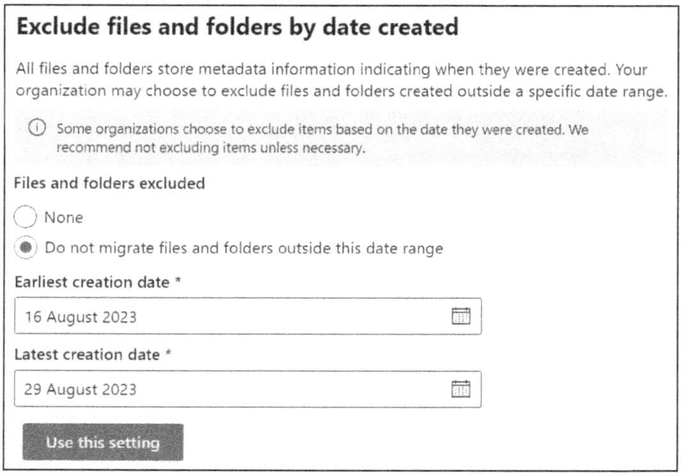

Figure 6.87: Exclude files and folders by date created

29. Similarly, you can select the option for category **Exclude files and folders by date modified**. Once all options are selected, then click on the option **Copy to Migrations**. You will get a confirmation like **Successfully copied** as seen in *Figure 6.88*. Click on the button **Go to Drive migrations**.

Figure 6.88: Successfully copied

30. You will be redirected to the third tab, drive migrations, and will find the status of column destination location as none found, as seen in *Figure 6.89*:

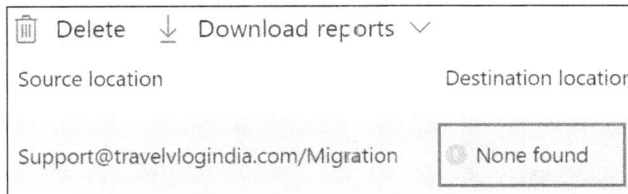

Figure 6.89: Destination location none found

31. Click on the drive. You will get a new dialog box with option tabs like **Overview, Folders, Files, Data, Settings** as seen in *Figure 6.90*. Click on **Edit** present under the field destination.

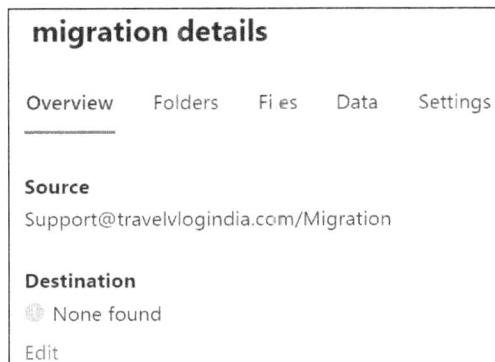

Figure 6.90: Migration details overview tab

32. You will get a new window, select the destination path, to select the destination path as **OneDrive**, **SharePoint**, or **Teams** as seen in *Figure 6.91*.

33. Select **OneDrive** as the destination. Enter an account under the field **Select a OneDrive account** and select one folder as the destination. Click on the button **Save path**.

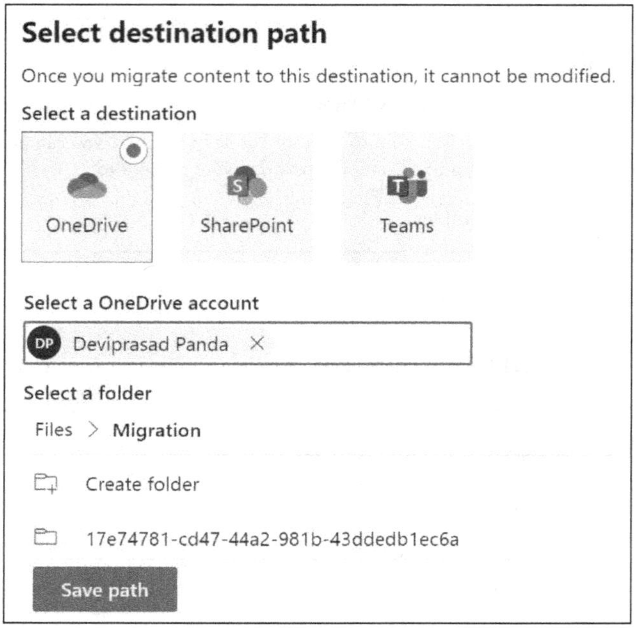

Figure 6.91: *Select OneDrive as destination*

34. Status of column **Destination location** will reflect a valid path now. Select the drive and click on the option **Migrate** from navigation. Refer to *Figure 6.92*:

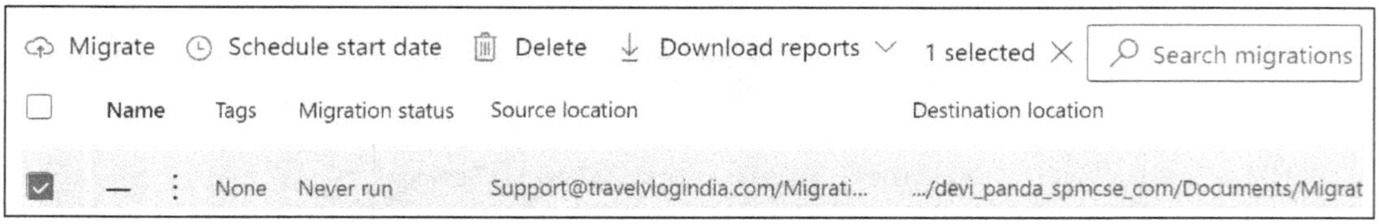

Figure 6.92: *Migration option in the navigation*

35. Click on the button **Migrate** from the next window. Migration will start and will be completed. Refer to *Figure 6.93*:

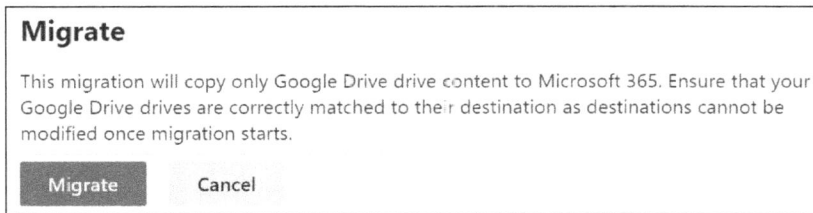

Figure 6.93: Click on Migrate button to start migration

36. Click on the drive once migration is completed. You will find details in the tabs **Overview, Folders, Files, Data. Settings**, like the details in Stream classic content migration.

We discussed migration from file share, stream, and Google Workspace. You will notice the common steps done in all cases are connect to source account, add source path, scan source content, copy to migrate, and migrate. We got scan reports for pre-analysis and migration. We got reports after the migration was completed. Similarly, we can migrate content from third-party applications like Egnyte, Box, and Dropbox to Microsoft 365. We can also migrate from SharePoint Server 2010, 2013, and 2016 to Microsoft 365. We will not discuss other applications here. The process and reports generated are nearly the same.

Conclusion

In this chapter, we had a glance at SharePoint migration. Understood the step-by-step procedure to install Microsoft 365 agent. We discussed the step-by-step procedure to migrate file share content to Microsoft 365. We also discussed how to migrate content from applications like Stream Classic Content, Google Workspace to Microsoft 365, and got information to migrate content from Egnyte, Box, and Dropbox to Microsoft 365.

In the next *Chapter 7, User Profiles Administration*, we will discuss administering the user profile service.

Points to remember

- Regular changes are applied in Office 365 and SharePoint Online. There may be changes in features with time.

Join our book's Discord space

Join the book's Discord Workspace for Latest updates, Offers, Tech happenings around the world, New Release and Sessions with the Authors:

https://discord.bpbonline.com

CHAPTER 7

User Profiles Administration

Introduction

In *Chapter 6, Migration*, we discussed how to migrate content from different data sources to Microsoft 365. In this chapter, we will discuss SharePoint user profiles and the settings available to manage user profiles. User profile is a service that holds user information of those who use SharePoint online. User profile is the central place to **Manage user properties**, **Manage user profiles**, **Manage audiences**, **Manage user permissions**, **Manage policies** and **Setup My Sites** in SharePoint online. This service is all about managing user information or properties using SharePoint. Any user accessing the SharePoint site must have a user profile present in the user profile service. Hence, it is very important to administer the user profile better. In this chapter, we will discuss the settings used to administer user profile and user properties.

Structure

In this chapter, we will discuss the following topics:

- User profiles under more features
- People management under user profiles
- My Site Settings management

Objectives

By the end of this chapter, you will get a clear understanding of user profiles in SharePoint. You will understand user properties and the step-by-step procedure to create and edit properties. You will get clarity on managing user profiles. You get a real-time view of managing audience, sub-types, and user permissions. You will get a clear understanding of the options available under My Site Settings to set up my sites and manage my sites.

User profiles under more features

Once you access SharePoint admin center, you will find an option named **More features** on the left navigation. Click on **More features**, and you will find SharePoint features or services like **User profiles**, **Search**, **Apps**, **BCS**, **Secure store**, **Records management**, **InfoPath**, **Hybrid picker**. So, User profiles is one of the services which is present under the left navigation More features. Click on the button **Open** present below the feature **User profiles**, as seen in the following figure:

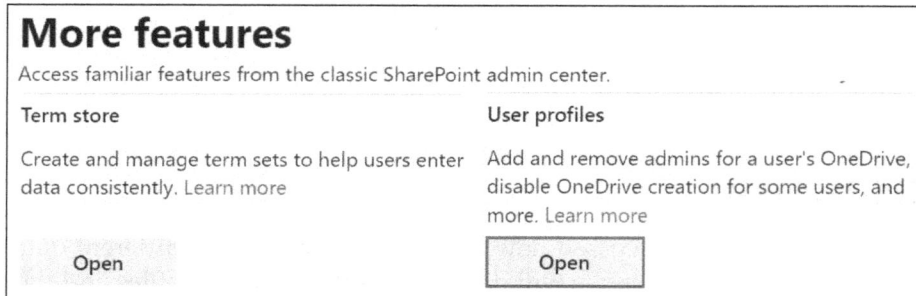

More features

Access familiar features from the classic SharePoint admin center.

Term store	User profiles
Create and manage term sets to help users enter data consistently. Learn more	Add and remove admins for a user's OneDrive, disable OneDrive creation for some users, and more. Learn more
Open	Open

Figure 7.1: User profiles under more features

People management under user profiles

Once you have accessed User profiles by clicking the button **Open** present below the feature **User profiles**, you will be redirected to the manage user profile service application page. You will find that the user profiles options are categorized as **People** and **My Site Settings**. Under the category **People**, you will find options, namely, **Manage User Properties**, **Manage User Profiles**, **Manage User Sub-types**, **Manage Audiences**, **Manage User Permissions**, and **Manage Policies**. The category **My Site Settings** holds the option **Setup My Sites**. Refer to *Figure 7.2*. Let us discuss the settings present under each category and understand how we can administer user profile.

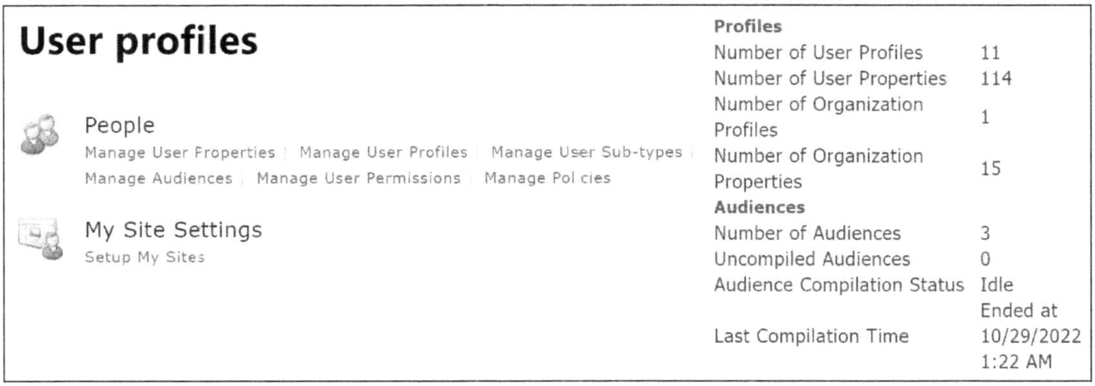

Figure 7.2: *User profiles settings*

Manage user properties

Manage user properties is the first option under the category people in user profile. This holds all the properties of a user. On clicking **Manage User Properties**, you will see all user properties like **Id**, **SID**, **First name**, **Last name**, **Work email**, **Mobile phone**, etc., as seen in *Figure 7.3*. User properties of specific types are categorized into sections. You will find that the user properties fall under sections like **Basic Information**, **Contact Information**, **Details**, **Delegation**, **Newsfeed Settings**, **Language and Region**, and **Custom Properties**.

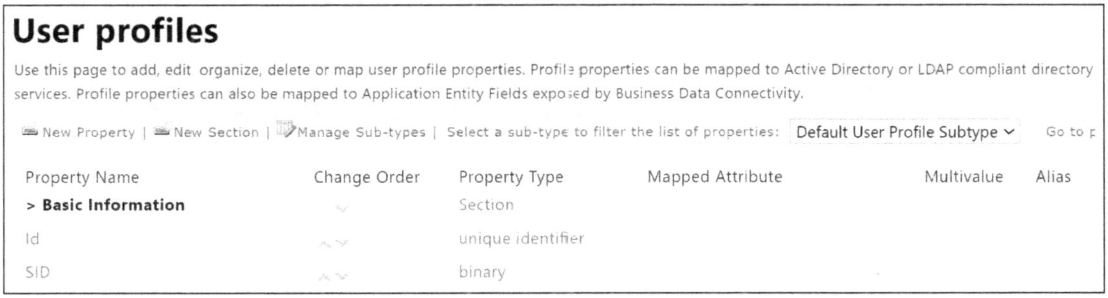

Figure 7.3: *Manage user properties*

Navigation is present at the top that holds options, namely, **New Property**, **New Section**, **Manage sub-types**, **Select a sub-type to filter the list of properties** to create new user profile properties, new sections, subtypes, and filter properties based on subtypes, respectively. Let us proceed to the following section to discuss the first navigation option, **New Property**, present under **Manage User Properties**, and understand the step-by-step procedure to create a new user property.

New property

SharePoint user profiles get synced from the Azure Active Directory to the SharePoint user profile service. User properties available in the Azure Active Directory will be available in the SharePoint user profile. Using the navigation option **New Property** from the SharePoint user profile end, we can create properties that will fall under the section **Custom Properties**. Let us perform the following steps to create a new user property:

1. Click on **New Property** from the navigation present under **Manage User Properties**.

2. You will find the category of options, namely, **Property Settings**, **Sub-type of Profile**, **User Description**, **Policy Settings**, **Edit Settings**, **Display Settings**, **Search Settings**, **Property Mapping for Synchronization**, and **Add New Mapping**.

3. The first category, **Property Settings**, holds information, namely, **Name**, **Display Name**, **Edit Languages**, **Type**, **Length**. Enter a unique name in the field **Name**. Enter **Display Name,** which will be visible to users.

4. Choose the data type from the option, **Type**, based on the type of property being created.

5. You can select the check box **Configure a Term Set to be used for this property** to use the team set.

6. Select one option from the **Sub-type of Profile**. Initially, the sub-type is selected as **Default User Profile Subtype**. Once you create new sub-types, those will be available here, and you will get more options to select. Refer to *Figure 7.4*:

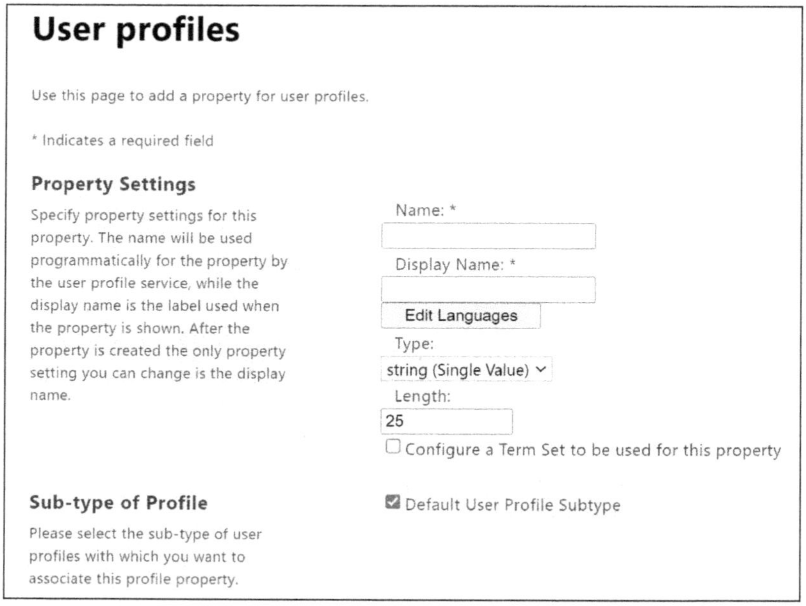

Figure 7.4: Create new user property and enter name, type

7. Enter property description in the field **User Description**. Refer to *Figure 7.5*.

8. Select one option out of **Required, Optional, Disabled** present under **Policy Setting** to apply the policy to user property.

9. Apply **Default Privacy Setting** by choosing **Only Me** or **Everyone**.

10. Select the checkbox option **User can override**, if you want to allow the user to change these settings.

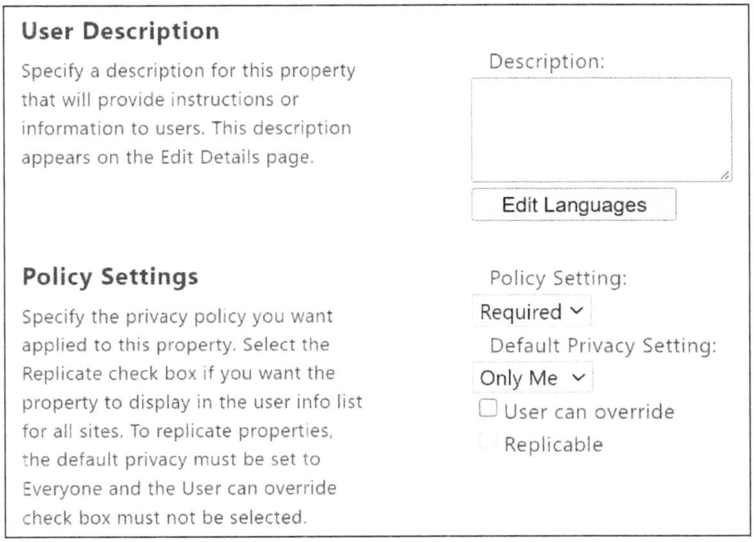

User Description

Specify a description for this property that will provide instructions or information to users. This description appears on the Edit Details page.

Description:

Edit Languages

Policy Settings

Specify the privacy policy you want applied to this property. Select the Replicate check box if you want the property to display in the user info list for all sites. To replicate properties, the default privacy must be set to Everyone and the User can override check box must not be selected.

Policy Setting:

Required ⌄

Default Privacy Setting:

Only Me ⌄

☐ User can override

☐ Replicable

Figure 7.5: Create new user property enter policy setting

11. Select the checkbox **Allow users to edit values for this property** present under **Edit Settings** if you want to allow users to change the value present in this property. Refer to *Figure 7.6*:

Edit Settings

Specify whether users can change the values for this property in their user profile. Users with the Manage Profile permission can edit any property value for any user.

☐ Allow users to edit values for this property

Figure 7.6: Create New User Property Select Edit Settings

12. Select the option present under **Display Settings** to configure the view settings of the property on My Site profile page. Select the checkbox **Show on the Edit Details page** to view the property in **Edit Details** page. Refer to *Figure 7.7*:

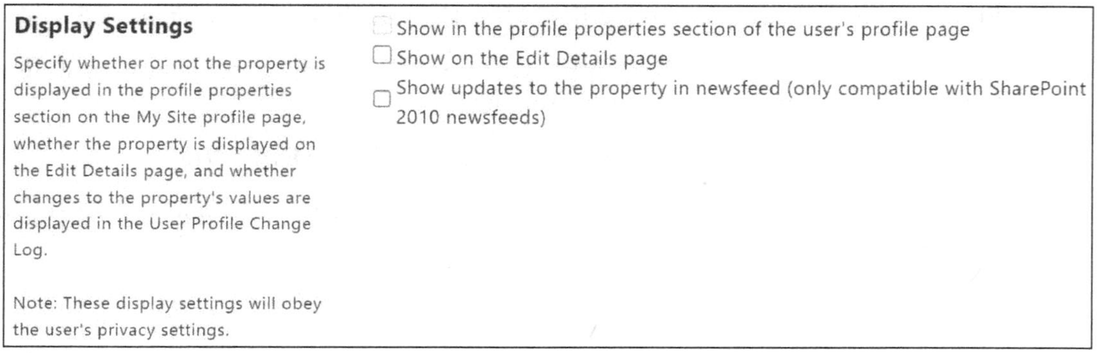

Display Settings

Specify whether or not the property is displayed in the profile properties section on the My Site profile page, whether the property is displayed on the Edit Details page, and whether changes to the property's values are displayed in the User Profile Change Log.

Note: These display settings will obey the user's privacy settings.

☐ Show in the profile properties section of the user's profile page
☐ Show on the Edit Details page
☐ Show updates to the property in newsfeed (only compatible with SharePoint 2010 newsfeeds)

Figure 7.7: Create new user property choose display settings

13. Select the checkbox **Indexed** to include the property under the search result applicable for all user profiles matching the property. Refer to *Figure 7.8*:

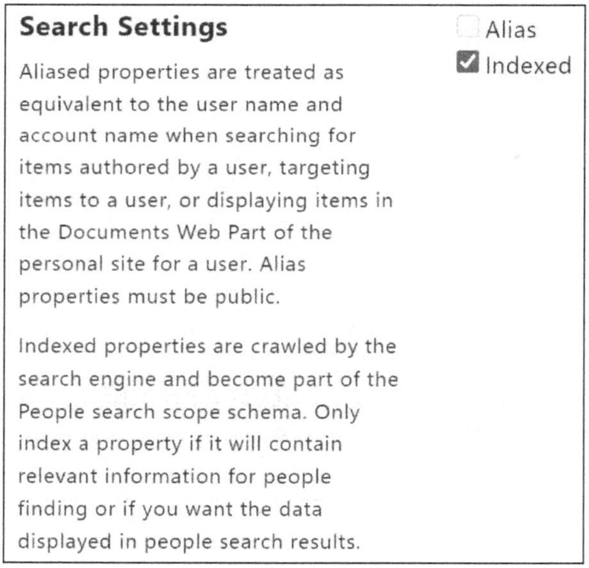

Search Settings

Aliased properties are treated as equivalent to the user name and account name when searching for items authored by a user, targeting items to a user, or displaying items in the Documents Web Part of the personal site for a user. Alias properties must be public.

Indexed properties are crawled by the search engine and become part of the People search scope schema. Only index a property if it will contain relevant information for people finding or if you want the data displayed in people search results.

☐ Alias
☑ Indexed

Figure 7.8: Create new user property choose search settings

14. Keep the rest of the properties mapping for synchronization and add new mapping as default, and click **OK**. Refer to *Figure 7.9*:

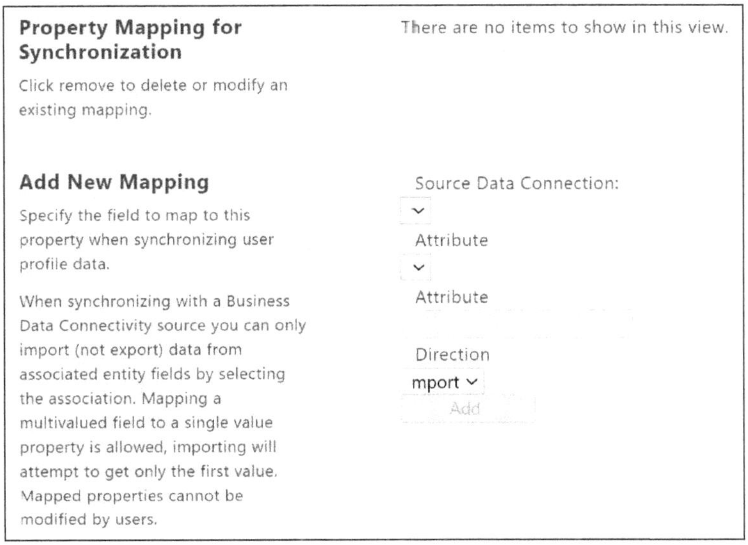

Property Mapping for Synchronization

Click remove to delete or modify an existing mapping.

There are no items to show in this view.

Add New Mapping

Specify the field to map to this property when synchronizing user profile data.

When synchronizing with a Business Data Connectivity source you can only import (not export) data from associated entity fields by selecting the association. Mapping a multivalued field to a single value property is allowed, importing will attempt to get only the first value. Mapped properties cannot be modified by users.

Source Data Connection:

⌄

Attribute

⌄

Attribute

Direction

mport ⌄

Add

Figure 7.9: Property mapping

15. You will find the new property created and added under the section **Custom Properties**. Refer to *Figure 7.10*.

16. You can edit or delete the property created. Select the drop-down icon present next to the property and click on **Edit** to edit it. Select the option **Delete** from drop-down if you want to delete the custom property.

> Custom Properties

OfficeGraphEnabled ▾

SPS-UserType 🗐 Edit

SPS-HideFromAddressLists ✕ Delete

Figure 7.10: Custom user property

We discussed the first navigation option, **New Property**, present under **Manage User Properties**. Let us proceed to the next section to discuss the second navigation option, **Manage Sub-types**, present under **Manage User Properties**, and understand the step-by-step procedure to create and manage sub-types.

Manage sub-types

While creating the new property above, we selected one sub-type of profile as described in *Step 6* above. We can create and manage sub-types using this option. This is the second navigation option present under Manage User Properties. Let us perform the following steps to understand the different options available under manage sub-types:

1. Click on **Manage Sub-types** from the navigation present under **Manage User Properties**.

2. You will be redirected to the **Manage Subtypes** page.

3. You will find options to create or remove sub-types following the option create new sub-types or remove existing sub-types.

4. Enter details like **Name for sub-type** and **Display Name for sub-type** present under the new sub-types.

5. Click on **Create** to create the new sub-type, shown as follows:

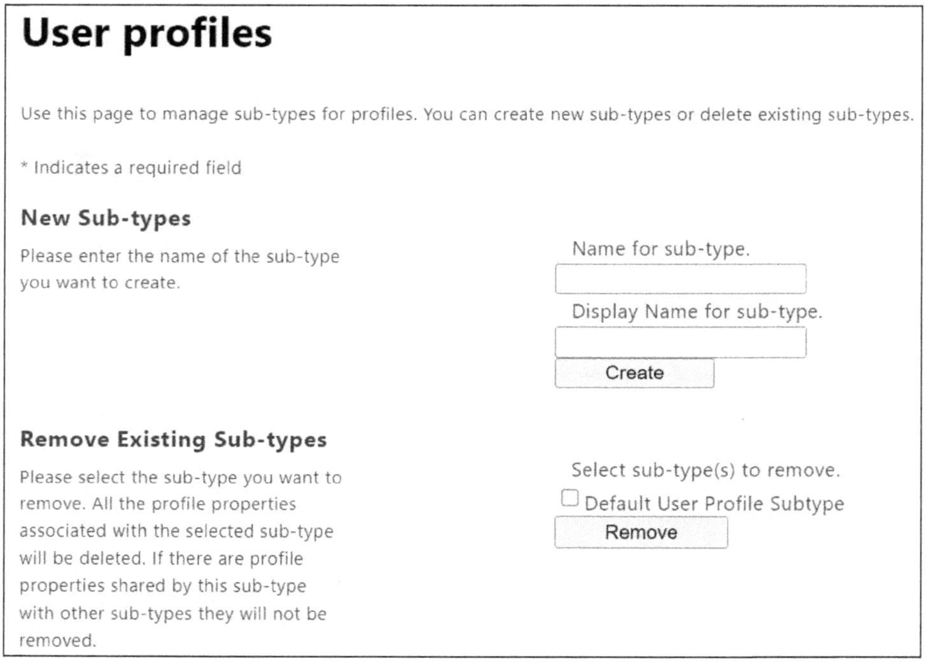

User profiles

Use this page to manage sub-types for profiles. You can create new sub-types or delete existing sub-types.

* Indicates a required field

New Sub-types

Please enter the name of the sub-type you want to create.

Name for sub-type.

Display Name for sub-type.

Create

Remove Existing Sub-types

Please select the sub-type you want to remove. All the profile properties associated with the selected sub-type will be deleted. If there are profile properties shared by this sub-type with other sub-types they will not be removed.

Select sub-type(s) to remove.
☐ Default User Profile Subtype
Remove

Figure 7.11: Create Sub-type

6. You will notice the new sub-type created.

7. The next time you open **Manage Sub-types** from navigation, you will see the new sub-type available under **Remove Existing Sub-types,** as seen in *Figure 7.11*.

8. Select one of the sub-types and click on **Remove** to delete the sub-type.

9. If there are multiple sub-types present, then you will find the option to choose one sub-type while creating a new user profile property, as seen in the following figure:

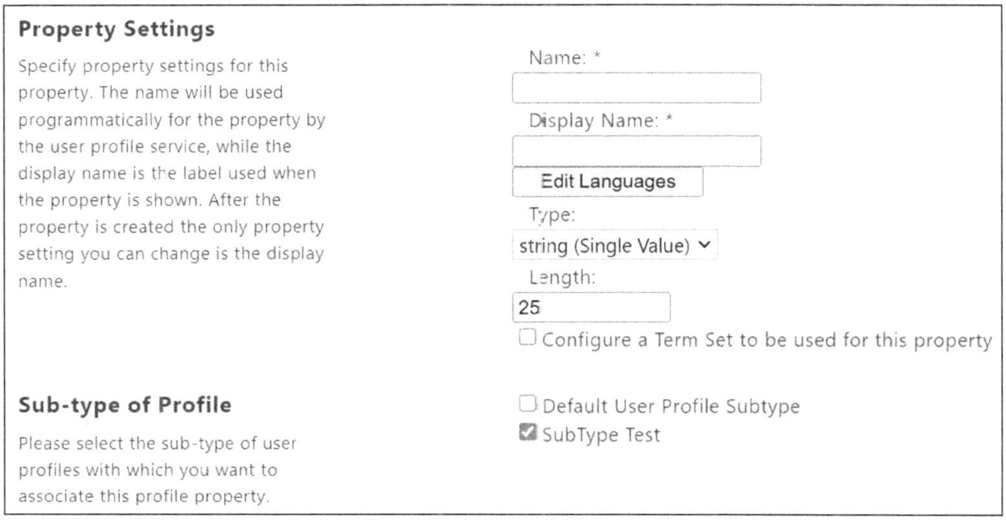

Property Settings

Specify property settings for this
property. The name will be used
programmatically for the property by
the user profile service, while the
display name is the label used when
the property is shown. After the
property is created the only property
setting you can change is the display
name.

Name: *

Display Name: *

Edit Languages

Type:

string (Single Value) ⌄

Length:

25

☐ Configure a Term Set to be used for this property

Sub-type of Profile

Please select the sub-type of user
profiles with which you want to
associate this profile property.

☐ Default User Profile Subtype
☑ SubType Test

Figure 7.12: *Sub-type option while creating new user property*

10. Under the navigation bar present within **Manage User Properties**, there is an option select a sub-type to filter the list of properties. The new sub-type will be added there so that properties can be filtered based on the sub-type. Refer to *Figure 7.13*:

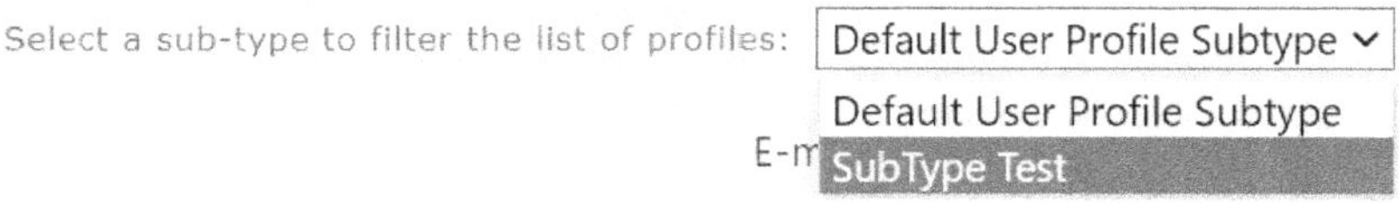

Select a sub-type to filter the list of profiles: Default User Profile Subtype ⌄

Default User Profile Subtype

E-m SubType Test

Figure 7.13: *Sub-type available under select a sub-type to filter the list of properties*

We discussed the second navigation option, Manage Sub-types, present under Manage User Properties. Let us proceed to the following section to discuss the third navigation option **New Section**, present under **Manage User Properties**, and understand the step-by-step procedure to create a new section.

New section

User profile properties are categorized into sections. Each section contains a specific type of property. We can create one custom section using the option new section present in the navigation. Let us perform the following steps to create a new section:

1. Click on **New Section** from the navigation present under **Manage User Properties**.

2. Enter the new section **Name** and **Display name**.

3. Choose one profile sub-type and click on **OK**. A new section will be added. Refer to *Figure 7.14*:

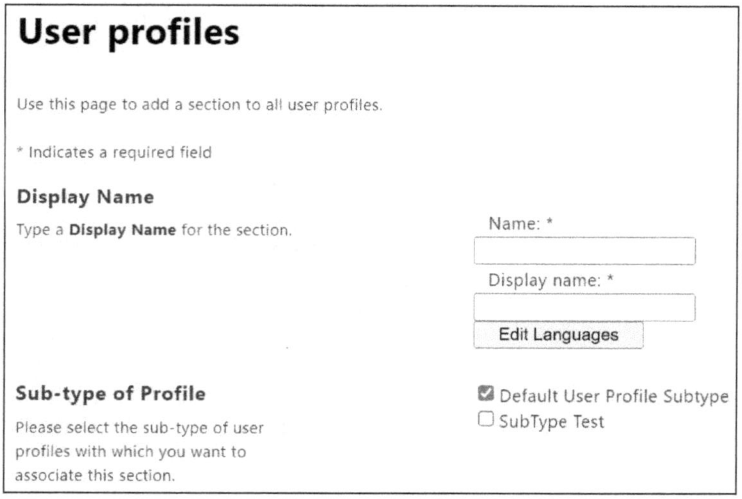

Figure 7.14: New section

We discussed the third navigation option, **New section**, present under Manage User Properties. So, we have covered the important options present under Manage User properties. This completes the first category of options present under People in User Profiles. Let us proceed to the next section to discuss the second category of options, Manage user Profiles present under People in user Profiles.

Manage user profiles

Manage user profiles is the second setting in the user profile service present under the category, **People**. Using this setting, the administrator can find the user profile, edit my profile, delete the profile, manage the personal site, and permissions. Let us discuss the option manage user profiles in detail to understand better.

Find profile

The number of users present in the user profile will be very high. There should be an option to quickly find user profile. The find profiles option is used to search the user present in the tenant. Let us perform the following steps to find a user profile:

1. Click on **Manage User Profile** present under the category **People**. You will be redirected to the profile management page. You will find a search box field named **Find Profiles**. Refer to *Figure 7.15*.

2. Enter the name, mail, or any relevant word and click on **Find**.

3. You will get user profiles present that match the search term.

4. You will find user profile columns like **Account name**, **Preferred name**, **E-mail address**. Refer to the *Figure 7.15*:

User profiles

Use this page to manage the user profiles in this User Profile Service Application. From this page you can also manage a user's personal site.

Total number of profiles: 11

Find profiles [deviprasad panda] [Find]

🖙 New Profile | ✕ Delete | View: [Active Profiles ∨] | 📝 Manage Sub-types | Select a sub-type to filter the list of profiles: [Default User Profile Subtype]

	Account name	Preferred name	E-mail address
☐	i:0#.f|membership|devi.panda@spmcse.com	Dev prasad Panda	Devi.Panda@spmcse.com

Figure 7.15: Find user profile

View

Under manage user profiles page navigation, you will find a drop-down option named **View**. Click on the drop-down and you will find two options, **Active Profiles** and **Profile Missing from Import**, to filter the user profile as seen in *Figure 7.16*. Click on the option **Active Profiles** to see active profiles. Click on the option **Profile Missing from Import** to see user profiles missing from import.

Find profiles [d]   [Find]

🖙 New Profile | ✕ Delete | View: [Active Profiles ∨]

 Account name

> Active Profiles
> **Profiles Missing from Import**

Figure 7.16: View user profile

Select a sub-type to filter

Under manage user profiles page navigation, you will find one drop-down option named **Select a sub-type to filter the list of profiles**. You can click on that option to filter user profiles based on the sub-type. Refer to *Figure 7.17*:

Select a sub-type to filter the list of properties: [Default User Profile Subtype ∨]

Property Type

> Default User Profile Subtype
> **SubType Test**

Figure 7.17: Select a sub-type to filter the list of profiles

Edit my profile

Edit my profile option allows you to make any change in user property details. Let us perform the following steps to edit My Profile:

1. Find the user profile as discussed in the previous section under the section **Find Profiles**.

2. You will get user profiles as a search result.

3. Once you hover over any user profile, you will notice one drop-down option on the side of that profile. Click on that drop-down option.

4. You will find drop-down options like **Edit My Profile**, **Delete**, **Manage Personal Site**, and **Manage site collection owners**. Click on the option **Edit My Profile**. Refer to *Figure 7.18*:

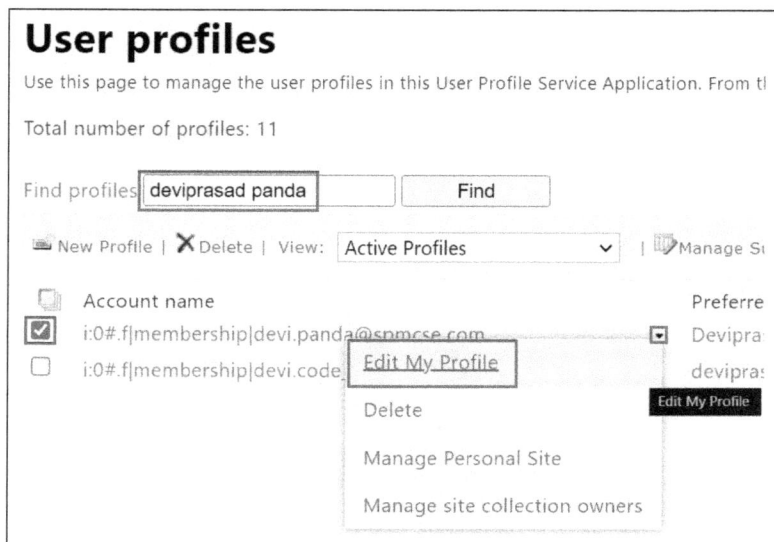

Figure 7.18: Edit my profile

5. You will be redirected to the edit profile page and can see user profile properties with policy settings like required properties marked with a star and default privacy settings, such as show to **Everyone** or **Only Me**. You can see that the properties **Name**, **Work phone**, **Department**, and **Title** are marked with a star. This means these properties are required fields. The privacy setting is shown as **Everyone**. This means these properties will be visible to everyone. You can see that the privacy setting for the property department is set as Only Me. Hence, the property will not be visible to everyone but will only be visible to the user whose profile it belongs to. Refer to *Figure 7.19*:

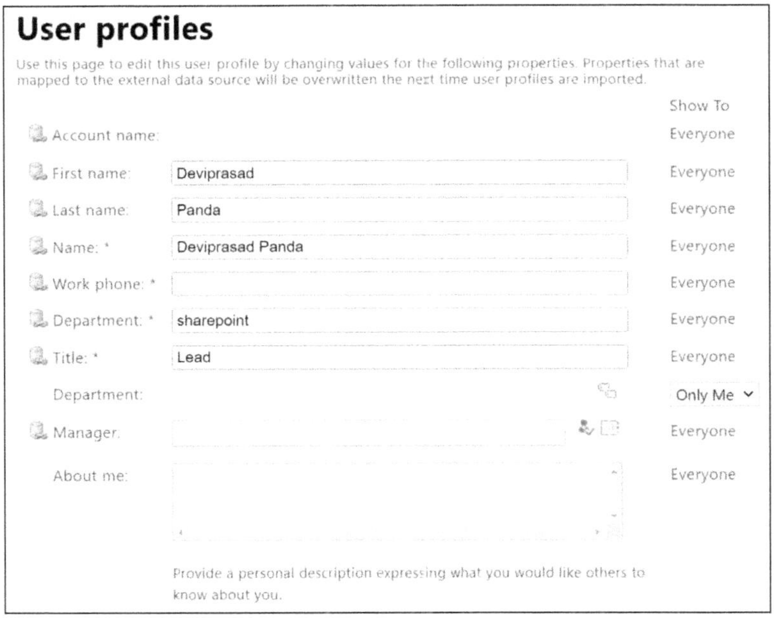

Figure 7.19: User profile properties

6. Similarly, you will find more properties like **Personal site URL, Profile picture, Web site, Job Title** as seen in *Figure 7.20*:

Figure 7.20: User profile properties

7. You will find more properties like **mobile number, mail id, fax number.** Refer to *Figure 7.21*. You can update the mobile number or fax number.

Figure 7.21: User profile properties

8. In the next step, you will find properties like **Skills**, **Birthday**, **Followed #Tags**, **Email Notifications** as seen in *Figure 7.22*:

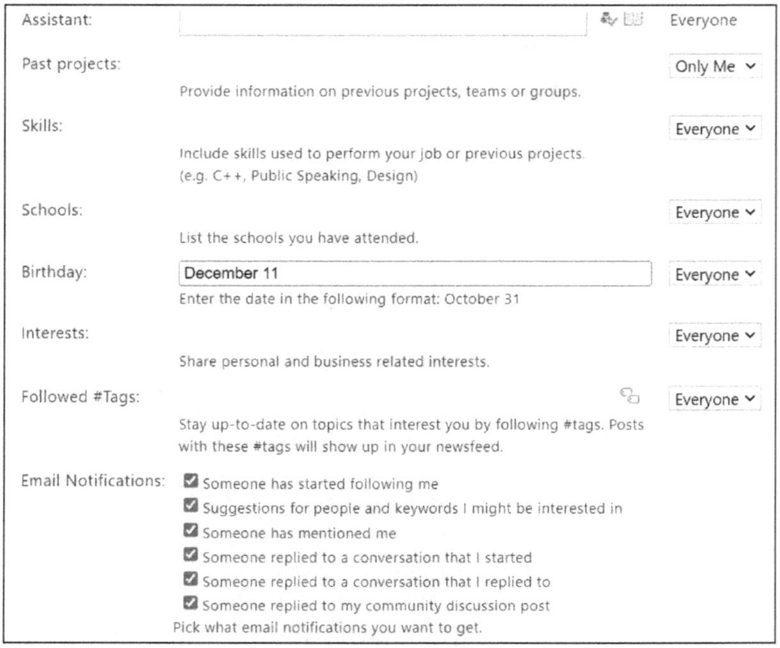

Figure 7.22: User profile properties

9. In the next step, you will find properties to follow activities in the newsfeed, as seen in *Figure 7.23*:

People I follow:	☑ Allow others to see the people you're following and the people following you when they view your profile.	Everyone
Activities I want to share in my newsfeed:	☑ Share all of them ⓘ ☑ Following a person ☑ Following a document or site ☑ Following a tag ☑ Tagging an item ☑ Birthday celebration ☑ Job title change ☑ Workplace anniversary ☑ Updating your "Ask Me About" ☑ Posting on a note board ☑ Liking or rating something ☑ New blog post ☑ Participation in communities Pick the activities you want to tell people about.	Everyone
Picture Timestamp:		Everyone
Picture Placeholder State:	0	Everyone
Picture Exchange Sync State:	1	Everyone

Figure 7.23: *User profile properties*

10. You can change the language of the user profile by setting **Language Preferences**, shown as follows:

🖳 Language Preferences:	**My Display Languages:** English (United States) ▲ ▼ ✕ Pick a new language ▼ [Add] ▾ Show Advanced Language Settings	Only Me ▾
Time Zone:	▾ Select the time zone for your current location. We will use this information to show the local time on your profile page.	Everyone ▾
Choose your settings:	◉ Always use regional settings defined by site administrators. ○ Always use my personal settings	Only Me ▾
Locale:	▾ Select a locale from the list to specify the way sites display numbers, dates, and time.	Only Me ▾
Set Your Calendar:	▾ ☐ Show week numbers in the Date Navigator. Specify the type of calendar.	Only Me ▾
Enable An Alternate Calendar:	▾ Specify a secondary calendar that provides extra information on the calendar features.	Only Me ▾

Figure 7.24: *User profile properties*

11. You can find more properties like **Time Zone, Define Your Work Week, Time format, use language and regional settings**, etc., as seen in *Figure 7.25*. Once you

update the user profile property that is to be changed, click on **Save and Close** to apply changes.

Figure 7.25: User profile properties

Delete

We can delete the user profile using the option **Delete**. Let us perform the following steps to delete the profile:

1. Find the user profile as discussed previously under the section **Find Profiles**.

2. You will find user profiles as the search result.

3. Once you hover over any user profile, you will notice one drop-down option next to that profile. Click on that drop-down option.

4. Click on the **Delete** option. Refer to *Figure 7.26*.

5. Another way to do this is by selecting the user profile and clicking on **Delete** from the navigation.

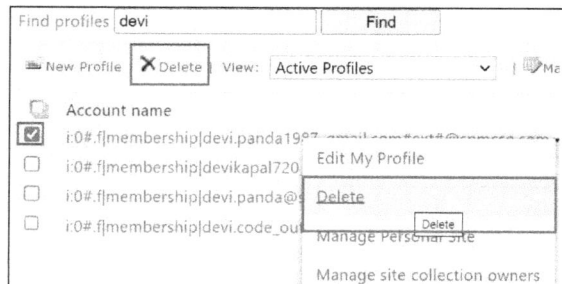

Figure 7.26: Delete my profile

Manage personal site

Personal sites can be managed from the personal site settings page. Let us perform the following steps to get personal site settings:

1. Find the user profile as discussed previously under the section **Find Profiles**.

2. You will find user profiles as a search result.

3. Once you hover over any user profile, you will notice one drop-down option on the side of that profile. Click on that drop-down option. Refer to *Figure 7.26*.

4. Click on the option **Manage Personal Site**.

5. You will be redirected to the personal site settings page, where you can change settings for a user's personal site, as seen in *Figure 7.27*:

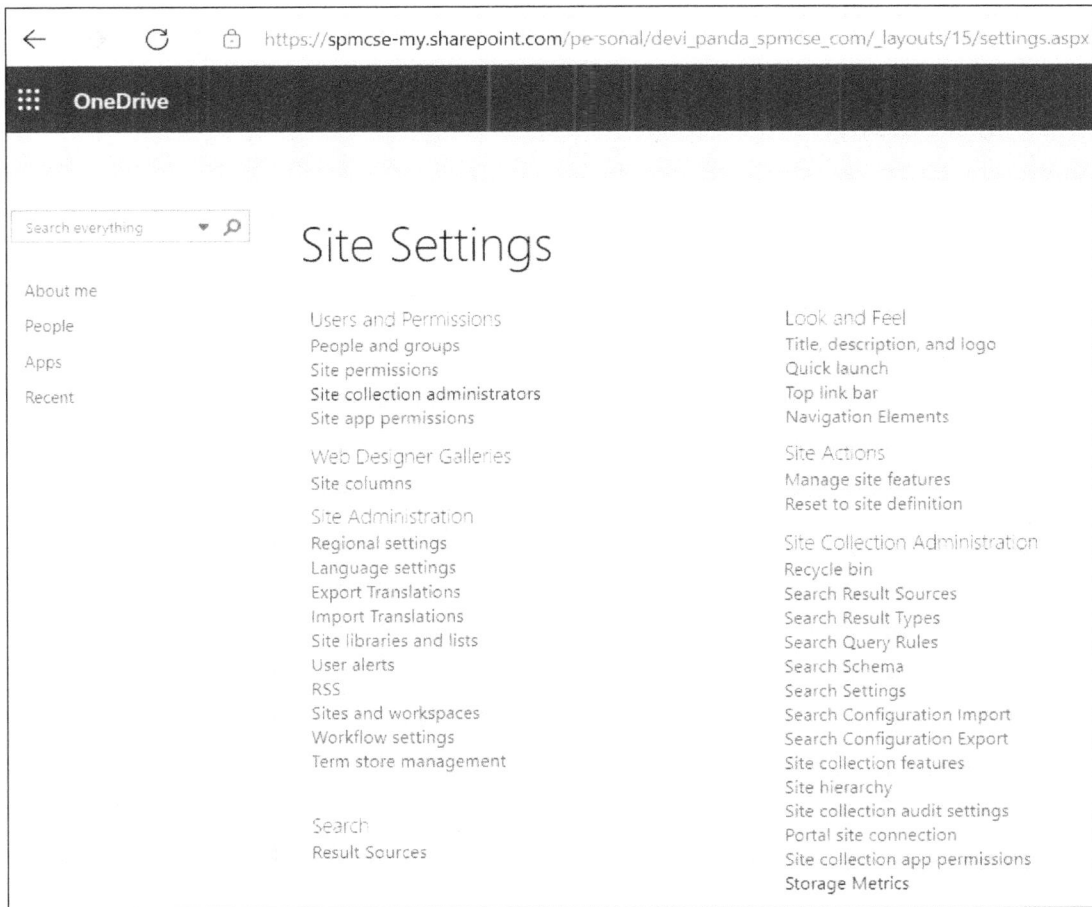

Figure 7.27: Manage personal site

Manage site collection owners

The option Manage site collection owner allows you to change the administrator of the My Site as well as the OneDrive. You should not remove the user as an admin from their own site and OneDrive. Let us perform the following steps to change the site collection owner:

1. Find the user profile as discussed above under the section **Find Profiles**.

2. You will find user profiles as a search result.

3. Once you hover over any user profile, you will notice a drop-down option on the side of that profile. Click on that drop-down option. Refer to *Figure 7.26*.

4. Click on the option **Manage site collection owners.**

5. You will get a new dialog box that will provide the options to change **Primary Site Collection Administrator** and **Site Collection Administrators** as seen in *Figure 7.28*.

6. Removing the user from here will remove the admin permission from the user's own OneDrive.

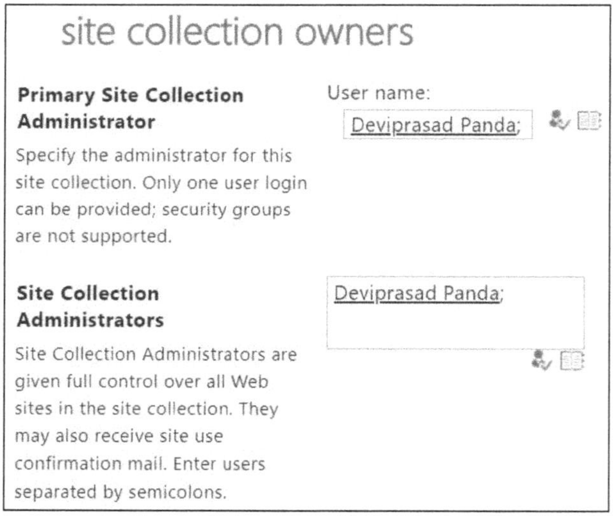

Figure 7.28: Manage site collection owners

Manage user sub-types

Manage user sub-types is the third option under the category people in user profile. We can create and manage sub-types using this option. We already discussed this under the section **Manage Sub-types** present under **Manage User Properties**. Follow the steps mentioned in the section **Manage Sub-types** present under **Manage User Properties** to create or remove sub-types. Refer to *Figure 7.29*:

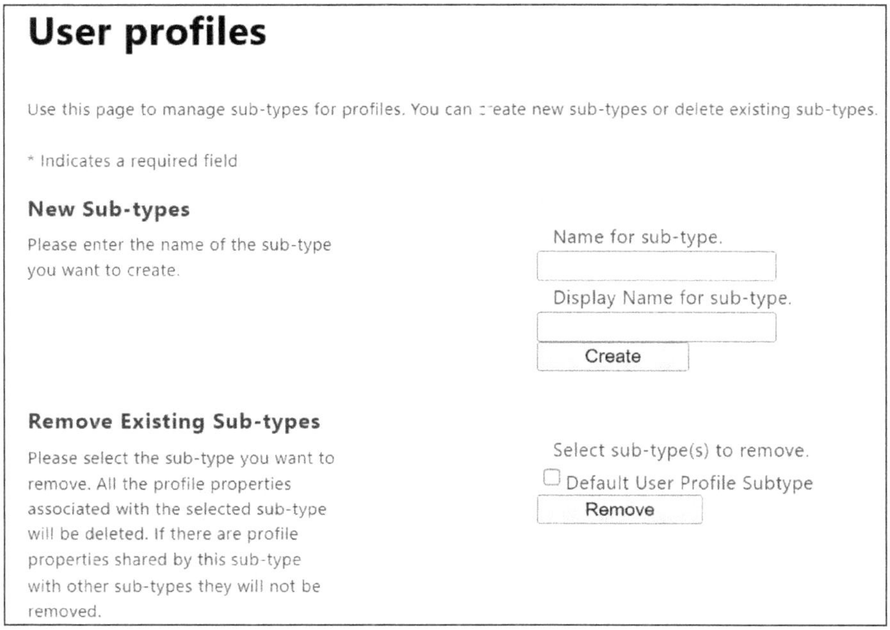

User profiles

Use this page to manage sub-types for profiles. You can create new sub-types or delete existing sub-types.

* Indicates a required field

New Sub-types

Please enter the name of the sub-type you want to create.

Name for sub-type.

Display Name for sub-type.

Create

Remove Existing Sub-types

Please select the sub-type you want to remove. All the profile properties associated with the selected sub-type will be deleted. If there are profile properties shared by this sub-type with other sub-types they will not be removed.

Select sub-type(s) to remove.

☐ Default User Profile Subtype

Remove

Figure 7.29: Create sub-types

Manage audiences

Audience is a group of users to whom specific contents are targeted. There are situations where specific content is shared with a specific group of people. In that situation, these audiences come into the picture. We can create an audience from SharePoint admin center and add rules to audiences as well. Click on **Manage Audiences** present under the category **People** in user profile. You will be redirected to view the audiences page, as seen in *Figure 7.30*. You will find different options, like **Find** audience, in the list. You see more options to create **New Audience**, **Delete**. Let us discuss each option in detail and see how we can manage audiences from SharePoint admin center.

User profiles

Use this page to view audience properties, add and edit audiences, and view audience membership.

Total audiences: 3
Uncompiled audiences: 0

Find audiences that start with:

[ ] Find

New Audience | ✕ Delete | View: All ▾   Go to page 1 ▾ of 1

	Audience Name	Description	Last Compiled	Last Compilation Status	Members
☐	All site users	All users who can access the site	Not applicable	Not applicable	Not applicable
☐	Digital Marketing		10/29/2022 1:22 AM	No error	
☐	New Joinees	new joined users Audience >= 3 yr	10/29/2022 1:22 AM	No error	

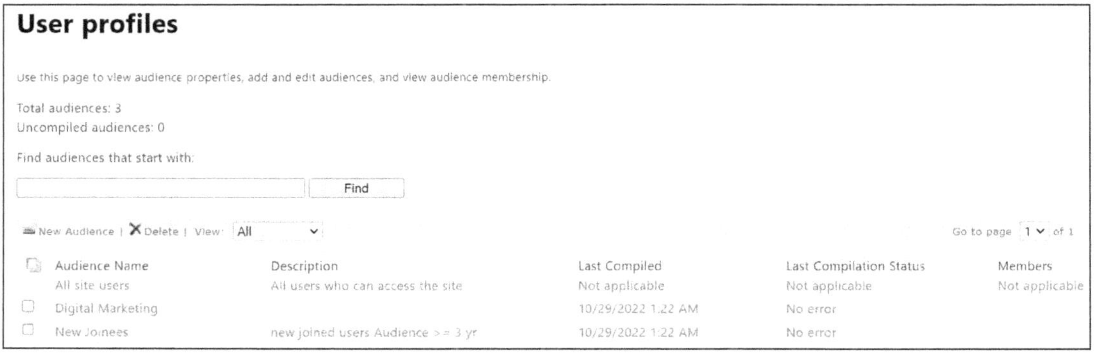

Figure 7.30: Manage Audience

New audience

As discussed previously, audience is a group of users to whom specific contents are targeted. We can create a new audience from the admin center by following the option New Audience. Let us perform the following steps to create an audience:

1. Click on **Manage Audiences** present under the category **People** in user profile. You will be redirected to view the audience page.

2. Click on the option **New Audience** from navigation, as seen in *Figure 7.30*. You will be redirected to another page.

3. Enter **Name** of the audience and describe something about the audience under the field **Description**. Refer to *Figure 7.31*.

4. Enter user details under the field **Owner,** who will own and manage the audience.

5. Select any one of the options, namely, **Satisfy all of the rules** or **Satisfy any of the rules**. Users satisfying this rule will be included in this audience.

6. Click on **OK** to proceed to the next step of audience creation.

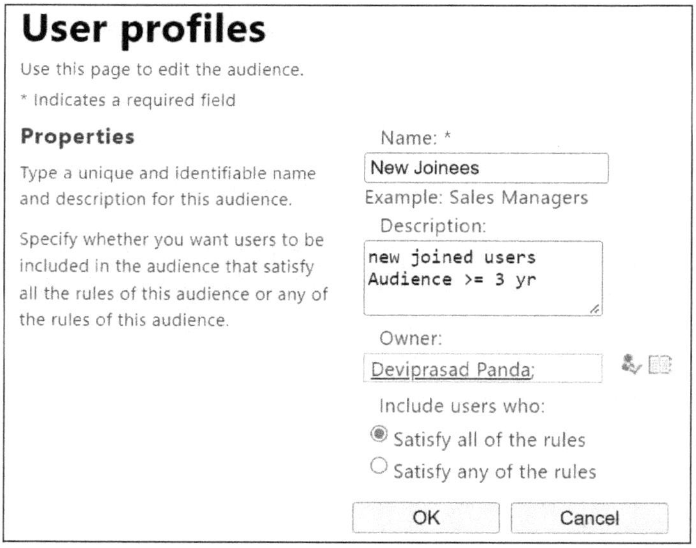

User profiles

Use this page to edit the audience.

* Indicates a required field

Properties

Type a unique and identifiable name and description for this audience.

Specify whether you want users to be included in the audience that satisfy all the rules of this audience or any of the rules of this audience.

Name: *

New Joinees

Example: Sales Managers

Description:

new joined users
Audience >= 3 yr

Owner:

Deviprasad Panda;

Include users who:

● Satisfy all of the rules
○ Satisfy any of the rules

OK   Cancel

Figure 7.31: Create new audience, enter name, description, owner

7. In the next window, you will find three categories of options, namely, **Operand**, **Operator**, and **Value**. Operand can be of type **User** or **Property**. Select the option **User** from **Operand** first.

8. Click on the drop-down option from the operator. You will see two options like **Reports Under** and **Member Of**. Select any one of the **Operator**. Refer to *Figure 7.32*:

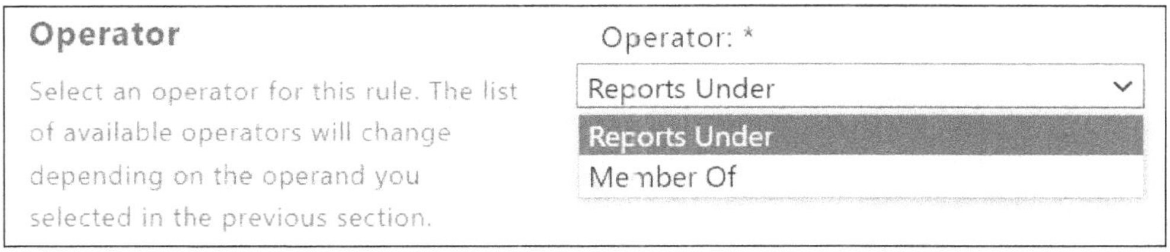

Figure7.32: *Create new audience select operator*

9. You will find the value will be a people picker field. Enter details about the Windows security group or distribution list.

10. Click on **OK** once all selection is done. This will create a rule based on the security group, distribution list, or organizational hierarchy. Refer to *Figure 7.33*:

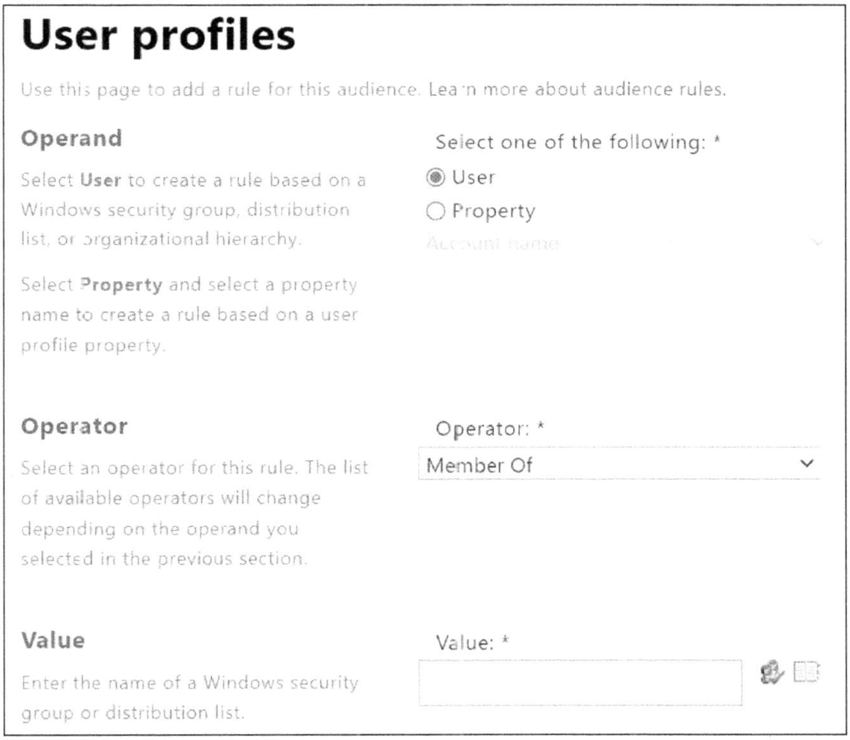

Figure7.33: *Create new audience using operand user*

11. If you are selecting **Operand** as **Property**, then you will find all user properties as a drop-down option. You need to select any of the property options to apply the rule. Refer to *Figure 7.34*:

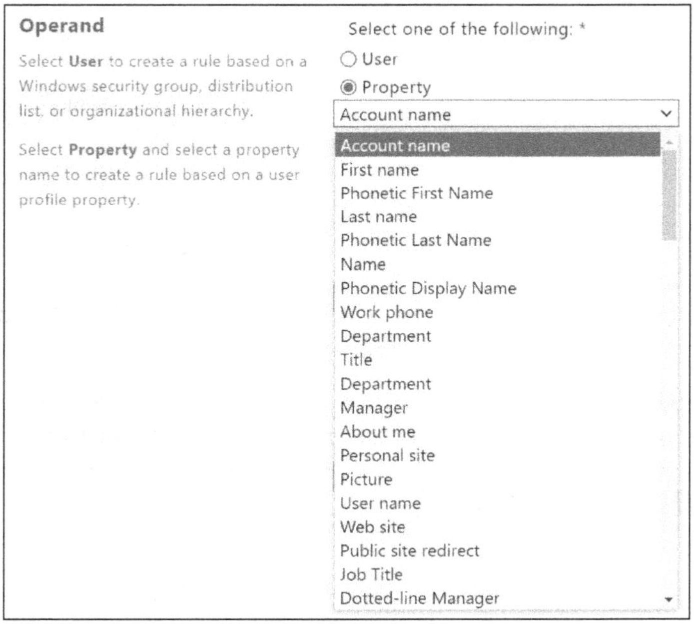

Figure7.34: *Different operand options*

12. Let us say you selected department as the **Operand** property.

13. Based on the property in operand selected, you will find related **Operators** such as **=**, **Contains**, **< >**, and **not Contains**. Select the operator contains, as shown in *Figure 7.35*:

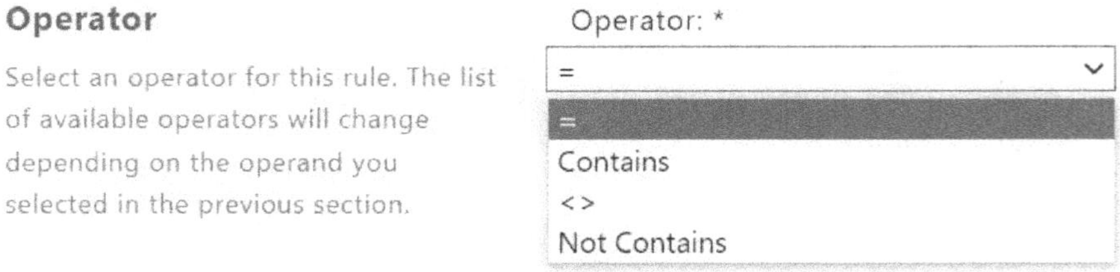

Figure 7.35: *Different operator in new audience*

14. Enter the value related to the department present in the organization. Refer to *Figure 7.36*:

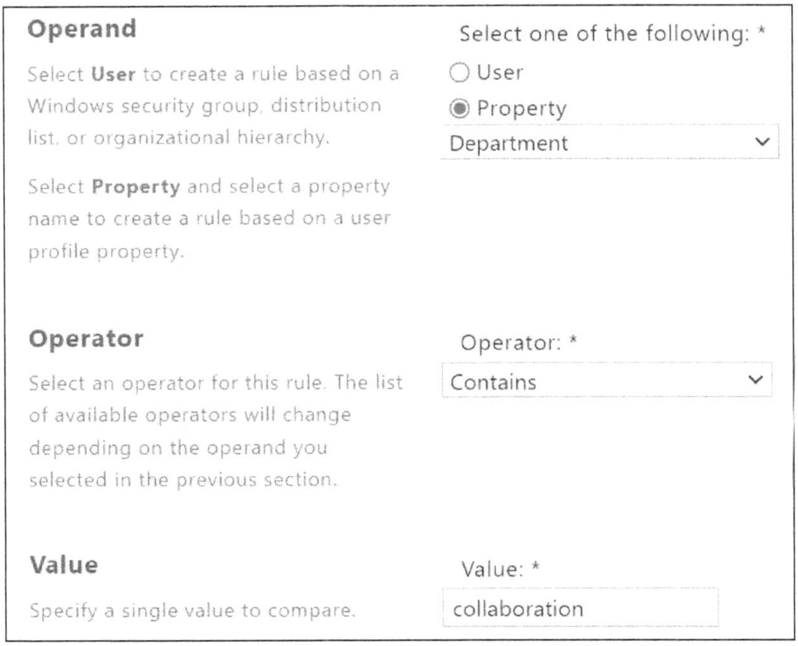

Operand

Select **User** to create a rule based on a Windows security group, distribution list, or organizational hierarchy.

Select **Property** and select a property name to create a rule based on a user profile property.

Select one of the following: *
○ User
◉ Property
Department ▾

Operator

Select an operator for this rule. The list of available operators will change depending on the operand you selected in the previous section.

Operator: *
Contains ▾

Value

Specify a single value to compare.

Value: *
collaboration

Figure 7.36: Contains operator in new audience

15. Similarly, you can select other user properties from operand, operator, and value to apply rules. Refer to *Figure 7.37*:

Operand

Select **User** to create a rule based on a Windows security group, distribution list, or organizational hierarchy.

Select **Property** and select a property name to create a rule based on a user profile property.

Select one of the following: *
○ User
◉ Property
Skills ▾

Operator

Select an operator for this rule. The list of available operators will change depending on the operand you selected in the previous section.

Operator: *
Contains ▾

Value

Specify a single value to compare.

collaboration

Figure 7.37: Applying operator contains and operand as skill property

16. Selecting property from **Operand** as **Manager**, you will find the value field as user ID, as seen in *Figure 7.38*. Selecting a different property from the operand will change the respective operator and value, as seen in *Figure 7.38*:

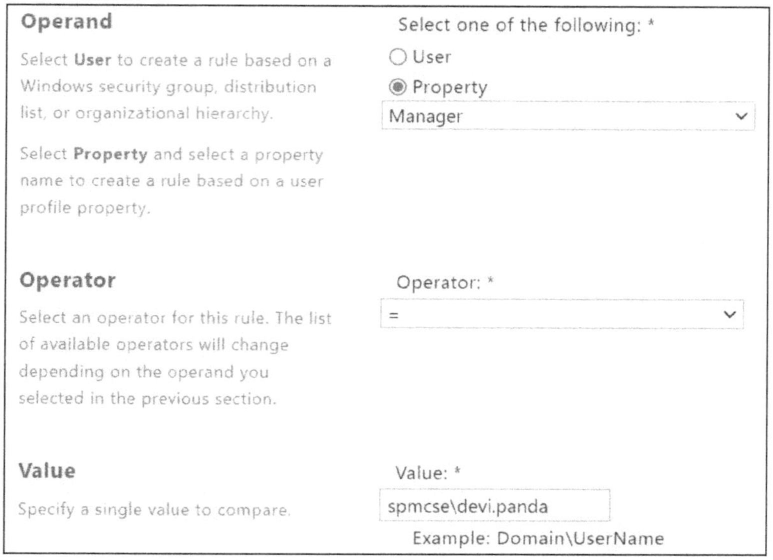

Figure 7.38: *Applying operator equal and operand as manager*

17. Click on **OK** once the selection is completed. Audience will be created, and you will notice the following page with audience details. Refer to *Figure 7.39*:

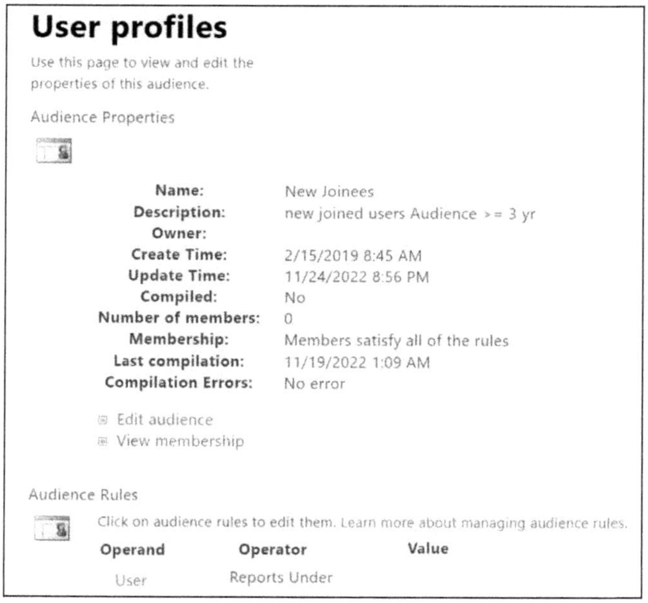

Figure 7.39: *New audience created*

Edit audience

We can edit the audience if there is any change in the future. Let us perform the following steps to edit audience:

1. Click on **Manage Audiences** present under the category **People** in user profile. You will be redirected to view the audience page. You will find existing audiences.

2. If you hover over the audience that you want to edit, you will notice the drop-down error side to it. Click on the drop-down arrow.

3. You will find drop-down options like **Edit**, **View Properties**, **Delete**, and **View membership**. Click on the option **Edit**. Refer to *Figure 7.40*:

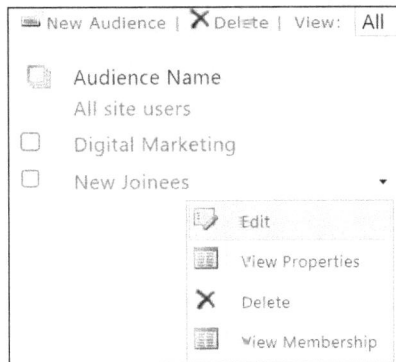

Figure 7.40: Edit audience

4. You will get the same page as you got while creating a new audience. Update the change required and press **OK**. Refer to *Figure 7.41*:

Figure 7.41: Edit audience

5. After pressing **OK**, you will be redirected to the same page as you got while creating a new audience, as discussed in *Step 17* of the preceding section, **New Audience**.

6. Click on the operand **User** present under **Audience Rules** to edit the rule. Refer to *Figure 7.42*:

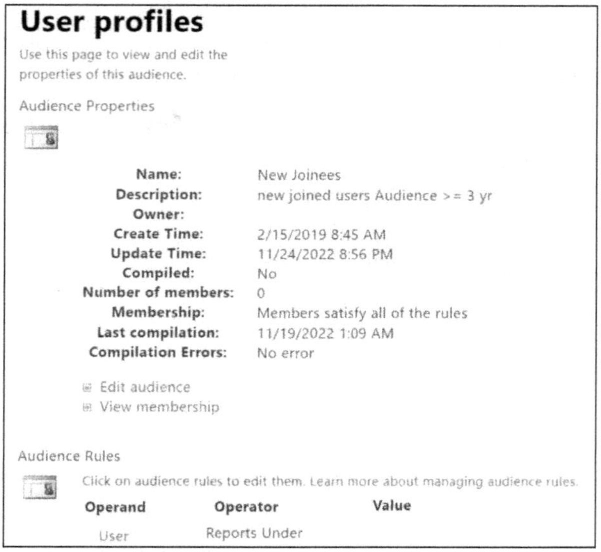

User profiles

Use this page to view and edit the properties of this audience.

Audience Properties

Name:	New Joinees
Description:	new joined users Audience >= 3 yr
Owner:	
Create Time:	2/15/2019 8:45 AM
Update Time:	11/24/2022 8:56 PM
Compiled:	No
Number of members:	0
Membership:	Members satisfy all of the rules
Last compilation:	11/19/2022 1:09 AM
Compilation Errors:	No error

⊞ Edit audience
⊞ View membership

Audience Rules

Click on audience rules to edit them. Learn more about managing audience rules.

Operand	Operator	Value
User	Reports Under	

Figure 7.42: Edit audience

7. You will be redirected to the Audience_DefRuleEdit page. Make necessary changes as required and click on **OK** to apply changes. Refer to *Figure 7.43*.

8. If you want to delete the rule, click on **Delete**. Refer to the following figure:

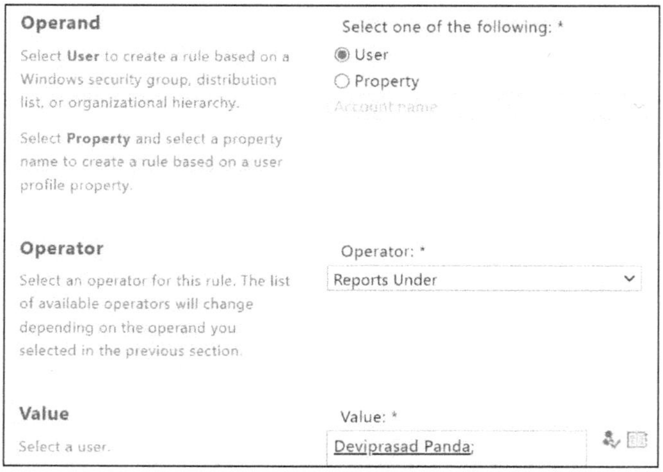

Operand

Select **User** to create a rule based on a Windows security group, distribution list, or organizational hierarchy.

Select **Property** and select a property name to create a rule based on a user profile property.

Select one of the following: *
◉ User
○ Property
Account name ⌄

Operator

Select an operator for this rule. The list of available operators will change depending on the operand you selected in the previous section.

Operator: *
Reports Under ⌄

Value

Select a user.

Value: *
Deviprasad Panda;

Figure 7.43: Delete audience rule

View properties

You can view the audience property by following the option View Properties. Let us perform the following steps to check the applications of **View Properties**:

1. Click on **Manage Audiences** present under the category **People** in user profile. You will be redirected to view the audience page, and you will find **existing audiences.**

2. If you hover over the audience that you want to edit, you will notice the drop-down arrow next to it. Click on the drop-down arrow.

3. You will find options like **Edit, View Properties, Delete,** and **View membership**. Click on the option **View Properties**.

4. You will be redirected to the page as seen in *Figure 7.44*. You can edit or delete the rules from here as well.

User profiles

Use this page to view and edit the properties of this audience.

Audience Properties

Name:	New Joinees
Description:	new joined users Audience >= 3 yr
Owner:	
Create Time:	2/15/2019 8:45 AM
Update Time:	11/24/2022 8:56 PM
Compiled:	No
Number of members:	0
Membership:	Members satisfy all of the rules
Last compilation:	11/19/2022 1:09 AM
Compilation Errors:	No error

▣ Edit audience
▣ View membership

Audience Rules

Click on audience rules to edit them. Learn more about managing audience rules.

Operand	Operator	Value
User	Reports Under	

Figure 7.44: View audience properties

View membership

You can check the membership of an audience by following the option View membership. Let us perform the following steps to check the application of view membership:

1. Click on **Manage audiences** present under the category **People** in user profile. You will be redirected to the View audiences page and find existing audiences.

2. If you hover over the audience that you want to edit, you will notice the drop-down arrow on the side. Click on the drop-down arrow.

3. You will find drop-down options like **Edit**, **View Properties**, **Delete**, and **View membership**. Click on the option **View membership**.

4. You will be redirected to the page, as seen in the following figure, which holds the members in this audience:

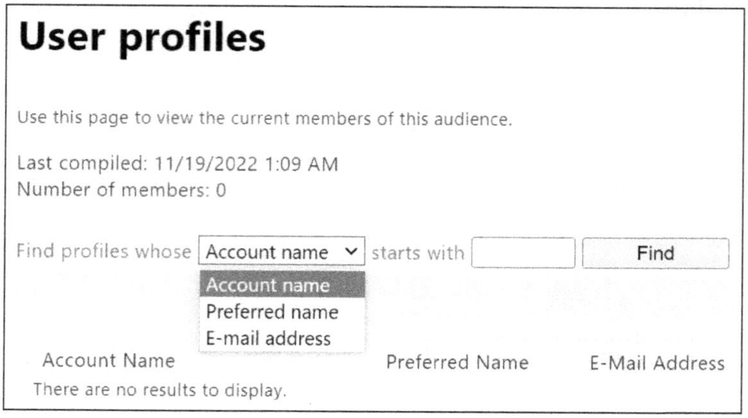

Figure 7.45: Find audience membership

5. You can find profiles by applying conditions like selecting **Account name**, **Preferred name**, and **E-mail address** from the drop-down field, **Find profiles whose**, and related details in the field **starts with**.

Delete

We can delete the audience as per our requirement. Select the audience and click on delete either from the drop-down or from the navigation option, as seen in *Figure 7.46*:

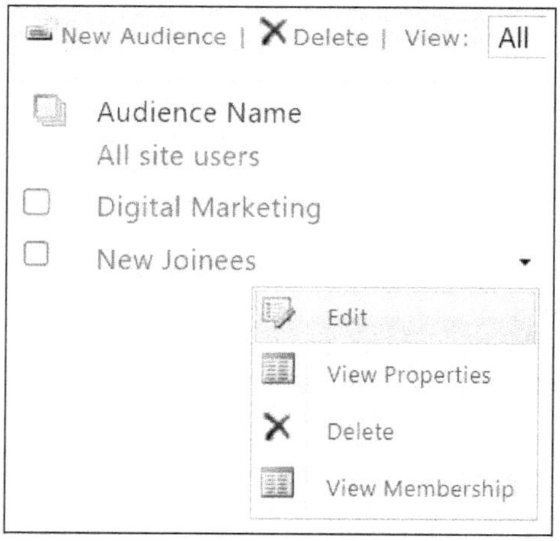

Figure 7.46: Delete audience

You will get a pop-up dialog to confirm the deletion of the audience. Once you click on **OK**, it will be deleted. Refer to *Figure 7.47*:

Figure 7.47: Delete audience confirmation

Manage user permissions

Everyone except external users has the permission to follow people, edit profiles, use tags and notes, and the permission to create a personal site that ultimately creates OneDrive as well. We can control these settings using the option **Manage User Permissions**. Let us perform the following steps to manage personal site, OneDrive, and other options available:

1. Click on **Manage User Permissions** present under the category **People** in user profile. A new dialog box will open. You will notice one group, **Everyone except external users,** is added. You will find another field, **Permissions for Everyone except external users,** which has checkbox options like **Create Personal Site (required for personal storage, newsfeed, and followed content)**, **Follow People and Edit Profile**, **Use Tags and Notes**, as seen in *Figure 7.48*.

2. By default, the group **Everyone except external users** has permission to **Create Personal Site** (OneDrive created to store followed sites, frequent sites), **Follow People and Edit Profile**, **Use Tags and Notes**. All three checkboxes are selected.

3. Select the group and click on the option **Remove** to remove the group and the permissions assigned.

4. Add any specific group and select the checkbox **Create Personal Site** only. This group of people can only create a personal site. Similarly, you can select other checkboxes, namely, **Follow People and Edit Profile** or **Use Tags and Notes** to assign those permissions to that group of people.

5. You can add multiple groups and assign any of the permissions by selecting the checkbox to control permissions.

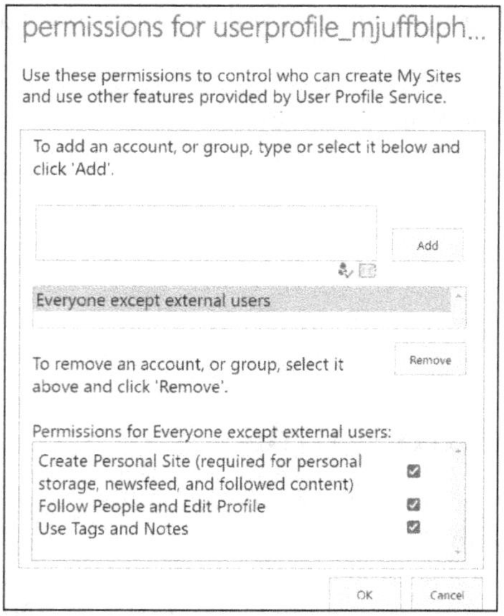

Figure 7.48: *Creaate Persoanl Site permission*

My Site Settings management

My Site Settings is the second category under user profile. You will find the option **Setup My Sites** under the category **My Site Settings** where we can check various settings applied to personal sites. Let us perform the following steps to see what the settings are applied exactly:

1. Click on **Setup My Sites** under the category **My Site Settings** in user profile. You will be redirected to the Personal Sites page.

2. The first setting under My Site Settings is **preferred search center**. You will find options like **Preferred Search Center**, **Search scope for finding people**, and **Search scope for finding documents**. You will also find the search center URL under the option Preferred Search Center. When someone searches for any user profile, the search result will be redirected to that page. **The search scope for finding people** is the drop-down field selected as **People**. The search scope for finding documents is the drop-down field, which is selected as **All Sites**. Document search results will be available from all sites. Refer to *Figure 7.49*:

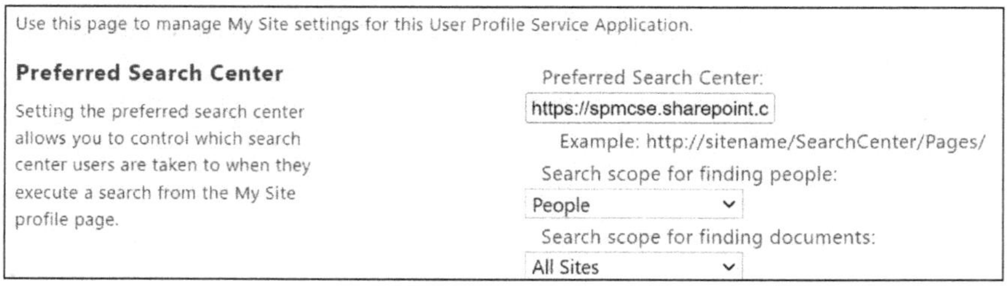

Figure 7.49: *Preferred Search Center*

3. The next option under **My Site Settings** is **My Site Host**. This field holds the URL of My Site Host location **http://<My Site Host Web Application Path>/** as seen in *Figure 7.50*:

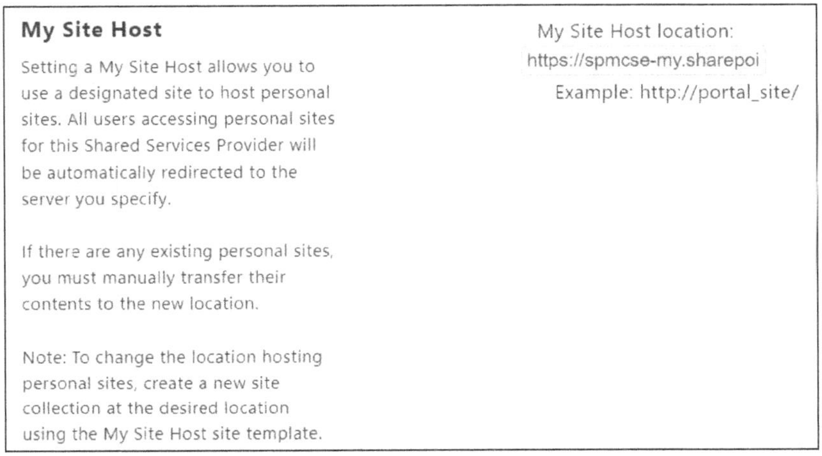

My Site Host

Setting a My Site Host allows you to use a designated site to host personal sites. All users accessing personal sites for this Shared Services Provider will be automatically redirected to the server you specify.

If there are any existing personal sites, you must manually transfer their contents to the new location.

Note: To change the location hosting personal sites, create a new site collection at the desired location using the My Site Host site template.

My Site Host location:
https://spmcse-my.sharepoi
Example: http://portal_site/

Figure 7.50: My Site Host

4. The next option is **Personal Site Location,** which is the managed path of My Site. Under the field **Location,** you will find that the managed path is set as personal. The Managed path is placed after **My Site Host** location **http://<My Site Host Web Application Path>/<My Site Managed Path>/**. Refer to *Figure 7.51*:

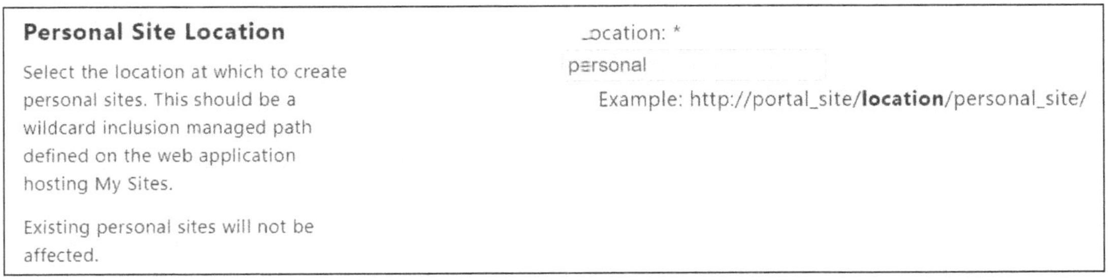

Personal Site Location

Select the location at which to create personal sites. This should be a wildcard inclusion managed path defined on the web application hosting My Sites.

Existing personal sites will not be affected.

Location: *
personal
Example: http://portal_site/**location**/personal_site/

Figure 7.51: Personal Site Location

5. The next option is **Site Naming Format,** which indicates the default My Site name format **http://<My Site Host Web Application Path>/<My Site Managed Path>/username/**, as shown in *Figure 7.52*:

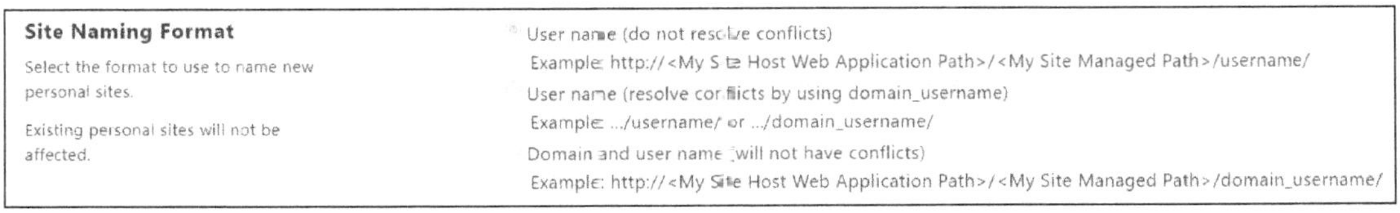

Site Naming Format

Select the format to use to name new personal sites.

Existing personal sites will not be affected.

User name (do not resolve conflicts)
Example: http://<My Site Host Web Application Path>/<My Site Managed Path>/username/
User name (resolve conflicts by using domain_username)
Example: .../username/ or .../domain_username/
Domain and user name (will not have conflicts)
Example: http://<My Site Host Web Application Path>/<My Site Managed Path>/domain_username/

Figure 7.52: Site Naming Format

6. The next option, **Read Permission Level**, allows giving read permission to a group, which can be modified as per requirement. Refer to *Figure 7.53*:

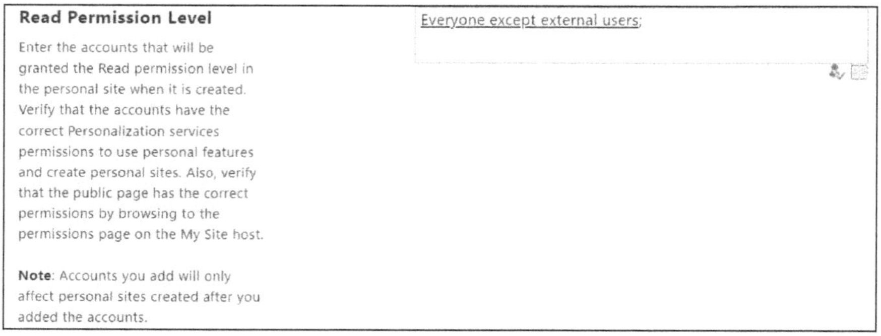

Read Permission Level	Everyone except external users;
Enter the accounts that will be granted the Read permission level in the personal site when it is created. Verify that the accounts have the correct Personalization services permissions to use personal features and create personal sites. Also, verify that the public page has the correct permissions by browsing to the permissions page on the My Site host. **Note**: Accounts you add will only affect personal sites created after you added the accounts.	

Figure 7.53: Read Permission Level

7. The option **Newsfeed** allows you to enable or disable the **My Site newsfeeds activities**. This allows the users to enable or disable activity notifications from people and content they follow. Refer to *Figure 7.54*:

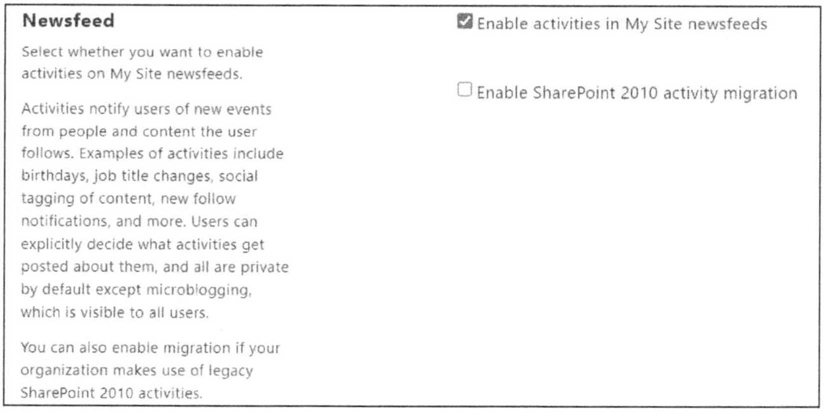

Newsfeed	☑ Enable activities in My Site newsfeeds
Select whether you want to enable activities on My Site newsfeeds. Activities notify users of new events from people and content the user follows. Examples of activities include birthdays, job title changes, social tagging of content, new follow notifications, and more. Users can explicitly decide what activities get posted about them, and all are private by default except microblogging, which is visible to all users. You can also enable migration if your organization makes use of legacy SharePoint 2010 activities.	☐ Enable SharePoint 2010 activity migration

Figure 7.54: Newsfeed

8. In the next option, **Email Notifications**, allows you to enable or disable newsfeed activities notifications by mail. Refer to *Figure 7.55*:

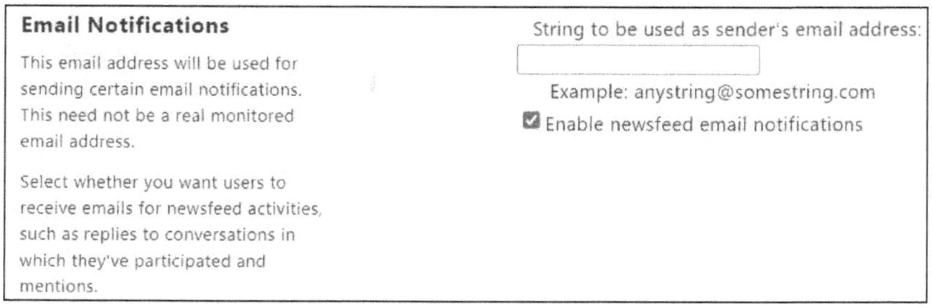

Email Notifications	String to be used as sender's email address:
This email address will be used for sending certain email notifications. This need not be a real monitored email address. Select whether you want users to receive emails for newsfeed activities, such as replies to conversations in which they've participated and mentions.	_____ Example: anystring@somestring.com ☑ Enable newsfeed email notifications

Figure 7.55: Email Notifications

9. In the next option, **My Site Cleanup**, provides an option to enable or disable access delegation to My Site. If any user leaves the organization or in case an account is deleted, then it is important to retrieve the contents related to a project on that site. By access delegation, a secondary owner can be granted permission to retrieve content from My Site. Usually, My Site will be permanently deleted after thirty days if the user profile is deleted. To avoid any data loss, this access delegation is applied. The secondary owner can retrieve the content within thirty days of time, if required. Refer to *Figure 7.56*:

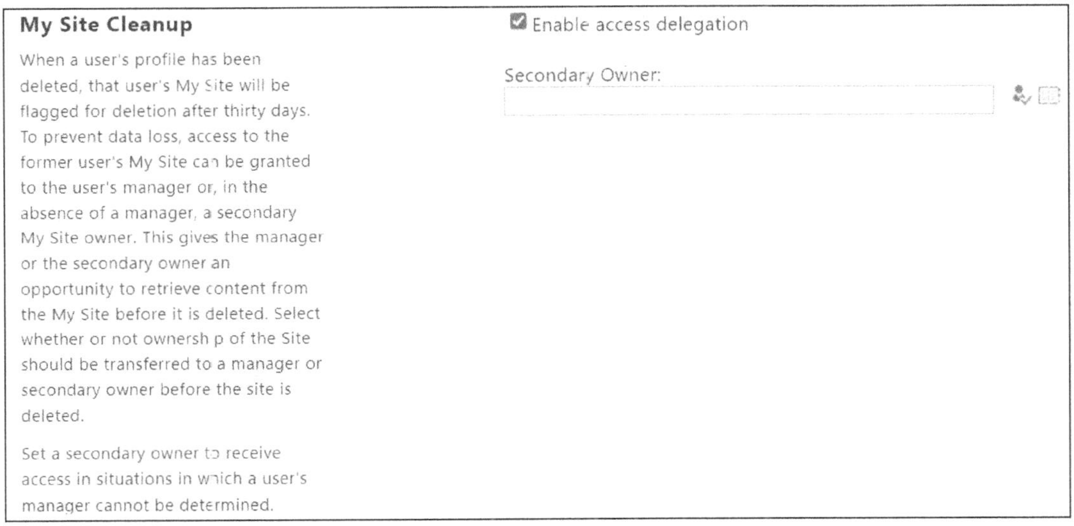

Figure 7.56: My Site Cleanup

10. Now, the next option, **My Site Secondary Admin**, allows adding any user or a group as an admin to all My Sites, who would like to have admin rights apart from my site owner. Refer to *Figure 7.57*:

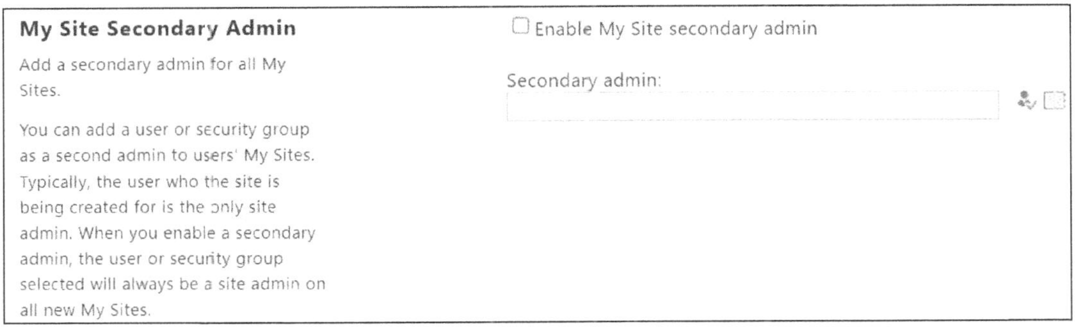

Figure 7.57: My Site Secondary Admin

11. The next option, **Privacy Settings**, allows making My Site public or keeping it Private. Making My Site public will allow anyone to see users' followers, users'

following, job title changes, birthdays, workplace anniversary, ask me about updates, new blog posts social tagging and rating of content. Refer to *Figure 7.58*:

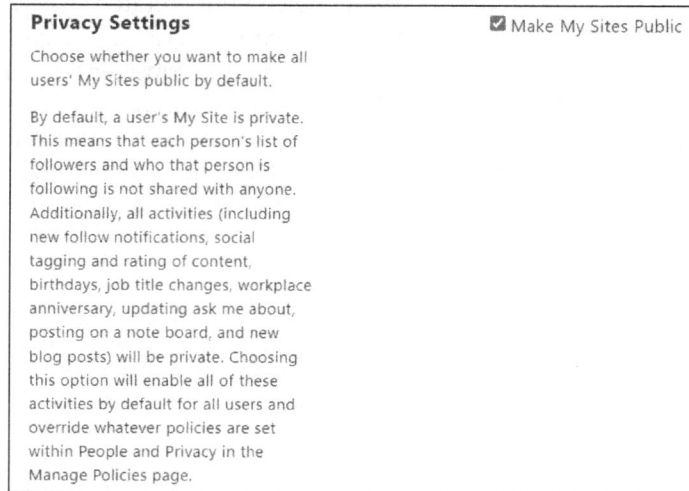

Figure 7.58: My Site Privacy Settings

Conclusion

In this chapter, we discussed user profile categories, people, and my site settings. We also looked at the different options to manage user properties, user profiles, user sub-types, audiences, user permissions, policies, and the various options available under my site settings.

In *Chapter 8, Search Administration*, we will explore search administration in SharePoint.

Points to remember

- Regular changes are applied in Office 365 and SharePoint Online. There may be changes in the template or some other features with time.

- Removing the user from here will remove the admin permission from user own OneDrive. Enable access delegation.

CHAPTER 8
Search Administration

Introduction

In *Chapter 7, User Profiles Administration*, we discussed SharePoint user profiles and settings available to manage user profiles. In this chapter, we will discuss SharePoint search and the settings available to manage search. SharePoint search is a service responsible for handling user search queries across the organization and providing the most relevant search results with a modern search experience. This is the center of SharePoint search. You will find settings like **Manage Search Schema**, **Manage Search Dictionaries**, **Manage Authoritative Pages**, **Query Suggestion Settings**, **Manage Result Sources**, **Manage Query Rules**, **Manage Query Client Types**, **Remove Search Results**, **View Usage Reports**, **Search Center Settings**, **Export Search Configuration**, **Import Search Configuration**, **Crawl Log Permissions** which together responsible to provide the best search result. As an administrator, you are responsible for managing these settings to provide the most relevant search results to users using SharePoint. In this chapter, we will discuss these settings to administer search.

Structure

In this chapter, we will discuss the following topics:

- Manage search schema
- Manage search dictionaries
- Query suggestion settings
- Manage result sources
- Manage query rules
- Remove search results
- View usage reports
- Search center settings
- Export search configuration
- Import search configuration
- Crawl log permissions

Objectives

By the end of this chapter, you will have a clear understanding of the search schema, crawled property, and managed property. You will learn about the search dictionaries by managing company inclusions, company exclusions, query spelling inclusions, and query spelling exclusions. You will understand what query suggestion is and how to manage the settings available under query suggestion. You will gain insights regarding result sources and the step-by-step procedure to manage the settings available under result source. You will get to know about query rules, settings available under query rules, and their application. You will gain a fair understanding of the settings to remove search results, view usage reports, search settings, crawl log permissions, and how to export and import search configuration.

Manage search schema

Manage search schema is the first setting present under search service. You can navigate to the setting from the SharePoint admin center by following the given steps:

1. Click on the option **More features** from the left navigation in SharePoint admin center. You will find multiple services in the result pane like **Term store, User profiles, Search, Apps, BCS, Secure store, Record management, InfoPath**, and **Hybrid picker**.

2. Identify the service **Search** as seen in the following figure. Click on **Open**. Refer to *Figure 8.1*:

More features

Access familiar features from the classic SharePoint admin center.

Search

Help users find what they're looking for. Learn more

Open

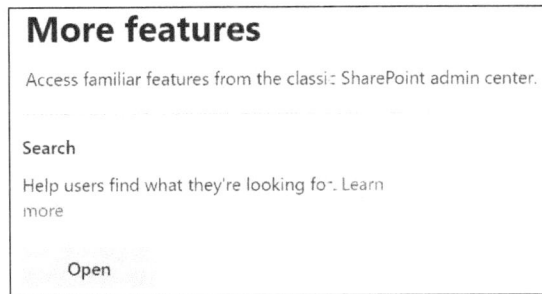

Figure 8.1: Identify search service from all services present under more features

3. You will be redirected to the Search administration page and will find all settings related to search administration.

4. Identify the first search setting, which is **Manage Search Schema,** as seen in *Figure 8.2*. Click on the option **Manage Search Schema**.

Search
Manage Search Schema
Create and modify search properties so that users can query these properties.

Figure 8.2: Manage search schema

5. You will be redirected to the managed properties page, where you will find options like **Managed Properties**, **Crawled Properties**, and **Categories** as top navigation. Under top navigation, you will find the filter properties field, and next to that, you will find all managed properties. We will discuss managed properties later, but let us discuss the crawled property first.

Crawled properties

Each item present in SharePoint has content and metadata associated with it. These properties are extracted during search crawl, and these extracted properties are called **crawled properties**. Follow the given step-by-step procedure to find different options present under crawled properties:

1. Click on **Crawled Properties** from the navigation option that we got on clicking **Manage Search Schema**. You will be redirected to **listcrawledproperties** page. You will find a list of crawled properties at the lowest zone of the page, as seen in *Figure 8.4*.

2. Next to top navigation, you will find the option **Filters,** which is used to filter and find any crawled properties from the crawled properties list. You see two more fields named **Crawled Properties** and **Category** present in the option **Filters,** as seen in *Figure 8.3*:

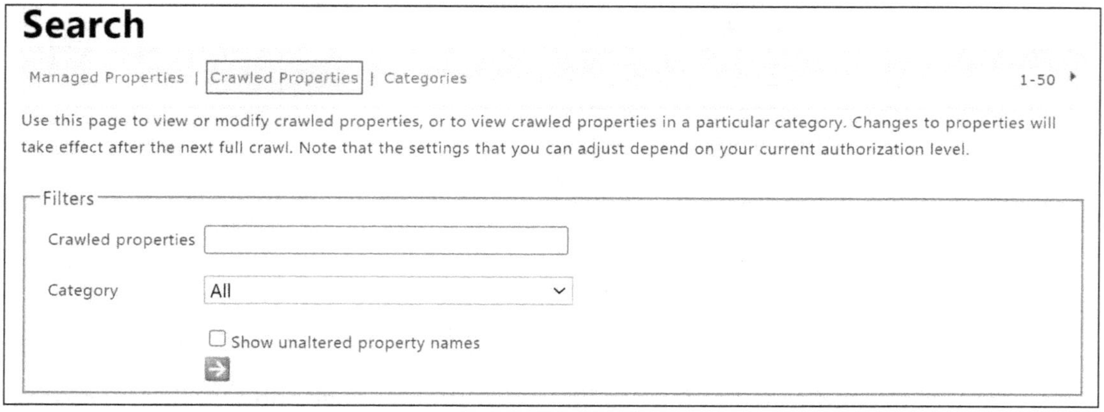

Search

Managed Properties | Crawled Properties | Categories   1-50 ▸

Use this page to view or modify crawled properties, or to view crawled properties in a particular category. Changes to properties will take effect after the next full crawl. Note that the settings that you can adjust depend on your current authorization level.

┌─ Filters ───┐
│   │
│   Crawled properties   [   ]   │
│   │
│   Category   [All   ∨]   │
│   │
│   ☐ Show unaltered property names   │
│   [→]   │
│   │
└──┘

Figure 8.3: Crawled properties navigation option

3. Next to **Filters**, you will find a list of crawled properties extracted from all content sources in SharePoint, as seen in the following figure. **Property Name** represents the name of the crawled property. Each crawled property should be mapped to one or more managed properties to get search results. You will find many crawled properties mapped to managed property automatically, and many more not mapped. Column **Mapped to Property** represents the mapped managed property with the crawled property. Refer to *Figure 8.4*:

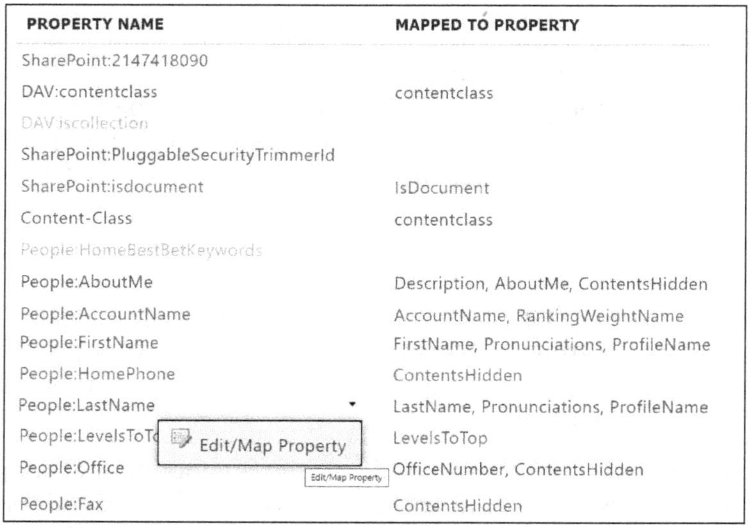

PROPERTY NAME	MAPPED TO PROPERTY
SharePoint:2147418090	
DAV:contentclass	contentclass
DAV:iscollection	
SharePoint:PluggableSecurityTrimmerId	
SharePoint:isdocument	IsDocument
Content-Class	contentclass
People:HomeBestBetKeywords	
People:AboutMe	Description, AboutMe, ContentsHidden
People:AccountName	AccountName, RankingWeightName
People:FirstName	FirstName, Pronunciations, ProfileName
People:HomePhone	ContentsHidden
People:LastName	LastName, Pronunciations, ProfileName
People:LevelsToTo [▤ Edit/Map Property]	LevelsToTop
People:Office [Edit/Map Property]	OfficeNumber, ContentsHidden
People:Fax	ContentsHidden

Figure 8.4: Crawled property

4. Click on the drop-down field **Category** present under **Filters,** as seen in the figure. You will find crawled property categories like **Basic, Business Date, Connector, Document Parser, Internal, Mail, MetadataExtractor, Notes, Office, People, SharePoint, Tiff, Web, XML.** This means that whatever crawled properties are

present in SharePoint must fall under any one of these categories. So, crawled property helps the crawler and defines what category of properties needs to be extracted from items in SharePoint. Refer to *Figure 8.5:*

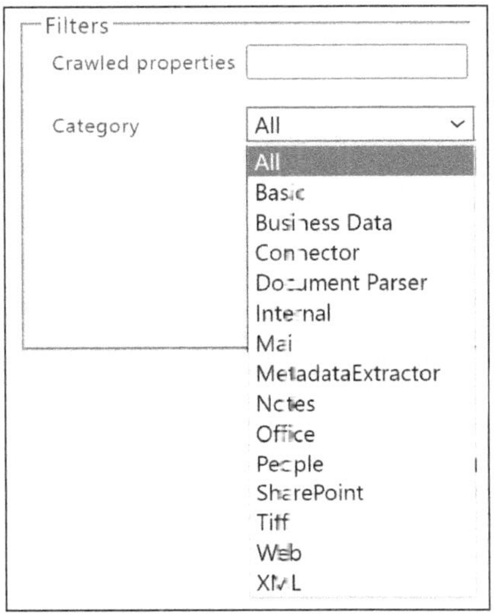

Figure 8.5: Crawled property category

5. Enter the name of the crawled property in the field **Crawled Properties** that you want to find. Select any category to filter, or select **All** from the drop-down menu and click on the arrow button to apply the filter and find. Hovering over the crawled property from the search result will show you one drop-down error option. Click on the **Arrow** and then select the option **Edit/Map Property** as seen in *Figure 8.6:*

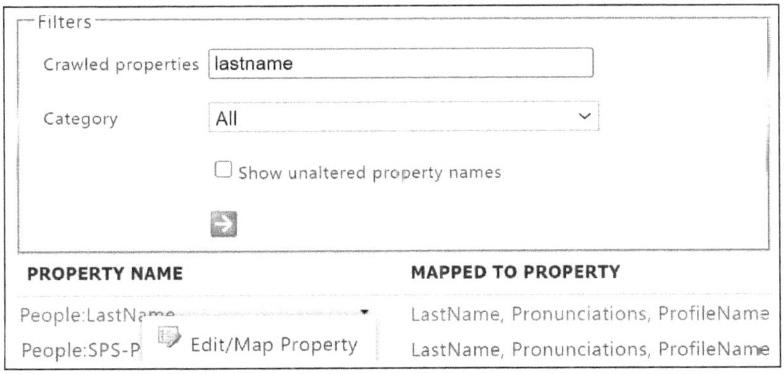

Figure 8.6: Edit or map crawled property

6. In the next page, you will find crawled property details like **Property Name**, **Category**, **Property Set ID**, and **Mappings to managed properties** to add or remove mapping, as seen in *Figure 8.7:*

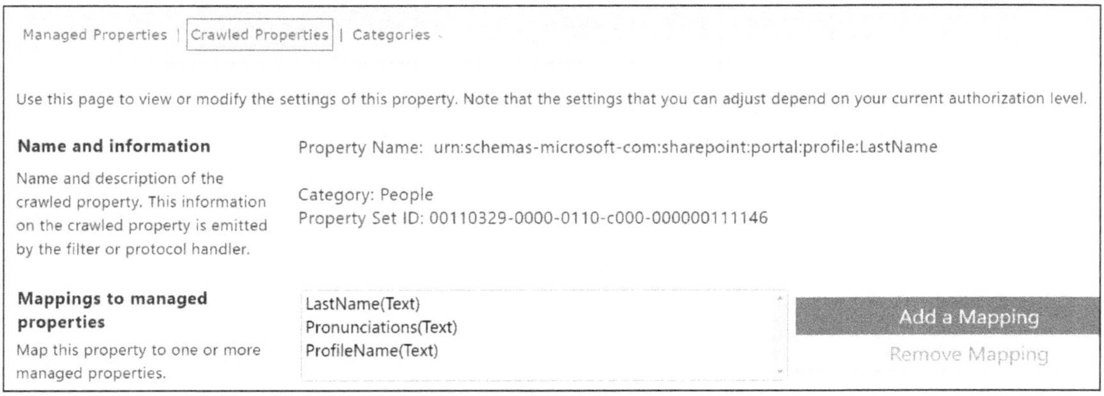

Figure 8.7: Add mapping crawled property

7. Click on the option **Add Mapping** if you need to map to the required managed property. Select the managed property and click on **OK** to apply changes, as seen in *Figure 8.8*:

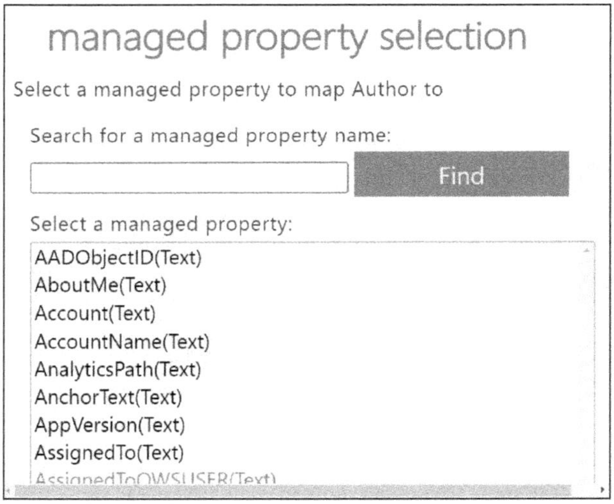

Figure 8.8: Managed property selection

8. The next option in crawled properties is **Include in full-text index**. This option is not selected by default, as seen in *Figure 8.9*, since the crawled property is already mapped to the managed property. You can select if that is required in search, but you do not find any relevant managed property to map.

Include in full-text index	☐ Include in full-text index
Include the content of this crawled property in the full-text index. This enables searching for the content of this crawled property without mapping to a managed property. Use this setting if the content of this property may be relevant for end-user queries, but you do not see a need for a managed property that contains this content.	

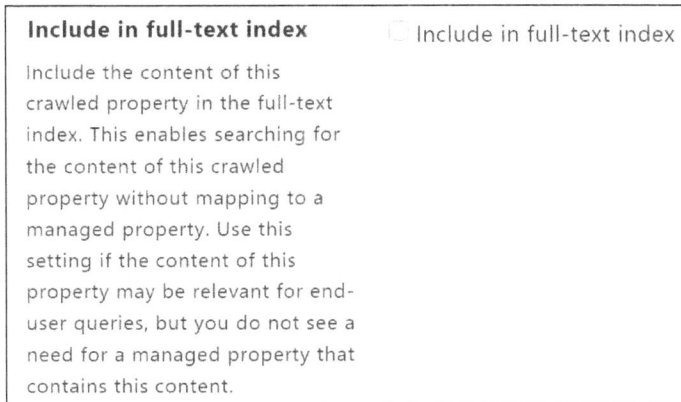

Figure 8.9: Include in full-text index

9. When you create a new site column in a list or library and that column contains value, crawled properties are created automatically after the crawling is completed. You will notice that **Crawled Property** will look like **ows_[SiteColumnInternalName]** (example: **ows_CustomColumn**). You may find one or more crawled properties like **ows_CustomColumn** and **ows_q_Text_CustomColumn**. Crawled Property **ows_CustomColumn** is used to map to managed property, whereas property **ows_q_Text_CustomColumn** got created automatically and should not be used.

Managed properties

There are predefined useful properties in search schema by default, which define what content can be displayed to the user as search results and how. Search results are retrieved from the search index. The search index includes metadata and content from managed properties. Managed properties must be mapped to one or more crawled properties to bring the content under the search result. Follow the given step-by-step procedure to find the different options present under managed properties:

1. Click on **Managed Properties** from the top navigation, as seen in the figure. You will be redirected to the **ta_listmanagedproperties** page and will see options like **Filter,** and next to it, you will find managed property.

2. You will find a few managed properties in gray, which are auto-generated. When you add a site column to a library or list that contains values, search automatically creates crawled and managed properties for that site column. Those managed properties are added automatically and seen as grey. Refer to *Figure 8.10:*

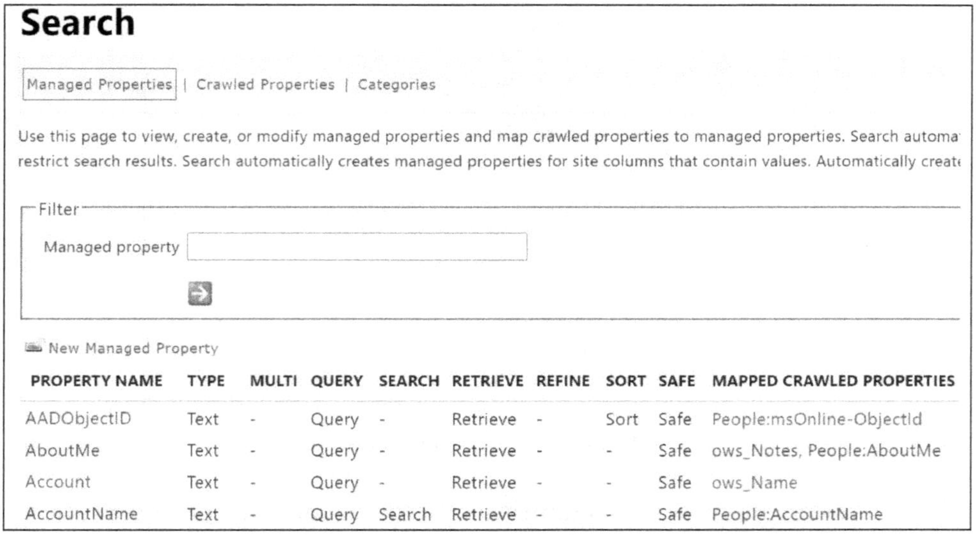

Search

Managed Properties | Crawled Properties | Categories

Use this page to view, create, or modify managed properties and map crawled properties to managed properties. Search automa restrict search results. Search automatically creates managed properties for site columns that contain values. Automatically create

─ Filter ─

Managed property [   ]

⤷

📖 New Managed Property

PROPERTY NAME	TYPE	MULTI	QUERY	SEARCH	RETRIEVE	REFINE	SORT	SAFE	MAPPED CRAWLED PROPERTIES
AADObjectID	Text	-	Query	-	Retrieve	-	Sort	Safe	People:msOnline-ObjectId
AboutMe	Text	-	Query	-	Retrieve	-	-	Safe	ows_Notes, People:AboutMe
Account	Text	-	Query	-	Retrieve	-	-	Safe	ows_Name
AccountName	Text	-	Query	Search	Retrieve	-	-	Safe	People:AccountName

Figure 8.10: Managed property page

3. Enter the property keyword (for example, title) that you want to search in the field **Managed property** and click on the arrow icon to apply. You will find relevant managed properties from the list, as seen in *Figure 8.11*:

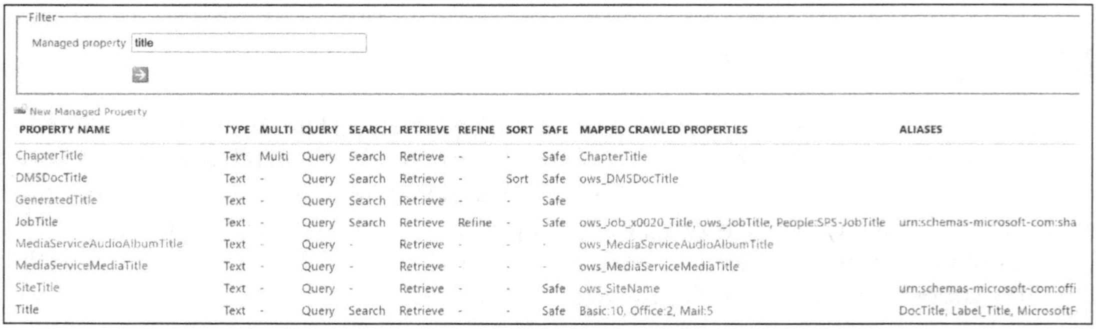

─Filter─

Managed property [title]

⤷

📖 New Managed Property

PROPERTY NAME	TYPE	MULTI	QUERY	SEARCH	RETRIEVE	REFINE	SORT	SAFE	MAPPED CRAWLED PROPERTIES	ALIASES
ChapterTitle	Text	Multi	Query	Search	Retrieve	-	-	Safe	ChapterTitle	
DMSDocTitle	Text	-	Query	Search	Retrieve	-	Sort	Safe	ows_DMSDocTitle	
GeneratedTitle	Text	-	Query	Search	Retrieve	-	-	Safe		
JobTitle	Text	-	Query	Search	Retrieve	Refine	-	Safe	ows_Job_x0020_Title, ows_JobTitle, People:SPS-JobTitle	urn:schemas-microsoft-com:sha
MediaServiceAudioAlbumTitle	Text	-	Query	-	Retrieve	-	-		ows_MediaServiceAudioAlbumTitle	
MediaServiceMediaTitle	Text	-	Query	-	Retrieve	-	-		ows_MediaServiceMediaTitle	
SiteTitle	Text	-	Query	-	Retrieve	-	-	Safe	ows_SiteName	urn:schemas-microsoft-com:offi
Title	Text	-	Query	Search	Retrieve	-	-	Safe	Basic:10, Office:2, Mail:5	DocTitle, Label_Title, MicrosoftF

Figure 8.11: Filter managed property

4. You will find that a few managed properties are mapped, and a few are not mapped. Hover over any one of the managed properties, let us say **JobTitle**. You will find an arrow icon; click on that arrow. You will get options to **Edit/Map Property** or **Delete** managed property, as seen in *Figure 8.12*. Click on **Edit/Map Property**.

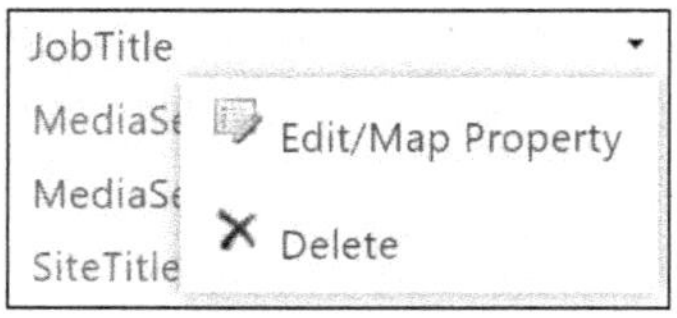

JobTitle   ▾
MediaS⸺ 📝 Edit/Map Property
MediaS⸺ ✕ Delete
SiteTitle

Figure 8.12: Edit or map property

5. The managed property will open and will show the **Name and description** of the managed property. Next, we will find the managed property **Type**. Managed properties of type **Text**, **Integer**, **Decimal**, **Date and Time**, **Yes/No**, **Double precision float**, and **Binary** are available. Currently, we have edited the managed property **JobTitle** and its type is **Text**, as seen in *Figure 8.13*:

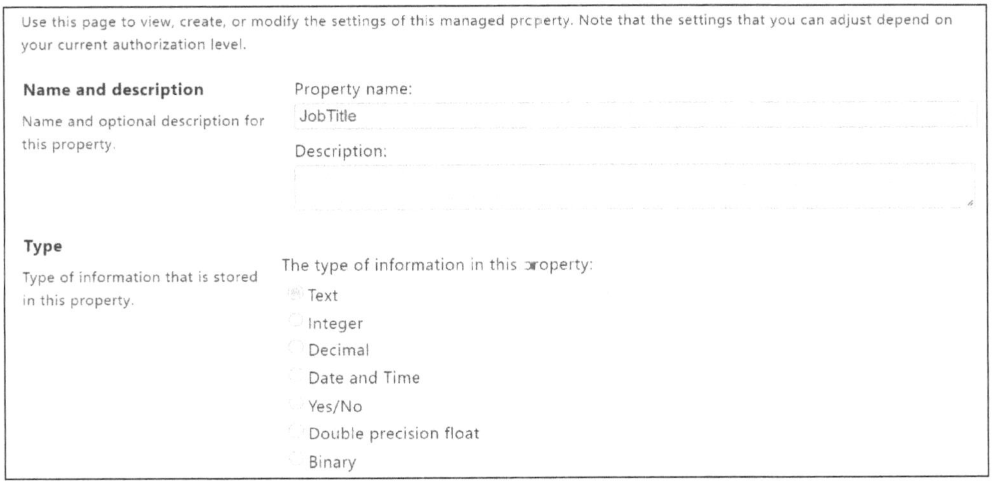

Figure 8.13: Name and description in managed property

6. The next field under managed property is **Searchable**. Turn this feature **ON** by selecting the checkbox to make the managed property searchable, as seen in *Figure 8.14*, if you are creating a new custom managed property. The property that opened here has already selected this searchable option. The next available option is **Advanced Searchable Settings**. Keep these settings as the default.

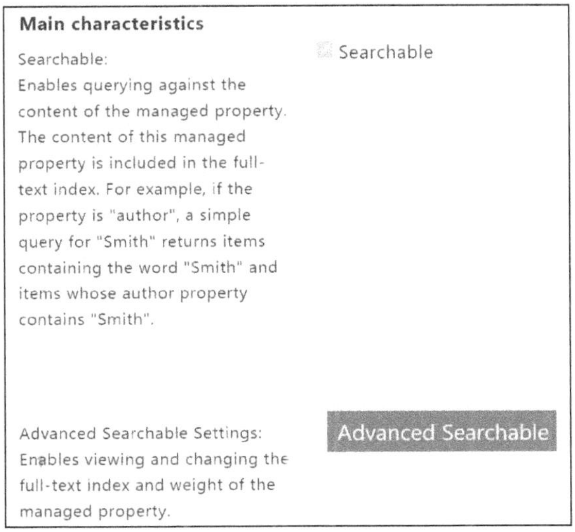

Figure 8.14: Searchable

7. The next option is **Queryable**. If you are creating a new managed property, then you can select the check box to enable and make the managed property queryable. Next to **Queryable**, you will find the option **Retrievable**. Select the check box to enable and bring the contents mapped to this property under the search result, as seen in *Figure 8.15*:

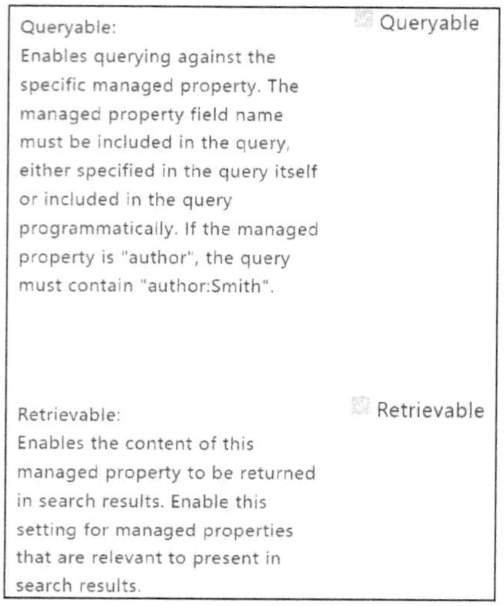

Figure 8.15: *Queryable and Retrievable*

8. The next option is **Allow multiple values**. Select the checkbox to allow multiple values of a managed property of the same type. The next option you will find is **Refinable**. This option is selected yes for the predefined managed property as seen in *Figure 8.16*:

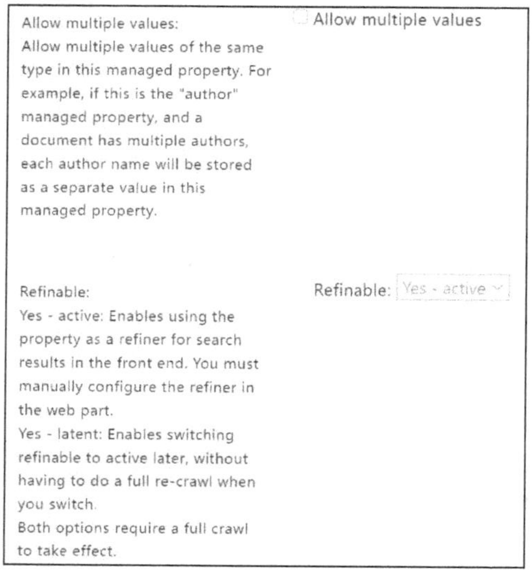

Figure 8.16: *Allow multiple values and Refinable*

9. The next option is **Sortable,** which is selected **No** by default for the current managed property, as seen in *Figure 8.17*. Selecting **Yes** will enable the sorting of search results based on this property. The next option is **Safe for Anonymous**. Enabling this option will mark this property as non-sensitive, and contents mapped to this property will be accessible by any user in SharePoint.

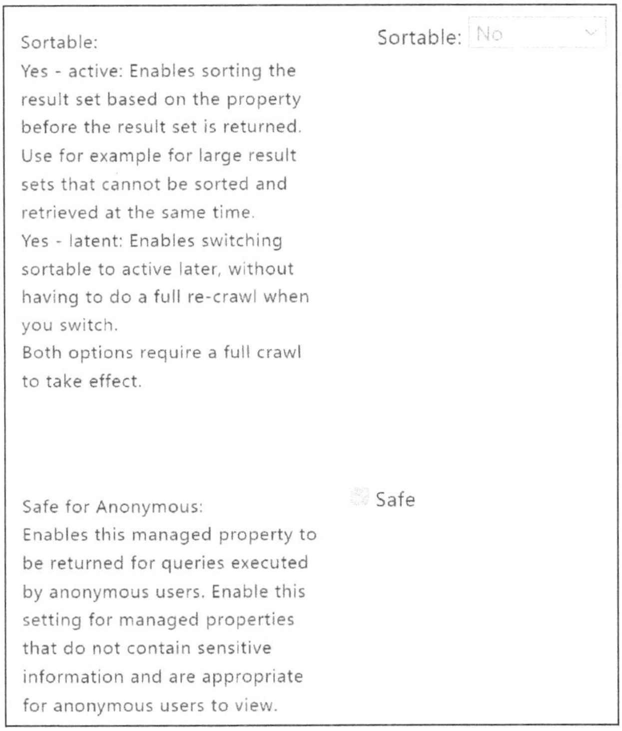

Sortable:
Yes - active: Enables sorting the result set based on the property before the result set is returned. Use for example for large result sets that cannot be sorted and retrieved at the same time.
Yes - latent: Enables switching sortable to active later, without having to do a full re-crawl when you switch.
Both options require a full crawl to take effect.

Sortable: No

Safe for Anonymous:
Enables this managed property to be returned for queries executed by anonymous users. Enable this setting for managed properties that do not contain sensitive information and are appropriate for anonymous users to view.

Safe

Figure 8.17: Sortable and Safe for Anonymous

10. The property is **Alias**. There are auto-created aliases for managed properties. You can create an alias for any managed property when needed. An alias is nothing but a short name representing the same managed property. If the property name is long or something odd, then you can add an alias to make it easier to find. You can add multiple aliases, but make sure each alias name is separated by semicolons.

11. In the next option, we have **Token Normalization**. This enables us to return results independent of letter casing and diacritics. Refer to *Figure 8.18*:

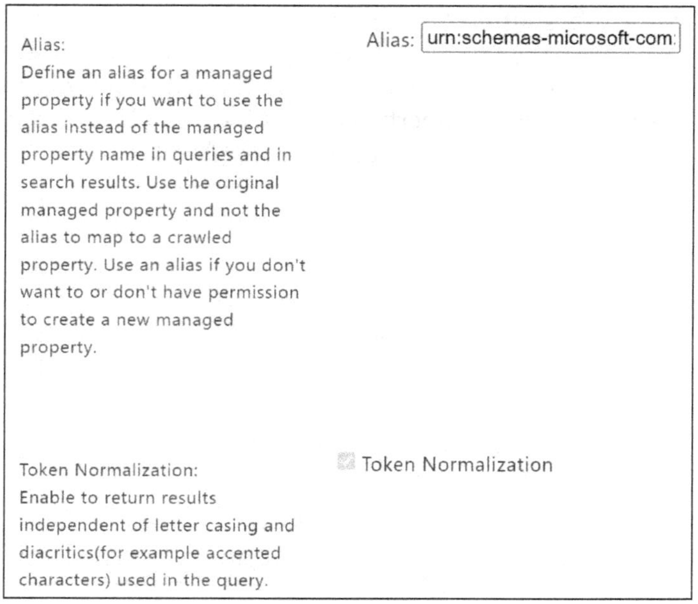

Alias:
Define an alias for a managed
property if you want to use the
alias instead of the managed
property name in queries and in
search results. Use the original
managed property and not the
alias to map to a crawled
property. Use an alias if you don't
want to or don't have permission
to create a new managed
property.

Alias: urn:schemas-microsoft-com:

Token Normalization:
Enable to return results
independent of letter casing and
diacritics(for example accented
characters) used in the query.

☑ Token Normalization

Figure 8.18: Alias and Token Normalization

12. The next option is **Complete Matching,** as seen in *Figure 8.19*. Users enter a value
in the field to search. The search will return results for the managed property and
its content matching partially or completely by default. If you are selecting the
checkbox option **Complete Matching,** the search will return results only if the
query value matches the managed property and its contents exactly. For example,
if the managed property **Title** contains the value **Contoso Site**, the search result
will return content if the user queries the exact value **Contoso Site**.

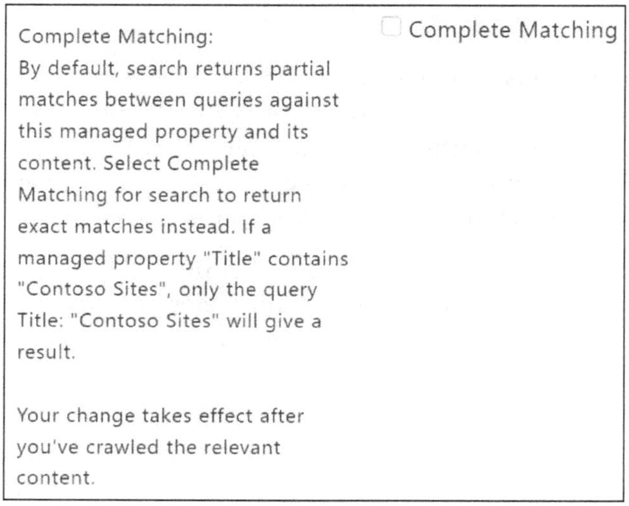

Complete Matching:
By default, search returns partial
matches between queries against
this managed property and its
content. Select Complete
Matching for search to return
exact matches instead. If a
managed property "Title" contains
"Contoso Sites", only the query
Title: "Contoso Sites" will give a
result.

Your change takes effect after
you've crawled the relevant
content.

☐ Complete Matching

Figure 8.19: Complete matching

13. The next option is **Language Neutral Tokenization,** as seen in *Figure 8.20*. If multilingual content is available, then this option can be enabled.

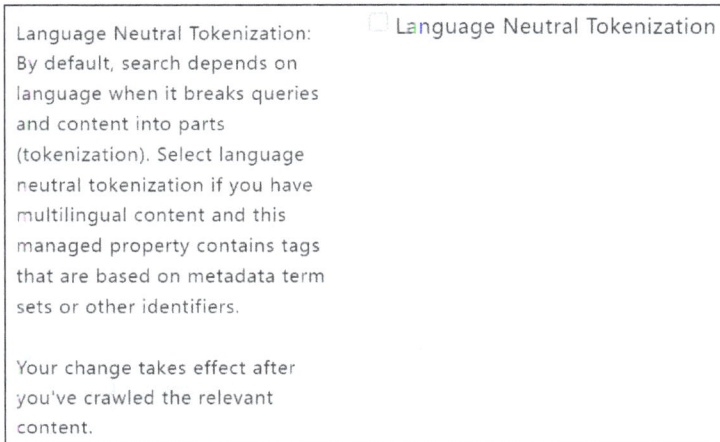

Language Neutral Tokenization:
By default, search depends on language when it breaks queries and content into parts (tokenization). Select language neutral tokenization if you have multilingual content and this managed property contains tags that are based on metadata term sets or other identifiers.

Your change takes effect after you've crawled the relevant content.

☐ Language Neutral Tokenization

Figure 8.20: Language neutral tokenization

14. The next option is **Finer Query Tokenization,** as seen in *Figure 8.21*. Managed property containing separators such as dots and dashes might not return search results for a partial match. For this reason, this option can be enabled for the managed property containing separators.

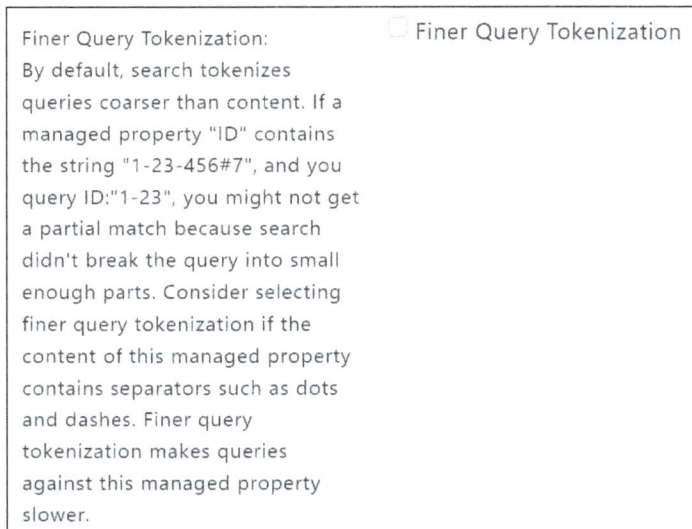

Finer Query Tokenization:
By default, search tokenizes queries coarser than content. If a managed property "ID" contains the string "1-23-456#7", and you query ID:"1-23", you might not get a partial match because search didn't break the query into small enough parts. Consider selecting finer query tokenization if the content of this managed property contains separators such as dots and dashes. Finer query tokenization makes queries against this managed property slower.

☐ Finer Query Tokenization

Figure 8.21: Finer Query Tokenization

15. The next option is **Mapping to crawled properties**. You can map managed property with crawled property or can remove mapping from the property by using this option. Click on the option **Add a Mapping** as seen in *Figure 8.22*:

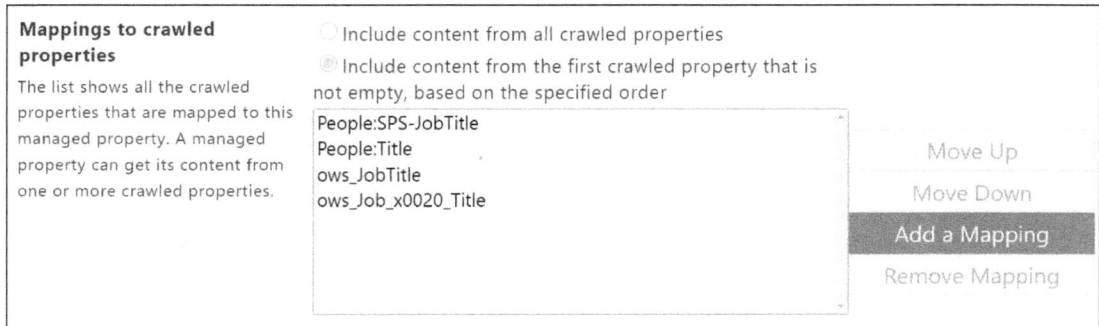

Figure 8.22: Add a mapping

16. You will get another window to find and select the crawled property and click **OK** to apply changes. Finally, click on **OK** to save and apply changes to the managed property. Refer to *Figure 8.23*:

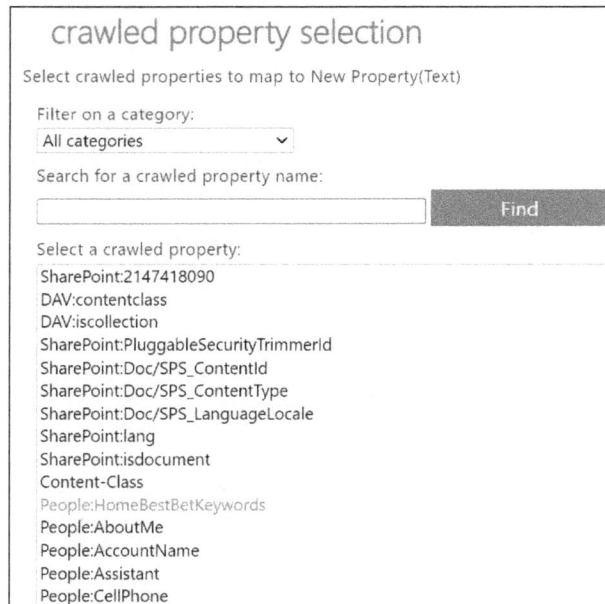

Figure 8.23: Crawled property selection

17. Similarly, you can move the mapped crawled property up and down using the **Move Up** and **Move Down** options, respectively. Select the crawled property and click on **Move Up**. Moving the crawled property up increases the priority of search results mapped to that property as well. Similarly, crawled properties present down have less priority compared to the top properties.

18. You will notice that if **Queryable** is enabled for a managed property, then **Searchable**, **Retrievable**, and **Token Normalization** are also enabled. We are not

allowed to create a new managed property that is **Refinable** or **Sortable**. There are predefined managed properties defined in the form **Refinable + Type of Column + Number** (for example, **RefinableString00, RefinableDate00,** etc.), which we can use. There are predefined, unused, and managed properties present in the managed property list, which you can use before creating new properties.

19. Identify one refinable managed property that is not mapped to any crawled property from the list. You can edit that existing refinable property following the steps described above. Add mapping with crawled property and wait for the search index refresh, which may take a few hours. Also, you can navigate to **Site settings | Search | Search and offline availability**. Click on **Reindex site** to make the edited refinable property update and ready to return search result.

Manage search dictionaries

In the previous section, we discussed managing search schema. The next setting under search is **Manage search dictionaries**. Search dictionaries are used to include or exclude company names from the contents of indexed documents, as well as **include** or exclude words for query spelling. Click on the option **Manage Search Dictionaries** from the search admin page. You will be redirected to the term store admin center. On the left navigation, you will find term groups, and **Search Dictionaries** is one of the term groups present by default. Refer to *Figure 8.24.* On expanding the term group, you will find four term sets: **Company Exclusions, Company Inclusions, Query Spelling Exclusions**, and **Query Spelling Inclusions**. Let us discuss each term set step by step.

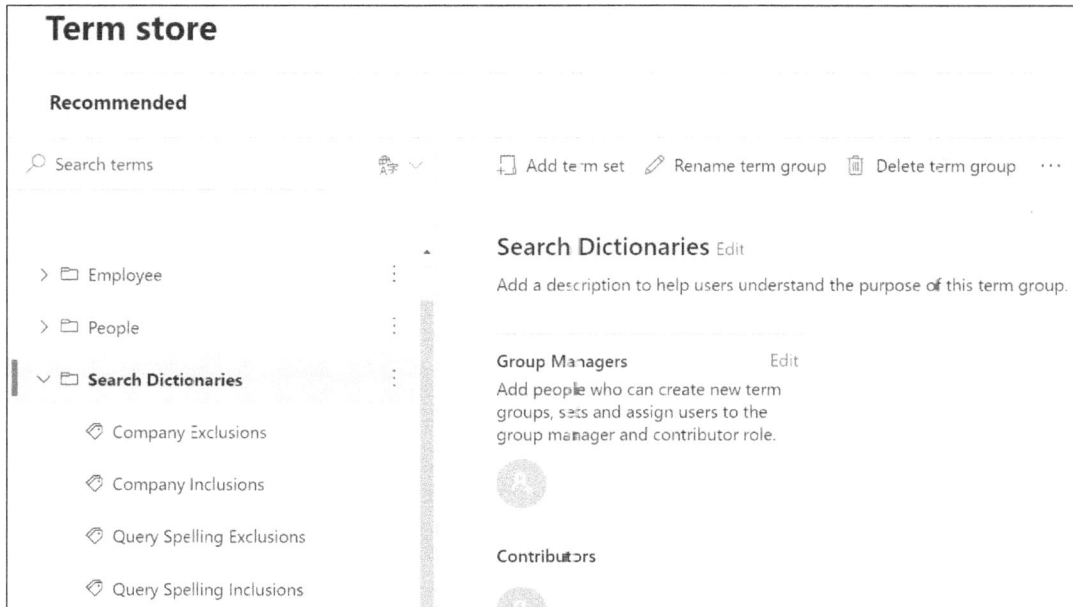

Figure 8.24: Search Dictionaries

Company inclusions and company exclusions

We need to **Add terms** under the term set **Company Inclusions** and **Company Exclusions** to include and exclude the company name from search results. Follow the given steps to include the company name in the search results:

1. Click on the action button present next to **Company Inclusion**.

2. Select **Add term**. Refer to *Figure 8.25*:

3. Enter the name of the company when the option to enter the name appears.

4. On successful configuration, the company name will appear in the search results. Refer to the following *Figure 8.25*:

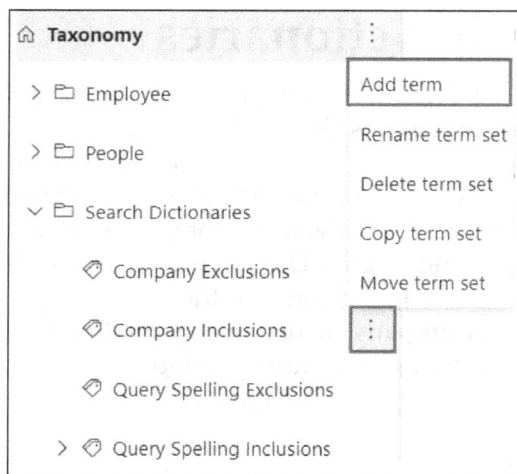

Figure 8.25: Add term in Company Inclusions or Company Exclusions

Similarly, you can create a term to exclude the company name from the search results.

Query spelling inclusions and query spelling exclusions

You can use this to add terms in query spelling inclusion. This added term will be used in the query spelling check. When you search for a word that has some spelling mistakes, then the search will suggest the correct word added as a term under **Query Spelling Inclusions**. You can add or remove the term following the same step under the term set **Query Spelling Inclusions**. You can add terms under **Query Spelling Exclusions** to exclude them from search results. Refer to *Figure 8.26*:

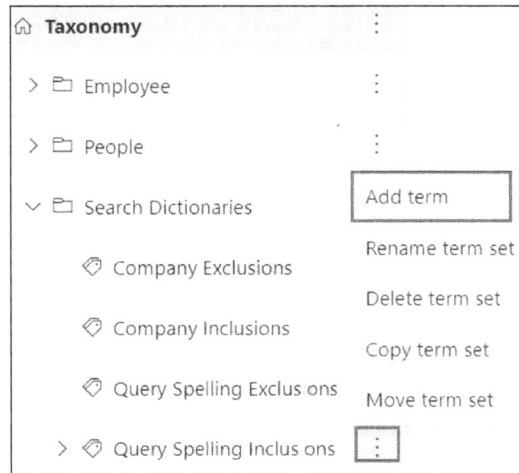

Figure 8. 26: Add tern in Query Spelling Inclusions or Query Spelling Exclusions

Query suggestion settings

SharePoint shows the search suggestions as users type in the search box. Let us say the user types SharePoint in the search box. Search suggestions will be SharePoint-related queries under the search box so that the user can select any one of the queries they are looking for. So, query suggestions help the users find necessary information quickly. Query suggestions are created automatically daily for each result source and site collection and are different for different result sources and site collections. Users can enter query details in the search box, and the search results related to the query will appear. When the user clicks on any of the search results related to the query, the search creates the suggestions automatically at least six times. Let us discuss the different options available in the query suggestion setting step by step:

1. Click on **Query Suggestion Settings** present in the search admin page. You will be redirected to **querysuggestionsettings** page.

2. The first option under **querysuggestionsettings** page will be **Search Suggestions**. Select the check box to enable query suggestions in the tenant, as seen in *Figure 8.27*:

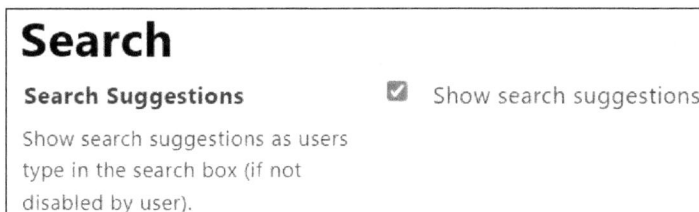

Figure 8.27: Search suggestions

3. The next option is the language for suggestion phrases. Select the **language** for suggestion, as seen in *Figure 8.28*:

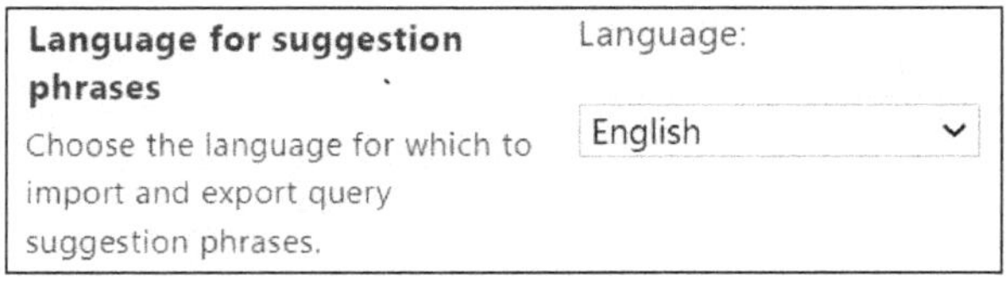

Figure 8.28: *Language*

4. For the next option, **Always suggest phrases**, click on **Import from text files** as seen in *Figure 8.29*:

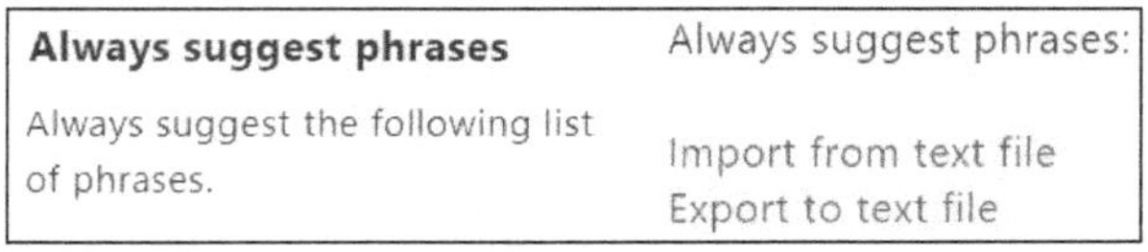

Figure 8.29: *Always suggest phrases*

5. Select the text file to import. The text file contains suggested words that will appear as query suggestions. For example, create a text file and enter words as seen in *Figure 8.30*:

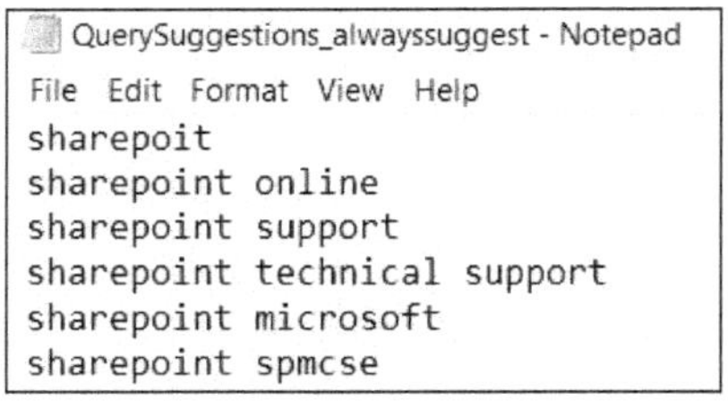

Figure 8.30: *Query suggestion text file*

6. Similarly, you can import the text file that contains words that are never suggested under query suggestions, as seen in *Figure 8.31*:

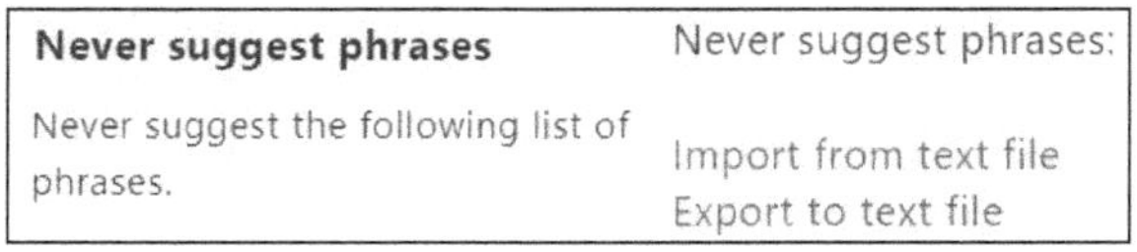

Figure 8.31: *Never suggest phrases*

Manage result sources

The result source is the source location. The search provider or source URL, like the search index, is from where search results come, with the help of protocol. The search scope is the specific set of contents that can be included or excluded from search results to further narrow the search results. The option manage search result creates or modifies the sources to scope search results. We are just filtering results by creating result sources. Let us follow the step-by-step procedure to create or modify the result source:

1. Click on the option **Manage Result Sources** present on the search admin page. You will be redirected to **ManageResultSources** page, as shown in *Figure 8.32*:

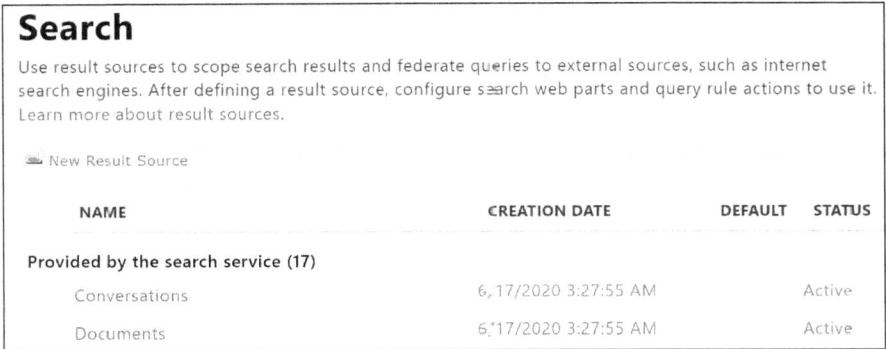

Search

Use result sources to scope search results and federate queries to external sources, such as internet search engines. After defining a result source, configure search web parts and query rule actions to use it. Learn more about result sources.

▬ New Result Source

NAME	CREATION DATE	DEFAULT	STATUS
Provided by the search service (17)			
Conversations	6, 17/2020 3:27:55 AM		Active
Documents	6, 17/2020 3:27:55 AM		Active

Figure 8.32: Result source page

2. You will find the list of result sources like Conversions, Documents, Items matching a content type, Items matching a tag, Items related to current user, Items with same keyword as this Item, Local People Results, Local Reports and Data Results, Local SharePoint Results, Local Video Results, Pages, Pictures, Popular, Recently changed items, Recommended Items, Schema Query Results, Wiki that are provided by search service by default, as seen in *Figure 8.33*:

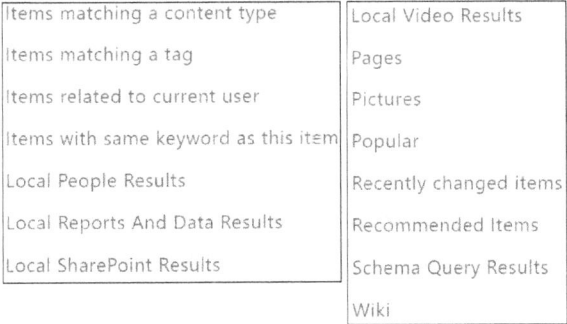

Items matching a content type	Local Video Results
Items matching a tag	Pages
Items related to current user	Pictures
Items with same keyword as this item	Popular
Local People Results	Recently changed items
Local Reports And Data Results	Recommended Items
Local SharePoint Results	Schema Query Results
	Wiki

Figure 8.33: Result source list

3. So, the result sources limit the search to certain content or a subset of search results. We can create new result sources. Click on the option **New Result Source** present at the top of the **ManageResultSources** page. You will be redirected to the **EditResultSource** page. Enter the **Name** and **Description** of the result source, as seen in *Figure 8.34*:

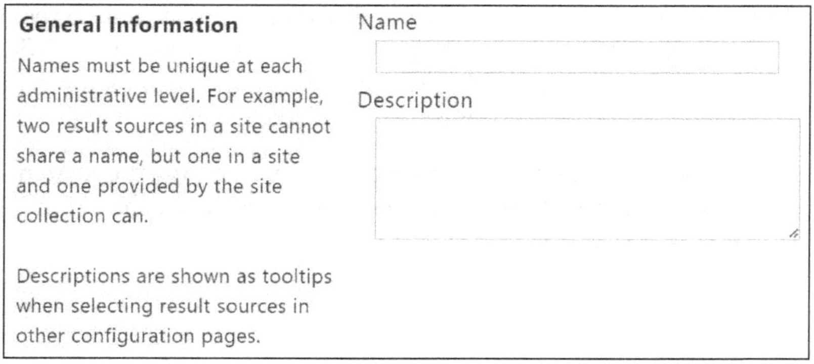

Figure 8.34: *General information while creating new result source*

4. Select the **Protocol** as **Local SharePoint** for results from SharePoint search index, as seen in *Figure 8.35*. Local SharePoint is the default protocol used to get search results from the search index of the local search service, which is the search index of the tenant. Remote SharePoint and OpenSearch 1.0/1.1 protocols are deprecated and will be removed from the configuration soon.

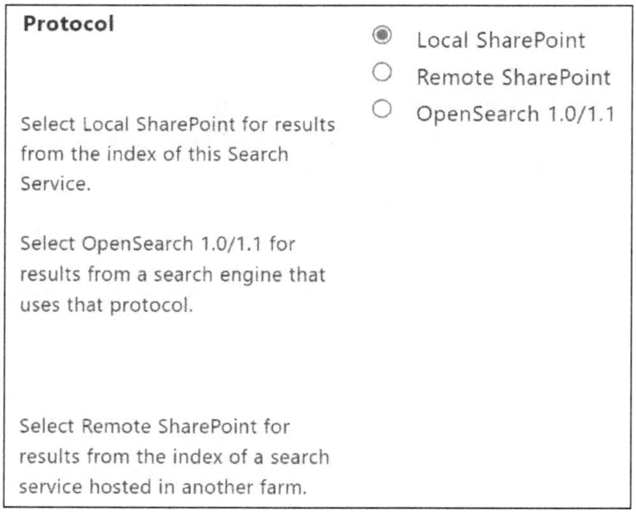

Figure 8.35: *Result source protocol*

5. Select the **Type** of search result, whether **SharePoint Search Results** to search over the entire search index, or **People Search Results** to search people. Select **SharePoint Search Results**, as seen in *Figure 8.36*:

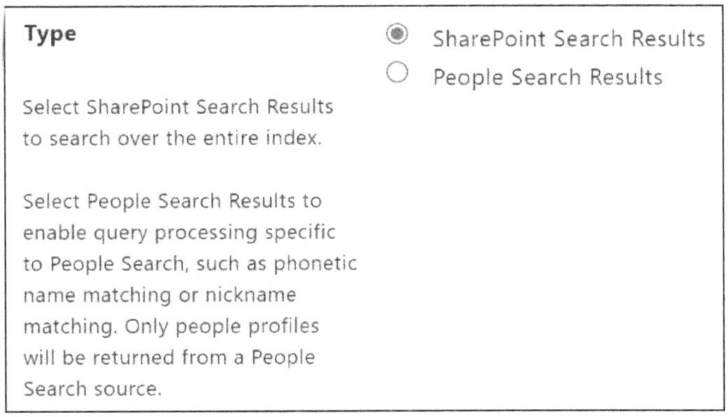

Figure 8.36: Result source type

6. The next option is **Search Results**. By default, partial search is enabled. You can select the checkbox **Don't show partial search results** to disable partial search, as seen in *Figure 8.37*. Partial search is when a user types a part of the term, like the beginning of the term, the end of the term, or the middle of the term, instead of the whole term in the search box to get search results.

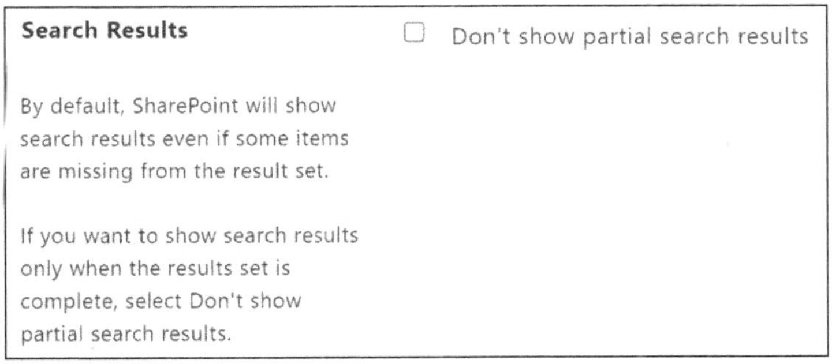

Figure 8.37: Search results

7. The next option is **Query Transform**. You can apply a custom query transform to get specific results from the result source. You can build your custom query transform using the query builder. Click on the option **Launch Query Builder** to open the query builder to build your own query transform as per the requirement. Currently, the selected query transform is **searchTerms,** as seen in *Figure 8.38*:

Query Transform

Change incoming queries to use this new query text instead. Include the incoming query in the new text by using the query variable "{searchTerms}".

Use this to scope results. For example, to only return OneNote items, set the new text to " {searchTerms} fileextension=one". Then, an incoming query "sharepoint" becomes "sharepoint fileextension=one". Launch the Query Builder for additional options.

{searchTerms}   Launch Query Build

Learn more about query transforms.

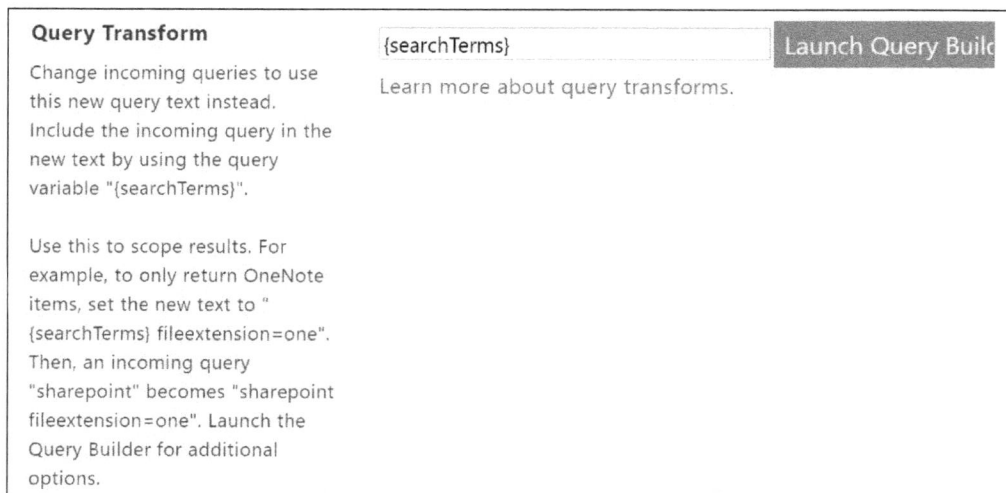

Figure 8.38: Query transform

8. The next option is **Credential Information**. There will be two options, namely **Default Authentication** and **Basic Authentication**. Select **Default Authentication** to use SharePoint authentication, as seen in *Figure 8.39*. **Basic Authentication** needs a username and a password.

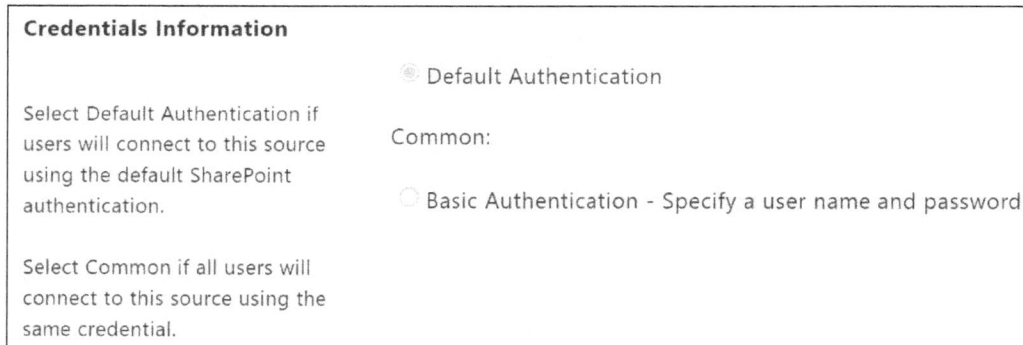

Credentials Information

Select Default Authentication if users will connect to this source using the default SharePoint authentication.

Select Common if all users will connect to this source using the same credential.

◉ Default Authentication

Common:

○ Basic Authentication - Specify a user name and password

Figure 8.39: Credential information

9. Finally, click on **Save**. The result source will be created and added to the list of result sources.

10. Once you hover over any result sources, you will get a drop-down option. Click on the drop-down and select the option **Set as Default** to make that content source the default content source, as seen in *Figure 8.40*:

Figure 8.40: Set the content source as default

11. Find predefined result sources and their respective query transforms in *Table 8.1*:

Result source	Query transforms
Conversations	{searchTerms?} (MicroBlogType:2 OR MicroBlogType:4 OR ContentTypeId:0x012002* OR ContentTypeId:0x0107* OR WebTemplate=COMMUNITY)
Documents	{?path:{Scope}} {?owstaxIdMetadataAllTagsInfo:{Tag}} (FileExtension:doc OR FileExtension:docx OR FileExtension:xls OR FileExtension:xlsx OR FileExtension:ppt OR FileExtension:pptx OR FileExtension:pdf) (IsDocument:"True" OR contentclass:"STS_ListItem")
Items matching a content type	{searchTerms?} {?path:{Scope}} {?owstaxIdMetadataAllTagsInfo:{Tag}} {?ContentTypeId:{ContentTypeId}}
Items matching a tag	{searchTerms?} {?path:{Scope}} {?owstaxIdMetadataAllTagsInfo:{Tag}} (IsDocument:"True" OR contentclass:"STS_ListItem")
Items related to current user	{?path:{Scope}} {?owstaxIdMetadataAllTagsInfo:{Tag}} {?ContentTypeId:{ContentTypeId}} People:{User} (IsDocument:"True" OR contentclass:"STS_ListItem")
Items with same keyword as this item	{searchTerms?} (size=-1 {?OR {ListItem.Keyphrases}}) AND (NOT path:{ListItem.QuotedUrl}) {?path:{Scope}} (ContentTypeId:0x01* AND NOT ContentTypeId:0x0120*)
Local People Results	{?{searchTerms} ContentClass=urn:content-class:SPSPeople}
Local Reports And Data Results	{?{searchTerms} (fileextension=xlsx OR fileextension=xls OR fileextension=xlsb OR fileextension=xlsm OR fileextension=odc OR fileextension=rdl OR IsReport=1 OR IsData=1)}
Local SharePoint Results	{?{searchTerms} -ContentClass=urn:content-class:SPSPeople}

Result source	Query transforms
Local Video Results	{searchTerms?} {?path:{Scope}} {?owstaxIdMetadataAllTagsInfo:{Tag}} (ContentTypeId:0x0120D520A808* OR ContentTypeId:0x010100F3754F12A9B6490D9622A01FE9D8F012* OR (SecondaryFileExtension=wmv OR SecondaryFileExtension=avi OR SecondaryFileExtension=mpg OR SecondaryFileExtension=asf OR SecondaryFileExtension=mp4 OR SecondaryFileExtension=ogg OR SecondaryFileExtension=ogv OR SecondaryFileExtension=webm OR SecondaryFileExtension=mov))
Pages	{?path:{Scope}} {?owstaxIdMetadataAllTagsInfo:{Tag}} ContentTypeId:0x010100C568DB52D9D0A14D9B2FDCC96666E9F2007948130EC3D-B064584E219954237AF39* (IsDocument:"True" OR contentclass:"STS_ListItem")
Pictures	{?path:{Scope}} {?owstaxIdMetadataAllTagsInfo:{Tag}} (ContentTypeId:0x0101009148F5A04DDD49cbA7127AADA5FB792B00AADE-34325A8B49cdA8BB4DB53328F214* OR ContentTypeId:0x010102*)
Popular	{searchTerms?} {?path:{Scope}} {?owstaxIdMetadataAllTagsInfo:{Tag}} {?ContentTypeId:{ContentTypeId}} (IsDocument:"True" OR contentclass:"STS_ListItem")
Recently changed items	{?path:{Scope}} {?owstaxIdMetadataAllTagsInfo:{Tag}} (IsDocument:"True" OR contentclass:"STS_ListItem")
Recommended Items	{searchTerms?} recommendedfor:{RecsURL} {?path:{Scope}} {?ContentTypeId:{ContentTypeId}} (IsDocument:"True" OR contentclass:"STS_ListItem")
Wiki	{?path:{Scope}} {?owstaxIdMetadataAllTagsInfo:{Tag}} (ContentTypeId:0x010100C568DB52D9D0A14D9B2FDCC96666E9F2007948130EC3D-B064584E219954237AF39004C1F8B46085B4d22B1CDC3DE08CFFB9C* OR ContentTypeId:0x010108*) (IsDocument:"True" OR contentclass:"STS_ListItem")

Table 8.1: Result source and Query transforms

Manage query rules

Query rules are nothing but conditions and their associated actions. SharePoint search performs actions based on the query rule when the user query meets the query rule conditions. We can promote search results to the top and influence search result ranking by applying query rules. Let us follow the step-by-step procedure to create query rules:

1. Click on the option **Manage Query Rules** present in the search admin page. You will be redirected to **listqueryrules** page as seen in *Figure 8.41*:

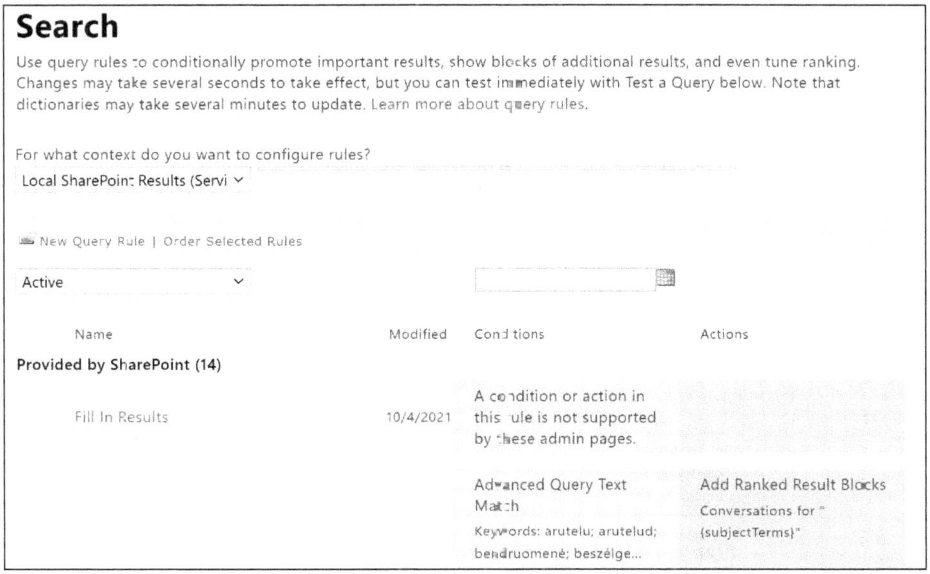

Search

Use query rules to conditionally promote important results, show blocks of additional results, and even tune ranking. Changes may take several seconds to take effect, but you can test immediately with Test a Query below. Note that dictionaries may take several minutes to update. Learn more about query rules.

For what context do you want to configure rules?
Local SharePoint Results (Servi ∨

New Query Rule | Order Selected Rules

Active ∨

Name	Modified	Conditions	Actions
Provided by SharePoint (14)			
Fill In Results	10/4/2021	A condition or action in this rule is not supported by these admin pages.	
		Advanced Query Text Match	Add Ranked Result Blocks
		Keywords: arutelu; arutelud; bendruomenė; beszélge...	Conversations for " {subjectTerms}"

Figure 8.41: Manage query rule page

2. You will notice a drop-down box, **Select a Result Source**, that defines the context for which you want to configure rules. Select the drop-down; you will get a list of all result sources, as seen in *Figure 8.42*. Select the result source **Local SharePoint Results** from the drop-down.

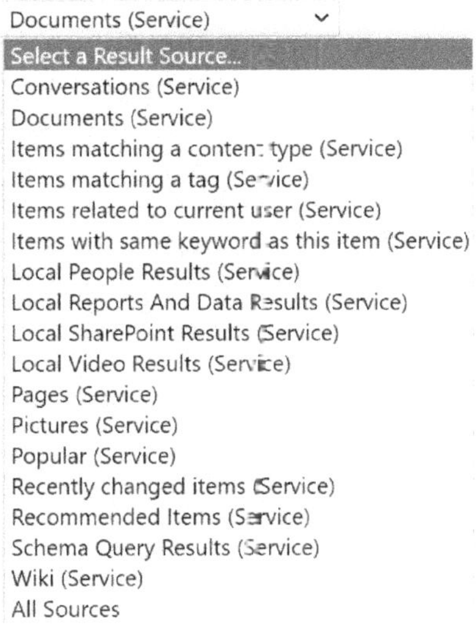

Documents (Service) ∨
Select a Result Source...
Conversations (Service)
Documents (Service)
Items matching a content type (Service)
Items matching a tag (Service)
Items related to current user (Service)
Items with same keyword as this item (Service)
Local People Results (Service)
Local Reports And Data Results (Service)
Local SharePoint Results (Service)
Local Video Results (Service)
Pages (Service)
Pictures (Service)
Popular (Service)
Recently changed items (Service)
Recommended Items (Service)
Schema Query Results (Service)
Wiki (Service)
All Sources

Figure 8.42: Result sources

3. Click on the option **New Query Rule** from the navigation. You will be redirected to **editqueryrule** page.

4. Enter the name of the query rule (e.g., sharepoint projects) in the field **Rule name** under the category **General Information**.

5. If you expand the category **Context**, you will find information regarding the content source. You can add or remove the result source by following the options **Add Source** and **remove**, respectively, as seen in *Figure 8.43*:

General Information	Rule name
	sharepoint projects
	Fires only on source Local SharePoint Results
◢ Context	
You can restrict this rule to queries performed on a particular result source. For instance, restrict a rule to the Local Video Results source so that it only fires in Video search.	Query is performed on these sources ○ All sources ◉ One of these sources 　　Local SharePoint Results remove Add Source

Figure 8.43: Query rule general information and context

6. The next option is **Query Conditions**. You can create rules that will fire only if the user's search query in the search box matches this rule. This ultimately limits and influences the search results. Click on the drop-down button present in the option **Query Conditions**. You will find options like **Query Matches Keyword Exactly**, **Query Contains Action Term**, and **Advanced Query Text Match**. Select the option **Advanced Query Text Match**, as seen in *Figure 8.44*.

7. You need to enter query phrases in the option **Query contains one of these phrases (semi-colon separated)**. You can enter a single phrase or multiple phrases separated by a semi-colon, as seen in *Figure 8.44*. Enter the possible key query phrases (Example: SharePoint, project) that are most relevant to the content.

Query Conditions	Advanced Query Text Match ⌄
Define when a user's search box query makes this rule fire. You can specify multiple conditions of different types, or remove all conditions to fire for any query text. Every query condition becomes false if the query is not a simple keyword query, such as if it has quotes, property filters, parentheses, or special operators.	◉ Query contains one of these phrases (semi-colon separated) 　sharepoint;project ☑ Entire query matches exactly ☑ Start of query matches, but not entire query ☑ End of query matches, but not entire query ◉ Assign the entire query to {subjectTerms} ○ Assign match to {subjectTerms}, unmatched terms to {actionTerms} ○ Assign match to {actionTerms}, unmatched terms to {subjectTerms} Remove Condition Add Alternate Condition

Figure 8.44: Query condition and query phrase

8. Next to it, you will find three checkboxes, namely, **Entire query matches exactly**, **Start of query matches but not entire query**, and **End of query matches but not entire query**. You can select any one or all three so that the rule will fire once it matches those conditions.

9. In the next step, you will find three more options, namely **Assign the entire query to {subjectTerms}**, **Assign match to {subjectTerms} unmatched terms to {actionTerms}, and Assign match to {actionTerms} unmatched terms to {subjectTerms}**. Keep the default selection as **Assign the entire query to {subjectTerms}** as seen in *Figure 8.44*.

10. The next Category is **Actions**. You will find the option **Add Promoted Result** to create **Promoted Results**. Another option is the **Add Result Block**, used to create **Result Blocks**. Click on the option **Add Promoted Results**, as seen in *Figure 8.45*:

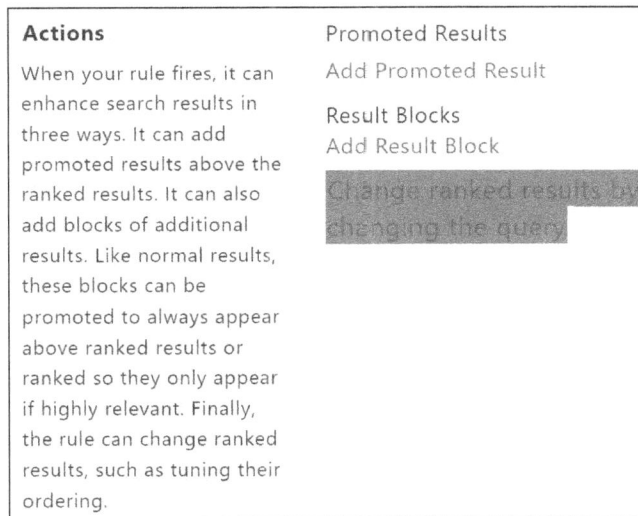

Actions	Promoted Results
When your rule fires, it can enhance search results in three ways. It can add promoted results above the ranked results. It can also add blocks of additional results. Like normal results, these blocks can be promoted to always appear above ranked results or ranked so they only appear if highly relevant. Finally, the rule can change ranked results, such as tuning their ordering.	Add Promoted Result
	Result Blocks
	Add Result Block
	Change ranked results by changing the query

Figure 8.45: Action category to add promoted result and result block

11. You will get a new dialog box to enter details like **Title**, **URL**, and **Description** for promoted results, as shown in the following figure. **URL** (e.g., **https://spmcse. sharepoint.com/sites/BPB-ModernTeamSite/SitePages/SharePoint-Projects. aspx**) will be a SharePoint site page that needs to be promoted.

12. Click on **Save** once all the details are filled, as seen in *Figure 8.46*. You can select the checkbox option **Render the URL as a banner instead of as a hyperlink** to display the promoted search result as a banner.

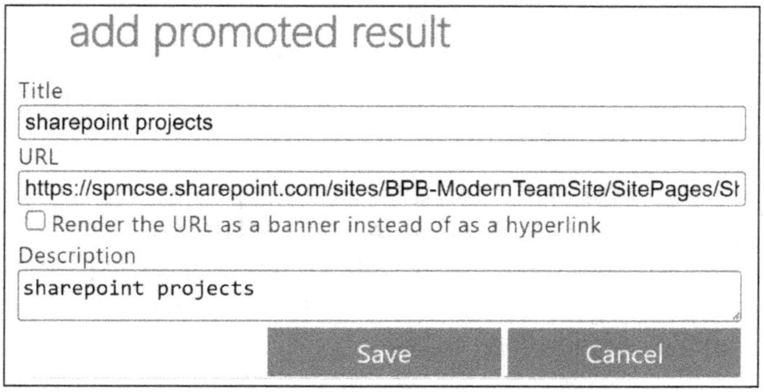

Figure 8.46: *Add promoted result details*

13. The next option is **Publishing**. You can select the **Start Date** on which the promotion of the search result will start. Select the **End Date** after which the promotion will stop, as seen in *Figure 8.47*. Finally, click on **Save**.

Figure 8.47: *Select publishing date*

14. A query rule with promoted search results is now created. Now, enter the query phrase project or SharePoint, which you configured while creating the query rule, in the search box. You will find the promoted search result at the top, as shown in *Figure 8.48*. Promoted search results will always be on top.

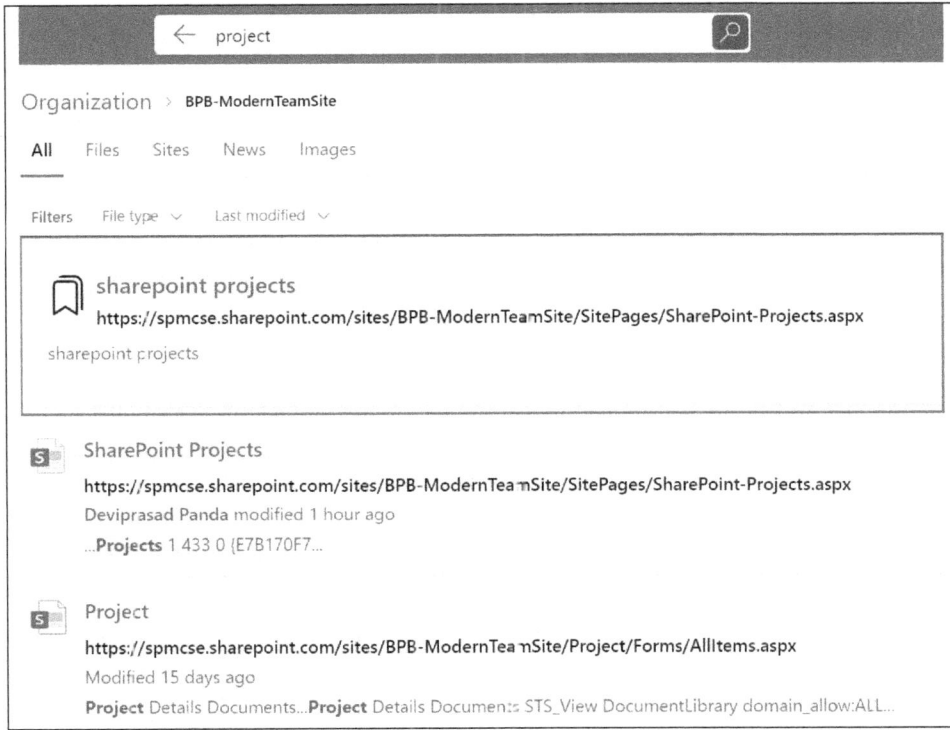

Figure 8.48: Promoted search result

15. Now, going back to *Step 5* described previously. You can create a new query rule and add **Local People Results** as a result source, as shown in *Figure 8.49*:

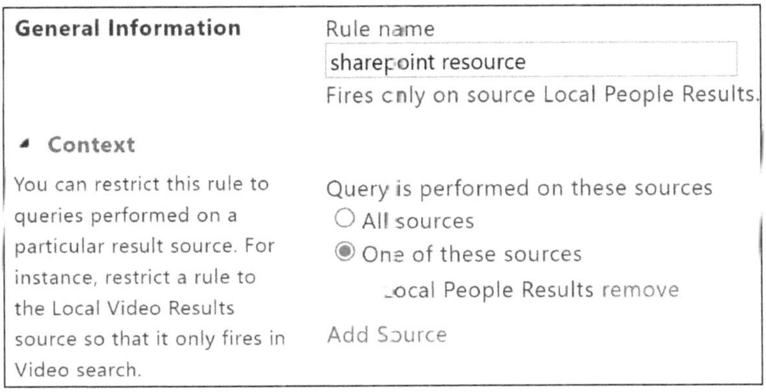

Figure 8.49: Add source in context

16. From the next option, **Query Conditions,** remove the condition.

17. The next category is **Actions**. Click on the option **Add Result Block**. You will get a dialog box, as seen in *Figure 8.50*. Click on the option **Launch Query Builder**.

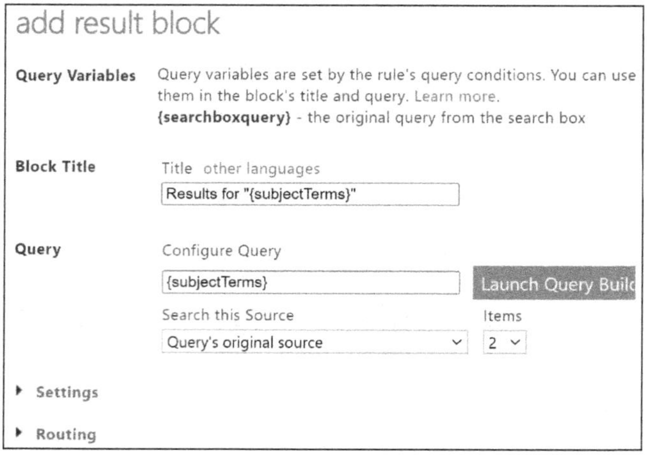

Figure 8.50: Add result block

18. From the next window, click on the drop-down option **Select a query** and select **Local People Results**. Refer to *Figure 8.51*.

19. In the next step, you will find drop-down fields under **Property Filter**. From the first drop-down, select the option **Show All Managed Properties** and select **Skills** from Managed Properties.

20. Select the option **Contains** from the drop-down next.

21. Select the option **Manual value** from the drop-down option next.

22. You will get an additional field where you need to enter **{subjectTerms}**.

23. Click on **Add property filter** and click on **OK**, as seen in *Figure 8.51*:

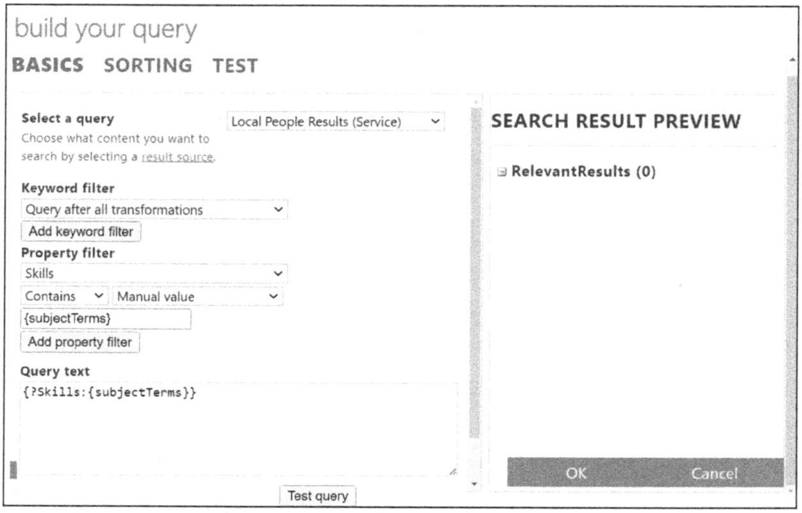

Figure 8.51: Add a property filter

24. You will find the query added, as seen in *Figure 8.52*:

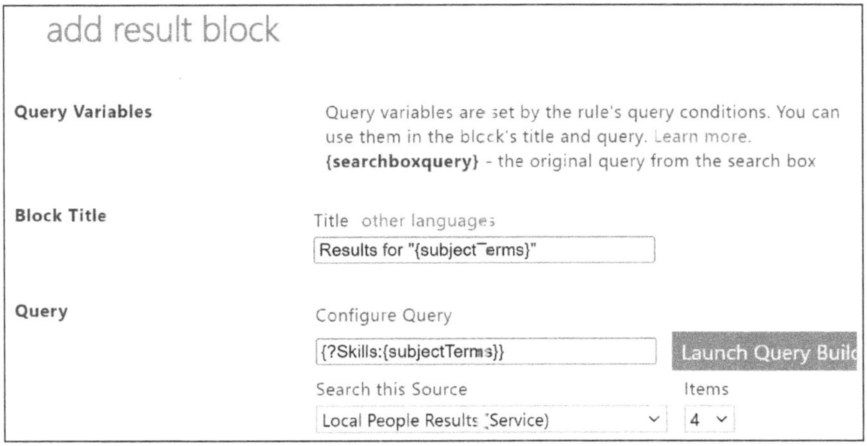

Figure 8.52: Added query in configure query field under result block

25. Expand the category **Settings** present in the result block. You can change the options as per requirement, as seen in *Figure 8.53*:

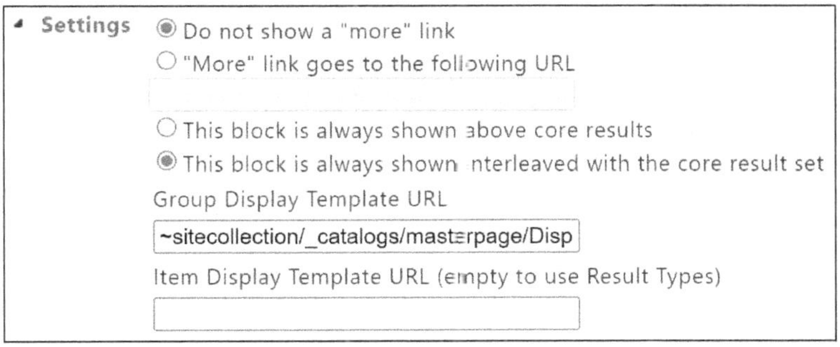

Figure 8.53: Result block settings

26. Finally, click on **Save**. A query rule will be created.

27. If you enter the query phrase in the search box now, you will get the details of people in the top blocks as a promoted result, which was a primary requirement of creating the result block.

Remove search results

You can exclude URLs from search results as per the requirement. Click on the option **Remove Search Results** from the search administration page. You will be redirected to the **searchresultremoval** page. Enter the URL that you want to exclude from search results in the field **URLs to remove** and click on **Remove Now**, as seen in *Figure 5.54*. You will notice that it will be excluded from the search results.

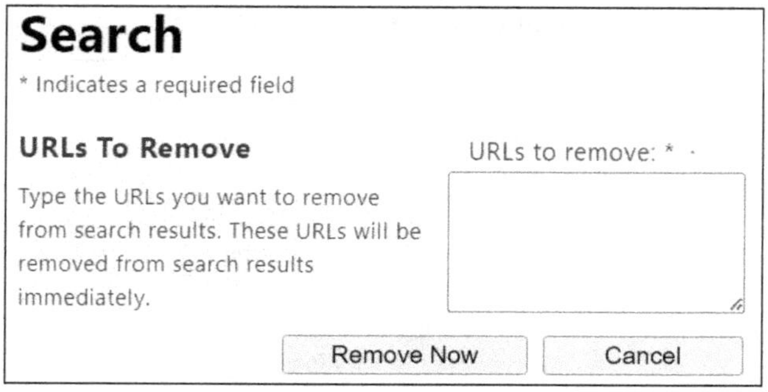

Figure 8.54: Remove search results

View usage reports

The next setting under search administration is view usage reports. Click on the option **View Usage Reports**. You will be redirected to reporting page and will find reports like **Number of Queries**, **Top Queries by Day**, **Top Queries by Month**, **Abandoned Queries by Day**, **Abandoned Queries by Month**, **No Result Queries by Day**, **No Result Queries by Month**, **Query Rule Usage by Day**, **Query Rule Usage by Month**. You will find details and analyze information like the number of queries, top queries, abandoned queries, and **no result queries** to modify search settings for better search results, as per the organization's requirements.

Search center settings

The next setting under the search administration page is search center settings. Click on the option **Search Center Settings**. You will be redirected to the **searchcentersettings** page. You will find two options, namely **Enter a URL for the global Search Center** and **Loading search results**. You can change the URL of the global search center to any custom page. Using this setting, enter a URL for the global search center and enter the custom search center page in the field **Search Center URL**, as seen in *Figure 8.55*:

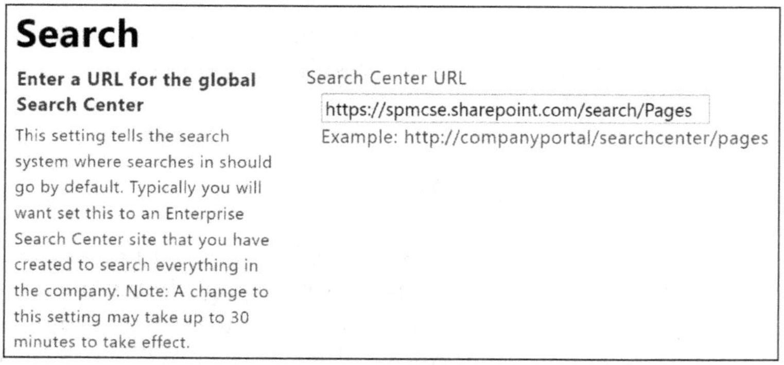

Figure 8.55: Search center URL

Keep the setting for **Loading search results** as the default option **Only asynchronous,** as seen in the following figure, and click on **OK** to finish the settings for the global search center. Tell where searches should go by specifying the location of your search center. Refer to the following figure:

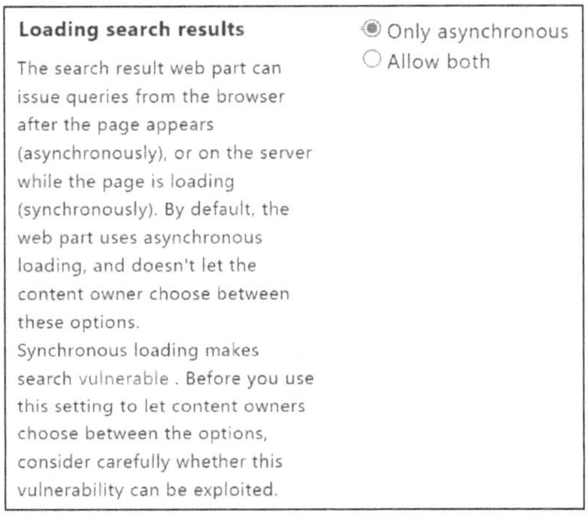

Loading search results   ◉ Only asynchronous
                              ○ Allow both

The search result web part can issue queries from the browser after the page appears (asynchronously), or on the server while the page is loading (synchronously). By default, the web part uses asynchronous loading, and doesn't let the content owner choose between these options. Synchronous loading makes search vulnerable . Before you use this setting to let content owners choose between the options, consider carefully whether this vulnerability can be exploited.

Figure 8.56: Loading search results

Export search configuration

The next setting under the search administration page is **Export Search Configuration**. By clicking on the option **Export Search Configuration**, it will create an xml file named `SearchConfiguration`. The XML file includes all customized query rules, result sources, result types, ranking models, and site search settings, but not any that shipped with SharePoint, in the current tenant, that can be imported to other tenants.

Import search configuration

The next option in the search administration page is **Import Search Configuration**. You can import search settings using this option. Click on **Choose File**, select the XML file, and click on **Import** as seen in *Figure 8.57*:

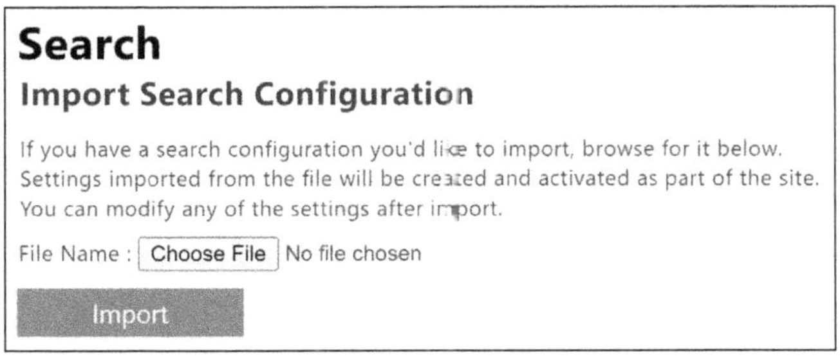

Search
Import Search Configuration

If you have a search configuration you'd like to import, browse for it below. Settings imported from the file will be created and activated as part of the site. You can modify any of the settings after import.

File Name : [Choose File] No file chosen

[Import]

Figure 8.57: Import Search Configuration

Crawl log permissions

The next option under the search administration page is **Crawl Log Permission**. You can grant users read access to crawl log information for this tenant, as seen in *Figure 8.58*:

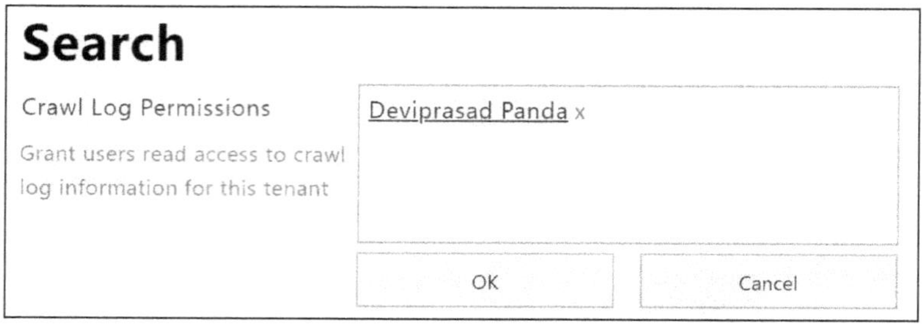

Search

Crawl Log Permissions	Deviprasad Panda x
Grant users read access to crawl log information for this tenant	

OK   Cancel

Figure 8.58: Crawl Log Permissions

Conclusion

In this chapter, we glanced at managed properties, crawled properties, and how to map managed properties with crawled properties. We understood the search dictionary and configured high-quality pages to improve search relevance. We also learned how to configure query phrases as suggestions during user searches and gained a clear understanding of result sources, how to create them, and query transforms. Additionally, we discussed the step-by-step procedure to create query rules, query conditions, promoted results, and result blocks. We learned how to exclude sites from search results and export search usage reports. We also discussed exporting and importing search settings and checked the possibility of assigning permissions to crawl logs for users.

In *Chapter 9, App Administration*, we will discuss administering apps in SharePoint.

Points to remember

- Regular changes are applied in Office 365 and SharePoint Online, by which you may notice small changes related to a template or some other features.

- The modern search experience gets results from the default result source. Switching from the default result source to another will impact both the classic and modern search experiences.

- Hybrid federated search retired from Microsoft 365. Remote SharePoint and OpenSearch 1.0/1.1 protocols are deprecated and will be removed from the configuration soon.

CHAPTER 9

App Administration

Introduction

In the previous *Chapter 8, Search Administration,* we discussed one of the service applications in SharePoint called search. In this chapter, we will discuss another service in SharePoint called **Apps**. The term web part, in the previous versions of SharePoint, is replaced with the term App. The app is the building block of SharePoint, under which content resides. Hence, all the services related to the SharePoint Apps are managed centrally by this setting called **Apps** present in the SharePoint admin center. You will find various options like **Manage Apps, App requests, More features, SharePoint Store,** and **API access** in **Apps** service to manage better. Let us discuss these Apps' settings step by step.

Structure

In this chapter, we will discuss the following topics:

- SharePoint store
- Manage apps
- API access
- App requests
- More features

Objectives

By the end of this chapter, you will get a clear understanding of SharePoint Apps, how to acquire Apps from the SharePoint store, and how to Manage Apps. You will also understand the management of API access and app requests. Additionally, you will learn a few more features related to the Apps.

SharePoint store

Apps are stand-alone and can perform tasks using services independently with improved performance. Apps are available in the SharePoint Store. Your organization can develop Apps, or you can get existing Apps developed by third-party developers that are available for purchase. SharePoint store is a marketplace where you can get third-party Apps. Follow this step-by-step procedure to get an app:

1. Open the **SharePoint admin center**.

2. Click on **More features** from the left navigation.

3. Click on **Open** present below the feature **Apps** as seen in the following figure:

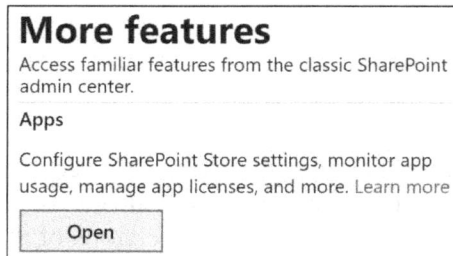

Figure 9.1: Click on Apps from More features

4. You will be redirected to the **tenantAppCatalog** page, and an option, **Manage apps**, will pop up. You will find options like **Manage apps**, **App requests**, **More features**, **SharePoint Store**, **API access,** and **SharePoint admin center** in the left navigation, as seen in the following figure. Click on the option **SharePoint Store**. We will discuss the option **Manage Apps** later; before that, let us understand the SharePoint store.

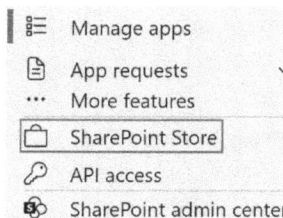

Figure 9.2: SharePoint Store option from left navigation

5. You will be redirected to the **Appstore** page, and the **SharePoint Store** option will be selected, as seen in *Figure 9.3*. You will find three options, such as **My Apps**, **SharePoint Store**, and **My requests**, in the top navigation. By default, SharePoint Store is the landing option. You will find different types of third-party Apps in the SharePoint store categorized as **Features Apps, Apps that complement Viva Connections, Popular Apps powered by SharePoint, All Apps**. You can acquire any app from these categories. There are Apps that need to use data sources or web services to read the data and, therefore, need organization-level permission. Approval is required from the Microsoft 365 admin or SharePoint administrator to install those Apps.

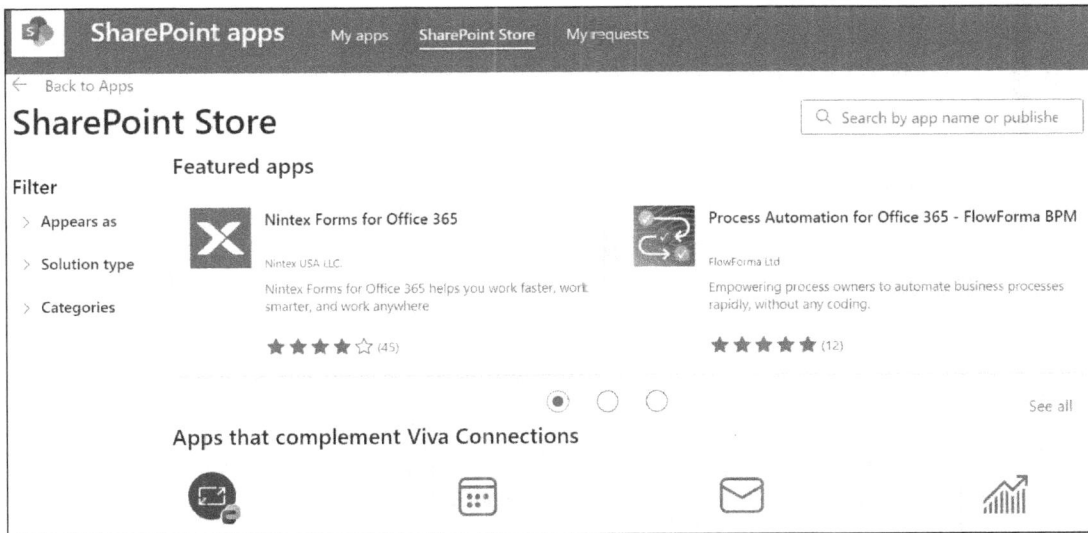

Figure 9.3: SharePoint Store in AppStore Page

6. Identify the app from the SharePoint store that suits your requirement and click on the app to acquire it, as seen in the following figure:

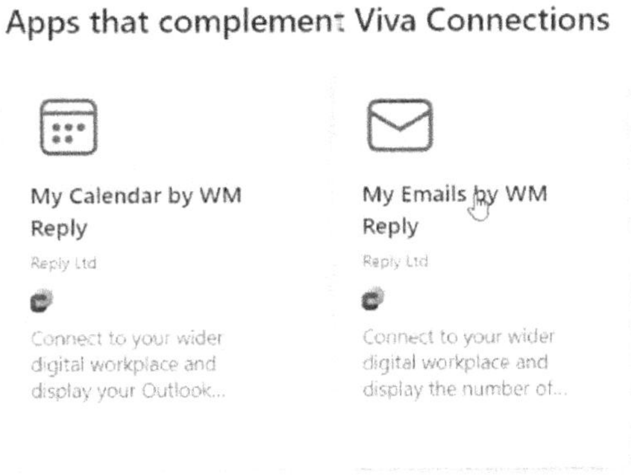

Figure 9.4: Identify and Select an App from SharePoint Store

7. You will be redirected to the **appDetail** page where you will find the app, details and support, and reviews. You will find a button named **Add to Apps site** just below the name of the app. Click on **Add to Apps site**, as shown in the following figure:

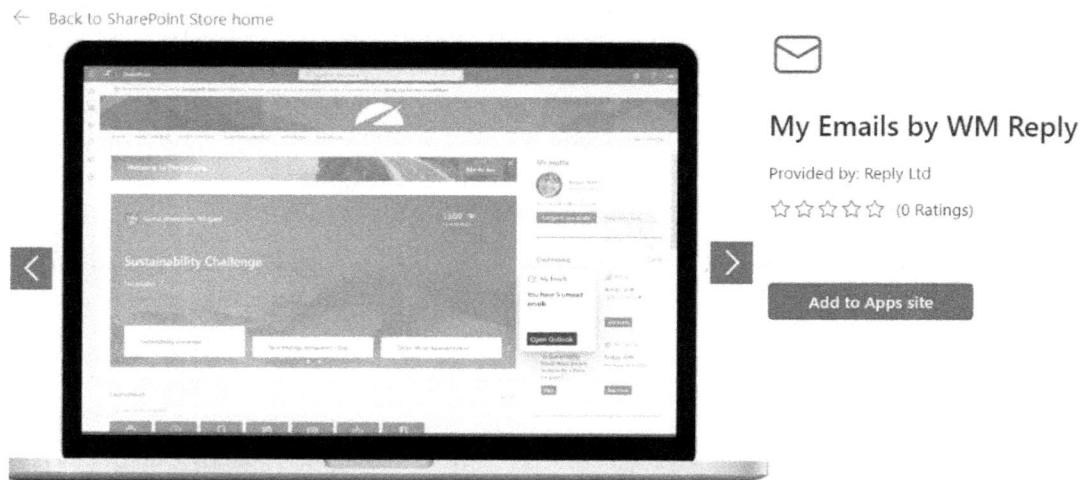

Figure 9.5: Add to Apps Site

8. You will get a **Confirm data access** dialog box that contains information about which data source this app gets data from, API access, and app availability. We can filter Apps into two categories. In the first category of Apps, you will find information like **This app gets data from** and **App availability** only. You will not find the information **API access that must be approved after you enable this app,** which means these Apps access SharePoint data only and do not need to consume any other web service using API. In the second category, you will find all information like **This app gets data from, API access that must be approved after you enable this app**, and **App availability**. This means these categories of Apps consume other services apart from SharePoint, which need the approval of API access.

9. Under the option **Apps availability**, you will find options like **Only enable this app**, and **Enable this app and add it to all sites**. If you select the option **Only enable this app,** then the app will be available to be added by site owners on their sites. If you select the option **Enable this app and add it to all sites,** then the app will be enabled and added to all sites. No site owner action is required to add the app from the My Apps page to the site. Refer to the following figure for an illustration of the same:

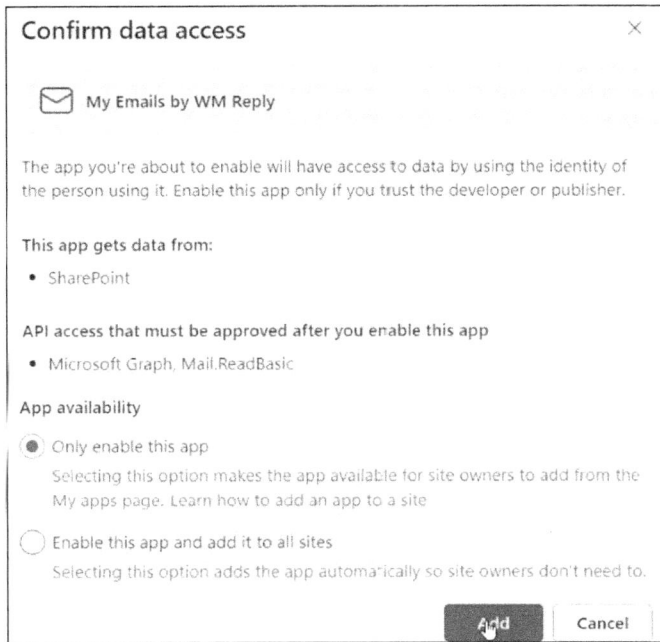

Figure 9.6: Confirm Data Access

10. In a few Apps, you will find another option, **Add to Teams,** as seen in the following figure:

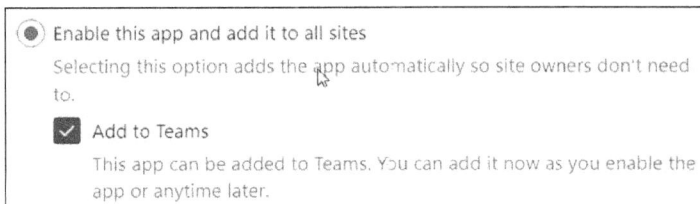

Figure 9.7: Add App to All Sites and Teams

11. After selecting the options, click on the button **Add,** as seen in *Figure 9.6.*

12. Two things are possible. If you select an app where no API permission is required, then the app will be added to the app page and will get a confirmation, as seen in the following figure:

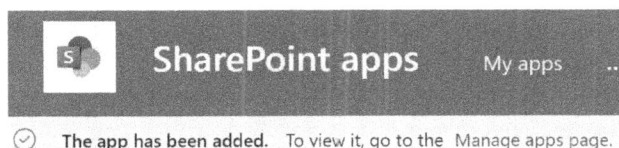

Figure 9.8: SharePoint app added

13. If you select an app that requires API permission, you will get a dialog box with a message like **Approve access so this app works as designed**. You can click on **I'll do it later** to approve the API later. If you are willing to approve the API right now, you need to click on the button **Go to API access page,** as seen in the following figure:

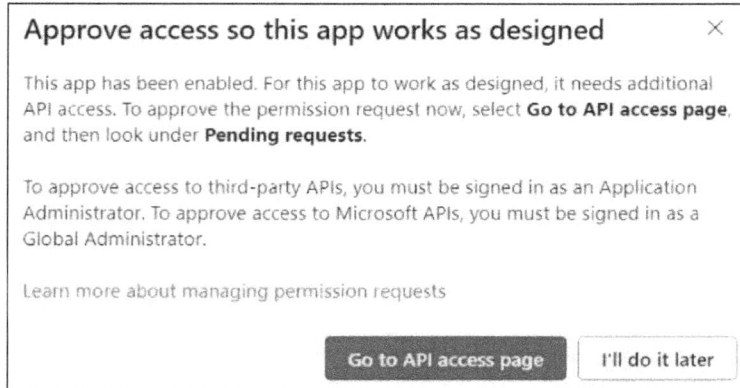

Figure 9.9: Go to API Access Page to grant API access permission

14. Before approving the API access, click on the option **My Apps** from the navigation present in the SharePoint store. You will find the app available under the section named **Apps you can add,** as seen in the following figure:

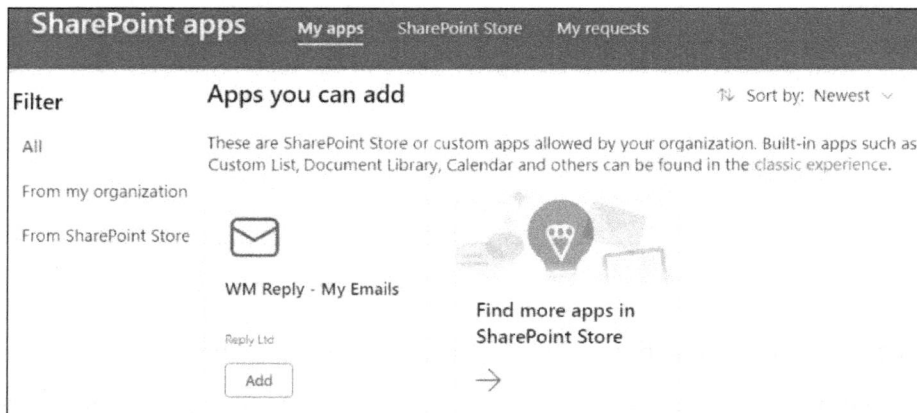

Figure 9.10: Apps You can add

15. Click on the button **Go to API access page,** as mentioned in *Step 8*. You will be redirected to **webApiPermissionManagement** to approve or reject the API access request. You will find the requests that are pending approval under the category **Pending requests**. Select the API request from this category and click on **Approve,** as seen in the following figure. Then the request will move from **Pending requests** to **approved requests**.

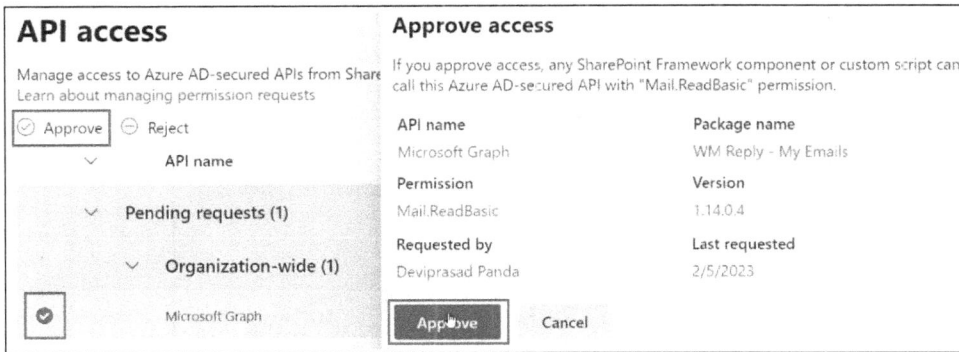

Figure 9.11: *Approve API access*

16. After approval, you will find the app under **Manage apps,** as shown in the following figure:

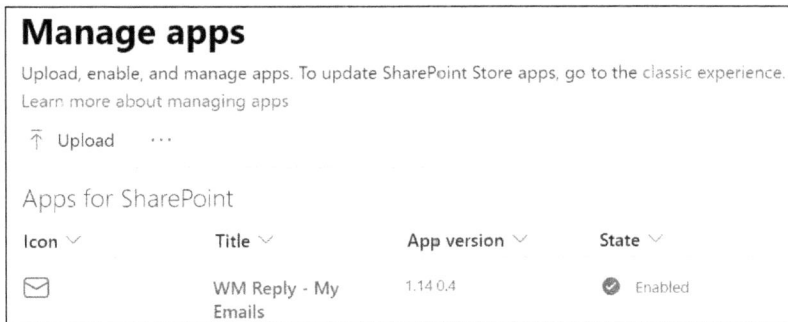

Figure 9.12: *App added under Manage Apps*

Now, you have acquired an app from the SharePoint store. Let us proceed to the next category of options called **Manage apps**.

Manage apps

Manage apps is the first category of options present in the left navigation once you open the **Apps** feature, shown as follows:

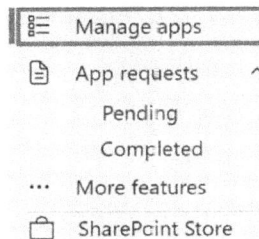

Figure 9.13: *Manage apps*

This holds all the Apps that are acquired from the SharePoint store or by adding custom Apps, as seen in the following figure. This is a location from which you can manage the Apps.

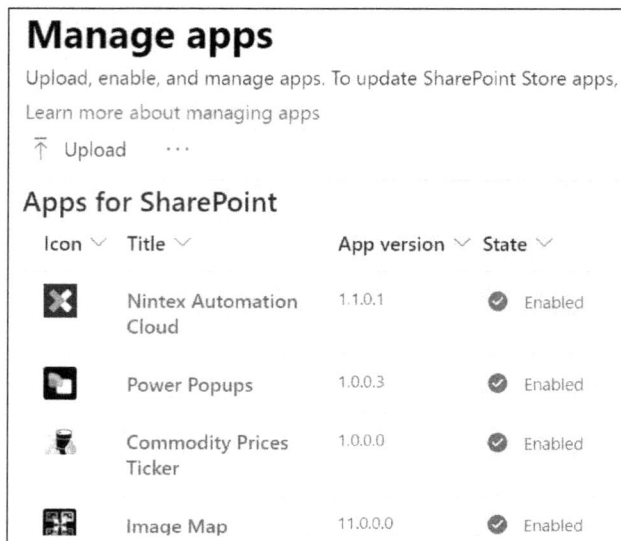

Figure 9.14: Manage Apps page

Let us follow the step-by-step procedure to understand each setting available under the category Manage apps:

1. On the **Manage apps** page, you will find options like **Upload** and **Show actions** in the navigation.

2. We can add a custom app using the **Upload** option. Click on **Upload**, as seen in the following figure:

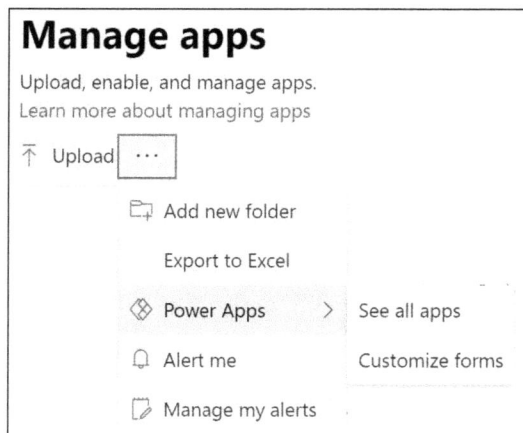

Figure 9.15: Navigation options

3. Select the custom app package with the file extension **.sppkg** from the system. The file will be uploaded, and you will find the dialog box **Enable app**. Click on the button **Enable app** to enable the custom app, as shown in the following figure. A custom app will be added.

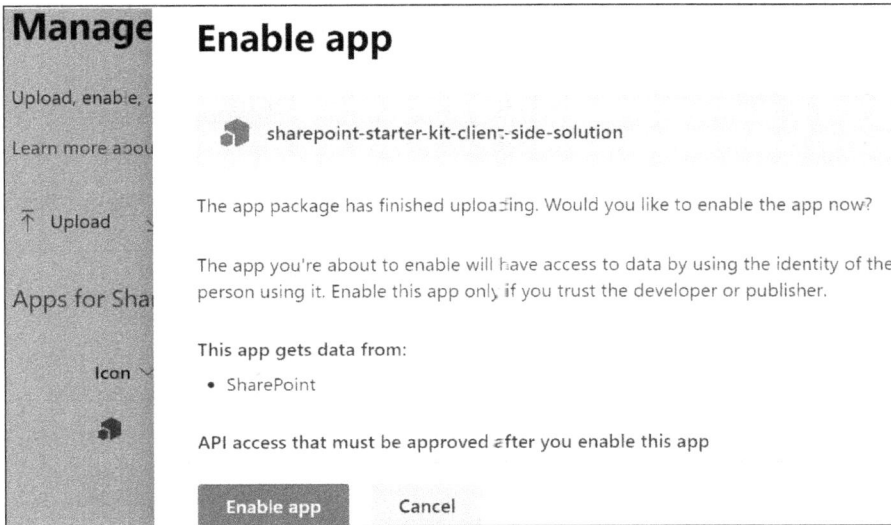

Figure 9.16: Enable app after uploading custom app

4. Click on the option **Show actions** present in navigation side to upload and click on the option **Add new folder** to create a new folder, as seen in *Figure 9.14*. You can upload the custom app package in that folder as well.

5. Click on the option **Show actions** present on the navigation side to upload, as seen in *Figure 9.14*, and click on the option **Export** to Excel. Information about all Apps will be exported to Excel. You will find app information and its status from columns like **Icon, Title, App version, State, Added to all sites, Available for, Valid app package, Modified, App type, Publisher, Client-side solution, Current Version Deployed, Deployed, Package Default Skip Feature Deployment, App package error message, Isolated Domain, Contains Teams Manifest, Supports Teams Tabs, Store ID, Name, Enabled, Contains Viva Manifest, Item Type** (Item/Folder), **Path** (sites/appcatalog/AppCatalog).

6. Click on the option **Show actions** on the navigation side to upload, as seen in *Figure 9.14*, and click on **Power Apps**. You will be redirected to the power app portal.

7. **Alert Me** and **Manage My alerts** are two other options present under **Show actions,** which are used to create and manage alerts.

8. There are certain settings you will notice once you select an app from the app list. You will find options like **Add to all sites, Add to Teams, View app details**,

Download, Delete, Properties, Move to, Add new folder, Version history, Alert me, and Manage my alerts in navigation, as seen in *Figure 9.17*.

9. Select one app and click on **Add to all sites** from the navigation. The app will be added to all sites. No site owner action is required to add the app from the My Apps page to the site.

10. Select the same app, and you will find an option to **Stop adding to new sites** in the navigation. Click on **Stop adding to new sites** and then **Confirm**. This will stop adding the app automatically to new sites.

11. You can add the app to Teams as well. Select the app that can be added to Teams and click on **Add to Teams** from the navigation.

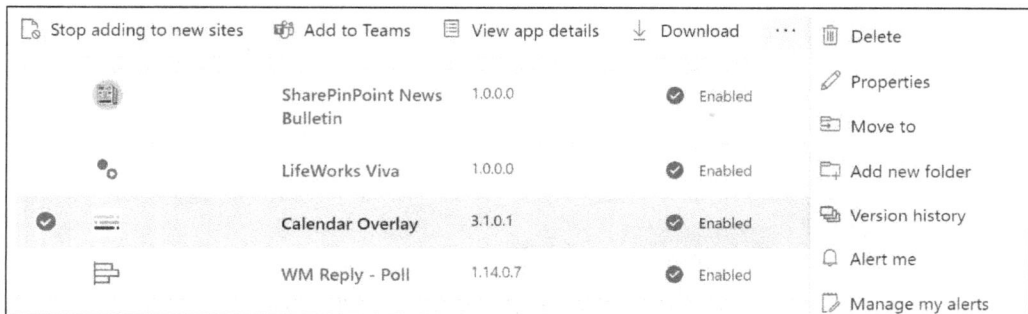

	Stop adding to new sites	Add to Teams	View app details	Download	⋯	Delete
		SharePinPoint News Bulletin	1.0.0.0		Enabled	Properties
		LifeWorks Viva	1.0.0.0		Enabled	Move to
✓		Calendar Overlay	3.1.0.1		Enabled	Add new folder
		WM Reply - Poll	1.14.0.7		Enabled	Version history

Alert me
Manage my alerts

Figure 9.17: App Properties under manage Apps

12. Select one app and click on **Delete** to remove the app from the Manage apps page. The app will be removed from the Manage apps page and will not be available to add for additional sites. Sites already using this app will remain unaffected and can continue using it. The deleted app will move to the recycle bin, as seen in the following figure:

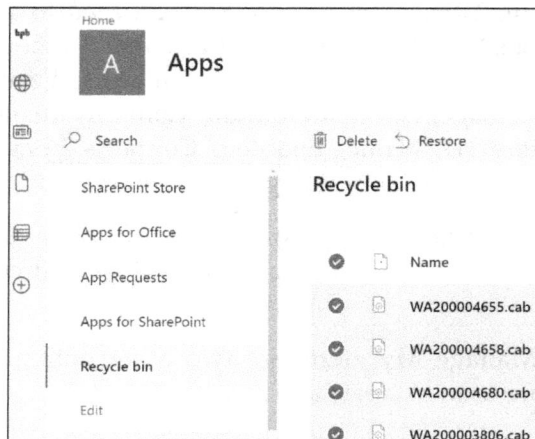

Figure 9.18: Recycle bin for App catalog page

13. If you want to check details about the Apps added, then select the app and click on the option **View app details** from the navigation. You will be redirected to the SharePoint Store, as seen in *Figure 9.5.*

14. You can download the app by selecting the app and clicking on **Download** from the navigation options. The **CAB** file will be downloaded. You can extract the package SPPKG file and reuse it by uploading it as discussed in *Step 2.*

15. Select the app now and click on **Properties** from the navigation bar. You can see properties related to the app like **Name, Title, Metadata Language, Default Metadata Language, Short Description, Description, Icon, Category, Publisher, Support URL, Image URL, Video URL, Enabled, Featured,** and **Apply label**. You can disable and enable the app by unselecting and selecting the check box, respectively.

16. You can move the app from the Manage apps page to another site. Select the app and click on **Move to** from the navigation options. Select the destination site and click **Move here,** as shown in the following figure. The cab file will be moved to the destination site location.

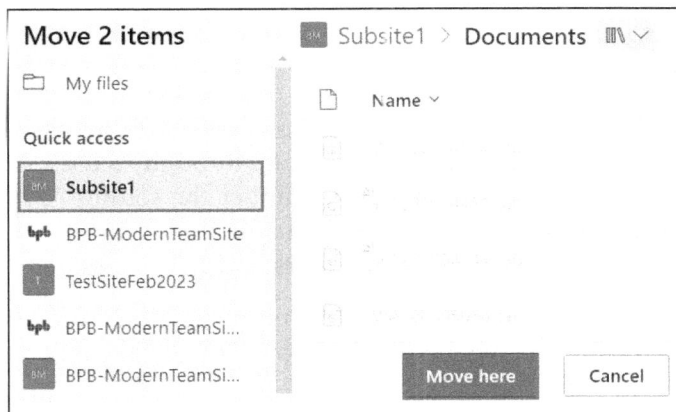

Figure 9.19: Move the App to a different Location

17. Select the app and click on **Version history** from the navigation. You will find different app versions available, as seen in the following figure:

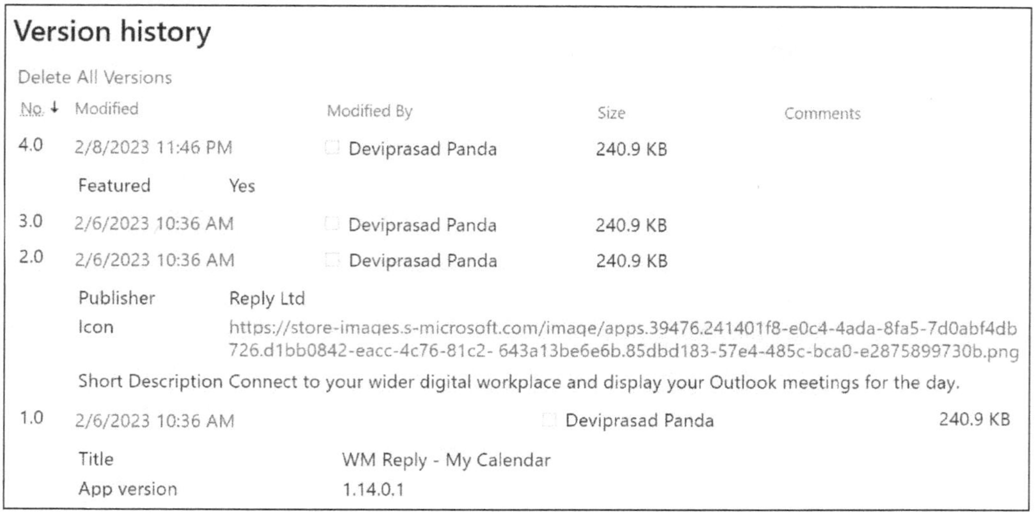

Version history

Delete All Versions

No. ↓	Modified	Modified By	Size	Comments
4.0	2/8/2023 11:46 PM	☐ Deviprasad Panda	240.9 KB	
	Featured　　　　Yes			
3.0	2/6/2023 10:36 AM	☐ Deviprasad Panda	240.9 KB	
2.0	2/6/2023 10:36 AM	☐ Deviprasad Panda	240.9 KB	

Publisher　　　　Reply Ltd

Icon　　　　https://store-images.s-microsoft.com/image/apps.39476.241401f8-e0c4-4ada-8fa5-7d0abf4db 726.d1bb0842-eacc-4c76-81c2- 643a13be6e6b.85dbd183-57e4-485c-bca0-e2875899730b.png

Short Description Connect to your wider digital workplace and display your Outlook meetings for the day.

1.0	2/6/2023 10:36 AM		☐ Deviprasad Panda	240.9 KB

Title　　　　WM Reply - My Calendar

App version　　　　1.14.0.1

Figure 9.20: App Version History

API access

Apps built-in with SharePoint framework solutions need **API access** when added from the SharePoint store. API provides a secure channel through Azure's Active Directory to access resources. API access requests are stored under the setting API access, which the administrator needs to act upon. We already discussed this in the *SharePoint* store section. Let us follow the step-by-step procedure to understand API access better:

1. Click on the option **API access** from the left navigation. You will be redirected to **webApiPermissionManagement** to approve or reject the API access request.

2. You will find the requests that are pending approval under the category **Pending requests**, as seen in the following figure:

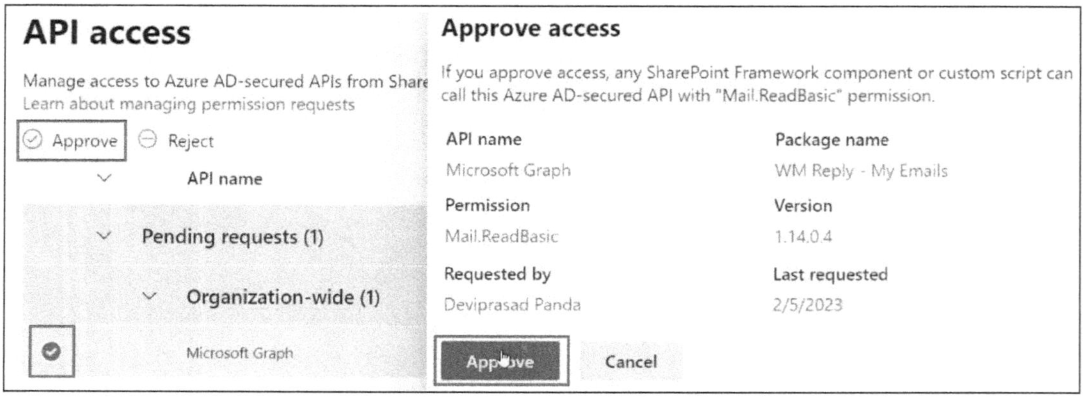

API access

Manage access to Azure AD-secured APIs from Share
Learn about managing permission requests

⊘ Approve　⊖ Reject

ˇ　　　API name

ˇ　　Pending requests (1)

　　ˇ　　Organization-wide (1)

●　　　　Microsoft Graph

Approve access

If you approve access, any SharePoint Framework component or custom script can call this Azure AD-secured API with "Mail.ReadBasic" permission.

API name	Package name
Microsoft Graph	WM Reply - My Emails
Permission	**Version**
Mail.ReadBasic	1.14.0.4
Requested by	**Last requested**
Deviprasad Panda	2/5/2023

[**Approve**]　Cancel

Figure 9.21: Approve API access

3. Select the API request from this category and click on **Approve,** as seen in *Figure 9.20*. Then the request will move from **Pending requests** to **Approved requests,** as shown in the following figure:

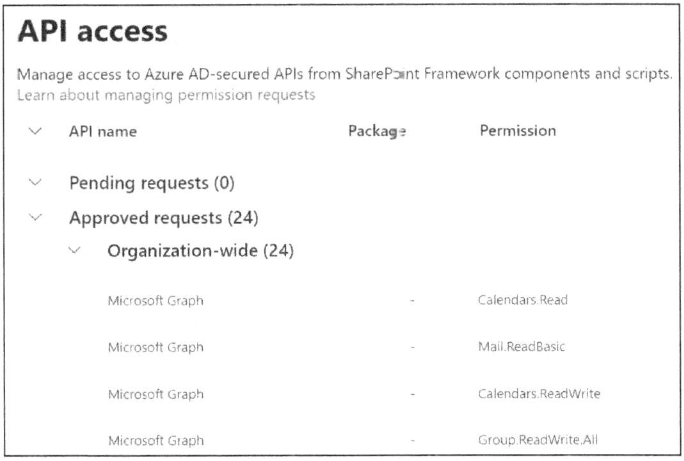

Figure 9.22: Pending requests and Approved requests in API Access

App requests

App requests is the second option in the SharePoint admin center left navigation in the **Tenant App Catalog** page. You will find the status of the requested Apps by following this navigation option. Follow this step-by-step procedure to understand each setting available under the category App requests:

1. Open **Apps** feature from the SharePoint admin center, shown as follows:

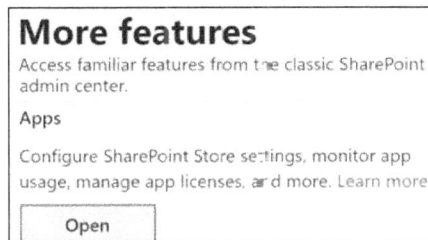

Figure 9.23: Open Apps feature from SharePoint admin center

2. Click on the option **App requests** from the left navigation. It will expand, and you will find two more options, **Pending** and **Completed**.

3. App requests pending approval will be found under the option **Pending**.

4. Once the action is taken by the administrator, the requested app status will be complete and will be reflected under the category **Completed**.

More features

A group of features is placed under one category of options called **More features**. Click on the option **More features** from the left navigation, and you will find a few more features, like **Tenant wide extensions, App permissions, Configure store settings**, and **Site contents**, as shown in the following figure:

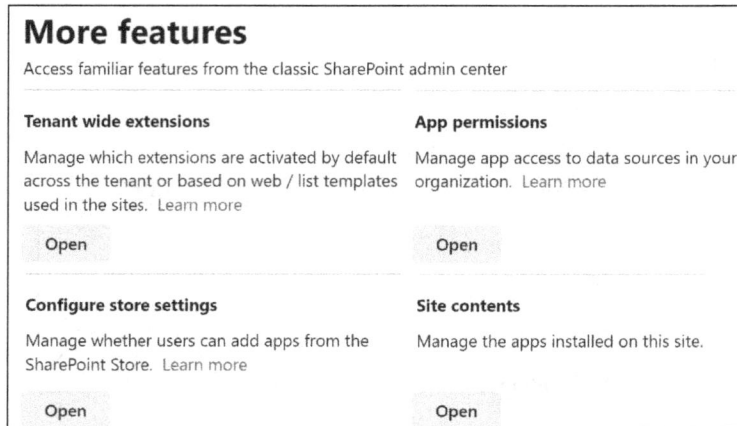

More features

Access familiar features from the classic SharePoint admin center

Tenant wide extensions	App permissions
Manage which extensions are activated by default across the tenant or based on web / list templates used in the sites. Learn more	Manage app access to data sources in your organization. Learn more
Open	Open
Configure store settings	**Site contents**
Manage whether users can add apps from the SharePoint Store. Learn more	Manage the apps installed on this site.
Open	Open

Figure 9.24: More features

Let us follow the step-by-step procedure to understand the settings better:

1. Click on the feature **Site contents**. You will be redirected to the **Site contents** page of the site **appcatalog**, as seen in the following figure. You will find lists like **App Requests, Apps for Office, Apps for SharePoint**, and **Tenant Wide Extension**.

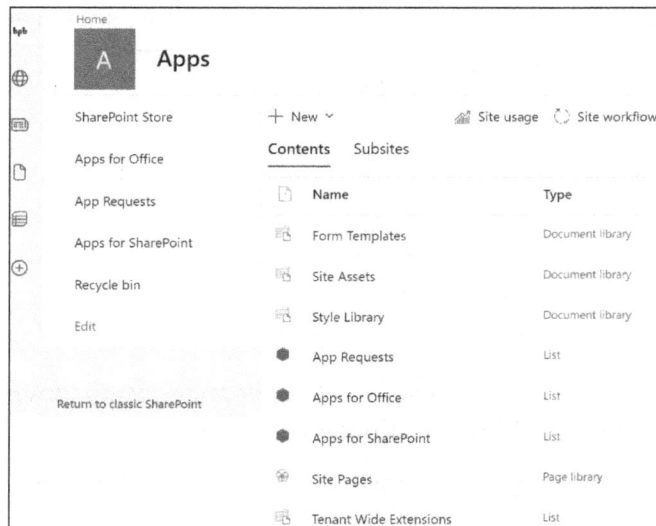

Figure 9.25: Site Content in App Catalog Site

2. Click on the feature **Tenant wide extensions** from **More features** in the left navigation, as seen in *Figure 9.22*. You will be redirected to a list called **Tenant Wide Extensions**, which is available under **Site contents** of the app catalog site. SharePoint framework extension can be provisioned and deployed to the app catalog to make the app available tenant-wide. After the deployment of the SharePoint framework extension tenant-wide, you will find an entry in the **Tenant Wide Extensions** list having columns like **Title**, **Component ID**, **Component Properties, Web Template**, and **List Template**. **Location (location of the customizer)**, **Sequence**, **Host Properties**, **Disabled,** as seen in the following figure:

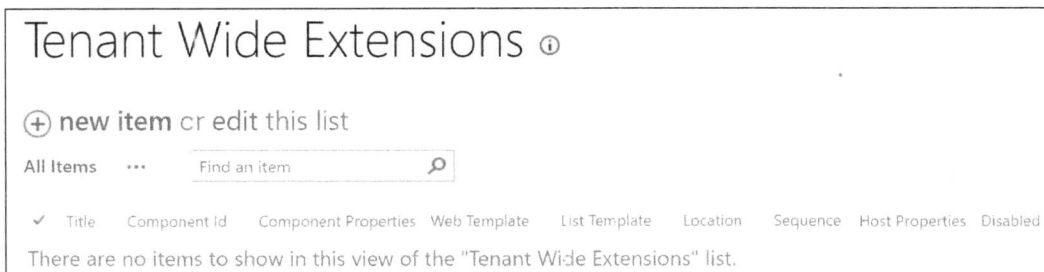

Figure 9.26: Tenant Wide Extensions

3. We can delegate permission (**Read, Write, Manage, FullControl**) to an app to access the SharePoint site and do certain activities on the site. Users can access the SharePoint site and its content through that app only, without exposing the credentials to the SharePoint site. SharePoint uses the OAuth protocol for authorization using a token, which is a combination of **Client ID** and **Client Secret**.

4. We need to call the page **appregnew.aspx** from any site which will be of format like **https://<site>/_layouts/15/appregnew.aspx**

   (e.g., **https://spmcse.sharepoint.com/sites/TestSiteFeb2023/_layouts/15/appregnew.aspx**). You will be redirected to the new app registration page.

5. Click on the **Generate** button next to the field **Client Id**. Copy this ID, which will be used in the future.

6. Click on the **Generate** button next to the field **Client Secret**.

7. Enter the title of the app in the **Title** field.

8. Fill the field **App Domain** as **www.localhost.com**.

9. Fill the details under the field **Redirect URL** as **https://www.localhost.com** and click on the button **Create**, as seen in the following figure:

Figure 9.27: Create app identifier

10. The app identifier will be created successfully, as seen in the following figure:

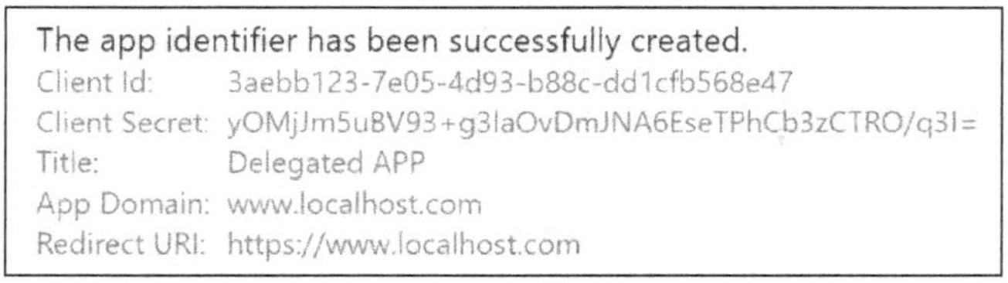

Figure 9.28: App identifier created

11. In the second stage, we need to authorize the app by granting permission using the **Client ID** and **Client Secret** generated from the app identifier, as seen in *Figure 9.25*.

12. Call the page **appinv.aspx** from the same site, which will have the format `https://<site>/_layouts/15/appinv.aspx`

(e.g., **https://spmcse.sharepoint.com/sites/TestSiteFeb2023/_layouts/15/appinv. aspx**)

13. Paste the **Client ID** generated (copied previously, as discussed in *Step 5)* in the field **App Id**. Click on **Lookup**.

14. **Title**, **App Domain**, and **Redirect URL** will be auto-populated from the app identifier.

15. In the field of **Permission Request XML**, we can enter details in XML format. Permission can be **Read**, **Write**, **manage**, **FullControl**.

Scope can be **http://sharepoint/content/sitecollection, http://sharepoint/content/ sitecollection/web,** **http://sharepoint/content/sitecollection/web/list,** **http:// sharepoint/content/tenant**

```
<AppPermissionRequests AllowAppOnlyPolicy="true">
 <AppPermissionRequest Scope="http://sharepoint/content/
sitecollection" Right="Read" />
 <AppPermissionRequest Scope="http://sharepoint/content/
sitecollection/web" Right="Read" />
 <AppPermissionRequest Scope="http://sharepoint/content/
sitecollection/web/list" Right="Read" />
</AppPermissionRequests>
```

16. Click on **Create** after entering all the details, as seen in the following figure:

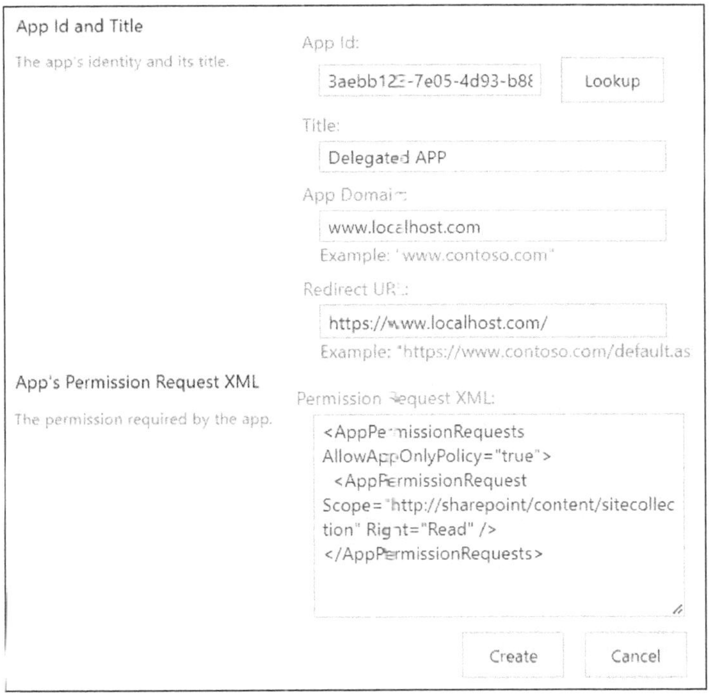

Figure 9.29: Delegate Permission to app

17. You will be prompted with a dialog box **Do you trust Delegated APP?** as seen in the following figure. Click on **Trust It**.

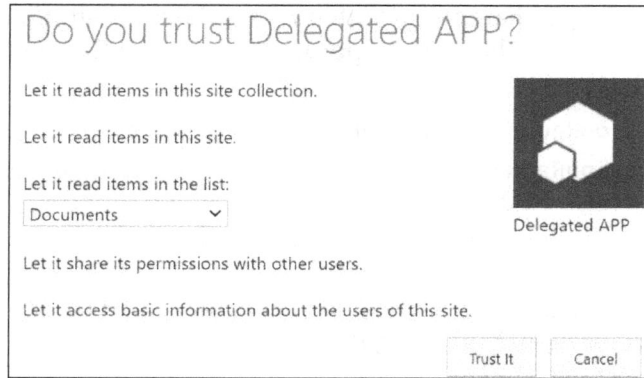

Figure 9.30: Trust the App during permission delegation

18. In the next stage, call the page **appprincipals.aspx** from the same site, which will have the format **https://<site>/_layouts/15/appprincipals. aspx** (e.g., **https://spmcse.sharepoint.com/sites/TestSiteFeb2023/_layouts/15/ appprincipals.aspx**). You will notice the **App Display Name** and **App identifier** created for the site collection, as seen in the following figure:

Figure 9.31: Site Collection App Permission granted and entry found

19. If the app principal is created with scope as tenant, you will notice similar entries like **App Display Name** and **App Identifier** under the setting **App permissions** present under **More features**, as seen in the following figure:

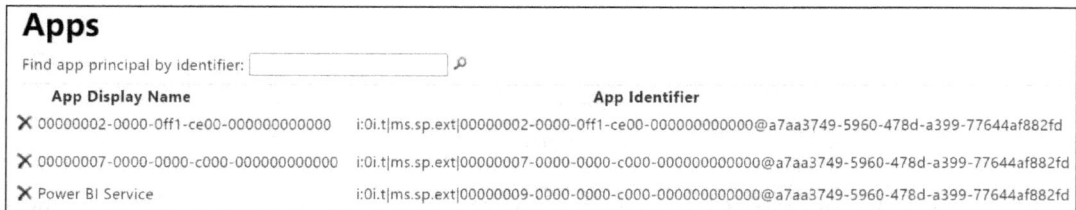

Figure 9.32: Entry related to permission delegation at tenant level

20. Now, click on the **Configuring Store Settings option** present under the **More feature**. You will be redirected to the manage marketplace Settings page, where you will find options like **App Purchases**, **App Requests**, and **Apps for Office from the Store**.

21. The option **App Purchases** prevents end users from getting Apps from the marketplace. You will find two options, **Yes** and **No**, as seen in the following figure. Selecting **Yes** will enable end users to add Apps from the marketplace. If you select **No,** then the end users cannot add Apps from the marketplace.

Apps

App Purchases	Should end users be able to get apps from the marketplace?
Specify whether end users can get free, trial or paid apps from the SharePoint Store.	◉ Yes ○ No

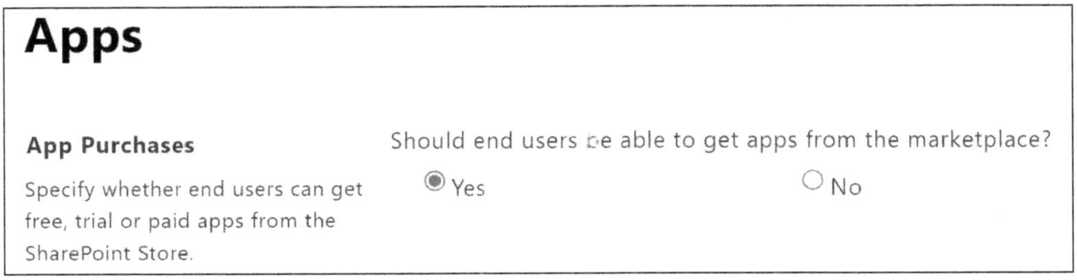

Figure 9.33: App Purchase in configuring store settings

22. The next option under **Configuring Store Settings** is **App Requests**, as shown in the following figure. Click on the link **Click here to view app requests,** and you will be redirected to the list of **App Requests** present on the app catalog site. You can find the status (New/Closed) of all app requests raised by the end user.

App Requests	Click here to view app requests
View the list of app requests. Users can request apps if they are unable or choose not to get apps directly from the SharePoint Store.	

Figure 9.34: App Requests in configuring store settings

23. The next option is **Apps for Office from the Store**. If you select **Yes**, then Office Apps from the store will start once the documents are opened. If you choose **No,** the Office Apps will not open when documents are opened. Refer to the following figure:

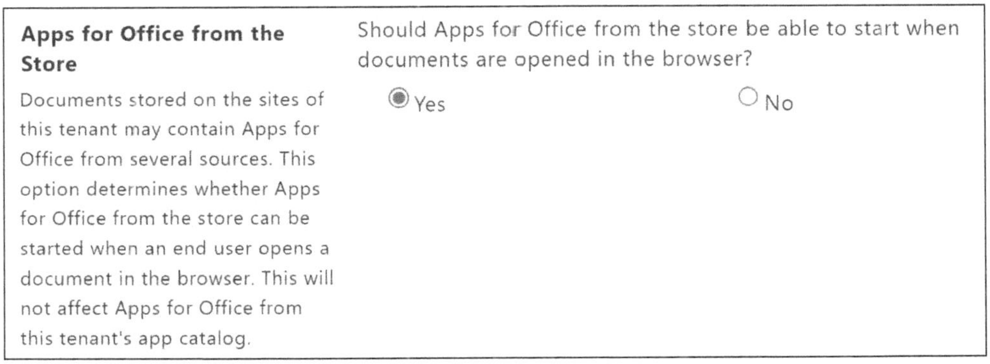

Apps for Office from the Store	Should Apps for Office from the store be able to start when documents are opened in the browser?
Documents stored on the sites of this tenant may contain Apps for Office from several sources. This option determines whether Apps for Office from the store can be started when an end user opens a document in the browser. This will not affect Apps for Office from this tenant's app catalog.	◉ Yes ○ No

Figure 9.35: Apps for Office from the Store in Configuring Store Settings

Conclusion

In this chapter, we learned about acquiring Apps from the SharePoint store and adding custom Apps in SharePoint. Furthermore, we understood the different options for managing Apps in SharePoint. We discussed adding Apps in all SharePoint sites as well as teams and understood how to manage app requests and app permissions. We also discussed a step-by-step procedure for managing tenant-wide extensions, API permissions, and configuring store settings.

In *Chapter 10, BCS Administration,* we will discuss how to create and manage external data sources in SharePoint.

Points to remember

- Regular changes are applied in Office 365 and SharePoint Online, and there may be slight changes in the template or some features.

Join our book's Discord space

Join the book's Discord Workspace for Latest updates, Offers, Tech happenings around the world, New Release and Sessions with the Authors:

https://discord.bpbonline.com

CHAPTER 10
BCS Administration

Introduction

In the previous *Chapter 9, App Administration.* we discussed how to manage apps in SharePoint from the admin center. In this chapter, we will discuss another service in SharePoint, the **Business Connectivity Service (BCS)**. BCS is used to create a connection to external data sources like SQL Azure database and WCF web services that are outside the SharePoint site. In this chapter, we will discuss how to connect with external data sources that exist online or on-premises.

Structure

In this chapter, we will discuss the following topics:

- Navigating BCS
- Manage BDC models and external content types
- Manage connections to online services
- Manage connections to on-premises services

Objectives

By the end of this chapter, you will understand how to import BDCM files, set object permissions, and set metadata store permissions. You will understand the step-by-step procedure to create and upgrade the profile page host, configure the profile page for the selected content type, and manage connections to online and on-premises services.

Navigating BCS

BCS is a SharePoint feature used to create and manage connections with external data sources. Let us perform the following steps to access the BCS feature from the SharePoint admin center:

1. Open **SharePoint Admin Center** and click on **More Features** from the left navigation.

2. Identify the feature **BCS** and click on **Open**, as seen in *Figure 10.1*:

More features

Access familiar features from the classic SharePoint admin center.

BCS

Manage connections to data sources like Azure SQL databases or WCF web services. Learn more

Open

Figure 10.1: Site settings

3. You will get three settings like **Manage BDC Models and External Content Types**, **Manage connections to online services**, and **Manage connections to on-premises services**, as shown in *Figure 10.2*:

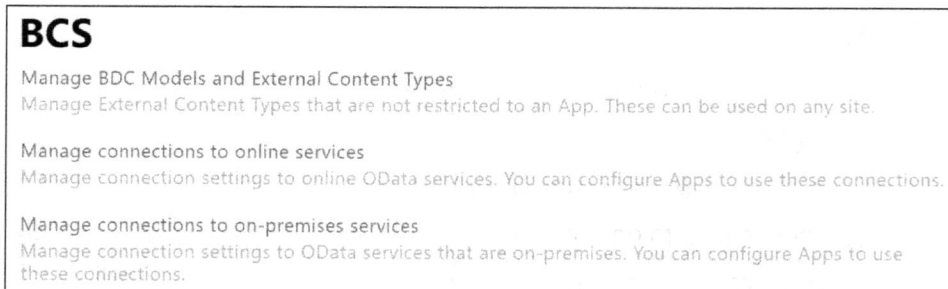

BCS

Manage BDC Models and External Content Types
Manage External Content Types that are not restricted to an App. These can be used on any site.

Manage connections to online services
Manage connection settings to online OData services. You can configure Apps to use these connections.

Manage connections to on-premises services
Manage connection settings to OData services that are on-premises. You can configure Apps to use these connections.

Figure 10.2: Settings present under more features BCS

Manage BDC models and external content types

Managing BDC models and external content types is the first category of options present under feature BCS. This includes settings to manage BDC models as well as external content types. Follow these steps to understand it:

1. Once we access the BCS feature, we can proceed to explore the first setting present under BCS.

2. Click on the first category of settings, **BCS Manage BDC Models and External Content Types**.

3. You will be redirected to the page **TA_ViewBDCApplication**. You will find a ribbon with multiple options categorized as **BDC Models**, **Permissions**, **Manage**, **Profile Pages**, **View**, as seen in the following figure.

4. Under the category **BDC Models**, you will find the option **Import**. The options **Set Object Permissions** and **Set metadata Store Permissions** are given under the category **Permissions**.

5. Under the **Manage** category, you will find the option **Delete**.

6. Under the category **Profile Pages**, you will find options like **Create/Upgrade** and **Configure**.

7. Under the category **View**, you will find three types of views, namely, **DBC Models**, **External Systems**, and **External Content Types**. Refer to *Figure 10.3*:

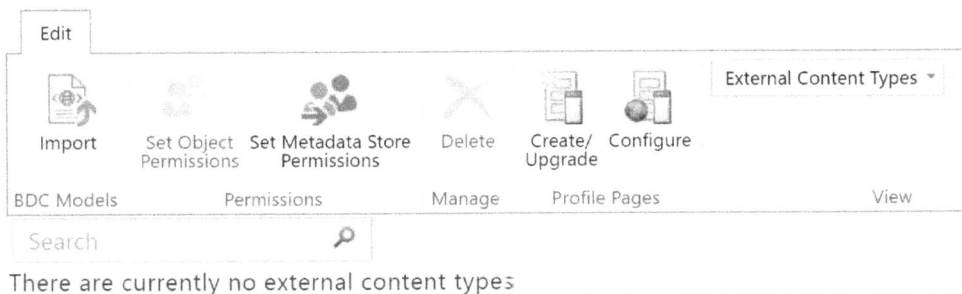

Figure 10.3: Ribbon under the settings BCS manage BDC Models and external content types

Import

Import is the first option in the ribbon, present under the setting **BCS Manage BDC Models and External Content Types**. We can create a connection with an external content type to an external system by importing BDCM files. The **Import** option from the ribbon allows you to import a BDCM file. Follow the given step-by-step procedure to import the BDCM file:

1. Click on the option **Import** from the ribbon present under the section **BDC Models**, as seen in *Figure 10.4*:

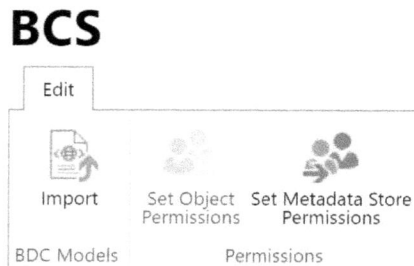

Figure 10.4: Import BDCM file

2. You will be redirected to the page **TA_AddBDCApplication**. Click on the option **Choose File** present under the first section, **BDC Model**. Select the **BDCM** file, as shown in *Figure 10.5*:

Figure 10.5: BDC Model File

3. In the section **File Type**, select the file type as **Model** or **Resource** that you want to import. File type **Model** exports the XML metadata, and file type **Resource** exports localized names, properties, and permissions. Refer to *Figure 10.6*:

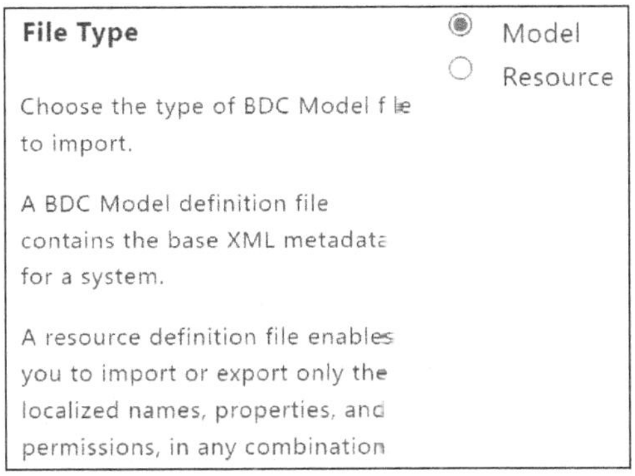

Figure 10.6: File Type

4. From the next section, **Advanced Settings**, choose one or more resources like **Localized names**, **Properties**, or **Permissions** to import. Refer to *Figure 10.7*:

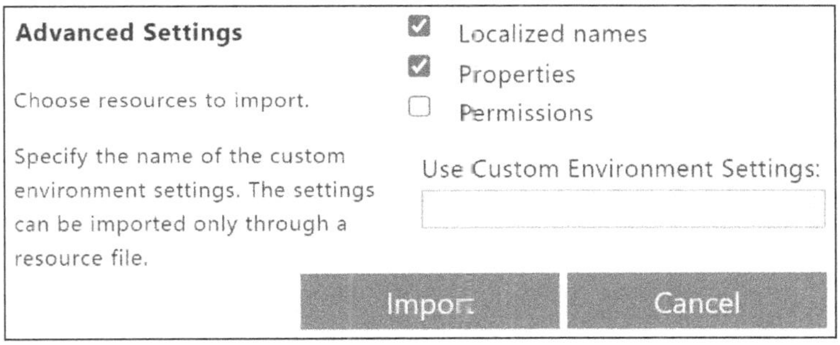

Figure 10.7: Advanced Settings

5. Finally, click on the **Import** button. The file will be uploaded. You will find an entry in **BDC** under the option **Models and External Content Types**.

In the following section, **Set Object Permissions**, we will discuss assigning object permissions that we just imported and added in **BDC** under the option **Models and External Content Types**.

Set object permissions

We can assign permission to specific content types by following the option set object permissions from the ribbon. Follow the given step-by-step procedure to set permission for specific external content type:

1. Select the check box present next to the external system or external content type present in **BDC** under the option **Models and External Content Types.**

2. Now, click on the option **Set Object Permissions** from the ribbon. Refer to *Figure 10.8*:

Set Object   Set Metadata Store
Permissions   Permissions

Permissions

Figure 10.8: Set Object Permissions

3. You will get a dialog box, as seen in *Figure 10.9*. Enter user or group details in the people picker to whom you want to give permission.

4. Click on **Add**. You can **Check Names** or **Browse** to find users or groups. Refer to *Figure 10.9*:

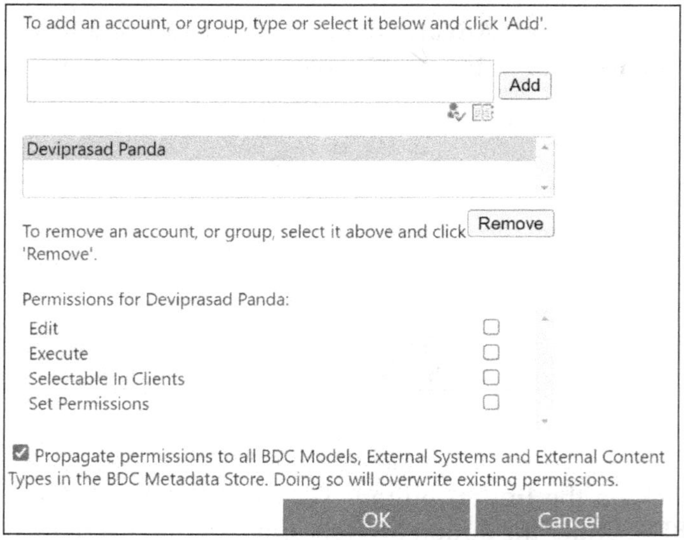

Figure 10.9: Types of permissions in set object permissions

5. After clicking **Add**, you will notice that additional options related to permission types will appear, as seen in *Figure 10.9*. You see four types of permissions, namely, **Edit**, **Execute**, **Selectable in Clients**, and **Set Permissions**. People with edit permission can create external systems and BDC models and import and export BDC models. **Edit** permission is assigned to highly privileged users. People with **Execute** permission can execute operations like read, create, delete, update, or query on external content types. People having permission **Selectable in Clients** can create external lists and view them in the external item picker. People having permission, **Set Permissions,** can set permissions on the Metadata Store. Assigned to highly privileged users.

6. Select the permission type that you want to assign to the user or group and click **OK** to apply changes.

Set metadata store permissions

We can assign permission globally to the whole BCS store by following the option **Metadata Store Permissions** from the ribbon. Permission assigned is applicable to all BDC Models, external systems, external content types, methods, and methods instances. Follow the given step-by-step procedure to assign permission globally to the whole BCS store:

1. Click on the option **Metadata Store Permissions** from the ribbon. Refer to *Figure 10.10*:

Figure 10.10: Set Metadata Store Permissions

2. You will get a dialog box, as seen in *Figure 10.11*. Enter **User or Group** details in the people picker to whom you want to give permission.

3. Click on **Add**. You can **Check Names** or **Browse** to find users or groups.

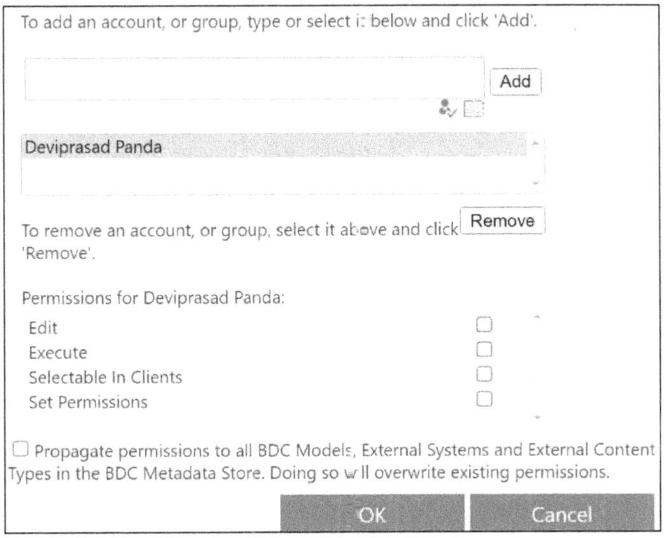

Figure 10.11: Types of permissions in Set Metadata Store Permissions

4. After clicking **Add**, you will notice additional options related to permission types will appear, as seen in *Figure 10.11*. You see four types of permissions: **Edit**, **Execute**, **Selectable in Clients**, and **Set Permissions**. People having **Edit** permission can create external systems and BDC models, and import and export BDC models.

Edit permission is assigned to highly privileged users. People with the **execute** permission can do all execute operations like read, create, delete, update, or query on external content types. People having permission **Selectable in clients** can create external lists and view them in the external item picker. People having the permission **Set permissions** can set permissions on the Metadata Store. It is assigned to highly privileged users.

5. Select the permission type that you want to assign to the user or group and click **OK** to apply changes.

Delete

The option **Delete** is used to delete any items present under **Manage BDC Models and External Content Types**. Select the check box present on the side of the item and click on the option **Delete** from the ribbon. Items will be removed from the list.

Configure

We can configure the external content type profile page host using the **Configure** option present in the ribbon. Once you click on the **Configure** option, you get a new dialog box. Select the checkbox option **Enable Profile Page Creation**. Enter the **URL** of the SharePoint site where profile pages of all external content types will be created. Finally, click on **OK** to apply the changes. Refer to *Figure 10.12*:

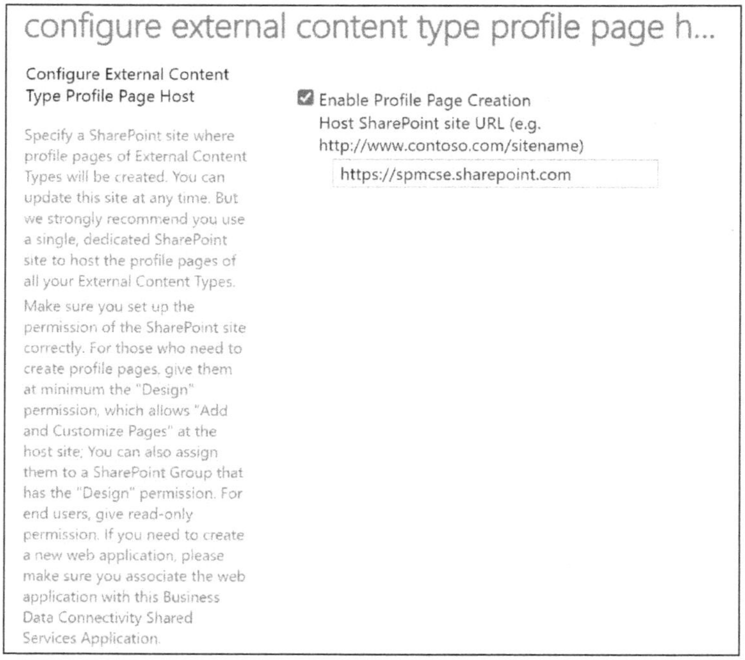

Figure 10.12: Configure external content type profile page host

Create or upgrade

We can create or upgrade the profile page for selected external content types using the option **Create or upgrade** from the ribbon. Click on **Create or upgrade**, as shown in *Figure 10.13*:

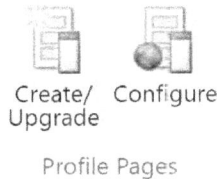

Create/ Configure
Upgrade

Profile Pages

Figure 10.13: Create or Upgrade

You will get a dialog box. Click on **OK** in that dialog box. You will get a confirmation message that the **Profile page creation succeeded**. A default action will be created for the external content type.

View

You can find the BCS connections in three different views, i.e., **External Content Types**, **BDC Models**, **External Systems**, as seen in *Figure 10.14*. The view **BDC Models** enables the options to export and import business data connections to recreate connections in a new environment. The view **External Systems** displays the BCS connection property **External Systems Name**. The view **External Content Types** displays Service Application Information like **Name**, **Display Name**, **Namespace**, **Namespace version**, and **External system name**.

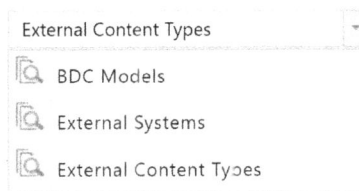

External Content Types

BDC Models

External Systems

External Content Types

Figure 10.14: Views

Manage connections to online services

Manage connections to online services is the second option in **BCS**. Using this option, you can manage connection settings to online OData services and configure apps to use these connections. Follow the step-by-step instructions to understand better.

1. Navigate to **SharePoint Admin Center** and click on **More Features** from navigation. Identify the feature **BCS** and click on **Open**, as seen in *Figure 10.15*:

More features

Access familiar features from the classic SharePoint admin center.

BCS

Manage connections to data sources like Azure SQL databases or WCF web services. Learn more

Open

Figure 10.15: Navigate to feature BCS

2. You will get settings like **Manage BDC Models and External Content Types, Manage connections to online services,** and **Manage connections to on-premises services,** as shown in *Figure 10.16*. Click on **Manage connections to online services:**

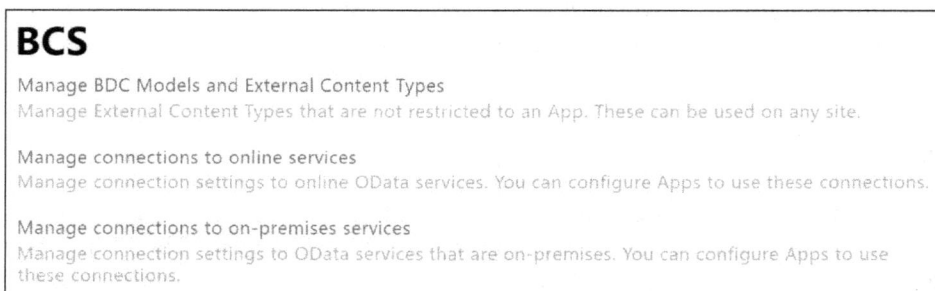

BCS

Manage BDC Models and External Content Types
Manage External Content Types that are not restricted to an App. These can be used on any site.

Manage connections to online services
Manage connection settings to online OData services. You can configure Apps to use these connections.

Manage connections to on-premises services
Manage connection settings to OData services that are on-premises. You can configure Apps to use these connections.

Figure 10.16: BCS settings

3. You will find options in the ribbon categorized as **Connections** and **Configure,** as shown in *Figure 10.17*:

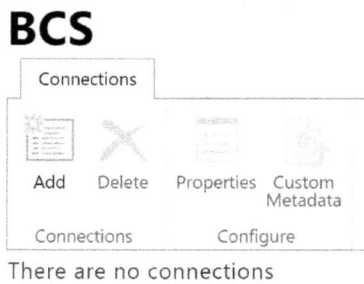

BCS

Connections

Add   Delete   Properties   Custom Metadata

Connections   Configure

There are no connections

Figure 10.17: Ribbon options under manage connections to online services

4. Click on the option **Add** under the category **Connections.** A new dialog box will appear, as seen in *Figure 10.18*. Enter the name of the connection in the **Title** field. Enter the OData service URL in the **Service Address** field. Select the **Authentication** type as **Use user's identity** or **Use credentials stored in SharePoint,** and click on **Create.**

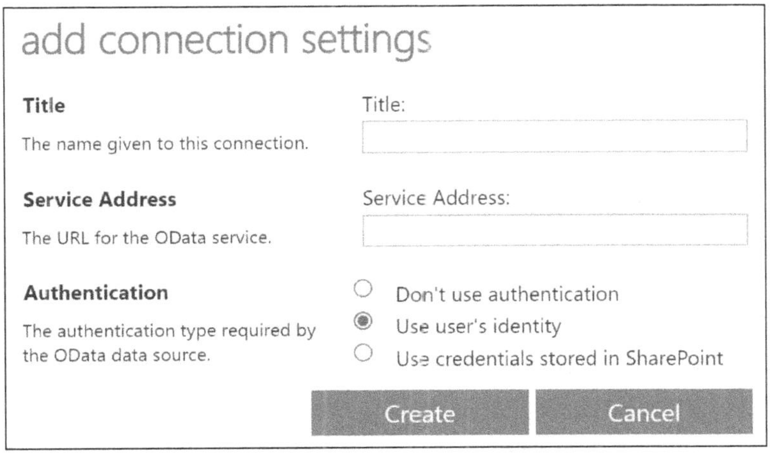

Figure 10.18: *Add connections to online services*

Manage connections to on-premises services

The **Manage connections to on-premises services** is the third option in **BCS**. You can manage connection settings to OData services that are in the on-premises environment using this option and can configure apps to use these connections. Refer to the following steps:

1. Navigate to **SharePoint Admin Center** and click on **More Features** from the left navigation pane.

2. Identify the feature **BCS** and click on **Open** as seen in *Figure 10.19*:

Figure 10.19: *Navigate to BCS feature*

3. You will get settings like **Manage BDC Models and External Content Types, Manage connections to online services,** and **Manage connections to on-premises services**. Click on **Manage connections to on-premises services**. Refer to *Figure 10.20*:

BCS

Manage BDC Models and External Content Types
Manage External Content Types that are not restricted to an App. These can be used on any site.

Manage connections to online services
Manage connection settings to online OData services. You can configure Apps to use these connections.

Manage connections to on-premises services
Manage connection settings to OData services that are on-premises. You can configure Apps to use these connections.

Figure 10.20: BCS feature settings

4. You will find options in the ribbon categorized as **Connections** and **Configure,** as seen in *Figure 10.21*:

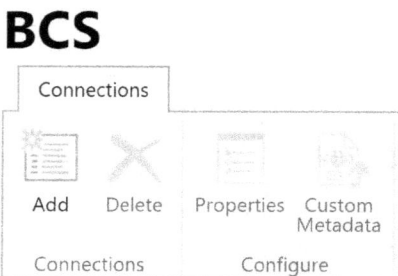

Figure 10.21: Ribbon options under manage connections to on-premises services

5. Click on the option **Add** under the category **Connections**. A new dialog box will appear, as seen in *Figure 10.22*. Enter the name of the connection in the **Title** field. Enter the on-premises OData service URL in the field **Service Address**. Select the **Authentication** type as **Use user's identity, User credentials stored in SharePoint on-premises,** or **Use OData Extension Provider**, as seen in the following figure:

Figure 10.22: Manage connections to on-premises services options like title, service address, authentication

6. Enter the internet-facing URL that Office 365 uses to connect to the **Service Address**, which is usually published by a Reverse Proxy, a Service Bus, or other Network Appliance in the field **Internet-facing URL**. Refer to *Figure 10.23*.

7. Enter the Secure Store Target Application ID for the SSL client certificate in the Secure Store Service that Office 365 uses to connect to the Internet-facing URL in the **Secure Store Target Application ID**. This must be pre-configured in Office 365 Secure Store Service.

Internet-facing URL

The internet facing URL that Office 365 uses to connect to the Service Address, and that is usually published by a Reverse Proxy, a Service Bus, or other Network Appliance.

Internet-facing URL:

Client Certificate

The Target Application ID for the SSL client certificate in the Secure Store Service that Office 365 uses to connect to the Internet facing URL. This must be pre-configured in the Office 365 Secure Store Service.

Secure Store Target Application ID:

Create   Cancel

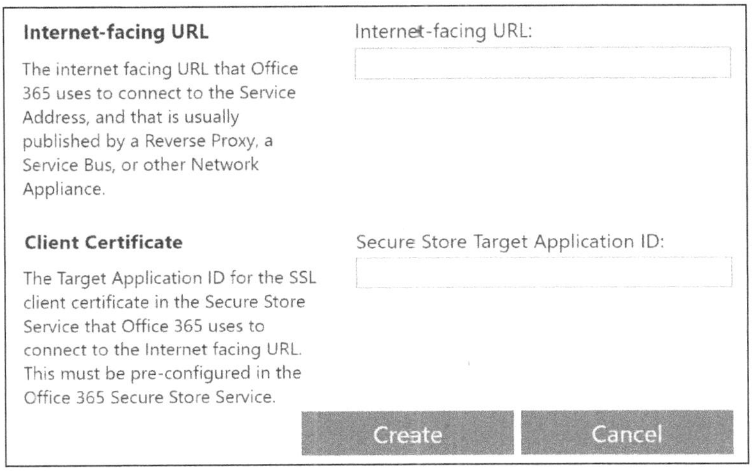

Figure 10.23: Manage connections to on-premises services options like internet-facing URL, client certificate

8. Finally, click on **Create** to create the connection.

Conclusion

In this chapter, we explored how to import BDCM files and understood how to set object permissions and metadata store permissions. We also understood how to create and upgrade the profile page host and how to configure the profile page for selected content types. We also gained clarity on how to manage connection settings to OData services that are in an on-premises environment or an online environment. In the next chapter, *Secure Store Administration*, we will discuss how to manage and administer a secure store service in SharePoint.

Points to remember

•   Regular changes are applied in Office 365 and SharePoint Online. There may be changes in features over time.

Join our book's Discord space

Join the book's Discord Workspace for Latest updates, Offers, Tech happenings around the world, New Release and Sessions with the Authors:

https://discord.bpbonline.com

CHAPTER 11

Secure Store Administration

Introduction

In the previous *Chapter 10, BCS Administration,* we discussed how to create and manage external data sources in SharePoint from the admin center. In this chapter, we will discuss another service in SharePoint, called the **secure store**. Secure store service stores credentials for the service accounts, which are used for communication between external systems or applications, like business connectivity services with SharePoint. While creating and configuring a connection to external target applications using business connectivity services to integrate external data with SharePoint, credentials stored in a secure store are used to provide a secure channel for retrieving data from external data sources. This chapter will discuss how to create and set the credentials for external target applications used for business connectivity service connections in the secure store feature.

Structure

In this chapter, we will discuss the following topics:

- Accessing secure store feature
- Creating a new target application

Objectives

By this chapter's end, you will clearly understand the secure store feature and its use. You will also learn how to create, edit, and delete a target application. You will also understand how to store credentials in a secure store. Additionally, you will learn how to use a secure store to access data from the SQL server database.

Accessing secure store feature

The secure store feature is one of the features in SharePoint, which can be managed and accessed from the SharePoint admin center. In this section, we will discuss the secure store access feature. Follow the step-by-step procedure for the same:

1. Navigate to SharePoint admin center.

2. Click on the option, **More features** from the left navigation.

3. Identify the option **Secure store** and click on **Open** as seen in *Figure 11.1*:

Figure 11.1: Access Secure Store feature

4. You will be redirected to manage the secure store service application page. You will find a ribbon with options, **New, Delete**, and **Edit** under the section **Manage Target Application.** You will also get an option **Set** under the section **Credentials,** as seen in *Figure 11.2*:

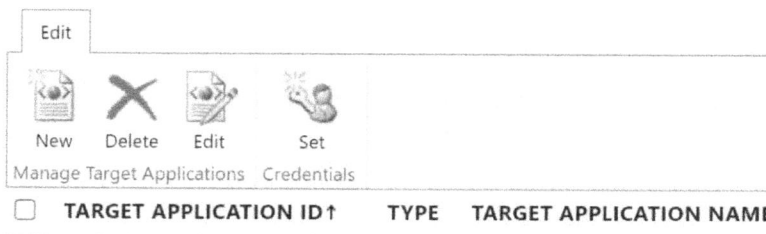

Figure 11.2: Secure store feature options in ribbon

Creating a new target application

Once you access the secure store feature, the next action is to create a target application. Follow the given step-by-step procedure to create a new target application:

1. Click on the option **New** present under the section **Manage Target Applications** in the ribbon.

2. You will be redirected to another page with sections like **Target Application Settings**, **Credential Fields**, **Target Application Administrators**, and **Members**.

3. Enter the details in the field **Target Application ID** (e.g., EmployeeTargetApp), **Display Name** (e.g., EmployeeTargetApp), **Contact E-mail**, **Target Application Type**, which is by default **Group Restricted**, in the section **Target Application Settings**, as seen in *Figure 11.3*:

Secure store

Target Application Settings

The Secure Store Target Application ID is a unique identifier. You cannot change this property after you create the Target Application.

The display name is used for display purposes only.

The contact e-mail should be a valid e-mail address of the primary contact for this Target Application.

Target Application ID

EmployeeTargetApp

Display Name

EmployeeTargetApp

Contact E-mail

Target Application Type

Group Restricted ∨

Figure 11.3: Target application settings options

4. The next section is **Credential Fields**, which defines the type of credentials stored in a secure store. You will find columns like **Field Name**, **Field Type**, **Masked**, and **Delete**. Under **Field Type**, you will see fields like **User Name**, **Password**, **Certificate**, and **Certificate Password**. Keep selecting the default field types, **User Name** and **Password**, which will be used for storing SQL server credentials. Click on the option **Add Field** to store credentials of field type certificate, **Certificate Password**, if required, else click on the option **Delete** to delete that field type. All these fields are stored encrypted with secure store database. Refer to *Figure 11.4*:

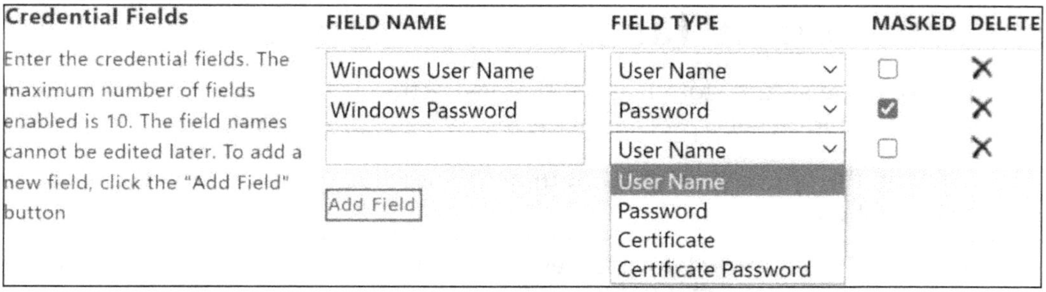

Credential Fields	FIELD NAME	FIELD TYPE	MASKED	DELETE
Enter the credential fields. The maximum number of fields enabled is 10. The field names cannot be edited later. To add a new field, click the "Add Field" button	Windows User Name	User Name ⌄	☐	✕
	Windows Password	Password ⌄	☑	✕
		User Name ⌄	☐	✕
	Add Field	User Name		
		Password		
		Certificate		
		Certificate Password		

Figure 11.4: Credential fields

5. In the next section, **Target Application Administrators**, we enter the administrator user or group who can manage and administer the target application settings. Refer to *Figure 11.5*:

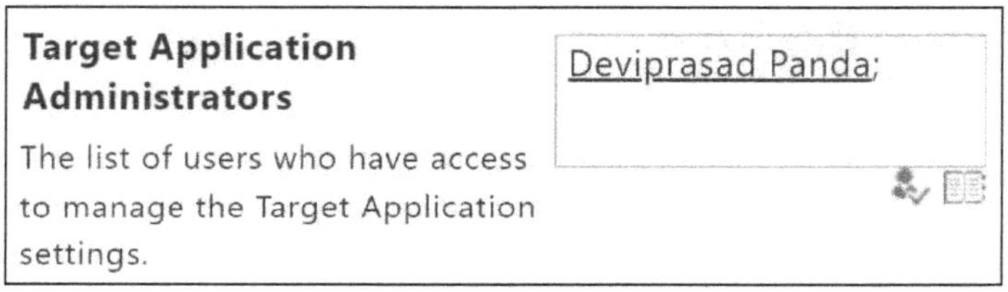

Target Application Administrators	Deviprasad Panda;
The list of users who have access to manage the Target Application settings.	

Figure 11.5: Target Application Administrators

6. The next section is **Members**. Members are authorized users who can access secure store credentials. Let us say there is one SQL server database (e.g., Employee) that needs to be accessed by users present in the security group (e.g., BPB-Online Members). In that case, you can add the group as **Members**. Refer to *Figure 11.6*.

7. Click on **OK** to apply the changes.

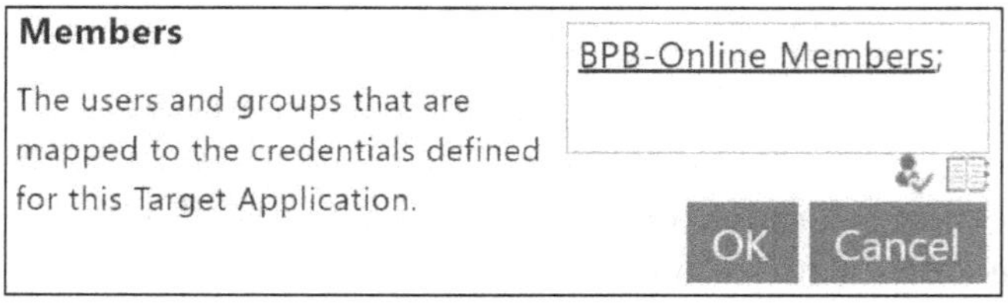

Members	BPB-Online Members;
The users and groups that are mapped to the credentials defined for this Target Application.	OK Cancel

Figure 11.6: Target Application members

8. You will find the target application created and added to the secure store feature, as shown in *Figure 11.7*. You will find the fields **Target Application ID**, **Group Type**, and **Target Application Name** added.

Secure store

Figure 11.7: Target application created

9. The next action is to set the actual credential stored in the secure store database. Select the target application just created (e.g., EmployeeTargetApp) and click on **Set** present under the section **Credential** in the ribbon. Refer to *Figure 11.7*.

10. You will find an additional dialog box. You will find **Credential Owners**. Next, you need to fill in the username and password that are stored in the secure store. These credentials are encrypted and cannot be seen by anyone. Using the target application, the credential owners are authorized to use the credentials. Services like business connectivity services use these credentials on behalf of the credential owner. Refer to *Figure 11.8*.

11. As discussed in *Step 6* above, there is one SQL server database, **Employee**. User account **BPB-OnlineAdmin** (having mail ID and password) has permission to the SQL server database Employee. You want to give access to the database, Employee, to a group of people in the security group BPB-Online Members.

12. Back to *Step 10,* where you get the dialog box to set credentials. In the aforementioned scenario, enter the **Windows User Name** (BPB-OnlineAdmin) and **Windows Password** (related to the account BPB-OnlineAdmin) with access to the SQL server, Employee. Refer to *Figure 11.8*. These passwords are encrypted and stored in secure store. We have already given permission to the users present in the security group **BPB-Online Members** by adding the group as the **Members** as discussed in *Step 6*.

13. Click on **OK** to save and apply changes.

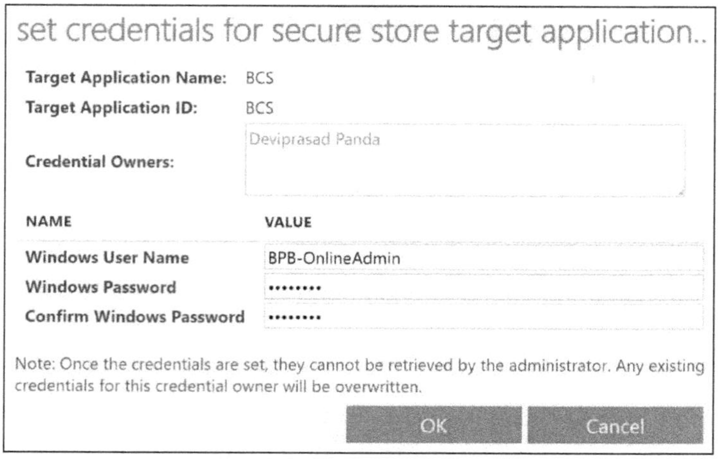

Figure 11.8: Set credentials for target application

Edit target application

You can edit the target application by selecting the required target application and clicking on the **Edit** option present under the section **Manage Target Applications** in the ribbon. Refer to *Figure 11.7*.

Delete target application

You can delete the application by selecting the required target application and clicking on **Delete** option present under the section **Manage Target Applications** in the ribbon. Refer to *Figure 11.7*.

Conclusion

In this chapter, we discussed what the secure store feature is all about and the purpose of using a secure store. Furthermore, we discussed how to create a new target application step-by-step, set credentials for the target application, and store it in a secure store. We also understood how to use credentials stored in a secure store to access data from the SQL server database and discussed the procedure to edit and delete the target application.

In the next *Chapter 12, Record Management Administration,* we will discuss how to manage and administer records in SharePoint.

Points to remember

- Regular changes are applied in Office 365 and SharePoint Online. There may be changes in features over time.

CHAPTER 12

Record Management Administration

Introduction

In the previous *Chapter 11, Secure Store Administration*, we discussed secure store service in SharePoint. In this chapter, we are going to discuss how to manage records in SharePoint using the service record management. **Record management** is one of the features in SharePoint that is used to create and manage **send to connection** settings. The content organizer feature in SharePoint manages a few library tasks automatically, which include routing documents to different libraries or folders, uploading all documents to a drop-off library, managing folder size, managing duplicate submissions, and maintaining audit logs. Hence, the content organizer sends documents to the specified document repository or record center, whose settings are defined and managed under send to connections. In this chapter, we will discuss creating and managing send to connections.

Structure

In this chapter, we will discuss the following topics:

- Create send to connections
- Edit or remove connections

Objectives

By the end of this chapter, you will get a clear understanding of record management. You will understand the step-by-step procedures to create, edit, and delete the send to connection.

Create send to connections

Send to connection defines the settings for a document repository or a records center. Send to connection allows content to be submitted to a document repository or a records center, manually or by configuring an information management policy. Let us follow the given steps to create a send to connection:

1. Open **SharePoint Admin Center** and click on **More Features** from the left navigation.

2. Identify the feature **Records management** and click on **Open** as shown in *Figure 12.1*:

More features

Access familiar features from the classic SharePoint admin center.

Records management

Manage records in a Records Center site that serves as an archive. Learn more

Open

Figure 12.1: More features

3. In the field **Send To Connections**, select **New Connection**, as shown in *Figure 12.2*:

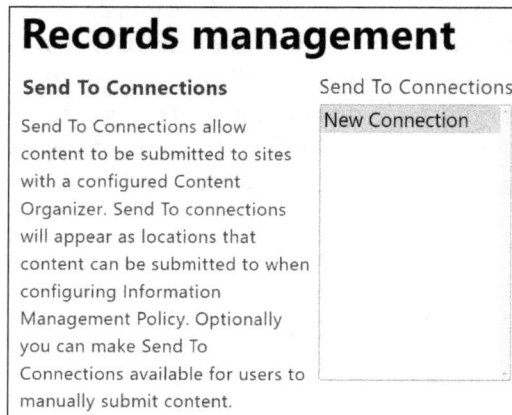

Records management

Send To Connections

Send To Connections allow content to be submitted to sites with a configured Content Organizer. Send To connections will appear as locations that content can be submitted to when configuring Information Management Policy. Optionally you can make Send To Connections available for users to manually submit content.

Send To Connections

New Connection

Figure 12.2: Send to connections

4. Enter the name of the connection in the field **Display name**. Refer to *Figure 12.3*.

5. Enter the destination site **Submission Points** web service URL (e.g., **https://spmcse. sharepoint.com/sites/BPB-ModernTeamSite/_vti_bin/OfficialFile.asmx**) in the field **Send To URL**. You can find the submission point URL on the destination site. Navigate to **Site Settings | Site Administration | Content Organizer Settings** from the destination site.

6. Select the checkbox option present next to **Allow manual submission from the Send To menu**, as shown in the following figure, which will enable users to submit records to the repository directly:

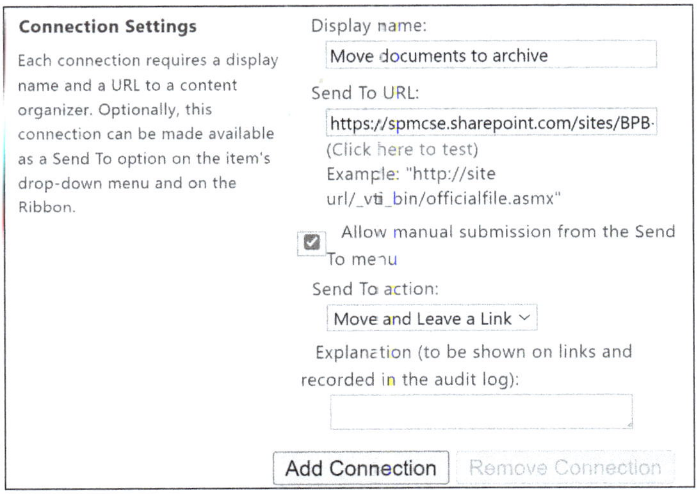

Figure 12.3: Connection Settings

7. Select **Send To action** as **Copy**, **Move**, or **Move and Leave a Link**. The action **Copy** will create a copy of the document and send it to the destination location. The action **Move** will move the document to its destination location. The action **Move and Leave a Link** will move the document to the destination location, leaving behind a reference link at the source location. The link at the source location holds the metadata and document URL.

8. In the field **Explanation**, enter additional information related to the connection.

9. Click on **Add Connection**.

Edit or remove connections

You can edit or remove a connection if you need any changes in the future. Follow the given step-by-step procedure to edit or remove the connection:

1. Navigate to feature **Records management** as discussed in *Step 1* and *Step 2* in the preceding section.

2. Select one connection you want to edit or update, as seen in *Figure 12.4*:

Figure 12.4: *Select Send to connections*

3. Click on **Remove Connection** from the **Connection Settings** category if you want to delete the connection. The connection will be removed from record management. Refer to *Figure 12.5*.

4. If you want to edit the connection, then change the **Display name,** the **Send To URL,** or the **Send To action** from the category **Connection Settings**, as per requirements.

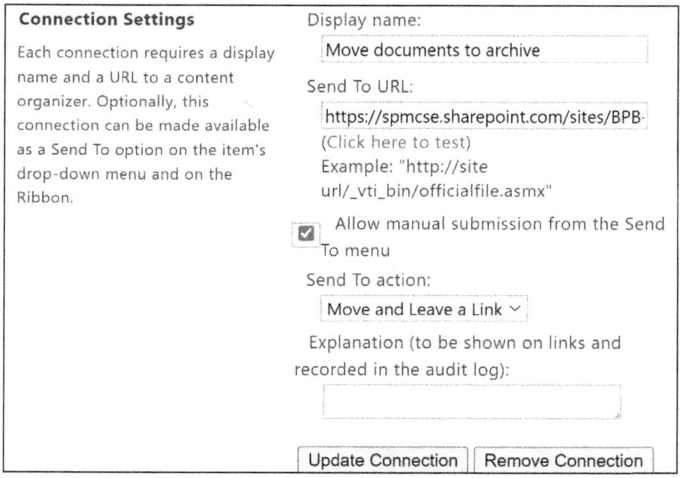

Figure 12.5: *Edit or Remove connection*

5. Click on **Update Connection** to apply the changes.

Conclusion

In this chapter, we discussed how to send a connection and its purpose of use. Furthermore, we also understood the role of the content organizer feature and discussed the step-by-step procedure to create a new sent-to connection and how to update or remove a connection.

In the next *Chapter 13, Hybrid Picker*, we will discuss different hybrid features and their functionalities.

Points to remember

- Regular changes are applied in Office 365 and SharePoint Online. There may be changes in features over time.

Hybrid Picker

Introduction

In *Chapter 12, Record Management Administration,* we discussed how to manage SharePoint records using service record management. In this chapter, we will discuss SharePoint hybrid features and their functionalities. Hybrid picker is one of the features in SharePoint online that provides a straightforward way to set up a connection with the SharePoint on-premises environment features to create a hybrid environment. **Hybrid picker** is a UI method to combine SharePoint on-premises services with online features.

Structure

In this chapter, we will discuss the following topics:

- Run hybrid picker
- Hybrid OneDrive
- Hybrid sites
- Hybrid app launcher
- Hybrid business to business sites
- Hybrid self-service site creation

- Hybrid taxonomy and content type
- Hybrid search

Objectives

By the end of the chapter, you will get a clear understanding of hybrid picker and how to run the hybrid picker. You will understand various hybrid features, namely OneDrive, sites, app launcher, business to business sites, self-service site creation, taxonomy and content type, search, and a step-by-step procedure to configure the hybrid features.

Run hybrid picker

A hybrid picker is a wizard that needs to run in the SharePoint farm to start the configuration process. You need to download the hybrid picker from the Microsoft 365 portal first. In this section, we will discuss how to run the hybrid picker and the various options available to set up hybrid features. Follow the given steps to combine SharePoint on-premises services with online features:

1. Open **SharePoint Admin Center** and click on **More features** from the left navigation.

2. Identify the feature **Hybrid picker** and click on **Open,** as shown in *Figure 13.1*:

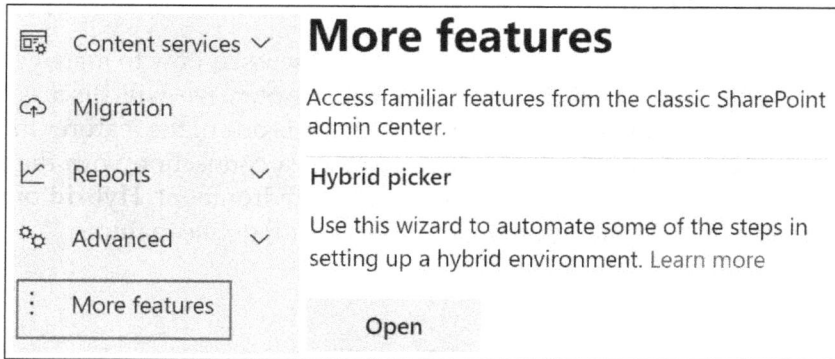

Figure 13.1: Hybrid picker feature

3. You will be redirected to the hybrid settings page. This page describes some hybrid features like **OneDrive, OneDrive and sites, App launcher, Extranet Business to business sites, Taxonomy**, and **Hybrid Self-Service site creation**. You can configure **cloud hybrid search**. In the hybrid settings page, you will notice two more options, namely, Prerequisites and **Go to Hybrid Picker Download Page**. There will be a prerequisite check for running a hybrid picker. The option **Go to Hybrid Picker Download Page** will download the SharePoint hybrid picker. Click on the option **Go to Hybrid Picker Download Page,** as shown in *Figure 13.2*:

Figure 13.2: SharePoint Hybrid Settings page to download hybrid picker

4. You will get an additional dialog to install **SharePoint Hybrid Configuration Wizard**, as shown in *Figure 13.3*. Click on **Install**.

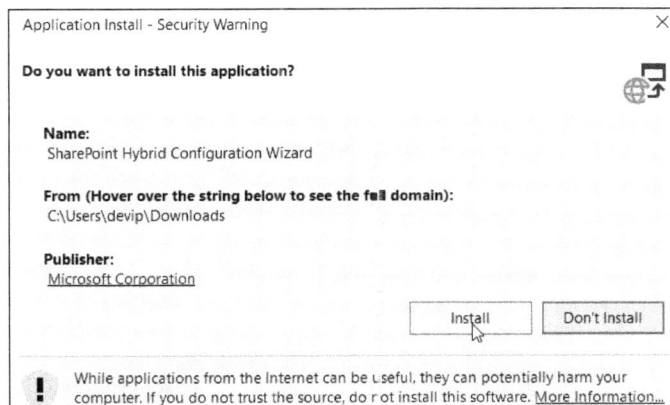

Figure 13.3: Install hybrid picker

5. You will get more information, like **run this wizard in SharePoint 2019, SharePoint 2016, or SharePoint 2013 server**, in the next dialog box, as shown in *Figure 13.4*. Click on **Next**.

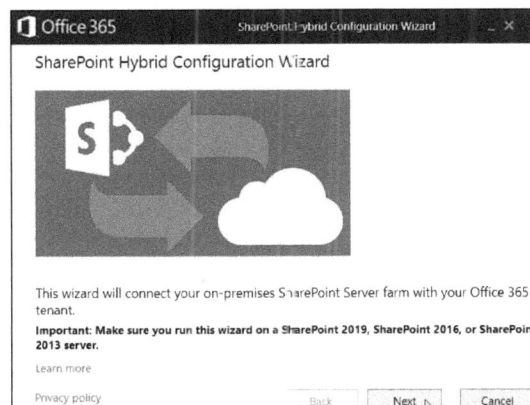

Figure 13.4: SharePoint Hybrid Configuration Wizard

6. In the next window, you will be asked to enter the credentials for the on-premises account as well as the Office 365 account. You will get two fields: **Enter your on-premises account credentials,** and **Enter your global administrator credentials for Office 365**. Since you are running the SharePoint Hybrid Configuration Wizard in an on-premises environment, the credentials for the option **Enter your on-premises account credentials** will be taken automatically. You need to enter the global administrator mail ID for Office 365 under the option **Enter your global administrator credentials for Office 365**.

7. Click on **Validate credentials** as shown in *Figure 13.5*:

Figure 13.5: Validate credentials

8. Enter Office 365 global administrator password in the next dialog box and click on **Sign in**, as shown in *Figure 13.6*:

Figure 13.6: Office 365 tenant admin credential validation

9. Once the credentials are validated successfully, you will get a window as shown in *Figure 13.7*. Click on the button **Close**.

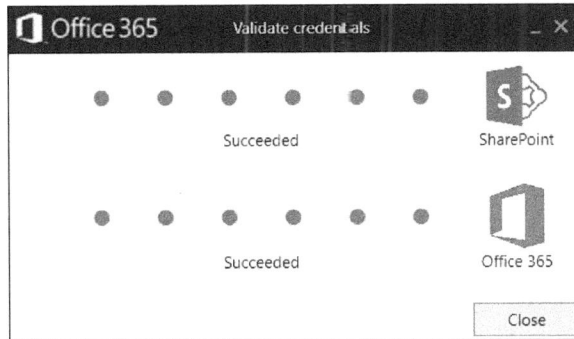

Figure 13.7: On-premises and Office 365 credentials validation successful

10. You will find that the button **Next** is enabled now. Click on **Next** as shown in *Figure 13.8*:

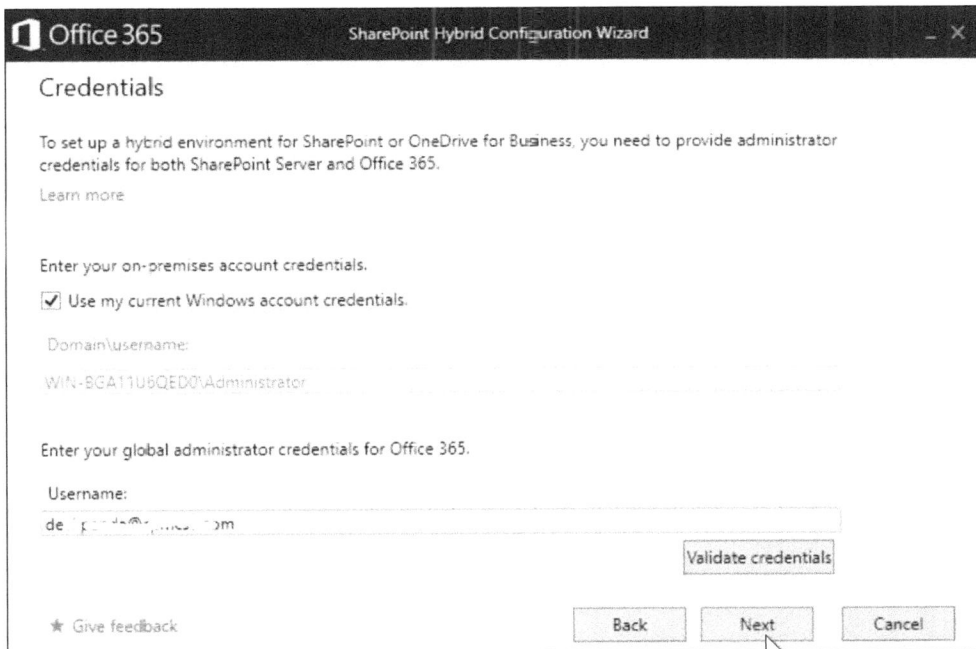

Figure 13.8: Post validation of credentials enabled the option Next

11. There will be a prerequisite check in the next window. It should be successful to proceed with the next step in the configuration process. You will find a green mark on the right side of each check, as shown in *Figure 13.9*. Click on **Next**.

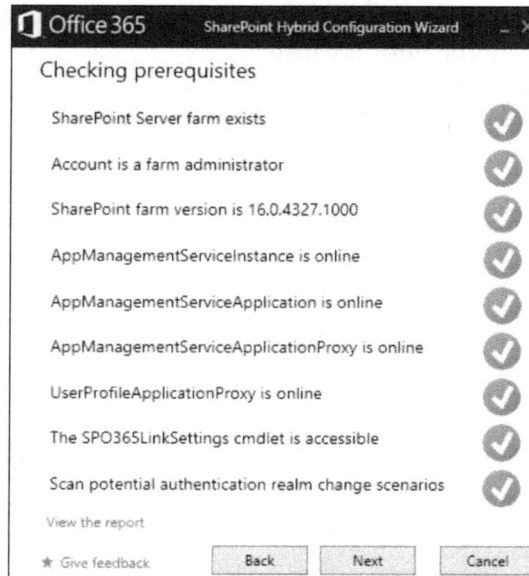

Figure 13.9: Prerequisite check

12. From the next window, **Authentication realm updates**, click on **Next**, as shown in *Figure 13.10*:

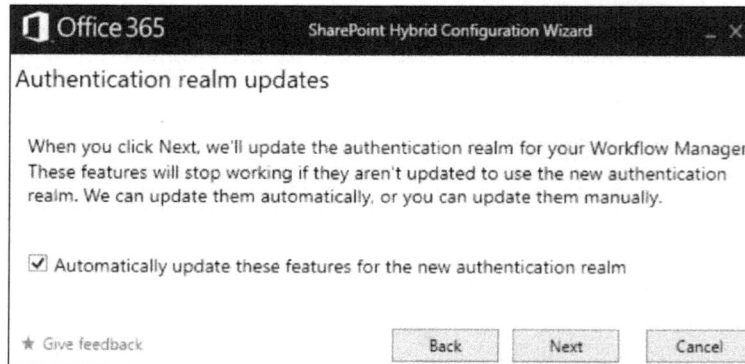

Figure 13.10: Authentication realm updates

13. In the next window, you need to select the feature you want to configure as hybrid, refer to *Figure 13.11*. You can configure **OneDrive**, **OneDrive and sites**, **Hybrid App launcher, Hybrid Business to business sites, Hybrid taxonomy and content type, Hybrid Self-Service site creation,** and **Hybrid search**. You can select any one of the features or multiple features at a time to configure. Refer to the following figure:

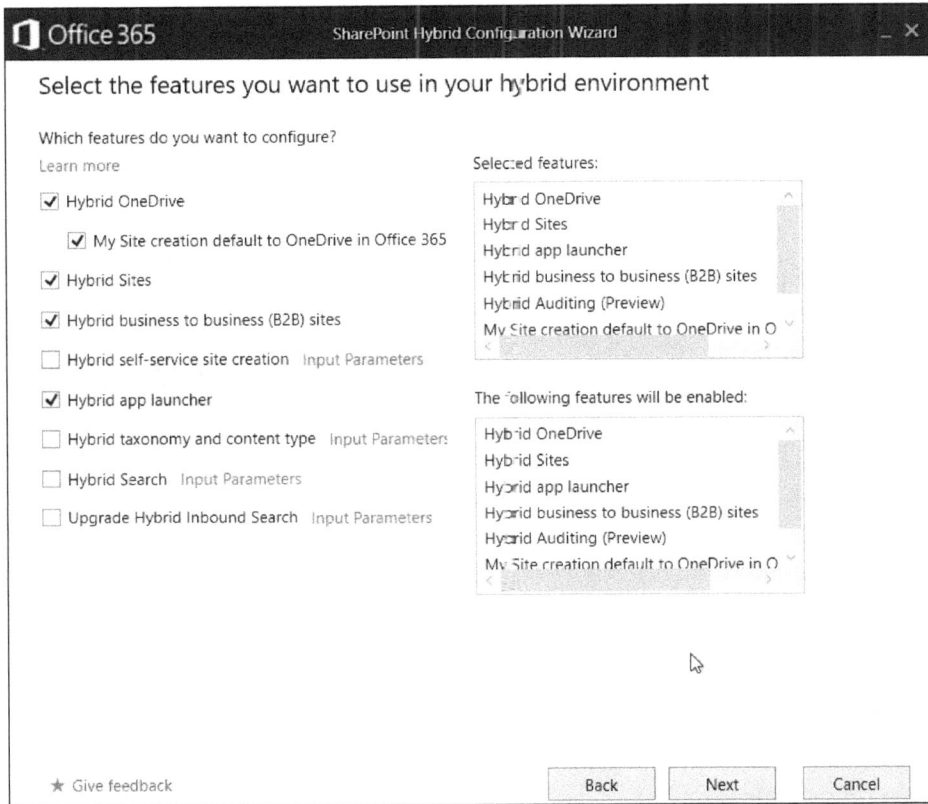

Figure 13.11: SharePoint hybrid features to configure

If you want to configure any hybrid features, you need to proceed till this step is completed. In the following section, we will discuss configuring each feature at a time.

Hybrid OneDrive

Once you open SharePoint 2013 or SharePoint 2016 on-premises environment and click on **OneDrive** from the app launcher, you will be redirected to on-premises OneDrive. Configure Hybrid OneDrive. Next, open SharePoint 2013 or SharePoint 2016 on-premises environment and click on **OneDrive** from the app launcher, and you will be redirected to Microsoft 365 OneDrive. Hence, by configuring hybrid OneDrive, we only redirect users from on-premises to Microsoft 365 OneDrive so that they can store files in the cloud directly. On-premises data will remain in the on-premises server, which can be migrated online using a migration tool, as needed.

In this section, we will discuss how to configure hybrid OneDrive. Follow these steps to configure hybrid OneDrive:

1. Follow *Step 1* to *Step 13* as discussed in the section *Run Hybrid Picker*.

2. Select the only feature **Hybrid OneDrive** in the SharePoint Hybrid Configuration Wizard, as shown in *Figure 13.12*.

3. On the right side of SharePoint Hybrid Configuration Wizard, you will notice the **Selected features** as **Hybrid OneDrive, Hybrid Auditing**. Under **Selected features**, you will see features like **Hybrid OneDrive, Hybrid app launcher**, and **Hybrid Auditing** that will be enabled.

4. If you are selecting the hybrid feature, **My Site creation default to OneDrive in Office 365**, then you will find one more option along with the other features to be enabled.

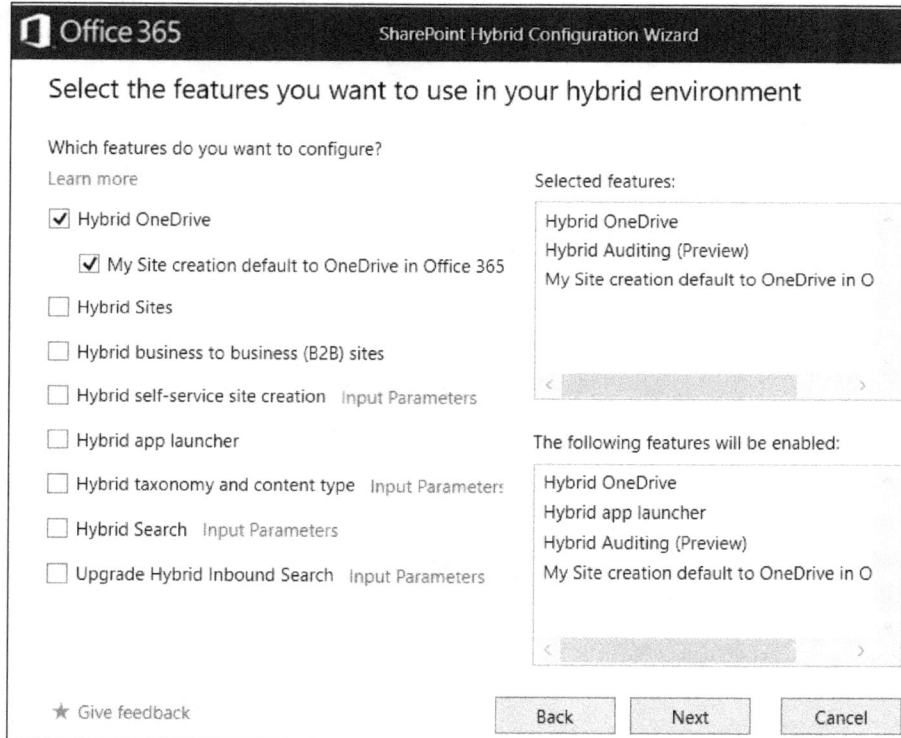

Figure 13.12: Hybrid OneDrive feature

5. Click on **Next**. The configuration will be completed automatically. You will get confirmation with a **Configuration summary**. Click on the **Close** button to close the Hybrid Configuration Wizard.

6. Now, navigate to the SharePoint on-premises central admin and click on **Office 365** from the left navigation.

7. Click on **Configure hybrid OneDrive and Site features**. You will get a window, as shown in *Figure 13.13*:

Figure 13.13: Configure hybrid OneDrive and Site features

8. You find the field **My Site URL,** which is auto-filled with the Office 365 tenant MySite URL, on successful configuration of hybrid OneDrive after running the Hybrid Configuration Wizard. Refer to *Figure 13.14*:

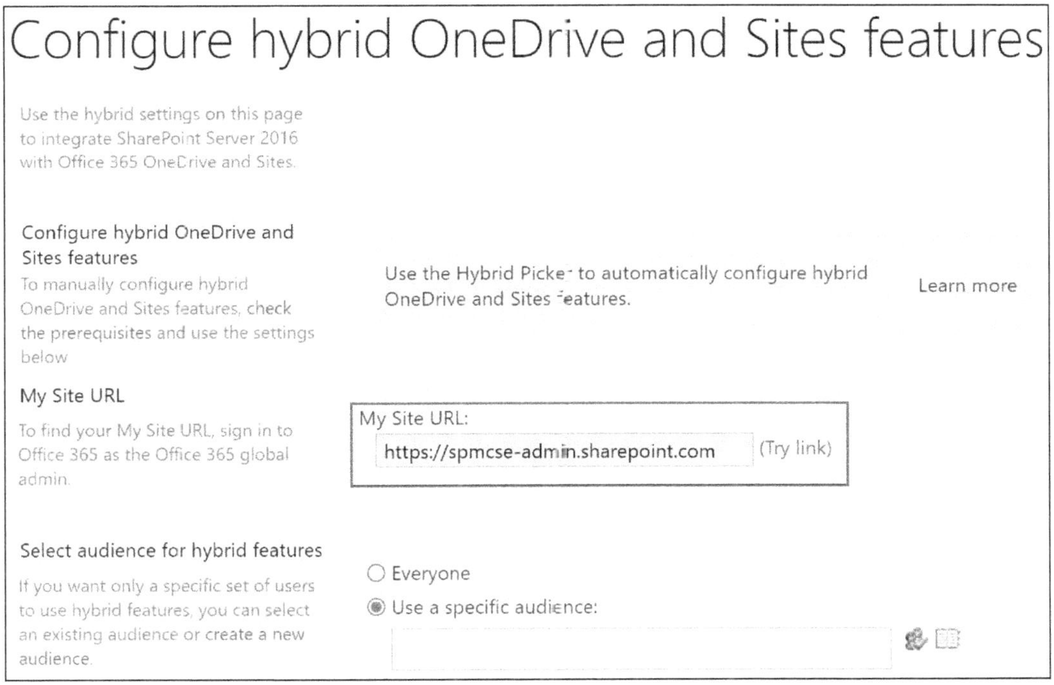

Figure 13.14: MySite URL of Office 365 tenant and hybrid feature audience targeting

9. The next field is **Select audience for hybrid features**. We can target hybrid features to a specific group of people. You will find two check boxes, **Everyone** and **Use a specific audience**, as shown in the preceding feature. Selecting **Everyone** will make the hybrid feature available to everyone in the organization. Select the option **Use a specific audience** and enter the group in the people picker, making the hybrid feature available for that group of people.

10. The next option is **Select hybrid features**. In this option, you will find three options under hybrid features, such as **OneDrive and sites, OneDrive only,** and **None**. Select the option **OneDrive only** and click on **OK** to complete hybrid OneDrive configuration, as shown in the following figure:

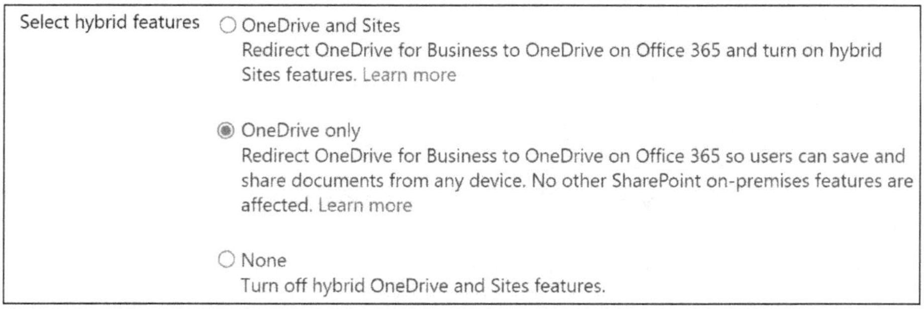

Select hybrid features ○ OneDrive and Sites
Redirect OneDrive for Business to OneDrive on Office 365 and turn on hybrid Sites features. Learn more

◉ OneDrive only
Redirect OneDrive for Business to OneDrive on Office 365 so users can save and share documents from any device. No other SharePoint on-premises features are affected. Learn more

○ None
Turn off hybrid OneDrive and Sites features.

Figure 13.15: OneDrive Only feature configuration

11. When you click on **OneDrive** from the app launcher in the on-premises environment, you will be redirected to Office 365 OneDrive.

Hybrid sites

Access the SharePoint on-premises environment. You can access any site and click on Follow present at the top right corner. You will find that the site is added to your on-premises followed site list. Now, open SharePoint online site and you will not find the on-premises followed site under SharePoint online followed site list. Next, follow any SharePoint online site, and you will find the site under SharePoint online followed site list. It is difficult for users who are using both on-premises and online sites in their day-to-day lives. Hence, by configuring hybrid sites, we can make all the followed sites (on-premises or online sites) available in one place in SharePoint online. On-premises site data will remain in the on-premises server. We are just building a connection so that we can access all sites from one place. Follow these steps to configure hybrid sites:

1. Follow *Step 1* to *Step 13* as discussed in the section *Run Hybrid Picker.*

2. Select the only feature, **Hybrid Sites**, in the SharePoint Hybrid Configuration Wizard as shown in *Figure 13.16*.

3. On the right side of SharePoint Hybrid Configuration Wizard, you will notice the **Selected features** as **Hybrid sites**, and **Hybrid Auditing**. Under the **Selected features**, you see features like **Hybrid OneDrive, Hybrid sites, Hybrid app launcher, Hybrid business to business (B2B) sites**, and **Hybrid Auditing**, will be enabled. Refer to the following figure:

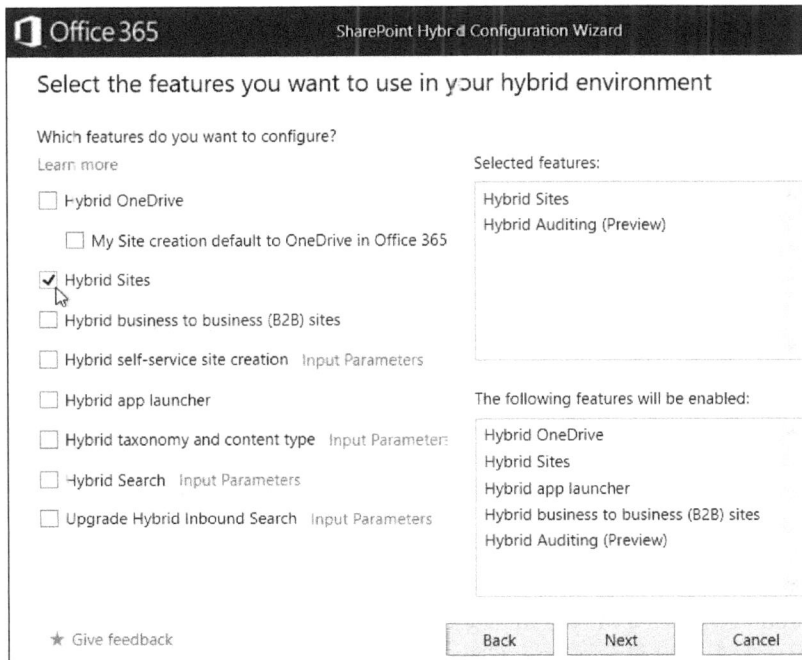

Figure 13.16: Hybrid sites

4. Click on **Next**. The configuration will be completed automatically, and you will get confirmation to close the Hybrid Configuration Wizard.

5. Next, navigate to SharePoint on-premises central admin and click on **Office 365** from the left navigation.

6. Click on **Configure hybrid OneDrive and Site features**.

7. Identify the option **Select hybrid features** from the net window. You will find three options under hybrid features, **OneDrive and sites**, **OneDrive only**, and **None**. Now you can select the option **OneDrive and sites** to use the feature. Refer to *Figure 13.17*.

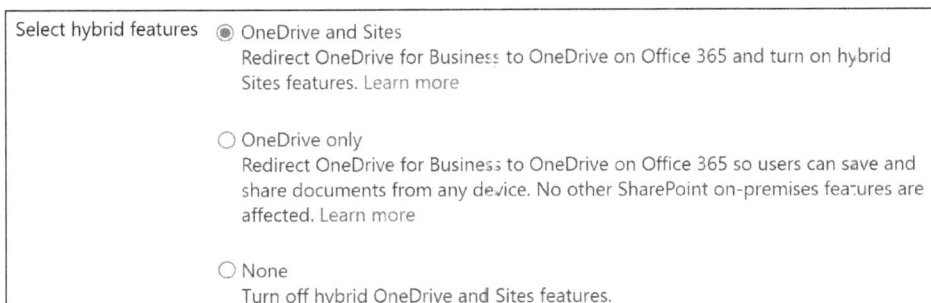

Figure 13.17: OneDrive and sites

Hybrid app launcher

Open SharePoint on-premises environment site and click on the app launcher from the top left corner of the site. You will find on-premises tiles like **Newsfeed, OneDrive,** and **sites.** By configuring the hybrid app launcher, you will notice additional tiles, such as **Delve, Office 365 video,** and **Custom apps,** along with the apps, such as **Newsfeed, OneDrive,** and **sites,** in the SharePoint on-premises site app launcher that are in sync with Office 365 app launcher. This means that the apps will be available both in Office 365 and on-premises sites app launcher. The users can easily navigate to the Office 365 apps while using the on-premises site and vice versa. This provides a better user experience for both on-premises and online sites. In this section, we will discuss how to configure the **Hybrid app launcher.** Refer to the following steps:

1. Follow *Steps 1 to 13,* as discussed in the *Run Hybrid Picker section.*

2. Only select the feature **Hybrid app launcher** in the SharePoint Hybrid Configuration Wizard, as shown in *Figure 13.18.*

3. On the right side of SharePoint Hybrid Configuration Wizard, you will notice the **Selected features** as **Hybrid sites.** Under **Selected features,** you will see features like **Hybrid OneDrive** and **Hybrid app launcher** will be enabled. Refer to the following figure:

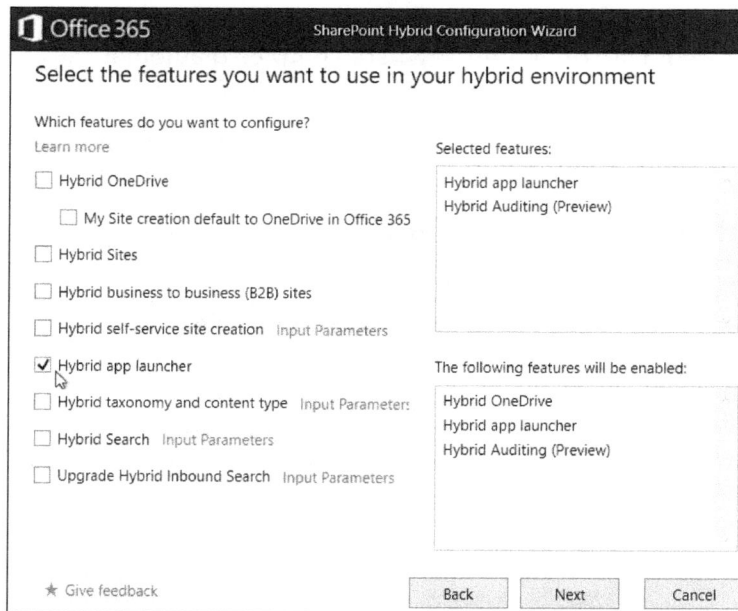

Figure 13.18: Hybrid app launcher

4. Click on **Next.** The configuration will be completed automatically, and you will get confirmation to close the Hybrid Configuration Wizard.

Hybrid business to business sites

Business to Business (B2B) site is nothing but an extranet site that is accessible by external users (other company users, vendors, stakeholders, etc.). There were a lot of configurations done in the on-premises SharePoint farm to provide site access to external users. SharePoint online makes onboarding and sharing content to external users simple by configuring a few settings from Azure Active Directory. By running the Hybrid Configuration Wizard, we can configure OAuth hybrid connection and the hybrid follow site features, so that the user can navigate across intranet sites in on-premises and extranet sites in SharePoint online by simply using the follow gesture in site pages. In the following steps, let us discuss how to configure Hybrid B2B sites:

1. Follow *Steps 1 to 13,* as discussed in the *Run Hybrid Picker section.*

2. Only select the **Hybrid Business to Business (B2B) sites** feature in the SharePoint Hybrid Configuration Wizard, as shown in *Figure 13.19.*

3. On the right side of SharePoint Hybrid Configuration Wizard, you will notice the **Selected features** as **Hybrid Business to Business (B2B) sites** and **Hybrid Auditing (Preview)**. Under that option, you will find another field with related features like **Hybrid OneDrive, Hybrid sites, Hybrid app launcher, Hybrid Business to Business (B2B) sites**, and **Hybrid Auditing (Preview)** that will be enabled.

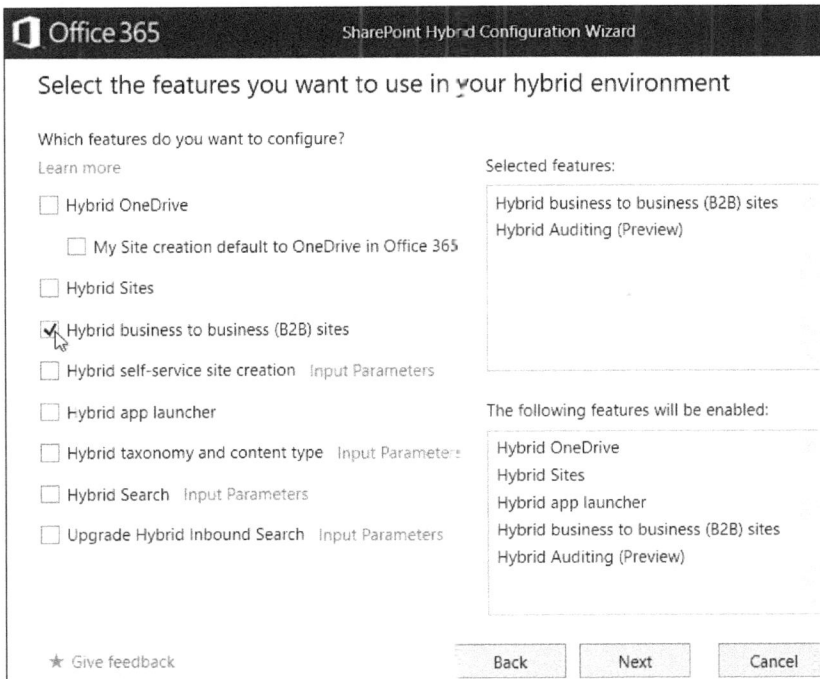

Figure 13.19: Hybrid Business to Business (B2B) sites

4. Click on **Next**. The configuration will be completed automatically, and you will get confirmation to close the Hybrid Configuration Wizard.

5. Now you can add guest users (external users) while creating SharePoint online site using SharePoint admin center.

Hybrid self-service site creation

In the SharePoint on-premises environment, site collection is created under a specific web application URL. Farm administrators can create a site collection. The **Self-Service Site Creation** feature enables users to create site collection under a specific web application URL. By default, the **Self-Service Site Creation** feature is turned off for end users. Farm administrators need to turn on this feature for a specific web application and assign specific permissions to the group so that only those users can create self-service site under a specific web URL.

Let us follow these steps to understand better:

1. Open central admin in SharePoint on-premises environment.

2. Click on **Manage web applications**. Select one web application that you want to enable self-service site creation and click on the option **Self-Service Site Creation** from the ribbon, as shown in the following figure:

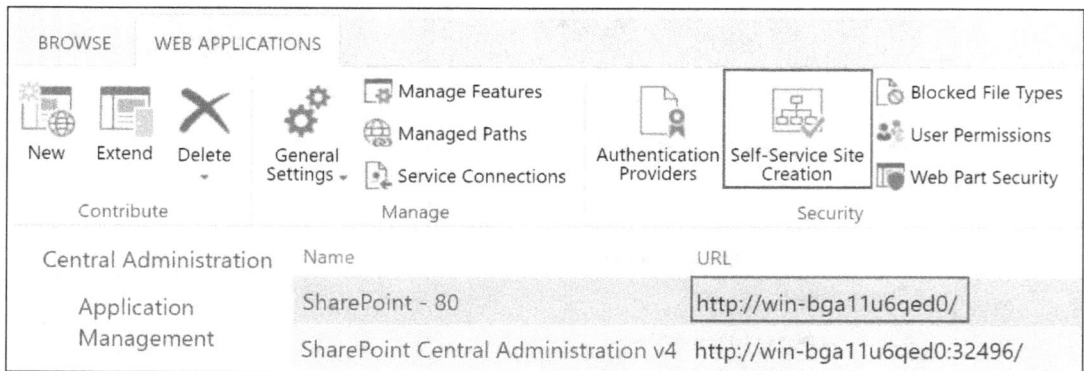

Figure 13.20: Self-Service Site Creation in on-premises

3. Enable the feature by selecting the option **on present** under **Site Collections**.

4. Select the path from the option **Start a Site**, under which the self-service site collection will be created. Refer to the following figure for an illustration of the same:

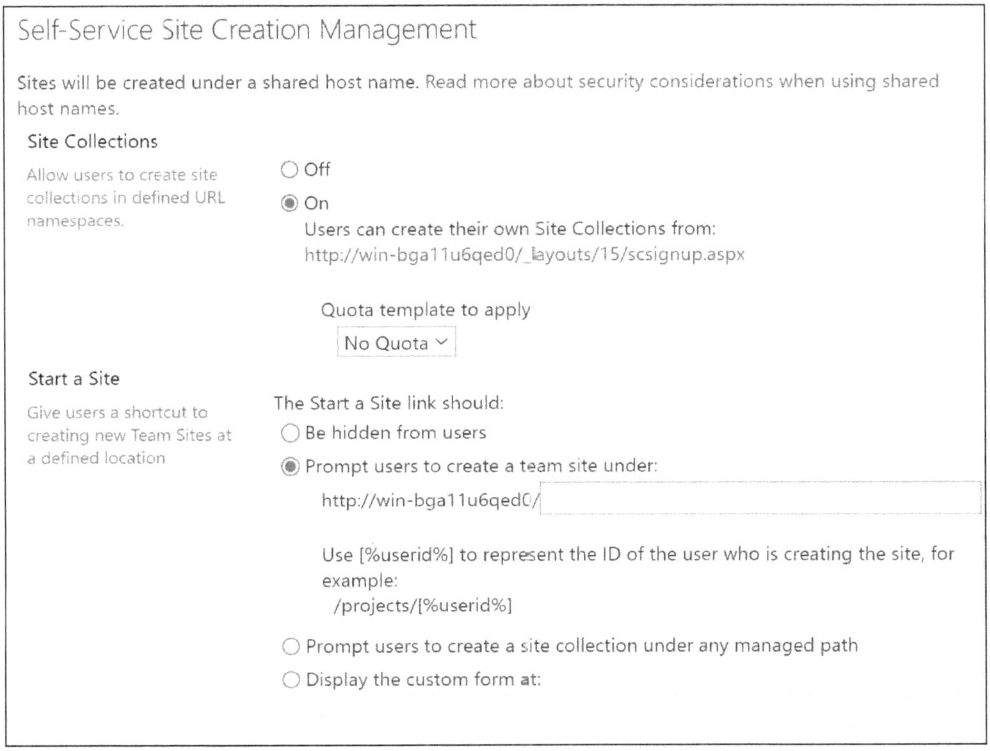

Self-Service Site Creation Management

Sites will be created under a shared host name. Read more about security considerations when using shared host names.

Site Collections

Allow users to create site collections in defined URL namespaces.

○ Off

◉ On

Users can create their own Site Collections from:
http://win-bga11u6qed0/_layouts/15/scsignup.aspx

Quota template to apply

[No Quota ∨]

Start a Site

Give users a shortcut to creating new Team Sites at a defined location

The Start a Site link should:

○ Be hidden from users

◉ Prompt users to create a team site under:

http://win-bga11u6qed0/ [   ]

Use [%userid%] to represent the ID of the user who is creating the site, for example:
/projects/[%userid%]

○ Prompt users to create a site collection under any managed path

○ Display the custom form at:

Figure 13.21: Enable Self-Service Site Creation for web application

5. By configuring hybrid self-service site creation, we are redirecting self-service site creation page from SharePoint server on-premises **(/_layouts/15/scsignup.aspx)** or **(/_layouts/16/scsignup.aspx)** to SharePoint online **(/sites or /teams)**.

This section will discuss how to configure hybrid self-service site creation. Follow the given steps to configure hybrid self-service site creation:

1. Follow *Steps 1 to 13*, as discussed in the *Run Hybrid Picker section*.

2. Select the only feature, **Hybrid self-service site creation**, in the SharePoint Hybrid Configuration Wizard, as shown in *Figure 13.22*.

3. On the right side of SharePoint Hybrid Configuration Wizard, you will notice the **Selected features** as **Hybrid Auditing (Preview)** and **Hybrid self-service site creation**. Under that option, you will find another field that contains related features, like **Hybrid Auditing (Preview),** which will be enabled.

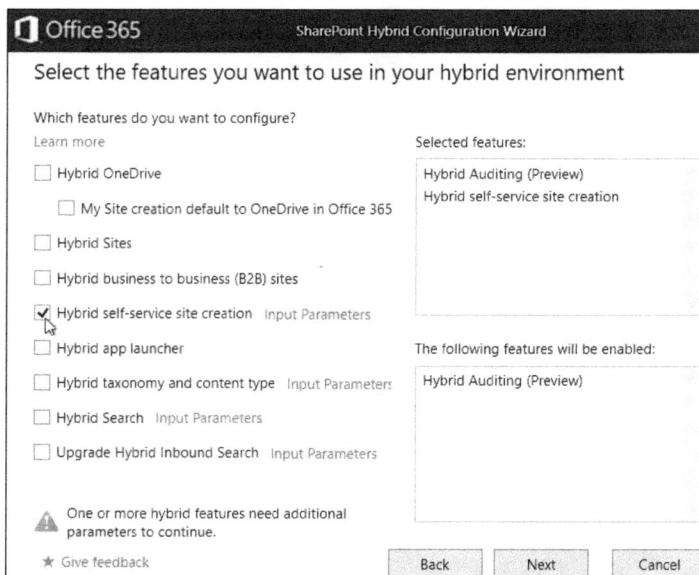

Figure 13.22: Hybrid self-service site creation

4. Click on the **Input Parameter** as shown in *Figure 13.22*. You will get another dialog box to **Select the web application to use with hybrid self-service site creation**. Select the web application from the drop-down option. Refer to *Figure 13.23*:

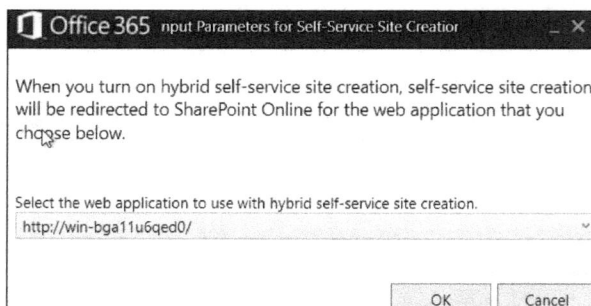

Figure 13.23: Select web application for self-service site creation

5. Click on **OK**. Then click on **Next**. The configuration will be completed automatically, and you will get confirmation to close the Hybrid Configuration Wizard.

Hybrid taxonomy and content type

SharePoint on-premises term sets are stored in the on-premises managed metadata service application taxonomy term store, and SharePoint online term sets are stored in the online admin center Term Store. By configuring Hybrid taxonomy, we can store and manage both on-premises and online taxonomy in one place. Configuring hybrid taxonomy and content type is a two-step process. First, we need to copy terms and content types from the on-premises platform to the online platform using PowerShell. Second, run the Hybrid Configuration Wizard to build a connection with the on-premises environment from the SharePoint online platform, so that terms and content types from online will replicate at the on-premises platform. Follow the given steps to configure hybrid taxonomy:

1. Open SharePoint on-premises **Central Administration**.

2. Click on **Manage Service Applications** present under **Application Management**.

3. Identify the service application **Managed Metadata Service**.

4. Copy the Local **Term Store Name** (**Managed Metadata Service**), as shown in *Figure 13.24*.

5. Copy the on-premises root site collection URL (e.g., **https://win-bga11u6qed0/**) under which the term group is created. That site collection URL will be the **Local Site URL**

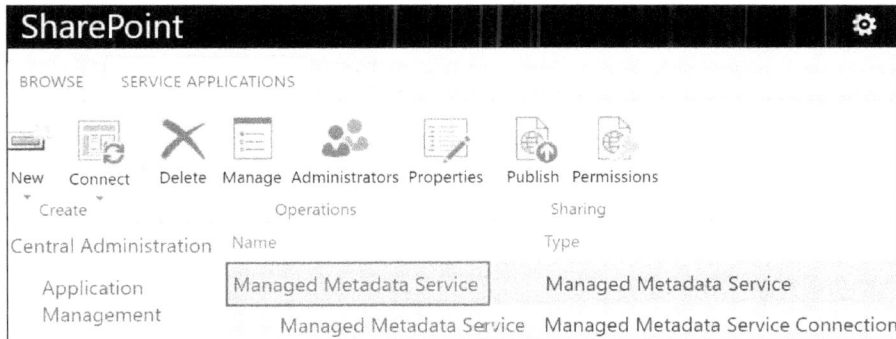

Figure 13.24: Term Store Name

6. Click on the service application **Managed Metadata Service**. You will see one term group **Employee**, as shown in *Figure 13.25*, which you want to copy from SharePoint on-premises to the SharePoint online platform. Copy that term group (**Employee**). Refer to the following figure:

Figure 13.25: Term group to be copied from on-premises environment

7. Open SharePoint online admin center (**https://spmcse-admin.sharepoint.com/**). Identify and open the primary online site collection (**https://spmcse.sharepoint. com/**), the destination site URL called **Remote Site Url** (**https://spmcse.sharepoint. com/**).

8. Now, you need to use the following PowerShell command to copy the taxonomy from on-premises to an online platform:

```
$credential = Get-Credential
Copy-SPTaxonomyGroups -LocalTermStoreName "Managed Metadata
Service Application Proxy" -LocalSiteUrl "<OnPremisesSiteURL>"
-RemoteSiteUrl "SharePointOnlineSiteURL" -GroupNames
"Group1","Group2" -Credential $credential
```

9. Use the details copied in the previous step (Local term store name, Local site URL, remote site URL, and Term group name) in the PowerShell command:

```
$credential = Get-Credential
Copy-SPTaxonomyGroups -LocalTermStoreName "Managed Metadata
Service" -LocalSiteUrl "https://win-bga11u6qed0/" -RemoteSiteUrl
"https://spmcse.sharepoint.com" -GroupNames "Employee" -Credential
$credential
```

10. Now, open the SharePoint online **admin center**.

11. Click on **Content services** from the left navigation.

12. Click on the **Term store**.

13. Now, you will find the SharePoint on-premises term group (**Employee**) in SharePoint online term store, as shown in *Figure 13.26*:

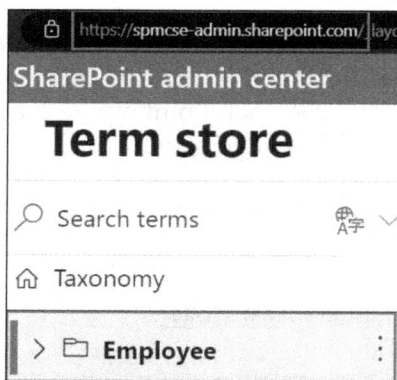

Figure 13.26: Term Group Copied to SharePoint Online

14. Similarly, we can copy SharePoint on-premises custom content type to SharePoint online content hub, using the following PowerShell command:

```
$credential = Get-Credential
Copy-SPTaxonomyGroups -LocalTermStoreName "Managed Metadata
Service Application Proxy" -LocalSiteUrl "<OnPremisesSiteURL>"
-RemoteSiteUrl "SharePointOnlineSiteURL" -GroupNames
"Group1","Group2" -Credential $credential
$credential = Get-Credential
Copy-SPContentTypes -LocalSiteUrl <OnPremSiteURL>
-LocalTermStoreName "managed metadata service application proxy"
-RemoteSiteUrl <OnlineSiteURL> -ContentTypeNames @("ContentTypeA",
"ContentTypeB") -Credential $credential
```

15. We can use the **Local Site URL** and the root site collection URL (**https://win-bga11u6qed0/**) in the on-premises server. This would be the same as discussed in *Step 5*.

16. The **Remote Site URL (https://spmcse.sharepoint.com/)** will be SharePoint online primary site collection URL, same as discussed in *Step 7*.

17. Identify the custom content type from the on-premises SharePoint content type hub site, that you want to copy to the online environment. Copy the name of that content type.

18. Enter parameters like **LocalSiteURL**, **LocalTermStoreName**, **RemoteSiteURL** and **ContentTypeName** in the PowerShell, as shown in the following command:

```
$credential = Get-Credential
Copy-SPContentTypes -LocalSiteUrl https://win-bga11u6qed0/
-LocalTermStoreName "managed metadata service" -RemoteSiteUrl
https://spmcse.sharepoint.com/ -ContentTypeNames @("Contact List")
-Credential $credential
```

19. Now, open the primary site in SharePoint online as discussed in *Step 7*.

20. Navigate to SharePoint online content type hub **https://spmcse.sharepoint.com/sites/contentTypeHub/_layouts/15/mngctype.aspx (https://<tenant>.sharepoint.com/sites/contentTypeHub/_layouts/15/mngctype.aspx)**.

21. You will find the source content type copied from on-premises.

22. We copied terms and content type from on-premises to online. Now we need to run the Hybrid Configuration Wizard to build a connection from online to on-premises so that online terms and content types will be available in the on-premises environment.

23. Follow *Steps 1* to *13*, as discussed in the *Run Hybrid Picker section*.

24. Select **Hybrid taxonomy** and content type in the SharePoint Hybrid Configuration Wizard, as shown in *Figure 13.27*.

25. On the right side of the SharePoint Hybrid Configuration Wizard, you will notice the **Selected features**, such as **Hybrid Auditing (Preview)**, **Hybrid taxonomy**, and **Hybrid content type**. Under that, you will find another field with related features like **Hybrid Auditing (Preview)** that will be enabled. Refer to the following figure:

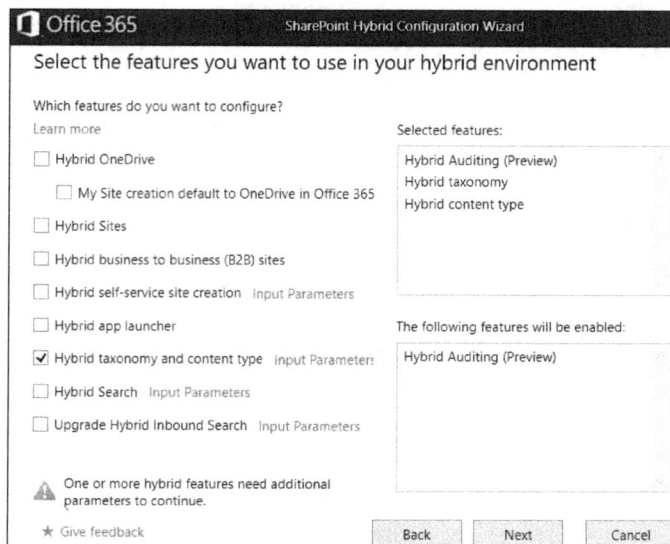

Figure 13.27: Hybrid taxonomy and content type

26. Click on **Input Parameters** as shown in *Figure 13.27*. You will get another dialog box. Enter the on-premises root site collection URL in the field **Local Site URL** as discussed in *Step 5*. Enter the name of the on-premises metadata service application in the field **Local Term Store Name**, which is **Managed Metadata Service** as discussed in *Step 4*.

27. All Groups and All Content Types under the field **Remote Group Names** and **Remote Content Type Names**, respectively, are selected by default.

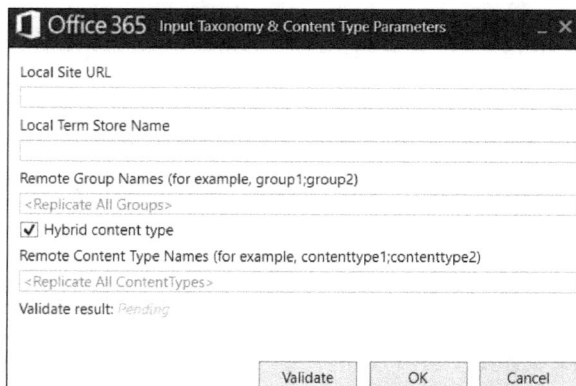

Figure 13.28: Hybrid taxonomy and content type Input Parameters

28. Click on **Validate**. You will get validation is successful. Click **OK** and then click **Next**.

29. The configuration will be completed automatically, and you will get confirmation to close the Hybrid Configuration Wizard.

30. Wait for 24 hours to run the timer jobs **Content Type Replication** and **Taxonomy Groups Replication**. Alternatively, you can run the timer job immediately from SharePoint on-premises server.

31. Now you can find SharePoint online terms in the on-premises environment managed term store.

32. SharePoint's online content type, which we copied using PowerShell, as discussed in *Step 14*, will not be seen in the on-premises content type hub. If you open on-premises content type hub **Site Settings** and click on **Content type publishing**, you will find the online content type hub page URL added here. Open any on-premises site collection, and open site content types, you will find the copied online content types. Hence, hybrid content type replicates SharePoint online content types to the site collections rather than to the content type hub.

Hybrid search

Traditionally, the SharePoint on-premises search index is stored on on-premises servers. If you are searching on-premises, the search result is queried from SharePoint on-premises content only, and similarly searching in SharePoint online site will display results from online content only. Hybrid search provides an option to store the search index of both on-premises and online content at one place in the cloud. Searching anything from SharePoint online will display both on-premises and online content at one place in SharePoint online.

Suppose an organization has sensitive data and does not want to store index data outside the on-premises server (not to store in a cloud environment). In that case, you can select the option **Upgrade Hybrid inbound Search** as shown in *Figure 13.29*. Hybrid inbound Search is a hybrid federated search which enables storing search index data in an on-premises environment. Searching anything on the SharePoint site will display results from both on-premises and online content at one place.

Microsoft recommends configuring hybrid search to get the most benefits of the search experience. Follow the step-by-step procedure to configure hybrid search:

1. Follow *Steps 1* to *13,* as discussed in the *Run Hybrid Picker section.*

2. Select the feature **Hybrid Search** in the SharePoint Hybrid Configuration Wizard as shown in *Figure 13.29*.

3. On the right side of SharePoint Hybrid Configuration Wizard, you will notice the **Selected features** as **Hybrid Auditing (Preview)** and **Hybrid Search**. Below you will find another field with related features like **Hybrid Auditing (Preview)** that will be enabled.

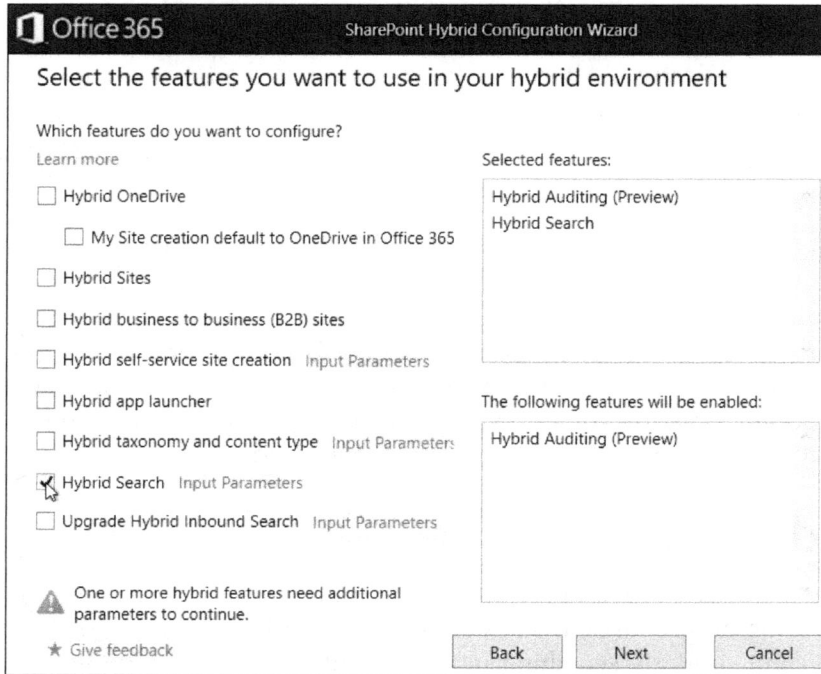

Figure 13.29: Hybrid Search

4. Click on **Input Parameters**. You will get another dialog box, as shown in *Figure 13.30*. Enter the name of the primary server under the field **Enter the name of the on-premises SharePoint server to host the cloud search service application**. This server will host cloud search.

5. If you have high availability configured, then enter the secondary server's name in the next field, else, leave it blank.

6. Enter the name of the on-premises SQL server in the field **Enter the name of the on-premises SQL database server to host search data**. That database server will host search data.

7. Enter the name of the cloud search service application in the field **Enter a name for the cloud Search service application that will be created,** made during this configuration process.

8. Select the checkbox **I have installed MSOnline AAD Powershell module** and click **OK**. Refer to the following figure:

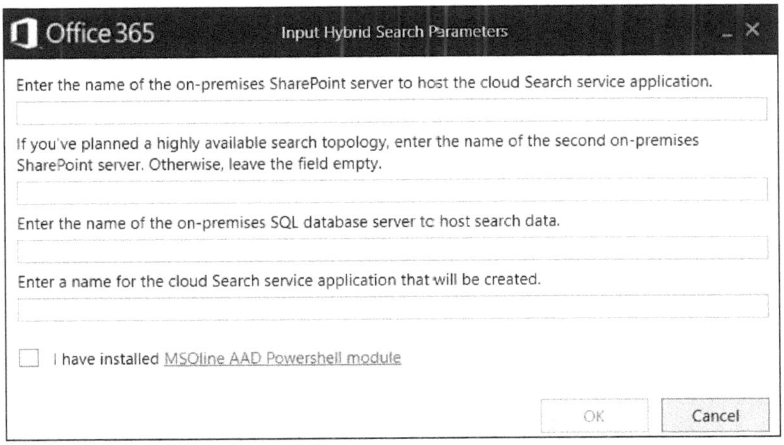

Figure 13.30: Hybrid Search Input Parameters

9. Click on **Next**. The configuration will be completed automatically, and you will get confirmation to close the Hybrid Configuration Wizard.

Conclusion

In this chapter, we glanced at the SharePoint hybrid feature, specifically the hybrid picker, and clearly understood the purpose of using hybrid features. We understood various hybrid features such as hybrid OneDrive, hybrid OneDrive and sites, hybrid app launcher, extranet business-to-business sites, hybrid taxonomy, hybrid search, and hybrid auditing. We discussed the step-by-step process to launch the hybrid picker and configure hybrid OneDrive, hybrid OneDrive and sites, and the hybrid app launcher. By running the SharePoint Hybrid Configuration Wizard, we understood the step-by-step procedure to configure extranet business-to-business sites, hybrid taxonomy, hybrid search, and hybrid auditing.

With this, we concluded the last chapter of the book. We have tried to cover all settings and configurations related to SharePoint online administration, with their screenshots. We hope you get a clear understanding of SharePoint online administration.

Points to remember

- Regular changes are applied in Office 365 and SharePoint online. There may be changes in features with time.

Join our book's Discord space

Join the book's Discord Workspace for Latest updates, Offers, Tech happenings around the world, New Release and Sessions with the Authors:

https://discord.bpbonline.com

Index

www.ingramcontent.com/pod-product-compliance
Lightning Source LLC
Chambersburg PA
CBHW061742210326
41599CB00034B/6770